Diversity and Self-Determination in International Law

The emergence of new states and independence movements after the Cold War has intensified the long-standing disagreement among international lawyers over the right of self-determination, especially the right of secession. Karen Knop shifts the discussion from the articulation of the right to its interpretation. She argues that the practice of interpretation involves and illuminates a problem of diversity raised by the exclusion of many of the groups that self-determination most affects.

Distinguishing different types of exclusion and the relationships between them reveals the deep structures, biases and stakes in the decisions and scholarship on self-determination. Knop's analysis also reveals that the leading cases have grappled with these embedded inequalities. Challenges by colonies, ethnic nations, indigenous peoples, women and others to the culture or gender biases of international law emerge as integral to the interpretation of self-determination historically, as do attempts by judges and other institutional interpreters to meet these challenges.

KAREN KNOP is Associate Professor of Law in the Faculty of Law, University of Toronto, where she teaches international law and issues of self-determination in international law. She is editor, with Sylvia Ostry, Richard Simeon and Katherine Swinton, of *Rethinking Federalism: Citizens, Markets, and Governments in a Changing World* (1995).

CAMBRIDGE STUDIES IN INTERNATIONAL AND COMPARATIVE LAW

Books in the series

Principles of the Institutional Law of International Organisations
C. F. Amerasinghe

Fragmentation and the International Relations of Micro-States
Jorri Duursma

The Polar Regions and the Development of International Law
Donald R. Rothwell

Sovereignty over Natural Resources
Nico Schrijver

Ethics and Authority in International Law
Alfred P. Rubin

Religious Liberty and International Law in Europe
Malcolm D. Evans

Unjust Enrichment
Hanoch Dagan

Trade and the Environment
Damien Geradin

The Changing International Law of High Seas Fisheries
Francisco Orrego Vicuña

International Organizations before National Courts
August Reinisch

The Right to Property in Commonwealth Constitutions
Tom Allen

Trusts
A Comparative Study
Maurizio Lupoi

On Civil Procedure
J. A. Jolowicz

Good Faith in European Contract Law
Reinhard Zimmerman and Simon Whittaker

Money Laundering
Guy Stessens

International Law in Antiquity
David J. Bederman

The Enforceability of Promises in European Contract Law
James Gordley

International Commercial Arbitration and African States
Amazu Asouzu

The Law of Internal Armed Conflict
Lindsay Moir

Diversity and Self-Determination in International Law
Karen Knop

Diversity and Self-Determination in International Law

Karen Knop
University of Toronto

CAMBRIDGE UNIVERSITY PRESS
Cambridge, New York, Melbourne, Madrid, Cape Town, Singapore, São Paulo

Cambridge University Press
The Edinburgh Building, Cambridge CB2 2RU, UK

Published in the United States of America by Cambridge University Press, New York

www.cambridge.org
Information on this title: www.cambridge.org/9780521781787

© Karen Knop 2002

This publication is in copyright. Subject to statutory exception
and to the provisions of relevant collective licensing agreements,
no reproduction of any part may take place without
the written permission of Cambridge University Press.

First published 2002
Reprinted 2003

A catalogue record for this publication is available from the British Library

Library of Congress Cataloguing in Publication data
Knop, Karen, 1960–
Diversity and self-determination in international law / Karen Knop.
    p.   cm.
Cambridge studies in international and comparative law; 20
Includes bibliographical references and index.
ISBN 0 521 78178 7
1. Self-determination, National.   2. Women (International law).   3. International
law.   I. Title.   II. Cambridge studies in international and comparative law
(Cambridge, England 1996); 20
KZ1269. K58   2002   341.26 – dc21   2001037639

ISBN-13 978-0-521-78178-7 hardback
ISBN-10 0-521-78178-7 hardback

Transferred to digital printing 2005

To my parents

Contents

Acknowledgments	*page* xi
Table of cases	xiii
Table of treaties	xviii
List of abbreviations	xxi
Introduction	1
Approach	5
Methodology	16

PART I Self-determination in post-Cold War international legal literature

1	**The question of norm-type**	29
	Rules and principles	30
	Change	38
	Participation	41
	The international community	45
2	**Interpretation and identity**	50
	Who is a 'people'?	51
	When does the right of self-determination entitle a people to choose independence?	65
3	**Pandemonium, interpretation and participation**	91
	Darkness visible	94
	On the perilous edge	95
	The apostate angel	102

PART II Self-determination interpreted in practice: the challenge of culture

4 **The canon of self-determination** — 109
   Western Sahara — 110
   EC Arbitration Commission Opinion No. 2 on Yugoslavia — 167
   East Timor — 190

5 **Developing texts** — 212
   Competing visions — 217
   International Labour Organization — 223
   UN Working Group on Indigenous Populations — 248

PART III Self-determination interpreted in practice: the challenge of gender

6 **Women and self-determination in Europe after World War I** — 277
   Collective self-determination — 281
   Individual self-determination — 309

7 **Women and self-determination in United Nations trust territories** — 327
   Self-determination and the UN trusteeship system — 329
   Equality and self-determination in the UN trusteeship system — 332
   Equality and self-determination in the UN Commission on the Status of Women — 344
   Petitions — 349

8 **Indigenous women and self-determination** — 358
   Equality — 360
   Lovelace's arguments — 362
   Views in Lovelace — 367

Conclusion — 373
   Patterns — 374
   Promise — 380

Bibliography — 382
Index — 421

Acknowledgments

It is a pleasure to acknowledge the input and assistance that I have received in the writing of this book.

Work on the book was funded by the Social Sciences and Humanities Research Council of Canada, the Connaught Fund of the University of Toronto and the Cecil A. Wright Foundation for Legal Scholarship of the University of Toronto Faculty of Law. Research for Chapter 5 at the International Labour Organization and the United Nations in Geneva was kindly made possible through the International Human Rights Programme of the University of Toronto Faculty of Law and Lee Swepston of the International Labour Office. The opportunity to sit in on the United Nations Working Group on Indigenous Populations at the final stages of its drafting of the declaration on the rights of indigenous peoples was particularly valuable. The librarians at the Bora Laskin Law Library at the University of Toronto have been unfailingly helpful. My appreciation also goes to Johanna (Myyra) Blom and Ira Parghi for their diligent research assistance on Chapters 6 and 7 respectively and Alissa Hamilton, Alison Symington and Julissa Reynoso for other assistance with the book.

For suggestions and support at key moments, I should like to thank Hilary Charlesworth, Rebecca Cook, Donald Fleming, Bruce Grant, David Kennedy, Martti Koskenniemi, Mayo Moran, Jennifer Nedelsky, Karen Nørregaard, Craig Scott and Saskia Sassen. The book has also benefited from the comments of participants in the Legal Studies Workshop at the University of Virginia School of Law, the International Law Workshop Series at the University of Michigan Law School and the Feminist Project at Harvard Law School, where I presented parts of the book in draft.

I owe a special debt to James Crawford, who supervised the doctoral dissertation out of which the book grew. His advice, expertise and encouragement have been a lifeline time and time again. Michael

Trebilcock and Robert Howse, who also supervised the dissertation, brought a breadth of mind and a warmth to their task that both pushed and sustained my efforts. Thomas Franck, Melissa Williams and Ed Morgan lent their support to the book in ways that went well beyond their original involvement as examiners of the dissertation. I should particularly like to thank Thomas Franck and New York University School of Law for giving me a home during the final year of my work on the book.

Above all, I am grateful to my parents, Osvald and Helga Knop, to whom this book is dedicated, and to Ralph Glass. Their example and their understanding have been an inspiration throughout. Ralph has made the journey with me from first word to last with love and patience. I thank him with the fullest and gladdest heart imaginable.

Table of cases

Aaland Islands, Report of International Committee of Jurists (Larnaude, Struycken, Huber), LNOJ Sp. Supp. No. 3 (October 1920) 3   *page* 21–2, 78
Aaland Islands, Report of the Commission of Rapporteurs (Beyens, Calonder, Elkus), LN Council Doc. B7/21/68/106 (16 April 1921)   21–2, 78–80, 86–7
Aegean Sea Continental Shelf (Greece v. Turkey), ICJ Reports 1978, p. 3; 60 ILR 511   160 n. 194
Canada AG v. Lavell (1973), [1974] SCR 1349   360, 362 n. 27, 365
Amendments to the Naturalization Provisions of the Constitution of Costa Rica, Advisory Opinion (Inter-American Court of Human Rights, 1984), 5 *Human Rights Law Journal* 161; 79 ILR 282   316
Application of the Convention on the Prevention and Punishment of the Crime of Genocide (Bosnia-Herzegovina v. Yugoslavia), Preliminary Objections, ICJ Reports 1996, p. 595; 115 ILR 1   109–10 n. 4
Barcelona Traction, Light and Power Company, Limited (Belgium v. Spain), ICJ Reports 1970, p. 3; 46 ILR 1   191 n. 322
Canevaro Case (Italy v. Peru) (1912), 11 Reports of International Arbitral Awards 397   189 n. 310
Certain Phosphate Lands in Nauru (Nauru v. Australia), ICJ Reports 1992, p. 240; 97 ILR 1   6 n. 12, 109 n. 4
Opinion and Award of the Arbitrator in the Matter of the Arbitration Between the Republic of Chile and the Republic of Peru, With respect to the Unfulfilled Provisions of the Treaty of Peace of October 20, 1883, under the Protocol and Supplementary Articles Signed at Washington, July 20, 1922,

4 March 1925, reprinted in S. Wambaugh, *Plebiscites Since the World War with a Collection of Official Documents* (2 vols., Washington: Carnegie Endowment for International Peace, 1933), vol. II, p. 282; 3 ILR 357   284, 303–5, 307–9

Delgamuukw v. British Columbia, [1997] 3 SCR 1010, 37 ILM 261; 115 ILR 446   132 n. 77

Dubai/Sharjah Border Arbitration, 19 October 1981, Court of Arbitration (Cahier, Simpson, Simmonds) (1993) 91 ILR 543   116, 131–2 n. 77, 140 n. 113, 150–8, 193, 379

East Timor (Portugal v. Australia), ICJ Reports 1995, p. 90; 150 ILR 226   11, 32 n. 12, 52 n. 10, 109, 190–211, 214–15, 327, 378

Frontier Dispute (Burkina Faso v. Republic of Mali), ICJ Reports 1986, p. 554; 80 ILR 440   177 n. 254

Greco-Bulgarian 'Communities', Advisory Opinion (1930), PCIJ Ser. B, No. 17; 5 ILR 4   63

Guerin v. The Queen, [1984] 2 SCR 335   201–2, 207

International Status of South-West Africa, Advisory Opinion, ICJ Reports 1950, p. 128; 17 ILR 47   199

Iran v. United States, Case No. A/18 (1984), 5 Iran–US Claims Tribunal Reports 251; 75 ILR 175   189 n. 310

Island of Palmas Case (Netherlands, USA) (1928), 2 Reports of International Arbitral Awards 829; 4 ILR *passim*   70 n. 84, 135, 160

Ivan Kitok v. Sweden (Communication No. 197/1985), GAOR, 43rd Sess., Supp. No. 40, UN Doc. A/43/40 (1988), p. 221; 96 ILR 637   22 n. 73, 369–70

Kugler v. (Austrian) Federal Ministry for the Interior (Austrian Administrative Court, 1921), reported in J. R. Williams and H. Lauterpacht (eds.), *Annual Digest of Public International Law Cases, Being a Selection from the Decisions of International and National Courts and Tribunals given during the Years 1919 to 1922* (London: Longmans, Green and Co., 1932), pp. 220–1 (Case No. 153)   311 n. 176

R. L. v. Canada (Communication No. 358/1989), GAOR, 47th Sess., Supp. No. 40, UN Doc. A/47/40 (1994), p. 358; 96 ILR 706   17 n. 52, 364 n. 32

Land, Island and Maritime Frontier Dispute (El Salvador v. Honduras, Nicaragua intervening), ICJ Reports 1992, p. 351; 97 ILR 112   375–6

Legal Status of Eastern Greenland (Denmark v. Norway) (1933), PCIJ Ser. A/B, No. 53; 6 ILR 95   135–7, 153 n. 173

Legality of the Threat or Use of Nuclear Weapons, Advisory
 Opinion, ICJ Reports 1996, p. 226; 110 ILR 1; 110 ILR 163   97 n. 31
Loizidou v. Turkey (Merits), European Court of Human Rights, 18
 December 1996, (1997) 18 *Human Rights Law Journal* 50;
 108 ILR 443   73–4, 77
Sandra Lovelace v. Canada (Communication No. 24/1977), Selected
 Decisions under the Optional Protocol, vol. I (New York:
 United Nations, 1985), UN Doc. CCPR/C/OP/1, p. 10
 (admissibility); 68 ILR 19   358
Sandra Lovelace v. Canada (Communication No. 24/1977), Selected
 Decisions under the Optional Protocol, vol. I (New York:
 United Nations, 1985), UN Doc. CCPR/C/OP/1, p. 37 (interim
 decision); 68 ILR 21   358
Sandra Lovelace v. Canada (Communication No. 24/1977, formerly
 Communication No. R.6/24), GAOR, 36th Sess., Supp. No. 40,
 UN Doc. A/36/40 (1981), p. 166 (merits); 68 ILR 25   11, 16 n. 52,
 24, 358–72, 380
Mabo v. Queensland (No. 2) (1992), 175 Commonwealth Law
 Reports 1 (High Court of Australia); 112 ILR 457   116, 128–9
Mackenzie v. Hare (1915) 239 US 299   317, 321 n. 214
Mergé Claim (US v. Italy) (1955), 22 ILR 443   189 n. 310
Military and Paramilitary Activities in and against Nicaragua
 (Nicaragua v. United States), Merits, ICJ Reports 1986, p. 14;
 76 ILR 349   194
Minquiers and Ecrehos (France v. United Kingdom), ICJ Reports
 1953, p. 47; 20 ILR 94   142–3, 160 n. 194, 204
Monetary Gold Removed From Rome in 1943 (Italy v. France,
 United Kingdom and United States), ICJ Reports 1954, p. 19;
 20 ILR 441   205 n. 394
L. S. N. v. Canada (Communication No. 94/1981), Selected Decisions
 of the Human Rights Committee under the Optional Protocol,
 vol. II (New York: United Nations, 1990), UN Doc. CCPR/C/OP/2,
 p. 6   362 n. 25
Namibia (South West Africa), Advisory Opinion, ICJ Reports 1971,
 p. 16; 49 ILR 2   22, 44, 52 n. 10, 114, 127 n. 65, 200, 330
Native Women's Association of Canada v. Canada, [1992] 3 Canada
 Federal Court Reports 192 (Federal Court of Appeal)   365
North Sea Continental Shelf Cases (Federal Republic of Germany
 v. Denmark; Federal Republic of Germany v. Netherlands), ICJ
 Reports 1969, p. 3; 41 ILR 29   379

Bernard Ominayak, Chief of the Lubicon Lake Band v.
    Canada (Communication No. 167/1984), GAOR, 45th Sess.,
    Supp. 40, UN Doc. A/45/40 (1990), vol. II, p. 1; 96 ILR 667   22 n. 73
Reference re Secession of Quebec, [1998] 2 SCR 217, (1998) 37 ILM
    1340; 115 ILR 536   1–3
Reparation for Injuries Suffered in the Service of the United
    Nations, Advisory Opinion, ICJ Reports 1949, p. 174; 16
    ILR 318   149–50
Rights of Passage Case (Second Phase), ICJ Reports 1962, p. 6
        129 n. 73
Salem Case (Egypt v. US) (1932), 2 Reports of International
    Arbitral Awards 1161; 6 ILR 188   189 n. 310
Sawridge Band v. Canada, [1996] 1 Canada Federal Court
    Reports 3 (Federal Court, Trial Division)   367 n. 45
Sawridge Band v. Canada, [1997] 3 Canada Federal Court
    Reports 580 (Federal Court of Appeal)   367 n. 45
South West Africa (Ethiopia v. South Africa; Liberia v. South Africa),
    Preliminary Objections, ICJ Reports 1962, p. 319;
    37 ILR 3   113–14
South West Africa (Ethiopia v. South Africa; Liberia v. South Africa),
    Second Phase, ICJ Reports 1966, p. 6; 37 ILR 243   113–14
South West Africa – Voting Procedure, Advisory Opinion, ICJ
    Reports 1955, p. 67; 22 ILR 651   203 n. 384
Temple of Preah Vihear (Cambodia v. Thailand), Merits, ICJ
    Reports 1962, p. 6; 33 ILR 48   153 n. 171
Territorial Dispute (Libyan Arab Jamahiriya v. Chad), ICJ
    Reports 1994, p. 6; 100 ILR 1   375–6
United States Nationals in Morocco, ICJ Reports 1952, p. 176; 19
    ILR 255   129 n. 73, 160 n. 194
Western Sahara, Advisory Opinion, ICJ Reports 1975, p. 12; 59
    ILR 30   11, 15–16, 18 n. 55, 44 n. 80, 52 n. 10, 66, 72,
    109–67, 192, 193, 206, 210–11, 273, 374–80
Conference on Yugoslavia, Arbitration Commission, Opinion
    No. 1 (1992) 31 ILM 1494; 92 ILR 162   170–1, 174
Opinion No. 2 (1992) 31 ILM 1497; 92 ILR 167   11, 109, 167–90, 192,
    193, 210, 378
Opinion No. 3 (1992) 31 ILM 1499; 92 ILR 170   171, 187
Opinion No. 4 (1992) 31 ILM 1501; 92 ILR 173   172, 187–8
Opinion No. 5 (1992) 31 ILM 1503; 92 ILR 178   172, 173–4, 187–8

Opinion No. 6 (1992) 31 ILM 1507; 92 ILR 182   172, 187–8
Opinion No. 7 (1992) 31 ILM 1512; 92 ILR 188   172, 187–8
Opinion No. 9 (1992) 31 ILM 1523; 92 ILR 203   174 n. 245
Opinion No. 11 (1993) 32 ILM 1587; 96 ILR 718   167 n. 222, 171

Table of treaties

Australia–Republic of Nauru Settlement of the Case in the International Court of Justice Concerning Certain Phosphate Lands in Nauru, Nauru, 10 August 1993, in force 20 August 1993, (1993) 32 ILM 1471   *page* 109 n. 4

Charter of the United Nations, 26 June 1945, 59 Stat. 1031, 145 BFSP (1943–5) 805 (1953)   6–7, 9, 11, 31, 34, 35 n. 29, 36, 51–3, 69 n. 83, 70, 72, 82, 84–5, 87–8, 99, 111, 191–2, 194 n. 331, 196, 197 n. 351, 199–200, 202–3, 206–10, 267, 269, 270, 278, 327–35, 343 n. 74, 344, 346–7, 356

Convention on Certain Questions Relating to the Conflict of Nationality Laws, The Hague, 12 April 1930, in force 1 July 1937, 179 LNTS 89   189 n. 310, 313 n. 186

Convention on Consent to Marriage, Minimum Age for Marriage and Registration of Marriages, New York, 10 December 1962, in force 9 December 1964, 521 UNTS 231   347

Convention on the Elimination of All Forms of Discrimination Against Women, New York, adopted, 18 December 1979, in force 3 September 1981, 1249 UNTS 13   279

Convention (No. 169) concerning Indigenous and Tribal Peoples in Independent Countries, Geneva, adopted by the International Labour Conference on 27 June 1989, in force 5 September 1991, 28 ILM 1382   11, 215, 217–48, 255, 259

Convention on the Nationality of Married Women, New York, adopted 29 January 1957, in force 11 August 1958, 309 UNTS 65   313 n. 186

Convention on the Nationality of Women, Montevideo,
26 December 1933, in force 29 August 1934, (1934) 28 *American
Journal of International Law Supplement* 61   313 n. 186
Convention on the Prevention and Punishment of the Crime of
Genocide, New York, adopted 9 December 1948, in force 12
January 1951, 78 UNTS 277   109 n. 4
Convention (No. 107) concerning the Protection and Integration of
Indigenous and Other Tribal and Semi-Tribal Populations in
Independent Countries, Geneva, adopted by the International
Labour Conference on 26 June 1957, in force 2 June 1959, 328
UNTS 247   223–4, 225–6, 227, 233, 234, 243–4
Convention (No. 144) concerning Tripartite Consultations to
Promote the Implementation of International Labour
Standards, Geneva, adopted by the International Labour
Conference on 21 June 1976, in force 16 May 1978, (1976)
15 ILM 1076   226
Covenant of the League of Nations, Versailles, 28 June 1919, in
force 10 January 1920, (1919) 112 BFSP 13   51, 196, 197 n. 351,
        198, 288–9, 296, 298, 328–30, 332
Declaration on the 'Guidelines on the Recognition of New States
in Eastern Europe and in the Soviet Union', Brussels, The
Hague, 16 December 1991, (1992) 31 ILM 1486   172–4, 187–8
Declaration on Yugoslavia, Brussels, 16 December 1991, (1992)
31 ILM 1485   172–4, 187–8
General Framework Agreement for Peace in Bosnia and
Herzegovina (Dayton Accords), Paris, 14 December 1995, in
force 14 December 1995, (1996) 35 ILM 75   189 n. 309
International Covenant on Civil and Political Rights, New York,
16 December 1966, in force 23 March 1976, 999 UNTS
171   16 n. 52, 22–3, 58–9, 80, 82, 85, 100–2, 169,
        174–5, 177, 178 n. 259, 213–14 n. 6, 222–3, 235,
        252, 265–70, 278, 358 n. 4, 360–2, 364, 368–71
International Covenant on Economic, Social and Cultural Rights,
New York, 16 December 1966, in force 3 January 1976, 993
UNTS 3   22 n. 69, 58, 80, 82, 169, 174–5, 177,
        213–14 n. 6, 235, 265–70
Optional Protocol to the International Covenant on Civil and
Political Rights, New York, 16 December 1966, in force
23 March 1976, 999 UNTS 171   22–3

Protocol and Additional Article Regarding the Settlement of the Question of Western Hungary, Venice, 13 October 1921, ratified by Austria on 28 December 1921 (ratification not required by the Hungarian constitution), 9 LNTS 203   283

Statute of the International Court of Justice, 26 June 1945, 59 Stat. 1179, 145 BFSP (1943–5) 832 (1953)   29 n. 2, 43, 193–4, 205

Treaty Between Australia and the Republic of Indonesia on the Zone of Cooperation in an Area Between the Indonesian Province of East Timor and Northern Australia (Timor Gap Treaty), Timor Sea, 11 December 1989, in force 9 February 1991, *Australian Treaty Series* 1991 No. 9   191, 209 n. 412

Treaty of Amsterdam, 2 October 1997, in force 1 May 1999, OJ 1997 No. C340, p. 1, (1998) 37 ILM 56   187, 189

Treaty on European Union, Maastricht, 7 February 1992, in force 1 November 1993, OJ 1992 No. C191, p. 1, (1992) 31 ILM 253   187, 189

Treaty of Peace Between the Allied and Associated Powers and Austria, St Germain-en-Laye, 10 September 1919, 226 Consol. TS 1 (Treaty of St Germain)   282, 297, 309–10, 311, 314

Treaty of Peace Between the Allied and Associated Powers and Germany, Versailles, 28 June 1919, 225 Consol. TS 188 (Treaty of Versailles)   225, 282–3, 297, 299, 309–10, 311–12, 314, 323–4

Treaty of Peace and Friendship Between Chile and Peru, signed at Ancón, 20 October 1883, 162 Consol. TS 453   283–4

Abbreviations

BFSP	British and Foreign State Papers
CHR Res.	Resolution of the Commission on Human Rights of the United Nations
Consol. TS	Consolidated Treaty Series
CSW	Commission on the Status of Women of the United Nations
CSW Res.	Resolution of the Commission on the Status of Women of the United Nations
ESCOR	Official Records of the Economic and Social Council of the United Nations
ESC Res.	Resolution of the Economic and Social Council of the United Nations
GAOR	Official Records of the General Assembly of the United Nations
GA Res.	Resolution of the General Assembly of the United Nations
Hague Recueil	Recueil des Cours, Collected Courses of the Hague Academy of International Law
ICJ Reports	Reports of Judgments, Advisory Opinions and Orders of the International Court of Justice
ILM	International Legal Materials
LN Council	Council of the League of Nations
LNTS	Treaties and International Engagements Registered with the Secretariat of the League of Nations
PCIJ	Permanent Court of International Justice
SCR	Canada Supreme Court Reports
SC Res.	Resolution of the Security Council of the United Nations

Stat.	United States Statutes at Large
TC	Trusteeship Council of the United Nations
TCOR	Official Records of the Trusteeship Council of the United Nations
TC Res.	Resolution of the Trusteeship Council of the United Nations
UNTS	Treaties and International Agreements Registered or Filed and Recorded with the Secretariat of the United Nations

Introduction

It is a commonplace that international lawyers differ on whether the right[1] of self-determination of peoples in international law includes a right of secession, and if so, in what circumstances. In the 1998 *Reference re Secession of Quebec*,[2] which put the question squarely to the Supreme Court of Canada, the Canadian government, the Quebec *amicus curiae*, and intervenors including the Nunavik Inuit,[3] the Ad Hoc Committee of Canadian Women on the Constitution, and the provincial government of Saskatchewan could all find support for their positions among international lawyers.[4] Indeed, the number of new states and self-determination movements to emerge from the end of the Cold War has only broadened the range of views on self-determination, some spying a new norm in these developments and others distinguishing them in various ways.

But beyond the fact of disagreement, the cross-section of opinions on secession in the Quebec reference brings home a feature of the international law discourse on self-determination that many international lawyers may register, but few engage: its unhelpful generality. The accounts of self-determination that compete in the literature are so neatly logical and linear as to either miss or generalize away much of what is involved in the actual interpretation of self-determination. One of

---

[1] As will be seen, some authors analyse self-determination as a legal right and others as a legal principle. The terms 'right' and 'principle' are used somewhat loosely in the Introduction, and this usage should not be seen as prejudging the issue of norm-type.
[2] *Reference re Secession of Quebec*, [1998] 2 SCR 217, (1998) 37 ILM 1340.
[3] The Nunavik Inuit were represented by the intervenor Makivik Corporation.
[4] The facta and accompanying expert opinions of the Attorney General of Canada and the Quebec *amicus curiae*, and the submissions of the Ad Hoc Committee of Canadian Women on the Constitution are reprinted in A. F. Bayefsky (ed.), *Self-Determination in International Law: Quebec and Lessons Learned* (The Hague: Kluwer Law International, 2000).

the few to criticize this body of literature, Nathaniel Berman dismisses its broad dichotomies as inadequate to the complex production of meaning in a concrete case.[5] Yet the habit of reading each new decision on secession as the validation of one simple definition over another perpetuates the international law discourse of self-determination as a contest of impervious generality or what James Crawford, another of its rare critics, slightingly calls the 'programmatic'.[6] Indeed, by reconstructing the specificity and historical context of the judgments that figure in the standard formulations of self-determination, Berman and Crawford do much to demonstrate the weaknesses of these formulations as description. Berman identifies patterns of imagination and invention in the judgments that undermine the predictive value of the competing rules, while Crawford stresses the relevance of colonialism inside and outside the International Court of Justice.

This book does not set out to establish a single best account of whether and when the right of self-determination of peoples in international law includes a right to independence. Nor, any more than Berman or Crawford do, does it simply aim to prove that the standard answers fail to capture the richness and detail of the key cases and events – which no summary could accomplish. Instead, it seeks to show that there is something important that these answers systematically ignore: the challenge of diversity for the interpretation of self-determination and – conversely – the implications of the interpretive history of self-determination, once seen in this light, for the challenge of diversity in international law and perhaps law more generally.

As a rough intuition, this relationship between diversity and self-determination is suggested too by the Quebec secession reference. What seemed troubling about the legal answers that the scholarship on self-determination offered the court was their starkness, because it was so unlikely to appear legitimate to the judges and, relatedly, to the full range of those implicated in the judgment: Canadians, Québecois,

[5] N. Berman, 'Sovereignty in Abeyance: Self-Determination in International Law' (1988) 7 *Wisconsin International Law Journal* 51 at 93–4. See similarly M. Koskenniemi, 'National Self-Determination Today: Problems of Legal Theory and Practice' (1994) 43 *International and Comparative Law Quarterly* 241 at 264–9.
 This is perhaps also implicit in complex case-studies of secession by international lawyers. See e.g. E. Stein, *Czecho/Slovakia: Ethnic Conflict, Constitutional Fissure, Negotiated Breakup* (Ann Arbor: University of Michigan Press, 1997).
[6] J. Crawford, 'The General Assembly, the International Court and Self-Determination' in V. Lowe and M. Fitzmaurice (eds.), *Fifty Years of the International Court of Justice. Essays in Honour of Sir Robert Jennings* (Cambridge: Grotius Publications, 1996), pp. 585–605 at p. 586.

indigenous peoples, minorities, women. Indeed, a number of the lawyers and experts involved in the case laboured to present the court with a less open-and-shut view of the international law of self-determination. And the innovative structure of the decision – the housing of much of it in the Canadian constitution, the development of the constitution's deep principles of federalism, democracy, constitutionalism and the rule of law and the protection of minorities, the appeal to an inclusive constitutional history and the finding of a duty to negotiate supported and informed by these principles and this history – seems to testify to the court's recognition that the broad legitimacy of the judgment required engagement with a diversity of perspectives and that the approach it took to interpretation was related to its ability to engage.

The problems posed by differences of culture and gender for the interpretation of international law are exceptionally acute for self-determination because its interpretation directly affects non-state groups as well as states. Moreover, the groups involved, including the colonized, ethnic nations and indigenous peoples and women within these groups, tend to be marginalized both internationally and domestically. As distinct from interest groups, these groups are generally characterized by an experience of membership as non-voluntary and immutable and correspond historically to patterns of social and political inequality and negative stereotyping.[7] For such groups, differences of power and voice often combine to exclude them unfairly from the making of the law, placing pressure on its interpretation to begin the work of inclusion. The book investigates the importance of one particular question of self-determination – when it gives rise to independence – as a place, perhaps without equal, where international law has had to contend with the challenge of diversity for interpretation. In this, it differs from Crawford's essay, which pursues the challenge only with respect to diversity among states and considers a fairly limited and statist set of interpretive responses. Berman's scholarship analyses how the verisimilitude of various international judgments and other influential writings on issues of nationalism derives from the author's image of the nationalist subject, be it peoples, nations or minorities, and the interaction of that sociological impression with the author's image of international law and institutions.[8] Berman's primary interest, however, is in exploring the

---

[7] I borrow here from M. S. Williams, *Voice, Trust, and Memory. Marginalized Groups and the Failings of Liberal Representation* (Princeton: Princeton University Press, 1998), pp. 15–16.

[8] See e.g. N. Berman, '"But the Alternative is Despair": Nationalism and the Modernist Renewal of International Law' (1993) 106 *Harvard Law Review* 1792; N. Berman, 'The

construction of the individual vision rather than its responsiveness to the claims of those it implicates.

As the challenge of diversity, the book distinguishes three ways in which groups affected by the right of self-determination of peoples may be included in or excluded from its interpretation: *participation*, *identity* and *interpretation*. What is meant by *participation* is whether these groups have a voice in the process. In addition to actual involvement in the determination of meaning, participation refers to other means of building in consideration of their perspectives. Whereas participation is concerned with the procedural possibilities to speak, *identity* relates to what is said. Identity refers to international law's construction of the identity of a group; the capacity of international law, as a type of language, to describe and thereby to help shape our perception of a group, its history and entitlements. This image that informs and is, in turn, reinforced by international law may or may not be consistent with the self-image of the group or its parts. So identity too involves inclusion or exclusion. *Interpretation*, the third form of responsiveness, signifies the room that the interpreter's theory of law, his model of law and legal reasoning, makes for argument and the kinds of arguments it recognizes as valid. The choice of an interpretive theory determines how to speak; it sets the limits and terms of the conversation about meaning that may be had in international law. As such, interpretation rules in or out the sorts of reasoning that resonate most strongly with the groups affected. Participation, identity and interpretation thus name different ways in which those who see themselves as subjects of self-determination might experience the process of formulating its meaning, negatively, as yet another imperial imposition or, more positively, as engagement. These three aspects of the challenge of diversity, while distinct, are also interrelated, and the book demonstrates the variableness and complexity of their interrelation.

It may already be evident that participation, identity and interpretation offer both a framework for analysis and a measure for legitimacy. As a set of questions about the scholarship and case-law on

International Law of Nationalism: Group Identity and Legal History' in D. Wippman (ed.), *International Law and Ethnic Conflict* (Ithaca: Cornell University Press, 1998), pp. 25–57; N. Berman, 'Legalizing Jerusalem or, Of Law, Fantasy, and Faith' (1996) 45 *Catholic University Law Review* 823; N. Berman, 'Modernism, Nationalism, and the Rhetoric of Reconstruction' (1992) 4 *Yale Journal of Law and the Humanities* 351; N. Berman, 'A Perilous Ambivalence: Nationalist Desire, Legal Autonomy, and the Limits of the Interwar Framework' (1992) 33 *Harvard International Law Journal* 353; Berman, 'Sovereignty in Abeyance'.

self-determination, they illuminate the deep structures, biases and stakes in the development of meaning in international law. As a standard, they suggest that the better interpretation of self-determination is one that engages on a basis of equality all those directly affected. While important recent work in legal and political theory argues in the abstract for a similar ideal of judgment[9] or the rule of law,[10] the intention of this book is a different one. The book shows that, historically, participation, identity and interpretation express some of the claims actually made by groups marginalized in the interpretation of self-determination and, as important, some of the responses crafted by judges and other institutional interpreters of self-determination. The development of self-determination in international law is thus of broader relevance because in it we may find glimmers of striving toward an ideal of interpretation for our age of diversity. While such moments may be downplayed as relatively few, minor or even unsuccessful by this very standard, their instructiveness lies in the attempt, and their hope, in the recognition of inclusion and equality as essential to interpretation.

The remainder of the Introduction expands on the book's approach to self-determination and methodology.

Approach

The international legal texts on self-determination, like all legal texts, assume and create a world.[11] And our recognition or acceptance of the

---

[9] See e.g. M. Minow, 'Identities' (1991) 3 *Yale Journal of Law and the Humanities* 97; M. Minow, *Making All the Difference. Inclusion, Exclusion and American Law* (Ithaca: Cornell University Press, 1990); J. Nedelsky, 'Embodied Diversity and the Challenges to Law' (1997) 42 *McGill Law Journal* 91; J. Nedelsky, 'Judgment, Diversity and Relational Autonomy', J. A. Corry Lecture, Queen's University, Canada, October 1995 (unpublished); M. C. Nussbaum, *Poetic Justice: The Literary Imagination and Public Life* (Boston: Beacon Press, 1995); E. Scarry, 'The Difficulty of Imagining Other Persons' in C. Hesse and R. Post (eds.), *Human Rights in Political Transitions: Gettysburg to Bosnia* (New York: Zone Books, 1999), pp. 277–309; C. R. Sunstein, *Legal Reasoning and Political Conflict* (New York: Oxford University Press, 1996); J. Tully, *Strange Multiplicity. Constitutionalism in an Age of Diversity* (Cambridge: Cambridge University Press, 1995).

[10] See e.g. D. Dyzenhaus, 'Recrafting the Rule of Law' in D. Dyzenhaus (ed.), *Recrafting the Rule of Law: The Limits of Legal Order* (Oxford: Hart Publishing, 1999), pp. 1–12 at pp. 5–10; N. MacCormick, 'Rhetoric and the Rule of Law' in *ibid.*, pp. 163–77.

[11] See J. B. White, 'Law as Rhetoric, Rhetoric as Law: The Arts of Cultural and Communal Life' (1985) 52 *University of Chicago Law Review* 684, reprinted in J. B. White, *Heracles' Bow: Essays on the Rhetoric and Poetics of the Law* (Madison, Wisc.: University of Wisconsin Press, 1985), pp. 28–48. See also J. B. White, *The Legal Imagination: Studies in the Nature of Legal Thought and Expression* (Boston: Little, Brown & Co., 1973), pp. 243–503.

world created in a particular reading of self-determination is part of what convinces us about that reading. In this sense, the texts on self-determination construct and are constructed on *identity*. The universe they define looks quite different, however, from the community of formally equal sovereign states posited by other international legal norms. Public international law overwrites everything with the narrative of sovereign sameness in order to establish a discourse where all states are equal.[12] In contrast, the subjects of self-determination are by definition not states, but communities and even cultures. By creating an image of non-state groups, including Islamic communities, nomadic tribes, the colonized, ethnic nations and indigenous peoples, and of women within these groups, the interpretation of self-determination introduces a diversity and particularity into international law. But this has also internalized assumptions about identity that perpetuate and justify inequalities of culture and gender.

In the vast United Nations documentation on colonies and their readiness for self-determination, for instance, the colonial world was constructed – exoticized and domesticated, marvelled at and pitied, recorded and reformed – in post-World War II international law. While dispatches from states administering colonies often took the tone of the sage imperialist, the UN visiting missions were latter-day explorers for the international legal system, their reports sometimes sprinkled with their excitement about the voyage[13] or allusions to children's stories of adventures and faraway places.[14] Whatever the authorial voice, the central narrative of these texts was progress. The UN Charter envisaged the exercise of self-determination by colonial populations, but only when they were judged sufficiently politically, economically, socially and educationally advanced. Until then, the colonies were to be administered by Western states as trust or non-self-governing territories

---

[12] See *Certain Phosphate Lands in Nauru (Nauru v. Australia)*, ICJ Reports 1992, p. 240 at p. 270 (Separate Opinion of Judge Shahabudeen). See generally B. Kingsbury, 'Sovereignty and Inequality' (1998) 9 *European Journal of International Law* 599.

[13] E.g. 'It was an exciting moment when, after flying for a day and part of the next day, at last the island appeared looking like a small ball of green and brown in the vast blue ocean,' wrote a UN visiting mission to the trust territory of Nauru in 1962. UN Visiting Mission to the Trust Territories of Nauru and New Guinea, 1962, Report on Nauru, UN TCOR, 29th Sess., Supp. No. 2, UN Doc. T/1603 (1962), para. 20.

[14] I. Parghi, 'Beyond Colonialism? Voice and Power in the UN Trusteeship System' (unpublished research paper, Faculty of Law, University of Toronto, 1997) 34 (citing references to the *Arabian Nights* and the famous story of the British explorer Stanley's remarkable sang-froid when he came upon Dr Livingstone lost in deepest Africa).

under UN supervision.[15] Because the Charter made the encouragement of respect for human rights without distinction as to sex a basic objective of the international trusteeship system,[16] the status of women in the trust territories was treated as a measure of a territory's readiness for self-determination.[17] In this way, the characterization of women became part of the story of progress told by the international law of self-determination. For example, the discussion of the Mututsi women in a report from the early 1950s by Belgium, which administered Ruanda-Urundi as a trust territory,[18] illustrates a keen eye for (if not also a hint of irritation at) the respect and authority some Mututsi women enjoyed in their own society, and a blind faith that European gender relations epitomized the goal of equality.

> The proud and haughty Mututsi women as a general rule never left the family compound; they did no manual work except for a little basket-making. They supervised the work of others. Then [sic] they travelled with their husbands, they were borne in litters. The mother of the Mwami played an important political role; a number of Batutsi women have governed *chefferies* and *sous-chefferies* with undisputed authority...
> ...
> Women, and especially mothers, are held in high esteem. Whereas in some parts of Central Africa, they are treated as beasts of burden, in Ruanda-Urundi they are almost on an equality with their husbands...
> Up to the present the indigenous women have shown little desire to give up their customary role of wife and mother. This apathy would not, however, have justified neglect of the question by the Administration... The status of women will be raised chiefly by means of slow and persevering action.
> Visits to hospitals and dispensaries and attendance at religious services have liberated the Mututsi women from the seclusion in which they lived. School education has sharpened the young girls' minds and awakened their intelligence. The presence of a number of European families, especially those of colonists, has given the Africans the example of real partnership between men and women and shown them what an important part women can play.[19]

If international law benevolently envisages those worthy of self-determination, it also contemplates, with apprehension, those who will clamour unwisely for it. It seems in part the prospect of controlling the

---

[15] Charter of the United Nations, 26 June 1945, 59 Stat. 1031, 145 BFSP (1943–5) 805 (1953), c. XI–XIII.
[16] *Ibid.*, Art. 76(c).   [17] See Chapter 7 below.
[18] The trust territory of Ruanda-Urundi became Rwanda and Burundi in 1962.
[19] Commission on the Status of Women, Information Concerning the Status of Women in Trust Territories, CSW, 7th Sess., UN Doc. E/CN.6/210 (1953), pp. 13–14.

excitable races that so alarmed Robert Lansing, Secretary of State to President Wilson, about any recognition of a right of self-determination. Before the peace conference ending World War I, Lansing wrote:

> The more I think about the President's declaration as to the right of 'self-determination,' the more convinced I am of the danger of putting such ideas into the minds of certain races. It is bound to be the basis of impossible demands on the Peace Congress and create trouble in many lands.
>
> What effect will it have on the Irish, the Indians, the Egyptians, and the nationalists among the Boers? Will it not breed discontent, disorder, and rebellion? Will not the Mohammedans of Syria and Palestine and possibly of Morocco and Tripoli not rely on it?...
>
> The phrase is simply loaded with dynamite.[20]

What is remarkable about Lansing's reasoning is not only the view of 'certain races', but the role of this assumption about *identity* in justifying his conclusion about the form of *interpretation*. In effect, Lansing argues that the hot-bloodedness of these races demands the clearest of rules. They cannot be trusted to acknowledge or respect legal distinctions among claimants for self-determination. So whatever the merits of a more nuanced rule or broader principle on self-determination, the rabidity of the Irish, the Indians, the Egyptians and others makes a simple 'no' rule the only prudent formulation.

While self-determination thus involves speaking about and to[21] nations, peoples and minorities, it has rarely involved speaking with them. States are the paradigmatic subjects of international law. The jumping-off point for most definitions of international law is that it is law made by states to govern relations between them. The recognition of other entities as limited subjects of international law has not led to a role for them in constructing international law. Hence, although peoples may have a right of self-determination, they have in fact been largely excluded from *participation* in the interpretation and development of the right.

---

[20] Note of 30 December 1918, quoted in R. Lansing, *The Peace Negotiations – A Personal Narrative* (New York: Houghton Mifflin Co., 1921), p. 97.

[21] This is true whether or not, as some writers have argued, the right of self-determination in international law is 'the right of State A to claim from State B that the latter State respect any peoples' self-determination' and whether or not a particular rule of self-determination is addressed to states. G. Arangio-Ruiz, 'Human Rights and Non-Intervention in the Helsinki Final Act' (1977-IV) 157 Hague Recueil 195 at 230. See the discussion in A. Cassese, *Self-Determination of Peoples: A Legal Reappraisal* (Cambridge: Cambridge University Press, 1995), pp. 141–7 and in R. Ranjeva, 'Peoples and National Liberation Movements' in M. Bedjaoui (ed.), *International Law: Achievements and Prospects* (Paris: UNESCO/Dordrecht: Martinus Nijhoff, 1991), pp. 101–12.

This attitude toward *participation* fits with an image of *identity*, much as Lansing's analytical argument about norm-type followed from his characterization of the groups likely to claim self-determination. Historically, the depiction of minorities and peoples as irrational, inferior or backward made it seem natural that they not participate in international law. Chris Tennant demonstrates generally how from 1945 to 1993, the representation of indigenous peoples in the international legal literature changed from ignoble to noble primitive and how this change in representational practices paralleled a change in the engagement of international institutions with indigenous peoples.[22]

Even when various individual and collective entitlements to petition international institutions did exist, the attitude toward the petitioners influenced the effectiveness of this participation. During the period of decolonization after World War II, for example, much use was made of a broad right to petition the United Nations concerning trust territories.[23] However, native petitioners tended to be regarded as objects of paternalism and well-meaning curiosity. A 1953 UN pamphlet on the United Nations' work for dependent peoples, as the inhabitants of trust and non-self-governing territories were termed, opened with a 'you are there' account of a petitioner from the French-administered Cameroons addressing the General Assembly. Having placed the reader in 'the public gallery of one of the great committee rooms' of the General Assembly, above the tiers of attentive delegates seated at 'curved and polished tables', the description, heavy with approving wonder, of the petitioner proceeded:

> It is an eloquent voice, expressing thoughts and ideas as fluently as might those who listen. It is also the voice of a practical mind...
>
> It is a man – a humble and modest man – who has made a long and costly journey from his native land to tell of the desire of his people to rise above their present low level of development and their political dependence.[24]

If assumptions about identity undermined such opportunities as there were for groups claiming self-determination to participate in, challenge or vindicate the construction of themselves and their right to choose their place in the international legal order, their *participation* could also

---

[22] C. Tennant, 'Indigenous Peoples, International Institutions, and the International Legal Literature from 1945–1993' (1994) 16 *Human Rights Quarterly* 1.
[23] UN Charter, Art.87(b).
[24] United Nations, *A Sacred Trust. The Work of the United Nations for Dependent People* (1953), p. 1.

be affected by the approach taken to *interpretation*. In resolving the issue of what self-determination means, an author validates or authorizes a theory of the interpretation of international law. The choice of an interpretive theory determines how to talk about the meaning of self-determination: it endorses one kind of reasoning and invites one kind of response to argument. In defining the sort of conversation we can have in international law about self-determination, an interpretive theory also contemplates and advantages a certain sort of speaker.[25] Consider, for example, the seemingly innocuous classification of self-determination as a legal rule or a legal principle.[26] As Lansing's note has already illustrated, such an analytical first step may have a profound effect on interpretation by establishing how and how far the meaning of self-determination can be developed. Michel Virally[27] argues that reasoning with rules is essentially conservative: this painstaking induction keeps time with a homogeneous and stable international society, such as the vanished world of European diplomacy prior to World War I. Principles, which add a deductive dimension to the interpretation of international law, respond to the imperatives of a diverse and changing international society. In addition, the classification of self-determination as rule or principle may establish who can speak effectively about its meaning. The elaboration of a rule tends to be a narrower and more technical exercise than the interpretation of a principle. To build an effective argument for the evolution of a rule requires an extensive knowledge of precedents, mastery of traditional methods of interpretation, and professional reputation. But, as between developed and developing world, state actors and non-state actors, there are obvious disparities in access to the necessary evidence of state practice and in the proficiency and stature needed to turn it to advantage. Moreover, the most readily available evidence of state practice is the national digests prepared by or with the government of the state concerned, which favours states with the resources and expertise to compile them.[28] In contrast, principles may, to quote Virally's warning, 'constituent une idée-force, accessible à tous, échappant, par

---

[25] See White, 'Law as Rhetoric', 697. See also J. B. White, *Justice as Translation: An Essay in Cultural and Legal Criticism* (Chicago: University of Chicago Press, 1990), especially pp. 97–102.

[26] See Chapter 1 below.

[27] M. Virally, 'Le rôle des "principes" dans le développement du droit international' in *Recueil d'études de droit international: En hommage à Paul Guggenheim* (Geneva: Faculté de droit de l'Université de Genève & Institut universitaire de hautes études internationales, 1968), pp. 531–54 at pp. 539–45.

[28] See Cassese, *Self-Determination of Peoples*, p. 93; V. Lowe, 'The Marginalisation of Africa' (2000) 94 *Proceedings of the American Society of International Law* (forthcoming);

conséquent, dans une large mesure, au contrôle des juristes et exerçant sur le fonctionnement des modes de formation du droit une action dynamique' ('constitute an idea-force, *accessible to all, largely escaping, as a consequence, the control of jurists* and dynamically affecting the functioning of the ways of creating law').[29]

From the examples given so far of the relationship between identity, participation and interpretation, we can begin to see why the process of giving meaning to the right of self-determination might seem alien or unfair to those who claim the right. Indeed, it becomes apparent that the persuasiveness of a particular meaning may rely on the interrelation of these three forms of exclusion. In this light, Part I of the book (Chapters 1–3) discusses the current debate in the international law literature over whether the right of self-determination of peoples in international law includes a right of secession, and Parts II (Chapters 4–5) and III (Chapters 6–8) look at cases where an international legal authority has been squarely confronted with some aspect of the debate. Part II examines anew those instances relied on by most authors of the post-Cold War period in their interpretation of self-determination: the 1975 International Court of Justice advisory opinion in *Western Sahara*, Opinion No. 2 issued in 1992 by the European Communities Conference on Yugoslavia Arbitration Commission, the 1995 International Court of Justice judgment in the *East Timor* case between Portugal and Australia, the adoption of ILO Convention (No. 169) concerning Indigenous and Tribal Peoples in Independent Countries and the preparation by the United Nations Working Group on Indigenous Populations of a draft declaration on the rights of indigenous peoples. Whereas the cases treated in Part II involve cultural difference, the series of cases in Part III are chosen to develop women's relationship to self-determination. Part III looks at women in the post-World War I plebiscites in Europe, women in trust territories administered under the UN Charter and indigenous women in the 1981 views of the UN Human Rights Committee in *Lovelace* v. *Canada*.

The value of the book's approach, it is hoped, lies not only in the richer and more precise understanding that its matrix of diversity gives of the current scholarly controversy over a right to secede and the precedents that figure in the controversy. It lies also in what this concrete case-study contributes, in turn, to the analysis of diversity in international law generally, starting with a new micro-history. Whereas the

O. Schachter, 'International Law in Theory and Practice' (1982-V) 178 Hague Recueil 9 at 61; O. Schachter, *International Law in Theory and Practice* (Dordrecht: Martinus Nijhoff, 1991), p. 36.

[29] (Translation and emphasis mine) Virally, 'Le rôle des "principes"', p. 543.

scholarship on self-determination treats the importance of judgments, arbitral decisions and other authoritative texts of self-determination as stepping stones in the development of the right, the book shows their importance as successive encounters with marginalized groups – from nomadic desert peoples to indigenous women – and their perspectives on international law.

To appreciate this shift in standpoint, we have only to think back to the petitioner from the French-administered Cameroons addressing the General Assembly. By depicting him as an anthropological curiosity under the delegates' attentive gaze, the UN pamphlet told us little of his own sense of self and reasons for being there. In fact, the petitioner was Guillaume Bissek, and he represented the political party *Evolution sociale camerounaise*.[30] For him and Ruben Um Nyobé, the petitioner heard as a representative of the *Union des Populations du Cameroun*,[31] the issues were independence and unification with the British-administered Cameroons. Bissek spoke mainly about the programme of reforms needed to prepare the French-administered Cameroons for independence, reforms that included the reorganization of traditional indigenous society to produce a hybrid of the French state apparatus and the traditional system of chiefdoms. The hearing of Bissek and Um Nyobé[32] led to a General Assembly resolution recommending that the Trusteeship Council give priority to the matter of the French-administered Cameroons, take the petitioners' positions into consideration and conduct a special study of the matter.[33]

Telling the history of self-determination in this way is valuable both in and of itself and because it destabilizes familiar accounts of international law. A landmark in the history of self-determination such as the plebiscites in Europe between the wars thus becomes significant as the first time that women had the right to participate in an international expression of popular sovereignty.[34] On a standard

---

[30] GAOR, 8th Sess., C.4, 388th Mtg., UN Doc. A/C.4/SR.388 (1953), pp. 493–6 (Oral statement of Guillaume Bissek). For the full text of the statement, see UN Doc. A/C.4/257.

[31] GAOR, 8th Sess., C.4, 393rd Mtg., UN Doc. A/C.4/SR.393 (1953), pp. 526–8 (Oral statement of Ruben Um Nyobé). For the full text of the statement, see UN Doc. A/C.4/261. See generally S. N. Grovogui, *Sovereigns, Quasi-Sovereigns, and Africans: Race and Self-Determination in International Law* (Minneapolis: University of Minnesota Press, 1996), p. 198 (discussing Um Nyobé's criticism of the United Nations system for providing such limited mechanisms for the participation of the colonized).

[32] GAOR, 8th Sess., C.4, 393rd and 394th Mtgs., UN Doc. A/C.4/SR.393-4 (1953), pp. 528–38.

[33] Hearing of Petitioners from the Trust Territory of the Cameroons under French Administration, GA Res. 758 (VIII) (1953).

[34] See Chapter 6 below.

account, the significance of these plebiscites, provided for in the peace treaties ending World War I, lies in the departure from the traditional international law on transfer of territory by giving the population of certain border areas the opportunity to choose between the two states disputing the territory. 'Peoples...are not to be bartered about from sovereignty to sovereignty as if they were mere chattels and pawns in a game,' declared President Wilson in 1918.[35] For women, this exercise in self-determination of peoples or 'selves' was also about whether women were included in the determining 'self'.[36] As such, the plebiscites introduced into international law the most important women's issue of the time: the vote for women. Women's groups were present at the 1919 Paris Peace Conference: international women's organizations already existed, several international conferences of women were held around this time with the goal of influencing the peace process, and women lobbied the delegations to the Peace Conference on women's rights and other issues concerning the peace treaties and proposed league of nations. Given that the treaties were negotiated when the tide had just begun to turn for women's suffrage, however, it is remarkable that women were given the vote in all the plebiscites held. Only two of the five powers that composed the Supreme Council at the Peace Conference, the United States and Britain, were even close to enfranchising women fully. The other three, France, Italy and Japan, did not extend the franchise to women for over two decades. Of the states involved in the plebiscites, five had given women the vote, but two would not do so for some time.

The practice of self-determination thus becomes a struggle for inclusion, not only a people's struggle to become part of the world of sovereign states, but their struggle to incorporate their own story into international law. Self-determination has always been seen as revolutionary. Whether or not it has actually become the acid test for the legitimacy of international law, as István Bibó maintains,[37] self-determination appears to give peoples a right to participate in the international legal order, an issue previously decided by the fact of power alone. Its

---

[35] 'Four Points' speech to Congress, 11 February 1918, quoted in S. Wambaugh, *Plebiscites Since the World War with a Collection of Official Documents* (2 vols., Washington: Carnegie Endowment for International Peace, 1933), vol. I, p. 11.

[36] The distinction between self and determining self is illustrated by the position of children: children belong to the self whose future is decided by the exercise of self-determination, but do not participate in that exercise.

[37] I. Bibó, *The Paralysis of International Institutions and the Remedies: A Study of Self-Determination, Concord Among the Major Powers, and Political Arbitration* (New York: John Wiley & Sons, 1976), pp. 17–34.

revolutionary potential may now also be seen in the place it provides for non-state groups and their members to contest the images of identity, exercise of participation and model of reasoning involved in the interpretation of self-determination. Self-determination serves, in John and Jean Comaroff's terms, to transform hegemony into ideology, where

> hegemony consists of constructs and conventional practices that have come to permeate a political community; ideology originates in the assertions of a particular social group. Hegemony is beyond direct argument; ideology is more likely to be perceived as a matter of inimical opinion and interest and hence is more open to contestation. Hegemony, at its most effective, is mute; ideology invites argument.[38]

Presenting an alternative account of self-determination as a series of challenges from the margins, as the book does in Parts II and III, reveals this counter-hegemonic function that self-determination has sometimes performed; operating not just as a norm to be applied, but as an opportunity to expose the exclusions and inequalities of international law. More broadly, the book introduces and develops the critiques of cultural and gender biases that emerged in this practice.

In addition to the historical and critical dimensions of diversity in international law, Parts II and III contribute to an appreciation of the reconstructive dimension by showing that international law and international institutions have sought to respond, if in ad hoc and partial fashion, to the diversity-based critiques raised in a number of key contests over the interpretation of self-determination.[39] The response is most visible in the meaning given to the 'self'[40] and the right of self-determination. But there may also be hints of a deeper change in the methods and processes of interpretation, aimed at redressing exclusion or inequality by developing a broader-based legitimacy for the meaning of self-determination or at persuading a more diverse community. Parts II and III explore the possibility of a deeper change, structured, like the critiques that provoked it, by some combination of *identity*, *participation*

---

[38] J. and J. Comaroff, *Ethnography and the Historical Imagination* (Boulder, Colo.: Westview Press, 1992), p. 29.

[39] Compare S. J. Anaya, *Indigenous Peoples in International Law* (New York: Oxford University Press, 1996), p. 4 (identifying as his 'central contention' that 'international law, although once an instrument of colonialism, has developed and continues to develop, however grudgingly or imperfectly, to support indigenous peoples' demands').

[40] In current international law, the subject of the right of self-determination is a 'people'. However, since I consider a longer and broader line of cases, I will often use the term 'self' instead of 'people'.

and *interpretation*. At their best, these shifts may all be seen as directed toward an ideal of legal interpretation for a world that is simultaneously integrating and diversifying, although they vary in which of identity, participation and interpretation they emphasize and how they do so. To give one example, what it might mean for international legal concepts to become valid across differences of identity, whether culture or gender, is powerfully demonstrated by Judge Dillard's separate opinion in the *Western Sahara* case.[41] One of the questions in *Western Sahara* was what the legal ties were between the territory of the Western Sahara and the Kingdom of Morocco and the Mauritanian entity in the late nineteenth century; what was, in Judge Dillard's words, 'the nature of legal ties in a time long past and in an area with its own peculiar attributes'.[42] How should international law treat a tie between the Sultan of Morocco and the marabout Ma ul-'Aineen or between the Emir of the Adrar and the chiefs of nomadic tribes?[43] Judge Dillard developed two approaches to the concept of 'law' and 'legal' ties, using the second to expose the cultural specificity of the first. On his first approach, a tie is legal 'if it expresses a *relationship* in which there is a *sense of obligation* of a special kind'.[44] While this sense of obligation need not be inspired by the fear of sanctions, it must be 'pervasively felt as part of the way of life of the people'.[45] It is not sufficient for the inhabitants of the territory to obey the wishes of the Sultan or the Emir out of a feeling of religious affiliation or courtesy; they must do so out of a sense of deferential obligation. The qualitative difference is between their sense that they must obey and that they merely ought to obey. Judge Dillard's second approach to the nature of legal ties criticizes the first approach as premised on a post-Reformation Western-oriented society and as inappropriate to a society such as existed in the Sahara. In societies influenced by the Reformation, the sense of obligation to the sovereign is 'focused on his secular authority which is not only paramount but permits a dissociation between obligations owed to the State and those owed to religious authority'.[46] This sharp distinction between modes of authority was not characteristic of the society and popular consciousness that prevailed in the Sahara. In a society that understood power as neither secular nor religious, Judge Dillard argued, it would be artificial to reject a tie as legal because it does not reflect a sense of obligation 'owed vertically to the secular power of someone in authority'.[47] Judge

---

[41] *Western Sahara*, Advisory Opinion, ICJ Reports 1975, p. 12 at p. 116. See Chapter 4 below.
[42] *Ibid.*, p. 125.   [43] *Ibid.*   [44] (Emphasis in original) *Ibid.*
[45] *Ibid.*   [46] *Ibid.*   [47] *Ibid.*, p. 126.

Dillard's alternative approach considers legal ties to be those that are experienced as belonging to a larger collectivity: 'The important thing is that the tribes criss-crossing in the Western Sahara felt themselves to be part of a larger whole, while also claiming rights in the territory focused on the intermittent possession of water-holes, burial grounds and grazing pastures'.[48] Judge Dillard's self-criticism illuminates both how deeply claims of difference and diversity challenge core concepts in the international law of self-determination and how judges may have the imagination needed to contend seriously with these claims.[49]

Understood as the expression of a changing relationship between interpretation, identity and participation, the historical practice of self-determination emerges in Parts II and III as more complex than the stands taken by international lawyers in the current debate over the meaning of self-determination and seen in Part I. Indeed, if we abandon the rigid optic of the scholarship on self-determination, we can see the fluidity of interpretive practice[50] and in it the shape of future possibilities.[51]

Methodology

In order to afford the fullest perspective on how the right of self-determination has been used in international law, the book considers an argument to be about self-determination if it is presented as such. The book also discusses certain decisions that are not framed in terms of self-determination,[52] where the decision involves an issue normatively

---

[48] Ibid.
[49] Compare L. V. Prott, *The Latent Power of Culture and the International Judge* (Abingdon: Oxon.: Professional Books, 1979), p. 232 (citing Judge Dillard's separate opinion in the *Western Sahara* case as an 'encouraging trend' in this respect).
[50] Compare A. Bunting, 'Particularity of Rights, Diversity of Contexts: Women, International Human Rights and the Case of Early Marriage' (SJD thesis, University of Toronto, 1999). (In contrast to the universalism/relativism impasse in the international human rights literature, variance and 'particularization' of rights already exist in practice.) See also A.-B. S. Preis, 'Human Rights as Cultural Practice: An Anthropological Critique' (1996) 18 *Human Rights Quarterly* 286.
[51] Compare D. Kennedy, 'A New Stream of International Law Scholarship' (1988) 7 *Wisconsin International Law Journal* 1 at 47–9 (on imagining 'a more thorough turn to the margins'); D. Otto, 'Subalternity and International Law: The Problems of Global Community and the Incommensurability of Difference' (1996) 5:3 *Social and Legal Studies* 337 (developing a related approach to the processes by which international law is formulated, as opposed to interpreted).
[52] Indeed, one of these decisions, *Sandra Lovelace v. Canada* (Communication No. 24/1977, formerly Communication No. R.6/24), GAOR, 36th Sess., Supp. No. 40, UN Doc. A/36/40

similar to one raised by self-determination and sheds light on the issue in the framework of self-determination.

Choice of literature

Over the past century, authors from the expert to the relatively untutored in international law have produced a steady stream of work on self-determination, with torrents of writing flowing from the breakup of empires from the Habsburg and Ottoman empires after World War I to the far-flung colonial empires after World War II to the Soviet Union in 1991.[53] While these torrents follow the contours of the preceding

(1981), p. 166, discussed in Chapter 8, would have been inadmissible if framed in terms of the right of self-determination of peoples under Article 1 of the International Covenant on Civil and Political Rights, New York, 16 December 1966, in force 23 March 1976, 999 UNTS 171, instead of the rights of minorities under Article 27. See below at note 73 and accompanying text. It is unclear, however, whether in making an argument under the article on 'minorities', Sandra Lovelace understood herself to be foreclosing the possibility of also identifying her community as a 'people'. See, for example, *R. L. v. Canada* (Communication No. 358/1989), GAOR, 47th Sess., Supp. No. 40, UN Doc. A/47/40 (1994), p. 358 at p. 361.

[53] Book-length treatments alone since the end of the Cold War include P. Aikio and M. Scheinin (eds.), *Operationalizing the Right of Indigenous Peoples to Self-Determination* (Turku/Åbo: Institute for Human Rights, Åbo Akademi University, 2000); Cassese, *Self-Determination of Peoples*; J. Castellino, *International Law and Self-Determination: The Interplay of the Politics of Territorial Possession with Formulations of Post-Colonial 'National' Identity* (The Hague: Martinus Nijhoff, 2000); T. Christakis, *Le droit à l'autodétermination en dehors des situations de décolonisation* (Paris: La documentation française, 1999); D. Clark and R. Williamson (eds.), *Self-Determination: International Perspectives* (New York: St Martin's Press, 1996); W. Danspeckgruber with A. Watts (eds.), *Self-Determination and Self-Administration: A Sourcebook* (Boulder, Colo.: Lynne Rienner, 1997); J. C. Duursma, *Fragmentation and the International Relations of Micro-States: Self-Determination and Statehood* (Cambridge: Cambridge University Press, 1996); E. Gayim, *The Principle of Self-Determination: A Study of its Historical and Contemporary Legal Evolution* (Oslo: Norwegian Institute of Human Rights, 1990); Grovogui, *Sovereigns, Quasi-Sovereigns, and Africans*; M. H. Halperin and D. J. Scheffer with P. L. Small, *Self-Determination in the New World Order* (Washington, D.C.: Carnegie Endowment for International Peace, 1992); H. Hannum, *Autonomy, Sovereignty, and Self-Determination: The Accommodation of Conflicting Rights* (rev. edn, Philadelphia: University of Pennsylvania Press, 1996); K. Henrard, *Devising an Adequate System of Minority Protection: Individual Human Rights, Minority Rights, and the Right to Self-Determination* (The Hague: Martinus Nijhoff, 2000); M.C. Lâm, *At the Edge of the State: Indigenous Peoples and Self-Determination* (Ardsley: N.Y.: Transnational Publishers, 2000); R. McCorquodale (ed.), *Self-Determination in International Law* (Aldershot: Ashgate/Dartmouth, 2000); T. D. Musgrave, *Self-Determination and National Minorities* (Oxford: Clarendon Press, 1997); M. Sellers (ed.), *The New World Order: Sovereignty, Human Rights and the Self-Determination of Peoples* (Oxford: Berg, 1996); Z. Skurbaty, *As If Peoples Mattered: A Critical Appraisal of 'Peoples' and 'Minorities' from the International Human Rights Perspective and Beyond* (The Hague: Martinus Nijhoff, 2000).

scholarship, each is shaped by the issues of its time. Certain issues that once structured the discussion of self-determination – for instance, whether the principle was even part of international law[54] – are now largely beyond dispute, and other issues have come to define the debate.

In the international legal literature of the post-Cold War period, the issue of self-determination, broadly stated, is whether the right of self-determination of peoples has been spent by overseas decolonization. It is common ground that the population of an overseas colony is a 'people',[55] that these peoples have a right of self-determination and that their right of self-determination gives them the choice of independent statehood. Controversy arises over who else is a 'people', whether other peoples have a right of self-determination, and if so, how they can exercise their right of self-determination. Discussion of these questions tends to be organized around the notions of external and internal self-determination, where external self-determination refers to the choice of international status and internal self-determination to some – authors differ as to what – range of political entitlements within the state. In the contemporary literature, the right of external self-determination is essentially the question of a right to secede.

Part I of the book, which discusses the post-Cold War scholarship on self-determination, focuses on the treatment of external self-determination. This should not be taken to mean that internal self-determination is not worth pursuing or that it can be strictly separated from external self-determination. Indeed, as will be seen in Chapter 2, some scholars interpret existing international law as predicating external self-determination on the failure of internal self-determination: a group's right to secede is triggered only where, depending on the particular scholar's view of internal self-determination, democracy, minority rights

---

For an indication of the periodical literature, see D. Turp, 'A Select Bibliography on the Right of Self-Determination of Peoples' in Clark and Williamson, *Self-Determination*, pp. 391–406.

There is also a considerable literature on self-determination and secession by non-international lawyers. Books include V. O. Bartkus, *The Dynamic of Secession* (Cambridge: Cambridge University Press, 1999); A. Buchanan, *Secession: The Morality of Political Divorce from Fort Sumter to Lithuania and Quebec* (Boulder, Colo.: Westview Press, 1991); M. Moore (ed.), *National Self-Determination and Secession* (New York: Oxford University Press, 1998).

[54] See Cassese, *Self-Determination of Peoples*, pp. 126–8, nn. 44–5. (The references that Cassese gives for the view that self-determination is a principle of international law are more recent by decades than those he provides for the opposite view.)

[55] The idea of a colonial population as a 'people' is discussed critically in Chapter 2 and in connection with the *Western Sahara* case in Chapter 4.

or autonomy within the state is insufficient to secure the group's well-being. The reason for the book's focus on external self-determination is rather that external self-determination has attracted the widest range of interpretation and best shows the nature and history of the debate. In comparison, the theory and practice of internal self-determination tend to fall within the European liberal tradition[56] and have only a short recent history in international law.[57]

Similarly, because the book's interest is exploring critically the dominant discourse of self-determination, which concentrates on political self-determination, it leaves aside important feminist and Third World critiques based on the interdependence of political and economic self-determination. Both feminist and Third World authors have observed that the political expression of self-determination receives much greater attention in international law than its economic, social or cultural expression. This observation is even more pertinent since the 'liberal' revolutions in Eastern Europe have prompted a number of international lawyers to turn their attention to internal political self-determination, often synonymous with an entitlement to liberal democracy, while the concomitant disappearance of the communist bloc has subtracted from the voices arguing that economic, as well as political, self-determination is necessary for a people to realize independent statehood.[58] In 'The Hunger Trap: Women, Food, and Self-Determination', Christine Chinkin and Shelley Wright criticize this hierarchy in the interpretation of self-determination as an international human right, arguing that 'food,

[56] Compare A. Michalska, 'Rights of Peoples to Self-Determination in International Law' in W. Twining (ed.), *Issues of Self-Determination* (Aberdeen: Aberdeen University Press, 1991), pp. 71–90 at pp. 83–4 (discussing differences between liberal and Marxist conceptions of internal self-determination).

[57] See e.g. G. H. Fox, 'Self-Determination in the Post-Cold War Era: A New Internal Focus?' (1995) 16 *Michigan Journal of International Law* 733; T. M. Franck, 'The Democratic Entitlement' (1994) 29 *University of Richmond Law Review* 1; T. M. Franck, 'The Emerging Right to Democratic Governance' (1992) 86 *American Journal of International Law* 46; K. Myntti, 'National Minorities, Indigenous Peoples and Various Modes of Political Participation' and P. Thornberry, 'Minorities, Indigenous Peoples, Participation' in F. Horn (ed.), *Minorities and Their Right of Political Participation* (Rovaniemi: Northern Institute for Environmental and Minority Law at the University of Lapland, 1996); A. Rosas, 'Internal Self-Determination', J. Salmon, 'Internal Aspects of the Right to Self-Determination: Towards a Democratic Legitimacy Principle?', and P. Thornberry, 'The Democratic or Internal Aspect of Self-Determination With Some Remarks on Federalism' in C. Tomuschat (ed.), *Modern Law of Self-Determination* (Dordrecht: Martinus Nijhoff, 1993).

[58] E.g. A. A. Kovalev, *Samoopredelenie i ekonomicheskaia nezavisimost' narodov* (Moscow: Mezhdunarodnye otnosheniia, 1988); N. A. Ushakov, 'Mezhdunarodno-pravovye aspekty obrazovaniia Soiuza SSR' [1972] *Sovetskii Ezhegodnik Mezhdunarodnogo Prava* 11 at 16.

shelter, clean water, a healthy environment, peace, and a stable existence must be the first priorities in how we define or "determine" the "self" of both individuals and groups'.[59] Third World critiques of self-determination include the lasting violence done to pre-colonial selves by the use of colonial borders to define the self,[60] the imposition of a Western idea of progress in the application of self-determination,[61] and the travesty of self-determination where formal independence is accompanied by continued economic dependence on developed states.[62] While the book discusses the first[63] and second[64] of these critiques as they played out in the interpretive practice of self-determination, it does not pursue the third.

In short, the book is not intended as an exhaustive treatment of the critiques or critical potential of self-determination, but as one contribution to what needs to be an ongoing interrogation of the concept from many perspectives.

Choice of case-studies

From the discussion in Part I of the debate over the interpretation of self-determination in the post-Cold War literature, Parts II and III turn

[59] C. Chinkin and S. Wright, 'The Hunger Trap: Women, Food, and Self-Determination' (1993) 14 *Michigan Journal of International Law* 262 at 294. See also H. Charlesworth and C. Chinkin, *The Boundaries of International Law: A Feminist Analysis* (Manchester: Manchester University Press, 2000), p. 163; R. McCorquodale, 'Secrets and Lies: Economic Globalisation and Women's Human Rights' (1998) 19 *Australian Year Book of International Law* 73 at 82.

[60] E.g. A. A. Mazrui, 'The African State as a Political Refugee: Institutional Collapse and Human Displacement' [July 1995] *International Journal of Refugee Law* Special Issue 21; M. wa Mutua, 'Putting Humpty Dumpty Back Together Again: The Dilemmas of the Post-Colonial African State' (1995) 21 *Brooklyn Journal of International Law* 505; M. wa Mutua, 'Why Redraw the Map of Africa: A Moral and Legal Inquiry' (1995) 16 *Michigan Journal of International Law* 1113; E. K. M. Yakpo, 'The African Concept of *Uti Possidetis* – Need for Change?' in E. Yakpo and T. Boumedra (eds.), *Liber Amicorum Judge Mohammed Bedjaoui* (The Hague: Kluwer Law International, 1999), pp. 271–90.

For the argument that international law's failure to articulate a right of self-determination beyond independence within the old colonial borders facilitated the repression of minorities within the new African states that emerged from decolonization, see e.g. I. A. Gambari with M. Uhomoibi, 'Self-Determination and Nation Building in Post-Cold War Africa: Problems and Prospects' in Danspeckgruber, *Self-Determination and Self-Administration*, pp. 273–82 at p. 273; O. C. Okafor, *Re-Defining Legitimate Statehood: International Law and State Fragmentation in Africa* (The Hague: Martinus Nijhoff, 2000), pp. 92–125.

[61] E.g. Grovogui, *Sovereigns, Quasi-Sovereigns, and Africans*.

[62] E.g. M. Bedjaoui, *Towards a New International Economic Order* (Paris: UNESCO, 1979), pp. 87–90; Gambari, 'Nation Building in Post-Cold War Africa', pp. 281–2.

[63] See Chapter 4 below.   [64] See Chapter 7 below.

to the practice of self-determination as it bears on that debate. The case-studies in Parts II and III are moments in the progressive interpretation of self-determination when an international legal authority is confronted with an issue of self-determination that relates to the current debate over meaning and tells us something about the underlying contest between different schools of interpretation and normative visions of self-determination.

The notion of interpretation used to select the case-studies is one that allows for some variation in the usual identification of the exercise with the application of existing norms to a controversy by a third party. Beyond the decisions of international courts and tribunals, the determination of what norms of international law exist and what follows from them in a specific context (not necessarily a single controversy) may be seen to occur in a variety of international settings. More important, since participants may disagree on the line between interpretation and legislation generally or on the objective of a specific international institution or process, a certain flexibility is needed in order to permit the most extensive consideration of self-determination as a contested relationship between interpretation, identity and participation. The third party in the case-studies is not always an adjudicator because the book takes the view that others may tend to function as third parties in particular institutional and procedural settings. That is, the book treats the existence of a third party and the disinterestedness of the third party as a matter of degree.[65] Although perhaps not standard, this view is familiar in international law from Georges Scelle's famous concept of *dédoublement fonctionnel*, whereby the individual identity and interests of states in the international system are tempered by their functional duality as advocate in their own cause and judge, in lieu of a flourishing international judiciary, of other states' actions.[66]

As will be apparent, Parts II and III leave out a few of the well-known decisions on self-determination. Cases that antedate the recognition of self-determination in international law (*Aaland Islands*)[67] or that

---

[65] Compare F. V. Kratochwil, *Rules, Norms, and Decisions. On the Conditions of Practical and Legal Reasoning in International Relations and Domestic Affairs* (Cambridge: Cambridge University Press, 1989), pp. 181–211.

[66] G. Scelle, *Précis de droit des gens. Principes et systématique* (Paris: Recueil Sirey, 1932) (Première Partie), pp. 50–7. See also B. H. Weston, R. A. Falk and A. A. D'Amato, *International Law and World Order: A Problem-Oriented Casebook* (St Paul: West, 1980), p. 245.

[67] *Report of International Committee of Jurists* (Larnaude, Struycken, Huber), LNOJ Sp. Supp. No. 3 (October 1920) 3; *Report of the Commission of Rapporteurs* (Beyens, Calonder, Elkus), LN Council Doc. B7/21/68/106 (16 April 1921).

are remarkable chiefly for that recognition (*Namibia*)[68] are excluded because they are not about the working out of the tensions in the international legal norm, although a case like the *Aaland Islands* will often enter into interpretations of self-determination that seek to recover a lost strand of meaning. While the interwar European plebiscites also antedate the recognition of self-determination in international law, the study of women and the plebiscites is included as an instance where self-determination was, in fact, given concrete legal effect. Although many writers on self-determination are attentive to the UN Human Rights Committee's interpretation of the right of self-determination in Article 1(1) of the International Covenant on Civil and Political Rights,[69] a case-study is not devoted to it because the Committee has not gone beyond the most general indication of what self-determination means in the Covenant. The Committee has had the opportunity to interpret Article 1 in the course of its two main functions: considering reports from and complaints against state parties. State parties are obliged to report periodically to the Committee.[70] In addition, they have the option of recognizing the Committee's competence to hear interstate 'communications' under the Covenant[71] and individual 'communications' under the Optional Protocol.[72] However, the Committee has made clear that Article 1 cannot be invoked under the Optional Protocol because the right of self-determination is a right of peoples, whereas the Optional Protocol mechanism only allows the Committee to hear claims by individuals concerning the violation of individual rights.[73] While it is nevertheless possible for the Committee's views on individual communications to shed light on Article 1 through its relationships to other articles, the Committee has not explicitly availed itself of this

---

[68] *Namibia (South West Africa)*, Advisory Opinion, ICJ Reports 1971, p. 16.

[69] International Covenant on Civil and Political Rights. The identical article is contained in the International Covenant on Economic, Social and Cultural Rights, New York, 16 December 1966, in force 3 January 1976, 993 UNTS 3, although this has received less attention.

[70] International Covenant on Civil and Political Rights, Art. 40. [71] *Ibid.*, Arts. 41–2.

[72] Optional Protocol to the International Covenant on Civil and Political Rights, New York, 16 December 1966, in force 23 March 1976, 999 UNTS 171.

[73] See *Bernard Ominayak, Chief of the Lubicon Lake Band* v. *Canada* (Communication No. 167/1984), GAOR, 45th Sess., Supp. 40, UN Doc. A/45/40 (1990), vol. II, p. 1; *Ivan Kitok* v. *Sweden* (Communication No. 197/1985), GAOR, 43rd Sess., Supp. No. 40, UN Doc. A/43/40 (1988), p. 221. See also General Comment No. 23(50) of the Human Rights Committee, Regarding Article 27, GAOR, 49th Sess., Supp. 40, UN Doc. A/49/40 (1994), vol. I, p. 107 para. 3.1.

possibility.⁷⁴ There is no restriction on the Committee's competence to hear interstate communications regarding the right of self-determination,⁷⁵ but an interstate communication has never been brought. Issued under its consideration of state reports,⁷⁶ the Committee's 1984 General Comment on self-determination⁷⁷ has been diplomatically described by former Committee member Torkel Opsahl as 'perhaps somewhat less helpful in providing guidance for practice' than the Committee's comments on less politically sensitive areas.⁷⁸ In so far as the Committee has publicized its understanding of self-determination, it has been through its concluding observations on the reports of individual states. However, even on Committee member Martin Scheinin's detailed analysis, the concluding observations have contained little or nothing on external self-determination other than in the least contentious cases of decolonization.⁷⁹

Finally, because the case-studies in Parts II and III are also episodes where groups traditionally marginalized in international law have used self-determination to oppose dominant representations of them and their rights in international law, something needs to be said about reading them as the pure expression of heroic resistance. It may be tempting to read the case-studies as the group's struggle to communicate its 'real' identity in opposition to the myths of international law. The voices heard in the case-studies are true in that the case-studies generally privilege the participants' own voices, through pleadings, petitions, statements, and sometimes interviews and other writings. In addition, the chapters on indigenous peoples (Chapter 5), colonial women (Chapter 7) and indigenous women (Chapter 8) touch on problems of voice; specifically, what speaking styles and modes of expression are required and whether

---

[74] Committee member Martin Scheinin identifies several cases where the Committee's views involve the interdependence of Article 1 and the article under direct consideration, but does not point to any actual mention of Article 1 or self-determination. M. Scheinin, 'The Right to Self-Determination under the Covenant on Civil and Political Rights' in Aikio and Scheinin, *Right of Indigenous Peoples*, pp. 179–99 at pp. 185, 187.

[75] M. Nowak, *UN Covenant on Civil and Political Rights: CCPR Commentary* (Kehl: N. P. Engel, 1993), p. 17.

[76] International Covenant on Civil and Political Rights, Art. 40(4).

[77] General Comment No. 12(21) of the Human Rights Committee, Regarding Article 1, GAOR, 39th Sess., Supp. 40, UN Doc. A/39/40 (1984), p. 142.

[78] T. Opsahl, 'The Human Rights Committee' in P. Alston (ed.), *The United Nations and Human Rights: A Critical Appraisal* (Oxford: Clarendon Press, 1992), pp. 369–443 at p. 414.

[79] Scheinin, 'The Right to Self-Determination under the Covenant on Civil and Political Rights', pp. 187–92, pp. 197–8.

they can do justice to participants' experiences. But beyond these problems of communication and communicability raised by international law, there are those that emanate from us as readers. The chapter on indigenous women, which centres on the *Lovelace* case, discusses the reductionism involved not only in the Human Rights Committee's views, but in subsequent interpretations of them. As such, it bears out Gayatri Chakravorty Spivak's observation that finding the subaltern is not as hard as actually entering into a two-way structure of responsibility with the subaltern: 'learning to learn without this quick-fix frenzy of doing good with an implicit assumption of cultural supremacy which is legitimized by unexamined romanticization'.[80]

Moreover, while sporadic access to the international legal system has enabled some traditionally marginalized groups to assert their self-understanding in opposition to the images of them created by international law, this participation is not unproblematic. If it improves on the practice of exclusion, it also raises issues of representation relative to the groups themselves. Just as the case-studies in Parts II and III dwell on what was and could be said, however, they concentrate on who was and could be present. An individual case-study does not step outside the parameters of interpretation to examine whose interests were really represented. Instead, Parts II and III seek to demonstrate these concerns through the order of presentation of the case-studies. Part II documents how marginalized groups commonly invoke the authenticity of the community with its own cultural traditions against the notions of equality and individual rights entrenched in international law, while Part III uses the example of women to show that identity is more complex and contingent than either of these representations. By examining, in so far as possible, women's own representations of their collective identity at different stages of self-determination, Part III problematizes the treatment of the self described in Part II. Within Part III, the movement, from European women in the plebiscites after World War I to Third World women during decolonization under the United Nations after World War II to indigenous women in connection with indigenous self-government, replicates the evolution of feminism[81]

---

[80] 'Subaltern Talk: Interview with the Editors' in D. Landry and G. MacLean (eds.), *The Spivak Reader: Selected Works of Gayatri Chakravorty Spivak* (New York: Routledge, 1996), pp. 287–308 at p. 293.

[81] Similarly, the structure of my 'Re/Statements: Feminism and State Sovereignty in International Law' (1993) 3 *Transnational Law and Contemporary Problems* 293 echoes the movement from liberal to cultural to post-modern feminism.

in response to critiques by Third World women[82] and women of colour.[83]

Despite this dialectical movement of the case-studies, they cannot hope to map identity in all its shifting complexity. On any approach to self-determination in international law, there will be identities that remain invisible. International law, despite the greater openness of international fora, increased savvy of international activists and growth of international civil society, remains predominantly an elite discourse and its institutions the precinct of state elites. This is particularly true of the case-studies here, which examine the interpretation of self-determination at the most elite and statist level. While the groups that figure in the case-studies are marginalized relative to the epicentre of international law, there is undoubtedly another story that could be told about who was marginalized by the representations made in the name of the group or even some cross-cutting or sub-group. As opposed to tracing the impact at the centre further out to the periphery, a story might be told about what is happening on the periphery, perhaps even quite independent of the goings-on at the centre.[84] An example might be the life that self-determination takes on at the grassroots level through the manifestos on self-determination by intellectuals in international civil society such as the 1976 Algiers Declaration of the Rights of Peoples.[85]

---

[82] E.g. T. T. Minh-ha, *Woman, Native, Other: Writing Postcoloniality and Feminism* (Bloomington: Indiana University Press, 1989); C. T. Mohanty, A. Russo and L. Torres (eds.), *Third World Women and the Politics of Feminism* (Bloomington: Indiana University Press, 1991); U. Narayan, *Dislocating Cultures. Identities, Traditions, and Third World Feminism* (New York: Routledge, 1997); V. Nesiah, 'Toward a Feminist Internationality: A Critique of US Feminist Legal Scholarship' (1993) 16 *Harvard Women's Law Journal* 189; J. Oloka-Onyango and S. Tamale, ' "The Personal is Political," or Why Women's Rights are Indeed Human Rights: An African Perspective on International Feminism' (1995) 17 *Human Rights Quarterly* 691.

[83] E.g. K. Crenshaw, 'Demarginalizing the Intersection of Race and Sex: A Black Feminist Critique of Antidiscrimination Doctrine, Feminist Theory and Antiracist Politics' [1989] *University of Chicago Legal Forum* 139; B. E. Hernández-Truyol, 'Borders (En)Gendered: Normativities, Latinas, and a LatCrit Paradigm' (1997) 72 *New York University Law Review* 882; b. hooks, *Feminist Theory: From Margin to Center* (Boston: South End Press, 1984); E. V. Spelman, *Inessential Woman: Problems of Exclusion in Feminist Thought* (Boston: Beacon Press, 1998).

[84] See A. Riles, *The Network Inside Out* (Ann Arbor: University of Michigan Press, 2000).

[85] Universal Declaration of the Rights of Peoples, Algiers, 4 July 1976, International Lelio Basso Foundation for the Rights and Liberation of Peoples, *Universal Declaration of the Rights of Peoples* (Paris: François Maspero, 1977); J. Crawford (ed.), *The Rights of Peoples* (Oxford: Clarendon Press, 1988), p. 187. Crawford glosses the Declaration as an 'unofficial declaration of scholars and publicists; basis for activities of Permanent Peoples' Tribunal, a private foundation'. *Ibid*. See generally F. Rigaux, *Pour une*

Or we might imagine that the right of self-determination of peoples takes on a local significance for parties to a dispute that has little to do with the familiar debate in international law. The book chooses to look at the central processes and institutions of international law because they have been heavily, and usually rightly, criticized, but often without much attention to whether they are actually impervious to change. It is as if each assault on the citadel is the first. But this erases, however inadvertently, whatever valiance and impact any earlier critical efforts may have had; it restores the original fortifications because international law, the target of criticism, is taken to remain the same. The book seeks instead to recuperate one history of critical engagement and the potential of this one history.

>déclaration universelle des droits des peuples: Identité nationale et coopération internationale (Lyon: Chronique Sociale, 1990).
>
>Other efforts include the Saskatoon Statement and Recommendations on Self-Determination, adopted on 6 March 1993 at the Martin Ennals Memorial Symposium on Self-Determination held in Saskatoon, Saskatchewan, published in Clark and Williamson, *Self-Determination*, App. 1–2; and the draft Convention on Self-Determination Through Self-Administration, which began as a Liechtenstein initiative at the UN in the early 1990s and later became part of the Liechtenstein Research Program on Self-Determination, Center of International Studies, Woodrow Wilson School of Public and International Affairs, Princeton University. For the draft Convention and associated research, see Danspeckgruber, *Self-Determination and Self-Administration*.

PART I • SELF-DETERMINATION IN POST-COLD WAR INTERNATIONAL LEGAL LITERATURE

1   The question of norm-type

'Un droit imprécis, voire marqué par la contradiction, est aussi un droit éminemment évolutif,' observes Michel Virally. ('A law that is imprecise, or even marked by contradiction, is also a law that is eminently evolutive.')[1] He connects the form that an international law norm takes to its ability to meet the needs of an international society in transition from a club of European states to a more equal and inclusive community. Virally's observation draws attention to an important but neglected point of contention in the debate among international lawyers over a right to secede – namely, how imprecise the law of self-determination is – and to the implications for diversity. This chapter pursues one particular aspect of this disagreement: the characterization of self-determination as a rule of international law, a principle of international law, or both.[2] To frame the discussion, the chapter uses Antonio Cassese's treatment of self-determination as both principle and rule in *Self-Determination of Peoples: A Legal Reappraisal*[3] and James Crawford's response in his review of the book.[4]

We need not accept Virally's mapping of the rule/principle distinction onto the dichotomies of conservative/progressive, disempowering/

---

[1] (Translation mine) M. Virally, 'Panorama du droit international contemporain' (1983-V) 183 Hague Recueil 9 at 175.

[2] It should be underscored that this is not the threadbare debate over whether self-determination is political principle or legal norm, but the lesser noticed question of legal norm-type. Nor are we in the realm of the 'general principles of law' recognized as a source of international law in Article 38(1)(c) of the *Statute of the International Court of Justice*. Statute of the International Court of Justice, 26 June 1945, 59 Stat. 1179, 145 BFSP (1943–5) 832 (1953).

[3] A. Cassese, *Self-Determination of Peoples: A Legal Reappraisal* (Cambridge: Cambridge University Press, 1995).

[4] J. Crawford, Book Review of *Self-Determination of Peoples: A Legal Reappraisal* by A. Cassese (1996) 90 *American Journal of International Law* 331.

empowering, homogeneous/heterogeneous.⁵ Indeed, we shall find that approaching self-determination as a principle is not necessarily always better suited to advancing substantive justice, procedural fairness and a thrivingly diverse international community. The proposition, however, provokes a set of questions that begin to reveal the structures at work in competing definitions of self-determination and the stakes in the choice of structure. Is there room in the interpretation of international law for a conversation about the meaning of self-determination? If so, what sort of conversation can we have? Who can participate? What does the conversation say about us as an international community? These are questions about the idea of *interpretation* that informs arguments about self-determination and the relationship of this idea to *participation* and *identity*. They tell us not what self-determination means, but how international lawyers say what they do about its meaning and how we, as readers and potential speakers, are implicated in it.

The first part of the chapter relates the categorization of self-determination as a norm-type to the openness and path of the interpretive process. The three subsequent parts correspond to three aspects of the significance that this categorization takes on in the context of international society: a mechanism for change, a practice of participation and a narration of the identity of that society.

Rules and principles

In the international law literature on self-determination, the tendency is to proceed as if self-determination could only be a rule. The result is either the formulation of a clear-cut rule, most often that only overseas colonies have the right of self-determination;⁶ or hand-wringing because no precise rule capable of guiding states and nationalists alike can be derived from practice, and international law is therefore sidelined in nationalist conflicts.⁷ For James Crawford, this search for a single,

---

⁵ M. Virally, 'Le rôle des "principes" dans le développement du droit international' in *Recueil d'études de droit international: En hommage à Paul Guggenheim* (Geneva: Faculté de droit de l'Université de Genève & Institut universitaire de hautes études internationales, 1968), pp. 531–54 at p. 539–45.

⁶ For a discussion of this position, see below Chapter 2, notes 13 and 14 and accompanying text.

⁷ M. Eisner, 'A Procedural Model for the Resolution of Secessionist Disputes' (1992) 33 *Harvard International Law Journal* 407 at 407–15; G. J. Simpson, 'The Diffusion of Sovereignty: Self-Determination in the Post-Colonial Age' in M. Sellers (ed.), *The New World Order: Sovereignty, Human Rights, and the Self-Determination of Peoples*

self-sufficient norm on self-determination is nonsensical. In his review of Antonio Cassese's *Self-Determination of Peoples*, he notes with approval that Cassese 'sees self-determination as consisting both of general principle and of particular rules', thereby avoiding the common mistake of looking for a single norm.[8]

On Cassese's analysis of the relationship between the principle and the rules of self-determination, the power of the principle is as the ground for interpreting a rule or as the sole ground for action in cases not covered by rules.[9] The General Assembly's use of the principle of self-determination to widen a rule on jurisdiction is an example of the former. A. Rigo Sureda discusses how, by grounding itself in the principle of self-determination contained in Article 1(2) of the United Nations Charter, the General Assembly was able to interpret its jurisdiction as extending beyond the determination of which territories are non-self-governing under Chapter XI of the Charter (a status treated as a precondition and preparation for the exercise of self-determination) to the more general determination of which territories are entitled to self-determination.[10] The other use that Cassese identifies for the principle of self-determination, principle as the ground for action where there are no applicable rules, is illustrated by Gaetano Arangio-Ruiz's view of the Charter principle of self-determination. Arangio-Ruiz maintains that being a treaty principle of universal scope, self-determination has not been circumscribed by the practice of applying it to colonial peoples only and remains a wellspring for the external and internal self-determination of any people, whether metropolitan or colonial.[11]

(Oxford: Berg, 1996), pp. 35–69 at p. 36, (1996) 32 *Stanford Journal of International Law* 255 at 255–60.

[8] Crawford, Book Review, 331.

I presume that Crawford is thinking primarily, as am I, of the Anglo-American literature. The Continental analytical tradition, to which Cassese belongs, is inclined to be more attentive to questions of normative structure in international law. See generally e.g. B. Graefrath, *Zur Stellung der Prinzipien im Gegenwärtigen Völkerrecht* (Berlin: Akademie-Verlag, 1968); G. Schwarzenberger, *The Inductive Approach to International Law* (London: Stevens & Sons, 1965), pp. 72–107; Virally, 'Le rôle des "principes"'. On self-determination, see S. Calageropoulos-Stratis, *Le droit des peuples à disposer d'eux-mêmes* (Brussels: Emile Bruylant, 1973), pp. 251–74.

[9] Cassese, *Self-Determination*, pp. 132–3. See also D. Thürer, 'Self-Determination' in R. Bernhardt (ed.), *Encyclopedia of Public International Law* (12 vols., Amsterdam: North-Holland, 1985), vol. VIII, pp. 470–6 at pp. 474–5.

[10] A. Rigo Sureda, *The Evolution of the Right of Self-Determination. A Study of United Nations Practice* (Leiden: A.W. Sijthoff, 1973), pp. 58–66.

[11] G. Arangio-Ruiz, 'Human Rights and Non-Intervention in the Helsinki Final Act' (1977-IV) 157 Hague Recueil 195 at 225–7. Arangio-Ruiz reads the Charter provisions

If self-determination is categorized as a principle as well as or instead of a rule, there is thus more room for its interpretation to evolve than if it is categorized as a rule only. In turn, the approach taken to principles in international law[12] controls how much more room and how it may be used; in particular, where there is space for argument, what kinds of argument and what authority they carry. This effect of the rule/principle distinction may be seen by comparing two of the main jurisprudential treatments of self-determination as a principle of international law: James Crawford's own[13] and that of Oscar Schachter.[14]

on self-determination as 'asserting self-determination in favour of any people subjected either to any form of foreign domination or to any form of despotism'. *Ibid.* at 225. To the same effect, see his more recent comments in the International Law Commission, Summary Records of the 2053rd Meeting, [1988] I *Yearbook of the International Law Commission* 62–3, paras. 21–4.

[12] The discussion of rules and principles in this chapter is limited to their treatment in the international law literature, particularly as it bears on self-determination. For the more developed discussion in domestic legal theory, see e.g. R. Dworkin, *Taking Rights Seriously* (Cambridge, Mass.: Harvard University Press, 1978); J. Raz, 'Legal Principles and the Limits of Law' (1972) 81 *Yale Law Journal* 823; C. R. Sunstein, *Legal Reasoning and Political Conflict* (New York: Oxford University Press, 1996). Some international lawyers and judges do, however, draw on this domestic law literature. See e.g. the discussion of Oscar Schachter in this part; *East Timor (Portugal v. Australia)*, ICJ Reports 1995, p. 90 at pp. 210–12 (Dissenting Opinion of Judge Weeramantry, adopting Dworkin).

[13] J. Crawford, *The Creation of States in International Law* (Oxford: Clarendon Press, 1979), pp. 84–118. Although dating from 1979, the treatment of self-determination as a legal principle in *The Creation of States* merits attention because the work continues to be referred to as authoritative. Crawford's later writing does not depart from this view of the norm structure of self-determination, and, in any event, the treatment is important as such. For Crawford's more recent work on self-determination, see J. Crawford, *State Practice and International Law in Relation to Unilateral Secession* (Expert Report for Canadian federal government, *Reference re Secession of Quebec*, [1998] 2 SCR 217, (1998) 37 ILM 1340), reprinted in A. F. Bayefsky (ed.), *Self-Determination in International Law: Quebec and Lessons Learned* (The Hague: Kluwer Law International, 2000), pp. 31–61; J. Crawford, Response to Expert Reports of the Amicus Curiae (*Reference re Secession of Quebec*), reprinted in Bayefsky, *Lessons Learned*, pp. 153–71; J. Crawford, 'State Practice and International Law in Relation to Secession' (1998) 69 *British Yearbook of International Law* 85 (based closely on the Expert Report); J. Crawford, 'The General Assembly, the International Court and Self-Determination' in V. Lowe and M. Fitzmaurice (eds.), *Fifty Years of the International Court of Justice: Essays in Honour of Sir Robert Jennings* (Cambridge: Grotius Publications, 1996), pp. 585–605; J. Crawford, 'The Rights of Peoples: "Peoples" or "Governments"?' in J. Crawford (ed.), *The Rights of Peoples* (Oxford: Clarendon Press, 1988), pp. 55–67; J. Crawford, 'The Rights of Peoples: Some Conclusions' in Crawford, *The Rights of Peoples*, pp. 159–75; J. Crawford, 'Self-Determination Outside the Colonial Context' in W. J. A. Macartney, ed., *Self-Determination in the Commonwealth* (Aberdeen: Aberdeen University Press, 1988), pp. 1–22.

[14] O. Schachter, 'Sovereignty – Then and Now' in R. St J. Macdonald (ed.), *Essays in Honour of Wang Tieya* (Dordrecht: Martinus Nijhoff, 1993), pp. 671–88 at pp. 681–4. See also

Whereas James Crawford is close in style and substance to the positivist tradition in international law, Oscar Schachter's affinity, although it has weakened over time,[15] is with the policy-oriented jurisprudence of Myres McDougal and Harold Lasswell.[16] Crawford and Schachter share, however, the conviction that international law is 'open-textured',[17] consisting of general principles as well as specific rules. Schachter has noted that 'the application of all general propositions – whether legal or not – to diverse facts and events has necessarily a substantial degree of uncertainty or ambiguity'.[18] Crawford too accepts that 'lawyering is an interpretive process',[19] though he is inclined to make less of this fact. Referring to Cassese's ambition in *Self-Determination of Peoples* to study 'self-determination as it exists in international law', the lex lata, and also to go '*beyond* the realm of law' and adopt a contextual approach 'in which history, politics and jurisprudence are all employed in the service of legal elucidation', Crawford queries 'why such a contextual approach takes one beyond the realm of law'.[20]

Crawford distinguishes political principle, legal principle and legal right in terms of generality, and argues that self-determination is all three.[21] While the political principle of self-determination has contributed to the international legal practice, 'this general ideal is too vague

---

O. Schachter, 'Micronationalism and Secession' in U. Beyerlin, M. Bothe, R. Hofmann and E.-U. Petersmann (eds.), *Recht zwischen Umbruch und Bewahrung. Festschrift für Rudolf Bernhardt* (Berlin: Springer-Verlag, 1995), pp. 179–86; O. Schachter, *International Law in Theory and Practice* (Dordrecht: Martinus Nijhoff, 1991), pp. 20–1; O. Schachter, 'International Law in Theory and Practice' (1982-V) 178 Hague Recueil 9 at 43–4; O. Schachter, 'The Relation of Law, Politics and Action in the United Nations' (1963-II) 109 Hague Recueil 169 at 191–4.

[15] Compare e.g. O. Schachter, 'Towards a Theory of International Obligation' (1968) 8 *Virginia Journal of International Law* 300 at 307 with Schachter, 'International Law', 40–73; Schachter, *Theory and Practice*, pp. 18–48. In this respect, Schachter's trajectory is not unlike that of Rosalyn Higgins. See below, pp. 95–102.

[16] See generally M. S. McDougal, H. D. Lasswell and W. M. Reisman, 'Theories About International Law: Prologue to a Configurative Jurisprudence' (1968) 8 *Virginia Journal of International Law* 188; M. S. McDougal and W. M. Reisman, 'International Law in Policy-Oriented Perspective' in R. St J. Macdonald and D. M. Johnston (eds.), *The Structure and Process of International Law: Essays in Legal Philosophy, Doctrine and Theory* (Boston: Martinus Nijhoff, 1983), pp. 103–29; J. N. Moore, 'Prolegomenon to the Jurisprudence of Myres McDougal and Harold Lasswell' (1968) 54 *Virginia Law Review* 662.

[17] Schachter uses the term in Schachter, 'The Relation of Law, Politics and Action', 189; Schachter, 'International Law', 43; Schachter, *Theory and Practice*, p. 20.

[18] Schachter, 'The Relation of Law, Politics and Action', 189. See also Schachter, 'International Law', 41; Schachter, *Theory and Practice*, p. 19.

[19] Crawford, Book Review, 332.

[20] Ibid. at 331, quoting Cassese, *Self-Determination*, pp. 2–3.

[21] Crawford, *The Creation of States*, pp. 85–102.

and ill-defined to constitute a legal principle, much less a positive legal rule'.²² But uncertainty of application in specific cases does not prevent the existence of a guiding legal principle; 'so long as there exists a "hard core" of reasonably clear cases, the status of the principle in question need not be doubted'.²³ The legal principle of self-determination has a core of clear meaning, which is coterminous with the legal right.

The distinction between the legal principle and the legal right of self-determination is not the content of self-determination, which Crawford takes to be a people's right to choose its own political organization, to be exercised without coercion on the basis of equality (one person, one vote). The exercise of self-determination may result in independence, or incorporation into or association with another state on a basis of political equality for that people. The difference between the principle and the right of self-determination in international law is the determinacy of the subject; that is, the definition of a 'people'. 'The notion of a right presupposes identification of the subject of the right.'²⁴ Thus the subject of the right of self-determination, unlike the subject of the principle, is fully determined: trust and mandated territories, and territories treated as non-self-governing under Chapter XI of the UN Charter are entitled to self-determination.²⁵ The principle applies to cases in which the subject does not come within the subject of the right; that is, within one of these definite categories. In such cases, an interpreter necessarily exercises discretion with regard to the subject – Crawford considers the question 'as much a matter of politics as law'²⁶ – and may choose to accept, for example, the additional category that Crawford terms *carence de souveraineté*:²⁷ 'territories forming distinct political-geographical areas, whose inhabitants do not share in the government either of the region or of the State to which the region belongs, with the result that the territory becomes in effect, with respect to the remainder of the State, non-self-governing'.²⁸

For Crawford, then, the legal principle of self-determination plays a residual role. In the absence of a right, the principle acts as a template for the translation of moral or political arguments into international law. The undefined subject, 'peoples', creates an opening through which certain of these arguments enter the interpretation of the principle.

Schachter's general treatment of rules and principles in international law is broadly similar to that reflected in Crawford's analysis of

---

²² Ibid., p. 88. ²³ Ibid., p. 98. ²⁴ Ibid., p. 88.
²⁵ Crawford also includes states and all other territories to which the parties agree to apply self-determination, but these categories do not concern us here. Ibid., p. 101.
²⁶ Ibid., p. 89. ²⁷ Ibid., pp. 86, 100. ²⁸ Ibid., p. 101.

self-determination. Where a rule is clear and clearly applicable to the case at hand, there is no place for principles in its interpretation. Where a rule is ambiguous, there is a choice of applicable rules or indeed no applicable rule, then principles govern the case.[29]

Schachter distinguishes principles from rules[30] in terms of their generality and the nature of the choices they require.[31] Principles are much more general than rules, with more abstract key terms. In addition, they are usually treated as higher than rules in the hierarchy of legal norms. Finally, principles are not dispositive: they carry weight rather than apply in an all-or-nothing fashion. Being general and fundamental, principles tend to clash with one another in concrete cases. An interpreter may therefore be faced with competing principles of equal legal status: 'abstractions, arrayed in intransigent hostility like robot sentinels facing each other across a border'.[32] A solution is reached by weighing and balancing these competing principles in light of the factual context and policies of international law,[33] thereby making them 'useful guardians on either hand in the climb to

---

[29] While this is the most likely reading of Schachter (Schachter, 'International Law', 44–51; Schachter, *Theory and Practice*, pp. 21–7), his real focus is the appropriate relationship between rules and policies. In some places, he contrasts principles and rules with policies; in others, he contrasts principles and policies with rules. Although principles and policies are distinct types of propositions, policies may be expressed legally in the form of principles. As a result, it is not always easy to tell which sense Schachter intends when he groups principles with policies.

Principles and policies differ as types of propositions used in legal reasoning in that principles give rise to claims of entitlement and policies do not. Policies are instead concerned with collective goals. Schachter, 'International Law', 44; Schachter, *Theory and Practice*, p. 21. Compare Dworkin, *Taking Rights Seriously*, p. 90. In positive international law, policies may sometimes be formulated as principles. The principle of self-determination in an international treaty, such as the UN Charter, may act as a principle (claim of entitlement) or a policy (claim of a different distributional character) depending on the context. Indeed, Schachter discusses self-determination as both in his recent writing. Schachter, 'International Law', 43, 48, 51; Schachter, *Theory and Practice*, p. 20, p. 25, p. 31.

[30] While Schachter's account of principles and rules has remained constant, his use of other categories of legal norms has varied with the discussion. Compare Schachter, 'The Relation of Law, Politics and Action', 188–98 (rules, principles, standards and doctrines) with Schachter, 'International Law', 40–57; Schachter, *Theory and Practice*, pp. 18–33 (rules, principles and policies).

[31] Schachter, 'The Relation of Law, Politics and Action', 189. See also Schachter, 'International Law', 43; Schachter, *Theory and Practice*, pp. 20–1.

[32] O. Schachter, 'Dag Hammarskjold and the Relation of Law to Politics' (1962) 56 *American Journal of International Law* 1 at 5, quoting P. A. Freund, 'Thomas Reed Powell' (1956) 69 *Harvard Law Review* 800 at 803.

[33] Schachter, 'The Relation of Law, Politics and Action', 191–3; Schachter, 'International Law', 43–4; Schachter, *Theory and Practice*, pp. 20–1.

truth'.³⁴ Writing about the interpretation of the UN Charter, Schachter explains that the emphasis in interpretation necessarily shifts from 'dictionary' and 'ordinary' meaning to 'an assessment of a complex factual situation and a consideration of the consequences of a decision in light of more basic values that are regarded as implicit in the Charter'.³⁵

Like Crawford, Schachter has consistently maintained, following H. L. A. Hart,³⁶ that principles are 'applicable to an indeterminate series of events, which may be viewed as extending outward from a "core meaning"';³⁷ principles have a core of certain application and a penumbra in which there are good reasons both to apply and not to apply them. Schachter is, earlier on, less true to Hart's distinction between core and penumbra, stating squarely in a 1968 piece that the issue of policy 'is not an issue that arises only in the "penumbral" case as H. L. A. Hart seems to suggest; it is far more central and common, at least on the international level, than that'.³⁸ Nevertheless, in important recent work,³⁹ he carefully distances himself from the pervasive policy-orientation of McDougal and Lasswell by emphasizing the areas of certainty in the interpretation of international law.

If Crawford and Schachter both give the impression of an obvious borderline between easy and hard cases, interpretation being straightforward in the easy cases, they differ on the nature of interpretation in the hard cases. Crawford seems to contemplate the exercise of relatively unstructured discretion in cases requiring a hard decision about the subject of the principle of sovereignty or self-determination,⁴⁰ whereas Schachter foresees the weighing and balancing of opposite principles with regard to the facts and the policies of international law.

---

³⁴ Schachter, 'Dag Hammarskjold', 5.
³⁵ Schachter, 'The Relation of Law, Politics and Action', 193. For an account of why an argument that one principle is preferable to another because it better advances a Charter purpose is nevertheless an argument of principle, see Dworkin, *Taking Rights Seriously*, p. 297.
³⁶ As, in different ways, do I. Brownlie in *Treaties and Indigenous Peoples. The Robb Lectures 1991* (Oxford: Clarendon Press, 1992), pp. 47–8 and 'The Rights of Peoples in Modern International Law' in Crawford, *The Rights of Peoples*, pp. 1–16 at pp. 4–5; and D. Z. Cass, 'Re-thinking Self-Determination: A Critical Analysis of Current International Law Theories' (1992) 18 *Syracuse Journal of International Law and Commerce* 21 at 22–3.
³⁷ Schachter, 'The Relation of Law, Politics and Action', 191–2. He earlier attributes 'core meaning' to H. L. A. Hart. *Ibid.*, 189, n. 11, citing H. L. A. Hart, *The Concept of Law* (London: Oxford University Press, 1961), p. 119. See also Schachter, 'International Law', 43; Schachter, *Theory and Practice*, p. 20.
³⁸ Schachter, 'Towards a Theory', 319.
³⁹ Schachter, 'International Law', 40–57; Schachter, *Theory and Practice*, pp. 18–33.
⁴⁰ Crawford, *The Creation of States*, pp. 88–9.

The difference between Crawford and Schachter is more marked in their interpretation of self-determination. Unlike Crawford, Schachter considers self-determination one of several major areas of international law in which rules are relatively thin on the ground and general principles dominate.[41] The interpretation of self-determination therefore proceeds from the opposition of two major principles of international law: the right of each people to self-determination as a choice of independence or autonomy, and the territorial integrity of states. Schachter reconciles these principles by interpreting self-determination as a human right, but prohibiting foreign states from forcibly intervening to support such action against the territorial sovereign.[42]

Moreover, Schachter maintains that the term 'people' is incapable of a core meaning. In his view, the determination of the subject of self-determination is so dependent on the individual and contingent facts of the cases that it can only be governed by a standard of reasonableness or appropriateness.[43] By 'standard', Schachter means generally 'highly general prescriptions which involve evaluating the individual features of events'. Compared to standards, rules and even to some degree principles 'assume a relatively uniform application, irrespective of individual characteristics'.[44] Schachter's recently formulated standards for determining the peoples entitled to independence are:

(1) The claimant community should have an identity distinct from the rest of the country and inhabit a region that largely supports separation in the given circumstances.
(2) The community has been subjected to a pattern of systematic political or economic discrimination.
(3) The central regime has rejected reasonable proposals for autonomy and minority rights of the claimant community.[45]

In substance, Crawford and Schachter are not far apart on self-determination: both propose an interpretation that makes the systematic denial of political rights to a community with an identity distinct from the rest of the state a condition for secession. The difference between the two lies in their picture of the interpretation of self-determination, and the place and authority of this proposal in it. For Crawford, there is an obvious difference between cases to which a right

---

[41] Schachter, 'International Law', 44; Schachter, *Theory and Practice*, p. 21.
[42] 'Schachter, 'Sovereignty – Then and Now', pp. 683–4.
[43] Schachter, 'The Relation of Law, Politics and Action', 193–4.   [44] Ibid., 193.
[45] Schachter, 'Sovereignty – Then and Now', p. 684.

of self-determination applies and cases governed by the principle of self-determination. It is clear that the peoples of trust and mandated territories and non-self-governing territories are 'peoples', and beyond this, unclear who else qualifies. In these hard cases, interpretation involves a politico-legal choice, and his category of *carence de souveraineté* is offered simply as one possible politico-legal choice that might be made. Schachter does not apply the notion of core and penumbra to the principle of self-determination; he does not separate the interpretation of the principle into easy and hard cases. The interpretation of self-determination in all cases is bounded by opposing principles and structured by the application of his tripartite reasonableness standard to the subject of self-determination, necessarily requiring consideration of basic values and the 'felt necessities of time and place'.[46]

Change

Antonio Cassese's analysis of self-determination as a principle of international law in *Self-Determination of Peoples* recalls the significance of the rule/principle distinction in the context of international society. In the 1960s, the role of principles was debated as a way for international law to keep pace with a world community that included a rapidly growing number of Third World states. Rules predominated in classical international law,[47] but many Third World states[48] and others saw rules as too slow a logic of change. The incrementalism of reasoning with rules was considered inadequate for the necessary reinterpretation of an international law formed in the encounter of colonizer with colonized. Mohammed Bedjaoui termed international lawyers' attachment to this old model of law 'legal paganism': the worship of an international law detached from the reality it governed and preserved as an idol.[49] He

---

[46] Schachter, 'The Relation of Law, Politics and Action', 194. The reference is presumably to O. W. Holmes, *The Common Law* (Boston: Little, Brown and Co., 1923), p. 1.

[47] David Kennedy characterizes the traditional intellectual history of international law from 1648 to 1918 as the expulsion of principle: the 'narrative of authority's triumph over principle is repeated – in the shift from natural law to principle, from naturalism to positivism, and finally from law to institutions in the post-World War One era'. D. Kennedy, 'Images of Religion in International Legal Theory' in M. W. Janis (ed.), *The Influence of Religion on the Development of International Law* (Dordrecht: Martinus Nijhoff, 1991), pp. 137–46 at p. 141.

[48] See A. Cassese, *International Law in a Divided World* (Oxford: Clarendon Press, 1986), pp. 119–21.

[49] M. Bedjaoui, *Towards a New International Economic Order* (Paris: UNESCO, 1979), p. 100.

argued that international law thus fetishized was not neutral. 'Totally cut off from international life', it would be

> a selective set of rules serving only to perpetuate one kind of reality and a certain type of unequal relationship. It would be a law of dominance, a law for the preservation of oligarchical privileges. A law of this kind, taken as a sacrosanct point of reference by its advocates, could not possibly be called 'neutral' because it is in fact the powerful expression of the interests of a certain group of States at a certain time.[50]

Moreover, international law, properly understood, had the capacity and the responsibility to change.[51] Whereas classical legal science 'was reduced to the mechanical establishment of the existence of the legal rule and a formalistic study of the mechanisms of its application', a concrete and authentic science of law would study, among other things, 'the mechanisms – including their possibilities and their limitations – by which the legal rule can adapt itself to change, both through its own flexibility and through modern methods of interpretation'.[52] The relevance of principles is evident here. The generality and plurality of principles introduce uncertainty, plasticity and contradiction into the law, giving them, in Cassese's words, 'great normative potential and dynamic force'.[53]

Michel Virally, whom Cassese cites,[54] argues in a 1968 essay that because it proceeds by induction, reasoning with rules is essentially conservative. This painstaking process of interpretation keeps time with a homogeneous and stable international society, such as the vanished world of European diplomacy prior to World War I. Principles, which add a deductive dimension to interpretation, respond to the imperatives of a diverse and changing international society.[55] The exchange between Georg Schwarzenberger and Wilfred Jenks[56] is typical of

---

[50] Ibid. [51] Ibid., pp. 104–15. [52] Ibid., p. 107.
[53] Cassese, Self-Determination, pp. 128–9.
[54] Ibid., p. 129, n. 49 (citing Virally, 'Panorama').
[55] Virally, 'Le rôle des "principes"', pp. 539–45. Virally distinguishes principles that innovate from those that generalize from existing rules, but observes that the difference between the two types of principle as a force for change can be overdrawn in so far as the former take on a life of their own and often blur in practice with the latter. Ibid., pp. 543, 545.
[56] See C. W. Jenks, The Prospects of International Adjudication (London: Stevens & Sons Ltd, 1964), pp. 617–62 (taking issue with the inductive approach formulated primarily by Schwarzenberger in, inter alia, two articles collected in Schwarzenberger, The Inductive Approach, pp. 8–71); Schwarzenberger, The Inductive Approach, pp. 115–64 (refuting Jenks point by point).

the period.⁵⁷ Schwarzenberger, inured to the slow tempo of the judicial development of international law, argued that new rules could not be deduced from principles without being inductively verified by reference to the sources of international law, namely, treaty, custom and general principles of law.⁵⁸ Jenks encouraged acceptance of such judicial boldness as a normal feature of 'the judicial practice of an age of political, economic and social change unprecedented in scale and rate'.⁵⁹ For Schwarzenberger, Jenks was a woolly-thinking 'representative *par excellence* of the eclectic and liberal-reformist treatment of international law'⁶⁰ who failed to appreciate the rigour and prudence of the inductive approach to international law. For Jenks, Schwarzenberger was not only hopelessly conservative, but positively dangerous to the already flimsy prospects of international adjudication.

If the sweep of principles and dynamism of their interaction with one another leads to the association of principles with progress, these very same qualities can be seen instead as allowing principles to be harnessed to conservative or even regressive tendencies. When appraised against the realities of power in international law, the flexibility of principles begins to look more like bias,⁶¹ and the hope for positive change through principles, naive. Oscar Schachter's interpretation of self-determination as a pervasive balancing of the principle of self-determination against other, status quo principles is no guarantee that the balance will be stable, let alone tip further toward the principle of self-determination. In comparison, James Crawford's understanding of the principle of self-determination may have more room for Realpolitik in its interpretation, but ensures the fixity of the right, or rule, of self-determination.

Nor may describing self-determination as a rule spell conservatism. In Virally's view, the need to develop rules by analogy makes them slow to change. But analogies may be broader or narrower depending on the comparison chosen. For example, the James Bay Cree, an indigenous people based in Quebec, have fortified their claim to self-determination

---

[57] See e.g. Cassese, *International Law in a Divided World*, pp. 105–25.
[58] Schwarzenberger, *The Inductive Approach*, pp. 5, 50–1, 72–107, 129–30. Besides furnishing hypotheses about rules, to be tested against the raw material of international law, principles could contribute convenient labels, *Ordnungsbegriffe*, for classifying, teaching and memorizing related rules that had been inductively verified. Schwarzenberger cautioned, though, that 'such classificatory concepts must not be abused for the purpose of deducing from them new rules'. *Ibid.*, p. 129.
[59] Jenks, *International Adjudication*, p. 621.
[60] Schwarzenberger, *The Inductive Approach*, p. 115.
[61] See D. Kennedy, 'Form and Substance in Private Law Adjudication' (1976) 89 *Harvard Law Review* 1685 at 1710 (illustrating the ability to describe any quality of rules or standards in either positive or negative terms).

with the argument that even if the right is limited to overseas colonies, their situation is analogous because they too are victims of European colonization.⁶² They have also argued that self-determination is a general, rather than a specific, rule and that it has simply been underapplied.⁶³ The virtue of these legal strategies, moreover, is that rules, unlike principles, are dispositive.

Participation

In helping define the sort of conversation we can have in international law about self-determination, the classification of self-determination as rule or principle contemplates and advantages a certain sort of speaker.⁶⁴ This connection between the rule/principle distinction and the ability to participate in interpretation is clear to a number of the authors under discussion in this chapter. In his 1968 essay on principles, Michel Virally points out that the elaboration of a rule tends to be a narrower and more technical exercise than the interpretation of a principle. An effective argument for the evolution of a rule depends on an extensive knowledge of precedents and on a mastery of traditional methods of interpretation, whereas, observes Virally, 'beaucoup des acteurs de la vie internationale sont dépourvus de toute formation juridique et ne disposent pas de services ayant une information et une expérience suffisantes dans le domaine du droit international pour les conseiller utilement sur ce point' ('many actors in international life are deprived of any legal training and do not have at their disposal a department with sufficient information and experience in the domain of international law to advise them usefully on this point').⁶⁵

In this connection, Georg Schwarzenberger and Wilfred Jenks both emphasize that an inductive, empirically-based approach to international

---

⁶² See Grand Council of the Crees (of Quebec), *Status and Rights of the James Bay Cree in the Context of Quebec's Secession from Canada*, Submission to the United Nations Commission on Human Rights (February 1992), pp. 23–33 (comparing 'internal' with 'external' colonialism).

⁶³ See T. Moses, 'The Right of Self-Determination and its Significance to the Survival of Indigenous Peoples' in P. Aikio and M. Scheinin (eds.), *Operationalizing the Right of Indigenous Peoples to Self-Determination* (Turku/Åbo: Institute for Human Rights, Åbo Akademi University, 2000), pp. 155–77 at pp. 157–66 (stressing 'all peoples').

⁶⁴ See J. B. White, 'Law as Rhetoric, Rhetoric as Law: The Arts of Cultural and Communal Life' (1985) 52 *University of Chicago Law Review* 684 at 697, reprinted in
J. B. White, *Heracles' Bow: Essays on the Rhetoric and Poetics of the Law* (Madison, Wisc.: University of Wisconsin Press, 1985), pp. 28–48. See also J. B. White, *Justice as Translation: An Essay in Cultural and Legal Criticism* (Chicago: University of Chicago Press, 1990), especially pp. 97–102.

⁶⁵ (Translation mine) Virally, 'Le rôle des "principes"', p. 541.

law was only made possible by what Schwarzenberger describes as a transition from monastic toilers to master builders to compulsive documentalists:

> the self-denying work of the eighteenth-century compilers, the monumental collections of Martens and Hertslet, the flow of State and parliamentary papers which, since the nineteenth century, grew to an unprecedented extent, the proceedings of numerous international conferences, and the paper-spilling organisations modelled on the League of Nations – not to speak of the multitude of decisions on international law by international and national courts.[66]

It follows that unequal access to these resources and unequal ability to mobilize them are greater disadvantages in the marshalling of an inductive argument about the existence or meaning of a rule than in constructing an argument about the interpretation of a principle.

Even if there were no disparity in access to the organized evidence or in the possession of the proficiency needed to turn it to one's legal advantage, the bias of these compilations and collections and their impact on the determination of the rules of international law would impose a considerable empirical burden on anyone seeking to establish a new rule or reinterpret an existing one. Schachter describes how, given the difficulty of determining the state practice and therefore the customary rule on a particular point, practitioners of the inductive method of international law have long relied heavily on the national digests of state practice prepared by or in close association with the government of the state concerned. Since not all states produce such digests, reliance on them gives a potentially biased and unrepresentative picture of state practice.[67] The first one hundred volumes of the *International Law Reports*, for example, include just over one hundred cases from sub-Saharan Africa (fifty-plus states, population around 800 million) as compared to around 320 cases from Austria (population 8.9 million).[68] To remedy this distortion in the ready-made data, however, would require

---

[66] Schwarzenberger, *The Inductive Approach*, p. 13. See also Jenks, *International Adjudication*, pp. 623–4.

[67] Schachter, 'International Law', 61; Schachter, *Theory and Practice*, p. 36. See also Cassese, *Self-Determination*, p. 93.

[68] V. Lowe, 'The Marginalisation of Africa' (2000) 94 *Proceedings of the American Society of International Law* (forthcoming). See also e.g. M. K. Nawaz, 'On the Ways and Means of Improving Research of International Law in India' in S. K. Agrawala, T. S. Rama Rao and J. N. Saxena (eds.), *New Horizons of International Law and Developing Countries* (International Law Association (Indian Branch), 1983), pp. 400–16 at p. 400 (deploring that although India has been sovereign and independent since 1947, it has yet to produce a digest of state practice).

extensive independent collection of information on state practice.[69] In comparison, the interpretation of a principle can be less dependent on evidence of state practice.[70] For example, in a case where it is accepted that there is an applicable principle, but no applicable rule, the interpretation of the principle may turn on the types of political, moral, factual and policy considerations that Crawford and Schachter mention.

In the context of self-determination, if self-determination is understood as an 'overseas colonies only' rule, then any alternative interpretation of the rule must account for all cases of independence or attempted independence worldwide over the last fifty years or so and states' reactions to them. If the interpretation of self-determination is instead seen to engage the balancing of the principles of self-determination and territorial integrity, then interpretation is not grounded in the exhaustive consideration of state practice.

The extensive reliance on collections and digests of state practice in determining the rules of international law is paralleled by the pride of place given to what publicists have written, despite the fact that the writings of even the most highly qualified publicists are, according to the Statute of the International Court of Justice,[71] no more than a 'subsidiary means for the determination of rules of law'. Since traditional international law is based on rules and developed by the more technical and empirical methods of induction and analogy, it is first of all, according to Virally, 'un droit de juristes' or lawyers' law. It privileges international lawyers, and states with a strong diplomatic tradition and experienced diplomatic corps, more than an international law that is also built on principles does.[72] This structural advantage magnifies the stature of eminent authors in international law and thereby increases the likelihood that an author's reputation may discourage any interrogation of his views and his name be enough for his opinions to influence the interpretation of international law.[73] In contrast, principles may, to quote Virally's warning, 'constituent une idée-force, accessible à tous, échappant, par conséquent, dans une large mesure, au contrôle des juristes et exerçant sur le fonctionnement des modes de formation du

[69] See Schwarzenberger, *The Inductive Approach*, p. 18.
[70] This would not always be true; for example, the deduction of a new rule from an existing principle might require the demonstration that the new rule is not contrary to state practice. See Cassese, *Self-Determination*, p. 129.
[71] ICJ Statute, Art.38(1)(d).   [72] Virally, 'Le rôle des "principes"', p. 540.
[73] Compare the implacable Schwarzenberger, *The Inductive Approach*, pp. 13–19 (mutual quotation clubs and 'ipsedixitism' rampant in the treatment of international law), cited by Schachter in Schachter, 'International Law', 63, n. 58.

droit une action dynamique' ('constitute an idea-force, *accessible to all, largely escaping, as a consequence, the control of jurists* and dynamically affecting the functioning of the ways of creating law').[74] Principles, by their nature and their broad appeal, resist the control of international lawyers.

This association of rules with disempowerment and principles with empowerment is no less questionable, however, than the association of rules/principles with conservatism/progress. The goal of an equal say in the interpretation of international law for all states does not always point to principles over rules. While principles help to broaden participation and to place participants on the same level, principles are not hard-and-fast norms and rules are. A democratization of rules – in particular, what counts as or toward a rule – may therefore seem preferable. In this vein, the debate over the legal value of General Assembly resolutions, which do not fit clearly into the traditional sources of international law,[75] is precisely about the recognition of norms based on a majority vote of all states. Such distinguished Third World figures as ICJ Judges Taslim Olawale Elias[76] and Kéba Mbaye[77] argued that GA resolutions should be accepted as a source of international law. Judge Elias wrote:

> The question surely is that most of the rules of customary international law were established in the last four centuries by only a handful of Western European States; the advocates of consent as the only basis of obligation for sovereign States are also the first to insist that the three-quarters of the world that took no part in its formation must be regarded as bound by it, consent or no consent.[78]

From this perspective, the International Court of Justice's reliance on GA resolutions in interpreting the right of self-determination in *Namibia*[79] and later cases[80] appears as an effort to enhance the legitimacy of international law and its own legitimacy by adopting a definition that reflects the equal participation of states.[81]

---

[74] (Emphasis and translation mine) Virally, 'Le rôle des "principes"', p. 543.
[75] See B. Sloan, *United Nations General Assembly Resolutions in our Changing World* (Ardsley-on-Hudson, N.Y.: Transnational Publishers, 1991), pp. 53–91, 123–30; Bedjaoui, *Towards a New International Economic Order*, pp. 131–92.
[76] T. O. Elias, *Africa and the Development of International Law* (2nd rev. edn, Dordrecht: Martinus Nijhoff, 1988), pp. 69–74.
[77] K. Mbaye, 'Le droit au développement en droit international' in J. Makarczyk (ed.), *Essays in International Law in Honour of Judge Manfred Lachs* (The Hague: Martinus Nijhoff, 1984), pp. 163–77 at p. 173.
[78] Elias, *Africa and the Development of International Law*, p. 72.
[79] *Namibia (South West Africa)*, Advisory Opinion, ICJ Reports 1971, p. 16 at p. 31.
[80] On *Western Sahara*, see Chapter 4 below.
[81] See Crawford, 'The General Assembly', p. 591 (discussed under the heading 'Decolonizing the Court?').

The international community

The rule/principle distinction is bound up with stories about international society, as well as with theories of interpretation and change and practices of participation. Antonio Cassese's definition of principles in *Self-Determination of Peoples* introduces the relationship between the rule/principle distinction and narratives of the international community:

> Principles do not differ from treaty or customary rules simply in that they are more general and less precise... Rather, principles differ from legal rules in that they are the expression and result of conflicting views of States on matters of crucial importance... In this respect, principles are a typical expression of the present world community, whereas in the old community – relatively homogenous and less conflictual – specific and precise rules prevailed.[82]

Cassese's definition of principles is perplexing in several ways. First, as a matter of legal theory, why are principles *by definition* 'the expression and result of conflicting views of States'? Without criticizing Cassese's definition outright, James Crawford comments in his review of *Self-Determination of Peoples* that 'presumably, if views did not conflict, the principle would soon crystallize into a "specific and precise" rule'.[83] I take the implicit criticism to be that as legal norm-types, principles and rules have a distinct existence and function, and one is not reducible to the other. Principles are not rules *manquées* nor vice versa. Principles differ from rules in their generality and application as 'directive principles' having weight rather than applying in an all-or-nothing fashion.[84] Logically, rules may elaborate, but not replace, principles; just as principles may summarize, but not replace, a body of rules.

Second, according to the usual intellectual history of international law,[85] the view of international law entrenched in the nineteenth century was the positivist one that international law consisted of empirically verifiable rules. In this light, Cassese's observation that rules prevailed in the old international community has a tautological flavour. International law was rules because only rules could be international law.

---

[82] Cassese, *Self-Determination*, p. 128. See also A. Cassese, 'The International Court of Justice and the Right of Peoples to Self-Determination' in V. Lowe and M. Fitzmaurice (eds.), *Fifty Years of the International Court of Justice: Essays in Honour of Sir Robert Jennings* (Cambridge: Grotius Publications, 1996), pp. 351–63 at p. 351.

[83] Crawford, Book Review, 331.   [84] *Ibid.*

[85] See note 47 above. But see D. Kennedy, 'International Law and the Nineteenth Century: History of an Illusion' (1996) 65 *Nordic Journal of International Law* 385.

These two difficulties with Cassese's definition of principles may be attributed to his conflation of principles as norm-type, an analytical category; and principles as a set of assumptions about the world we live in, a sociological construct. That is, his rhetoric of rules and principles is traceable to a story of the world community.[86] Cassese emphasizes rules as a reflection of unity of values and harmony. Rules are possible because the homogeneity of international society makes precise agreement possible. In a fractured, conflictual world,[87] generalities are the best we can do. A heterogeneous international society can only agree on vague formulations. Principles become placeholders for rules; they come to represent the possibility of reaching agreement on rules, the hope of shared values in the future. A procedural version of this story may be found in the international legal literature that sees particularly the principles of sovereignty and self-determination as a meeting place, a language for speaking across difference. The promise of principles there is as an ongoing process, the dream of communication that leads to understanding, rather than as a stand-in for substance.[88]

Approaching the rule/principle distinction as a story of the international community offers a context for Cassese's definition of principles. It also leads us to think about how different stories of the international community would support different analyses of rules and principles, in particular, as applied to self-determination. For Cassese, principles must be the 'expression and result' of deadlock among states over fundamentals. He assumes that states opposed in ideology and

---

[86] Compare Kennedy, 'Form and Substance', 1712; C. M. Rose, 'Crystals and Mud in Property Law' in C. M. Rose, *Property and Persuasion: Essays on the History, Theory and Rhetoric of Ownership* (Boulder: Westview Press, 1994), pp. 199–232.

[87] Self-determination, and international law generally, in an ideologically divided world has long been a theme of Cassese's scholarship. On self-determination, see A. Cassese, 'Article 1, Paragraphe 2' in J.-P. Cot and A. Pellet (eds.), *La Charte des Nations Unies* (2nd edn, Paris: Economica, 1991), pp. 39–55; A. Cassese, 'The Helsinki Declaration and Self-Determination' in T. Buergenthal (ed.), *Human Rights, International Law and the Helsinki Accord* (New York: Universe Books, 1977), pp. 83–110; A. Cassese, 'Political Self-Determination – Old Concepts and New Developments' in A. Cassese (ed.), *UN Law/Fundamental Rights: Two Topics in International Law* (Alphen aan den Rijn: Sijthoff & Noordhoff, 1979), pp. 137–65; A. Cassese, 'The Self-Determination of Peoples' in L. Henkin (ed.), *The International Bill of Rights. The Covenant on Civil and Political Rights* (New York: Columbia University Press, 1981), pp. 92–113. On international law generally, see Cassese, *International Law in a Divided World*.

[88] E.g. C. Scott, 'Dialogical Sovereignty: Preliminary Metaphorical Musings' (1992) 21 *Proceedings of the Canadian Council on International Law* 267; C. Scott, 'Indigenous Self-Determination and Decolonization of the International Imagination: A Plea' (1996) 18 *Human Rights Quarterly* 814.

interests are more inclined to reach agreement on general principles than on specific rules.[89] Such agreement seems plausible to John Rawls, who constructs a law of peoples from the idea of an overlapping consensus on basic principles among diverse societies.[90] On this assumption, the principle of self-determination in international law should be highly abstract and quicksilver, sliding away like mercury to the touch, when attempts are made to formulate rules.

Yet one can just as easily imagine that in a politically diverse world, rules are a more likely outcome than principles; that is, that rules are congenial to heterogeneity and principles to homogeneity, instead of the other way around. Indeed, Cass Sunstein argues that the law's strategy for dealing with the fact of pluralism domestically is to seek 'incompletely theorized agreements'. Rather than applying controversial moral and political theories to legal problems, legal reasoners rely on rules and low-level principles of law to settle them.[91] This would suggest that international law has developed self-determination as an 'overseas colonies only' rule because this rule is one on which states can agree for different moral and political reasons.

Even if we accept Cassese's position that 'principles are a typical expression of the present world community', the nature of the agreement among states on principles is variable. With the greater specificity of rules, the likelihood increases that agreement on them will be substantive, whereas agreement on principles might be anything including genuine agreement in the abstract, tacit agreement to reach a common meaning progressively or to a process of dialogue over meaning, disagreement veiled for reasons of entente[92] or the cynical creation of agitprop.

---

[89] Compare B. Ferencz, *Defining International Aggression. The Search for World Peace: A Documentary History and Analysis* (2 vols., Dobbs Ferry, N.Y.: Oceana Publications, 1975), vol. II, pp. 48–9.
[90] J. Rawls, 'The Law of Peoples' in S. Shute and S. Hurley (eds.), *On Human Rights: The Oxford Amnesty Lectures 1993* (New York: Basic Books, 1993), pp. 41–82.
[91] Sunstein, *Legal Reasoning and Political Conflict*.
[92] See F. C. Iklé, *How Nations Negotiate* (New York: Harper & Row, 1964), p. 15. Iklé takes as an example the following passage from L. B. Pearson, *Diplomacy in the Nuclear Age* (Cambridge, Mass.: Harvard University Press, 1949), pp. 47–8:

> I know that there have been occasions, and I have been concerned with one or two, when, as the lesser of two evils, words were used in recording the results of negotiations or discussion whose value lay precisely in the fact that they were imprecise, that they could be interpreted somewhat freely and therefore could be used not so much to record agreement as to conceal a disagreement which it was desired to play down and which, it was hoped, would disappear in time. It is a practice, however, which is only rarely justified.

More important than premises about the typical level of generality of agreement between states and the typical nature of that agreement is the basic narrative of the international community in the rule/principle distinction. As we have seen, Cassese associates rules with the relatively homogeneous and stable old international community and principles with the fragmented and conflict-prone modern international community. Rules are equated with unity and harmony;[93] principles with diversity and tension, but with the potential to give way to rules reflecting a new unity and harmony. In contrast to this narrative of redemption,[94] a narrative of the fallen world can be identified in the work of some authors who identify self-determination as a rule.[95] On their Hobbesian account, rules are the last bastion of certainty that protects international society from chaos, whereas the vagueness of principles invites argument, dissimulation, demagoguery and, ultimately, violence.

Through the study of one architectural detail, this chapter has sought to begin the task of understanding and evaluating the literature on self-determination. In this, it has embarked upon an account that differs from the existing accounts of what is 'really' going on in the debate among international lawyers over whether the right of self-determination includes a right of secession. The more doctrinal explanations do the useful diagnostic work of localizing the disagreement.[96] Taxonomies of the underlying normative models of self-determination and their interplay in the development of self-determination in international law make promising connections between the debate in

---

[93] Cassese is presumably using a baseline of nineteenth-century positivism, since principles reflected a single worldview in the earlier period when international law was informed by Christian theology or natural law. See M. W. Janis, 'Religion and the Literature of International Law: Some Standard Texts' in Janis, *The Influence of Religion*, pp. 61–84; M. Forsyth, 'The Tradition of International Law' in T. Nardin and D. R. Mapel (eds.), *Traditions of International Ethics* (Cambridge: Cambridge University Press, 1992), pp. 23–41.

[94] Compare Kennedy, 'Images of Religion' (tracing the structural similarities among stories told by international law and religion). Like Kennedy, I am referring to narrative homologies and not, more literally, to the use of the Bible in international relations. On the latter, see M. G. Cartwright, 'Biblical Argument in International Ethics' in Nardin and Mapel, *Traditions of International Ethics*, pp. 270–96.

[95] See Chapter 3 below.

[96] See R. G. Steinhardt, Book Review (1994) 88 *American Journal of International Law* 831 at 832 (describing the 'conventional' diagnosis).

international law and its counterparts in political and moral theory.[97] Conversely, the value of explanations that trace the stand-off over the meaning of self-determination to such fundamental oppositions in international law as statism/globalism and law/politics is that they remind us of the distinctness of the international and the legal context.[98] This chapter has been closest to the last sort of explanation. (The next will be more akin to the other two sorts.) But there is an important difference. In focusing closely on the question of norm-type and what flows from it, the chapter intended to draw attention to interpretation as an activity and to the ethics of that activity.[99] By exploring the links between the rule/principle distinction and ideas of change, participation and identity in international society, it sought to sharpen our awareness not only of initial interpretive decisions about the definition of self-determination, but of the fact that these decisions are embedded in contexts of inequality and exclusion.

[97] E.g. G. Binder, 'The Kaplan Lecture on Human Rights: The Case for Self-Determination' (1993) 29 *Stanford Journal of International Law* 223; Simpson, 'The Diffusion of Sovereignty'.
[98] Steinhardt, Book Review, 832.
[99] See O. Korhonen, 'The Place of Ethics of International Law' (1998) 21:80 *Retfærd* 3, especially at 13–15 (distinguishing 'interpretationist', exemplified by this book's approach as articulated in an early draft, from other styles of ethics in international law).

2 Interpretation and identity

As the previous chapter illustrated, there are different structural ways to interpret the right of external self-determination broadly in international law. This chapter examines the two general approaches taken in the post-Cold War literature and their implications for the identity of groups claiming self-determination. Some authors take what I call here the 'categories' approach. They broaden the interpretation of self-determination by establishing the independent existence of new categories and rules. Others achieve the same result by imposing coherence through global definitions, consistent rationales, overarching principles and other unifying devices. I call this the 'coherence' approach. Whereas the categories approach does not need to tell one story about decolonization and whatever other situations might give rise to a right to independence, the coherence approach imparts a single powerful story of identity. And since different authors create categories and coherence differently, the result is an emerging rivalry between and among hodgepodges and grand narratives of self-determination.

The object of this chapter is not to evaluate, whether doctrinally or normatively, the strengths and weaknesses of these competing understandings.[1] It is to introduce the range of legally defensible interpretations of self-determination and the relationship of *interpretation* to *identity* that they instantiate. As such, the chapter develops further the practice of reading begun in Chapter 1, which situates the activity of interpretation in an international community that historically has marginalized precisely the groups for whom the concept of self-determination has the greatest significance. The chapter seeks to show

---

[1] For an early attempt by this author to evaluate the competing normative models of self-determination, see R. Howse and K. Knop, 'Federalism, Secession, and the Limits of Ethnic Accommodation: A Canadian Perspective' (1993) 1 *New Europe Law Review* 269.

how the process of giving meaning to self-determination is a process of constituting these human communities in distinctive ways, and therefore in ways that we or they may find disturbing or comforting, alien or familiar, strategic or genuine, respectful or demeaning.

The chapter follows the standard organization of the post-Cold War international law literature on external self-determination.[2] The first part deals with the definition of a 'people', and the second part, with the determination of when the right of self-determination entitles a people to choose their external political status.

Who is a 'people'?

Colonies

International lawyers virtually all agree that whatever else the term 'peoples' may mean, it means the colonial categories of trust territories and non-self-governing territories established by the United Nations Charter.[3] Trust territories, covered by Chapter XII of the Charter, were primarily territories held previously under the League of Nations mandate system.[4] At the end of World War I, territories were taken from Germany and the Ottoman Empire, now Turkey, and administered as mandated territories by one of the victorious states on conditions agreed with the League of Nations.[5] By the early days of the UN Charter, some of the mandated territories – Iraq, Jordan, Lebanon and Syria – had become independent. The remaining ones, apart from the British mandate of Palestine and the South African mandate of South West Africa, were brought under the UN trusteeship system. Additional territories could be placed under the trusteeship system, but the only such trust territory was Italian Somaliland, present-day Somalia. In the case of each trust territory, an authority, which could be one or more states or the United

---

[2] The discussion in this chapter is limited to general international law. In the regional context, see e.g. R. N. Kiwanuka, 'The Meaning of "People" in the African Charter on Human and Peoples' Rights' (1988) 82 *American Journal of International Law* 80 (African Charter on Human and Peoples' Rights); J. Salo, 'Self-Determination: An Overview of History and Present State with Emphasis on the CSCE Process' (1991) 2 *Finnish Yearbook of International Law* 268 at 310–40 (Organization for Security and Cooperation in Europe).

[3] Charter of the United Nations, 26 June 1945, 59 Stat. 1031, 145 BFSP (1943–5) 805 (1953).

[4] For a summary of League mandates and United Nations trusteeships, see J. Crawford, *The Creation of States in International Law* (Oxford: Clarendon Press, 1979), App. 2.

[5] Covenant of the League of Nations, Versailles, 28 June 1919, in force 10 January 1920, (1919) 112 BFSP 13, Art. 22.

Nations itself, administered the territory pursuant to an individual trusteeship agreement. The United Nations supervised the administration of trust territories through a system of reporting by administering authorities, examination of petitions and periodic visits by UN missions.[6]

Non-self-governing territories are dealt with in Chapter XI of the Charter.[7] In the words of that Chapter, non-self-governing territories are 'territories whose people have not yet attained a full measure of self-government'. Initially, these territories were identified by the states responsible for them. Australia, Belgium, Denmark, France, the Netherlands, New Zealand, the United Kingdom and the United States all voluntarily listed certain of their territories as non-self-governing. However, Portugal's and Spain's refusal to declare any of their colonies as non-self-governing territories and thereby bring them within the reporting system of Chapter XI led the General Assembly to specify criteria for non-self-governing territories.[8] Using these criteria, the General Assembly found Southern Rhodesia and certain French territories, as well as certain overseas territories of Portugal and Spain, to be non-self-governing.[9]

While the UN Charter envisaged progress toward self-government for trust territories and non-self-governing territories, it made no mention of self-determination. It is generally accepted, however, that the subsequent development of international law gave these territories a right of self-determination[10] which they were free to exercise by the establishment of an independent state, their association or integration with

---

[6] UN Charter, c. XIII.

[7] For a summary of non-self-governing territories from 1946 to 1977, see Crawford, *The Creation of States*, App. 3.

[8] Principles Which Should Guide Members in Determining Whether or Not an Obligation Exists to Transmit the Information Called for Under Article 73e of the Charter: Annex, GA Res. 1541 (XV) (1960). For the history of these criteria, see A. Rigo Sureda, *The Evolution of the Right of Self-Determination: A Study of United Nations Practice* (Leiden: A.W. Sijthoff, 1973), pp. 54–8.

[9] See J. Crawford, *State Practice and International Law in Relation to Unilateral Secession* (Expert Report for Canadian federal government, *Reference re Secession of Quebec*, [1998] 2 SCR 217, (1998) 37 ILM 1340), reprinted in A. F. Bayefsky (ed.), *Self-Determination in International Law: Quebec and Lessons Learned* (The Hague: Kluwer Law International, 2000), pp. 31–61 at p. 38. See also J. Crawford, 'State Practice and International Law in Relation to Secession' (1998) 69 *British Yearbook of International Law* 85 at 88–9 (based closely on Crawford, Expert Report).

[10] See e.g. *Namibia (South West Africa)*, Advisory Opinion, ICJ Reports 1971, p. 16 at pp. 31–2; *Western Sahara*, Advisory Opinion, ICJ Reports 1975, p. 12 at pp. 31–3; *East Timor (Portugal v. Australia)*, ICJ Reports 1995, p. 90 at pp. 102–3, 105–6. The *Western Sahara* and *East Timor* cases are discussed in Chapter 4 below.

another state or the transition to any other freely chosen political status. All trust territories have now exercised their right of self-determination. Except for a few territories – most notably, Western Sahara – all non-self-governing territories have also achieved self-determination. The exercise of self-determination has most often resulted in independence, creating almost one hundred new states.[11]

Categories and coherence

Both generally accepted categories of 'peoples', trust territories and non-self-governing territories, were colonies in the sense of being dependent on and subordinate to a geographically separate state. The current controversy over 'peoples'[12] in international law is whether the term means more than just the population of colonies in this particular historical sense. As is evident from the expert opinions solicited in the debate over Quebec's right to secede from Canada, the established view continues to be that it does not.[13] At its narrowest and most positivist, the argument

---

[11] See Crawford, Expert Report, pp. 38–40. See also Crawford, 'State Practice', 89–91.

[12] It should be remembered that the discussion is limited to 'peoples' having the right to *external* self-determination.

[13] This view is taken by five eminent international lawyers from France (Alain Pellet), Germany (Christian Tomuschat), the United Kingdom (Rosalyn Higgins and Malcolm Shaw) and the United States (Thomas Franck) in a joint report prepared for a Quebec commission studying questions related to Quebec's accession to sovereignty. T. Franck, R. Higgins, A. Pellet, M. Shaw and C. Tomuschat, 'L'intégrité territoriale du Québec dans l'hypothèse de l'accession à la souveraineté' in Commission d'étude des questions afférentes à l'accession du Québec à la souveraineté, *Les attributs d'un Québec souverain, Exposés et études,* vol. I (1992), pp. 377–461, translated as 'The Territorial Integrity of Québec in the Event of the Attainment of Sovereignty' in Bayefsky, *Lessons Learned,* pp. 241–303. In connection with a reference to the Supreme Court of Canada regarding Quebec's right to secede, the federal government retained James Crawford (Australia) as an expert in international law. Crawford's report takes the same position on external self-determination. Crawford, Expert Report. See also Crawford, 'State Practice'. The international law experts consulted by the *amicus curiae* for Quebec essentially share Crawford's view that outside the colonial context, the right of self-determination does not include a right to independence. They argue, however, that to focus on the absence of a right in this 'hard' legal sense is misleading because international law does not prohibit secession, and, indeed, the international community often recognizes states formed by secession. See the expert reports of Thomas M. Franck, Alain Pellet and Malcolm N. Shaw, reprinted in Bayefsky, *Lessons Learned* at Part II(B) and replies at Part II(D). In the Quebec context, see also N. Finkelstein and G. Vegh, *The Separation of Quebec and the Constitution of Canada* (Background Studies of the York University Constitutional Reform Project, Study No. 2) (North York, Ont.: York University Centre for Public Law and Public Policy, 1992), pp. 49–51, but see N. Finkelstein, G. Vegh and C. Joly, 'Does Québec Have the Right to Secede at International Law?' (1995) 74 *Canadian Bar Review* 225.

is that self-determination entered international law only as a rule of decolonization, and its formulation and application in international law preclude any definition of 'peoples' broader than colonies.[14]

This section next introduces and compares the two ways that authors have structurally expanded the definition of 'peoples' beyond the colonial categories of trust territories and non-self-governing territories. One way is to establish a general definition of 'peoples' that makes sense of the colonial identity (the coherence approach), and the other is to demonstrate that international law has recognized additional categories of 'peoples' (the categories approach).

> More generally, see also J. Castellino, 'Order and Justice: National Minorities and the Right to Secession' (1999) 6 *International Journal on Minority and Group Rights* 389 at 391, 410; O. Corten, 'Le droit à l'autodétermination en dehors des situations de décolonisation, de Théodore Christakis. A propos d'un désormais "classique"' (1999) 32 *Revue belge de droit international* 329; L. S. Eastwood, 'Secession: State Practice and International Law After the Dissolution of the Soviet Union and Yugoslavia' (1993) 3 *Duke Journal of Comparative and International Law* 299; M. H. Halperin and D. J. Scheffer with P. L. Small, *Self-Determination in the New World Order* (Washington, D. C.: Carnegie Endowment for International Peace, 1992), pp. 16–25, 53; H. Quane, 'A Right to Self-Determination for the Kosovo Albanians?' (2000) 13 *Leiden Journal of International Law* 219; H. Quane, 'The United Nations and the Evolving Right to Self-Determination' (1998) 47 *International and Comparative Law Quarterly* 537; C. Saladin, 'Self-Determination, Minority Rights, and Constitutional Accommodation: The Example of the Czech and Slovak Federal Republic' (1991) 13 *Michigan Journal of International Law* 172; R. G. Steinhardt, *International Law and Self-Determination* (Occasional Paper Series) (Washington, D.C.: Atlantic Council of the United States, November 1994), pp. 9–24; W. T. Webb, 'The International Legal Aspects of the Lithuanian Secession' (1991) 17 *Journal of Legislation* 309 at 325–8; J. Wilson, 'Ethnic Groups and the Right to Self-Determination' (1996) 11 *Connecticut Journal of International Law* 433; E. K. M. Yakpo, 'The African Concept of *Uti Possidetis* – Need for Change?' in E. Yakpo and T. Boumedra (eds.), *Liber Amicorum Judge Mohammed Bedjaoui* (The Hague: Kluwer Law International, 1999), pp. 271–90 at pp. 274–7, 280.

[14] Although the argument for a 'colonies only' interpretation of self-determination varies from author to author, the most common steps of the argument are (1) self-determination was not recognized in international law prior to the development of a right of self-determination for colonies; (2) when the right of self-determination did enter international law, it was formulated in such a way as to deny the right to any peoples other than colonial peoples; (3) the principle of *uti possidetis*, which preserves existing boundaries upon independence, reinforces the principle of territorial integrity for newly independent states by prohibiting any exercise of self-determination by groups within the state; and (4) the interpretation of the right of self-determination as limited to colonial peoples is consistent with post-World War II practice because few if any of the new states to emerge from processes other than decolonization were the result of unilateral secession, and this precedent was far outweighed by the lack of international support for the numerous other attempts at secession.

Coherence

While trust territories and non-self-governing territories give a technical legal meaning to 'peoples', it is unclear what idea of identity underlies them and, hence, what more abstract definition of 'peoples' would encompass them. Colonies corresponded to neither *demos* nor *ethnos*, the two ideas of the nation current in European political thought since the eighteenth century.[15] In the 1882 lecture, 'Qu'est-ce qu'une Nation?', Ernest Renan expressed the idea of *demos*, the political nation, as summarized by the tangible fact of 'consent, the clearly expressed desire to continue a common life'.[16] On this view, the nation embodies a common consciousness derived primarily from shared lives and shared ideals. United by the historical fact of imperial conquest, however, the population of the colonies had never consented to an existence in common, and did not originally possess a collective consciousness or hold shared ideals.

For the German Romantic thinkers, the nation was an *ethnos*, a cultural community based on a common language. Johann Gottfried Herder, who is often regarded as the intellectual father of ethnic nationalism,[17] wrote that providence 'has wonderfully separated nationalities not only by woods and mountains, seas and deserts, rivers and climates, but more particularly by languages, inclinations and characters'.[18] But since the colonies were often patchwork quilts of different tribes, colonial populations did not necessarily have a common ethnicity or language.

While colonies were neither *demos* nor *ethnos* in origin, their international legal recognition as 'peoples' might nevertheless have registered a sociological identity forged by colonialism. Charles Chaumont postulates that a colonial population became a people through its development of a collective awareness of oppression and exploitation by the imperial power and through its common fight for liberation. Tribal rivalries inside the generally artificial colonial borders of Africa,

---

[15] On these two concepts of nation, see e.g. A. Cobban, *The Nation State and National Self-Determination* (rev. edn, New York: T. Y. Crowell, 1969), pp. 118–25.

[16] E. Renan, 'What is a Nation?', M. Thom (trans.) in H. K. Bhabha (ed.), *Nation and Narration* (London: Routledge, 1990), pp. 8–22 at p. 19. For a similar definition, see J. S. Mill, 'Considerations on Representative Government' in J. S. Mill, *On Liberty and Other Essays*, J. Gray (ed.) (Oxford: Oxford University Press, 1991), pp. 205–467 at p. 427.

[17] See e.g. R. R. Ergang, *Herder and the Foundations of German Nationalism* (New York: Columbia University Press, 1931), pp. 239–66.

[18] Quoted in *ibid.*, p. 244.

according to Chaumont, sometimes masked this awareness until it arose from the unifying force of combat.[19] Other international legal scholars maintain that cultural devices – ranging from the European production of knowledge about the colonies[20] in such forms as census, map and museum[21] to the creation of a fictional common history or ethnicity by African writers[22] – could lead colonial populations to imagine themselves as 'peoples'.[23] However, the complex and contradictory relationship between colonialism and nationalism[24] makes any generalization about colonial identity problematic. Quite apart from whether colonial nationalism is authentic,[25] we are left with the extensive variations in its form, expression and power.

Rather than as corresponding to a sociological fact, we might justify the colonial categories of 'peoples' as a normative designation. Whether or not a trust territory or non-self-governing territory had some identity apart from the purely administrative, its population was normatively joined together as a 'people' by virtue of suffering the collective

---

[19] C. Chaumont, 'Le droit des peuples à témoigner d'eux-mêmes' (1976) 2 *Annuaire du Tiers Monde* 15 at 27.

[20] See B. Maurer, 'Writing Law, Making a "Nation": History, Modernity, and Paradoxes of Self-Rule in the British Virgin Islands' (1995) 29 *Law and Society Review* 255; D. Otto, 'Subalternity and International Law: The Problems of Global Community and the Incommensurability of Difference' (1996) 5:3 *Social and Legal Studies* 337 at 348–54 (applying Subaltern Studies scholarship on nationalism in India to international law).

[21] See B. Anderson, *Imagined Communities: Reflections on the Origin and Spread of Nationalism* (rev. edn, London, Verso, 1991), pp. 163–85. See also C. Young, 'Ethnicity and the Colonial and Post-Colonial State in Africa' in P. Brass (ed.), *Ethnic Groups and the State* (Totowa, New Jersey: Barnes and Noble Books, 1985), pp. 57–93 at pp. 73–82.

[22] In the case of Kenya, see E. M. Morgan, 'The Imagery and Meaning of Self-Determination' (1988) 20 *New York University Journal of International Law and Politics* 355.

[23] But see Y. Ghai, 'Reflections on Self-Determination in the South Pacific' in D. Clark and R. Williamson (eds.), *Self-Determination: International Perspectives* (New York: St. Martin's Press, 1996), pp. 173–99 at pp. 177–8.

[24] See P. Chatterjee, *Nationalist Thought and the Colonial World: A Derivative Discourse* (Minneapolis: University of Minnesota Press, 1986).

[25] See the debate of the 1960s and 1970s in the African and Asian context between 'primordialists', who stressed the resistance of natural groupings of kinship, religion, language and custom to the civic identity necessary to the newly independent colonial states; and 'instrumentalists', who argued that identity is created by interested leaders, elite groups or the political system. The debate is usefully excerpted in J. Hutchinson and A. D. Smith (eds.), *Nationalism* (Oxford: Oxford University Press, 1994) at pp. 29–34 (C. Geertz, 'Primordial and Civic Ties') and pp. 83–9 (P. R. Brass, 'Elite Competition and Nation-Formation'). More recent scholarship on nationalism argues that any national identity is a cultural construction. Anderson, *Imagined Communities*; H. K. Bhabha, 'Introduction' in Bhabha, *Nation and Narration*, pp. 1–7.

injury of colonialism. That is, they were defined by the wrong. On this approach, the question remains which of the many wrongs instantiated by colonialism is definitive. Among the principles violated by colonialism, Karl Doehring lists 'the protection of human rights, the equality of states, the prohibition of discrimination on account of race, language, and religion, freedom from oppression by foreign powers, protection against exploitation, and the preservation of peace among peoples'.[26]

A different normative way of looking at colonial identity is to see the notion of 'peoples' as flowing from the principle that whenever the future of a territory falls to be determined – regardless of the reason – it is for the population of the territory to make that determination. In President Wilson's famous words, 'peoples... are not to be bartered about from sovereignty to sovereignty as if they were mere chattels and pawns in a game'.[27] From this perspective, a 'people' need have no fellow feeling. A 'people' is *au fond* a community of fate, the inhabitants of a territory defined by forces beyond their control. Their identity is as a collection of individuals each entitled to vote on the future of the territory, and their collective will is the majority of their individual wills. In the case of border territories, for example, the identity of the 'people' may be spent by the redrawing of the border in response to the democratically determined will of the majority.

Despite the uneasy fit with colonial identity, the general definitions of 'peoples' found in the post-Cold War international law literature on external self-determination usually revolve around the ideas of *demos* and *ethnos*. For Daniel Turp, a 'people' is a democratically constituted community: a 'group of individuals who choose to determine their own future... A common language, culture, and religion play a determining role in the process of self-definition, but the collective desire to live together better defines a people'.[28]

---

[26] K. Doehring, 'Self-Determination' in B. Simma (ed.), *The Charter of the United Nations: A Commentary* (Munich: C. H. Beck, 1994), pp. 56–72 at p. 61.

[27] Woodrow Wilson, 'Four Points' speech to Congress, 11 February 1918, quoted in S. Wambaugh, *Plebiscites Since the World War with a Collection of Official Documents* (2 vols., Washington: Carnegie Endowment for International Peace, 1933), vol. I, p. 11. See also his earlier address to the Senate, 22 January 1917, quoted in *ibid.*, p. 5 ('No right anywhere exists to hand peoples about from sovereignty to sovereignty as if they were property.').

[28] D. Turp, 'Quebec's Democratic Right to Self-Determination: A Critical and Legal Reflection' in S. H. Hartt, A. L. C. de Mestral, J. McCallum, V. Loungenarath, D. Morton and D. Turp, *Tangled Web: Legal Aspects of Deconfederation* (Toronto: C. D. Howe Institute, 1992), pp. 99–124 at p. 110. See also D. Turp, 'Le droit à la sécession: l'expression du principe démocratique' in A.-G. Gagnon and F. Rocher (eds.), *Répliques aux détracteurs*

Turp derives his definition of peoples in international treaty law[29] from common Article 1 of the 1966 International Covenants on Human Rights, which begins 'All peoples have the right of self-determination. By virtue of that right they freely determine their political status and freely pursue their economic, social and cultural development'.[30] According to Turp, the ordinary meaning of these words, the contexts of Article 1 and of the Covenants as a whole, and the *travaux préparatoires* all show that this right of self-determination belongs to 'all peoples' and includes a right of secession. While the Covenants do not actually define 'peoples', Turp argues, they also 'ne contiennent aucune disposition permettant de circonscrire la notion de peuples et d'interpréter restrictivement celle-ci; le libellé de cet article premier tend au contraire à conférer au terme peuples une définition extensive' ('contain no provision permitting the notion of peoples to be circumscribed and interpreted restrictively; the wording of this first article tends on the contrary to confer an extensive definition on the term peoples').[31] Turp originally anticipates that the Human Rights Committee, the body of experts established under the International Covenant on Civil and Political Rights, will give meaning to the term 'peoples' in the course of interpreting that Covenant.[32] As this has not happened,[33] Turp now asserts that the silence in international law 'tend à suggérer que les peuples doivent témoigner d'eux-mêmes et que la qualité de peuple résulte dès

---

de la souveraineté du Québec (Montreal: VLB Editeur, 1992), pp. 49–68 at p. 55; D. Turp, Expert Testimony before the Commission d'étude des questions afférentes à l'accession du Québec à la souveraineté, Assemblée Nationale, Journal des débats, No. 5 (9 Oct. 1991), pp. 128–42 at p. 129; D. Turp, 'Exposé-réponse (Processus d'accession à la souveraineté)' in Commission d'étude des questions afférentes à l'accession du Québec à la souveraineté, *Les attributs d'un Québec souverain, Exposés et études*, vol. I (1992), pp. 655–86 at p. 660.

[29] D. Turp, 'Le droit de sécession en droit international public' (1982) 20 *Canadian Yearbook of International Law* 24 at 45–54. In this article, Turp takes the position that there is neither a right of nor prohibition on secession in international customary law. *Ibid.*, 54–76. More recently, he has argued that state practice shows a new openness toward a right of self-determination. See *e.g.* D. Turp, 'L'émergence de nouveaux états et le droit des peuples à disposer d'eux-mêmes' (1992) 21 *Proceedings of the Canadian Council on International Law* 25.

[30] International Covenant on Civil and Political Rights, New York, 16 December 1966, in force 23 March 1976, 999 UNTS 171; International Covenant on Economic, Social and Cultural Rights, New York, 16 December 1966, in force 3 January 1976, 993 UNTS 3. For the drafting history of the International Covenant on Civil and Political Rights, see M. J. Bossuyt, *Guide to the 'Travaux Préparatoires' of the International Covenant on Civil and Political Rights* (Dordrecht: Martinus Nijhoff, 1987).

[31] (Translation mine) Turp, 'Le droit de sécession', 52.

[32] *Ibid.*, 52.   [33] See pp. 22–3 above.

lors d'un processus d'autoqualification' ('tends to suggest that peoples must bear witness to themselves and that that quality of a people is from that moment on the result of a process of self-description').[34] For him, this definition of a 'people' is the 'more plausible' one.[35]

Why 'more plausible'? Turp does not spell out an answer, but his recent writing and testimony indicate where we might look for one. Turp's reference to the object and purpose of the International Covenant on Civil and Political Rights may locate the importance of collective choice in the liberal democratic values of that Covenant; for example, the right to freedom of association in Article 22 and the right of political participation in Article 25.[36] But this does not account for the precedent of trust territories and non-self-governing territories in so far as conquest and not choice was originally responsible for the contours of the community. Here, Turp's citation to Charles Chaumont[37] is apposite because Chaumont argued that resistance to colonialism actually constituted a people, thereby both removing the problem of the original lack of choice (a people having come together in the struggle) and expressing a current choice (the desire to live together free of colonial rule).

A closer reading of Turp and Chaumont, however, suggests that although both interpret 'peoples' by reference to the 'reality' of action, they present very different visions of that reality. Chaumont's theory of law anticipates and embraces the violence of identity formation, whereas Turp's example of Quebec suggests that he seeks to transmute this embrace. Chaumont's interpretation of 'peoples' presupposes a theory of international law that sees international law as based on social reality.[38] For Chaumont, the relationship between them is dialectical.

> Le droit international... n'est pas destiné à planer au-dessus des réalités, et par là même à les camoufler, et en fin de compte à permettre aux Etats d'agir librement à l'abri d'une façade de généralités. Il est une tentative continue de mutation des contradictions réelles, et il accomplit la double tâche de traduire ces contradictions et en même temps de les surmonter.

---

[34] (Translation mine) Turp, 'Exposé-réponse', p. 660.
[35] Turp, 'Quebec's Democratic Right', p. 110.
[36] Turp, 'L'expression du principe démocratique', p. 55. See also Turp, 'Quebec's Democratic Right', p. 110. (The English-language article refers to 'subject and purpose'.)
[37] Turp, 'L'expression du principe démocratique', p. 55, n. 30; Turp, 'Exposé-réponse', 660, n. 13; Turp, 'Quebec's Democratic Right', p. 110, n. 29, citing Chaumont, 'Le droit des peuples'.
[38] Chaumont, 'Le droit des peuples', 16.

[International law... is not destined to hover above realities, in this way even to camouflage them, and, in the end, to permit states to act freely under shelter of a facade of generalities. It is a continuous attempt to transform real contradictions, and it accomplishes the dual task of translating these contradictions whilst at the same time surmounting them.][39]

Just as international law is based on the realities of international life, the right of peoples rests on the reality of those peoples,[40] where that reality is demonstrated by the people itself in action.[41] What Chaumont has in mind is the material reality of armed resistance. The legal and political acts that Turp presents as evidence of a Québécois people do not belong to this material base, but to the ideological superstructure. For Turp, the laws and public statements of a democratically elected majority government are enough to prove the self-affirmation of a people. Among the acts of Quebec self-assertion he identifies are Quebec legislation establishing various commissions on Quebec's political future, the provincial *Chartre de la langue française*, a speech by the former Quebec premier Robert Bourassa referring to the 'intérêt supérieur du peuple québécois' and a series of motions and resolutions passed by the Quebec legislature.[42] In contrast, Chaumont, writing at the height of national liberation movements in the Third World, assumes that violence will testify to the existence of a people:

Et de même que l'histoire d'un homme, par l'achèvement de la mort, prend sa signification totale, étant entièrement accompli, même si ses caractéristiques dominantes restent en partie mystérieuses, de même la mort des personnes en tant que parties d'un peuple constitue l'affirmation historique suprême.
  L'enjeu de la mort est ainsi l'élément probatoire le plus déterminant pour un peuple, comme pour une personne.

[And just as the story of a man assumes its total signification from its culmination in death, having been wholly accomplished, even if its dominant characteristics remain in part mysterious, so the death of persons as part of a people constitutes the supreme historical affirmation.

---

[39] (Translation mine) C. Chaumont, 'Cours général de droit international public' (1970–I) 129 Hague Recueil 333 at 363.
[40] Chaumont, 'Le droit des peuples', 16, 26, 29.
[41] *Ibid.*, 17–23.
[42] Turp, 'Quebec's Democratic Right', pp. 110–12; Turp, 'L'expression du principe démocratique', pp. 55–6; Turp, 'Exposé-réponse', pp. 660–1; Turp, Expert Testimony, pp. 129–30.

The stakes of death are thus the most determinative probative element for a people as for a person.]⁴³

Other general definitions of 'peoples'⁴⁴ found in the literature tend to combine objective elements, such as language, religion or ethnicity, with the subjective element of a common will to live together.⁴⁵ Whereas most authors who produce these coherent definitions rely on the interpretation of international customary law and the writings of publicists, Ian Brownlie differs in explicitly invoking a notion of the coherence of international law.

For Brownlie, the principle of self-determination of peoples has a core meaning, which is 'the right of a community which has a distinct character to have this character reflected in the institutions of government under which it lives'.⁴⁶ The distinct character of a community does not hinge on a single criterion, but depends on a sufficient cluster of criteria being present. Brownlie considers one of the more important to be race

---

[43] (Translation mine) Chaumont, 'Le droit des peuples', 17.
[44] Unlike Turp, other authors who define 'peoples' in general terms do not subscribe to an absolute right of secession of peoples.
[45] J. Woehrling, 'Les aspects juridiques d'une éventuelle sécession du Québec' (1995) 74 *Canadian Bar Review* 293 at 316; Finkelstein, Vegh and Joly, 'Does Québec Have the Right?', 248–9; J. Woehrling 'Les aspects juridiques de la redéfinition du statut politique et constitutionnel du Québec' in Commission sur l'avenir politique et constitutionnel du Québec, *Éléments d'analyse institutionnelle, juridique et démolinguistique pertinents à la révision du statut politique et constitutionnel du Québec* (Document de travail, No. 2) (M. Bélanger and J. Campeau chairs, 1991), pp. 1–110 at pp. 86–7; R. F. Iglar, 'The Constitutional Crisis in Yugoslavia and the International Law of Self-Determination: Slovenia's and Croatia's Right to Secede' (1992) 15 *Boston College International and Comparative Law Review* 213 at 225–6.

For an instance where an ethno-cultural definition of 'people' was essentially asserted, see R. A. Falk, Testimony before the Commission d'étude des questions afférentes à l'accession du Québec à la souveraineté, Assemblée Nationale, Journal des débats, No. 24 (4 Feb. 1991), pp. 705–14 at p. 705 (Professor of International Law at Princeton University testifying on behalf of the Algonquin people); M. E. Turpel, 'Does the Road to Québec Sovereignty Run Through Aboriginal Territory?' in D. Drache and R. Perin (eds.), *Negotiating with a Sovereign Quebec* (Toronto: James Lorimer & Co., 1992), pp. 93–106 at pp. 100–1; M. E. Turpel, 'The Cultural Non-Homogeneity of Québec: Secessionism, Indigenous Legal Perspectives and Inseparability' in Clark and Williamson, *Self-Determination*, pp. 284–90 at p. 287.
[46] I. Brownlie, 'The Rights of Peoples in Modern International Law' in J. Crawford (ed.), *The Rights of Peoples* (Oxford: Clarendon Press, 1988), pp. 1–16 at p. 5. See also I. Brownlie, 'An Essay in the History of the Principle of Self-Determination' in C. N. Alexandrowicz (ed.), *Grotian Society Papers: Studies in the History of the Law of Nations, 1968* (The Hague: Martinus Nijhoff, 1970), pp. 90–9 at p. 90; I. Brownlie, *Treaties and Indigenous Peoples: The Robb Lectures 1991* (Oxford: Clarendon Press, 1992), pp. 47–8.

or nationality, which he disaggregates into culture, language, religion and group psychology. At the same time, he notes that the physical indicia of race or nationality are not essential to national identity.[47] While acknowledging that his definition is not generally accepted, Brownlie nevertheless seems to present it as descriptive of the actual coherence of international law, a coherence obscured by the usual typology. In particular, he observes that the categories of 'nationalities', 'peoples', 'minorities' and 'indigenous populations' all involve essentially the same idea.[48]

Categories and coherence compared

In contrast to the coherence approach to expanding the interpretation of 'peoples' beyond trust territories and non-self-governing territories, the categories approach treats colonies as a legal artefact. Rather than abstracting a new definition of peoples from some feature of the colonial identity or formulating a new definition that encompasses that feature, the categories approach establishes new categories of peoples independent of the old colonial categories. Karl Doehring is a good example. For Doehring, the historical development of self-determination in international law yields three distinct meanings for 'peoples'.[49]

To the generally accepted category of colonial populations, Doehring adds a second category, the population of sovereign states, which he associates with the right of self-determination as a defence against foreign domination. Doehring's third category, ethnic minorities, stems from the

[47] Brownlie, 'The Rights of Peoples', p. 5. Compare A. A. An-Na'im, 'The National Question, Secession and Constitutionalism: The Mediation of Competing Claims to Self-Determination' in I. G. Shivji (ed.), *State and Constitutionalism: An African Debate on Democracy* (Harare: SAPES, 1991), pp. 101–19 at pp. 107–8 (relying on Brownlie, among others, to define 'peoples' as ethnic, religious or linguistic minorities).

[48] Brownlie, 'The Rights of Peoples', p. 16. Compare B. Kingsbury, 'Claims by Non-State Groups in International Law' (1992) 25 *Cornell International Law Journal* 481 at 481 ('The separate structure of each of these domains has obscured the overlap (if not the identity) of underlying justificatory purposes among these different domains.') Both Brownlie and Kingsbury make prescriptive, as well as descriptive, arguments for a coherent approach to groups and group rights in international law. For Kingsbury, however, a coherent approach only becomes imperative where categorization makes a difference to the outcome; that is, where a problem of commensurability or reconciliation between conflicting categories must be resolved. In B. Kingsbury, 'Reconciling Five Competing Conceptual Structures of Indigenous Peoples' Claims in International and Comparative Law' in P. Alston (ed.), *Peoples' Rights* (Oxford: Oxford University Press, 2001), pp. 69–110, Kingsbury rounds out his analysis with a discussion of the advantages otherwise offered by the possibility of multiple categorization.

[49] Doehring, 'Self-Determination', pp. 63–4.

end of World War I. Although the principle of self-determination was not then part of ordinary international law, the idea that ethnicity was nature's blueprint for political organization played a role in the creation of new states and the settlement of boundaries by the peace treaties, and in the establishment of an ambitious inter-war international legal regime for the protection of ethnic minorities in a number of European states.[50] Doehring takes this third definition of 'peoples' from the advisory opinion of the Permanent Court of International Justice in the *Greco-Bulgarian 'Communities'* case:

a group of persons living in a given country or locality, having a race, religion, language and traditions of their own and united by this identity of race, religion, language and traditions in a sentiment of solidarity, with a view to preserving their traditions, maintaining their form of worship, ensuring the instruction and upbringing of their children in accordance with the spirit and traditions of their race and rendering mutual assistance to each other.[51]

Contemporary evidence of such a category may be found in the 1970 UN Declaration on Principles of International Law Concerning Friendly Relations and Cooperation Among States in Accordance with the Charter of the United Nations (Declaration on Friendly Relations) (GA Resolution 2625 (XXV)). Although the final paragraph of the principle of equal rights and self-determination of peoples in the Declaration on Friendly Relations prohibits the disruption of the territorial integrity of a state, the preceding paragraph has been read by Doehring and others as making an exception for the secession of racial and religious minorities in cases of extreme discrimination.[52]

Categories authors like Doehring thus reject a 'one size fits all' definition of peoples.[53] Moreover, because they treat any non-colonial category of peoples independent of the colonial categories, the narratives of identity in the technical definition of colonial peoples as trust territories and non-self-governing territories are left unexamined. The colonial identity remains ambiguous rather than being distilled to some essential trait, as it is by the coherence approach to 'peoples'. This contrast is

---

[50] See D. Thürer, 'Self-Determination' in R. Bernhardt (ed.), *Encyclopedia of Public International Law* (12 vols., Amsterdam: North-Holland, 1985) vol. VIII, pp. 470–6 at pp. 470–1. But see e.g. Cobban, *The Nation State*, pp. 57–84 (arguing that it passed virtually without notice that the peace negotiations substituted for self-determination 'a belief in small states as a justifiable part of the international order, a belief in the equality of states, great or small, and a belief in the right of absolute national sovereignty').

[51] *Greco-Bulgarian 'Communities'*, Advisory Opinion (1930), PCIJ Ser. B, No. 17, p. 21.

[52] Doehring, 'Self-Determination', p. 66.

[53] Doehring, 'Self-Determination', p. 64.

illustrated by the discussion in the literature of peoples subject to alien domination or foreign occupation.

Support for the position that peoples subject to alien domination or foreign occupation are entitled to self-determination comes from the 1960 UN Declaration on the Granting of Independence to Colonial Countries and Peoples (Declaration on the Independence of Colonial Peoples) (GA Resolution 1514 (XV)), which states that 'the subjection of peoples to alien subjugation, domination and exploitation' constitutes a denial of human rights, violation of the UN Charter and impediment to peace;[54] and from the Declaration on Friendly Relations, which spells out that such subjugation contravenes the principle of self-determination.[55] Further support is found in UN resolutions invoking the right of self-determination in the case of apartheid South Africa, an independent state where a white formerly colonial minority dominated a black majority; and in the case of occupied territories, including Afghanistan and Palestine.[56]

Among those authors who recognize peoples subject to alien domination or foreign occupation as having a right of self-determination, some organize the definition of 'peoples' into colonial (trust territories and non-self-governing territories) and non-colonial (peoples subject to alien domination or foreign occupation) categories, and others formulate a single definition of 'peoples'. Rosalyn Higgins[57] and Anna Michalska,[58] for example,[59] simply document the existence of a separate category of

---

[54] Declaration on the Granting of Independence to Colonial Countries and Peoples, GA Res. 1514 (XV) (1960), para. 1.

[55] Declaration on Friendly Relations, fifth principle (the principle of equal rights and self-determination of peoples), second paragraph.

[56] R. Higgins, 'International Law and the Avoidance, Containment and Resolution of Disputes' (1991–V) 230 Hague Recueil 9 at 159–60; R. Higgins, *Problems and Process: International Law and How We Use It* (Oxford: Clarendon Press, 1994), pp. 115–16.

[57] *Ibid.*

[58] A. Michalska, 'Rights of Peoples to Self-Determination in International Law' in W. Twining (ed.), *Issues of Self-Determination* (Aberdeen: Aberdeen University Press, 1991), pp. 71–90 at pp. 78–83.

[59] See also A. Eide, 'In Search of Constructive Alternatives to Secession' in C. Tomuschat (ed.), *Modern Law of Self-Determination* (Dordrecht: Martinus Nijhoff, 1993), pp. 139–76 at p. 153; A. Eide, *Possible Ways and Means of Facilitating the Peaceful and Constructive Solution of Problems Involving Minorities*, Report to the Sub-Commission on Prevention of Discrimination and Protection of Minorities, UN Doc. E/CN.4/Sub.2/1993/34 (1993), p. 16; H. Hannum, *Autonomy, Sovereignty, and Self-Determination: The Accommodation of Conflicting Rights* (rev. edn, Philadelphia: University of Pennsylvania Press, 1996), pp. 46–9, 497–9; M. N. Shaw, 'Peoples, Territorialism and Boundaries' (1997) 8 *European Journal of International Law* 478 at 480–4.

peoples subject to alien domination or foreign occupation. Neither of them goes behind the colonial and non-colonial categories because they are satisfied that each category can be established independently in positive international law. In defining colonial peoples only in the technical sense of trust territories and non-self-governing territories, they leave the colonial categories as political fiat made law and thereby open to multiple narratives of colonial identity.

Unlike Higgins and Michalska, W. Ofuatey-Kodjoe[60] develops a unified definition of the peoples entitled to self-determination as subjugated, by which he means 'those non-self-governing, those occupied, those under foreign rule and those deprived of a previous independent condition'.[61] Ofuatey-Kodjoe's view that a people is defined in terms of alien domination or foreign occupation also seems to inform the Vienna Declaration and Programme of Action produced by the 1993 UN World Conference on Human Rights ('peoples under colonial and *other* forms of alien domination or foreign occupation').[62] By lending consistency to the definition of 'peoples', Ofuatey-Kodjoe makes the identity of all peoples in international law, including colonial peoples, that of the collective victim of subjugation by a foreign power.

When does the right of self-determination entitle a people to choose independence?

In the previous part of this chapter, we saw how the interpretation of 'people' creates an image of a people and their history in international law. This part examines how the interpretation of the right of self-determination contributes to that image, whether by strengthening it or by altering it.

---

[60] See also F. Przetacznik, 'The Basic Collective Human Right to Self-Determination of Peoples and Nations as Prerequisite for Peace' (1990) 8 *New York Law School Journal of Human Rights* 49.

[61] W. Ofuatey-Kodjoe, 'Self-Determination' in O. Schachter and C. C. Joyner (eds.), *United Nations Legal Order* (2 vols., Cambridge: American Society of International Law and Grotius Publications of Cambridge University Press, 1995), vol. I, pp. 349–89 at p. 375. His full definition of a 'people' is 'a self-conscious, politically coherent community that is currently under the political subjugation and domination of another community separate and distinct from itself'. *Ibid.*, p. 376. For his earlier work on self-determination, see W. Ofuatey-Kodjoe, *The Principle of Self-Determination in International Law* (New York: Nellen Publishers, 1977).

[62] (Emphasis mine), United Nations World Conference on Human Rights, Vienna Declaration and Programme of Action, adopted 25 June 1993, (1993) 32 ILM 1661 at pt. I. 2, para. 2.

Colonialism and freely expressed will

On the traditional equation of 'peoples' with colonies, all peoples have the right of self-determination. The right of self-determination is to be exercised by the establishment of an independent state, the free association or integration with another state or the emergence into any other political status freely chosen by the people.[63] Its essence, as expressed by the International Court of Justice in the *Western Sahara* case, is 'the need to pay regard to the freely expressed will of peoples'.[64]

In *Western Sahara*, the court traces the rhetoric of free choice in the key UN resolutions on self-determination.[65] GA Resolution 1541, which lists the modes of self-government[66] as independence, free association or integration, spells out that 'free association should be the result of a free and voluntary choice by the peoples of the territory concerned expressed through informed and democratic processes'.[67] The resolution further specifies that integration constitutes an exercise of self-determination only where it is 'the result of the freely expressed wishes of the territory's peoples acting with full knowledge of the change in their status, their wishes having been expressed through informed and democratic processes, impartially conducted and based on universal adult suffrage'.[68] In providing that a people may also opt for some political status other than statehood, association or integration, the later Declaration on Friendly Relations requires that such status be 'freely determined by a people'.[69] More generally, the Declaration places a duty on states to promote self-determination in order to 'bring a speedy end to colonialism, having due regard to the freely expressed will of the peoples concerned'.[70]

Although traditionally associated with decolonization, freedom of choice is not as such dependent on a particular history. Antonio Cassese formulates the principle as the 'need to pay regard to the freely

---

[63] Declaration on Friendly Relations, fifth principle, fourth paragraph.
[64] *Western Sahara*, p. 33.   [65] *Ibid.*, pp. 32–3.
[66] The notion of self-government, which summarizes the various possible choices for a people, sometimes obscures the fact that the right of self-determination is about free choice and not about the particular choices. Ofuatey-Kodjoe, for example, defines the right of self-determination as the right to attain full self-government, but analyses it in terms of free choice. Ofuatey-Kodjoe, 'Self-Determination', pp. 372–3, 377. Compare S. J. Anaya, *Indigenous Peoples in International Law* (New York: Oxford University Press, 1996), p. 80 (distinguishing remedies from substance).
[67] GA Res. 1541, principle VII(a).   [68] *Ibid.*, principle IX(b).
[69] Declaration on Friendly Relations, fifth principle, fourth paragraph.
[70] Declaration on Friendly Relations, fifth principle, second paragraph, (b).

expressed will of peoples' each time the fate of peoples is at issue.[71] Daniel Turp goes further, seeing consent as the ongoing basis for political association. He defines a 'people' as 'a group of individuals who choose to determine their own future' and likewise maintains that the right of self-determination gives any such people an unlimited choice.[72] But even if international law does not support Turp's view of a people as a 'daily plebiscite',[73] the description of the right of self-determination as freedom of choice projects a generic liberal identity back onto whatever view of 'peoples' international law does contain. It superimposes the image of a collection of liberal monads inhabiting a territory, interchangeable exercisers of free will whose aggregate choice will determine the fate of the territory. Although asserting that the principle does not define the units of self-determination,[74] Cassese refers to 'conglomerates of individuals whose wishes and aspirations must be taken into account and given legal force as much as possible'.[75] In this sense, the effect is to de-historicize and de-particularize identity.[76]

---

[71] A. Cassese, *Self-Determination of Peoples: A Legal Reappraisal* (Cambridge: Cambridge University Press, 1995), pp. 128, 319–20.

[72] Turp, 'Quebec's Democratic Right', pp. 109–10; Turp, 'L'expression du principe démocratique', pp. 54–5; Turp, 'Exposé-réponse', pp. 659, 660, 663; Turp, Expert Testimony, p. 129. See also L. Beaudoin and J. Vallée, 'La reconnaissance internationale d'un Québec souverain' in Gagnon and Rocher, *Répliques aux détracteurs*, pp. 181–205 at p. 184 (relying on J. Brossard, *L'accession à la souveraineté et le cas du Québec* (Montreal: Les Presses de l'Université de Montréal, 1976), p. 191); Y. de Montigny, 'Exposé constitutionnel' in Commission sur l'avenir politique et constitutionnel du Québec, *Les avis des spécialistes invités à répondre aux huit questions posées par la Commission* (Document de travail, No. 4) (M. Bélanger and J. Campeau chairs, 1991), pp. 249–68 at p. 267.

[73] Renan, 'What is a Nation?', p. 19.   [74] Cassese, *Self-Determination of Peoples*, p. 128.

[75] A. Cassese, 'The International Court of Justice and the Right of Peoples to Self-Determination' in V. Lowe and M. Fitzmaurice (eds.), *Fifty Years of the International Court of Justice: Essays in Honour of Sir Robert Jennings* (Cambridge: Grotius Publications, 1996), pp. 351–63 at p. 361.

[76] But compare J. M. Woods, 'The Fallacy of Neutrality: Diary of an Election Observer' (1997) 18 *Michigan Journal of International Law* 475 at 480, 524 (describing South Africa's first democratic and internationally observed elections in 1994 as engaged in the liberal project of obliterating history) with H. G. West, 'Creative Destruction and Sorcery of Construction: Power, Hope and Suspicion in Post-War Mozambique' (1997) 20 *Political and Legal Anthropology Review* 13; R. J. Coombe, 'Identifying and Engendering the Forms of Emergent Civil Societies: New Directions in Political Anthropology' (1997) 20 *Political and Legal Anthropology Review* 1 at 2–3 (giving an account of how Mozambique's UN-supervised 1994 multi-party elections were used by one local populace to articulate performatively a new set of relationships between state and society in the idioms of a precolonial political cosmology).

Categories and coherence

The strict consensualism of Turp's interpretation of the right of self-determination of peoples points to what seems to be the inconsistency of defining the right of self-determination as the 'need to pay regard to the freely expressed will of peoples', yet limiting the right to colonial peoples. Why should the populations of overseas colonies be the only groups entitled to choose their political status? Indeed, the line drawn at colonies is widely thought to be normatively arbitrary. For some international lawyers, as we saw with the definition of 'peoples', this arbitrariness is irrelevant. Positive international law simply has the categories it has, although it may prove to have more categories of self-determination than just the absolute freedom of choice given to the populations of overseas colonies.

There are others, however, who feel what Robert Cover described as the insistent demand of every prescription 'to be located in a discourse – to be supplied with history and destiny, beginning and end, explanation and purpose'.[77] For them, international law contains an explanation both for the international community's support for decolonization and for its usual lack of support for secession. Such explanations most often revolve around the nature of the wrong, the impediment to human well-being or the minimization of violence. I deal with each in turn. And, once one of these more abstract accounts of the entitlement to external self-determination is given, as with the more abstract accounts of 'peoples', the possibility exists that situations other than overseas colonization will satisfy the account.[78]

Corrective justice and history

A few international lawyers argue that decolonization is distinguishable from secession in terms of corrective justice.[79] Private law, which is

---

[77] R. Cover, 'Nomos and Narrative' in M. Minow, M. Ryan and A. Sarat (eds.), *Narrative, Violence, and the Law: The Essays of Robert Cover* (Ann Arbor: University of Michigan Press, 1992), pp. 95–172 at p. 96.

[78] It should be noted that an author's interpretive approach to the definition of a 'people' may differ from her interpretive approach to the determination of when international law entitles a people to secede. She may define 'peoples' by unrelated, even inconsistent, categories, yet take a coherent approach to the meaning of the right of self-determination, or vice versa. Nor, where a coherence approach is taken to the interpretation of both, is it necessarily the same normatively.

[79] On corrective justice, see generally E. J. Weinrib, 'Aristotle's Forms of Justice' in S. Panagiotou (ed.), *Justice, Law and Method in Plato and Aristotle* (Edmonton, Alta.: Academic Printing & Publishing, 1987), pp. 133–52.

informed by corrective justice, has traditionally been a jurisprudential wellspring for international law. By substituting the state in international law for the individual in private law, the international law of territory can proceed by analogy with the law of property,[80] international treaty law can borrow from contract law, and so on. On an analogy between the collective subject of international law – not necessarily the state – and the individual in private law, the right of self-determination can be seen as restoring power or territory to the rightful sovereign, just as private law requires the restoration of wrongfully taken property to its owner.[81] In contrast to the story of a freely chosen future, this story of self-determination is of a past wrong; the bonds of identity it underwrites, those of historical deprivation. 'One loves in proportion to the sacrifices to which one has consented, and in proportion to the ills that one has suffered,' Renan observed of nations.[82]

It should be noted that quite apart from the right of self-determination, international law prohibits the acquisition of territory by conquest, or forcible taking of territory. The Iraqi invasion of Kuwait is a textbook example.[83] For these principles on acquisition of territory

---

[80] D. P. O'Connell maintains that the property conception of territory dominates Anglo-American thinking and is also found in French and Italian doctrine. D. P. O'Connell, *State Succession in Municipal Law and International Law* (2 vols., Cambridge: Cambridge University Press, 1967), vol. I, p. 22. For an account of this and other schools of thought, see E. Szlechter, *Les options conventionnelles de nationalité à la suite de cessions de territoires* (Paris: Recueil Sirey, 1948), pp. 27–57; W. Schœnborn, 'La nature juridique du territoire' (1929–V) 30 Hague Recueil 85 at 91–125.

[81] Although not found in the international legal literature, another corrective justice model of self-determination would be breach of pact. Asbjørn Eide hints at such a model. Eide, 'In Search of Constructive Alternatives to Secession', pp. 153–4. For possible examples, see R. Cohen, 'Legal Problems Arising From the Dissolution of the Mali Federation' (1960) 36 *British Yearbook of International Law* 375 at 375–82 (Senegal's position); G. H. Tesfagiorgis, 'Self-Determination: Its Evolution and Practice by the United Nations and Its Application to the Case of Eritrea' (1987) 6 *Wisconsin International Law Journal* 75 at 104, 107–8, 115–17 (Eritrea's position); Howse and Knop, 'Federalism, Secession', 296–303 (Quebec's position); Z. M. Necatigil, *The Cyprus Question and the Turkish Position in International Law* (Oxford: Oxford University Press, 1989), pp. 189–93 (Turkish Cypriots' position).

[82] Renan, 'What is a nation?', p. 19.

[83] The initial UN Security Council resolution failed to condemn the invasion as a violation of Article 2(4) of the Charter. SC Res. 660 (1990) reprinted in E. Lauterpacht, C. J. Greenwood, M. Weller and D. Bethlehem (eds.), *The Kuwait Crisis: Basic Documents* (Cambridge: Grotius Publications, 1991), p. 88. However, statements made in the Security Council indicate that the invasion was considered in those terms. UN Doc. S/PV.2932 (1990), excerpted in Lauterpacht, *The Kuwait Crisis*, pp. 99–102. This impression is reinforced by subsequent resolutions' preambles, which mention the need to restore sovereignty, independence and territorial integrity to Kuwait. SC Res.

and use of force to apply, however, the victim must be a sovereign state. Moreover, title acquired by conquest before the mid-twentieth century is shielded by the doctrine of intertemporal law. The first branch of the doctrine requires that a title's validity be judged by the law contemporaneous with its acquisition,[84] and the prohibition on the use of force only dates to Article 2(4) of the United Nations Charter in 1945 or, at most, a decade or two before. Finally, even if a state or some part of its territory is forcibly annexed in violation of Article 2(4), the international community may elect to recognize the wrongful taking; that is, to treat it as a *fait accompli*.[85]

However, if the wrongful taking argument is sheltered instead under the legal roof of self-determination, then it does not matter whether the people were a state or whether the taking was legal at the time. Interpreted as corrective, the right of self-determination of peoples restores power or territory to a people on the grounds that the taking was wrongful in a deeper sense. The case of the Baltic states[86] has been analysed as a wrongful taking both in the formal, inter-state sense and in this sense of self-determination.[87] While some scholarly commentary bases the Baltics' right to independence on the conclusion that the 1940 Soviet

---

661 (1990), SC Res. 662 (1990), SC Res. 665 (1990), SC Res. 674 (1990), all reprinted in Lauterpacht, *The Kuwait Crisis*. Although there is no overt reference to Article 2(4), Oscar Schachter regards this as merely a strategic omission. O. Schachter, 'United Nations Law in the Gulf Crisis' (1991) 85 *American Journal of International Law* 452 at 453.

But see L. M. Frankel, 'International Law of Secession: New Rules for a New Era' (1992) 14 *Houston Journal of International Law* 521 at 552; R. E. Frankel, 'Recognizing Self-Determination in International Law: Kuwait's Conflict with Iraq' (1992) 14 *Loyola of Los Angeles International and Comparative Law Journal* 359 (analysing the Gulf War in terms of the Kuwaiti people's right of self-determination).

[84] See *Island of Palmas Case* (Netherlands, USA) (1928), 2 *Reports of International Arbitral Awards* 829 at 845. While such title may be challenged under the second branch of intertemporal law, which subjects it to developments in international law, it cannot be challenged in this first sense. On the operation of the intertemporal law doctrine, see below, pp. 158–67.

[85] See S. J. Anaya, 'The Capacity of International Law to Advance Ethnic or Nationality Rights Claims' (1990) 75 *Iowa Law Review* 837 at 838–41, (1991) 13 *Human Rights Quarterly* 403 at 404–7, in W. Kymlicka (ed.), *The Rights of Minority Cultures* (New York: Oxford University Press, 1995), pp. 321–30 at pp. 322–4.

[86] See generally C. Gray, 'Self-Determination and the Break-up of the Soviet Union' (1992) 12 *Yearbook of European Law* 465 at 477–84; R. Pullat, 'The Restauration [sic] of the Independence of Estonia 1991' (1991) 2 *Finnish Yearbook of International Law* 512.

[87] The discussion here is limited to interpretations of Baltic independence based on wrongful taking. For an overview of different frameworks applied to the Baltics, see W. C. Allison, 'Self-Determination and Recent Developments in the Baltic States' (1991) 19 *Denver Journal of International Law and Policy* 625 at 627–30.

annexation was wrongful under the international legal principles of the time on the acquisition of territory and the use of force,[88] other work regards the wrongful taking instead as underlying the Baltic peoples' international legal right of self-determination.[89]

R. S. Bhalla's[90] and Lea Brilmayer's[91] work offer two well-developed interpretations of the right of self-determination as a wrongful taking. Both authors argue that this interpretation makes intelligible international law's limitation of the right to colonies. Bhalla and Brilmayer differ, though, in their characterization of what is taken. For Bhalla, the loss is the population's control over their own political, social and economic structures.[92] For Brilmayer, the object of the wrongful taking is the territory.

Bhalla interprets self-determination as the simple restoration of the power of determination that has been taken from the self[93] and belongs naturally to it.[94] He writes:

Colonisation is an exercise of brute force. Its illegality lies in the very denial of civilised behaviour which both socially and morally implies that people are left to exercise their own free will in their own affairs. Therefore, colonisation is a trespass... Until the trespass is vacated, it continues by analogy with the very simple principle of the tort of trespass.[95]

If we see the right of self-determination as corrective justice, Bhalla argues, we discover a defensible line between colonial populations, which

---

[88] See R. Yakemtchouk, 'Les républiques baltes en droit international. Échec d'une annexation opérée en violation du droit des gens' (1991) 37 *Annuaire français de droit international* 259; V. Rudrakumaran, 'The Legitimacy of Lithuania's Claim for Secession' (1992) 10 *Boston University International Law Journal* 33.

[89] I. Grazin, 'The International Recognition of National Rights: The Baltic States' Case' (1991) 66 *Notre Dame Law Review* 1385; Salo, 'An Overview of History', 330–5, relying on S. P. Sinha, 'Self-Determination in International Law and its Applicability to the Baltic Peoples' in A. Sprudzs and A. Rusis (eds.), *Res Baltica: A Collection of Essays in Honor of the Memory of Dr Alfred Bilmanis (1887–1948)* (Leyden: A. W. Sijthoff, 1968), pp. 256–85.

[90] R. S. Bhalla, 'The Right of Self-Determination in International Law' in Twining, *Issues of Self-Determination*, pp. 91–101.

[91] L. Brilmayer, 'Secession and Self-Determination: A Territorial Interpretation' (1991) 16 *Yale Journal of International Law* 177. See also L. Brilmayer, 'Secession and Self-Determination: One Decade Later' (2000) 25 *Yale Journal of International Law* 283.

[92] Bhalla, 'The Right of Self-Determination in International Law', pp. 91–2.

[93] *Ibid.*, p. 92. [94] *Ibid.*, p. 95.

[95] *Ibid.*, p. 99. Bhalla extends the trespass analogy to define as a people 'the people trespassed upon... the indigenous people and not the later transplants, the selves who came after colonisation'. *Ibid.* Precisely because the 'colonial power's obligation [is] towards those from whom the colony was seized', the right of self-determination should not be exercised jointly by natives and newcomers. *Ibid.*, pp. 99–100.

have a right to independence, and national groups in established states, which do not. Namely, national groups, unlike colonial populations, are demanding a new right.[96]

In identifying the nub of self-determination as eliminating the imposition of a 'foreign will' upon a people,[97] Jorri Duursma's interpretation is similar to Bhalla's. It differs, however, in emphasizing the restoration of the people's will, as opposed to the restoration of their historical independence, which is what permits Bhalla to distinguish colonies from sub-state groups. From this broader conception of what is taken, it follows that Duursma extends the meaning of self-determination beyond colonies[98] to other peoples placed in a position of subordination such as East Pakistan (which separated from West Pakistan to become the state of Bangladesh).[99] She is unusual in grounding the consistency of her interpretation, her rejection of a double standard, in the formulation of self-determination in the UN Charter and the Declaration on Friendly Relations.[100] For her, the word 'equal' in 'the principle of equal rights and self-determination of peoples' signifies that the principle of self-determination applies equally, although its application may in practice be limited by a countervailing principle.[101]

Brilmayer's interpretive argument[102] is also that corrective justice better explains the right of self-determination in international law.[103] She argues that the standard interpretation of self-determination[104] focuses on peoples rather than places and has therefore obscured the coherence of how international law actually deals with secessionist claims. If we reverse Judge Dillard's nostrum in the *Western Sahara* case – 'it is for the people to determine the destiny of the territory and not the territory the destiny of the people'[105] – we can see that the international community has, in fact, recognized a right of self-determination in the form

---

[96] *Ibid.*, p. 92. But see notes 88–89 (Baltic states' right to secede from the USSR based on corrective justice).

[97] J. C. Duursma, *Fragmentation and the International Relations of Micro-States: Self-Determination and Statehood* (Cambridge: Cambridge University Press, 1996), p. 78.

[98] *Ibid.*, pp. 82–3.   [99] *Ibid.*, p. 83.   [100] *Ibid.*, pp. 12–16, 19–26, 78.

[101] *Ibid.*, pp. 79, 83–8 (discussing the balance of self-determination and territorial integrity in the case of colonial enclaves) and 89–103 (arguing that the balance has not yet yielded clear rules in the case of secession).

[102] As the subject of the current work is interpretation, I do not present the political theory portions of Brilmayer's argument.

[103] Brilmayer, 'Secession and Self-Determination', 193.

[104] Brilmayer describes the standard account of secession as pitting the principle of self-determination, whereby a nation or people has a right to determine its own destiny, against the principle of territorial integrity. *Ibid.*, 177–84.

[105] *Western Sahara*, p. 122 (separate opinion of Judge Dillard).

of secession only where the secessionists have had the better territorial claim.

To demonstrate the descriptive superiority of her territorial interpretation of self-determination, Brilmayer points out how the 'colonies only' practice of self-determination is anomalous on the standard account, but consistent with her account.[106] The usual interpretation of self-determination, predicated on the status and rights of peoples, cannot explain the distinction made in international law between colonial and non-colonial situations: if the nature of the group or its mistreatment at the hands of the state is the same, how can international law draw a defensible line at colonies? On Brilmayer's account, the answer is that the historical grievance is particularly clear in colonial situations: 'Colonialism represents a special case because the colonial powers were particularly lacking in justification for their original territorial conquest. Colonial powers possessed no colorable claims to the territories they conquered. Once conquered, the colonies were not incorporated into the nation but were retained as overseas possessions'.[107] Apart from a few cases, such as the Baltic states where a right to secede was recognized based on the Soviet annexation, the majority of non-colonial claims to secede do not attract international support because the historical grievance is different. The general lack of support for independence movements in African and Asian states, for example, is explainable by the fact that decolonization, and not territorial conquest, is what gave these states sovereignty over minorities. Indeed, some of the secessionist minorities even participated in the anti-colonial struggle.

Rights, *demos* and *ethnos*

In *Loizidou v. Turkey*, a 1996 judgment of the European Court of Human Rights, Judge Wildhaber identifies an emerging consensus that the right of self-determination, more specifically secession, should be interpreted as remedial for certain human rights abuses:

Until recently in international practice the right to self-determination was in practical terms identical to, and indeed restricted to, a right to decolonisation. In recent years a consensus has seemed to emerge that peoples may also exercise a right to self-determination if their human rights are consistently and flagrantly violated or if they are without representation at all or are massively underrepresented in an undemocratic and discriminatory way. If this description is

---

[106] Brilmayer, 'Secession and Self-Determination', 195–7.   [107] *Ibid.*, 195–6.

correct, then the right to self-determination is a tool which may be used to re-establish international standards of human rights and democracy.[108]

As Judge Wildhaber attests, there is increasing agreement among authors that the right of self-determination provides the remedy of secession to a group whose rights have been consistently and severely abused by the state. We shall see that while some authors rely narrowly on the 1970 UN Declaration on Friendly Relations to establish this qualified right to secede, other authors trace the right further back in international law. Moreover, as with the definition of 'peoples', authors either treat this type of interpretation as a new non-colonial category or anchor it with decolonization in a theory of the coherence of international law. We shall also see that despite the emerging consensus that secession is instrumental to human rights, authors continue to differ over which human rights: civil or political, individual or collective, guarantors of *demos* or protectors of *ethnos*.

The penultimate paragraph of the principle of equal rights and self-determination of peoples in the Declaration on Friendly Relations has become the interpretive touchstone for a remedial right of secession because it seemingly makes an exception to the principle of the territorial integrity of states where a racial or religious group within the state is unrepresented or severely under-represented in government or their human rights are consistently and flagrantly violated and where the state's intransigence leaves secession as the only remedy.[109] The principle of territorial integrity goes hand-in-hand with the principle of self-determination in the 1960 Declaration on the Independence of Colonial Peoples (GA Resolution 1514) and the later Declaration on Friendly Relations. The Declaration on the Independence of Colonial Peoples gives all peoples the right to self-determination,[110] but prohibits the disruption of a state's territorial integrity.[111] Yet it requires that immediate

---

[108] *Loizidou v. Turkey* (Merits), European Court of Human Rights, 18 December 1996, (1997) 18 *Human Rights Law Journal* 50 at 59 (concurring opinion of Judge Wildhaber, joined by Judge Ryssdal). In his academic capacity, see L. Wildhaber, 'Territorial Modifications and Breakups in Federal States' (1995) 33 *Canadian Yearbook of International Law* 41 at 42; L. Wildhaber, Expert Report (*Reference re Secession of Quebec*, [1998] 2 SCR 217, (1998) 37 ILM 1340), reprinted in Bayefsky, *Lessons Learned*, pp. 63–5 at pp. 64–5. See also *Reference re Secession of Quebec*, 285–6 (SCR), 1372–3 (ILM).

[109] E.g. Iglar, 'Constitutional Crisis in Yugoslavia', 228–9 (non-representation in government or unequal treatment); An-Na'im, 'Mediation of Competing Claims', p. 110 (deprivation of basic human rights).

[110] Declaration on the Independence of Colonial Peoples, para. 2.

[111] *Ibid.*, para. 6.

steps be taken to transfer all powers unconditionally to the peoples of trust and non-self-governing territories and all other territories not yet independent in accordance with their freely expressed will and desire, thereby clarifying that decolonization is consistent with the principle of territorial integrity.[112] The reason that the self-determination of colonies does not violate the state's territorial integrity is that international law gives colonies a status separate and distinct from the state. GA Resolution 1541, passed shortly after the Declaration on the Independence of Colonial Peoples, defines a non-self-governing territory prima facie as 'a territory which is geographically separate and is distinct ethnically and/or culturally from the country administering it'.[113] Geographically separate has, in practice, meant separated by an ocean, the international lawyers' shorthand being 'blue water' or 'salt water' colonialism.[114] The Declaration on Friendly Relations reaffirms that the right of all peoples to self-determination[115] cannot violate the principle of territorial integrity,[116] but that a colony or other non-self-governing territory has a separate and distinct territorial status.[117] The principle of territorial integrity thus prohibits secession, but not decolonization. However, the penultimate paragraph on self-determination in the Declaration on Friendly Relations has been read as establishing remedial secession as an exception. It reads:

> Nothing in the foregoing paragraphs shall be construed as authorizing or encouraging any action which would dismember or impair, totally or in part, the territorial integrity or political unity of sovereign and independent States conducting themselves in compliance with the principle of equal rights and self-determination of peoples as described above and thus possessed of a government representing the whole people belonging to the territory without distinction as to race, creed or colour.[118]

---

[112] *Ibid.*, para. 5.   [113] GA Res. 1541, principle IV.
[114] See P. Thornberry, *International Law and the Rights of Minorities* (Oxford: Clarendon Press, 1991), pp. 16–18; P. Thornberry, 'Self-Determination, Minorities, Human Rights: A Review of International Instruments' (1989) 38 *International and Comparative Law Quarterly* 867 at 873–5.
[115] Declaration on Friendly Relations, fifth principle, first paragraph.
[116] *Ibid.*, fifth principle, eighth paragraph.   [117] *Ibid.*, fifth principle, sixth paragraph.
[118] *Ibid.*, fifth principle, seventh paragraph. See also Vienna Declaration and Programme of Action, pt. I. 2, para. 3. The UN Committee on the Elimination of Racial Discrimination makes reference to this paragraph in its general recommendation on self-determination, but leaves ambiguous whether it might justify a right to secede under certain circumstances. Committee on the Elimination of Racial Discrimination, General Recommendation XXI on Self-Determination, UN Doc. CERD/48/Misc.7/Rev.3 (1996), para. 6 ('International law has not recognized a general right of peoples to unilaterally declare secession from a State.').

Thus the principle of territorial integrity prohibits secession, but only if the state complies with the principle of self-determination.

It is unclear exactly what compliance with the principle of self-determination requires. One school of thought, picking up on the phrasing 'and *thus* possessed of a government representing the whole people', argues that the principle of self-determination is satisfied by representative government. Although the tendency in international law is to equate representative government with democracy, particularly constitutional parliamentary democracy, the Declaration on Friendly Relations does not explicitly make this equation.[119] Indeed, the wording of the paragraph has lent support to the argument that the principle of self-determination may require more than just formally equal representation in government for racial and religious groups within the state. 'In compliance with the principle of... self-determination of peoples as described above' directs us to the preceding paragraphs. As modes of implementing self-determination, the fifth paragraph lists independent statehood, free association or integration with an independent state or any other political status freely determined by the people. While this paragraph arguably refers to decolonization and the penultimate paragraph refers to secession, nothing actually excludes it from the ambit of 'as described above'. On the assumption that these modes of implementation are germane, the principle of self-determination obliges a state to recognize more than a group's equal right of representation in government; it requires a state to contemplate varying degrees of governmental autonomy for groups within the state.[120] José Woehrling interprets the Declaration on Friendly Relations as granting a right to secede where there is a denial of this option,[121] as well as where there is an absence

---

[119] Even if it did, some authors criticize the insistence on a traditional Western-style parliamentary system on the grounds that it is an ineffective guarantee of representation for minorities and amounts to democratic imperialism. R. McCorquodale, 'Self-Determination: A Human Rights Approach' (1994) 43 *International and Comparative Law Quarterly* 857 at 865, n. 47. See also M. C. Lâm, 'The Legal Value of Self-Determination: Vision or Inconvenience?' in International Centre for Human Rights and Democratic Development, *People or Peoples; Equality, Autonomy and Self-Determination: The Issues at Stake of the International Decade of the World's Indigenous People* (Essays on Human Rights and Democratic Development, Paper No. 5) (Montreal, 1996), pp. 79–142 at p. 119.

[120] Woehrling, 'Une éventuelle sécession', 316; Woehrling, 'La redéfinition', p. 90.

[121] Woehrling cites in support Jacques Brossard's interpretation of the Declaration on Friendly Relations. Woehrling, 'Une éventuelle sécession', 317; Woehrling, 'La redéfinition', p. 89, citing J. Brossard, *L'accession à la souveraineté*, p. 101. See also J. Brossard, 'Le droit du peuple québécois de disposer de lui-même au regard du droit international' (1977) 15 *Canadian Yearbook of International Law* 84 at 107–8.

of representative government, unequal and discriminatory treatment or the violation of human rights.[122] In so far as this interpretation relies on reading the fifth paragraph into the penultimate one, however, the difficulty is that the fifth paragraph also refers to independent statehood. But if this mode of self-determination is also read in, then the result would be that secession is prohibited (by the principle of territorial integrity) so long as secession is allowed (by the state's compliance with the principle of self-determination).

Another school of thought interprets the principle of self-determination in the Declaration on Friendly Relations as requiring the observance of certain human rights, as distinct from some notion of representative government. Judge Wildhaber in *Loizidou* characterizes self-determination as a means to secure both; he describes self-determination as 'a tool which may be used to re-establish international standards of human rights and democracy'.[123]

The language of nondiscrimination ('without distinction as to race, creed or colour') in the penultimate paragraph on self-determination in the Declaration on Friendly Relations gives some support to the view of secession as the remedy of last resort for gross inequality of treatment. A higher benchmark for the state's responsibility to racial and religious groups, and hence a lower threshold for secession, is set via the third paragraph. (On the same logic as before, this earlier paragraph can be read into the meaning of compliance with the principle of self-determination in the penultimate one because the latter refers to compliance with the principle 'as described above'.) The third paragraph places a duty on states to promote 'universal respect for and observance of human rights and fundamental freedoms in accordance with the Charter'.

Writers have also traced the interpretation of self-determination as remedial for the abuse of a racial or religious minority's rights beyond the

---

This is also Daniel Turp's fall-back interpretation of self-determination in international law. Turp, 'Quebec's Democratic Right', pp. 113–14; Turp, 'L'expression du principe démocratique', pp. 57–8; Turp, 'Exposé-réponse', pp. 663–4. Another author who conditions a right of secession on the failure of internal arrangements including equality, minority protection, autonomy and federal structures is O. Kimminich, 'A "Federal" Right of Self-Determination?' in Tomuschat, *Modern Law of Self-Determination*, pp. 83–100.

[122] Woehrling, 'Une éventuelle sécession', 316–17; Woehrling, 'La redéfinition', pp. 88–9.

[123] *Loizidou*, p. 59. See also T. D. Musgrave, *Self-Determination and National Minorities* (Oxford: Clarendon Press, 1997), pp. 188–92, 209 (arguing that the Declaration on Friendly Relations makes oppression and non-representation in government two distinct bases for secession). But see *ibid.*, p. 258 (mentioning only oppression).

Declaration on Friendly Relations: from the *Aaland Islands* case through the UN Charter concept of non-self-governing territories to the contemporary cases of secession. In the 1921 *Aaland Islands* case, a League of Nations Commission of Rapporteurs found on the merits that the Swedish-speaking population of the Aaland Islands did not have the right to detach the Islands from Finland and join them to Sweden. However, the Commission also stated that 'the separation of a minority from the State of which it forms a part and its incorporation in another State can only be considered as an altogether exceptional solution, a last resort when the State lacks either the will or the power to enact and apply just and effective guarantees.'[124] This statement is often cited in support of a right of secession in the situation James Crawford terms *carence de souveraineté*:[125] misgovernment of a territory so extreme that the territory is effectively alienated from the state. Language to a similar effect is found in the *Aaland Islands* decision on jurisdiction. An earlier League of Nations commission determined that the League of Nations had jurisdiction because Finland was not definitively constituted as a state at the time the dispute arose and therefore could not assert domestic jurisdiction against the League. Nevertheless, the earlier commission explicitly reserved the question of whether a fully constituted state could claim domestic jurisdiction in circumstances where it had engaged in 'a manifest and continued abuse of sovereign power, to the detriment of a section of the population of a State'.[126]

By characterizing the hypothetical situations mentioned by the League of Nations commissioners in the *Aaland Islands* as misgovernance, international lawyers[127] are able to find a common thread from this post-World War I case dealing with minorities to the post-World War II system of non-self-governing territories. At the time James Crawford identified this thread, Bangladesh was the only possible instance of a right of secession recognized on the basis of *carence de souveraineté*.[128] Crawford

---

[124] *Report of the Commission of Rapporteurs* (Beyens, Calonder, Elkus), LN Council Doc. B7/21/68/106 (16 April 1921) at 28.
[125] Crawford, *The Creation of States*, p. 86.
[126] *Report of International Committee of Jurists* (Larnaude, Struycken, Huber), LNOJ Sp. Supp. No. 3 (October 1920) 3 at 5.
[127] Crawford, *The Creation of States*, pp. 85–7, 99–101. See also M. Sellers, 'Republican Principles in International Law' (1996) 11 *Connecticut Journal of International Law* 403 at 424–5; Thürer, 'Self-Determination', p. 473; S. A. Williams, *International Legal Effects of Secession by Quebec* (Background Studies of the York University Constitutional Reform Project, Study No. 3) (North York, Ont.: York University Centre for Public Law and Public Policy, 1992), pp. 13–14, 19–20 (citing Crawford).
[128] Crawford, *The Creation of States*, p. 100.

continues to regard Bangladesh as the only instance,[129] but other international lawyers now also cite the cases of the Baltic states, and Croatia, Slovenia and Bosnia-Herzegovina.[130]

Like the Declaration on Friendly Relations, international legal practice is open to different rights-based interpretations of self-determination. The *Aaland Islands* case may stand for the proposition that self-determination is instrumental not to equal representation in government, but to protection for minority identity. That is, a right of secession acts as the ultimate guarantee not of the individual rights of political participation associated with a democratic polity, but of a complex of rights recognizing *ethnos* and ranging from linguistic, cultural and religious rights of minorities to a right of autonomy or self-government. In the *Aaland Islands* case, the Commission of Rapporteurs was prepared to consider incorporation of the Aaland Islands with Sweden as a solution had Finland been unready to grant the guarantees necessary to preserve the Aalanders' ethnic heritage:

> the Aaland population, by reason of its insular position and its strong tradition, forms a group apart in Finland, not only distinct from the Finnish population, but also in certain respects distinct from the Swedish-speaking population. They deserve all the more protection and support in that they are, because of their great remoteness from the Finnish mainland, left to themselves, so to speak, in their struggle for the preservation of their ethnical heritage. We admit also that the fear fostered by the Aalanders of being little by little submerged by the Finnish invasion has good grounds,[131] and that effective measures should be taken with a view to eliminating this danger. If it were true that incorporation with Sweden was the only means of preserving its Swedish language for Aaland, we should not have hesitated to consider this solution. But such is not the case. There is no need for a separation. The Finnish State is ready to grant the inhabitants satisfactory guarantees and faithfully to observe the engagement which it will enter into with them: of this we have no doubt.[132]

The guarantees required of Finland by the Rapporteurs pertained to education (Swedish-only primary school and technical school education),

---

[129] Crawford, Expert Report, pp. 42–3; Crawford, 'State Practice', 95–6.
[130] Finkelstein, Vegh and Joly, 'Does Québec Have the Right', 245–7 (arguing that these cases are analogous to colonialism because the group seeking self-determination is politically disempowered and discriminated against).
[131] The Commission of Rapporteurs noted that the threat to the Aalanders' language and culture is not the result of a policy of oppression, but of 'quite exceptional conditions'. *Report of the Commission of Rapporteurs*, p. 28.
[132] *Ibid.*, pp. 28–9.

territorial property (a right of pre-emption in the native inhabitants with respect to offers to purchase property by those foreign to the Islands) and politics (the grant of the franchise to newcomers only after a five-year period and the requirement that the governor of the Aaland Islands be chosen from a list of three candidates presented by the General Council of the Aaland Islands).[133] The Rapporteurs concluded:

> However, in the event that Finland, contrary to our expectations and to what we have been given to understand, refused to grant the Aaland population the guarantees which we have just detailed, there would be another possible solution, and it is exactly the one which we wish to eliminate. The interest of the Aalanders, the interests of a durable peace in the Baltic, would then force us to advise the separation of the islands from Finland, based on the wishes of the inhabitants which would be freely expressed by means of a plebiscite.[134]

Whereas some authors treat a rights-based interpretation of secession as a new non-colonial category of external self-determination,[135] other scholars including Ian Brownlie, Oscar Schachter, Robert McCorquodale and, most of all, Thomas Franck appeal to a broader coherence. Brownlie and Schachter each describe the international legal standards governing self-determination as a synthesis of the principle of self-determination and the rights of groups in international human rights law. The recognition of group rights usually takes the form of a basic standard of equality or nondiscrimination (as in the International Covenants on Human Rights) and the form of the guarantee of the maintenance of group identity (as in Article 27 of the International Covenant on Civil and Political Rights). For Brownlie, the core of the principle of self-determination is 'the right of a community which has a distinct character to have this character reflected in the institutions of government under which it lives',[136] where that reflection may take a variety of forms. The recognition of group rights, especially rights relating to territory and regional autonomy, are 'the practical and internal working out of the concept of self-determination'.[137] Brownlie does not go so far as to present secession as the last resort where a government does not and will not reflect the distinct character of a community within the state, although it would

---

[133] *Ibid.*, pp. 32–3.   [134] *Ibid.*, p. 34.
[135] E.g. Doehring, 'Self-Determination', pp. 64–9 (decolonization, defence by people of state against foreign domination, right of secession of minority subject to oppression); Eide, *Possible Ways and Means*, pp. 16–19 (colonial territories; alien, illegal occupation; minority without representation in government); Williams, *International Legal Effects of Secession*, pp. 13–22 (colonial or alien domination, *carence de souveraineté*).
[136] Brownlie, 'The Rights of Peoples', p. 5.   [137] *Ibid.*, p. 6.

seem to flow from his analysis. In comparison, Schachter explicitly rationalizes the UN declarations along these lines, identifying three standards for secession:

(1) The claimant community should have an identity distinct from the rest of the country and inhabit a region that largely supports separation in the given circumstances.
(2) The community has been subjected to a pattern of systematic political or economic discrimination.
(3) The central regime has rejected reasonable proposals for autonomy and minority rights of the claimant community.[138]

Brownlie's and Schachter's interpretations of self-determination as instrumental to the protection of minority identity create a normative synthesis of the public international law principle of self-determination and the gamut of international human rights relevant to minority identity. With the same effect, Robert McCorquodale argues that the right of self-determination must be interpreted within the positive law framework of international human rights.[139] McCorquodale provides three reasons why the right of self-determination belongs properly to international human rights law. First, the purpose of the right of self-determination – to protect communities and groups from oppression and thus to empower them – is similar to that of the international human rights law framework. International human rights seek to protect the individual from oppression and thereby protect the communities and groups to which the individual belongs. The rights to freedom of religion, freedom of assembly and freedom of association are all exercised by individuals together with other individuals. Coupled with the right to freedom from discrimination and the rights of minorities, these rights protect the conditions for the existence of groups.[140] Second, as the UN Human Rights Committee stated in its General Comment on the right of

---

[138] O. Schachter, 'Sovereignty – Then and Now' in R. St J. Macdonald (ed.), *Essays in Honour of Wang Tieya* (Dordrecht: Martinus Nijhoff, 1994), pp. 671–88 at 684. For further discussion of Schachter's position, see Chapter 1 above. See also D. Murswiek, 'The Issue of a Right of Secession – Reconsidered' in Tomuschat, *Modern Law of Self-Determination*, pp. 21–39.

[139] McCorquodale, 'A Human Rights Approach'. See also R. McCorquodale, 'Human Rights and Self-Determination' in M. Sellers (ed.), *The New World Order: Sovereignty, Human Rights and the Self-Determination of Peoples* (Oxford: Berg, 1996), pp. 9–34. See also S. J. Anaya, 'Self-Determination as a Collective Human Right under Contemporary International Law' in P. Aikio and M. Scheinin (eds.), *Operationalizing the Right of Indigenous Peoples to Self-Determination* (Turku/Åbo: Institute for Human Rights, Åbo Akademi University, 2000), pp. 3–18.

[140] McCorquodale, 'A Human Rights Approach', 872.

self-determination,[141] the right of self-determination is an essential condition for the protection of individual rights because without freedom from oppression, individual rights cannot be effectively guaranteed.[142] Third, international human rights law has proved able to adjudicate group rights in the economic, social and cultural context; for example, rights protecting employees and families. The European Communities Conference on Yugoslavia Arbitration Commission has also demonstrated that a minority's entitlement to self-determination can be judged within a human rights framework.[143] For these three reasons, argues McCorquodale, the right of self-determination can be explained wholly within international human rights law.

Within the positive law framework of international human rights, the right of self-determination must be interpreted as justifying secession only where there is no less drastic means to free a people from oppression by others. International human rights law generally incorporates limitations on rights to protect other rights and to protect the general interests of society.[144] In particular, the right of self-determination of peoples in common Article 1(1) of the International Covenants on Human Rights, while couched in absolute terms, is subject to common Article 5(1), which provides that 'nothing in the present Covenant may be interpreted as implying for any State, group or person any right to engage in any activity or perform any act aimed at the destruction of any of the rights and freedoms recognized herein'. As well, common Article 1(3) requires states to respect the right of self-determination 'in conformity with the provisions of the Charter of the United Nations', which are designed to maintain international peace and security.[145] Since secession involves major structural and institutional change to a state and to the international community of states, it makes sense that the costs of transition and the potentially lasting effects on individuals and groups within the original and the breakaway states be created only if no less drastic means is available.

Thomas Franck's rights-based interpretation of self-determination in *The Power of Legitimacy Among Nations*[146] and 'The Emerging Right

---

[141] General Comment No. 12(21) of the Human Rights Committee, Regarding Article 1, GAOR, 39th Sess., Supp. 40, UN Doc. A/39/40 (1984), p. 142.
[142] McCorquodale, 'A Human Rights Approach', 872.
[143] Ibid., 873.   [144] Ibid., 873–5.   [145] Ibid., 875–83.
[146] T. M. Franck, *The Power of Legitimacy Among Nations* (New York: Oxford University Press, 1990).

to Democratic Governance'[147] is particularly illuminating for two reasons.[148] First, while authors such as Brownlie, Schachter and McCorquodale appeal to the coherence of international law in their interpretations of self-determination, Franck develops and applies a larger theory of the legitimacy of international legal rules[149] in which coherence plays a central role. Franck's theory explains a rule's legitimacy, by which he means the likelihood that it will be obeyed by states, as produced by the interaction between four of its properties. Coherence is one property, the others being the rule's determinacy, its symbolic validation through ritual and pedigree, and its adherence to a normative hierarchy. Among those authors who interpret self-determination within a matrix of rights, Franck therefore gives the strongest example of the trend toward coherence and thus towards a single grand narrative. Second, Franck's different analyses of self-determination in *The Power of Legitimacy Among Nations* and 'The Emerging Right to Democratic Governance' show how the same rights-based model can be narrated as either the vestige of *ethnos* or the emergence of *demos*.

In *The Power of Legitimacy Among Nations*, Franck uses self-determination as a case-study of coherence.[150] Told from the perspective of coherence, the story of self-determination in international law is one of 'gradual descent... into unprincipled incoherence'.[151] Franck's narration is based on the Romantic conception of national self-determination as the right

---

[147] T. M. Franck, 'The Emerging Right to Democratic Governance' (1992) 86 *American Journal of International Law* 46.

[148] Franck has written extensively on the right of self-determination, especially in recent years, and has progressively refined his interpretation. While not far removed from Franck's current thinking on self-determination, the two accounts of self-determination discussed here have been chosen more as illustrations of a trend toward coherence analysis than as most representative of Franck's present position on self-determination. For the latter, see T. M. Franck, *Fairness in International Law and Institutions* (Oxford: Clarendon Press, 1995), pp. 83–169; T. M. Franck, 'Fairness in the International Legal and Institutional System' (1993-III) 240 Hague Recueil 9 at 99–149. Franck's analysis of the interplay of collective and individual self-determination is developed in T. M. Franck, *The Empowered Self: Law and Society in the Age of Individualism* (New York: Oxford University Press, 2000).

[149] Franck, *Fairness in International Law*, pp. 25–46; Franck, 'Fairness', 41–61; T. M. Franck, 'Legitimacy in the International System' (1988) 82 *American Journal of International Law* 705; Franck, *The Power of Legitimacy*. For Franck's newer theory on fairness in international law and institutions, which analyses legitimacy as procedural fairness, see Franck, *Fairness in International Law*; Franck, 'Fairness'.

[150] Franck, *The Power of Legitimacy*, pp. 153–76. See also Franck, 'Legitimacy in the International System', 743–9.

[151] Franck, *The Power of Legitimacy*, p. 163.

of all ethnic nations to choose their political status. His description of the victories, compromises and failures for self-determination in the negotiations on new borders in Europe at the World War I peace conference assumes that ethnicity was central to the enterprise. Franck highlights President Wilson's inclusion of historians, geographers and ethnologists in the American delegation to the peace conference, and the delegation's extensive use of data on demographics and the ethnic sentiments of the various populations.[152] As applications of the principle of self-determination, Franck cites the creation of Czechoslovakia – characterized as 'a dramatic victory' – and the resurrection of an independent Poland. Secretary of State Lansing is quoted on America's desire to free all branches of the Slav race from German and Austrian rule, as is President Wilson on his public commitment in the Fourteen Points to an independent Polish state encompassing indisputably Polish-populated territories.[153] Nevertheless, as Franck shows, the principle of self-determination was imperfectly applied in the inter-war period. Article 1(2) of the 1945 United Nations Charter is therefore significant for its casting of the principle as universal and its recognition of the importance of ethnicity by its use of the term 'peoples'. The monumental process of decolonization under United Nations auspices confirms how seriously the obligation of self-determination was taken by the international community.[154] In this story of self-determination, the decline of self-determination into unprincipled conceptual incoherence begins with the betrayal of the universal principle by GA Resolution 1514, which constructively limits secession to overseas colonies.[155] The subsequent state practice – self-determination for Algeria, for example, but not Biafra – can only be made coherent by refining the universal principle of self-determination. Accordingly, Franck now grounds the right to secede on unequal treatment:[156] a distinct group in a specific region has the right to independence if they are a minority in the larger political unit from which they seek independence, are politically disempowered and can separate without unduly depriving the remaining inhabitants of their economic prospects or national security.[157]

The events narrated as *ethnos* in the story of self-determination's coherence in *The Power of Legitimacy Among Nations* are re-narrated as *demos* in the story of self-determination's pedigree in 'The Emerging

[152] Ibid., p. 154.   [153] Ibid., pp. 156-7.   [154] Ibid., pp. 160-1.   [155] Ibid., pp. 163-4.
[156] Ibid., p. 170.   [157] Ibid., p. 171.

Right to Democratic Governance'.[158] Franck begins with a formulation of the principle that makes no reference to nation or ethnic group: 'Self-determination postulates the right of a people organized in an established territory to determine its collective political destiny in a democratic fashion'.[159] The presence of historians, geographers and ethnologists on the American delegation to the World War I peace conference permitted the Americans to draw on demographic and ethnographic data 'in advocating free choice by "peoples"'.[160] It is the seeds of internationally validated political consultation – the wishes of the Danes of Schleswig, full consultation with Slavic representatives in the creation of Czechoslovakia, the will of the Rheinish Germans – that took root in the boundary settlements.[161] While the United Nations Charter universalized the principle of self-determination, what it universalized was a duty owed by all governments to their peoples; that is, Franck implies, a duty of democratic governance. Decolonization recorded the steady ascent of self-determination as the requirement of 'democratic consultation with colonial peoples, legitimated by an international presence at elections immediately preceding the creative moment of independence'.[162] GA Resolution 1514 marked the extension of self-determination from the conquered lands of post-World War I Europe to colonies, not the end of its halcyon days. If the coherence story of self-determination in *The Power of Legitimacy Among Nations* told of the principle's spectacular rise and ignominious fall, the pedigree story is one of its slow and gruelling rise.

Tracing the determinacy of self-determination, Franck concludes that with the coming into force of the International Covenant on Civil and Political Rights,

> the right of self-determination entered its third phase of enunciation: it ceased to be a rule applicable only to specific territories (at first, the defeated European powers; later, the overseas trust territories and colonies) and became a right of everyone. It also, at least for now, stopped being a principle of exclusion (secession) and became one of inclusion: the right to participate. The right now entitles peoples in all states to free, fair and open participation in the democratic process of governance freely chosen by each state.[163]

An international legal entitlement to secession may only re-emerge where a people satisfying the GA Resolution 1541 requirements of

---

[158] Franck, 'Democratic Governance', 52–6. See also T. M. Franck, 'The Democratic Entitlement' (1994) 29 *University of Richmond Law Review* 1 at 9–12.
[159] Franck, 'Democratic Governance', 52.   [160] *Ibid.*, 53.   [161] *Ibid.*   [162] *Ibid.*, 55.
[163] *Ibid.*, 58–9. See also Franck, 'The Democratic Entitlement', 12–14.

geographical separateness and ethnic or cultural distinctness has been subordinated by the denial of political participation.[164]

Peace and violence

In determining whether the Aaland Islanders had a right of self-determination, the League of Nations Commission of Rapporteurs examined the consequences of its determination for the security of the two states involved, Sweden and Finland, and for political stability and peace in the region. Describing their journey by steamer to the Aaland Archipelago, 'a continuous succession of islands, islets and skerries of a reddish colour, very close to one another, most of which are covered with a hardy vegetation of pines and firs growing amongst the rocks',[165] the Rapporteurs observed that 'it is impossible to visit the Aaland Islands without being struck by their strategic importance' for both Sweden and Finland.[166] Given the immediate proximity to the Swedish capital, Stockholm, the Aaland Archipelago was 'a dagger which is always raised ... against the heart of Sweden'.[167] The Islands were key to Finland's security as well because Finland in winter was joined to the Aaland Islands by ice, thereby providing an invader with easy access.[168]

In support of their legal conclusion that Finland's sovereignty over the Aaland Islands must prevail, the Rapporteurs argued that from a strategic point of view, the position of Finland and Sweden was about the same.[169] Politically, though, the Rapporteurs were anxious to reward Finland for resisting the Russian Bolshevik attack and thereby preventing the expansion of Communism into Scandinavia:[170]

> it is in the general interest to hasten the consolidation of the States which have freed themselves from the Empire of the Czars to live an independent existence, and to help them to live and to prosper. Finland, in particular, is one of these bulwarks of peace in Northern Europe. We can only wish that she will grow strong ... and that she will enter into the constellation of the Scandinavian States.... It will have been an honourable task for us to have contributed to this restoration of peace and at the same time to win still more sympathy for a State

---

[164] But compare D. F. Orentlicher, 'Separation Anxiety: International Responses to Ethno-Separatist Claims' (1998) 23 *Yale Journal of International Law* 1 at 44–62, especially 48–9 (suggesting that the consistency of Franck's democratic entitlement demands, and international law supports, that this right of secession not be limited to peoples satisfying GA Resolution 1541).
[165] *Report of the Commission of Rapporteurs*, p. 2.   [166] Ibid., p. 3.   [167] Ibid.   [168] Ibid.
[169] Ibid., p. 30.   [170] Ibid.

which has made such noble endeavours to rank among the most energetic, the most hard-working and the most cultivated of nations.[171]

The Rapporteurs cautioned, however, that if Finland did not grant the Aaland population the necessary minority rights guarantees, then the interest of the Aalanders and those of 'a durable peace in the Baltic' would force the Rapporteurs to recommend a plebiscite on the separation of the islands from Finland.[172]

The UN Charter can also be interpreted as incorporating the considerations of good relations among states and peace into the principle of self-determination. Article 1(2) reads:

The Purposes of the United Nations are:
...
2. To develop friendly relations among nations based on respect for the principle of equal rights and self-determination of peoples, and to take other appropriate measures to strengthen universal peace;[173]

If the Article means that international relations must respect the principle of self-determination of peoples – self-determination cannot be sacrificed for the sake of world harmony[174] – then self-determination is an end in itself and not a means to some other end. Accordingly, the reference to '*friendly* relations' has no significance for the interpretation of self-determination. At most, it reflects an empirical prediction about the effects of self-determination. The assumption is that self-determination will promote peace and goodwill among nations, but even when it does not, nations must still respect self-determination in their dealings with one another because principle is paramount.

Alternatively, '*other* appropriate measures to strengthen universal peace' means that the conception of self-determination in Article 1(2) is instrumental: respect for the principle of self-determination is only a tool for peace-building and may therefore be disregarded where

---

[171] *Ibid.*, p. 31. The disarmament and neutralization of the Aaland Islands are treated as separate issues. *Ibid.*, pp. 34–7.
[172] *Ibid.*, p. 34.
[173] The following discussion assumes that the self-determination of peoples means something other than non-interference in the internal affairs of states. For the contrary view, see p. 99 below.
[174] See e.g. M. Bedjaoui, 'Article 1 (commentaire général)' in J.-P. Cot and A. Pellet (eds.), *La Charte des Nations Unies* (2nd edn, Paris: Economica, 1991), pp. 23–30 at pp. 25–6 (Article 1(2) reflects the ambition of the architects of San Francisco to found peace on justice); *East Timor*, p. 194 (Dissenting Opinion of Judge Weeramantry).

compliance would cause or exacerbate conflict.¹⁷⁵ Article 55 can similarly be read as making self-determination instrumental to friendly relations among states and international peace.

Support for such an interpretation of self-determination is also found in the Declaration on Friendly Relations. As enunciated in the Declaration, the principle of self-determination requires states to promote realization of the principle in order 'to promote friendly relations and co-operation among states'. The preamble to the Declaration states that 'the subjection of peoples to alien subjugation, domination and exploitation constitutes a major obstacle to the promotion of international peace and security' and that the effective application of the principle of self-determination is of 'paramount importance for the promotion of friendly relations among States, based on respect for the principle of sovereign equality'.

During and after the Cold War, a few influential authors advocated the adoption of this approach to self-determination, building in the pull of power against normativity, minimum against optimum world order,¹⁷⁶ violence against identity,¹⁷⁷ or stability against representative democracy.¹⁷⁸ In the post-Cold War international legal literature on self-determination, there are those who argue that contemporary state practice already evidences this type of approach. Using the two key variables

---

[175] See e.g. A. Cassese, 'Article 1, Paragraphe 2' in Cot and Pellet, *La Charte des Nations Unies*, pp. 39–55 at p. 43 (The principle can legitimately not be observed if it creates friction); H. Thierry, 'L'Evolution de droit international' (1990–III) 222 Hague Recueil 9 at 159.

[176] L.-C. Chen, 'Self-Determination and World Public Order' (1991) 66 *Notre Dame Law Review* 1287; L.-C. Chen, 'Self-Determination as a Human Right' in W. M. Reisman and B. H. Weston (eds.), *Toward World Order and Human Dignity: Essays in Honor of Myres S. McDougal* (New York: Free Press, 1976), pp. 198–261, influencing J. Claydon and J. D. Whyte, 'Legal Aspects of Quebec's Claim for Independence' in R. Simeon (ed.), *Must Canada Fail?* (Montreal: McGill-Queen's University Press, 1977), pp. 259–80 at p. 280, n. 1 (citing Chen); M. R. Islam, 'Secession Crisis in Papua New Guinea: The Proclaimed Republic of Bougainville in International Law' (1991) 13 *University of Hawaii Law Review* 453 at 468–72; R. Müllerson, *International Law, Rights and Politics: Developments in Eastern Europe and the CIS* (London: Routledge/LSE, 1994), p. 86, but see pp. 3–4 (limitations of the policy science approach to international law); R. Müllerson, 'Self-Determination of Peoples and the Dissolution of the USSR' in Macdonald, *Wang Tieya*, pp. 567–85 at pp. 580–1; E. Suzuki, 'Self-Determination and World Public Order: Community Response to Territorial Separation' (1976) 16 *Virginia Journal of International Law* 779, modified by V. Nanda, 'Self-Determination Under International Law: Validity of Claims to Secede' (1981) 13 *Case Western Reserve Journal of International Law* 257 at 275–6; E. Suzuki, Book Review (1980) 89 *Yale Law Journal* 1247.

[177] L. C. Buchheit, *Secession: The Legitimacy of Self-Determination* (New Haven: Yale University Press, 1978), pp. 216–45 (a work still cited).

[178] Halperin, *New World Order*, pp. 71–93.

he identifies in the Declaration on Friendly Relations and the Vienna Declaration, Frederic Kirgis asserts that for a claim to secession (or any type of self-determination claim), 'the relationship is inverse between the degree of representative government, on the one hand, and the extent of destabilization that the international community will tolerate in a self-determination claim, on the other'.[179] This means that if a government is highly democratic, a claim to secede will only be given international credence if it has a very minimal destabilizing effect, where destabilization depends on factors including the plausibility of the historical claim to territory and the presence of dissident minority groups within the territory. Conversely, the international community may well recognize a claim to secede from a repressive dictatorship even if the secession would cause serious destabilization.

In a similar vein, Rein Müllerson sees emerging 'a guideline which establishes that secession is tolerated or at certain stages even supported by the world community of states when it leads, or there are reasonable grounds to believe that it may lead, to considerably greater protection of human rights and fundamental freedoms without constituting unreasonable risk for regional or even for world stability'.[180] Among the factors for a successful secession that Gregory Marchildon and Edward Maxwell derive from state practice are 'minimal disruption of national unity and international harmony; occurrences of violence; and denial of human rights or democratic process'.[181]

While some authors go about expanding the right of self-determination of peoples beyond decolonization by establishing the existence of additional legal categories, there are increasingly others who perceive a single coherent narrative in the law. But each author's interpretation inevitably reflects and creates an image or images of those seeking

---

[179] F. L. Kirgis, Jr., 'The Degrees of Self-Determination in the United Nations Era' (1994) 88 *American Journal of International Law* 304 at 308. See also T. N. Tappe, 'Chechnya and the State of Self-Determination in a Breakaway Region of the Former Soviet Union: Evaluating the Legitimacy of Secessionist Claims' (1995) 34 *Columbia Journal of Transnational Law* 255.

[180] Müllerson, *Law, Rights and Politics*, p. 72; Müllerson, 'Dissolution of the USSR', p. 575.

[181] G. Marchildon and E. Maxwell, 'Quebec's Right of Secession under Canadian and International Law' (1992) 32 *Virginia Journal of International Law* 583 at 608. See also T. Becker, 'Self-Determination in Perspective: Palestinian Claims to Statehood and the Relativity of the Right to Self-Determination' (1998) 32 *Israel Law Review* 301 at 333–4 (arguing that balancing the principle of self-determination against other factors, including international stability, has generated distinct categories of rights to external self-determination and of right-holders).

self-determination, the character that makes them worthy or unworthy. In the chapters that follow, I suggest that the understanding of identity contained in a particular interpretation of self-determination is also part of that interpretation's appeal – be it for international lawyers (in Chapter 3) or disputants (in Parts II and III) – and therefore part of the challenge of adjudicating self-determination.

3 Pandemonium, interpretation and participation

Chapters 1 and 2 introduced the different formulations of external self-determination found in the post-Cold War international law literature. In so doing, the two chapters sought to draw attention to the corresponding difference in approaches to interpretation and the consequences for participation in the activity of interpretation and for the narration of identity. Who could speak with authority? Whose image of self and society found expression? The emphasis thus far has been on participation and identity as the results of a choice about what interpretation involves, as generated by adherence to some general view of international law and its workings. This chapter explores the opposite relationship. It suggests that the implications for *participation* and *identity* may, in part, be responsible for the persuasiveness of one vision of *interpretation* over another. Thus, the interlocutors and the claimants anticipated by one rendition of self-determination may be part of why that rendition is more convincing to us than another.

The chapter uses the interpretation of self-determination by two well-known authors, Thomas Franck and Rosalyn Higgins, to develop this suggestion. It shows how the image each author creates of a world on the verge of pandemonium[1] may blind us to internal inconsistencies in their analysis of secession. That is, our recognition or acceptance of the imminence of pandemonium helps persuade us of the rightness of their interpretation and the propriety of their analysis.

Pandaemonium – the capital of Satan in Milton's 'Paradise Lost' – is the title of Daniel Patrick Moynihan's post-Cold War study of ethnicity in

---

[1] Compare D. Kennedy, 'A New Stream of International Law Scholarship' (1988) 7 *Wisconsin International Law Journal* 1 at 12. (The entire rhetorical apparatus of international law and society exists within and against a margin composed of such things as chaos and war.)

international politics.² In 'Paradise Lost', *Pandaemonium* is a place of both darkness and demagoguery. Having raised impious war in heaven, Satan and his host of rebel angels are hurled by the Almighty from the ethereal sky down into bottomless perdition, where, although a great furnace burns, 'yet from those flames/ No light, but rather darkness visible'.³ In his account of the dismantling of the Habsburg and Romanov empires after World War I, and with them the modest village structures of tolerance and coexistence between their many ethnic groups, Moynihan evokes the long fall from heaven into chaos.⁴ He also calls up the image of *Pandaemonium* as the setting for Satan's consultation with his followers on how to regain heaven. Among Satan and his infernal peers, argument is intemperate and recklessly ambitious. Alluding to the dangerousness of debate, Moynihan writes of ethnic conflict: 'For the moment the more pressing matter is simply to contain the risk, to restrain the tendency to hope for too much, either of altruism or of common sense. Pandaemonium was inhabited by creatures quite convinced that the great Satan had their best interests at heart.'⁵ Satan exemplifies too the treachery of certain interlocutors, vowing to Beëlzebub:

> If then his Providence
> Out of our evil seek to bring forth good,
> Our labour must be to pervert that end,
> And out of good still to find means of evil.⁶

The first part of this chapter compares Thomas Franck's interpretation of self-determination in two influential articles: 'The Emerging Right to Democratic Governance'⁷ and 'Postmodern Tribalism and the Right of Secession'.⁸ It contrasts the construction of *demos* as enlightenment in 'The Emerging Right to Democratic Governance' with that of *ethnos*

---

² D. P. Moynihan, *Pandaemonium: Ethnicity in International Politics* (New York: Oxford University Press, 1993).
³ J. Milton, 'Paradise Lost' in J. T. Shawcross (ed.), *The Complete Poetry of John Milton* (rev. edn, New York: Anchor Books, 1971), pp. 249–517 at pp. 252–3.
⁴ Moynihan, *Pandaemonium*, pp. 24, 140. See also the titles of chapters 4 ('Before the Fall') and 5 ('Order in an Age of Chaos').
⁵ *Ibid.*, pp. 173–4. See also A. Roberts, 'Foreword' in *ibid.*, p. vii, at pp. viii–ix (on nationalism as Satan, raised 'to that bad eminence').
⁶ Milton, 'Paradise Lost', p. 255.
⁷ T. M. Franck, 'The Emerging Right to Democratic Governance' (1992) 86 *American Journal of International Law* 46.
⁸ T. M. Franck, 'Postmodern Tribalism and the Right to Secession' in C. Brölmann, R. Lefeber and M. Zieck (eds.), *Peoples and Minorities in International Law* (Dordrecht: Martinus Nijhoff, 1993), pp. 3–27.

as pandemonium in 'Postmodern Tribalism and the Right of Secession.' The contention here is that these opposite worlds play a part in persuading us of Franck's composite interpretation of self-determination and in obscuring the inconsistency of the line he draws between politics and law.

Apart from their impact,[9] one reason for focusing on these particular articles by Franck[10] is that the two belong to the same historical moment, a few years after the end of the Cold War, and may therefore fairly be compared. The other is that since these articles were penned before the victory of liberal democracy and escalation of ethnic conflict had coalesced in the international legal imagination,[11] they provide the clearest example of the rhetoric.

The second part of the chapter discusses Rosalyn Higgins's most recent writing on self-determination. It demonstrates that her interpretation of self-determination is based on a shift from her general theory of international law as policy oriented and broadly participatory[12] to a theory of international law as rigid rules and international legal interpretation as

---

[9] See e.g. S. Marks, *The Riddle of All Constitutions: International Law, Democracy and the Critique of Ideology* (Oxford: Oxford University Press, 2000); Panel Discussion, 'National Sovereignty Revisited: Perspectives on the Emerging Norm of Democracy in International Law' (1992) 86 *Proceedings of the American Society of International Law* 249.

[10] Franck has written extensively on issues of individual and collective self-determination in international law. See also T. M. Franck, 'Clan and Superclan: Loyalty, Identity and Community in Law and Practice' (1996) 90 *American Journal of International Law* 359; T. M. Franck, 'The Democratic Entitlement' (1994) 29 *University of Richmond Law Review* 1; T. M. Franck, *The Empowered Self: Law and Society in the Age of Individualism* (New York: Oxford University Press, 2000); T. M. Franck, *Fairness in International Law and Institutions* (Oxford: Clarendon Press, 1995), pp. 83–169; T. M. Franck, 'Fairness in the International Legal and Institutional System' (1993-III) 240 *Hague Recueil* 9 at pp. 99–149; T. M. Franck, 'Legitimacy in the International System' (1988) 82 *American Journal of International Law* 705 at 743–9; T. M. Franck, *The Power of Legitimacy Among Nations* (New York: Oxford University Press, 1990), pp. 153–76; T. M. Franck, 'The Stealing of the Sahara' (1976) 70 *American Journal of International Law* 694. T. M. Franck and P. Hoffman, 'The Right of Self-Determination in Very Small Places' (1976) 8 *New York University Journal of International Law and Politics* 331;

[11] Franck's later account of self-determination synthesizes the phenomena of modernism and postmodern tribalism. Franck, *Fairness in International Law and Institutions*, pp. 140–69. On the antecedents of this distinction between good *demos* and bad *ethnos* in international legal thought, see N. Berman, 'Nationalism "Good" and "Bad": The Vicissitudes of an Obsession' (1996) 90 *Proceedings of the American Society of International Law* 214.

[12] R. Higgins, 'International Law and the Avoidance, Containment and Resolution of Disputes' (1991-V) 230 *Hague Recueil* 9 at 23–41, later published as R. Higgins, *Problems and Process: International Law and How We Use It* (Oxford: Clarendon Press, 1994), pp. 1–16.

the province of experts.¹³ The relevance of this shift from policy to rules is not so much Higgins's narrow interpretation of the right to secede – a similarly restrictive interpretation might be justified on policy grounds – but the implications for the transformative potential of interpretation. Higgins effectively seeks to end any conversation that we might have in international law about the meaning of self-determination or, at least, to exclude from the conversation those who do not accept its formalism. The third and final part of the chapter suggests how Higgins's insistence on rules corresponds to the fear of pandemonium as both chaos and debased discussion.

Darkness visible[14]

Thomas Franck's 'The Emerging Right to Democratic Governance'[15] argues that we are witnessing the transformation of self-determination in international law from the right of overseas colonies to independence into a right of all to participate in democratic governance, while his 'Postmodern Tribalism and the Right of Secession'[16] staunches the interpretation of self-determination so as to preclude a right of secession.

Both pieces begin with the sweep of historical events. In the opening pages of 'Democratic Governance', there are two large, magnificent historical events: the failed August 1992 coup in Moscow, and the decisive international action taken in immediate response to the overthrow of President Aristide of Haiti in September 1991. While Franck presents these events as political, more than legal, progress for democracy,[17] he implies that the distinction is unimportant because political principle will march triumphantly into international law. Indeed, in the space of three pages the word 'triumph' is applied to both President Yeltsin's victory and the ideas of Hume, Locke, Jefferson and Madison.[18]

The early paragraphs of 'Postmodern Tribalism', in contrast, crowd together the manifestations of nationalism that Franck calls 'postmodern tribalism'.[19] However neutral Franck's definition of postmodern tribalism

---

[13] Higgins, 'Avoidance, Containment and Resolution of Disputes', 154–74; Higgins, *Problems and Process*, pp. 111–28; R. Higgins, 'Postmodern Tribalism and the Right to Secession, Comments' in Brölmann, Lefeber and Zieck (eds.), *Peoples and Minorities*, pp. 29–35.

[14] Milton, 'Paradise Lost', p. 253.   [15] Franck, 'Democratic Governance'.
[16] Franck, 'Postmodern Tribalism'.   [17] Franck, 'Democratic Governance', 47.
[18] *Ibid.*, 47–9.
[19] For the argument that the analogy between nationalism and tribalism is at best unenlightening and at worst misleading, see E. Kedourie, *Nationalism* (4th edn, Oxford: Blackwell, 1993), p. 69.

as the promotion of a political and legal environment conducive to the break-up of a multinational or multicultural state in order to form a new state composed of a single nationality or culture,[20] his use of the term 'tribalism' strongly implies the primitiveness of such designs.[21]

Postmodern tribalism is presented as 'everywhere', the examples ranging across the age (old, nineteenth century and new) and place (Europe, the Americas and the Third World) of nations to reinforce this impression. Omnipresent, it is also uniform, 'manifest[ing] itself in efforts to break up, equally,' and undifferentiated in its lack of apology and open flaunting 'with zealously raised arms and firearms'.[22] No distinction is made between nationalist movements that generally work within the political and legal system, such as Scottish and Québécois nationalists, and those that have degenerated into unrest, violence or war. Whereas political principle flowed smoothly into international law in 'Democratic Governance', a scrupulous separation is observed in 'Postmodern Tribalism', and a thicket of policy obstacles planted between the 'undeniable political trend towards secessionist post-colonial "tribal" states'[23] and an international legal right to secede.

If 'Democratic Governance' creates an enlightened universe of *demos* that helps persuade us to recognize a right to democratic governance originating in self-determination, 'Postmodern Tribalism' summons a dark underworld of *ethnos* that plays to our fears of interpreting self-determination to include a right of secession.

On the perilous edge[24]

In the abstract, Rosalyn Higgins is unequivocal in choosing a policy-oriented approach to international law as process over a more formalist

---

[20] Franck, 'Postmodern Tribalism', p. 4.
Indeed, Franck himself acknowledges elsewhere the inferiorizing implications of the term 'tribalism'. Franck, *The Empowered Self*, p. 16.

[21] Consider further Michael Reisman's characterization in the course of a roundtable discussion of *uti possidetis*: 'In practice, this would mean that when group elites come forward, whether in former Czechoslovakia, former Yugoslavia, or some other state that is about to become a former state, *beating the tom-toms of ethnicism, tribalism or subnationalism*, the international community's response may be: "Sorry, the boundaries here are not subject to change"'. (Emphasis mine) Panel Discussion, 'Communities in Transition: Autonomy, Self-Governance and Independence' (1993) 87 *Proceedings of the American Society of International Law* 248 at 258. See also M. Reisman, 'Designing and Managing the Future of the State' (1997) 8 *European Journal of International Law* 409 at 413 (contrasting 'the language of the global scientific civilization' with 'the throbbing tom-toms of tribalism whose hypnotic rhythms communicate, at levels far below overt consciousness, the virtues of the old modes of identification and operation').

[22] Franck, 'Postmodern Tribalism', p. 3.   [23] *Ibid.*, p. 13.

[24] Milton, 'Paradise Lost', p. 258.

approach to international law as rules, and is dismissive of those who attempt to reconcile the two.[25] This part of the chapter shows that Higgins's formulation of the right of self-determination relies on an approach very much like the rules-based approach she criticizes, and examines how, compared to the processual approach, this restricts the kinds of arguments that can be made about the meaning of self-determination and who can make them.

In the first lecture of her general course on public international law given at the Hague Academy of International Law in 1991, Higgins firmly declares her approach to international law as 'process' and not 'just rules'.[26] Rather than regarding international law as the impartial application of rules, the process approach conceives of international law as 'the entire decision-making process, and not just the reference to the trend of past decisions which are termed "rules". There inevitably flows from this definition a concern, especially where the trend of past decisions is not overwhelmingly clear, with policy alternatives for the future'.[27]

In an argument familiar from American legal realism,[28] Higgins maintains that judges do not 'find the rule', but actually determine what the relevant rule is. Adjudication involves choice, and choice requires a consideration of the humanitarian, moral and social purposes of the law.[29] Since reference to rules can neither eliminate the need for choice nor guide a consideration of policy, Higgins concludes that policy factors should be dealt with systematically and openly by the decision-maker.[30]

---

[25] Higgins, 'Avoidance, Containment and Resolution of Disputes', 31–2; Higgins, *Problems and Process*, p. 8.

[26] Higgins, 'Avoidance, Containment and Resolution of Disputes', 24–37; Higgins, *Problems and Process*, pp. 2–12.

[27] R. Higgins, 'Policy Considerations and the International Judicial Process' (1968) 17 *International and Comparative Law Quarterly* 58 at 59, quoted in Higgins, 'Avoidance, Containment and Resolution of Disputes', 25; Higgins, *Problems and Process*, p. 2.

[28] See Note, "Round and 'Round the Bramble Bush: From Legal Realism to Critical Legal Scholarship' (1982) 95 *Harvard Law Review* 1669. Myres McDougal and Harold Lasswell, whose approach to international law appears to have influenced Higgins, regard American legal realism as an antecedent to their own scholarship. M. S. McDougal and H. D. Lasswell, *Jurisprudence for a Free Society* (2 vols., Dordrecht: Martinus Nijhoff, 1992), vol. I, pp. 249–67. See also R. A. Falk, 'Casting the Spell: The New Haven School of International Law' (1995) 104 *Yale Law Journal* 1991 at 1991–2; Higgins, 'Policy Considerations and the International Judicial Process', 58–63.

[29] Higgins, 'Avoidance, Containment and Resolution of Disputes', 25–6; Higgins, *Problems and Process*, p. 3.

[30] Higgins, 'Avoidance, Containment and Resolution of Disputes', 28–9; Higgins, *Problems and Process*, p. 5.

One consequence of analysing international law as process is that the distinction between international law as it is (*lex lata*) and as it ought to be (*lex ferenda*) becomes less important. Higgins states: 'If law as rules requires the application of outdated and inappropriate norms, then law as process encourages interpretation and choice that is more compatible with values we seek to promote and objectives we seek to achieve.'[31]

Another consequence is that the focus of inquiry into what international law is widens to include such varied phenomena as claims and counterclaims, state practice and decisions by a variety of authorized decision-makers. International law is no longer identified with what the International Court of Justice would say on a given matter, but reflects the entire range of claimants and decision-makers in the international system.

In theme, method and lexicon, Higgins's approach to international law strongly resembles[32] the policy science approach developed by Myres McDougal and Harold Lasswell.[33] However, the contrast between rules and process, stasis and dynamism, past and future, fixity and fluidity, noun and gerund that structures Higgins's introductory lecture detracts attention from the ways in which she narrows its ambit. The first lecture makes explicit that Higgins considers her process approach appropriate to cases where an ambiguous rule falls to be interpreted[34] or no rule covers the situation at hand (*non liquet*).[35] Her treatment of self-determination and the use of force in the later lectures indicates that she sees the process approach as applicable also where a more expansive

---

[31] Higgins, 'Avoidance, Containment and Resolution of Disputes', 34; Higgins, *Problems and Process*, p. 10. See also *Legality of the Threat or Use of Nuclear Weapons*, Advisory Opinion, ICJ Reports 1996, p. 226 at p. 592 (Dissenting Opinion of Judge Higgins) ('The judicial lodestar, whether in difficult questions of interpretation of humanitarian law, or in resolving claimed tensions between competing norms, must be those values that international law seeks to promote and protect'.)

[32] See Falk, 'Casting the Spell', 2006, n. 66.

[33] See generally M. S. McDougal, H. D. Lasswell and W. M. Reisman, 'Theories About International Law: Prologue to a Configurative Jurisprudence' (1968) 8 *Virginia Journal of International Law* 188; M. S. McDougal and W. M. Reisman, 'International Law in Policy-Oriented Perspective' in R. St J. Macdonald and D. M. Johnston (eds.), *The Structure and Process of International Law: Essays in Legal Philosophy, Doctrine and Theory* (Boston: Martinus Nijhoff, 1983), pp. 103–29; J. N. Moore, 'Prolegomenon to the Jurisprudence of Myres McDougal and Harold Lasswell' (1968) 54 *Virginia Law Review* 662.

[34] Higgins, 'Avoidance, Containment and Resolution of Disputes', 30 ('Where there is ambiguity or uncertainty, the policy directed choice can properly be made'). See also *ibid.*, 323 ('facts must be looked at, and legal views applied in context. But I also believe such policy choices are appropriate when the legal norms leave open alternative possibilities'). Higgins, *Problems and Process*, pp. 7, 253.

[35] Higgins, 'Avoidance, Containment and Resolution of Disputes', 34; Higgins, *Problems and Process*, p. 10.

interpretation of a clear rule is contemplated,[36] but not as justifying a new interpretation that would contradict that rule – in such cases non-compliance is the only route.[37]

To differentiate cases in which policy-directed choices can properly be made from those in which they have no role to play, Higgins must assume that clear rules can be separated from ambiguous rules; and that deviations from the written text that develop and elaborate rather limited statements of principle – such as self-determination – can be distinguished from deviant practices that are prohibited by the written text and must therefore be beyond justification by it.[38] This necessarily commits her to a strongly determinate view of language and law. She has written elsewhere, 'I believe that legal ideas develop, and that that is proper. But that is not to say that they can mean simply whatever those using them want them to mean.'[39] Meaning is one thing and development is another.

It is not apparent how Higgins reconciles this view of determinacy with the premises of the process approach. If there is, as she states, no 'real international law that all men of good faith can recognize, that is rules that can be neutrally applied, regardless of circumstance and context',[40] then how can we distinguish between clear and ambiguous rules and between deviations that expand the written text and those that contradict it? In modelling law as process, Higgins retains from the rules model the notion that international law has a core predictability.[41] How extensive is this core and how does it differ from 'rules that can be neutrally applied'?

In distancing her own process approach from the charge of apologism levelled at those who used a policy science approach to justify the Reagan administration's foreign policy,[42] Higgins introduces a tension

---

[36] Higgins, 'Avoidance, Containment and Resolution of Disputes', 156; Higgins, *Problems and Process*, p. 113; Higgins, 'Postmodern Tribalism', p. 30.
[37] Higgins, 'Avoidance, Containment and Resolution of Disputes', 322–3; Higgins, *Problems and Process*, pp. 252–3.
[38] Higgins, 'Avoidance, Containment and Resolution of Disputes', 156; Higgins, *Problems and Process*, p. 113.
[39] Higgins, 'Postmodern Tribalism', p. 30.
[40] Higgins, 'Avoidance, Containment and Resolution of Disputes', 30–1; Higgins, *Problems and Process*, p. 7.
[41] Higgins, 'Avoidance, Containment and Resolution of Disputes', 32; Higgins, *Problems and Process*, p. 8.
[42] Higgins, 'Avoidance, Containment and Resolution of Disputes', 29; Higgins, *Problems and Process*, p. 6. The troubling tendency of McDougal's and his followers' legal appraisals of controversial issues in US foreign policy to coincide with the

between process and rules. Policy is still there, but it is relegated to the ambiguities, the interstices and the margins of interpretation. Yet in her Hague lecture on self-determination – perhaps the most controversial and most dynamic norm in international law – policy is largely excluded. As we shall see, Higgins retreats to a walled city of interpretation whose bastions are rules and categories. Whether in defending the existing rule against attack by infidels or advancing a new interpretation, she relies on rules rather than policy or principle.

In Higgins's view, it is clear that what the UN Charter says about self-determination refers to the right of the people of one state to be protected from interference by other states, and that the chapters on dependent territories use neither the term 'self-determination' nor the concept as we now know it. 'Popular mythology'[43] is simply wrong in tracing the origins of self-determination to the Charter.[44]

More generally, Higgins assumes that each successive stage in the development of self-determination corresponds to a rule with a single meaning so that it makes sense to speak, as she does in her commentary on Franck's 'Postmodern Tribalism', of the 'misapplication of legal terms'.[45] This assumption permits her to criticize as wrong and irresponsible those who appeal to a different interpretation of the rule. In that commentary, she dwells on 'the importance of using concepts with some care... I am of course very aware that there are those who use the armoury of words in full knowledge of what they do.'[46] Her Hague lecture dismisses as confused rhetoric the fashion among political leaders to invoke self-determination as the right of minorities to secede[47] and ends with the admonition that self-determination cannot be all things to all men.[48] Even if Higgins's discussion of the original meaning of self-determination in the UN Charter and her scrupulous separation of

Administration's outlook has been commented on more generally. E.g. B. S. Chimni, *International Law and World Order: A Critique of Contemporary Approaches* (New Delhi: Sage Publications, 1993), pp. 73–145; O. Schachter, Remarks in Panel Discussion, 'McDougal's Jurisprudence: Utility, Influence, Controversy' (1985) 79 *Proceedings of the American Society of International Law* 266 at 272–3; Falk, 'Casting the Spell', 2001.

[43] Higgins, 'Avoidance, Containment and Resolution of Disputes', 154; Higgins, *Problems and Process*, p. 111.
[44] On the interpretation of the UN Charter, see also Higgins, 'Postmodern Tribalism', pp. 29–30.
[45] *Ibid.*, p. 35.   [46] *Ibid.*, pp. 34–5.
[47] Higgins, 'Avoidance, Containment and Resolution of Disputes', 170; Higgins, *Problems and Process*, p. 124.
[48] Higgins, 'Avoidance, Containment and Resolution of Disputes', 174; Higgins, *Problems and Process*, p. 128.

political vogue from legal meaning now is a prelude to a policy analysis of the directions that the rule should take – which turns out not to be the case – it is at odds with the rapprochement between *lex lata* and *lex ferenda* that follows from viewing international law as process.

If rules have a clear meaning and it is wrongheaded and irresponsible to use them in a different sense, then how can Higgins account for changes in meaning? Part of the answer that emerges from her lecture on self-determination is that international law is a high priesthood and the interpretation of texts is the province of high priests and ecclesiastical scholars. 'Popular' mythology and 'all' men are just that, and the claims of political leaders fickle and unsound. This may explain in part why the Human Rights Committee's interpretation of the right of self-determination in the International Covenant on Civil and Political Rights[49] is presented as, rather than shown to be, preferable to rival interpretations, even by other publicists. The mission of international lawyers is to safeguard the purity of the rule, eschewing 'current fashion when it is intellectually unsound'.[50] Here again, the dynamic of claims and counterclaims by a broad range of participants in the international legal system seems to have shifted to one of authoritative and expert interpretation.

Apart from its authority, why is the Human Rights Committee's development of the right of self-determination right and the interpretation of the right advanced by politicians, nations and minorities wrong? The justification that Higgins provides for the Committee's interpretation relies on a chain of reasoning with rules and categories. Nevertheless, without a larger normative context, she is hard pressed to prove why each link is the only one that can be made.

The Human Rights Committee, according to Higgins, considers that the right of self-determination gives the population of a territory still subject to colonialism, alien domination or occupation the right to choose its external status, be it independent statehood, free association or integration with an independent state, or any other political status freely determined by that population (external self-determination). Under any other circumstances, the right requires only that the population of a state be given the continuing opportunity to choose their system of government within the state in order that they can determine

---

[49] International Covenant on Civil and Political Rights, New York, 16 December 1966, in force 23 March 1976, 999 UNTS 171.
[50] Higgins, 'Avoidance, Containment and Resolution of Disputes', 174; Higgins, *Problems and Process*, p. 128.

their economic, social and cultural development (internal self-determination).⁵¹ The alternative interpretations that Higgins seeks to refute take the general form that even beyond colonialism, alien domination and occupation, certain subgroups of a population have the right to choose their political status under certain conditions.

Higgins begins by arguing that the right of self-determination in international law has never simply meant independence, but has always meant the free choice of peoples as to political status. That it also means the free choice of government follows from the wording of Article 1(1) of the Covenant 'and freely pursue their economic, social and cultural development'. But it would seem equally plausible to read this phrase as no more than the right of a newly independent population or indeed – consistent with her interpretation of Article 1(2) of the UN Charter – any population to be free of outside interference.⁵²

Higgins argues next that her interpretation of self-determination in Article 1 is not inconsistent with Article 25, which provides that every citizen shall have the right to take part in the conduct of public affairs, to vote and to be elected at periodic elections on the basis of universal suffrage, and to have access to public service in his country. The overlap between the internal self-determination envisaged by Article 1 and the rights of political participation guaranteed by Article 25, she maintains, is not fatal to such an interpretation of Article 1 because the two Articles are complementary.⁵³ Article 25 provides more detail on how free choice is to be implemented as well as covering matters beyond those covered by Article 1.

Without more, Higgins takes quite the opposite view of the relationship between Article 1 and Article 27. In her commentary on Franck's 'Postmodern Tribalism', she asserts that the Covenant provides for two discrete rights. This means that minorities, who have the minority rights guaranteed by Article 27, cannot also be peoples with some right of external self-determination under Article 1.⁵⁴ In addition, the possibility

---

⁵¹ Higgins, 'Avoidance, Containment and Resolution of Disputes', 165; Higgins, *Problems and Process*, p. 120.
⁵² Compare e.g. C. Tomuschat, Summary Records of 2060th Meeting, [1988] I *Yearbook of the International Law Commission* 110, para. 56. Tomuschat's view on self-determination is of particular relevance because both he and Higgins have been members of the UN Human Rights Committee.
⁵³ *Contra*, see e.g. *ibid*.
⁵⁴ Higgins, 'Postmodern Tribalism', p. 32. *Contra*, see e.g. D. McGoldrick, *The Human Rights Committee: Its Role in the Development of the International Covenant on Civil and Political*

that minorities might be peoples with an entitlement to secede is excluded, she argues in her Hague lectures, by the emphasis on the importance of territorial integrity in all the relevant instruments and in state practice.[55] But this neglects the argument that the penultimate paragraph of the UN Declaration on Friendly Relations[56] conditions the protection of a state's territorial integrity on its having 'a government representing the whole people belonging to the territory without distinction as to race, creed or colour', thereby contemplating the secession of racial or religious minorities where the state does not and will not meet the condition.[57]

In summary, Higgins's lecture on self-determination comes remarkably close to the assumptions about international law with which she takes issue in the introductory lecture: 'that "the correct legal view" is to be discerned by applying "rules" – the accumulated trend of past decisions, regardless of context or circumstance – and that "the correct legal view" has nothing to do with applying past decisions to current contexts by reference to objectives (values) that the law is designed to promote'.[58]

The apostate angel

Rosalyn Higgins's treatment of self-determination thus departs in two important ways from her general statement that the

> persuasive character of legal jurisprudence... is the necessary stuff of our very existence in community with others. Everyone is entitled to participate in the identification and articulation as to what they perceive the values to be promoted. Many factors, including the responsive chords struck in those to whom the argument is made, will determine whether particular suggestions prevail.[59]

First, her presentation of the right of self-determination as a set of clear-cut rules leaves no room for interpretation and, consequently, none for

---

Rights (Oxford: Clarendon Press, 1991), p. 250; J. Crawford, 'Self-Determination Outside the Colonial Context' in W. J. A. Macartney (ed.), *Self-Determination in the Commonwealth* (Aberdeen: Aberdeen University Press, 1988), pp. 1–22 at p. 6.

[55] Higgins, 'Avoidance, Containment and Resolution of Disputes', 170; Higgins, *Problems and Process*, p. 124.

[56] Declaration on Principles of International Law Concerning Friendly Relations and Cooperation Among States in Accordance with the Charter of the United Nations, GA Res. 2625 (XXV) (1970).

[57] See pp. 74–7 above.

[58] Higgins, 'Avoidance, Containment and Resolution of Disputes', 27; Higgins, *Problems and Process*, p. 4.

[59] Higgins, 'Avoidance, Containment and Resolution of Disputes', 34; Higgins, *Problems and Process*, p. 10.

the consideration of values. Second, her reliance on authority and disparagement of popular claims about self-determination are hard to reconcile with a broad entitlement to participate in interpretation and even harder to reconcile with a dialogic understanding of interpretation, whereby the interpretation should be persuasive to the parties concerned.

It is significant that not only could Higgins's limitation of the right of self-determination to colonial peoples and peoples under alien domination or foreign occupation be justified on her general approach to international law as process, but that she herself has in the past taken this type of approach to self-determination. In an article written in 1983,[60] she argues that the contest between a state's claim to the reintegration of territory based on sovereignty and a claim to independence by the territory's inhabitants based on the right of self-determination is resolved by contextual analysis, taking into consideration the variables of history, cultures, local wishes, human rights record and existence of a democratic government.[61]

Why, then, does Higgins ground her interpretation of self-determination in rules rather than process? And why might her analysis be persuasive? The glimpses she gives us of pandemonium, particularly at the end of her comment on Franck's 'Postmodern Tribalism', offer two tentative answers. A first answer lies in pandemonium as the spectre of uncontrollable disintegration that Higgins summons in rejecting a right of secession for minorities: Yugoslavia; Bosnia-Herzegovina; the Bosnian Serbs; if the Serbian areas of Bosnia are forcibly integrated into a greater Serbia, then the Muslim and Croat populations of these areas; 'and so on, *ad infinitum*'.[62] This answer is that the right of self-determination must be treated as a determinate rule because darkness is visible. If the content of self-determination were instead to depend on the conclusion of an argument of policy or principle, then international society would be inviting chaos. There are echoes here of Thomas Hobbes's command theory of law, which holds that positive law is always legitimate because it is imperative that the law be beyond challenge. According to Hobbes, the risk of making the

---

[60] R. Higgins, 'Judge Dillard and the Right to Self-Determination' (1983) 23 *Virginia Journal of International Law* 387.
[61] *Ibid.*, 392. In her 1991 Hague lecture on self-determination, however, she states categorically that the territorial claim comes first. Higgins, 'Avoidance, Containment and Resolution of Disputes', 174; Higgins, *Problems and Process*, p. 127.
[62] Higgins, 'Postmodern Tribalism', p. 35.

content of the law dependent on moral argument is no less than civil war.[63]

Implicit in Higgins's analysis of self-determination is another image of pandemonium: the debased rhetoric of Satan and his infernal peers. We have already seen that Higgins is strongly critical of those who, in her view, deliberately misappropriate the international legal language of self-determination. She writes of this linguistic mischief: 'the move to uninational and unicultural states that constitutes postmodern tribalism is profoundly illiberal. The attempt to legitimate these tendencies by the misapplication of legal terms runs the risk of harming the very values that international law is meant to promote.'[64] The image of the apostate angel in pandemonium, arguing without regard for reason or morality, allows us to see Higgins's analysis of self-determination as correct on rhetorical, as opposed to Hobbesian, grounds. Granting that interpretation involves inter-subjective argument – as Higgins puts it, 'the responsive chords struck in those to whom the argument is made' – a consensus may nevertheless be unavailable in reality. In this case, one of the rhetorical strategies advocated by Aristotle is to restrict the type of participants in the discussion. Friedrich Kratochwil quotes the following advice from Aristotle's *Topica*:

> You ought not to discuss with everybody... for with some people argument is sure to deteriorate; for with a man who appears to try every means to escape from the right (conclusion) you are justified in trying everything to come to such a conclusion; however, this is not a seemly proceeding. You should, therefore, not readily join issue with casual persons; this can only result in a debased sort of discussion; for those who are practicing cannot forbear from disputing contentiously.[65]

Higgins implicitly makes the same argument by creating an opposition between the international legal establishment, with its cultures of formal legal reason and neutrality, and the demagogues, who flout these

---

[63] T. Hobbes, *Leviathan*, C. B. MacPherson (ed.) (London, Penguin, 1968). For the argument that H. L. A. Hart's legal positivism cannot escape its origin in Hobbes's command theory of law, see D. Dyzenhaus, 'Law and Public Reason' (1993) 38 *McGill Law Journal* 366. Given the weak enforcement mechanisms in international law, certainty may be seen to take on even more importance than in Hobbes's domestic law framework. See T. Baty, *The Canons of International Law* (London: Murray, 1930); Franck, *The Power of Legitimacy Among Nations*; R. Y. Jennings, 'Closing Address' in Brölmann, Lefeber and Zieck, *Peoples and Minorities*, pp. 341–7 at pp. 344–5.

[64] Higgins, 'Postmodern Tribalism', p. 35.

[65] Aristotle, *Topica*, 165b8–10, quoted by F. V. Kratochwil, *Rules, Norms and Decisions. On the Conditions of Practical and Legal Reasoning in International Relations and Domestic Affairs* (Cambridge: Cambridge University Press, 1989), p. 230.

conventions. Seen through this image of pandemonium as debased discussion, Higgins's retreat to rules is not an attempt to deny any need for the interpretation of self-determination, as on the image of pandemonium as chaos, but an attempt to exclude irrationality and passion from its interpretation by narrowing the community of interpreters.[66]

John Comaroff has written that from the perspective of Euro-nationalism, with its ideal of civic identity, 'all ethno-nationalisms appear primitive, irrational, magical and, above all, threatening; in the eyes of ethno-nationalism – which appears perfectly "rational" from within – Euro-nationalism remains inherently colonizing, lacking in humanity or social conscience'.[67] In this chapter, I have suggested that while the Euro-nationalist perspective of Thomas Franck and Rosalyn Higgins does not find direct expression in their legal arguments about the meaning of self-determination, it translates into the underlying theme of pandemonium that helps to make their legal arguments seem internally consistent and therefore plausible. Without the narrative of a world plunged into violence and chaos by postmodern tribalism, Franck's anticipation of the passage of a right to democratic governance from politics into law might seem inconsistent with his reluctance to acknowledge an emerging right to secede. In Higgins's work, this narrative similarly supports the presentation of self-determination as a fixed rule, despite her general approach to international law as process. Alternatively, the narrative of inflamed discussion reinforces her implicit retreat from a broadly participatory interpretive process to a more traditional reliance on authority.

---

[66] Interestingly, the term 'barbarous nationalisms' coined by Carol A. L. Prager in 'Barbarous Nationalism and the Liberal International Order: Reflections on the "Is", the "Ought", and the "Can"' in J. Couture, K. Nielsen and M. Seymour (eds.), *Rethinking Nationalism* (Calgary, Alta.: University of Calgary Press, 1998), pp. 441–62 also contains the idea of incommunicability because incomprehensible, non-Greek and inferior are among the earliest senses of 'barbarous'. J. Kristeva, *Etrangers à nous-mêmes* (France: Gallimard, 1988), pp. 74–7.

[67] J. L. Comaroff, 'Ethnicity, Nationalism and the Politics of Difference in an Age of Revolution' in J. L. Comaroff and P. C. Stern (eds.), *Perspectives on Nationalism and War* (Luxembourg: Gordon and Breach, 1995), pp. 243–76 at p. 263.

PART II • SELF-DETERMINATION INTERPRETED IN PRACTICE: THE CHALLENGE OF CULTURE

4 The canon of self-determination

The significance of the major international decisions on the meaning of self-determination – the 1975 International Court of Justice *Western Sahara* advisory opinion,[1] *Opinion No. 2* issued in 1992 by the European Communities Conference on Yugoslavia Arbitration Commission[2] and the 1995 ICJ judgment in *East Timor (Portugal v. Australia)*[3] – goes beyond their importance as building blocks in the different accounts of external self-determination discussed in Part I.[4] The larger significance of these

---

[1] *Western Sahara*, Advisory Opinion, ICJ Reports 1975, p. 12.

[2] Conference on Yugoslavia, Arbitration Commission, *Opinion No. 2* (1992) 31 ILM 1497.

[3] *East Timor (Portugal v. Australia)*, ICJ Reports 1995, p. 90. See also H. Krieger (ed.), *East Timor and the International Community: Basic Documents* (Cambridge: Grotius Publications, 1997).

[4] It should be noted that two other ICJ cases might have turned on the right of self-determination. *Certain Phosphate Lands in Nauru (Nauru v. Australia)*, ICJ Reports 1992, p. 240, concerning the right of the people of Nauru to the rehabilitation of certain phosphate lands mined out during the period when Australia administered Nauru as a trust territory, was settled before it reached the merits stage. See A. Anghie, '"The Heart of My Home": Colonialism, Environmental Damage, and the Nauru Case' (1993) 34 *Harvard International Law Journal* 445. For the settlement, see Australia–Republic of Nauru Settlement of the Case in the International Court of Justice Concerning Certain Phosphate Lands in Nauru, Nauru, 10 August 1993, in force 20 August 1993, (1993) 32 ILM 1471. In *Application of the Convention on the Prevention and Punishment of the Crime of Genocide (Bosnia-Herzegovina v. Yugoslavia)*, one of Yugoslavia's preliminary objections was that Bosnia was not qualified to become a party to the Convention on the Prevention and Punishment of the Crime of Genocide, New York, adopted 9 December 1948, in force 12 January 1951, 78 UNTS 277 (Genocide Convention) because it had acquired independent statehood by acts violating the principle of self-determination and that the court consequently did not have jurisdiction under the Genocide Convention. Verbatim Record, CR 96/5 (29 April 1996) at pp. 12–43. The court dismissed this objection on the grounds that an independent Bosnia had become a UN member, Article 11 of the Genocide Convention opens the Convention to any UN member and the circumstances of Bosnia's accession to independence were therefore of no consequence for its

cases lies in the actors, the arguments and the judicial reasoning and values. This chapter shows in some detail how the interpretation of self-determination in the cases has served as a point of entry into international law for newcomers, the newly returned and even the absent, and for their challenges to international law's marginalization of them. What emerges from the decisions is not a uniform judicial method, but a pattern of creativity that may be seen as responsive to these challenges. In particular, concepts are broadened so as to make room for the inclusion of new identities and relationships within international law. The approach to their interpretation attempts not only to include, but also to equalize, whether by mediating between insider and outsider perspectives or by expanding participation through the choice of sources, doctrine of interpretation over time or determination of meaning. While the method of *interpretation* may vary from one judgment to another, the commitment in them to *identity* and *participation* as dimensions of equality is constant. This is not to say that the three decisions discussed here are necessarily successful by the very standard that this chapter discerns in them. It is to say, however, that the recognition of this standard holds promise for the interpretation of 'universal' laws that were made without universal participation and that systematically operate, whether intentionally or not, to the disadvantage of those excluded from their making.

Western Sahara

The United Nations General Assembly's request to the International Court of Justice in 1974 for an advisory opinion on Western Sahara originated in objections by Morocco and Mauritania to the referendum on decolonization that Spain planned to hold in Western Sahara.[5] Spain

> succession to the Convention. *Preliminary Objections*, ICJ Reports 1996, p. 595 at p. 611.
> Despite the potential relevance of self-determination to issues of territory, the analysis in this chapter cannot be extended to the series of ICJ cases characterized *ab initio* as territorial disputes. See pp. 374–6 below.

[5] For background to the request, see *Western Sahara*, pp. 25–7. See generally M. Barbier, *Le conflit du Sahara Occidental* (Paris: Editions l'Harmattan, 1982); T. Hodge, 'The Western Sahara' [1984] *International Commission of Jurists Review* 25; B. Jacquier, 'L'autodétermination du Sahara espagnol' (1974) 78 *Revue générale de droit international public* 683; E. H. Riedel, 'Confrontation in Western Sahara in the Light of the Advisory Opinion of the International Court of Justice of 16 October 1975. A Critical Appraisal' (1976) 19 *German Yearbook of International Law* 405 at 407–18.

had colonized Western Sahara in 1884. Since 1961, it had administered Western Sahara as a non-self-governing territory under Chapter XI of the UN Charter, thereby recognizing the right of the territory's inhabitants to self-determination. The referendum was intended to implement this right of self-determination. The objections of Morocco and Mauritania, both neighbouring states, were based on the status of Western Sahara at the time of its colonization by Spain. Morocco claimed that

> For commentary on the advisory opinion, see H. A. Amankwah, 'Self-Determination in the Spanish Sahara: A Credibility Gap in the United Nations' Practice and Procedure in the Decolonisation Process' (1981) 14 *Comparative and International Law Journal of Southern Africa* 34; Barbier, *Le conflit du Sahara Occidental*, pp. 132–54; N. Berman, 'Sovereignty in Abeyance: Self-Determination in International Law' (1988) 7 *Wisconsin International Law Journal* 51 at 99–103; L. E. Blaydes, 'International Court of Justice Does Not Find "Legal Ties" of Such a Nature to Affect Self-Determination in the Decolonization Process of Western Sahara' (1976) 11 *Texas International Law Journal* 354; A. Cassese, 'The International Court of Justice and the Right of Peoples to Self-Determination' in V. Lowe and M. Fitzmaurice (eds.), *Fifty Years of the International Court of Justice. Essays in Honour of Sir Robert Jennings* (Cambridge: Grotius Publications, 1996), pp. 351–63; J. Castellino, *International Law and Self-Determination: The Interplay of the Politics of Territorial Possession with Formulations of Post-Colonial 'National' Identity* (The Hague: Martinus Nijhoff, 2000), pp. 173–258; J. Chappez, 'L'avis consultatif de la Cour Internationale de Justice du 16 octobre 1975 dans l'affaire du Sahara occidental' (1976) 80 *Revue générale de droit international public* 1132; M. Chemillier-Gendreau, 'La Question du Sahara Occidental' (1976) 2 *Annuaire du Tiers Monde* 270; J. Crawford, *The Creation of States in International Law* (Oxford: Clarendon Press, 1979), especially pp. 181, 358, 378–84, 415; J. Crawford, 'The General Assembly, the International Court and Self-Determination' in Lowe and Fitzmaurice (eds.), *Fifty Years of the International Court of Justice*, pp. 585–605; M. Flory, 'L'Avis de la Cour Internationale de la Justice sur le Sahara Occidental (16 Octobre 1975)' (1975) 21 *Annuaire français de droit international* 253; R. Higgins, 'Judge Dillard and the Right to Self-Determination' (1983) 23 *Virginia Journal of International Law* 387; M. W. Janis, 'The International Court of Justice: Advisory Opinion on the Western Sahara' (1976) 17 *Harvard International Law Journal* 609; J.-F. Prévost, 'Observations sur l'avis consultatif de la Cour Internationale de Justice relatif au Sahara occidental ("terra nullius" et autodétermination)' (1976) 103 *Journal du droit international* 831; Riedel, 'Confrontation in Western Sahara'; M. Shaw, *Title to Territory in Africa: International Legal Issues* (Oxford: Clarendon Press, 1986), especially pp.12–13, 34–7, 52–8, 92–8, 187–91; M. Shaw, 'The Western Sahara Case' (1978) 49 *British Yearbook of International Law* 119; M. A. Smith, 'Sovereignty Over Unoccupied Territories – The Western Sahara Decision' (1977) 9 *Case Western Reserve Journal of International Law* 135.
> On the aftermath of the case, see L. Condorelli, 'Le droit international face à l'autodétermination du Sahara occidental' in G. Amato, A. Cassese, J. Echeverría, V. Gerratana, G. Haupt, L. Matarasso, O. Negt, F. Rigaux, S. Rodotá and A. Soboul (eds.), *Marxism, Democracy and the Rights of Peoples: Homage to Lelio Basso* (Milan: Franco Angeli Editore, 1979), pp. 653–62; T. M. Franck, 'The Stealing of the Sahara' (1976) 70 *American Journal of International Law* 694; Y. H. Zoubir, 'The Western Sahara Conflict: A Case Study in Failure of Prenegotiation and Prolongation of Conflict' (1996) 26 *California Western International Law Journal* 173.

Western Sahara was then part of the Sherifan State, and Mauritania that it formed part of the 'Mauritanian entity' or Bilad Shinguitti.[6]

Accordingly, the General Assembly requested an advisory opinion on two questions:

> I Was Western Sahara (Rio de Oro and Sakiet el Hamra) at the time of colonization by Spain a territory belonging to no one (*terra nullius*)?
>
> If the answer to the first question is in the negative,
>
> II What were the legal ties between this territory and the Kingdom of Morocco and the Mauritanian entity?[7]

By construing 'legal ties' as those relevant to the decolonization of Western Sahara, the court turned these otherwise historical questions about Western Sahara at the time of colonization by Spain into a modern problem of self-determination. Since 'legal ties' was not a technical term in international law, the court looked for its meaning in the object and purpose of the General Assembly resolution that decided to request the advisory opinion.[8] That resolution repeatedly situated the request in the context of the right of self-determination of the Western Saharan population in accordance with the 1960 UN Declaration on the Granting of Independence to Colonial Countries and Peoples (Declaration on the Independence of Colonial Peoples) (GA Resolution 1514 (XV)), leading the court to conclude that 'legal ties' meant legal ties

> of such a nature as might affect the application of resolution 1514 (XV) in the decolonization of Western Sahara and, in particular, of the principle of self-determination through the free and genuine expression of the will of the peoples of the Territory.[9]

In this way, the court established 'the free and genuine expression of the will of the peoples of the Territory' as the dominant narrative of self-determination and 'legal ties' as a source of counter-narratives.[10] Among the states that appeared before the court in *Western Sahara*, Spain and Algeria cleaved to the dominant narrative. They maintained that the population of the Western Sahara was entitled to exercise its right of self-determination through a referendum on independence, regardless

---

[6] On the overlap between the two claims, as resolved in the course of the case, see *Western Sahara*, pp. 65–7.

[7] GA Res. 3292 (XXIX) (1974), quoted in *Western Sahara*, p. 13.

[8] *Western Sahara*, p. 40.   [9] *Western Sahara*, p. 68. See also *ibid*., pp. 40–1.

[10] These are among the narratives found in the contemporary international law scholarship on external self-determination. See Chapter 2 above.

of whether Morocco or Mauritania could establish a precolonial claim to the territory. Through the counter-narrative of 'legal ties', Morocco and Mauritania argued that the wrongful taking of their territory by Spain and the historical patterns of cultural identity in the Sahara justified the restoration of the precolonial situation.[11]

Other than Spain, the states that made submissions in *Western Sahara* were all African states that had been subject to European colonialism. Part of Morocco had been controlled by Spain since the nineteenth century, and the rest had come under French rule in the twentieth century. Since becoming independent in the late 1950s, Morocco had acquired sovereignty over the Spanish enclave of Ifni by cession. Mauritania had been a French protectorate from the turn of the century until its independence in 1960. Algeria had fought a war of independence against France. Zaire (now the Democratic Republic of the Congo) was formerly the Belgian Congo. Morocco, Mauritania and Algeria, moreover, were Muslim states.

The appearance of these African states before the International Court of Justice was made more remarkable by the Third World's general disenchantment with the court following its 1966 judgment in the *South West Africa* case. Brought by Ethiopia and Liberia against South Africa, the case regarded the self-determination of Namibia; specifically, the continued existence of the mandate for what was then South West Africa and the duties and performance of South Africa as the mandatory.[12] In both this

---

[11] For a discussion of other such conflicts, see e.g. Amankwah, 'Self-Determination in the Spanish Sahara'; S. K. N. Blay, 'Self-Determination *versus* Territorial Integrity in Decolonization' (1986) 18 *New York University Journal of International Law and Politics* 441; Crawford, *The Creation of States*, pp. 377–84; T. M. Franck and P. Hoffman, 'The Right of Self-Determination in Very Small Places' (1976) 8 *New York University Journal of International Law and Politics* 331; J. F. Gravelle, 'The Falklands (Malvinas) Islands: An International Law Analysis of the Dispute Between Argentina and Great Britain' (1985) 107 *Military Law Review* 5; J. R. Maguire, 'The Decolonization of Belize: Self-Determination v. Territorial Integrity' (1982) 22 *Virginia Journal of International Law* 849; T. D. Musgrave, *Self-Determination and National Minorities* (Oxford: Clarendon Press, 1997), pp. 239–55; V. Rudrakumaran, 'The "Requirement" of Plebiscite in Territorial Rapprochement' (1989) 12 *Houston Journal of International Law* 23 at 41–5;
M. A. Sánchez, 'Self-Determination and the Falkland Islands Dispute' (1983) 21 *Columbia Journal of Transnational Law* 557; A. Schwed, 'Territorial Claims as a Limitation to the Right of Self-Determination in the Context of the Falklands Islands Dispute' (1983) 6 *Fordham International Law Journal* 443.

[12] See A. O. Adede, 'Judicial Settlement in Perspective' in A. S. Muller, D. Raič and J. M. Thuránszky (eds.), *The International Court of Justice: Its Future Role After Fifty Years* (The Hague: Martinus Nijhoff, 1997), pp. 47–81 at pp. 50–5; M. Shahabuddeen, 'The World Court at the Turn of the Century' in Muller, Raič and Thuránszky, *The International Court of Justice*, pp. 3–29 at pp. 3–20. See contra

and its 1962 judgment on South West Africa,[13] a technical issue of jurisdiction divided the court according to different ideas of international law and interpretation.[14] In the 1962 judgment, favourable to the court's jurisdiction, the minority judges adhered to the strict separation of international law and politics, and the construction of treaties according to original intent. The majority considered a rigid division between law and politics impossible to sustain and was prepared to read treaty commitments in light of the progressive development of international law, as necessary to give full effect to their purpose. The 1966 decision became a *cause célèbre* when chance[15] transformed the 1962 minority judges into the majority. Based on their theory of international law, the new majority declined jurisdiction and thereby effectively reversed the earlier decision. The 1966 decision was greeted with outrage by many states, particularly in the Third World,[16] and has been credited with the sea-change in judicial approach, starting with the 1971 *Namibia* advisory opinion, that James Crawford has titled 'decolonizing the Court'.[17]

R. P. Anand, 'Attitude of the "New" Asian-African Countries Toward the International Court of Justice' in F. E. Snyder and S. Sathirathai (eds.), *Third World Attitudes Toward International Law* (Dordrecht: Martinus Nijhoff, 1987), pp. 163–77 (not addressing this historical period in particular, but arguing generally that Asian and African states are no more or less reluctant than other states to submit their disputes to third-party settlement).

[13] *South West Africa (Ethiopia v. South Africa; Liberia v. South Africa), Preliminary Objections*, ICJ Reports 1962, p. 319; *South West Africa (Ethiopia v. South Africa; Liberia v. South Africa), Second Phase*, ICJ Reports 1966, p. 6. See generally E. Klein, 'South West Africa/Namibia (Advisory Opinions and Judgments)' in R. Bernhardt (ed.), *Encyclopedia of Public International Law* (12 vols., Amsterdam: North-Holland, 1981), vol. II, pp. 260–70.

[14] Crawford, 'The General Assembly', p. 587. For contemporaneous commentary, see e.g. C. J. R. Dugard, 'The South West Africa Cases, Second Phase, 1966' (1966) 83 *South African Law Journal* 429; R. A. Falk, 'The South West Africa Cases: An Appraisal' (1967) 21 *International Organization* 1; W. G. Friedmann, 'The Jurisprudential Implications of the South West Africa Case' (1967) 6 *Columbia Journal of Transnational Law* 1.

[15] Not only had the composition and presidency of the court changed, but Judge Zafrulla Khan did not sit (it was suspected that South Africa had objected to his participation); Judge Bustamente fell ill; Judge Badawi died while the case was being heard; and the casting vote was exercised by the new President, Sir Percy Spender, who had been in the minority in 1962. L. C. Green, 'South West Africa and the World Court' (1966–7) 22 *International Journal* 39 at 58–9. For information indicating that Sir Percy Spender actively engineered the disqualification of Judge Zafrulla Khan, see Adede, 'Judicial Settlement in Perspective', pp. 52–3.

[16] G.-M. Cockram, *South West African Mandate* (Cape Town: Juta & Co., 1976), pp. 327–43; T. O. Elias, *The International Court of Justice and Some Contemporary Problems: Essays on International Law* (The Hague: Martinus Nijhoff, 1983), p. 347; G. Fischer, 'Les réactions devant l'arrêt de la Cour Internationale de Justice concernant le Sud-Ouest africain' (1966) 12 *Annuaire français de droit international* 144.

[17] Crawford, 'The General Assembly', p. 587. Commentators also credit the case with affecting the next round of elections to the court. Green, 'South West Africa and the

Indeed, beyond the competing narratives of self-determination, *Western Sahara* required the court to deal with the centrality of European colonialism in international law.[18] In interpreting classical international law, how should the court navigate the straits of Eurocentrism and imperial expediency? In using self-determination to dismantle the colonial apparatus in modern international law, should the court provide a new way forward based on the free will of the colonized, taking colonialism as a fact, or should it look backwards to the precolonial situation, treating colonialism as an injustice done to the previous sovereigns? The African states that appeared in *Western Sahara* answered these larger questions differently. Morocco and Mauritania took the position that nineteenth-century international law should be interpreted so as to recognize the patterns of identity that existed in the Western Sahara and that these identities should be restored. For Algeria, the venality of nineteenth-century international law had to be openly admitted and remedied by a new international law based on the equal participation of old and new states alike and on the participation of peoples through the exercise of self-determination. Zaire made a limited appearance in *Western Sahara*; it agreed with Algeria that the notion of *terra nullius* reflected a European perspective on the world, but argued that it should be reinterpreted in a way authentic to Africa rather than dismissed as a colonial relic in international law.

On the facts of *Western Sahara*, the court retained the dominant account of self-determination as the free will of the population. The court found it unnecessary to consider whether this account, espoused by Spain and Algeria, should be modified by the Moroccan and Mauritanian accounts of self-determination as a wrongful taking of territory or a historical cultural identity. This was because neither Mauritania nor Morocco had persuaded the court of the underlying claim; that is, the sufficiency of its legal ties to the Western Sahara. On the first question, the court found that according to the international law then in force, Western Sahara was not *terra nullius* because the territory was inhabited by tribes having a social and political organization. Proceeding therefore to the second question, the court concluded that at the time of Spanish colonization, both Morocco and the Mauritanian entity had legal ties to the territory of Western Sahara. Ties of allegiance existed between the Sultan of Morocco and some of the tribes living in the territory of Western Sahara. Likewise, legal ties between the Mauritanian entity and the

World Court', 66; E. McWhinney, *Judge Manfred Lachs and Judicial Law-Making. Opinions on the International Court of Justice, 1967–1993* (The Hague: Martinus Nijhoff, 1995), p. 15.

[18] See generally Chemillier-Gendreau, 'La Question du Sahara Occidental'.

territory existed in the form of rights, including some rights relating to land. None of these legal ties, however, was of such a nature as to affect the decolonization of Western Sahara.[19]

This chapter argues, however, that the significance of the court's judgment should not be restricted to its conclusion on self-determination. In its interpretation and application of the concepts involved in the determination of the historical legal ties (*terra nullius*, legal ties, legal entity) and its dicta regarding the possible effect of such ties on the exercise of free choice by the population, the court engaged not only the specific challenges made to the account of self-determination as free choice, but also the more general problems of the interpretation of a historically Eurocentric international law and the appropriate international legal remedy for colonialism. Although this larger significance has been lost from view in the scholarship on self-determination, it is underlined by the treatment of *Western Sahara* in later cases. *Mabo v. Queensland (No. 2)*, the landmark 1992 decision of the High Court of Australia recognizing common law aboriginal title, is a powerful example. In *Mabo*, two of the judges used the ICJ's analysis of *terra nullius* to reverse the long held position that Australia had been *terra nullius* at the time of white settlement and that there could therefore be no title in Australian aboriginal peoples originating in their prior occupation of the land.[20] And the discussion of *Western Sahara* in the 1981 *Dubai/Sharjah* boundary arbitration[21] highlights the ICJ's efforts to relate the notion of sovereignty to historical ties between non-Western communities. Paradoxically, the arbitral tribunal does so by distinguishing the resulting notion of sovereignty in *Western Sahara* as nevertheless too Western to be legitimate in a territorial dispute between the emirates of Dubai and Sharjah.

Past

The questions referred to the International Court of Justice by the General Assembly in *Western Sahara* are remarkable, in and of themselves, for their treatment of the past. In classical international law, where colonization was justifiable, the issue would have been whether Spain had acquired good title to Western Sahara. The court, along with the

---

[19] *Western Sahara*, pp. 68–9.
[20] *Mabo v. Queensland (No. 2)* (1992), 175 Commonwealth Law Reports 1 (High Court of Australia) at 33–4, 40–1 (Brennan J.), 181–2 (Toohey J.).
[21] *Dubai/Sharjah* Border Arbitration, 19 October 1981, Court of Arbitration (Cahier, Simpson, Simmonds) (1993) 91 International Law Reports 543.

General Assembly and all the parties, explicitly set this issue aside.[22] Instead, the court's task was to determine the legalities of the precolonial situation and their relevance for the present (postcolonial-to-be) situation. In this sense, the framework of self-determination, as accepted in the case, bracketed Spain's colonization of Western Sahara. While it was colonization that gave rise to the people's right of self-determination, colonization was superficially expunged from the application of the right.

But the law that governed the court's historical task was nevertheless classical international law since the doctrine of intertemporal law requires facts to be assessed in light of the international law of the time. And the relevant classical international law was modelled on the European state and its territorial expansion.[23] The basic concepts in the reference questions – *terra nullius*, legal ties, legal entity, all of which concerned the degree of recognition to be given to patterns of identity – were based on European norms of political and social organization and on the relationship of European to non-European. Thus, although the questions concerned non-European communities and the relationships that existed between them prior to European colonization, the applicable international law was colonial and, as will be seen, worked against the recognition of non-European communities and their claims.

The interpretation given to self-determination by the court in *Western Sahara* also projected the colonial backwards onto the precolonial in so far as it made the colonial population the self and thereby consigned any historical claims to the category of territorial. The court adopted the General Assembly's view of self-determination as 'the right of the population of Western Sahara to determine their future political status by their own freely expressed will'.[24] 'It is for the people to determine the destiny of the territory', Judge Dillard wrote more plainly in his

---

[22] *Western Sahara*, p. 28.
[23] See e.g. A. Anghie, 'Finding the Peripheries: Sovereignty and Colonialism in Nineteenth Century International Law' (1999) 40 *Harvard International Law Journal* 1; A. Anghie, 'Francisco de Vitoria and the Colonial Origins of International Law' (1996) 5 *Social and Legal Studies* 321; Anghie, 'The Heart of My Home' 491–9; A. Anghie, 'Time Present and Time Past: Globalization, International Financial Institutions and the Third World' (2000) 32 *New York University Journal of International Law and Politics* 243 at 275–89. See also A. Carty, *The Decay of International Law? A Reappraisal of the Limits of Legal Imagination in International Affairs* (Manchester: Manchester University Press, 1986), pp. 49–50 (asserting that the international law doctrine and scholarship on the acquisition of territory had to do only with non-European territory and a different, often extra-legal, analysis was used for European territory).
[24] *Western Sahara*, p. 36.

separate opinion, 'and not the territory the destiny of the people'.[25] The assumption that the colonial population was the self and the referendum an exercise of their right to self-determination forced Morocco and Mauritania to base their arguments for the restoration of the precolonial situation on a claim to territory. To succeed, Morocco and Mauritania had to show that they had precolonial legal ties to the territory[26] and that these ties required the return of the territory regardless of the will of its population. Since an appeal to 'territory' generally lacks the power of an appeal to 'self',[27] this put Morocco and Mauritania at a rhetorical disadvantage.

Although the court treated the population of Western Sahara as the legal 'self', it is significant that it did not validate any such sociological finding. While the court did not accept Morocco's appeal to the salience of an ethnic, cultural and religious self that united Western Sahara with Morocco,[28] neither did it endorse Spain's view that the Sahrawi, the inhabitants of Western Sahara, formed a coherent and distinct self at the time of colonization;

> that what is the present territory of Western Sahara was the foundation of a Saharan people with its own well-defined character, made up of autonomous tribes, independent of any external authority; and that this people lived in a fairly well-defined area and had developed an organization and a system of life in common, on the basis of collective self-awareness and mutual solidarity.[29]

As far as the court was concerned, the self effectively took its identity from the referendum and not vice versa. The referendum constituted the population within the colonial borders as a conglomerate of choosers, indistinguishable from any other conglomerate of choosers. Through the process of the referendum, international law imprinted the uniformity of a democratic citizenry onto the particularity of whatever ethnic,

---

[25] *Ibid.*, p. 122 (Separate Opinion of Judge Dillard).
[26] *Ibid.*, p. 41 (burden of proof on Morocco and Mauritania).
[27] L. Brilmayer, 'Secession and Self-Determination: A Territorial Interpretation' (1991) 16 *Yale Journal of International Law* 177 at 177–9, 183.
[28] *Western Sahara*, p. 45. See also *ibid.*, pp. 57–8 (Mauritania). On this type of claim generally, see Crawford, *The Creation of States*, p. 382, No. 5; Franck and Hoffman, 'The Right of Self-Determination in Very Small Places', 369.
[29] *Western Sahara*, p. 62. See also 'Oral Statement of José M. Lacleta' (22 July 1975), *Western Sahara*, ICJ Pleadings, vol. V, p. 112 at pp. 114, 134–9. Contra e.g. T. K. Smith, in Panel: 'Self-Determination: The Cases of Fiji, New Caledonia, Namibia, and the Western Sahara' (1988) 82 *American Society of International Law Proceedings* 439 at 439 ('A Sahrawi identity emerged following the Second World War when Spain began to pursue a more active interest in its Saharan possession').

cultural or religious communities might ultimately find expression through the process.

The self/territory dichotomy projected backwards by colonialism also created concrete problems of proof for Morocco and Mauritania that it would not have created for a European state because traditionally Morocco's and Mauritania's political organization was ethnically rather than territorially based. To this effect, Morocco quoted from a turn-of-the-century account of Morocco by a French writer who had made several expeditions to the Moroccan south:

Il y a entre nous et les musulmans de l'Afrique du Nord une différence radicale dans la façon dont s'est construite dans notre esprit et dans le leur l'idée d'empire. Pour nous, l'élément dominant dans cette idée est la limite et c'est là ce qu'elle a d'essentiellement romain et cette notion de limite nous a empêchés de comprendre ce qu'est un empire maghrébin. Les musulmans de l'Afrique du Nord n'ont pas une conception territoriale de leur empire, mais bien une conception ethnique. L'élément principal, chez eux, dans cette conception, n'est pas l'idée de limites d'un territoire mais l'idée de sujétion d'une population.

Les Européens, géographes ou hommes politiques, ont toujours considéré le Maroc sous la forme d'un Etat européen; ils se trompaient et comme ils ne lui trouvaient pas de limites et qu'il leur en fallait quand même, ils en inventaient.

[Between us and the North African Muslims there is a radical difference in the way that the idea of empire is constructed in our mind and theirs. For us, the dominant element in this idea is the limit – and this is what is essentially Roman – and this notion of limit has prevented us from understanding what a Maghreb empire is. The North African Muslims do not have a territorial conception of their empire, but rather an ethnic conception. The principal element for them, in this conception, is not the idea of limits of a territory but the idea of the subjection of a population.

The Europeans, geographers or politicians, have always considered Morocco under the form of a European state; they are mistaken and as they did not find limits for it and needed limits all the same, they invented them.][30]

The fullness of the court's response to the dilemmas of applying an international law tailored to Europe and European colonialism to the precolonial Sahara emerged in the court's interpretation of three concepts: *terra nullius*, legal ties and legal entity.

[30] (Translation mine) E. Douté (1901), quoted in 'Oral Statement of Mr. Isoart' (2 July 1975), *Western Sahara*, ICJ Pleadings, vol. IV, p. 252 at p. 257. See also M. Flory, 'La notion de territoire arabe et son application au problème du Sahara' (1957) 3 *Annuaire français de droit international* 73.

Terra Nullius

A l'instar de la plupart des systèmes juridiques de droit privé et de la plupart des codes civils, qui disposent que les biens qui n'ont pas de maître appartiennent à l'Etat, l'on a procédé par l'application séculaire de la théorie de la *terra nullius* à une réification, à une 'chosification' des peuples de la planète, comme si le déterminisme géographique qui les avait placés hors d'Europe devait leur valoir de basculer douloureusement dans le néant pour des siècles.

[In the manner of most private law systems and most civil codes, which provide that goods without an owner belong to the state, one proceeded by the secular application of the theory of *terra nullius* to a reification or 'thingification' of the people of the planet, as if the geographic determinism that placed them outside Europe had earned them their painful fall into nothingness for centuries.]

Mohammed Bedjaoui, representing Algeria in *Western Sahara*[31]

Il est évident que l'Afrique consciente ne peut plus se rallier au concept de *terra nullius* tel qu'élaboré par les juristes occidentaux... La Cour internationale de Justice ne doit donc pas interpréter et envisager la notion de *terra nullius* selon l'authenticité et la conception occidentales; elle devra plutôt l'adapter, l'aborder compte tenu des réalités africaines.

[It is clear that an aware Africa can no longer rally to the concept of *terra nullius* as elaborated by Western jurists... Thus, the International Court of Justice must not contemplate and interpret the notion of *terra nullius* according to a Western conception and a Western authenticity, rather it must approach and adapt it so as to take account of African reality.]

Mr. Bayona-Ba-Meya, representing Zaire in *Western Sahara*[32]

Pourrait-on demander à la Cour de ne pas en tenir compte parce que, tout compte fait, c'est de la comédie, une farce, et de se contenter dès lors de reconnaître et de donner effet à la réalité crue, c'est-à-dire la domination ou la zone d'influence?

C'est pourtant à cela que l'on aboutit pour les notions juridiques de 1885 si on écarte les concepts humanistes de nécessité du consentement et de reconnaissance de la souveraineté des tribus qui faisaient le pendant à celui de *terra nullius*.

[Could one ask the court to disregard [*terra nullius*] because, all things considered, it is a joke and a farce and, from that moment, to be content to recognize and give effect to the crude reality; that is, domination and zones of influence?

---

[31] (Translation mine) 'Oral Statement of Mohammed Bedjaoui' (14 July 1975), *Western Sahara*, ICJ Pleadings, vol. IV, p. 448 at p. 452.

[32] (Translation mine) 'Oral Statement of Mr. Bayona-Ba-Meya' (14 July 1975), *Western Sahara*, ICJ Pleadings, vol. IV, p. 439 at pp. 440, 445.

This is nevertheless where one ends up with the legal notions of 1885 if one moves away from the humanist concepts of the need for consent and the recognition of the sovereignty of tribes which were paired with that of *terra nullius*.]

Jean Salmon, representing Mauritania in *Western Sahara*[33]

The first question put to the International Court of Justice in *Western Sahara* was whether Western Sahara (Rio de Oro and Sakiet el Hamra) was at the time of colonization by Spain a territory belonging to no one (*terra nullius*). Since this had to be judged in light of the law then in force,[34] the question required the court to decide what the concept of *terra nullius* meant in 1884, when Spain colonized the region.[35]

Some of the judges considered the question of *terra nullius* irrelevant since none of the interested states had actually relied on the proposition that Western Sahara was *terra nullius* at the time of colonization.[36] Whether strictly relevant or not, its significance was that it enabled the court to determine whether the international law of the late nineteenth century had cognizance of the tribes that inhabited the Western Sahara and to what extent the general practice of this period was 'de nier sa personalité pour mieux le conquérir'; that is, to deny international legal personality to non-European communities the better to conquer them.[37] According to the classical modes of acquiring sovereignty over territory, only sovereignty over a *terra nullius* could be acquired through acts of occupation. Sovereignty over other territory was acquired through cession, conquest or prescription.[38] Hence, to the extent that international law relegated territories inhabited by non-Europeans to the status of *terra nullius*, it erased the inhabitants from international law and opened the territory to acquisition through European settlement.

Mohammed Bedjaoui, the representative of Algeria, urged the court to acknowledge that nineteenth-century international law was a game played by European states and that Western Sahara would have been *terra nullius* under these rules. At that time, any territory not belonging to a 'civilized' state was *terra nullius*, just as any territory not belonging to a Christian sovereign had been during the Age of Discovery and any

---

[33] (Translation mine) 'Oral Statement of Jean Salmon' (28 July 1975), *Western Sahara*, ICJ Pleadings, vol. V, p. 253 at p. 265.

[34] See below at note 194 and accompanying text.   [35] *Western Sahara*, pp. 38–9.

[36] *Ibid.*, pp. 74–5 (Declaration of Judge Gros), 113 (Separate Opinion of Judge Petrén), 123 (Separate Opinion of Judge Dillard).

[37] Compare M. Shahabuddeen, 'Developing Countries and the Idea of International Law' in R. St J. Macdonald (ed.), *Essays in Honour of Wang Tieya* (Dordrecht: Martinus Nijhoff, 1994), pp. 721–36 at p. 728.

[38] *Western Sahara*, p. 39.

non-Roman territory had been in ancient Rome.³⁹ The secular civilizing mission simply replaced the bringing of Christianity as the ideology of colonialism, thereby imparting a new ideological content to *terra nullius*.⁴⁰ Bedjaoui argued before the court:

Chaque époque ... produit ses alibis et ses instruments de camouflage. C'est ainsi que l'on a colonisé pour lutter contre les infidèles et pour les évangéliser, alors que ce fut pour les réduire en esclavage et exploiter leurs richesses. On colonisa plus tard pour apporter des lumières de la civilisation et dispenser les bienfaits.

Dans cette perspective, on est toujours le 'sauvage' d'un autre, dès lors que l'on ne partage pas avec lui ses systèmes de références éthiques, politiques, philosophiques ou religieux. Si l'on décrète que le territoire doit revenir à la puissance coloniale candidate, il faut bien, de quelque manière, en rendre incapables de possession ou de souveraineté ses propres habitants. Il faut bien les décréter inhabiles à sa gestion. Suprême raffinement, si les 'sauvages' sonts inaptes à la gestion souveraine de leurs affaires publiques, c'est parce qu'ils sont même incapables de discerner leur propre bien et leur propre salut. Ils sont réduits à la condition de mineurs qu'heureusement la puissance coloniale portera un jour à l'âge de raison et à la qualité de responsables.

[Every era ... produces its alibis and its instruments of camouflage. It is thus that one colonized to fight the infidels and to evangelize them, when it was actually to reduce them into slavery and to exploit their riches. One colonized later to bring the enlightenment of civilization and to dispense its benefits.

From this perspective, one is always the 'savage' of another from the moment that one does not share his ethical, political, philosophical or religious system of reference. If one decrees that the territory must return to the candidate colonial power, one must effectively, in some manner, render its own inhabitants incapable of possessing it or having sovereignty over it. One must effectively decree them to be without the skills for its management. Supreme refinement – if the 'savages' are inapt at the sovereign management of their public affairs, it is because they are even incapable of discerning their own good and their own salvation. They are reduced to the condition of minors that happily the colonial power will one day bring to the age of reason and to the quality of responsible adults.]⁴¹

Bedjaoui's claim was not finally that the concept of *terra nullius* was used to justify all European colonizations of the nineteenth century,⁴²

---

³⁹ 'Oral Statement of Mohammed Bedjaoui' (14 July 1975), pp. 455–6, elaborated at pp. 456–73.
⁴⁰ To similar effect, see S. N. Grovogui, *Sovereigns, Quasi-Sovereigns, and Africans: Race and Self-Determination in International Law* (Minneapolis: University of Minnesota Press, 1996); R. A. Williams, Jr., *The American Indian in Western Legal Thought: The Discourse of Conquest* (New York: Oxford University Press, 1990).
⁴¹ (Translation mine) 'Oral Statement of Mohammed Bedjaoui' (14 July 1975), p. 475.
⁴² On treaties of cession, see *ibid.*, pp. 475–8.

but that lacking a rigorous definition and simultaneously animated by reference to the European system of states, it became an uncontrollable weapon in the hands of the colonial states, which they had the discretion to use according to their needs.[43] However scientific the application of *terra nullius* might have been in theory, in practice the distinction between *terra nullius* and *terra non nullius* was made by states based not only on a European idea of the state but also on their own interests in the circumstances.[44]

On Bedjaoui's approach to the interpretation of *terra nullius*, the court had to recognize that *terra nullius* signified the exclusion of non-European peoples from classical international law. For Bedjaoui,[45] the remedy for this long injustice lay in the development and application of a new international law, which revised the exclusionary concept of *terra nullius* through the inclusionary right of peoples to self-determination.

While the representative of Zaire, Mr. Bayona-Ba-Meya, shared Bedjaoui's view of *terra nullius* as the subject of Western ideology, he maintained that the time had come for it to become the subject of an African counter-ideology. Africans could not countenance the Western concept of *terra nullius*, even as an artefact of international law's venality at the time. To do so would, first of all, insult the memory of those Africans who had died in the ongoing struggle against colonialism and neo-colonialism.[46] Second, the Western concept did not reflect an African world view:

La conception foncière de l'homme occidental est purement utilitariste en ce sens que la mise en valeur économique est considérée comme le signe effectif d'occupation et d'utilisation du sol, la non-occupation de la terre pendant un certain temps étant sanctionnée par la perte de son droit de propriété foncière. Chez nous, en Afrique, dans notre mentalité traditionnelle authentique, la terre n'est pas un bien qui répond exclusivement à une fonction économique, à savoir fournir à l'homme ce dont il a besoin pour sa subsistance; la terre ... est une des composantes de la mère nature, elle constitue un cadre médiateur et protecteur, en raison de la communion spirituelle qui existe entre les vivants et les morts, tant il est vrai que les morts ne sont pas morts, car ils sont le souffle de la vie, invisibles mais toujours présents, pour assumer leur rôle de médiation et de protection. Ainsi donc, les ancêtres sont pour nous, Africains, un facteur d'enracinement, de rattachement au sol où ils reposent.

---

[43] 'Oral Statement of Mohammed Bedjaoui' (29 July 1975), *Western Sahara*, ICJ Pleadings, vol. V, p. 302 at p. 308.
[44] *Ibid.*   [45] See pp. 160–2 below.
[46] 'Oral Statement of Mr. Bayona-Ba-Meya' (14 July 1975), p. 441.

[The basic conception of Western man is purely utilitarian in the sense that economic exploitation is considered as the effective sign of occupation and utilization of the soil, the non-occupation of the land for a certain time being penalized by the loss of one's right of basic proprietorship. For us in Africa, in our authentic traditional mentality, the land is not a good that responds exclusively to an economic function, to know how to furnish man with what he needs for his subsistence; the land...is one of the components of mother nature, it constitutes a mediating and protective setting by reason of the spiritual communion that exists between the living and the dead, which only goes to show that the dead are not dead for they are the breath of life, invisible but always present to assume their role of mediation and protection. So in this way, ancestors are for us Africans a factor of rootedness and attachment to the soil where they rest.][47]

Given this fundamental difference between European and African world views, argued Bayona-Ba-Meya, the concept of *terra nullius* applied to Africa should be one that corresponds to an African sensibility, especially in a case where two of the three interested parties were African states. Indeed, a relationship between Europe and Africa based on cultural equality depended on this revision of *terra nullius*.[48]

Applying an African concept of *terra nullius*, Bayona-Ba-Meya concluded that Western Sahara was not *terra nullius* at the time of colonization because 'les ancêtres des peuples marocains et mauritaniens y sont nés, y ont fondé des civilisations propres et y ont été enterrés, créant ainsi entre les vivants et les morts une communauté spirituelle immémorable et inaliénable, qui a donné naissance à une implantation vitale foncière conforme à l'authenticité de ces deux peuples frères concernés' ('the ancestors of the Moroccan and Mauritanian peoples were born there, founded their own civilizations there and were buried there, thus creating an immemorial and inalienable spiritual community between the living and the dead which gave birth to a vital, basic and authentic establishment of these two brother peoples').[49]

Morocco[50] and Mauritania[51] disagreed with Bedjaoui's account of *terra nullius* as any territory not belonging to a European state or to a state that Europeans recognized because of its fundamental acceptance of the European philosophy of the state. This was true, Mauritania maintained, only of the later colonial period. And, even then, the purpose

---

[47] (Translation mine) *Ibid.*, p. 444. [48] *Ibid.*, p. 445.
[49] (Translation mine) *Ibid.*, pp. 445–6.
[50] 'Oral Statement of Georges Vedel' (24 July 1975), *Western Sahara*, ICJ Pleadings, vol. V, p. 151 at pp. 172–4.
[51] 'Oral Statement of Jean Salmon' (28 July 1975), pp. 264–9.

of *terra nullius* was to settle disputes among the European powers over territory and not to negate as such the sovereignty or international legal personality of the inhabitants.[52] According to Mauritania, the international legal doctrine and practice during the relevant period were best summed up as recognizing the international legal personality of local tribes and therefore excluding their territories from the ambit of *terra nullius*.[53]

On the facts of the case, Morocco's position was that Western Sahara was not *terra nullius* at the time of colonization because Morocco had sovereignty over the territory. Since Morocco was a recognized state at the time, its sovereignty over the territory would equally have been recognized.[54] Mauritania took the position that Western Sahara was not *terra nullius* because it was inhabited by tribes having a political organization and political authority, as evidenced by the fact that Spain entered into agreements with them.[55]

Whereas Bedjaoui's approach to the interpretation of *terra nullius* was to entomb it as the subject of colonial ideology and Bayona-Ba-Meya's to make it the subject of a new African counter-ideology, Jean Salmon, on behalf of Mauritania, presented *terra nullius* as the subject of a liberal ideology that could be turned to the advantage of the colonized. Salmon contended that at the relevant time, *terra nullius* embodied a contradiction between the territorial appetite of the European states and the humanist philosophy and liberal ideas of the European ruling classes. If the content of *terra nullius* fed and justified the appetite for empire, its humanist protection required the consent of the local population through their recognized leaders and under conditions that did not render that consent meaningless.[56] While acknowledging that these requirements were sometimes no more than formalities masking a brutal reality, Salmon argued that to take Bedjaoui's approach and reduce *terra nullius* to a cynical fiction did a disservice to peoples by dismissing these legal safeguards which, however slim, were a people's only defence. Similarly, Bayona-Ba-Meya's approach ignored the fact that these safeguards were already part of international law. The best approach to

---

[52] 'Oral Statement of Jean Salmon' (10 July 1975), *Western Sahara*, ICJ Pleadings, vol. IV, p. 425 at pp. 427–8.
[53] *Ibid.*, p. 425.
[54] See generally 'Written Statement of Morocco', *Western Sahara*, ICJ Pleadings, vol. III, p. 125 at pp. 125–204.
[55] 'Written Statement of Mauritania', *Western Sahara*, ICJ Pleadings, vol. III, p. 3 at pp. 28–57; 'Oral Statement of Jean Salmon' (10 July 1975), pp. 425–9.
[56] 'Oral Statement of Jean Salmon' (28 July 1975), p. 264.

the interpretation of *terra nullius* was instead to actualize this humanist impulse: 'Si chaque notion juridique a sa part importante de fonction idéologique, cette arme peut se retourner contre celui qui l'a forgée et la fiction devenue réalité se transforme en un instrument de lutte pour les peuples qui en ont été les victimes.' ('If an important part of every legal notion is its ideological function, this weapon can be turned against its maker, and the fiction made reality transforms itself into an instrument of struggle for the people who have been its victims.)'[57]

In accord with Mauritania, the International Court of Justice concluded that international law did not regard territories inhabited by tribes or peoples having a social or political organization as *terrae nullius*.[58] As a result, Western Sahara was not *terra nullius* because the evidence showed that the territory was 'inhabited by peoples which, if nomadic, were socially and politically organized in tribes and under chiefs competent to represent them'.[59] Since this conclusion afforded a complete answer to the first question, the court did not deal with the proposition that Western Sahara was not *terra nullius* because it belonged to Morocco or Mauritania.[60]

The court's answer to the first question thus established that late nineteenth-century international law regarded local tribes, in particular those of the Western Sahara, as the occupants of their territory such that their territory was not a *terra nullius* which could be acquired through occupation. It remained an open question, however, whether the same international law also regarded them as sovereign. Some commentators argue that given the court's findings that Western Sahara was not *terra nullius* (in answer to the first question) and that Morocco and Mauritania did not have sovereignty over the territory (in answer to the second question), it follows logically that the tribes of Western Sahara must themselves have been sovereign. But the court left the possibility that there was simply no sovereign in the classical legal sense.[61] Its references to 'independent tribes'[62] may be read as a historical description rather than the legal recognition of sovereignty. Nor can the sovereignty of local rulers be derived from the court's treatment of the legal status of their agreements with European states. While the court held that such

---

[57] (Translation mine) *Ibid.*, p. 266.   [58] *Western Sahara*, p. 39.   [59] *Ibid.*
[60] *Ibid.*, p. 40.
[61] See Crawford, *The Creation of States*, p. 179 ('it is one thing to deny an entity statehood on grounds such as lack of independence or coherent organization, and another to determine that the territory on which the entity is established is *terra nullius*').
[62] *Western Sahara*, pp. 48, 63, 67 (*per curiam*), 75 (Declaration of Judge Gros), 124 (Separate Opinion of Judge Dillard), 171 (Separate Opinion of Judge de Castro).

agreements were derivative roots of title, as opposed to original titles obtained by occupation of a *terra nullius*, its qualification 'whether or not considered as an actual "cession" of the territory'[63] prevented the blanket conclusion that local rulers had sovereignty to cede. The court also explicitly refrained from judging the legal character or the legality of the titles which led to Spain becoming the administering power of the Western Sahara.[64] Later on in the advisory opinion, the court was similarly circumspect about the configuration of Mauritanian sovereignty. Having found that the tribes, confederations and emirates of the Bilad Shinguitti, precursor to the modern state of Mauritania, did not constitute an international legal entity with some form of sovereignty, the court did not proceed to determine where, if anywhere, sovereignty over Mauritanian territory lay.

In a separate opinion, Judge Ammoun reached the same conclusion as the court on *terra nullius*, but used a different approach to interpretation.[65] Although the court presented its definition of *terra nullius* as historically accurate, some scholars have characterized it as revisionist.[66] And, indeed, Mauritania urged the court to make nineteenth-century international law truer to its liberal ideology than it may historically have been. In contrast, Judge Ammoun sought an interpretation of *terra nullius* that represented not a truer version of liberalism, but a sort of overlapping consensus.[67] As opposed to pushing a 'universal' approach to become more universal and therefore more legitimate, Judge Ammoun may be seen as building a universal approach from the commonalities of different cultures, those traditionally excluded from international law and those traditionally included.

Judge Ammoun accepted Bedjaoui's periodization of *terra nullius*, whereby *terra nullius* was used successively by ancient Rome, Christian nations and European states to deny the existence of the Other and to legitimate the acquisition of the Other's territory.[68] He also accepted Bedjaoui and Bayona-Ba-Meya's criticism that this conception of *terra nullius* was not universally valid. Nevertheless, Judge Ammoun's interpretation of *terra nullius* did not simply adopt Bayona-Ba-Meya's argument

[63] Ibid., p. 39.   [64] Ibid., pp. 39–40.
[65] *Western Sahara*, pp. 85–7 (Separate Opinion of Judge Ammoun). For other readings of Judge Ammoun, see Berman, 'Sovereignty in Abeyance', pp. 96–103 (*Namibia* and *Western Sahara*); L. V. Prott, *The Latent Power of Culture and the International Judge* (Abingdon, Oxon.: Professional Books, 1979), pp. 166–7 (*Namibia*).
[66] See e.g. Chemillier-Gendreau, 'La Question du Sahara Occidental', p. 277.
[67] Compare J. Rawls, 'The Domain of the Political and Overlapping Consensus' (1989) 64 *New York University Law Review* 233.
[68] *Western Sahara*, p. 86 (Separate Opinion of Judge Ammoun).

that *terra nullius* must take its meaning for Africa from Africa. Instead, it seemed to reflect the idea that *terra nullius* must be interpreted in a way that would resonate not only with Africa, but also with Europe. In this vein, Judge Ammoun began by remarking on the similarity of Bayona-Ba-Meya's presentation of the link between human being and nature in African thought to the Greek philosophy of Zeno of Sidon or Citium and his Stoic school. According to Judge Ammoun, Bayona-Ba-Meya's views were also reminiscent of African Bantu spirituality, which Judge Ammoun quoted Father Placide Tempels's *Philosophie bantoue* as analogizing to Catholicism.[69] By presenting Bayona-Ba-Meya's account of the African spiritual tie to the land, Greek Stoicism, African Bantu beliefs and Catholicism as fundamentally similar, Judge Ammoun predisposed us to believe that a notion of *terra nullius* common to them might be found. The definition he then proposed was that of Emmerich de Vattel, who restricted the notion of *terra nullius* to land empty of inhabitants. Traceable earlier to Francisco de Vitoria, this definition belonged to the Western international legal tradition. Being as narrow as, if not narrower than, Bayona-Ba-Meya's idea of *terra nullius*,[70] it should also, Judge Ammoun seemed to reason, be acceptable to Africa. As such, the interpretation of *terra nullius* in the advisory opinion represented 'a considerable step' along the common path marked out by Vitoria, Vattel, Bedjaoui and Bayona-Ba-Meya.[71]

It is striking that in *Mabo*, where the High Court of Australia broke with precedent to hold that Australia had not been *terra nullius* at the time of white settlement, two of the judges quoted from Judge Ammoun's separate opinion in *Western Sahara*, as well as from the *per curiam* opinion.[72] Still more striking is that the passage that each of them quoted from Judge Ammoun was the passage describing Bayona-Ba-Meya's view of *terra nullius* and the agreement of his view with Vattel's. In a society with a colonial history like Australia, as in international society, the value of Judge Ammoun's reasoning, over and above that of the court as a whole, would seem to be that it demonstrated the overlap in the perspectives of colonized and colonizer.

By defining *terra nullius* narrowly, the International Court of Justice in *Western Sahara* affirmed that to some degree, classical international law recognized the subjecthood of the nomadic peoples of Western Sahara and of non-European peoples generally.[73] The court thus made the tribes

---

[69] *Ibid*., pp. 85–6.   [70] *Ibid*., p. 86.   [71] *Ibid*., p. 87.
[72] *Mabo*, pp. 33–4, 40–1 (Brennan J.), 181–2 (Toohey J.).
[73] In James Crawford's view, 'the Court has been consistent in upholding the legal

themselves central to its story of identity in the precolonial Sahara. Had the court chosen instead to answer the question of *terra nullius* by way of the question of legal ties – finding that Western Sahara was not *terra nullius* because Morocco, Mauritania or both had legal ties to the territory – then the original status of the territory's inhabitants in classical international law might have remained uncertain and they in the half-light of international law past. Alternatively, had the court adopted Bedjaoui's broad definition of *terra nullius* in the last century, the local population would have been entirely effaced. Moreover, while this effacement would be remediable by the right of self-determination of peoples in *Western Sahara*, this would not always be the case. In *Mabo*, for instance, had the High Court of Australia upheld the view that Australia was *terra nullius*, the land rights of Australian aboriginal peoples would have remained unrecognized at common law and the right of self-determination would have been too controversial to provide an alternative legal basis for recognition.

In addition to the recognition of identity reflected in the International Court of Justice's treatment of *terra nullius*, Judge Ammoun's treatment may represent an expansion of participation in the process of giving historical meaning to international law. While it is possible to characterize his discussion of Greek Stoicism, Bayona-Ba-Meya's account of the African spiritual tie to the land, African Bantu beliefs and Catholicism simply as extra support for one historical insider's definition of *terra nullius* (Vattel's) over another (Fiore's), it is equally possible to see in it the application of a different doctrine of sources: less precise, but more communal.[74]

Sovereignty and legality

L'Etat marocain se rapproche de l'Etat européen du XIXe siècle, non pas parce qu'il est un Etat-nation, mais parce qu'il est un Etat national. De fait la structure gouvernementale est autochtone, c'est-à-dire, née de la terre marocaine, l'infrastructure est populaire et nationale. La solidarité certes est religieuse,

---

personality or, where relevant, the statehood of entities outside Europe in the eighteenth and nineteenth centuries, and thus indirectly the idea of the universality of international law'. Crawford, 'The General Assembly', p. 597, n. 52. In addition to *Western Sahara*, he cites as examples *United States Nationals in Morocco*, ICJ Reports 1952, p. 176 at pp. 185, 188; *Rights of Passage Case (Second Phase)*, ICJ Reports 1962, p. 6 at p. 38.

[74] Compare P. Glenn, 'Persuasive Authority' (1987) 32 *McGill Law Journal* 261 at 297. Compare also C. G. Weeramantry, 'Symposium. International Law and the Developing World: A Millennial Analysis. Keynote Address' (2000) 41 *Harvard International Law Journal* 277 at 281.

elle est aussi politique car le Maroc vit, depuis le XVᵉ siècle, sous la menace permanente de l'intervention étrangère.

Mais l'Etat marocain s'éloigne de l'Etat européen car il est musulman. Dès lors il sera construit sur deux principes, le principe égalitaire à la base, les tribus restant toujours administrées par leur autorités naturelles et leur chef, qui reçoit l'investiture du Sultan. Le caïd est donc à la fois le défenseur des intérêts locaux et le représentant du pouvoir central, mais à côté de ce principe égalitaire de base, il convient de faire figurer le principe hiérarchique qui place, au-dessus de l'organisation tribale, le chef spirituel et temporel avec son administration, son makhzen.

[The Moroccan state comes close to the European state of the nineteenth century not because it is a nation-state, but because it is a national state. Owing to the fact that the governmental structure is indigenous, that is to say, born of the Moroccan soil, the infrastructure is popular and national. The solidarity is certainly religious, but it is also political, for Morocco lived since the fifteenth century under permanent threat of foreign intervention.

But the Moroccan state distances itself from the European state because it is Muslim. From that moment, it will be constructed on two principles, the egalitarian principle at the base, the tribes always remaining administered by their natural authorities and their chief, who receives the investiture of the Sultan. The caid is thus at the same time the defender of local interests and the representative of the central power, but beside this egalitarian basic principle must figure the hierarchical principle that places, above the tribal organization, the spiritual and temporal chief with his administration, his Makhzen.]

Mr Isoart, representing Morocco in *Western Sahara*[75]

Le seule sujet de droit digne de considération est l'Etat, les autres formes d'organisation sociale étant méprisées, qualifiées de barbares ou de sauvages, voire complètement ignorées. Parmi ces collectivités préétatiques ou paraétatiques, les groupements nomades ont connu le sort le plus défavorable – et cela n'a rien d'étonnant. En effet, on peut dire sans exagérer que l'Etat est

---

[75] (Translation mine) 'Oral statement of Mr. Isoart' (2 July 1975), p. 262. As applied to the Western Sahara, many aspects of this description were contested by Spain. For example, Morocco pointed to evidence that the Sultan of Morocco appointed caids for the Western Sahara, whereas Spain maintained not only that these appointments did not relate to the Western Sahara, but that they were conferred on sheikhs already elected by their own tribes and were merely honorary titles bestowed on existing and effectively independent local rulers. *Western Sahara*, p. 45. According to Judge Ammoun, the appointment as caid of an individual having local influence or family or tribal connections did not mean that the title tended to be an honorary one. He observed that 'it is a practice current in quite a number of countries, in the absence of a centralized authority, to choose persons to govern who have the qualifications which enable them to make their authority felt and carry out their tasks'. *Ibid.*, p. 93 (Separate Opinion of Judge Ammoun).

l'ennemi héréditaire des nomades. Si le nomade vit à l'intérieur de ses frontières, il est considéré par l'Etat comme un élément de trouble; il échappe à son contrôle administratif, à sa justice, à ses collecteurs d'impôts... Si, au contraire, le nomade vit en dehors de son territoire... il représente souvent pour l'Etat un danger d'incursion ou de razzia... l'idéologie classique, longtemps dominante, a engendré des représentations déformées du nomadisme et a tendu à nier ce phénomène en tant que réalité juridique.

[[In international law,] the only legal subject worthy of consideration is the State, other forms of social organization being scorned, qualified as barbarous or savage, or even completely ignored. Among these pre-State or para-State collectivities, nomadic groups have known the most unfavourable fate – and this is not surprising. In effect, one can say without exaggeration that the State is the hereditary enemy of nomads. If the nomad lives inside its frontiers, the State considers him an element of trouble; he escapes its administrative control, its justice, its tax collectors... if on the contrary the nomad lives outside of its territory... he often represents for the State a danger of incursion or raid... the classical ideology, long dominant, has generated distorted representations of nomadism and has tended to deny this phenomenon as a legal reality.]

Jean Salmon, representing Mauritania in *Western Sahara*[76]

Since the International Court of Justice found that Western Sahara was not *terra nullius* at the time of colonization by Spain, it proceeded to the second question asked by the General Assembly: the existence and nature of the legal ties between the territory of Western Sahara and the Kingdom of Morocco and the Mauritanian entity respectively. In the case of the Kingdom of Morocco, which was a state at the time, the court needed only to give meaning to the concept of legal ties. In the case of the Mauritanian entity, which all parties agreed was not then a state, the court had first to define the notion of legal entity.[77]

---

[76] (Translation mine) 'Oral Statement of Jean Salmon' (10 July 1975), pp. 432–3.

[77] This chapter does not deal with the contest over the existence and significance of historical facts in *Western Sahara*: for example, did Sultan Hassan I visit the southern area of the Souss in 1882 and 1886, and if so, was the visit to maintain and strengthen his authority in the southern part of his realm? *Western Sahara*, pp. 45–6.

Such historical determinations raise problems of objectivity related to those encountered in the legal determinations treated here. European maps, the descriptions of European scholars, explorers and travellers, and the interpretation of treaties with European powers all raise problems of knowledge and perspective. In a comment on the *Dubai/Sharjah* boundary arbitration, discussed in the next section of this chapter, D. W. Bowett contrasts the tribunal's stated preference for written documents over witnesses' statements with the 'the traditions of the Arab world [which] do not lean toward documentary records, but rely heavily on oral testimony'. D. W. Bowett, 'The Dubai/Sharjah Boundary Arbitration of 1981' (1994) 65

Unlike *terra nullius*, legal ties was not a term of art in international law. In interpreting legal ties as those that might affect the General Assembly's decolonization policy in the Western Sahara, the court could rely on the object and purpose of the General Assembly resolution to request the advisory opinion. But international law gave the court little guidance on what that range of legal ties might include and what significance to give to the various ties that it found in the precolonial Sahara.

The court construed legal ties broadly as more than just ties of territorial sovereignty. To confine its consideration to sovereignty, it reasoned, would have been 'to ignore the special characteristics of the Saharan region and peoples' and also to disregard the possible relevance of other legal ties for the decolonization process.[78] Moreover, by rejecting the view that legal ties should be limited to those 'established directly with the territory and without reference to the people who may be found in it',[79] the court blurred the line between 'self' and 'territory' arguments that it had drawn by equating the right of self-determination with the free

---

British Yearbook of International Law 103 at 111, n. 21, referring to *Dubai/Sharjah*, 590.

An instructive comparison is provided by Canadian case-law, which has developed different principles of interpretation for agreements between colonial officials and aboriginal peoples. For a brief overview, see P. Macklem, 'The Impact of Treaty 9 on Natural Resource Development in Northern Ontario' in M. Asch (ed.), *Aboriginal and Treaty Rights in Canada: Essays on Law, Equality, and Respect for Difference* (Vancouver: University of British Columbia Press, 1997), pp. 97–134 at pp. 98–100. In addition, the Supreme Court of Canada in *Delgamuukw v. British Columbia*, [1997] 3 SCR 1010, 37 ILM 261 expressed a different attitude toward oral testimony by aboriginal witnesses in cases concerning the existence of aboriginal land rights. See also Australian Law Reform Commission, *The Recognition of Aboriginal Customary Laws* (Report No. 31) (2 vols, Canberra: Australian Government Publishing Service, 1986), vol. I, pp. 401–507 (Problems of Evidence and Procedure).

In the context of indigenous peoples, Chapter 5 discusses some of the issues raised by inter-cultural participation in the international legal process.

[78] *Western Sahara*, p. 64. The final paragraph of the advisory opinion nevertheless implies that only ties of sovereignty would have affected self-determination. The paragraph reads in part:

the Court's conclusion is that the materials and information presented to it do not establish any tie of territorial sovereignty between the territory of Western Sahara and the Kingdom of Morocco or the Mauritanian entity. Thus the Court has not found legal ties of such a nature as might affect the application of resolution 1514 (XV) in the decolonization of Western Sahara and, in particular, of the principle of self-determination through the free and genuine expression of the will of the people of the Territory.

(Emphasis mine) *Ibid.*, p. 68. See Crawford, *The Creation of States*, pp. 382–3, nos. 6, 7(a).
[79] *Western Sahara*, p. 41.

will of the colonial population, and legal ties with precolonial claims to territory. Hence, the concept of legal ties became a way to recognize relationships other than sovereignty in international law and to tell a more complex legal story about identity in *Western Sahara*.

The court thus had to determine not only whether a tie was sovereign, the strongest underwriting of its power by international law, but also whether a tie was legal, the indicium of its existence in international law. In late nineteenth-century international law, these fundamental concepts – sovereignty and legality – were based on the European state. The rules on acquisition of sovereignty over territory similarly assumed that the subject was a European state and the object of acquisition a non-European territory.

Although Western Sahara was colonized by Spain in 1884, it was Morocco's and Mauritania's prior sovereignty over the territory, not the sovereignty acquired by Spain, which had to be determined in the case. The court was therefore not dealing with the European colonial paradigm that informed the rules on the acquisition of sovereignty over territory. Morocco and Mauritania were non-European subjects and exercised non-European forms of authority over territory. Any ties they had to Western Sahara were inscribed in a common culture, but a culture outside the mind's eye and the conscience of *fin-de-siècle* international law. What relevance did this culture have for the court's interpretation of sovereignty and legality within international law? To use Judge Dillard's example of the quandary, how should international law treat a tie between the Sultan of Morocco and the marabout Ma ul-'Aineen or between the Emir of the Adrar and the chiefs of nomadic tribes?[80]

Spain argued against any cultural particularization of international law, warning that to depart from the idea of a unique international law would be to lose a common legal language without which states would be unable to reach true agreement.[81] In contrast, Algeria proposed the application of nineteenth-century Islamic public law, thereby underlining that classical international law was the unique international law only among Europeans.[82]

---

[80] *Ibid.*, p. 125 (Separate Opinion of Judge Dillard).
[81] E.g. 'Oral Statement of Fernando Arias-Salgado' (18 July 1975), *Western Sahara*, ICJ Pleadings, vol. V, p. 51 at p. 58.
[82] 'Oral Statement of Mohammed Bedjaoui' (15 July 1975), *Western Sahara*, ICJ Pleadings, vol. IV, p. 467 at p. 489. Bedjaoui later clarified that this was not the keystone of his argument. 'Oral Statement of Mohammed Bedjaoui' (29 July 1975), *Western Sahara*, ICJ Pleadings, vol. V, p. 302 at p. 304.

While the court applied international law, and not Islamic public law, to the question of legal ties, it also began by explicitly situating its analysis in the context of Western Sahara and the social and political organization of its population.[83] The advisory opinion depicted Western Sahara as an arid and sparsely populated part of the vast Sahara desert that stretches across North Africa. At the time of colonization by Spain, its population consisted mostly of nomadic tribes, who pastured their animals or grew crops wherever the conditions were favourable. These tribes crossed the deserts along fairly regular routes determined by the seasons or the available water-holes. Particularly significant for the case was that the pattern of low rainfall and the scarcity of the resources forced the nomadic tribes to cover very wide areas of the desert. All of the routes crossed from the Western Sahara into some neighbouring area, whether southern Morocco, present-day Mauritania, Algeria or beyond. The right of pasture was generally held in common by these tribes, while areas that could be cultivated were governed to a greater extent by separate rights. Although perennial water-holes could be used by all tribes, they were in principle considered the property of the tribe that had made them functional. Many tribes were thought to have recognized burial grounds, to which they and their allies rallied. All the nomadic tribes were of the Islamic faith and the territory that they travelled lay wholly within Dar al-Islam. Within a tribe, authority was generally vested in a sheikh, subject to an assembly of the tribe's leading members, and the law applied was a combination of Koranic law and the tribe's own customary law. Tribes sometimes had ties of dependence or alliance with other tribes. These ties were not territorial so much as inter-tribal.[84]

The court thus pointed to profound differences between a European state, which concentrated power territorially, and the society of Western

---

For an Islamic perspective on self-determination and secession, see S. H. Hashmi, 'Self-Determination and Secession in Islamic Thought' in M. Sellers (ed.), *The New World Order: Sovereignty, Human Rights, and the Self-Determination of Peoples* (Oxford: Berg, 1996), pp. 117–51. On other areas of international law, see M. Bedjaoui, 'The Gulf War of 1980-1988 and the Islamic Conception of International Law' in I. F. Dekker and H. H. G. Post (eds.), *The Gulf War of 1980–1988: The Iran–Iraq War in International Legal Perspective* (Dordrecht: Martinus Nijhoff, 1992), pp. 277–99; A. E. Mayer, 'War and Peace in the Islamic Tradition and International Law' in J. Kelsay and J. T. Johnson (eds.), *Just War and Jihad: Historical and Theoretical Perspectives on War and Peace in Western and Islamic Traditions* (New York: Greenwood Press, 1991), pp. 195–226; D. A. Westbrook, 'Islamic International Law and Public International Law: Separate Expressions of World Order' (1993) 33 *Virginia Journal of International Law* 819.

[83] *Western Sahara*, p. 42.   [84] *Ibid.*, pp. 41–2.

Sahara. Territorially, the population was nomadic, followed routes that took them beyond the Western Sahara, and acknowledged few exclusive rights or priorities over territory. Power respected both tribal and religious lines. The tribes were relatively autonomous with their own tribal law, there were certain inter-tribal laws, tribes might have various relationships with other tribes and yet they were all part of an even wider Islamic community and obeyed its law.

This contextualization by the court, however, did not necessarily signal a departure from traditional international law. Although the notion of sovereignty in international law abstracted from the European state and European forms of authority over territory, local culture was relevant in so far as it factored into the practicability of European control over the territory. In Max Huber's musty paternalism from the *Island of Palmas* case: 'the manifestations of sovereignty over a small and distant island, inhabited only by natives, cannot be expected to be frequent'.[85] There was a sliding scale of control that, in effect, assimilated the people and their culture to the climate, geography and other physical features of the territory.

Whether the court in *Western Sahara* intended more than this traditional contextualization of the object of sovereignty becomes clearer from its treatment of the subject of sovereignty. For in *Western Sahara*, subject, no less than object, differed from the European state. Any exercise of sovereignty by Morocco inevitably reflected the non-European character of the Sherifan state. To the extent that Morocco was unable or unwilling to conform its claim to Western Sahara to the European pattern of the rules on acquisition of sovereignty, it had to persuade the court to interpret those rules in a way that contextualized both subject and object.[86]

Along 'universal' lines, Morocco claimed Western Sahara based on Morocco's immemorial possession of the territory; in particular, its public display of sovereignty, uninterrupted and uncontested, for centuries.[87] In so far as Morocco relied on displays of authority that the court judged to be of a 'far-flung, spasmodic and often transitory character',[88] Morocco cited the sliding scale of control used by the Permanent Court of International Justice in the *Legal Status of Eastern Greenland*

---

[85] *Island of Palmas Case* (Netherlands, USA), (1928), 2 Reports of International Arbitral Awards 829 at 867.
[86] The claim of Mauritania, which had the additional difficulty of not having been a state in 1884, is treated below at pp. 144–50.
[87] *Western Sahara*, p. 42.   [88] *Ibid.*

case.[89] In *Eastern Greenland*, the court recognized that, particularly in the case of claims to sovereignty over uninhabited or sparsely populated areas, 'very little in the way of the actual exercise of sovereign rights' might suffice in the absence of superior claims.[90] Denmark, the colonial power in western Greenland, successfully claimed sovereignty over eastern Greenland based upon a continued display of authority, despite being unable to show more than notional authority over the eastern part of the island. Morocco argued that given the desert character of Western Sahara, its geographical contiguity to Morocco and Morocco's having been for a long time the only independent state in northwest Africa, the historical evidence sufficed to establish Morocco's title to Western Sahara on the same principles as in *Eastern Greenland*.[91]

It should be emphasized that Morocco's 'universal' line of argument was universal only from the cultural perspective of international law. By relying on the *Eastern Greenland* case, Morocco implicitly adopted the Permanent Court of International Justice's utter disregard for the possibility that the native inhabitants of Greenland might have had sovereignty or that, at the very least, their presence might have precluded the classification of the island as *terra nullius*.[92] The court's treatment of the disappearance in the fifteenth century of the Nordic settlements in Greenland was particularly revealing.[93] Even though attacks by the native Greenlanders were thought to have destroyed the settlements, the court gave no consideration to whether this show of force might have demonstrated native sovereignty or occupation of the island.[94] On the court's reasoning, either the end of these settlements

---

[89] *Legal Status of Eastern Greenland (Denmark v. Norway)* (1933), PCIJ Ser. A/B, No. 53.

[90] *Ibid.*, p. 46.

[91] *Western Sahara*, p. 42. The court distinguished *Eastern Greenland* on the facts. It found that while both Eastern Greenland and Western Sahara were thinly populated, the Western Saharan population differed in that it covered the area more actively and aggressively. In addition, the geographic contiguity of Western Sahara with Morocco was debatable, whereas it was uncontroversial in *Eastern Greenland*. Nor would the assumption of contiguity help Morocco's case, the court reasoned, since it would raise the expectation of evidence of displays of authority by Morocco. *Ibid.*, p. 43.

[92] Denmark's claim to sovereignty over eastern Greenland depended on Greenland's having been *terra nullius* and Norway's argument was explicitly that eastern Greenland was *terra nullius* as late as 1931 such that Norway could acquire sovereignty by occupation. *Eastern Greenland*, p. 44.

[93] *Ibid.*, pp. 46–7. See also S. J. Anaya, *Indigenous Peoples in International Law* (New York: Oxford University Press, 1996), p. 23.

[94] *Eastern Greenland*, p. 47. See also *ibid.*, pp. 83 (Dissenting Opinion of Judge Anzilotti), 97 (Dissenting Opinion of Judge *ad hoc* Vogt).

had returned Greenland to the status of *terra nullius* or Denmark had later consolidated its sovereignty through further displays of state authority. The picture of the original inhabitants that emerges from the documentary evidence is one of vulnerability to the predatoriness of European traders and the spread of disease brought by the white races.[95] And that vulnerability offered a pretext for Danish sovereignty.

While Morocco relied on the universal rules for the acquisition of sovereignty, it also sought to persuade the International Court of Justice that the interpretation of the rules should be particularized so as to take account of the special structure of the Sherifan state.[96]

In line with its interpretation of *terra nullius*, the International Court of Justice's interpretation of sovereignty in *Western Sahara* made full use of international law's liberal inspiration. Consistent with the idea of sovereignty as the state's sphere of autonomy, analogous to the individual's sphere of autonomy in liberalism, the court reasoned that international law did not dictate the structure of a state. States were free to choose the form that their sovereign authority would take. The fact alone that a state was not organized along European lines did not mean that it did not have sovereignty over the territory in question.

Moreover, understanding how a state elected to exercise its sovereignty might be useful in assessing whether it had established sovereignty over a particular territory. The structure of a state might, in the court's words, 'be a relevant element in appreciating the reality or otherwise of a display of State activity adduced as evidence of that sovereignty'.[97] An awareness of culture could help in the appreciation of the evidence.

Whereas the court thus recognized that states might exercise sovereignty differently (the bounded cultural diversity permitted by liberalism) and that an appreciation of those differences was important (cultural diversity as fact-enhancement), it did not modify the requirement that a state must exercise sovereignty effectively: 'the special character of the Moroccan State and special forms in which its exercise of sovereignty may, in consequence, have expressed itself, do not dispense the Court from appreciating whether at the relevant time Moroccan sovereignty was effectively exercised or displayed in Western Sahara'.[98] However

---

[95] *Ibid.*,
   pp. 29, 37, 48, 53, 79, 108, 114, 121.
[96] *Western Sahara*, p. 43. Compare Flory, 'L'Avis', 272 (Morocco using, on the one hand, the specificity of its state organization to explain what was not recognizable in a common law and relying, on the other hand, on the consequences of its being the only sovereign state in the region in the nineteenth century).
[97] *Western Sahara*, p. 44.   [98] *Ibid.*

sovereignty was expressed in a particular culture, it had to amount to effective control over territory in order to qualify as sovereignty in international law.[99]

The court found, on the facts, that the Moroccan state circa 1884 consisted of the Bled Makhzen, areas actually subject to the Sultan of Morocco, and the Bled Siba, areas where the tribes were de facto not submissive to the Sultan.[100] Western Sahara fell within the Bled Siba.[101] According to Morocco, the Bled Makhzen and the Bled Siba simply expressed two different relationships between the Moroccan local authorities and the central power, the Bled Siba being more decentralized than the Bled Makhzen. Because the Sultan's spiritual authority was always accepted throughout, this difference did not affect the unity of Morocco.[102]

The court accepted that the Sherifan state was based on 'the common religious bond of Islam existing among the peoples and on the allegiance of various tribes to the Sultan, through their caids or sheikhs', as opposed to on the notion of territory.[103] According to the court, allegiance was more likely than common religious bonds to signify sovereignty. To amount to sovereignty, however, that allegiance had to be manifested in the effective display of authority. In the territory of Western Sahara, Morocco could establish allegiance, but not control, and its claim to sovereignty over the territory therefore failed.

In their separate opinions, Judge Forster, Judge *ad hoc* Boni and Judge Ammoun disagreed with the court's conclusion that there were no ties of territorial sovereignty between the territory of Western Sahara and the Kingdom of Morocco. All three maintained that the court had not given enough importance to the geographical, social and temporal context of the problem.[104] It is somewhat unclear from their opinions what required further contextualization: the evidence going to sovereignty or the test for sovereignty. Was it that the evidence, if put in proper context, actually met the test of effective control? Or was it that because the effective control test abstracted from the European context, it was the wrong test? Central to either form of contextualization, however, is a sort of cultural functionalism or understanding that relationships can only be evaluated and compared in terms of the function they perform in a particular culture.

---

[99] Compare Flory, 'L'Avis', 270 (describing the court's approach as innovative for its acceptance that account must be taken of the specific structure of the Sherifan state, but as not following through on this innovative approach).
[100] *Western Sahara*, p. 44.   [101] *Ibid.*, p. 45.   [102] Ibid., p. 44.   [103] *Ibid.*
[104] See *ibid.*, p. 103 (Separate Opinion of Judge Forster).

According to Judge Forster, the court's perspective on the notions of 'state' and 'sovereignty' should have been the reality of the Sahara, and the specific structure and traditional system of the Moroccan state. Appreciated in terms of their function in that time and place, the ties of allegiance found by the court indicated 'the existence of State power and exercise of political administration analogous to a tie of sovereignty'.[105] Judge *ad hoc* Boni wrote similarly:

> As regards Morocco, insufficient emphasis has been placed on the religious ties linking the Sultan and certain tribes of the Sakiet El Hamra. For these tribes, the Sultan was Commander of the Faithful, that is to say, the Steward of God on earth for all matters, whether religious or not. He was thus regarded not only as religious leader but as director of their temporal affairs. The legal ties between them were thus not only religious – which no one denies – but also political, and had the character of territorial sovereignty.[106]

Like Judge Forster and Judge *ad hoc* Boni, Judge Ammoun grounded his conclusion that Morocco had ties of territorial sovereignty to Western Sahara on cultural functionalism. His opinion began and ended with the argument that in the Sahara of the late nineteenth century, allegiance to the Sultan was equivalent to allegiance to the state because the Sultan personified the state and exercised all of its powers. At 'the end of the nineteenth century, the Sultan combined in his person the legislative and executive powers, to which was added the spiritual power. He exercised those powers by means of dahirs, which were issued – a significant fact – under his sole signature.'[107] However, Judge Ammoun also rested his conclusion on universal international law. The bulk of his discussion of legal ties was devoted to detailing Morocco's activity in Western Sahara in order to demonstrate that even under the rules of 'universal' international law, Morocco had established that it manifested sovereignty over Western Sahara.[108] In this connection, Judge Ammoun did not insist on the local significance of the religious tie between the Sahrawi and Moroccans, but described it as a neglected element of the legal tie which found expression in their common recourse to holy war over the holy places of Christendom or Islam[109] and later, in the same spirit, in their common resistance to the Christian colonial powers.[110] By taking a

---

[105] *Ibid.* [106] *Ibid.*, p. 173 (Separate Opinion of Judge *ad hoc* Boni).
[107] *Ibid.*, pp. 83, 102 (Separate Opinion of Judge Ammoun).
[108] *Ibid.*, pp. 87–92 ('Recognition by the International Community of the Legal Ties Between Morocco and Western Sahara'), pp. 92–9 ('Internal Manifestations of Moroccan Authority Over Western Sahara').
[109] *Ibid.*, p. 98. [110] *Ibid.*, pp. 97–8, 101.

traditional as well as a functional approach to sovereignty, Judge Ammoun courted a greater diversity of viewpoints than Judge Forster and Judge *ad hoc* Boni. And it is in this presentation of an overlapping consensus that his treatment of the legal ties between the Kingdom of Morocco and the territory of Western Sahara resembles his treatment of *terra nullius*.[111]

While the court concluded that Morocco and Mauritania had neither ties of territorial sovereignty nor any other legal ties that might influence the exercise of self-determination by the Western Saharan population, it found that each had some legal ties to Western Sahara. The Sultan of Morocco had ties of allegiance to some of the tribes living in the territory of Western Sahara, while the Mauritanian entity had ties to other tribes in the territory in the form of rights, including some rights relating to land. The court was vague as to why these ties qualified as legal. By reading the court's finding in light of the discussion of legality and legal ties by individual judges, however, we can understand it as part of the court's efforts throughout the judgment to grapple with the partiality of international law.

The problem of partiality is well illustrated by Judge Gros's position that ties of allegiance and shared rights did not amount to legal ties. In his declaration, Judge Gros dismissed them as merely ethnic, religious or cultural.[112] Because allegiance took its legal meaning from European feudalism, he reasoned, it could not be used to describe the less formal and less hierarchical relationships found between the Sultan of Morocco and some of the tribes in Western Sahara.[113] The court's conclusion that legal ties of allegiance existed between Morocco and Western Sahara was therefore inaccurate. We might read Judge Gros here as ignoring, whether intentionally or unintentionally, any concerns about applying a European standard of legality to relationships between non-European communities. Yet, the Africa of former times should not be arbitrarily required to produce carbon copies of European institutions, as Judge Forster put it.[114]

There is, however, another possible reading of Judge Gros; namely, that it was precisely this artificiality that concerned him. 'If the desert is a separate world,' he wrote, 'it is an autonomous world in the conception

---

[111] See above at pp. 127–8.
[112] *Western Sahara*, p. 75 (Declaration of Judge Gros). See similarly *ibid.*, pp. 114–15 (Separate Opinion of Judge Petrén).
[113] Compare *Dubai/Sharjah*, 637, 639 (using the historical European concept of vassalage to analyse the situation of a nomadic desert tribe inhabiting an area disputed between the emirates of Dubai and Sharjah).
[114] *Western Sahara*, p. 103 (Separate Opinion of Judge Forster).

of its relationships with those who have a different way of life.'[115] This may be an analytical nicety; it may instead or also be a point about authenticity. Because Judge Gros concluded that allegiance in the legal sense of the word was unknown among the Saharan communities of the period, such a finding would not only be inaccurate, but inauthentic. Not only did their relationships fall short of the standard for legality, but the standard was not theirs.

Moreover, Judge Gros's charge that the advisory opinion had idealized the Sahara desert and the nomadic way of life in 1884 demonstrates the fundamental challenge to any interpretation of legality aimed at remedying this inauthenticity: the unknowability of the Other. Whether the court romanticized the Other (as it may have done) or barbarized the Other (as Judge Gros may have done),[116] it could only project its own vision onto the Other.[117]

Read as such, Judge Gros's objections to the court's finding of legal ties are not the result of indifference to culture, but exactly the opposite. This position, however, prompts several criticisms. We might begin by questioning, as Mohamed Shahabudeen and others have done, the readiness of Western international lawyers to find that developing countries were strangers to the idea of international law. In this, sensitivity to Eurocentrism coincides troublingly with the earlier attitude of European superiority. 'From the fact that the received jurisprudence was developed in one part of the world, it did not follow that the basic institutions, to which the jurisprudence related, were unknown to political collectivities in other parts of the world, or that rules regulating relations among such collectivities had somehow altogether failed to germinate before the coming of Grotius.'[118]

Second, to hold that 'our' relationships were legal and 'theirs' were non-legal meant that theirs were not cognizable and therefore not protected by international law. Paradoxically, the very respect for culture that would justify a finding of no legal ties – the reluctance to

---

[115] *Western Sahara*, p. 76 (Declaration of Judge Gros).
[116] Compare C. Tennant, 'Indigenous Peoples, International Institutions, and the International Legal Literature From 1945–1993' (1994) 16 *Human Rights Quarterly* 1 at 6–24 (on the representation of indigenous peoples in international law as the ignoble and the noble primitive successively).
[117] In contrast, Judge Petrén saw the court's limitations as a result of the fact that the court's only information was that submitted by interested states and it did not have the assistance of assessors expert in Islamic law or Northern African history. *Western Sahara*, pp. 112–14 (Separate Opinion of Judge Petrén). See also *ibid.*, pp. 141–2 (Separate Opinion of Judge de Castro).
[118] Shahabuddeen, 'Developing Countries and the Idea of International Law', p. 724.

impose an understanding foreign to that culture – results in an absence of respect, legally, for that culture's relationships. It thereby perpetuates the exclusion of the Other and its perspective from international law.

A final criticism is that the determination of which societies are Other and therefore unknowable is not neutral. Judge Gros clearly did not recognize European feudal society as Other, yet, as Claude Lévi-Strauss observed, the basic problem of perspective is the same whether a society is remote from ours in time or remote in space, or even culturally heterogeneous.[119] If Judge Gros accused the court in *Western Sahara* of romanticizing the conception of relationships in Saharan society, the discussion of French feudal society in the *Minquiers and Ecrehos* case[120] suggests that Judge Gros might just as easily be accused of romanticizing the notion of allegiance in European feudalism. In *Minquiers and Ecrehos*, France traced its original title to Minquiers and Ecrehos, two small groups of islets lying between the British Channel Island of Jersey and the coast of France, to the feudal relationship between the King of England and the King of France. France derived its original title from the fact that the Dukes of Normandy were the vassals of the Kings of France. Even after William, Duke of Normandy, became King of England in 1066, he and his successors continued to hold the Duchy of Normandy in the capacity of Duke of Normandy and therefore in fee of the French King. France contended that Minquiers and Ecrehos were held of the French King because the Channel Islands, including Minquiers and Ecrehos, were added to the Duke of Normandy's fief in 933 when William Longsword received the Islands in fee of the King of France, and William and his successors did homage to the French King for the whole of Normandy.[121] In his criticism of the court's finding in *Western Sahara* that legal ties of allegiance existed between the Sultan of Morocco and some of the tribes living in the territory of Western Sahara, Judge Gros wrote:

How can one speak of a legal tie of allegiance, a concept of feudal law in an extremely hierarchical society, in which allegiance was an obligation which was assumed formally and publicly, which was known to all, was relied on by both sides, and was backed by specific procedures and not merely by the force of arms... To give the term allegiance its traditional sense, more would have to

---

[119] C. Lévi-Strauss, *Structural Anthropology*, C. Jacobson and B. G. Schoepf (trans.) (New York: Basic Books, 1963), pp. 16–17.
[120] *Minquiers and Ecrehos (France v. United Kingdom)*, ICJ Reports 1953, p. 47.
[121] *Ibid.*, p. 56.

be said than that it was possible that the Sultan displayed some authority over some unidentified tribes of the desert.[122]

The United Kingdom argued in *Minquiers and Ecrehos*, however, that the homage due to the French King in respect of the fief of Normandy was purely nominal and rendered solely as suited the vassal.[123] Judge Levi Carneiro agreed, summarizing the evidence as showing that in this period, the authority of the Princes, Dukes and Counts in some forty feudal states was increasing, so that the authority of the King of France over the great fiefs was purely nominal. According to one historian, the Duke of Normandy in particular wielded unlimited power: he declared war and made peace, minted money and acted as 'the sole great judge in his Duchy'. In effect, the Duchy of Normandy was practically an independent state and its Duke 'one of the most absolute sovereigns of the Middle Ages'.[124]

Since the International Court of Justice in *Western Sahara* did not explain its finding of legal ties, we do not know whether the court differed from Judge Gros in finding that Morocco's ties to Western Sahara amounted to legal ties of allegiance in his European sense or whether the court conceived of legality differently. Its approach to the interpretation of *terra nullius* and sovereign ties make the former more probable. There the court's approach was basically to maximize the space that international law traditionally allowed for diversity, thus maximizing international law's respect for the autonomy of peoples and states, and to try to appreciate the facts. But the court did not absorb the critique that because the legal concepts at issue were based on Europe and a European world-view, they would systematically favour Europeans. On this critique, it was not enough that the concepts left room for diversity; the concepts themselves had to reflect it.

Judge Dillard's reasons for supporting the court's finding of legal ties are remarkable in that they both accepted this critique and were the most explicit in working through cultural functionalism as a response. Perhaps even more remarkable is the structure of the reasons, which trace the judicial thought process of attempting to identify and overcome the limitations of the judge's own initial understanding in order to construct a sounder judgment. Because he persuaded himself that the

---

[122] *Western Sahara*, p. 76 (Declaration of Judge Gros).
[123] *Minquiers and Ecrehos*, p. 85 (Individual Opinion of Judge Levi Carneiro).
[124] *Ibid.*, p. 86, relying on P. Gaxotte, *Histoire des français*, vol. I, pp. 126, 324–5 and Glasson, *Histoire du droit et des institutions de la France*, vol. IV, pp. 487, 497–8, 504–7, 508. But see *Minquiers and Ecrehos*, p. 75 (Individual Opinion of Judge Basdevant).

concept of legality was dependent on the logic of the prevailing cultural forms and therefore potentially a matter for judicial reconsideration, Judge Dillard did not vote against the existence of legal ties between Western Sahara and Morocco and Mauritania respectively. With reference particularly to Mauritania, he developed two approaches to the concept of legality and legal ties, using the second to expose the cultural specificity of the first.[125] On his first approach, a tie was legal 'if it expresses a *relationship* in which there is a *sense of obligation* of a special kind'.[126] While this sense of obligation need not be inspired by the fear of sanctions, it must be 'pervasively felt as part of the way of life of the people'.[127] It was not sufficient for the inhabitants of the territory to obey the wishes of the Sultan or the Emir out of a feeling of religious affiliation or courtesy; they had to do so out of a sense of deferential obligation. The qualitative difference was between their sense that they had to obey and that they merely ought to obey. Judge Dillard's second approach to the nature of legal ties criticized the first approach as premised on a post-Reformation Western-oriented society and as inappropriate to a society such as existed in the Sahara. In societies influenced by the Reformation, the sense of obligation to the sovereign was 'focused on his secular authority which is not only paramount but permits a dissociation between obligations owed to the State and those owed to religious authority'.[128] This sharp distinction between modes of authority was not characteristic of the society and popular consciousness that prevailed in the Sahara. In a society that understood power as neither secular nor religious, Judge Dillard argued, it would be artificial to reject a tie as legal because it did not reflect a sense of obligation 'owed vertically to the secular power of someone in authority'.[129] Judge Dillard's alternative approach considered legal ties to be those that are experienced as belonging to a larger collectivity:

the *relation* between those in power in the Mauritanian entity on the one hand and the wandering tribes, on the other hand, is of secondary importance. The important thing is that the tribes criss-crossing the Western Sahara felt themselves to be part of a larger whole, while also claiming rights in the territory focused on the intermittent possession of water-holes, burial grounds and grazing pastures.[130]

This approach resembled the approach taken to the interpretation of legal entity by Mauritania. Unlike Morocco, Mauritania was not a state

---

[125] Compare Flory, 'La notion', 75.
[126] (Emphasis in original) *Western Sahara*, p. 125 (Separate Opinion of Judge Dillard).
[127] *Ibid.*   [128] *Ibid.*   [129] *Ibid.*, p. 126.   [130] *Ibid.*

in 1884, when Spain colonized Western Sahara. This meant that while Mauritania might have been able to claim ties of sovereignty to Western Sahara, it could not claim ties of state sovereignty.[131]

Not only were the ties of sovereignty that Mauritania alleged existed between the Mauritanian entity and Western Sahara not ties of state sovereignty, that being impossible, they were not even vertical ties of subject to object akin to ties of state sovereignty. At the time of colonization, the Mauritanian entity was, according to Mauritania, 'a people formed of tribes, confederations and emirates jointly exercising co-sovereignty over the Shinguitti country'.[132] Its relationship to Western Sahara was a horizontal one of inclusion;[133] some of the Western Saharan tribes were part of the ensemble of tribes, confederations and emirates.

For the Mauritanian entity to have had these encompassing legal ties of sovereignty to some of the Western Saharan tribes, it would have had to have been a legal entity with some form of sovereignty. Mauritania's position therefore depended on the meaning of legal entity in the international law of the period. In particular, it revolved around whether the very concept of sovereignty, as opposed to merely the rules for a state to acquire sovereignty over territory, could accommodate cultural difference. Whereas Morocco's legal ties retained the distinction between the non-European subject, Morocco, and the non-European object, Western Sahara, the two merged in the analysis of the Mauritanian entity.

Mauritania built its argument for the international legal subjectivity of the Mauritanian entity on two theses about international law. The first was that international law reflected material reality: if the Mauritanian entity could be shown to have had a real existence which international law misrepresented or excluded due to cultural bias, then international law had to recognize its existence. The second thesis, which also informed Mauritania's interpretation of *terra nullius*,[134] was that there was a humanist tradition in nineteenth-century international law that could be recovered: specifically, nineteenth-century international law included peoples among its subjects and was therefore capable of recognizing a Mauritanian people as sovereign.

Thus, on Mauritania's first thesis, the Mauritanian entity, while not a state, was sociologically 'une réalité, à l'époque, avec des caractéristiques propres, l'indépendance et l'unité de droit, l'application du droit saharien' ('a reality at the time, with its own characteristics, independence and unity of law, the application of Saharan law').[135] Geographically,

[131] *Ibid.*, p. 57.   [132] *Ibid.*, p. 60.   [133] *Ibid.*   [134] See above at pp. 125–6.
[135] (Translation mine) 'Oral Statement of Jean Salmon' (10 July 1975), p. 431.

culturally and socially, it was a coherent community. Although covering a vast region, it was treated as geographically distinct by its inhabitants and by the other Arabo-Islamic communities. Culturally, the Mauritanian entity was distinguished by a common language, way of life and religion. Its social structure was also uniform, built on three 'orders' of tribes: warrior tribes which held political power, marabout tribes which engaged in religious, teaching, cultural, judicial and economic activities, and tribes which were under the protection of a warrior or marabout tribe. In addition, the much freer status of women and the renown of its marabout scholars differentiated the Mauritanian entity socially from the neighbouring Islamic societies.[136]

In terms of political authority, however, the Mauritanian entity was heterogeneous. The constituent tribes, confederations and emirates differed internally in the complexity of their political integration. Moreover, the political organization of the whole was horizontal; there was no common vertical hierarchy. Each tribe and emirate was autonomous and independent. Within its territory, each was sovereign, protecting its own subjects and others who sought protection while in its territory. Between the various tribes and emirates, alliances and wars had the character of relations among equals.[137]

Despite this political diversity, Mauritania maintained, the Mauritanian entity formed a coherent community internally by virtue of its common laws, as well as its geographic, cultural and social distinctness from neighbouring communities. This common Saharan law dealt with the use of water-holes, grazing lands and agricultural lands, the regulation of inter-tribal hostilities and dispute settlement. Externally, the Mauritanian entity had demonstrated its independence in times of threat from outside, exhibiting a common front, for example, against the French.[138]

The Mauritanian entity was not only a sociological reality, it was the functional equivalent of a sovereign state. Prior to the colonial era, the Mauritanian entity succeeded in assuring its coherence and independence without recourse to the form of the state and thus succeeded in achieving the supreme goal of the state without adopting state structures.[139] Having satisfied the purpose of a state, it had to constitute a legal entity in international law. Mauritania argued:

---

[136] *Western Sahara*, pp. 57–8.   [137] *Ibid.*, pp. 58–9.   [138] *Ibid.*, p. 59.
[139] 'Oral Statement of Jean Salmon' (28 July 1975), p. 296.

Qu'un ensemble ait naguère formé ou non un Etat tel que nous l'entendons aujourd'hui, peu importe. L'essentiel réside dans la question de savoir s'il constituait une communauté cohérente, apte à assurer l'indépendance d'un peuple vis-à-vis l'extérieur et à adopter, à l'intérieur de ses limites territoriales, une organisation qui permette à ce peuple d'y vivre selon sa personnalité propre et dans son authenticité.

[It matters little whether or not an entity has formerly formed a state as we understand the concept today. The essential question is whether it constitutes a coherent community capable of ensuring the independence of a people vis-à-vis the exterior and of adopting within its territorial limits an organization that permits this people to live there in accordance with its own personality and in its authenticity.][140]

To the extent that international law had not given international legal personality to nomadic societies such as those of the Sahara, Mauritania attributed it to international law's enduring Eurocentrism, which had created a distorted image of nomadic societies and tended to deny them legal reality. How, Mauritania asked rhetorically, could international law consider as a legal reality a group represented as anarchic and ephemeral, the negation of the ideal of the strongly structured and centralized state?[141] But sociologically, all nomadic peoples 'ont conscience d'appartenir à un groupe humain bien identifié, tous ont développé au plus haut point la notion de territoire, tous ont élaboré des institutions et un système juridique parfois fort complexe' ('are conscious of belonging to a well-identified human group, all have developed the notion of territory to its highest point, and all have elaborated institutions and legal systems that are often extremely complex').[142] Seen in context, the social development and political effectiveness exhibited by nomadic peoples were functionally and morally equivalent to a strongly structured state with a settled population.

If classical international law pathologically misrepresented or excluded the reality of nomadic life, its categories of subject could nevertheless accommodate that reality. Mauritania's historical thesis was that a category of people or nation existed in nineteenth-century international law and was appropriate to the Mauritanian entity and nomadic peoples more generally. According to Mauritania, the notion of a people or nation flourished in late nineteenth-century international

[140] (Translation mine) *Ibid.*, p. 297.
[141] 'Oral Statement of Jean Salmon' (10 July 1975), p. 433.
[142] (Translation mine) *Ibid.*

law, but was displaced around 1900 by a state centrism that lasted until the right of self-determination of peoples achieved prominence around 1960.[143] As examples of the idea of a people-nation in nineteenth-century international law, Mauritania cited the emergence of an independent Greece and Bulgaria in 1830, a Western consciousness that Christian subjects of the Sublime Porte had a right to self-determination, a unified Italy and Germany, recognition for an independent Romania, Serbia and Montenegro at the 1878 Congress of Berlin and a number of plebiscites of the same period.[144]

Spain characterized Mauritania's approach to the interpretation of legal entity as incorporating an element of legal particularism by inviting the court to distance itself from the general international law rules and categories in order to retain particular legal facts.[145] In response, Mauritania referred to the coexistence of general public international law in the nineteenth century with various particular legal orders – Latin American international law, relations among members of the British Commonwealth, the law of Dar al-Islam – and in the twentieth century with various regional legal systems such as that among European states and formerly among socialist states.[146] But the coexistence of general with regional international law would not appear to have been the gist of Mauritania's approach to the interpretation of legal entity.[147] Mauritania's interpretive approach seemed not so much that general law yielded to the particular law in certain cases, as that general law had to be made truly general. Where a 'general' international legal concept had been developed by abstracting from what was, in fact,

---

[143] *Ibid.*, pp. 427, 436.   [144] 'Oral Statement of Jean Salmon' (28 July 1975), p. 297.

[145] 'Oral Statement of Mr. Martínez Caro' (22 July 1975), *Western Sahara*, ICJ Pleadings, vol. V, p. 141 at p. 145. It should be noted that Spain's argument against the recognition of the Mauritanian entity as a legal entity is both ultra-universalist and ultra-particular. On a universalist understanding of legal entity, Spain argues that the Mauritanian entity is so loose as to have no legal existence. On a particularist understanding, it merges into the larger Islamic world. *Western Sahara*, p. 61.

[146] 'Oral Statement of Jean Salmon' (28 July 1975), p. 298.

[147] For this type of approach to the interpretation of legal entity, see Flory, 'L'Avis', pp. 273–4. Maurice Flory argues from an appreciation of Dar al-Islam as a heterogeneously organized geographical space. According to Flory, from the moment that one leaves the Western legal universe for the legal universe of Dar al-Islam, the Bilad Shinguitti must be accepted as a legal entity. The fact that the court recognized Morocco simultaneously as a sovereign state and a part of Dar al-Islam should not have prevented it from recognizing the existence of entities that were not included in the Moroccan state but were nevertheless part of Dar al-Islam and that maintained cultural, religious and economic links with a neighbouring entity, among them the Moroccan state.

the particularity of European experience, its generality had to be tested against the particularity of other cultural experiences. It had to be abstracted across particularities so that it was general in some broader sense. The concept of legal entity should therefore be interpreted functionally: the question was not whether an entity looked like a state, but whether it performed the essential functions of a state in the relevant culture.

Spain rejected both Mauritania's interpretive thesis that sociological fact had an impact on legal interpretation and its historical thesis that peoples were represented in nineteenth-century international legal thought. Whereas Mauritania quoted the sentence from the *Reparation for Injuries Suffered in the Service of the United Nations* case[148] 'the subjects of law in any legal system are not necessarily identical in their nature or in the extent of their rights',[149] Spain reminded the court of the end of that sentence: 'and their nature depends upon the needs of the community'. That is, Mauritania relied on the *Reparation* case for its recognition of the potential diversity of international legal subjects and argued that the sociological fact of diversity was relevant to the interpretation of international legal subjecthood. Spain pointed instead to the *Reparation* case's derivation of international legal personality from the necessities of the international legal community in a given historical period and stressed the limits of interpretation.[150] Spain also criticized Mauritania's historical account of a nineteenth-century international law configured on peoples as inaccurate and inconsistent with the fact that states were and continued to be the basis for the rules of international law.[151]

In determining whether the Mauritanian entity was a legal entity capable of including the Western Saharan tribes, the court explicitly gave 'full weight' to the observation in the *Reparation* case that 'the subjects of law in any legal system are not necessarily identical in their nature or in the extent of their rights, and their nature depends upon the needs of the community', and to the 'special characteristics of the Saharan region and peoples'. Adopting the test used to decide the status of the United Nations in the *Reparation* case, it quoted the essential test for a legal entity as whether the group in question was in 'such a

---

[148] *Reparation for Injuries Suffered in the Service of the United Nations*, Advisory Opinion, ICJ Reports 1949, p. 174 at p. 178.
[149] 'Oral Statement of Jean Salmon' (10 July 1975), p. 427.
[150] 'Oral Statement of José M. Lacleta' (30 July 1975), *Western Sahara*, ICJ Pleadings, vol. V, p. 324 at pp. 354–5.
[151] *Ibid.*, pp. 352–3.

position that it possesses, in regard to its Members, rights which it is entitled to ask them to respect'.¹⁵² On this test, the court found that given the independence of the emirates and tribes from one another and the absence of even the most minimal common institutions, the Bilad Shinguitti was not, in another phrase from the *Reparation* case, 'an entity capable of availing itself of obligations incumbent upon its Members' and therefore not an entity enjoying some form of sovereignty in Western Sahara.¹⁵³

Western Sahara considered: The Dubai/Sharjah boundary arbitration

The discussion of *Western Sahara* thus far has dwelt on the differences between the treatment of cultural diversity by the court as a whole and its treatment by various individual judges. I next use the consideration of *Western Sahara* in the 1981 *Dubai/Sharjah* boundary arbitration to bring out an important similarity between these treatments.

In *Dubai/Sharjah*, the arbitral tribunal cited *Western Sahara* as support for its general statement that to apply the rules of international law relating to boundary disputes, which are essentially the rules concerning sovereignty over territory, 'to peoples which have had, until very recently, a totally different conception of sovereignty would be highly artificial'.¹⁵⁴ The tribunal concluded that the international law to be applied had to be adapted to the special conditions of the region.¹⁵⁵ When it came to the specific analysis of legal ties in *Dubai/Sharjah*, however, the tribunal distinguished *Western Sahara* as too Eurocentric to be relevant to its determination of the internal boundary, the segment that ran through the desert territory of the nomadic Bani Qitab tribe. 'In the present case,' wrote the tribunal, 'it is not a question of applying a Western notion of sovereignty, which was unknown in the area.'¹⁵⁶

Derrick Bowett has described the tribunal's reasoning as 'orthodox and fully consistent with established law', but criticized its distinguishing of *Western Sahara* as 'somewhat lacking in conviction'.¹⁵⁷ Bowett's criticism follows, since the tribunal's rejection of the concept of sovereignty applied in *Western Sahara* undermines his characterization of the award as 'fully consistent with established law'. I will attempt to show, however, that Bowett's is not the only possible reading of the *Dubai/Sharjah* boundary award. In particular, it may be that the tribunal's distinguishing of

¹⁵² *Western Sahara*, p. 63, quoting from *Reparation*, p. 178.
¹⁵³ *Ibid.*   ¹⁵⁴ *Dubai/Sharjah*, 587.   ¹⁵⁵ *Ibid.*, 590.   ¹⁵⁶ *Ibid.*, 641.
¹⁵⁷ Bowett, 'Boundary Arbitration', 133. See also *ibid.*, 123–4.

Western Sahara is not a minor flaw in an otherwise orthodox treatment of sovereignty, but a sign that the tribunal intended to break with established law by giving greater importance to cultural diversity in the interpretation of sovereignty.

Until the mid-twentieth century, the region disputed between the emirates of Dubai and Sharjah was largely desert and sparsely populated. Apart from a fringe of settlements along the coast, its population was nomadic or semi-nomadic. The local world of these peoples was the routes that they travelled. Until the 1930s, the territorially bounded state was alien to the political notion of the rulers and tribes of this area. Instead, the political order was built on the allegiance owed by tribes to a ruler. While these ties of allegiance were the way that a ruler established sovereignty over an area populated by nomadic tribes, the strength of the ties, and hence the ruler's control, varied from tribe to tribe.[158] In a passage quoted by the tribunal, Mohammed Morsy Abdullah wrote of the emirates at that time:

> Political boundaries were dependent on tribal loyalties to particular shaikhs and consequently were subject to frequent change. Therefore, the frontier between the Trucial States and Sultanate of Muscat and the inter-state boundaries changed frequently during the nineteenth and twentieth centuries as it was based on the *dirah* of the tribes. *Dirah* in Arabia at this time was a flexibly defined area, changing in size according to the strength of the tribe which wandered within it. In addition, a tribe's loyalty was determined by its own interests and could, and at this time often did, alter.[159]

In this light, the tribunal identified allegiance and control as the two determinants of the legal situation. It recognized, moreover, that the weight and importance to be given to each had to vary with the period and the region under consideration.[160] With the economic and political development of the emirates, allegiance decreased in importance. Boundaries became easier to identify as the nomadic lifestyle became gradually less prevalent. The corollary was an increase in the significance of control, which had played a variable, even nominal, role in the earlier period. The criteria of allegiance and control also applied differently to the different segments of the disputed boundary. In the interior, which remained a desert region with a nomadic population, the criterion of control gained very little in importance. Control was of

---

[158] *Dubai/Sharjah*, 587–8.
[159] M. Morsy Abdullah, *The United Arab Emirates: A Modern History* (London: Barnes & Noble, 1978), p. 291, quoted in *ibid.*, 588.
[160] *Dubai/Sharjah*, 589.

much greater significance in the coastal area because its population was more settled and closely linked to two nearby towns. As their population grew and economy developed, the towns also exerted greater control.[161]

The parties' arguments regarding the internal boundary[162] presented the arbitral tribunal with a choice between allegiance and control. Sharjah claimed the area because the Bani Qitab, the nomadic tribes to whom the territory belonged, owed allegiance to Sharjah and were subject to Sharjah's control. Dubai argued that Sharjah's control over the Bani Qitab existed only in theory and even the tribe's allegiance was intermittent. While Dubai asserted that the Bani Qitab had on several occasions allied themselves with Dubai,[163] the basis of Dubai's claim was that it exercised effective control over the area.[164]

The tribunal found on the facts that the only possible basis for Sharjah's sovereignty over the interior was the bond of allegiance.[165] Always a powerful tribe, the Bani Qitab tended, at the end of the nineteenth century and the beginning of the twentieth century, to act as an independent tribe and changed alliances several times. In 1927, they participated in a plot against the ruler of Sharjah.[166] Indeed, Sharjah itself acknowledged that its influence over the Bani Qitab varied considerably over time.[167] Nevertheless, given the evidence as a whole, the tribunal concluded that this bond of allegiance was 'generally formally maintained even if it was not always close'.[168] In the longer narrative of allegiance, the Bani Qitab's brief alliances with other rulers and opposition to the rule of Sharjah were only short episodes.

Relying on *Western Sahara*, Dubai argued that allegiance alone was not enough to substantiate Sharjah's claim to sovereignty. In particular, Dubai relied on a passage from *Western Sahara*: 'Political ties of allegiance to a ruler... to afford indications of the ruler's sovereignty, must clearly be real and manifested in acts evidencing acceptance of his political authority. Otherwise, there will be no genuine display or exercise of State authority'.[169]

The tribunal disagreed with Dubai, distinguishing *Western Sahara* on the inapplicability of its Western notion of sovereignty, as well as on the facts.[170] It awarded the internal boundary to Sharjah, thereby recognizing that allegiance might be a sufficient basis for sovereignty.

---

[161] Ibid.   [162] Treated in *ibid.*, 635–52.
[163] A change of alliance is not taken to signify a change of allegiance. See *ibid.*, 637, 644.
[164] *Ibid.*, 636.   [165] *Ibid.*, 637–8.   [166] *Ibid.*, 637.   [167] *Ibid.*, 636.   [168] *Ibid.*, 643.
[169] *Western Sahara*, p. 44, quoted in *ibid.*, 640.   [170] *Dubai/Sharjah*, 641.

On Bowett's reading, the award was nevertheless consistent with the notion of sovereignty in *Western Sahara*. In determining which emirate had sovereignty over the interior, the tribunal was, in fact, using the ordinary measuring-stick of control.[171] The distinction it made between allegiance and control was really a distinction between 'different kinds of evidence of control'.[172] In basing its award of sovereignty to Sharjah on allegiance, it was therefore basing it on a lesser kind of evidence of control, but evidence of control nonetheless. In addition, Dubai did not claim allegiance and could not substantiate its claim of control, so Sharjah had the better evidence of control.

Finally, Bowett saw the *Dubai/Sharjah* award as consistent with the results in previous cases of competing claims to sovereignty over uninhabited or sparsely inhabited areas,[173] in which international law has been satisfied with much less evidence of control. Bowett thus added the *Dubai/Sharjah* boundary arbitration to a string of cases that conditioned the requirement of control on the European colonial paradigm, accepting less evidence of control over territory that, to the nineteenth-century European mind, was unimportant, inaccessible, or otherwise impractical to bring under strong control. To this way of thinking, the culture of the territory's inhabitants was simply one relevant factor, along with a harsh climate, forbidding geography and other physical features of the territory, in the determination of what display of sovereignty could reasonably be expected.

---

[171] Bowett, 'Boundary Arbitration', 110–11. It should be noted that Bowett regards the conduct of the parties, more specifically Dubai's lack of protest and Sharjah's quick action to exclude persons from Dubai, as decisive. *Ibid.*, 125. For a cultural critique of the international legal interpretation of protests in a somewhat different context, see *Temple of Preah Vihear (Cambodia v. Thailand)*, Merits, ICJ Reports 1962, p. 6 at pp. 128–9 (Dissenting Opinion of Sir Percy Spender), 90–1 (Dissenting Opinion of Judge Wellington Koo); Prott, *The Latent Power of Culture*, pp. 158–61.

[172] Bowett, 'Boundary Arbitration', 111.

[173] *Ibid.* Bowett footnotes the *Eastern Greenland* case in this regard. To the extent that he regards *Dubai/Sharjah* as factually similar to *Western Sahara* and his footnote suggests that *Dubai/Sharjah* is also factually similar to *Eastern Greenland*, it is interesting to note that the International Court of Justice in *Western Sahara* rejected the argument that *Western Sahara* is on all fours with *Eastern Greenland*. 'Western Sahara, if somewhat sparsely populated, was a territory across which socially and politically organized tribes were in constant movement and where armed incidents between these tribes were frequent'. *Western Sahara*, p. 43. The explanation for why *Dubai/Sharjah* might bear a greater similarity to *Eastern Greenland* than *Western Sahara* does is presumably that *Dubai/Sharjah* and *Eastern Greenland* were both construed as a choice between the sovereignty of two states, whereas *Western Sahara* was not.

Since Dubai could prove neither allegiance nor control, Bowett might well be correct that the internal boundary awarded in Sharjah's favour stood for the proposition that some evidence of control, in the form of allegiance, was superior to none.[174] But it is also possible to read the award for, as Jean Salmon put it on behalf of Mauritania in *Western Sahara*, the lesson of modesty that the ethnographer can teach the lawyer, the lesson that the only legal systems of worth are those to which individuals adhere.[175] On this reading, the tribunal's upholding of the bond of allegiance might represent an approach to interpretation similar to Zaire's position in *Western Sahara* that *terra nullius* had to take its meaning for Africa from Africa and directly responsive to Judge Gros's point that international law's European-derived view of legality was completely separate from Saharan society's own view. On such an approach, it becomes important whether the international legal concept of sovereignty is interpreted such that it is plausible within the culture of the sovereign subject and object. This idea would explain the tribunal's concern that to apply international law's rules on the acquisition of sovereignty 'to peoples which have had, until very recently, a totally different conception of sovereignty would be highly artificial', and its observation that a Western concept of sovereignty was unknown in the interior. On Bowett's reading, it would presumably be immaterial whether the requirement of control was natural or familiar, so long as it was capable of application.

The tribunal's reliance on the British view of the legal situation in the interior during the period of the British protectorate over the emirates and on the British method for ascertaining the legal situation also supports a reading of the *Dubai/Sharjah* boundary arbitration that gives greater importance to cultural authenticity. The tribunal stressed that the British authorities always recognized the territory of the Bani Qitab as part of Sharjah and that 'it would be unfair to the sense of the realities which the British authorities habitually showed' to think that the British authorities would not sooner or later have recognized the Bani Qitab as totally independent of Sharjah had this been so.[176]

---

[174] Nor did the coastal zone of Al Mamzer present a choice between allegiance and control. In the mid-nineteenth century, Sharjah had title on the basis of allegiance, but from the turn of the century onward Sharjah could not rely on allegiance because the population of the area was mixed and occasional, and could not rely on control since it had lost effective control to Dubai. *Dubai/Sharjah*, 595–635, especially 610.
[175] 'Oral Statement of Jean Salmon' (10 July 1975), p. 436.   [176] *Dubai/Sharjah*, 641.

By giving credence to the British 'sense of the realities', the tribunal indirectly adopted the British approach to interpreting reality in legal terms. As well, the tribunal came closer to a direct endorsement of the British approach by presenting it as a response to the question 'How may one ascertain to whom these territories belong?'[177] and by drawing the criteria of allegiance and control from a longer list of criteria compiled by the British officials who had earlier investigated the boundary.[178] In determining to whom a given territory belonged, the British authorities took account of 'the special characteristics of the region and of the fact that Western criteria for the establishment of frontiers could not be applied in this period'.[179] Instead of requiring direct control by the ruler over the territory, they required allegiance to the ruler by the tribe that effectively controlled the territory.

The tribunal's characterization of the British approach as recognizing the inapplicability of Western rules concerning sovereignty over territory and its virtual adoption of this approach suggest a greater responsiveness to cultural diversity than Bowett grants. At the same time, it may mean that the tribunal's award was motivated less by concern for validity within the culture of the region and more by regard for a contemporaneous European perspective. It is noteworthy that despite the Bani Qitab's control of the interior, the tribunal ruled out the possibility that the Bani Qitab might have had sovereignty over the disputed territory because the British authorities never recognized the Bani Qitab as an emirate.[180] Even if, given the relationship between Britain and the emirates, a new emirate could not come into existence without formal British recognition, this should not have meant that the Bani Qitab were entirely without international legal personality. In *Western Sahara*, the International Court of Justice held that a territory inhabited by tribes or peoples having a social or political organization was not *terra nullius*. Yet the tribunal raised the possibility that if not part of Dubai or Sharjah, the territory of the Bani Qitab was *terra nullius*. 'If these lands did not belong to Sharjah and the Bani Qitab, as has been shown, did not constitute an Emirate,' it asked, 'must then the territory be considered *terra nullius*?'[181]

Moreover, the tribunal defended the British assessment of the legal situation in the interior against Dubai's argument that it reflected British interests. Dubai maintained that British dealings with the ruler of Sharjah regarding the negotiation of the oil concession in the territory

[177] *Ibid.*, 642.   [178] *Ibid.*, 588–9.   [179] *Ibid.*, 642–3.   [180] *Ibid.*, 642.   [181] *Ibid.*

of the Bani Qitab were not evidence of Sharjah's authority over the Bani Qitab, but were attributable to their preference for dealing with the rulers in the region rather than with a series of tribal chiefs.[182] The tribunal reasoned that even if the British authorities' preference was expressed as 'the fewer the Shaikhs that we have to deal with...the better',[183] their information-gathering and sense of fair play would have compelled them to recognize eventually the total independence of the Bani Qitab from Sharjah, had that come about.

Nevertheless, the *Dubai/Sharjah* boundary arbitration can be read as differing from *Western Sahara* in the relevance it gives to culture in interpretation. In *Dubai/Sharjah*, the arbitral tribunal appeared concerned with the authenticity of its interpretation of sovereignty for the communities involved. The concern that the meaning of sovereignty ring true in the time and place in question led the tribunal essentially to take the meaning as it was (or was seen by the British to be) then and there. Indeed, the tribunal seemed unconcerned with whether this established that the interpretation of sovereignty would always be the local understanding and consequently that no general understanding, however minimal, might be possible.

In contrast, even those judges in *Western Sahara* who were most receptive to arguments from cultural diversity appeared to retain some standard that did not vary from one locale to another. Judge Ammoun contextualized the facts, but kept the familiar conception of sovereign ties as effective control (political ties of allegiance to the Sultan *were* ties of sovereignty because the Sultan personified executive, legislative and religious power). While Judge Dillard contextualized the actual conception of legal ties (replacing the idea of a sense of obligation owed vertically to the secular power of someone in authority with the experience of belonging to a larger collectivity), his reasoning suggests that he traced legality to some unarticulated universal function that took different forms in different cultures. Judge Dillard stressed the artificiality of the Western understanding of legality not in terms of its inauthenticity, but in terms of its unworkability. Because the sharp distinction between different modes of authority central to the Western concept of legal ties did not exist in the nineteenth-century Sahara, the concept could not be applied. Any application would bear little relationship to the reality. Judge Dillard therefore sought instead to express abstractly the form that legality took in that culture. What implicitly justifies his

[182] *Ibid.*, 641.   [183] *Ibid.*

interpretation is its ability to capture the sociological reality of the culture. Accordingly, his references to the 'consciousness of the people' and to the 'notion of law then prevalent in time and space' were part of the reality to be analysed. Judge Dillard's sense of the artificiality of applying a Western notion of sovereignty thus differs from the arbitral tribunal's sense of artificiality as unfamiliarity and the latter's implication that to be legitimate the interpretation of sovereignty should be the community's own notion.

Stepping back from the detail of the International Court of Justice's engagement with the different cultural critiques of international law framed by Algeria, Mauritania, Morocco and Zaire, we can see a more general pattern of response in its advisory opinion on *Western Sahara*. The court throughout used a broad concept of legality to domesticate the exotic relationships of the Sahara, bringing them inside international law by recognizing them as legal. Simultaneously, its narrow concept of sovereignty denied these relationships equal status with the European master's by refusing to consider them as sovereign. This double movement of acceptance and rejection, legality and sovereignty, was characteristic of the court's interpretation of legal ties and legal entity, just as it had been of its interpretation of *terra nullius*. The court's treatment of *terra nullius* recognized the legal existence of the tribes that inhabited Western Sahara, but was silent on their sovereignty. Its view of legal ties encompassed the ties of allegiance between some Western Sahara tribes and Morocco, but did not consider them ties of sovereignty. While Mauritania was found to have had legal ties to other Western Sahara tribes in the form of shared rights over land, Mauritania was not found to have been a sovereign entity that included those tribes. Although the court's analysis of legal entity acknowledged a variety of international legal subjects, it did not recognize the Mauritanian entity as such. The double movement of the advisory opinion was accentuated by the separate opinions. On the one hand, the court's model of legality broadened the European model defended by Judge Gros. On the other, the court's essentialist idea of sovereignty represented a rejection of the cultural functionalism variously reflected in the reasons of Judge Forster, Judge *ad hoc* Boni, Judge Ammoun and Judge Dillard.

Implicit in the interplay of sovereignty and legality, it can be argued, is the endeavour to legitimate international law through the more faithful representation and recognition of identity. Through the intermediate concept of legality, the court presented the precolonial identity of the Western Sahara as complex and overlapping, while its sovereignty was left obscure. In so far as Western Sahara was not *terra nullius* because it was inhabited by socially and politically organized tribes, the local tribes had a legal identity in nineteenth-century international law. The recognition as legal of ties between some tribes and Morocco, and other tribes and the Mauritanian entity, added other layers of identity.

Present

For Morocco and Mauritania's claim to corrective justice to prevail over 'the right of the population of the Western Sahara to determine their future political status by their own freely expressed will',[184] it was not enough for Morocco and Mauritania to demonstrate that they had legal ties to Western Sahara. They also had to establish that these ties were of such a nature as to affect the exercise of self-determination and that that effect was to require the return of their territory regardless of the will of the territory's population. (Since legal ties could conceivably modify the exercise of self-determination either procedurally or substantively, it did not follow that because legal ties had some effect, that effect would be to require the return of the territory regardless of the will of its population.)

This normative conflict in *Western Sahara* between consent-based and corrective justice-based interpretations of self-determination, between the determination of a future identity by popular consultation and the restoration of a past identity, might or might not create a temporal conflict as well. To the extent that the normative conflict was within the complex of modern international legal rules on self-determination, the problem of legal interpretation was not intertemporal. The rules on self-determination might be normatively Janus-faced, but both the forward- and the backward-looking rules belonged to modern international law. If, instead, the right of self-determination was seen as central to a new international law reflecting a new world order and the claim of legal ties as remaining from an old international law made by Europe for Europe, then the problem of legal interpretation became a more general intertemporal one. International law has a doctrine of intertemporal law, which applies in cases where the governing legal rules have changed over time so that the original rules and the later rules require different results.[185] In addition to the application of this legal doctrine, the broader-based participation behind modern international law would

[184] *Western Sahara*, p. 36.   [185] See below at note 194 and accompanying text.

be a normative reason for it to take precedence over clubby[186] traditional international law.

Morocco and Mauritania both argued that the conflict between the right of the Western Saharan population to choose their future political status and the restoration of Morocco's and Mauritania's territorial integrity was a conflict within the modern international legal rules on self-determination. To this effect, they cited the Declaration on the Independence of Colonial Peoples, which provided that 'all peoples have the right to self-determination' (paragraph 2), but also that 'any attempt at the partial or total disruption of the national unity and the territorial integrity of a country is incompatible with the purposes and principles of the Charter of the United Nations' (paragraph 6).[187] By interpreting the prohibition on the disruption of territorial integrity as protecting past territorial integrity,[188] Morocco and Mauritania were able to argue that contemporary international law gave the restoration of their precolonial territorial integrity precedence over the right of the Western Saharan population to self-determination.

According to Morocco, what had actually emerged was an international law of decolonization, where decolonization was accomplished by diverse legal principles and techniques. The practice of decolonization resolved into three types of cases, each of which achieved a different balance between the principle of self-determination, understood as the people's right to choose freely, and the principle of territorial integrity.[189] In those cases where an internationally recognized state was dismembered by colonization, as Morocco was by the Spanish colonization of Western Sahara, the principle of territorial integrity outweighed the principle of self-determination such that the precolonial state was made whole again. Mauritania was less categorical, relying instead on a contextual interpretation of self-determination,[190] as

un ensemble de règles complexes qui fait une place importante à l'intégrité territoriale, le poids d'un facteur ou d'un autre dépend de toute une série

---

[186] 'Oral Statement of Mohammed Bedjaoui' (15 July 1975), p. 493 (a European club). See also H. Charlesworth, 'Transforming the United Men's Club' (1994) 4 *Transnational Law and Contemporary Problems* 421 (a men's club).

[187] *Western Sahara*, pp. 29–30 (arguments of Morocco and Mauritania).

[188] On paragraph 6 generally, see Musgrave, *Self-Determination and National Minorities*, pp. 239–55; Sánchez, 'Falkland Islands Dispute', 564–74.

[189] 'Oral Argument of René-Jean Dupuy' (26 June 1975), *Western Sahara*, ICJ Pleadings, vol. IV, p. 140 at pp. 158–77.

[190] 'Oral Argument of Jean Salmon' (4 July 1975), *Western Sahara*, ICJ Pleadings, vol. IV, p. 310 at p. 312.

d'éléments sociologiques, économiques, politiques, juridiques, historiques. Ces facteurs ne sont pas morts. Ils vivent et, comme dans un kaléidoscope, leur mélange peut être bouleversé à chaque instant.

[an ensemble of complex rules that gives an important place to territorial integrity; the weight of one factor or another depends on a whole series of sociological, economic, political, legal and historical elements. These factors are not dead. They live and, as in a kaleidoscope, their mixture can be upset at each moment.][191]

Spain and Algeria maintained that regardless of whether Morocco or Mauritania could establish precolonial legal ties, the population of the Western Sahara was entitled to exercise its right of self-determination through a referendum on independence. While Spain took the position that the General Assembly was already committed to this result,[192] Algeria relied on the doctrine of intertemporal law.[193]

The most frequently quoted account of the doctrine of intertemporal law is that of the arbitrator Max Huber in the *Island of Palmas* case.[194] Huber's exposition of the doctrine of intertemporal law has two branches. The first requires that a legal fact be judged in light of the law in force at the time the fact occurred, as opposed to the law in force at the time the dispute arose or its settlement is contemplated. The second branch provides that the existence or maintenance of a right depends on the conditions set by evolving international law. Applying the doctrine of intertemporal law, Algeria argued that Spain originally acquired good title to Western Sahara by colonization. Because the broad and self-serving interpretation of *terra nullius* by European states excluded non-European peoples from international law, Western Sahara would have been *terra*

---

[191] (Translation mine) *Ibid.*, p. 332.
[192] 'Oral Statement of José M. Lacleta' (17 July 1975), *Western Sahara*, ICJ Pleadings, vol. V, p. 21 at pp. 25-30.
[193] 'Oral Statement of Mohammed Bedjaoui' (15–16 July 1975), pp. 490–6. Algeria further argued that self-determination must take precedence as a *jus cogens* norm. *Ibid.*, p. 493.
[194] In the *Island of Palmas Case*, 845, Huber described this doctrine as follows: 'As regards the question which of different legal systems prevailing at successive periods is to be applied in a particular case (the so-called intertemporal law), a distinction must be made between the creation of rights and the existence of rights. The same principle which subjects the act creative of a right to the law in force at the time the right arises, demands that the existence of the right, in other words its continued manifestation, shall follow the conditions required by the evolution of law.'
  See also *Minquiers and Ecrehos*; *United States Nationals in Morocco*; *Aegean Sea Continental Shelf (Greece v. Turkey)*, ICJ Reports 1978, p. 3.

nullius, and therefore open to acquisition by colonization.[195] Although valid when acquired, Spain's title to Western Sahara was subsequently invalidated by the development of a right of self-determination of peoples in international law. Since Spain had title to Western Sahara and that title had become subject to the population's exercise of self-determination, neither Morocco nor Mauritania could have any title to the territory.

As normative support for the doctrine of intertemporal law in this case, Algeria emphasized the greater legitimacy of modern international law, based on broader and more diverse participation. Counsel for Algeria, Mohammed Bedjaoui, described classical international law as

n'avait par ailleurs d'international que le nom. Elaboré progressivement depuis quatre siècles par et pour l'Europe, applicable seulement aux pays européens à l'exclusion des colonies, protectorats et pays dits non civilisés, c'était un droit de la famille européenne, inspiré par des valeurs européennes, expression d'une époque, d'une hégémonie et d'un complexe d'intérêts économiques et autres.

[international only in name. Elaborated progressively over four centuries by and for Europe, applicable only to European countries to the exclusion of colonies, protectorates and so-called uncivilized countries, it was a law of the European family, inspired by European values, the expression of an era, of a hegemony and of a complex of economic and other interests.][196]

In comparison, the emergence of new states through decolonization had led to what Charles Chaumont would designate as transitional international law[197] or Richard Falk would call an emerging international law of participation.[198] Not only did modern international law therefore have greater legitimacy generally than classical international law, the

---

[195] See above at pp. 121–3.
[196] (Translation mine) 'Oral Statement of Mohammed Bedjaoui' (15 July 1975), pp. 493–4. Among those who took issue with Bedjaoui's characterization of classical international law was Charles Alexandrowicz, who maintained that many of the states that emerged from decolonization 'had a presence in the pre-colonial Family of Nations and must be considered as participants in law-making in the classic period'. C. H. Alexandrowicz, 'Empirical and Doctrinal Positivism in International Law' (1975) 47 *British Yearbook of International Law* 286 at 289. See also C. H. Alexandrowicz, 'The Afro-Asian World and the Law of Nations (Historical Aspects)' (1968-I) 163 Hague Recueil 125; C. H. Alexandrowicz, 'New and Original States: The Issue of Reversion to Sovereignty' (1969) 45 *International Affairs* 465. See generally Grovogui, *Sovereigns, Quasi-Sovereigns, and Africans*, pp. 11–42 on this debate.
[197] 'Oral Statement of Mohammed Bedjaoui' (14 July 1975), *Western Sahara*, ICJ Pleadings, vol. IV, p. 448 at p. 451, citing C. Chaumont, 'Cours général de droit international public' (1970-I) 129 Hague Recueil 333 at 367.
[198] 'Oral Statement of Mohammed Bedjaoui' (15 July 1975), p. 493.

right of self-determination carried even greater legitimacy within modern international law because it entitled peoples, as well as states, to participate.[199]

Morocco argued that the theory of intertemporal law put forward by Algeria was mutilated and lacking the logical equilibrium of Huber's formulation in *Island of Palmas*. It objected that intertemporal law affected not just existing titles, but also the rights that were sacrificed to create them. In the context of *Western Sahara*, intertemporal law operated to invalidate Spain's title to the territory without simultaneously destroying the title lost by Morocco at that time. Second, Morocco objected that intertemporal law could not be reduced to the ultimate date in the chronology and had to do justice to all the legal facts concerning the Western Sahara, from oldest to newest.[200]

Since the International Court of Justice did not find 'legal ties of such a nature as might affect... the principle of self-determination through the free and genuine expression of the will of the peoples of the Territory',[201] it did not need to consider whether and how legal ties of sovereignty or some other stronger nature would have affected the principle of self-determination. Nevertheless, it can be inferred from the structure of the court's *ratio decidendi* that ties of sovereignty, if not also other legal ties, would have had some effect on the decolonization of Western Sahara.[202]

More difficult to decipher are the court's various indications as to exactly what that effect would have been. By detailing the General Assembly's different treatment of Western Sahara and Ifni,[203] the court registered, if not necessarily approved,[204] that in some cases, decolonization would respect the status quo ante. While both Western Sahara and Ifni were non-self-governing territories administered by Spain and claimed by Morocco, the General Assembly resolutions envisaged the decolonization of Western Sahara through a referendum and the decolonization of Ifni by transfer to Morocco.

One possibility is that the court did not consider cases such as Ifni to be cases of self-determination. This simply would not tell us whether there could be cases of self-determination where the interpretation of

---

[199] Compare L. Berat, 'The Evolution of Self-Determination in International Law: South Africa, Namibia, and the Case of Walvis Bay' (1990) 4 *Emory International Law Review* 251 at 278–89.
[200] 'Oral Statement of Georges Vedel' (24 July 1975), *Western Sahara*, ICJ Pleadings, vol. V, p. 151 at pp. 176–7.
[201] *Western Sahara*, p. 68.   [202] See above, note 78 and accompanying text.
[203] *Western Sahara*, pp. 34–5.
[204] See Crawford, *The Creation of States*, p. 383, n. 138 (approval at least by inference).

self-determination as the consent of the territorial population conflicted with its interpretation as the correction of a historical wrong done to the former territorial sovereign. The other possibility is that the court did regard Ifni as a case of self-determination. If so, then its tacit approval of Ifni's retrocession to Morocco indicated that the tension between past and present in the interpretation of self-determination would sometimes be resolved in favour of the past.

In an earlier passage of the advisory opinion, the court indicated that there were cases that looked like self-determination, but actually did not qualify as such and therefore did not require the inhabitants of the territory to be consulted. In the same sentence, it also referred to cases of self-determination where 'special circumstances' dispensed with the usual need to ascertain the will of the people. Left open is whether this exception was made for procedural or substantive reasons: was it because some equivalent procedure had already taken place or because it was subject to some substantive exception?

The validity of the principle of self-determination, defined as the need to pay regard to the freely expressed will of the people, is not affected by the fact that in certain cases the General Assembly has dispensed with the requirement of consulting the inhabitants of a given territory. Those instances were based either on the consideration that a certain population did not constitute a 'people' entitled to self-determination or on the conviction that a consultation was totally unnecessary, in view of special circumstances.[205]

On a proceduralist reading, the instances of self-determination where consultation would be unnecessary would be those where the inhabitants' wishes had already been made known through some other process of consultation, for example, through free and fair elections held in the territory.[206] If this is the meaning of 'special circumstances', then the interpretation of self-determination as 'free and genuine expression of the will of the peoples of the Territory' is intact. Since no referendum or equivalent was held in the case of Ifni, it could therefore only have been that the population of Ifni was not considered a 'people' entitled to self-determination.

On an alternative reading of the passage, consultation might be unnecessary to the exercise of self-determination not because it would be superfluous, but because it would be irrelevant to the disposition of the territory. This meaning of 'special circumstances' would be consistent

---

[205] *Western Sahara*, p. 33.
[206] See *ibid.*, p. 81 (Separate Opinion of Judge Nagendra Singh).

with the interpretation of self-determination as favouring corrective justice between states over the consent of the people in certain cases. On this interpretation of self-determination, the retrocession of Ifni could have represented an exercise of self-determination. This substantivist reading would support the view that the court had watered down the interpretation of self-determination as the free expression of the people's will.

The court's final passage of note also reads as either procedural or substantive:

> The right of self-determination leaves the General Assembly a measure of discretion with respect to the forms and procedures by which that right is to be realized... As to the future action of the General Assembly, various possibilities exist, for instance with regard to consultations between the interested States, and the procedures and guarantees required for ensuring a free and genuine expression of the will of the people.[207]

From a procedural perspective,[208] the import of the passage would be that proof of sovereign ties does not eliminate the need to determine the will of the people, but it might require a vote on the reintegration of the territory (the 'forms' by which the right of self-determination is to be realized)[209] or the negotiation by interested states of safeguards against the coercion or intimidation of the voters (the 'procedures' by which the right of self-determination is to be realized).

From a substantive perspective,[210] it could be argued that the 'form' of self-determination would dictate the 'procedure'. Where the appropriate form of self-determination was found to be the return of the territory, then the appropriate procedure was the negotiation of the transfer of sovereignty. On this scenario, the relevant course of action would be 'consultations between the interested States' regarding the details of the handover instead of the procedures and guarantees for a free and fair referendum.

While the court thus did give some indication of the extent to which legal ties could affect the principle of self-determination, it was silent on whether this was contemplated by the modern international legal framework for self-determination or resulted from the application of intertemporal law.

---

[207] *Ibid.*, pp. 36–7.
[208] E.g. Shaw, *Title to Territory in Africa*, p. 55; Shaw, 'The *Western Sahara* Case', 143–4.
[209] See Morocco's fall-back position quoted in *Western Sahara*, p. 79 (Declaration of Judge Nagendra Singh).
[210] E.g. Crawford, *The Creation of States*, pp. 382–3.

In comparison, the separate opinions were more forthcoming on the resolution of the normative and temporal conflict in the interpretation of self-determination. Toward the substantive end of the spectrum, Judge Nagendra Singh partly adopted Morocco and Mauritania's conception of the interpretive conflict. Like Morocco and Mauritania, Judge Nagendra Singh located the conflict within the modern international legal rules on self-determination; specifically, the relationship in the Declaration on the Independence of Colonial Peoples between the right of self-determination (paragraph 2) and the prohibition on the disruption of territorial integrity (paragraph 6).[211] In Judge Nagendra Singh's view, the Declaration's prohibition on the disruption of territorial integrity required the restoration of a state's territorial integrity upon decolonization where the state historically had sovereignty over the territory to be decolonized.[212] Judge Nagendra Singh otherwise considered the consultation of the people of the territory to be 'an inescapable imperative'.[213] At most, legal ties short of sovereignty might 'point in the direction of the possible options which could be afforded to the population in ascertaining the will of the population';[214] that is, to procedure rather than substance.

Judge Dillard was more emphatically proceduralist in that he explicitly set aside the relationship between paragraph 2 and paragraph 6 of the Declaration on the Independence of Colonial Peoples[215] and developed a proceduralist reading of the court's opinion:

> It hardly seems necessary to make more explicit the cardinal restraint which the legal right of self-determination imposes. That restraint may be captured in a single sentence. It is for the people to determine the destiny of the territory and not the territory the destiny of the people. Viewed in this perspective, it becomes almost self-evident that the existence of ancient 'legal ties' of the kind described in the Opinion, while they may influence some of the projected procedures for decolonization, can have only a tangential effect in the ultimate choices available to the people.[216]

At the other end of the spectrum from Judge Nagendra Singh, Judge de Castro applied the Algerian framework of analysis to the court's resolution of the temporal and normative conflict in the interpretation of

---

[211] *Western Sahara*, pp. 79–80 (Declaration of Judge Nagendra Singh). See also *ibid.*, p. 110 (Separate Opinion of Judge Petrén).
[212] *Ibid.*, pp. 80, 81 (Declaration of Judge Nagendra Singh).
[213] *Ibid.*, p. 81.   [214] *Ibid.*, p. 80.
[215] *Ibid.*, p. 120 (Separate Opinion of Judge Dillard).   [216] *Ibid.*, p. 122.

self-determination. Judge de Castro read the court as stating that 'whatever the existing legal ties with the territory may have been at the time of colonization by Spain, *legally* those ties remain subject to intertemporal law and... as a consequence, they cannot stand in the way of the application of the principle of self-determination'.[217] Similarly, Judge *ad hoc* Boni found that while the ties that existed between Morocco and Western Sahara did have the character of territorial sovereignty, consultation of the inhabitants of Western Sahara was nevertheless obligatory.[218]

In his separate opinion, Judge Ammoun was less sanguine that the process of participation could give expression to the authentic identity of the colonial population. He reasoned that the violence done by colonialism to the identity of the colonized cast doubt on any such expression. By seeking in stages to alter the culture and consciousness of the colonized, colonialism fostered a false solidarity.

> It let the local and regional languages, literature and civilization fall into decay, including the Arab civilization of the Maghreb, upon whose philosophical and scientific sources Europe drew from the Middle Ages up until the beginning of the Renaissance.
>
> In a second stage, the colonizers sought to win over the colonized peoples to their own civilization, in order to bind them more closely to themselves.
> ...
> If this is indeed the explanation for the origin of a certain autonomous way of life on the part of the tribal populations in Western Sahara, one can similarly suppose that the present separatist tendencies... are also the result of a foreign presence.[219]

In light of the court's story of identity in the late nineteenth-century Sahara, what is essential about its treatment of self-determination in the present is not whether the balance it struck in dicta between corrective justice for the former sovereign of the territory and the exercise of free choice by the current territorial population was procedural or substantive, the outcome of a conflict in the modern legal rules or of the application of intertemporal law. The essential is that the fact of a balance

---

[217] *Ibid.*, p. 171 (Separate Opinion of Judge de Castro). For commentators that subscribe to this view, see L. Berat, *Walvis Bay. Decolonization and International Law* (New Haven, Conn.: Yale University Press, 1990), p. 164; Crawford, *The Creation of States*, p. 383, No. 8; H. Gros Espiell, Study on Implementation of United Nations Resolutions Relating to the Right of Peoples under Colonial and Alien Domination to Self-Determination, UN Doc. E/CN.4/Sub. 2/377, pp. 20–1 (1976).

[218] *Western Sahara*, pp. 173–4 (Separate Opinion of Judge *ad hoc* Boni).

[219] *Ibid.*, p. 84 (Separate Opinion of Judge Ammoun). Interestingly, Ammoun does see national liberation struggles as authentic, adding them to the 'special circumstances' that would make consultation unnecessary. *Ibid.*, p. 99.

means that the court did not confine its recognition of the historical identities distorted by colonialism to narration, but created the possibility that they might affect the participatory exercise of the present day.

As a story about participation, the court's use of UN General Assembly resolutions to establish the right of self-determination in international law implicitly subscribed to the legitimacy that came from the vote of all UN member states, new and old alike, on GA resolutions. Not only did GA resolutions instantiate the emerging international law of participation heralded generally by Algeria, but the formal equality of one state-one vote lessened the power imbalance between developed and developing states reflected in international customary and treaty law. As discussed in Chapter 1, decolonization had introduced a debate, primarily between the newly independent states of Africa and Asia and the Western states, over the sources of international law. Developing states tended toward the position that resolutions passed by the General Assembly, where they formed the democratic majority, should be recognized as a new source, whereas Western states resisted this expansion of the established sources.[220] In this light, the court's reliance on the GA resolutions on self-determination lent strength to the position of the developing states.[221]

EC Arbitration Commission Opinion No. 2 on Yugoslavia[222]

If the 1975 advisory opinion of the International Court of Justice in *Western Sahara* is the *locus classicus* on the interpretation of self-determination, the controversial modern classic is the 1992 opinion of an arbitration commission established by the European Communities Conference for Peace in Yugoslavia.[223] The question put to the Arbitration Commission

---

[220] See p. 44 above.
[221] *Western Sahara*, pp. 31–3. See Crawford, 'The General Assembly', p. 591.
[222] The original Arbitration Commission, which issued ten opinions including *Opinion No. 2*, was established by the EC Conference on Yugoslavia. The International Conference on the Former Yugoslavia subsequently changed the Arbitration Commission's composition and terms of reference. This reconstituted Arbitration Commission issued a further series of opinions, of which only *Opinion No. 11* is discussed here. Reference throughout is to the 'EC Arbitration Commission' and the 'Conference on Yugoslavia'.
[223] In addition to the international legal literature on the former Yugoslavia discussed below, see generally M. Bothe and C. Schmidt, 'Sur quelques questions de succession posées par la dissolution de l'URSS et celle de la Yougoslavie' (1992) 96 *Revue générale de droit international public* 811; J. Charpentier, 'Les Déclarations des Douze sur la Reconnaissance des Nouveaux États' (1992) 96 *Revue générale de droit international public*

by the Republic of Serbia in *Opinion No. 2* was whether the Serbian populations in Croatia and Bosnia-Herzegovina had the right to self-determination.[224] Behind this question by Serbia about the Serbian minorities in neighbouring republics was the revival of the idea of self-determination traceable to the eighteenth-century German Romantic thinkers on nationalism: the idea that every ethnic nation should have its own state.[225] While this tradition of self-determination had influenced statecraft in Europe after World War I, it had been muted in post-World War II international law by the equation of self-determination with overseas decolonization.[226] In *Opinion No. 2*, the Arbitration

---

343; J. Crawford, 'The Dissolution of Yugoslavia and the Emergence of its Constituent Republics', Attachment 11 to *State Practice and International Law in Relation to Unilateral Secession* (Expert Report for Canadian federal government, *Reference re Secession of Quebec*, [1998] 2 SCR 217, (1998) 37 ILM 1340); T. M. Franck, *Fairness in International Law and Institutions* (Oxford: Clarendon Press, 1995), pp. 162–8; K. Knop, 'The "Righting" of Recognition: Recognition of States in Eastern Europe and the Soviet Union' in Y. Le Bouthillier, D. M. McRae and D. Pharand (eds.), *Selected Papers in International Law: Contribution of the Canadian Council on International Law* (The Hague: Kluwer, 1999), pp. 261–90; R. Müllerson, *International Law, Rights and Politics: Developments in Eastern Europe and the CIS* (London: Routledge/LSE, 1994), pp. 125–35; Musgrave, *Self-Determination and National Minorities*, pp. 113–24, 141–3, 170–1, 200–7, 229–37; R. Rich, 'Recognition of States: The Collapse of Yugoslavia and the Soviet Union' (1993) 4 *European Journal of International Law* 36; D. Türk, 'Recognition of States: A Comment' (1993) 4 *European Journal of International Law* 66; M. Weller, 'The International Response to the Dissolution of the Socialist Federal Republic of Yugoslavia' (1992) 86 *American Journal of International Law* 569.

On the Arbitration Commission, see M. C. R. Craven, 'The European Community Arbitration Commission on Yugoslavia' (1995) 66 *British Yearbook of International Law* 333; A. Pellet, 'L'Activité de la Commission d'arbitrage de la Conférence européenne pour la paix en Yougoslavie' (1992) 38 *Annuaire français de droit international* 220; A. Pellet, 'L'Activité de la Commission d'arbitrage de la Conférence internationale pour l'ancienne Yougoslavie' (1993) 39 *Annuaire français de droit international* 286; A. Pellet, 'Note sur la Commission d'arbitrage de la Conférence européenne pour la paix en Yougoslavie' (1991) 37 *Annuaire français de droit international* 329 (until August 1993, Alain Pellet acted as expert consultant to the Arbitration Commission); M. Ragazzi, 'Conference on Yugoslavia Arbitration Commission: Opinions on Questions Arising from the Dissolution of Yugoslavia: Introductory Note' (1992) 31 ILM 1488.

[224] See also the Socialist Federal Republic of Yugoslavia's position, reprinted in (1992) 43 (No. 1001) *Review of International Affairs* 21 ('The right of self-determination can only be exercised by a people in the sense of the nation and not in the sense of "demos"').

[225] See Musgrave, *Self-Determination and National Minorities*, pp. 230–1. On this idea of self-determination, see p. 55 above. But see R. Ratković, 'Two Concepts of the National Question in the Serbian Political Doctrine' (1995) 46 (Nos. 1035–6) *Review of International Affairs* 25 (arguing that historically, a democratic concept of the Serbian national question coexisted with the nationalist concept).

[226] Although in *Western Sahara* Morocco and Mauritania based their claim to Western Sahara on historical patterns of identity in the region, they relied primarily on corrective justice.

Commission had to determine what expression, if any, international law gave to ethnic nationalism in the right of self-determination of peoples and how this expression interacted with the dominant paradigm of democracy and independence within the old colonial borders.

The Arbitration Commission held that post-Cold War international law did not underwrite the Romantic ideal of the ethnic nation-state. According to the Arbitration Commission, the right of self-determination of peoples could never justify changes to the frontiers existing at the time of independence. The entitlement of ethnic, religious and linguistic communities, such as the Serbian populations in Croatia and Bosnia-Herzegovina, was limited to minority rights within the state. Potentially farther reaching, however, was the Arbitration Commission's finding that ethnic, religious and linguistic communities had a right to the recognition of their identity under international law. Moreover, the right of self-determination in Article 1 of the International Covenants on Human Rights[227] gave individuals the right to choose their ethnic, religious or linguistic community. In the case of the Serbian population in Croatia and Bosnia-Herzegovina, the Arbitration Commission indicated that the right to choose one's community might include the right to choose one's nationality, where that right could be recognized by agreement between the states concerned.

After introducing the Arbitration Commission's opinion in more detail, this part of the chapter shows how the categories and coherence approaches taken by most scholars of self-determination narrow or prevent the consideration of the opinion's conceptual originality: its refusal to confine the recognition of identity in international law within the territory of the state. Although the right to choose one's nationality was framed as a right of individual choice, the aggregate of these choices by members of the Serbian minorities outside Serbia might well be to give legal existence, through a common nationality, to a Serbian nation overlapping the states of Yugoslavia, Croatia and Bosnia-Herzegovina.

Thus, like the International Court of Justice's advisory opinion in *Western Sahara*, the Arbitration Commission's opinion involved the creative use and interpretation of legal concepts to produce in international law a more complex and, presumably the Arbitration Commission hoped, a truer picture of identity. Like *Western Sahara*, I go on to argue, the opinion should also be read broadly as inclusory in aspiration. In *Opinion*

---

[227] International Covenant on Civil and Political Rights, New York, 16 December 1966, in force 23 March 1976, 999 UNTS 171; International Covenant on Economic, Social and Cultural Rights, New York, 16 December 1966, in force 3 January 1976, 993 UNTS 3.

No. 2, the attempt is to integrate Yugoslavia into modern Europe by restructuring the right of self-determination from the superiority of *demos* over *ethnos* to their transnational or postnational reconciliation in the intellectual vein of the European Union.

The opinion

The Arbitration Commission's opinion on the right of self-determination of the Serbian population in Croatia and Bosnia-Herzegovina began with the familiar position that the right of self-determination cannot involve changes to borders.

> The Commission considers that international law as it currently stands does not spell out all the implications of the right of self-determination.
> However, it is well established that, whatever the circumstances, the right to self-determination must not involve changes to existing frontiers at the time of independence (*uti possidetis juris*) except where the States concerned agree otherwise.

Although this limitation is a leitmotif in the international legal interpretation of self-determination, its import here is unclear. Some read it as balancing the right of self-determination against the principles of territorial integrity and the stability of borders. Others see it as balancing one right of self-determination against another: that of the Serbian minority against that of the population of Croatia or Bosnia-Herzegovina as a whole.[228] These meanings potentially take on different shadings, moreover, depending on whether Croatia and Bosnia-Herzegovina were independent states at the time of the opinion. *Opinion No. 1* had found that the Socialist Federal Republic of Yugoslavia was in the process of

---

[228] For the purposes of this discussion, it is not necessary to engage the more technical debate about whether Yugoslavia is a case of dissolution or secession and what that implies. Compare e.g. J. Crawford, *State Practice and International Law in Relation to Unilateral Secession* (Expert Report for Canadian federal government, *Reference re Secession of Quebec*, [1998] 2 SCR 217, (1998) 37 ILM 1340), reprinted in A. F. Bayefsky (ed.), *Self-Determination in International Law: Quebec and Lessons Learned* (The Hague: Kluwer Law International, 2000), pp. 31–61 at pp. 48–50 and J. Crawford, Response to Expert Reports of the *Amicus Curiae* (*Reference re Secession of Quebec*), reprinted in Bayefsky, *Lessons Learned*, pp. 153–71 at p. 163 (Yugoslavia is a case of dissolution and has no implications for self-determination) with T. M. Franck, 'Opinion Directed at Response of Professors Crawford and Wildhaber' (Additional Expert Report of the *Amicus Curiae*, *Reference re Secession of Quebec*), reprinted in Bayefsky, *Lessons Learned*, pp. 179–83 at p. 181 (dissolution being in practice no more than 'multiple concurrent secessions', the case of Yugoslavia establishes that a group that does not have a right of self-determination is nevertheless not prohibited by international law from seceding and will be recognized as a state if it meets certain standards.).

dissolution,²²⁹ which suggests that no new states had emerged by the time that *Opinion No. 2* was issued. However, *Opinion No. 11* dated Croatia's statehood to before *Opinion No. 2* and Bosnia-Herzegovina's statehood to after.²³⁰

If the Arbitration Commission's reference to *uti possidetis* was shorthand for the principle of territorial integrity, then, on the assumption that Croatia and Bosnia-Herzegovina were states, it simply repeats the legal mantra of decolonization that the right of self-determination cannot disrupt the territorial integrity of a state.²³¹ If Croatia, Bosnia-Herzegovina or both had not yet become states, then *uti possidetis* means something else. As opposed to simply protecting the territorial integrity of a state that already exists, it determines territorially the entity that is eligible to somehow become a state. This quandary over the implications for territory and borders reappears in *Opinion No. 3*, which expanded the Arbitration Commission's reference to *uti possidetis* in *Opinion No. 2*. Similarly ambiguous in its timeframe, *Opinion No. 3* held that the stability of borders was a general principle of international law and, as applied to Yugoslavia, transformed the internal borders between republics under the old Socialist Federal Republic of Yugoslavia into the international boundaries of the new states.²³²

As previously mentioned, the Arbitration Commission's reference to the stability of borders might not stand for the priority international law gives to the existing territorial configuration, but instead for the priority it gives to the self-determination of their populations. If the stability of borders reflects some such idea of self-determination, then what might it be? On the assumption again that Croatia and Bosnia-Herzegovina were already states, it might be no more than the conservative side of the self-determination coin: the right of a state's population to be free from territorial incursions. Istvan Bibó calls this the stabilizing force of self-determination. But for Bibó, the stabilizing force of self-determination could only follow from its destabilizing force: self-determination only protected the territorial integrity of a state where that state had been created by an exercise of self-determination.²³³ Along

---

[229] Conference on Yugoslavia, Arbitration Commission, *Opinion No. 1* (1992) 31 ILM 1494 at 1497.

[230] Conference on Yugoslavia, Arbitration Commission, *Opinion No. 11* (1993) 32 ILM 1587 at 1589.

[231] See Declaration on the Independence of Colonial Peoples.

[232] Conference on Yugoslavia, Arbitration Commission, *Opinion No. 3* (1992) 31 ILM 1499.

[233] I. Bibó, *The Paralysis of International Institutions and the Remedies: A Study of Self-Determination, Concord Among the Major Powers, and Political Arbitration* (New York: John Wiley & Sons, 1976), pp. 17–34.

these lines, it might be that regardless of whether Croatia and Bosnia-Herzegovina had already achieved statehood, the Arbitration Commission saw their borders as becoming legitimate through the de jure or de facto exercise of self-determination.[234]

To the extent that the statehood of Croatia and Bosnia-Herzegovina was regarded as the result of self-determination, the pattern was that of colonial self-determination. As peoples, they were defined by their old federal borders, just as colonial peoples were defined by their old colonial borders. Their recognition as new states was also consonant with the definition of self-determination in *Western Sahara* as 'the need to pay regard to the freely expressed will of the people'.[235] In *Opinions Nos. 4 to 7*,[236] dealing with whether Bosnia-Herzegovina, Croatia, Macedonia and Slovenia respectively had complied with the EC Declaration on Yugoslavia[237] and Guidelines on the Recognition of New States in Eastern Europe and in the Soviet Union,[238] the Arbitration Commission required the demonstration of popular support for independence. In the case of Bosnia-Herzegovina, where the Serbian population had expressed its opposition to an independent Bosnia-Herzegovina through a separate plebiscite, a resolution of an 'Assembly of the Serbian people of Bosnia-Herzegovina' and ultimately a declaration of an independent Serbian Republic of Bosnia-Herzegovina, the Arbitration Commission held that Bosnia-Herzegovina did not qualify for recognition because the will of the people of Bosnia-Herzegovina to constitute a sovereign and independent state could not be held to have been fully established. However, it was prepared to review its assessment of the situation if there were, for example, an internationally supervised referendum on independence in which all citizens voted.[239]

---

[234] See R. Bieber, 'European Community Recognition of Eastern Europe: A New Perspective for International Law?' (1992) 86 *Proceedings of the American Society of International Law* 374 at 377; A. Cassese, 'Self-Determination of Peoples and the Recent Break-up of USSR and Yugoslavia' in R. St J. Macdonald (ed.), *Essays in Honour of Wang Tieya* (Dordrecht: Martinus Nijhoff, 1994), pp. 131–44 at p. 144.
[235] *Western Sahara*, p. 33.
[236] Conference on Yugoslavia, Arbitration Commission, *Opinion No. 4* (1992) 31 ILM 1501; Conference on Yugoslavia, Arbitration Commission, *Opinion No. 5* (1992) 31 ILM 1503; Conference on Yugoslavia, Arbitration Commission, *Opinion No. 6* (1992) 31 ILM 1507; Conference on Yugoslavia, Arbitration Commission, *Opinion No. 7* (1992) 31 ILM 1512.
[237] Declaration on Yugoslavia, Brussels, 16 December 1991, (1992) 31 ILM 1485.
[238] Declaration on the 'Guidelines on the Recognition of New States in Eastern Europe and in the Soviet Union', Brussels, The Hague, 16 December 1991, (1992) 31 ILM 1486.
[239] *Opinion No. 4*, 1503.

As opposed to some notion of the external self-determination of the republics' populations, the Arbitration Commission's insistence on the existing borders might be informed by Croatia and Bosnia-Herzegovina's international obligations to give effect to internal self-determination in the form of democratic government.[240] That is, whatever else the borders represented or represent, they defined a democratic community. All Yugoslav republics seeking recognition as independent states were required by the EC Declaration on Yugoslavia to accept the commitments in the EC Guidelines on the Recognition of New States in Eastern Europe and in the Soviet Union, among them 'respect for the provisions of the Charter of the United Nations and the commitments subscribed to in the Final Act of Helsinki and in the Charter of Paris, especially with regard to the rule of law, democracy and human rights'.

The Arbitration Commission's opinion on the right of self-determination of the Serbian population in Croatia and Bosnia-Herzegovina thus upheld the territorial status quo. It went on to find, however, that the Serbian population was entitled to minority rights within the state, a right of identity and a right of self-determination that gave them the right to choose their community beyond the state through nationality.

Extensive minority rights were already among the EC's conditions for the recognition of new states in Yugoslavia. In addition to the minority rights contained in the Conference on Security and Cooperation in Europe (CSCE) commitments required of all new states in Eastern Europe and the Soviet Union,[241] the Yugoslav republics were required to guarantee the more extensive minority rights provided for in a draft convention then under consideration by the EC Conference on Yugoslavia.[242] In *Opinion No. 5*,[243] the Arbitration Commission found that Croatia did not satisfy the EC conditions for recognition to the extent that its new constitutional law did not fully reflect the article of the draft convention

---

[240] See Bieber, 'A New Perspective', 377; Cassese, 'Break-up of USSR and Yugoslavia', p. 144.

[241] See generally J. Helgesen, 'Protecting Minorities in the Conference on Security and Cooperation in Europe (CSCE) Process' in A. Rosas and J. Helgesen (eds.), *The Strength of Diversity: Human Rights and Pluralist Democracy* (Dordrecht: Martinus Nijhoff, 1992), pp. 159–86; J. Wright, 'The OSCE and the Protection of Minority Rights' (1996) 18 *Human Rights Quarterly* 190.

[242] For the relevant provisions of the 4 November 1991 draft convention, see P. C. Szasz, 'Protecting Human and Minority Rights in Bosnia: A Documentary Summary of International Proposals' (1995) 25 *California Western International Law Journal* 237 at 259–63.

[243] *Opinion No. 5*, 1505.

giving a special status of autonomy to areas in which persons belonging to a national or ethnic group formed a majority.

The Arbitration Commission went further in its opinion on the right of self-determination. It found controversially that minority rights were *jus cogens*, or peremptory norms of general international law, and therefore that independent of any minority rights obligations that Croatia and Bosnia-Herzegovina had voluntarily assumed, they were bound by 'every right accorded to minorities under international conventions as well as national and international guarantees consistent with the principles of international law and the provisions of Chapter II of the draft Convention'.[244] In classifying minority rights as *jus cogens*, the Arbitration Commission cited its *Opinion No. 1*, which held that 'respect for the fundamental rights of the individual and the rights of peoples and minorities' were all *jus cogens*.[245]

The Arbitration Commission's conclusion that the Serbian population in Croatia and Bosnia-Herzegovina were entitled to minority rights did not disturb the orthodox view that ethnic groups were 'minorities' with minority rights and not 'peoples' with a right of self-determination in international law. Its paragraphs 2 and 3, however, may be read as complicating these categories. The second paragraph prefaced its discussion of the minority rights of the Serbian population with the statement: 'where there are one or more groups within a State constituting one or more ethnic, religious or language communities, they have the right to recognition of their identity under international law'.[246] On the one hand, this right of ethnic, religious and linguistic communities to the recognition of their identity might simply be a general description of minority rights. On the other, the identity entitled to recognition might be not only that of the minority ethnic, religious or linguistic community within the state, but also that of the broader trans-state community formed by the ethnicity, religion or language.

The third paragraph had similar potential to alter the categories of people and minority. From the right of self-determination of peoples in Article 1 of the International Covenants on Human Rights, the Arbitration Commission derived the principle that the right of self-determination serves to safeguard human rights. 'By virtue of that right', the Arbitration Commission continued, 'every individual may choose

---

[244] *Opinion No. 2*, 1498.
[245] *Opinion No. 1*, 1496. See also Conference on Yugoslavia, Arbitration Commission, *Opinion No. 9* (1992) 31 ILM 1523 at 1524.
[246] *Opinion No. 2*, 1498.

to belong to whatever ethnic, religious or language community he or she wishes.'[247] Some commentators treat this right to choose one's community as unconnected or mistakenly connected to the right of self-determination. But if the Arbitration Commission regarded the right of self-determination of peoples as a means to secure other human rights, then it would be logical to tailor the concepts of self-determination and peoples to that end. In particular, the concepts could be open to modification through the choice of individuals belonging to ethnic, religious and linguistic communities on the assumption that this would further the rights of those communities and their members. At the end of the third paragraph the Arbitration Commission raised the possibility that the people of Croatia and Bosnia-Herzegovina would not be exhaustively defined by the territorial borders or the self-determination represented by the territorial state or its government:

> one possible consequence of this principle might be for the members of the Serbian population in Bosnia-Hercegovina and Croatia to be recognized under agreements between the Republics as having the nationality of their choice, with all the rights and obligations which that entails with respect to the States concerned.[248]

Two schools of criticism

The Arbitration Commission's interpretation of self-determination in *Opinion No. 2*, opaquely presented in the concise formulations of the French legal tradition,[249] has provoked considerable criticism. In general, critics have taken one of the two approaches to self-determination described in Chapter 2. For 'categories' critics, the importance of the opinion was limited by its amateurish treatment of international law. Whether the Arbitration Commission, headed by the President of the French *Conseil Constitutionnel* Robert Badinter and composed originally of five presidents of Western European courts,[250] was simply ill informed about international law or actually disingenuous in its statement of the law,[251] the extravagance of the mistakes in its presentation of

---

[247] Ibid.   [248] Ibid.   [249] Pellet, 'Note', 337.
[250] Matthew Craven regards the fact that the Arbitration Commission initially contained European constitutional court judges as a sign that the *lex arbitri* was intended to be Yugoslav law and that the Arbitration Commission was to enquire, among other things, into the legitimacy and effects of the secession of Slovenia and Croatia under the Yugoslav Constitution. Craven, 'Arbitration Commission on Yugoslavia', 340, n. 44.
[251] See J. A. Frowein, 'Self-Determination as a Limit to Obligations under International Law' in C. Tomuschat (ed.), *Modern Law of Self-Determination* (Dordrecht: Martinus

self-determination was seen to diminish the value of the opinion. This approach, illustrated by Matthew Craven's discussion of *Opinion No. 2*,[252] catalogues the liberties that the Arbitration Commission took with the international legal rules relating to self-determination, discussing each rule in isolation from the others. Hurst Hannum's evaluation[253] provides the most extensive example of the 'coherence' approach, which sees the amateurism of the Arbitration Commission also in its ad hoc and unprincipled approach to self-determination. Hannum measures the model of self-determination that can be built from the Arbitration Commission's opinions against the standard of coherence set by a model that sees self-determination as furthering some single principle or policy, and finds that it falls far short of this standard. I argue here that both types of criticism obscure the reconceptualization of identity implicit in the Arbitration Commission's interpretation of self-determination.

Behind Craven's analysis of the Arbitration Commission's opinion seems to be the idea that the international law of self-determination

---

Nijhoff, 1993), pp. 211–23 at p. 217 (commenting on the Arbitration Commission, 'one wonders whether lawyers should automatically declare, as legally prescribed, what they consider to be the most appropriate solution in political terms').

[252] Craven, 'Arbitration Commission on Yugoslavia'.

[253] H. Hannum, Book Review of *Self-Determination in the New World Order* by M. H. Halperin and D. J. Scheffer with P. L. Small (1993) 33 *Virginia Journal of International Law* 467; H. Hannum, 'Postscript' in H. Hannum, *Autonomy, Sovereignty and Self-Determination: The Accommodation of Conflicting Rights* (rev. edn, Philadelphia: University of Pennsylvania Press, 1996), pp. 495–507; H. Hannum, 'Rethinking Self-Determination' (1993) 34 *Virginia Journal of International Law* 1; H. Hannum, 'Self-Determination, Yugoslavia, and Europe: Old Wine in New Bottles?' (1993) 3 *Transnational Law and Contemporary Problems* 57 (a modified excerpt of 'Rethinking Self-Determination'); H. Hannum, 'Synthesis of Discussion' in C. Brölmann, R. Lefeber and M. Zieck (eds.), *Peoples and Minorities in International Law* (Dordrecht: Martinus Nijhoff, 1993), pp. 333–9. Reference will be made primarily to Hannum, 'Rethinking Self-Determination'.

See also R. Falk, 'The Relevance of the Right of Self-Determination of Peoples under International Law to Canada's Fiduciary Obligations to the Aboriginal Peoples of Quebec in the Context of Quebec's Possible Accession to Sovereignty' in S. J. Anaya, R. Falk and D. Pharand, *Canada's Fiduciary Obligation to Aboriginal Peoples in the Context of Accession to Sovereignty by Quebec* (Papers prepared as part of the Research Program of the Royal Commission on Aboriginal Peoples) (Minister of Supply and Services Canada, 1995), pp. 41–80 at p. 65 and R. A. Falk, 'The Right of Self-Determination under International Law: The Coherence of Doctrine Versus the Incoherence of Experience' in W. Danspeckgruber with A. Watts (eds.), *Self-Determination and Self-Administration: A Sourcebook* (Boulder, Colo.: Lynne Rienner, 1997), pp. 47–63 at p. 57 (quoting Hannum's conclusion in 'Old Wine in New Bottles?' at 69 that the members of the Arbitration Commission 'appear to have based their judgments on geopolitical concerns and imaginary principles of international law, not on the unique situation in Yugoslavia' and describing Hannum's critique of the Arbitration Commission's opinions as 'devastating').

consists of discrete and determinate rules that develop through practice and not interpretation. He meticulously describes the ways in which the Arbitration Commission's interpretation of each rule conforms and does not conform to the current state of international law, prudently qualifying what he takes to be the Arbitration Commission's misstatements and overstatements of the rule. Consistent with the idea that rules develop through the practice and not the interpretation of international law, Craven does not examine whether the Arbitration Commission's interpretation of a particular rule could be grounded in, for example, the fabric of the rules or the principles or purposes that run through international law.

In this vein, Craven argues that the Arbitration Commission has been cavalier with the rules governing self-determination. By using *uti possidetis* to establish that the right of self-determination cannot change the borders that exist on independence, the Arbitration Commission had, for the first time, applied the principle of the stability of borders outside the historical frame of decolonization and possibly to the time period prior to independence.[254] It had strengthened rights within the borders of the state by elevating the right of self-determination, minority rights and basic human rights to the status of *jus cogens*, although there is scant support for calling the right of self-determination and basic human rights *jus cogens* and none for minority rights.[255] In addition to elevating them to *jus cogens*, the Arbitration Commission had gone beyond the traditional approach to these categories of human rights by effecting a synthesis of the categories.[256] Nor does its interpretation of the right of self-determination in Article 1 of the Covenants as giving individuals the right to choose their ethnic, religious or linguistic community have any basis in the jurisprudence of the committees responsible for monitoring and interpreting the Covenants.[257] In so far as the Arbitration Commission further derived the right of individuals belonging to ethnic, religious and linguistic communities to choose

[254] Craven, 'Arbitration Commission on Yugoslavia', 385–90. With respect to the Arbitration Commission's use of the ICJ case of *Frontier Dispute (Burkina Faso v. Republic of Mali)*, ICJ Reports 1986, p. 554 to support its interpretation of *uti possidetis*, compare M. N. Shaw, 'Peoples, Territorialism and Boundaries' (1997) 8 *European Journal of International Law* 478 at 496–501 with S. Ratner, 'Drawing a Better Line: Uti Possidetis and the Borders of New States' (1996) 90 *American Journal of International Law* 590 at 614.
[255] Craven, 'Arbitration Commission on Yugoslavia', 381–3, 390–1. With respect to minority rights as *jus cogens*, compare Craven with Shaw, 'Peoples, Territorialism and Boundaries', 505, n. 130 and Pellet, 'Note', 339.
[256] Craven, 'Arbitration Commission on Yugoslavia', 392–3.   [257] Ibid., 393.

their nationality, Craven's search for authority in international treaty and custom reveals only the faint possibility of a right of expatriation or a right of option.[258]

Ironically, Craven's quickness to discard much of the Arbitration Commission's opinion on self-determination as unwarranted innovation causes him to miss the full extent of its innovation. Since international legal practice is his school for imagination, as well as his test of soundness, he is inclined to understand the Arbitration Commission's interpretation of self-determination through the stock of ideas that already exist in international legal practice. The only glimmer of authority that Craven finds for the right of the Serbian population in Croatia and Bosnia-Herzegovina to the nationality of their choice is a right of expatriation or a right of option. But a right of expatriation returns to the classical liberal framework which the Arbitration Commission's attention to ethnicity sought to modify, and the right of option conjures up the ethnic ideal which informed the Republic of Serbia's question and which the Arbitration Commission's vision of democracy within stable borders dismissed.

Craven defines a right of expatriation by reference to the right not to be arbitrarily deprived of one's nationality nor denied the right to change one's nationality in Article 15 of the Universal Declaration of Human Rights.[259] As such, the right of expatriation assimilates the choice of nationality to a range of other isolated choices made by individuals. It is both indifferent to the ethnic community motivating the individual's choice of nationality and oblivious to the possibility that the whole may be greater than the sum of the parts: the outcome of these individual choices may actually be a new trans-border nationality which gives expression to that ethnic community. In contrast, the right of option historically reflected the strength of ethnic ties in that it gave the inhabitants of a territory which had changed sovereignty the right to opt for a nationality other than that of the new sovereign.[260] Under the right of option, however, the state that acquired sovereignty over the territory was entitled to demand the withdrawal of those individuals who opted and the removal of their property.[261] By tracing the Serbian population's

---

[258] *Ibid.*, 394–5.
[259] As 'somewhat less direct' support for a right of expatriation, Craven cites Article 12 of the International Covenant on Civil and Political Rights. *Ibid.*, 395, n. 364.
[260] See J. L. Kunz, 'L' option de nationalité' (1930–I) 31 Hague Recueil 107; D. P. O'Connell, *State Succession in Municipal Law and International Law* (2 vols., Cambridge: Cambridge University Press, 1967), vol. I, pp. 529–36.
[261] See O'Connell, *State Succession*, pp. 532–3.

right to choose their nationality to a right of option, Craven rhetorically introduces the possibility of large-scale transfers of ethnic populations destined to enhance the ethnic homogeneity of the states involved.[262]

Like Craven, Hannum finds the Arbitration Commission's presentation of the positive international law governing self-determination to be inaccurate. But whereas Craven notes discreetly that the Arbitration Commission's assertions about the right of self-determination cannot 'be accepted in an unqualified form',[263] Hannum is more scathing, accusing the Arbitration Commission of basing its judgments on 'imaginary principles of international law'.[264] Hannum's main criticism, however, is that even if the Arbitration Commission's statement of the law were correct, it would be normatively incoherent. Not only can its opinion on self-determination 'charitably be described as unclear',[265] it fobs international law off with shoddy geopolitical relativism in place of a sound theory of self-determination, with a 'non-response'[266] for a response. Hannum summarizes the approach taken to the Yugoslav conflict by the European Communities, including the EC Arbitration Commission, as

a one-time-only reaction to secessionist demands based on no discernible criteria other than the desire of some territorially based population to secede. The principle that borders should not be altered except by mutual agreement has been elevated to a hypocritical immutability and contradicted by the very act of recognizing secessionist states. New minorities have been trapped, not by any comprehensible legal principle, but by the historical accident of administrative borders drawn by an undemocratic government. Ethnic issues are ignored.[267]

Since the gist of Hannum's criticism is that the Arbitration Commission's opinion is incoherent, it is important to understand what he means by incoherence. Throughout his recent writings on self-determination, Hannum distinguishes between the coherent theory of

---

[262] Because the right of option required the individual who exercised the right to emigrate to the state for which he had opted, some publicists of the time saw the right as *demos* in the service of *ethnos*. E. Maxson Engeström wrote that 'le but des traités de paix de 1919–1920 a été d'appliquer purement et simplement ce principe [des nationalités], en réunissant sur le territoire les hommes de même race, de même langue et de même civilisation' (translation mine: 'the goal of the peace treaties of 1919–1920 was to apply this principle [of nationalities] pure and simple in reuniting on the territory the men of the same race, the same language and the same civilization'). E. M. Engeström, *Les Changements de Nationalité d'après les Traités de Paix de 1919–1920* (Paris: A. Pedone, 1923), p. 8.
[263] Craven, 'Arbitration Commission on Yugoslavia', 385.
[264] Hannum, 'Old Wine in New Bottles?', 69.
[265] Hannum, 'Rethinking Self-Determination', 54.   [266] Ibid., 54.   [267] Ibid., 55–6.

secession and what he calls 'the geopolitical non-theory of secession',[268] as if this distinction were self-evident. Yet even the provocative passage from Jonathan Swift's *Gulliver's Travels* which introduces Hannum's article 'Rethinking Self-Determination' can be used to show that coherence requires a context. Hannum opens with a quotation from *Gulliver's Travels* in which a doctor at the Grand Academy of Lagado proposes to reconcile violent parties in a state by exchanging half of the brain of each man with half of his political opponent's:

> For he argued thus; that the two half Brains being left to debate the Matter between themselves within the Space of one Scull, would soon come to a good Understanding, and produce that Moderation as well as Regularity of Thinking, so much to be wished for in the Heads of those, who imagine they come into the World only to watch and govern its Motion.[269]

In the paragraph that follows, Hannum implicitly classifies the doctor's proposal as a political compromise aimed at conflict resolution (which literally splits the difference). But, in the realm of satire, the proposal could just as easily be described as normatively coherent in the sense that Acton commended the heterogeneous state as the best guarantee of minimum government and negative rights because it frustrates any consensus on what more the government should do.[270]

Coherence relies on cultural, as well as normative, context. Discussing the meaning of self-determination that emerged from decolonization, Hannum does not criticize the practice of limiting the right of independence to colonies, without regard for the minorities trapped in the new states by the historical accident of borders drawn by the imperial power. On the contrary, Hannum defends United Nations practice from charges of 'hypocrisy' and 'inconsistency', arguing that such charges mistakenly assume that the right of self-determination of all peoples was intended to be absolute. The United Nations has always, he maintains, interpreted the right of self-determination of all peoples such that only the populations of classical colonies had an absolute right to immediate independence. Outside classical colonialism, the international community has balanced the right of self-determination against other rights in the manner of United States constitutional

---

[268] *Ibid.*, 49.
[269] J. Swift, *Gulliver's Travels*, P. Turner (ed.) (1726) (Oxford: Oxford University Press, 1986), p. 189, quoted by Hannum, 'Rethinking Self-Determination', 1–2.
[270] J. E. E. Dalberg-Acton (First Baron Acton), 'Nationality' (1862) in J. E. E. Dalberg-Acton, *Essays on Freedom and Power* (Glencoe, Illinois: The Free Press, 1948), pp. 166–95 at p. 185.

jurisprudence.[271] Particularly to an American audience, this description of a 'pragmatic, balancing approach'[272] lacks the unsavouriness of Realpolitik that Hannum gives to his descriptions of other balancing exercises in self-determination. Indeed, later in the discussion, he favourably contrasts 'the absolutist anti-colonial advocacy of the United Nations General Assembly' with 'the relativist geopolitical calculations of the victors at Versailles' after World War I.[273]

Moving from decolonization to the Yugoslav crisis, Hannum observes that the Arbitration Commission's upholding of the old federal borders between republics as the new international frontiers is consistent with the post-1945 emphasis on territory in decolonization. As applied to Yugoslavia, however, Hannum is quick to point out the inconsistencies and weaknesses of 'this neo-decolonization territorial approach'.[274] Even assuming that it was the most appropriate approach to the Yugoslav crisis, he argues, it is inconsistent to recognize the federal republics as new states, but not lesser federal subdivisions, such as the ethnically Albanian province of Kosovo. Moreover, even remedying this inconsistency would not deal with the problem of minorities created by the breakup of Yugoslavia.

But if Hannum's criticisms of the 'neo-decolonization territorial approach' taken to Yugoslavia are well founded, then why did he not also make them of the approach as originally taken to Africa and Asia? In his recent writing on the crisis of the African state, Makau wa Mutua argues that the numerous failed states in Africa are a result of the preservation of the colonial borders and makes the case for a radical new map of Africa that would better reflect its history and ethnography.[275] Alternatively, if the colonial borders in Africa and Asia can be defended, for example, as an identity created by imperial line-drawing that gradually became real to the population,[276] then why did Hannum not consider whether the borders of the Yugoslav republics might similarly have become defensible as the primary civic identity of their inhabitants?

It thus becomes apparent that the terms peppering Hannum's criticisms of the Arbitration Commission's opinion on self-determination –

---

[271] Hannum, 'Rethinking Self-Determination', 33.   [272] Ibid.   [273] Ibid., 48.
[274] Ibid., 38.
[275] M. wa Mutua, 'Putting Humpty Dumpty Back Together Again: The Dilemmas of the Post-Colonial African State' (1995) 21 *Brooklyn Journal of International Law* 505; M. wa Mutua, 'Why Redraw the Map of Africa: A Moral and Legal Inquiry' (1995) 16 *Michigan Journal of International Law* 1113.
[276] See pp. 55–6 above.

hypocritical, contradictory, unprincipled – depend on context and culture for their bite. Is Swift's doctor proposing a political saw-off or a design for the protection of negative liberty? Why does the denial of a right of secession to tribes within a former colony strike a balance worthy of the US constitutional tradition and its denial to ethnic minorities within a former Yugoslav republic raise issues of consistency and fairness?

Given that Hannum puts Harry Beran's theory of secession[277] in the camp of consistency, theory and universalism and Lee Buchheit's[278] and Lung-Chu Chen's[279] theories in the camp of inconsistency, non-theory and geopolitical relativism, a comparison of the two types of theory may explain how Hannum makes these judgments.

On Beran's liberal theory of secession, the liberal 'commitment to the freedom of self-governing choosers to live in societies that approach as closely as possible to voluntary schemes, requires that the unity of the state itself be voluntary and, therefore, that secession by part of a state be permitted where it is possible'.[280] Beran's liberal logic permits any territorially concentrated group within the state to secede if the majority of the group so chooses, which, for Hannum, has 'the appeal of consistency'.[281] Yet Hannum does not dwell on the fact that Beran limits secession to the morally and politically possible, and thereby introduces conditions that are not necessarily justifiable in liberal terms. Among these conditions are that the group be sufficiently large to assume the basic responsibilities of an independent state, that it occupy an area which is not culturally, economically or militarily essential to the existing state, and that it occupy an area which does not have a disproportionately high share of the economic resources of the existing state.[282]

The balance between the importance of secession for the group and the consequences for other communities is central to both Buchheit's

---

[277] H. Beran, 'A Liberal Theory of Secession' (1984) 32 *Political Studies* 21; H. Beran, 'A Philosophical Perspective' in W. J. A. Macartney (ed.), *Self-Determination in the Commonwealth* (Aberdeen: Aberdeen University Press, 1988), pp. 23–35.
[278] L. C. Buchheit, *Secession: The Legitimacy of Self-Determination* (New Haven: Yale University Press, 1978).
[279] L.-C. Chen, 'Self-Determination and World Public Order' (1991) 66 *Notre Dame Law Review* 1287; L.-C. Chen, 'Self-Determination as a Human Right' in W. M. Reisman and B. H. Weston (eds.), *Toward World Order and Human Dignity: Essays in Honor of Myres S. McDougal* (New York: Free Press, 1976), pp. 198–261.
[280] Beran, 'A Liberal Theory of Secession', 25.
[281] Hannum, 'Rethinking Self-Determination', 44.
[282] Beran, 'A Liberal Theory of Secession', 30–1.

and Chen's theories of secession. For Buchheit, a claim to secession made by a distinct group should basically be permitted unless it is outweighed by the disruption to the international community.[283] Chen similarly seeks to achieve the optimal combination of minimum world order, defined in terms of unauthorized coercion and violence, and optimum world order, defined in terms of human dignity.[284]

Hannum's comparison of Buchheit's and Chen's theories of secession with Beran's 'philosophically absolutist approach of permitting any secession supported by a majority of the seceding people'[285] suggests a variety of ways in which Hannum might distinguish between coherence and incoherence. First of all, Hannum sees Buchheit's and Chen's theories as different from Beran's because they do not enable us to say anything about a right to secede in the abstract: 'The very flexibility that characterizes pragmatism leaves unanswered the fundamental question of whether ethnic homogeneity is a legitimate criterion for statehood'.[286] Yet this distinction seems shaky, given that we could reformulate Buchheit's theory as the right of an ethnic group to secede subject to a limitation and that Beran's right to secede is also subject to a limitation. A related distinction made by Hannum is that Buchheit's and Chen's theories of secession lack predictability: 'unfortunately the proposed criteria provide no readily manageable norm against which to judge the legitimacy of secessionist claims'.[287] If this is a point about the need for interpretation, then certainly there is no less need for interpretation in the application of Beran's conditions of viability as an independent state, the territory in question not being culturally, economically or militarily essential to the existing state and the territory not representing a disproportionately high share of the economic resources of the existing state. Perhaps, then, Hannum's distinction is not about intelligibility in the abstract, but about structure. Deontological and teleological theories of secession seem not to capture his critical distinction completely, though, because he ultimately proposes that we view self-determination teleologically, where the *telos* is 'a democratic participatory political and economic system in which the rights of individuals and the identity of minority communities are protected'.[288] More likely is that Hannum also distinguishes between the kinds of ends to which self-determination is a means. Hannum compares Buchheit's

---

[283] Buchheit, *Secession*, pp. 225–45, 249.
[284] Chen, 'Self-Determination and World Public Order', 1293.
[285] Hannum, 'Rethinking Self-Determination', 48. [286] Ibid. [287] Ibid.
[288] Ibid., 66.

determination of whether a potential secession would promote 'general international harmony' to 'the relativist geopolitical calculations of the victors at Versailles'. But surely this comparison is overdrawn. A theory that subordinates a right of secession to the goal of international peace and security is not reducible to a political decision about secession which reflects the self-interest of the decision-makers. In this respect, Hannum's description of the approach to self-determination developed by Morton Halperin and David Scheffer in *Self-Determination in the New World Order*[289] as 'somewhat similar'[290] to Buchheit's and Chen's approaches to self-determination disregards the fact that Halperin and Scheffer's enterprise was the development of a new US foreign policy on self-determination, an enterprise in which US interests might legitimately be considered. In Buchheit's or Chen's analysis of secession, it would presumably be illegitimate to consider, for instance, whether American multinational corporations stood to gain from a secession. We are left with the impression that Hannum's distinctions between consistent/inconsistent, theory/non-theory and universalism/geopolitical relativism in theories of secession depend largely on an unarticulated distinction between legitimate and illegitimate considerations, where any consideration of international peace and security is illegitimate.

In this light, it appears that Hannum's dismissal of the Arbitration Commission's opinion on self-determination as incoherent is informed by his view of the Arbitration Commission's true motives as geopolitical[291] and therefore illegitimate. But by comparing Hannum's preferred theory of self-determination with the Arbitration Commission's opinion, we can see that not only may they be similarly inspired, but that the Arbitration Commission's opinion may be more far-sighted.

On Hannum's theory of self-determination, the right of self-determination is one means of achieving a participatory democracy that protects the rights of individuals and the identity of minority communities. As such, it gives all individuals the right to democratic governance and gives minorities the rights necessary to their identity as a community, whether cultural, religious and linguistic rights, a right of autonomy or even a right of self-government.[292] Only where the state

---

[289] M. H. Halperin and D. J. Scheffer with P. L. Small, *Self-Determination in the New World Order* (Washington, D.C.: Carnegie Endowment for International Peace, 1992).
[290] Hannum, 'Rethinking Self-Determination', 48, n. 191.
[291] Hannum, 'Old Wine in New Bottles?', 69.
[292] Hannum, 'Rethinking Self-Determination', 66. On the right of autonomy, see Hannum, *Autonomy, Sovereignty and Self-Determination*.

has irremediably failed to respect the rights of a minority does the right of self-determination give that minority a right to secede.²⁹³

If we adopt Roland Bieber's reading of the Arbitration Commission's opinion on self-determination, a remedial right to secede is the only difference between Hannum's theory of self-determination and the Arbitration Commission's opinion. Bieber identifies the primary aim of the Western European states in Yugoslavia as 'establishing solid foundations for states based on democratic government, wherein pressure for separation is counterbalanced by adequate means for participation in the democratic process and by efficient instruments for the protection of minorities',²⁹⁴ an idea of the state very similar to Hannum's. In so far as the Arbitration Commission framed the right of self-determination of the Serbian minority as a right of identity, including a wide range of minority rights, it envisaged self-determination as achieving this idea of the state just as Hannum does. The Arbitration Commission clearly did not share Hannum's view that self-determination justified the secession of a minority as a last resort where its right of identity was not realized within the state. Its opinion started with the primacy of territorial integrity and the stability of borders over the right of self-determination. But, Bieber argues, the Arbitration Commission gave this traditional primacy a 'consolidated justification'; namely, 'in an effective democratic system, coupled with the rule of law and protection of human rights, the right of self-determination of individuals and minorities is sufficiently achieved in as much as it enables each individual to maintain and practice an identity.'²⁹⁵ And the 'consolidated justification' Bieber finds in the Arbitration Commission's opinion is identical to Hannum's theory of secession, except in those few extreme cases where Hannum would allow secession and the Arbitration Commission would uphold the territorial status quo. Moreover, these cases become even rarer if one assumes, with Bieber, that the EC approach to Yugoslavia increases the overall responsibility of the international community for the internal affairs of states.²⁹⁶

Hannum's idea of coherence thus prevents him from seeing the Arbitration Commission's opinion on self-determination as fundamentally similar to his own theory of self-determination. It similarly prevents him from appreciating that while the Arbitration Commission's interpretation of self-determination does not give minorities a remedial right

---

²⁹³ Hannum, 'Rethinking Self-Determination', 63–9.
²⁹⁴ Bieber, 'A New Perspective', 377.   ²⁹⁵ Ibid.   ²⁹⁶ Ibid., 377–8.

to secede, it designs new alternatives to secession. Discussing general trends in self-determination, Hannum notes with approval that 'as self-determination is expressed in increasingly diverse relationships between central and sub-state entities, the relevance of international frontiers to the lives of most people will continue to diminish'.[297] Indeed, for him, one of the tragic ironies of Yugoslavia is that the borders fetishized in the conflict will be made largely irrelevant by the inevitable desire of the Yugoslav republics to join the European Union. Nevertheless, Hannum deems the Arbitration Commission's interpretation of self-determination as the right to choose one's community through nationality a confused 'non-response', instead of seeing that it might further diminish the relevance of international frontiers by adding trans-state identifications to the sub-state, state and potentially supra-state identifications.

A new geometry of identity

Hannum's assumption that the Arbitration Commission had confused the individual right to choose one's nationality with the collective right of self-determination,[298] like Craven's precedent of a right of expatriation, causes him to disregard the Arbitration Commission's suggestion that in the former Yugoslavia, the concept of nationality could be used to recognize a Serbian identity which cut across state borders. Although Craven's other precedent, the right of option, could result in a Serbian community living on Croatian or Bosnian territory while opting for Serbian nationality, the right of option would not prevent Croatia or Bosnia-Herzegovina from realigning identity with the state by requiring those who opted to leave the territory.

In contrast to Craven and Hannum, Alain Pellet reads the right to choose one's nationality as part of the new geometry of identity created for Yugoslavia by the Arbitration Commission's interpretation of self-determination, describing it as

> une dissociation très remarquable entre la nationalité et la territorialité, certainement féconde pour l'avenir et d'autant plus indispensable que l'imbrication des ethnies est telle, dans certaines Républiques – surtout en Bosnie-Herzégovine – , que de nouveaux découpages territoriaux semblent totalement irréalistes.
>
> [a very remarkable dissociation of nationality and territoriality, certainly fruitful for the future and even more indispensable since the ethnic groups are so

---

[297] Hannum, 'Rethinking Self-Determination', 65.   [298] Ibid., 54.

interwoven in certain republics – above all in Bosnia-Herzegovina – that the carving out of new territories seems totally unrealistic.][299]

From Pellet's perspective, no configuration of states in the former Yugoslavia can do equal justice to all ethnic groups. By dissociating nationality from territoriality, the Arbitration Commission introduced the possibility of using nationality to recognize an ethnic identity independent of territory and thereby help transcend the limitations inherent in any territorial settlement in the former Yugoslavia. Over and above their identity as citizens or residents of a multicultural Croatia or Bosnia-Herzegovina, the Serbian minority could have an identity as Serbian nationals. Pellet[300] uses the example of the European Union citizenship established by the 1992 Maastricht Treaty,[301] which the 1997 Amsterdam Treaty[302] describes as complementing but not replacing the nationality of the EU member states. The analogy may be not only to the complementarity of citizenship and nationality in the European Union, but also to their relationship as theorized by some EU scholars. One school of thought on EU citizenship sees the civic virtues represented by EU citizenship as a moderating influence on the nationalism embodied in member states' nationality: in Joseph Weiler's words, Civilization taming *Eros*.[303]

In all, Pellet sees the geometry of identity in the Arbitration Commission's opinions as having a state, a sub-state and a trans-state dimension. In terms of the state, *Opinion No. 2* starts with two ideas about self-determination. The first, developed further in *Opinion No. 3*, is that the right of self-determination of peoples cannot disturb the territorial integrity of the state and the stability of borders.[304] The second idea, that the right of self-determination of peoples is the right of the population of the state to democratic governance, follows from the EC guidelines

---

[299] (Translation mine) Pellet, 'Note', 341. See also A. Pellet, 'The Opinions of the Badinter Arbitration Commission: A Second Breath for the Self-Determination of Peoples' (1992) 3 *European Journal of International Law* 178 at 180.

On the history of international legal schemes for European minorities, see N. Berman, ' "But the Alternative is Despair": Nationalism and the Modernist Renewal of International Law' (1993) 106 *Harvard Law Review* 1792.

[300] Pellet, 'Note', 340–1; Pellet, 'A Second Breath', 179–80.

[301] Treaty on European Union, Maastricht, 7 February 1992, in force 1 November 1993, OJ 1992 No. C191, p. 1, (1992) 31 ILM 253.

[302] Treaty of Amsterdam, 2 October 1997, in force 1 May 1999, OJ 1997 No. C340, p. 1, (1998) 37 ILM 56.

[303] J. H. H. Weiler, 'To Be a European Citizen: Eros and Civilization' in J. H. H. Weiler, *The Constitution of Europe: 'Do the New Clothes Have an Emperor?' and Other Essays on European Integration* (Cambridge: Cambridge University Press, 1999), pp. 324–57.

[304] Pellet, 'A Second Breath', 180.

on recognition applied in *Opinions Nos.* 4 to 7, which make democracy a condition for the recognition of new states in Yugoslavia. One dimension of identity is thus the democratic community of the state.

By treating minority rights as part of the Serbian population's right of self-determination, the Arbitration Commission may be signalling that a 'people' need not be the legally homogeneous population of a state, but can include cultural minorities with a right of identity in the form of minority rights, and that the right of self-determination can accordingly mean the right to multicultural democracy.[305] The alternative to this conception of the multicultural *demos* is the view that 'peoples' means separately the *demos* represented by the state and the *ethnos* within the state. On the alternative conception, the self-determination of the whole is realized by individual rights of political participation and the self-determination of the parts by minority rights.[306]

In addition to the state and sub-state dimensions of identity given expression by self-determination, the Arbitration Commission interprets self-determination as potentially expressing a trans-state dimension. Through the right to choose their nationality, individuals belonging to the Serbian minority in Croatia and Bosnia-Herzegovina would effectively expand Serbian nationality beyond the inhabitants of the Republic of Serbia to ethnic Serbs throughout the successor states to Yugoslavia. In other words, Serbian nationality would constitute the Serbian *ethnos* in international law. Technically, Pellet assumes that those individuals living in Croatia and Bosnia-Herzegovina who choose Serbian nationality would retain only assured residency status in those states.[307] He describes the ultimate objective as 'to allow those persons who so wish to, to declare themselves as Serbs while retaining certain civil and political rights in the territories of Bosnia-Herzegovina and Croatia – for example, the right to vote in local elections – without thereby questioning

---

[305] See e.g. W. Kymlicka, *Multicultural Citizenship: A Liberal Theory of Minority Rights* (Oxford: Clarendon Press, 1995); I. M. Young, *Justice and the Politics of Difference* (Princeton: Princeton University Press, 1990).

[306] See Pellet, 'A Second Breath', 179. But compare J. C. Duursma, *Fragmentation and the International Relations of Micro-States: Self-Determination and Statehood* (Cambridge, Cambridge University Press, 1996), pp. 70–2. (Although it is unclear whether the Arbitration Commission sees the 'people' entitled to self-determination as the Serbian minorities in Croatia and Bosnia-Herzegovina or the Serbian nation as a whole, its definition of 'people' is ethnic.)

[307] See also B. Kingsbury, 'Claims by Non-State Groups in International Law' (1992) 25 *Cornell International Law Journal* 481 at 508. ('Although the Commission is not explicit, it is presumed that choice of Serbian nationality would not entail loss of the right of residence in whichever state the individual lived.')

the sovereignty of the State'.³⁰⁸ By analogy to EU citizenship, the other possibility would be to allow dual nationality³⁰⁹ and perhaps tailor to the former Yugoslavia the international legal rules regarding the rights of the one state of nationality vis-à-vis the other.³¹⁰

Pellet also provides a broader context for the Arbitration Commission's interpretation of self-determination which resonates with the interpretation of self-determination in *Western Sahara*. Not only do both decisions use interpretation to construct a complex understanding of identity in international law, both expand the relevant community of international law. By this, I mean that it is possible to see the Arbitration Commission's interpretation of self-determination as other than curiously stitched together from various legal categories or jerry-built by Western Europe to deal with the political problems of Eastern Europe. Pellet connects the Arbitration Commission's thinking on self-determination with the European project of identity. With the establishment of EU citizenship in the 1992 Maastricht Treaty came a renewed interest in how European identity should be conceived. To the old alternatives of building a common 'European fatherland' or preserving a 'Europe of fatherlands' was added the alternative of European constitutional patriotism.³¹¹ Whereas the common 'European fatherland' strives for a single European nationality and the 'Europe of fatherlands' holds fast to the nationality of the individual European states, European constitutional patriotism decouples citizenship

---

³⁰⁸ Pellet, 'A Second Breath', 180.
³⁰⁹ Article I(7)(d) of the Constitution of Bosnia and Herzegovina contained in Annex 4 to the General Framework Agreement for Peace in Bosnia and Herzegovina (Dayton Accords), Paris, 14 December 1995, in force 14 December 1995, (1996) 35 ILM 117 at 119 provides: 'Citizens of Bosnia and Herzegovina may hold the citizenship of another state, provided that there is a bilateral agreement, approved by the Parliamentary Assembly in accordance with Article IV(4)(d), between Bosnia and Herzegovina and that state governing this matter. Persons with dual citizenship may vote in Bosnia and Herzegovina and the Entities only if Bosnia and Herzegovina is their country of residence.'
³¹⁰ See Convention on Certain Questions Relating to the Conflict of Nationality Laws, The Hague, 12 April 1930, in force 1 July 1937, 179 LNTS 89, Art. 4; *Canevaro Case (Italy v. Peru)* (1912), 11 Reports of International Arbitral Awards 397; *Iran v. United States, Case No. A/18* (1984), 5 Iran–US Claims Tribunal Reports 251; *Mergé Claim (US v. Italy)* (1955), 22 International Law Reports 443; *Salem Case (Egypt v. US)* (1932), 2 Reports of International Arbitral Awards 1161.
³¹¹ The alternatives are taken from R. Bauböck, Citizenship and National Identities in the European Union, Harvard Jean Monnet Working Paper No. 4/97, http://www.jeanmonnetprogram.org/papers/97/97-04--4.html (visited 11 October 2001). Bauböck traces the concept of European constitutional patriotism to Dolf Sternberger and Jürgen Habermas.

from nationality. This decoupling makes it possible to theorize different types of identifications with different communities. On Joseph Weiler's version, 'the invitation is to embrace the national in the in-reaching strong sense of organic-cultural identification and belongingness and to embrace the European in terms of European transnational affinities to shared values which transcend the ethno-national diversity'.[312] The European is not intended to replace the national, but rather to encourage in it the virtues of tolerance and humanity by subordinating it to certain broader values and decision-making processes.[313] On Pellet's reading, the Arbitration Commission's interpretation of self-determination may harbour a similar hope: that by decoupling Serbian nationality from citizenship or residency in a multicultural Croatia and Bosnia-Herzegovina, nationality can recognize legally the importance of ethnicity, and the values of democracy and pluralism legally required of the territorial state can temper the excesses of ethnic nationalism.

East Timor

The treatment of self-determination in the 1995 judgment of the International Court of Justice in *East Timor (Portugal v. Australia)*[314] has been seen as timid in comparison to that in earlier cases.[315] Prior to the invasion of East Timor by Indonesia in 1975, Portugal had administered East Timor as a non-self-governing territory under Chapter XI of the UN

[312] Weiler, 'Eros and Civilization', p. 346.   [313] *Ibid.*, pp. 346–7.
[314] For commentary on the *East Timor* case, see C. Chinkin, 'The East Timor Case (*Portugal v. Australia*)' (1996) 45 *International and Comparative Law Quarterly* 712; C. Chinkin, 'East Timor Moves into the World Court' (1993) 4 *European Journal of International Law* 206; Crawford, 'The General Assembly', p. 605; Duursma, *Fragmentation and the International Relations of Micro-States*, pp. 62–3; N. S. Klein, 'Multilateral Disputes and the Doctrine of Necessary Parties in the *East Timor* Case' (1996) 12 *Yale Journal of International Law* 305; M. C. Maffei, 'The Case of East Timor before the International Court of Justice – Some Tentative Comments' (1993) 4 *European Journal of International Law* 223; Musgrave, *Self-Determination and National Minorities*, pp. 88–90, 242–3; I. Scobbie, 'The East Timor Case: Implications of Procedure for Litigation Strategy' (1991) 9 *Oil & Gas Law and Taxation Review* 273; G. J. Simpson, 'Judging the East Timor Dispute: Self-Determination at the International Court of Justice' (1994) 17 *Hastings International and Comparative Law Review* 323; J.-M. Thouvenin, 'L'Arrêt de la CIJ du 30 juin 1995 rendu dans l'affaire du Timor Oriental (Portugal c. Australie)' (1995) *Annuaire français de droit international* 328.

For a select bibliography on East Timor generally, see Krieger, *East Timor: Basic Documents*, pp. 487–9.
[315] R. Higgins, 'The International Court of Justice and Africa' in E. Yakpo and T. Boumedra (eds.), *Liber Amicorum Judge Mohammed Bedjaoui* (The Hague: Kluwer Law International, 1999), pp. 343–69 at p. 361.

Charter.[316] In *East Timor*, Portugal brought proceedings against Australia over the 1989 Timor Gap Treaty between Australia and Indonesia.[317] The treaty established a provisional arrangement for the exploration and exploitation of the resources of the undelimited part of the continental shelf between Australia and East Timor, which was known as the 'Timor Gap'.[318] Portugal maintained that by negotiating, concluding and implementing the treaty, Australia had infringed the rights of the people of East Timor to self-determination and permanent sovereignty over their natural resources, and the rights of Portugal as the administering power.[319] By a majority of fourteen to two, the court held that it could not exercise jurisdiction in the case because 'in order to decide the claims of Portugal, it would have to rule, as a prerequisite, on the lawfulness of Indonesia's conduct in the absence of that State's consent'.[320] The court, however, also upheld[321] the interpretation of self-determination in *Western Sahara* as 'the right of the population... to determine their future political status by their own freely expressed will'. Indeed it recognized the right of self-determination as *erga omnes*:[322] a right that all states are obliged to respect and in the observance of which all states have a legal interest.

Since the court dismissed the *East Timor* case on the ground that Indonesia was a necessary third party, it had no need to deal[323] with another issue of self-determination that arose on the facts: how to reconcile the trust relationship that Chapter XI of the UN Charter created between the state administering a non-self-governing territory (Portugal) and the people of the territory (East Timor) with the right of self-determination of colonial peoples developed in UN General Assembly resolutions from the 1960 Declaration on the Independence

---

[316] *East Timor*, pp. 95–6.
[317] Treaty between Australia and the Republic of Indonesia on the Zone of Cooperation in an Area between the Indonesian Province of East Timor and Northern Australia (Timor Gap Treaty), Timor Sea, 11 December 1989, in force 9 February 1991, *Australian Treaty Series* 1991 No. 9.
[318] *East Timor*, p. 98.   [319] *Ibid.*   [320] *Ibid.*, p. 105.
[321] *Ibid.*, pp. 103, 105–6. In fact, this interpretation of self-determination was not in dispute because the parties agreed that 'the Territory of East Timor remains a non-self-governing territory and its people has the right to self-determination'. *Ibid.*, p. 103.
[322] *Ibid.*, p. 102. On the formulation of the concept of *erga omnes* by the International Court of Justice, see *Barcelona Traction, Light and Power Company, Limited (Belgium v. Spain)*, ICJ Reports 1970, p. 3 at p. 32.
[323] The court did find, however, that the relevant UN resolutions did not establish a duty of third states, such as Australia, to treat exclusively with Portugal as regards the continental shelf of East Timor. *East Timor*, p. 104.

of Colonial Peoples (GA Resolution 1514) onward. Whereas trusteeship was predicated on cultural inferiority and the consequent irrelevance of the people's wishes until they were deemed advanced enough to make decisions for themselves, self-determination was based on equality and the need to consult the people on their future political status. The interpretation and application of trusteeship therefore implicated broadly both the portrayal of colonial peoples in international law and the relationship of this image of identity to the structure and meaning of participation in cases between states that directly concern colonial peoples.

Judge Vereshchetin, however, focused his separate opinion in *East Timor* on Portugal's role as the administering power of a non-self-governing territory, and Judge Weeramantry and Judge *ad hoc* Skubiszewski addressed the issue in their dissenting opinions.[324] This part of the chapter seeks to show the significance of their different approaches to interpretation and the continuity with *Western Sahara* and the EC Arbitration Commission's *Opinion No. 2* on Yugoslavia in the underlying concern for identity and participation as dimensions of equality.

Before examining the opinions of Judge Vereshchetin, Judge Weeramantry and Judge *ad hoc* Skubiszewski and the relevant arguments made by Portugal and Australia, this part describes the barriers to equality represented by the rules of court and the traditional idea of the trust.

Rules of court

Although behind the *East Timor* case was the military invasion of East Timor by Indonesia, the parties to the case were not the people of East Timor and the state of Indonesia. Instead, it was Portugal that brought the case against Australia. Portugal alleged that it had standing as the administering power in East Timor despite the fact that the Portuguese authorities had withdrawn from East Timor in 1975 and had not exercised control over the territory since then. But as a non-state group, the people of East Timor could not have initiated or intervened in the case – just as the Sahrawi in *Western Sahara*, the Bani Qitab in the

---

[324] Apart from the duties of the administering power of a non-self-governing territory to the territory's inhabitants, the 'sacred trust' in *East Timor* raised other issues of interpretation (notably, what the rights of the administering power were and what the duties of third states, such as Australia, were to the people and to the administering power) and application (in what sense Portugal was still the administering power and, depending on the interpretation given to trusteeship, how to determine which East Timorese group or groups represented the East Timorese people).

Dubai/Sharjah boundary arbitration[325] and the ethnic groups of the former Yugoslavia in the EC Arbitration Commission's *Opinion No. 2* were all excluded from direct participation in those cases. The rules of adjudication in international law, whether the ICJ Statute and Rules[326] or the procedures for arbitral tribunals, preclude peoples from participating directly in the adjudication of their right to self-determination, and thus from participating directly in the the development of self-determination and international law through interpretation by international judges and arbitrators.

Under the ICJ Statute and Rules, only states can be parties[327] or interveners[328] in a contentious proceeding such as the *East Timor* case between Portugal and Australia. While the ICJ Statute allows the court to request information relevant to a contentious case from 'public international organizations' and to receive relevant information submitted by 'public international organizations' on their own initiative,[329] the ICJ Rules define such organizations narrowly as international organizations of states.[330]

In an advisory proceeding, like *Western Sahara*, which may be initiated by the General Assembly, Security Council or such other UN bodies as

---

[325] In the *Dubai/Sharjah* boundary arbitration, the Tribunal, despite its usual caution with respect to statements made in the case, did emphasize the importance of a statement made by two paramount chiefs, seventeen chiefs and three elders of the Bani Qitab. *Dubai/Sharjah*, 639.

[326] See generally D. Shelton, 'The Participation of Nongovernmental Organizations in International Judicial Proceedings' (1994) 88 *American Journal of International Law* 611 at 619–28. See also 'Increasing the Use and Appeal of the Court' in C. Peck and R. S. Lee (eds.), *Increasing the Use and Effectiveness of the International Court of Justice* (Proceedings of the ICJ/UNITAR Colloquium to Celebrate the 50th Anniversary of the Court) (The Hague: Martinus Nijhoff, 1997), pp. 42–76, especially Professor Christine Chinkin's presentation at pp. 43–56.

[327] Statute of the International Court of Justice, 26 June 5, 59 Stat. 1179, 145 BFSP (1943–5) 832 (1953), Art. 34(1). Indigenous peoples have tried unsuccessfully to invoke the jurisdiction of the court on the ground that they constitute nations.
J. G. S., 'Access of Individuals to International Court of Justice' (1978) 52 *Australian Law Journal* 523 at 523.

[328] ICJ Statute, Arts. 62–3.   [329] *Ibid.*, Art. 34(2).

[330] Rules of the International Court of Justice, adopted 14 April 1978, (1979) 73 *American Journal of International Law* 748, Art. 69(4). On the drafting history of the term 'public international organizations', see Shelton, 'The Participation of Nongovernmental Organizations', 620–1. In the *Asylum* case, the Registrar of the Court rejected a request by an international human rights organization to participate on the grounds that it could not 'be characterized as a public international organization as envisaged by Statute'. *Asylum Case (Columbia v. Peru)*, ICJ Pleadings 1950, vol. II, pp. 227, 228 (International League for the Rights of Man).

may be authorized,[331] the ICJ Statute contemplates the appearance of all states so entitled[332] and of relevant 'international organizations',[333] a term potentially broader than 'public international organizations'. The court's granting early on of a request from an international human rights organization to submit information in the 1950 *International Status of South West Africa* proceedings[334] demonstrates that international organizations need not be organizations of states, but the denial of similar requests in later advisory proceedings[335] indicates that the court is generally reluctant to expand participation to non-governmental organizations. Moreover, its rulings have made clear that national groups[336] and individuals[337] cannot submit information in advisory proceedings.

Independent of other parties and interveners, the only opportunities for a people to participate directly in either a contentious or advisory proceeding would therefore seem to be[338] the Statute's provision for expert opinions[339] and the court's recognition in *Military and Paramilitary Activities in and against Nicaragua* that information could come to it 'in ways and by means not contemplated by the Rules'.[340]

Trusteeship

Not only could a colonial people not bring or intervene in a case like *East Timor*, the state administering the colonial territory did not even need the consent of the territory's inhabitants to do so. What had made this

---

[331] ICJ Statute, Art. 65(1); Charter of the United Nations, 26 June 1945, 59 Stat. 1031, 145 BFSP (1943-1945) 805 (1953), Art. 96(1).
[332] ICJ Statute, Art. 66(1).
[333] Ibid., Art. 66(2). On the drafting history of the term 'international organizations', see Shelton, 'The Participation of Nongovernmental Organizations', 621-3.
[334] *International Status of South West Africa*, Advisory Opinion, ICJ Pleadings 1950, pp. 324, 325, 327, 343-4, 346. (The International League for the Rights of Man was permitted to submit written information only, but failed to do so within the time-limit.)
[335] *Namibia (South West Africa)*, Advisory Opinion, ICJ Pleadings 1970, vol. II, p. 639-40, 678, 679 (International League for the Rights of Man); Shelton, 'The Participation of Nongovernmental Organizations', 624.
[336] *Namibia* Pleadings, vol. II, pp. 643, 644-5, 647, 649-50, 652 (American Committee on Africa).
[337] Ibid., pp. 636-7, 638-9 (Professor Michael Reisman), 677, 678 (four indigenous inhabitants of Namibia).
[338] Shelton, 'The Participation of Nongovernmental Organizations', 627-8.
[339] ICJ Statute, Art. 50.
[340] *Military and Paramilitary Activities in and against Nicaragua (Nicaragua v. United States)*, Merits, ICJ Reports 1986, p. 14 at p. 25.

arrangement seem right, sensible and, indeed, noble was some combination of trusteeship and tutelage. The conception of political power as a trust, whereby the government exercised power for the benefit of the governed and was accountable to them, blended with the concept of guardianship, whereby power was exercised for the benefit of someone incapable of managing his own affairs. In international law the interwar mandate territories supervised by the League of Nations and the post-World War II dependent territories under the United Nations were treated as a 'sacred trust'. Accordingly, the state administering the territory had certain duties toward the people of the territory. These duties were traditionally analogized to a trustee's duty to act in the interests of the beneficiary, supplemented by the assumption that colonial peoples, like children, were not yet capable of judging what was in their own interests. The structure of participation represented by the 'sacred trust' thus carried a meaning informed by the image of colonial peoples as backward, but educable.

The idea that colonialism was a trust exercised by the colonizer for the benefit of the colonized has a very long history in international law.[341] However, the idea that found expression in the League of Nations system of mandate territories and later in the United Nations system of trust and non-self-governing territories is traced back by its mid-twentieth-century chroniclers, such as Duncan Hall[342] and Charmian Toussaint,[343] only as far as Edmund Burke's 1783 speech in the British House of Commons on the principles of colonial rule in India:

All political power which is set over men, and ... all privilege claimed or exercised in exclusion of them, being wholly artificial, and for so much a deregation [sic] from the natural equality of mankind at large, ought to be in some way or other exercised ultimately for their benefit.

If this is true with regard to every species of political dominion, and every description of commercial privilege, none of which can be original self-derived rights, or grants for the benefit of the holders, then such rights or privileges,

---

[341] See D. Rauschning, 'United Nations Trusteeship System' in R. Bernhardt (ed.), *Encyclopedia of Public International Law* (12 vols., Amsterdam: North-Holland, 1983), vol. V, pp. 369–76 at p. 369; *South West Africa, Second Phase*, p. 265 (Dissenting Opinion of Judge Tanaka). The idea of the trust also seems to be inexhaustible in international law. For the more recent debate, see e.g. G. B. Helman and S. R. Ratner, 'Saving Failed States' (Winter 1992–3) *Foreign Policy* 3; R. E. Gordon, 'Some Legal Problems with Trusteeship' (1995) 28 *Cornell International Law Journal* 301.

[342] H. D. Hall, *Mandates, Dependencies and Trusteeship* (Washington: Carnegie Endowment for International Peace, 1948).

[343] C. E. Toussaint, *The Trusteeship System of the United Nations* (New York: Frederick A. Praeger, 1956).

or whatever else you choose to call them, are all, in the strictest sense, a trust; and it is of the very essence of every trust to be rendered accountable; and even totally to cease, when it substantially varies from the purposes for which alone it could have a lawful existence.[344]

Five years later, in the impeachment trial of the Governor-General of India, Warren Hastings, before the House of Lords, Burke would charge Hastings with breach of the colonial trust, impeaching him in the name of the people of India.[345] Hall, in his 1948 work on mandates, dependencies and trusteeship, groups the trial of Warren Hastings with the struggle for the abolition of the slave trade and slavery as the progressive forces that gave birth to the national trusteeship systems and, later, the international mandate and trusteeship systems of the twentieth century.[346]

In this sense, the idea of the colonial trust represented an extension of liberalism[347] to the British colonies: the application to the colonies of Locke's conception of political power as a trust.[348] The reference to the well-being of the inhabitants of the mandate territories as a 'sacred trust' in Article 22 of the League Covenant echoes Locke's idea, as do the opening words of Article 73 of the UN Charter:

> Members of the United Nations which have or assume responsibilities for the administration of territories whose peoples have not yet attained a full measure of self-government recognize the principle that the interests of the inhabitants of these territories are paramount, and accept as a sacred trust the obligation to promote to the utmost, within the system of international peace and security established by the present Charter, the well-being of the inhabitants of these territories.

Postcolonial writers on international law[349] narrate the history of trusteeship differently, tending to view it as structuring the justification

---

[344] Hansard, *Parliamentary History* (1783), vol. XXIII, cols. 1316–7, quoted in Toussaint, *The Trusteeship System*, p. 6. See also Hall, *Mandates, Dependencies and Trusteeship*, pp. 92, 98.
[345] *The Writings and Speeches of Edmund Burke* (Little, Brown, 1901), vol. X, pp. 144–5, quoted in Toussaint, *The Trusteeship System*, pp. 6–7. See also Hall, *Mandates, Dependencies and Trusteeship*, pp. 33, 99.
[346] Hall, *Mandates, Dependencies and Trusteeship*, p. 99.
[347] Compare Mauritania's argument on *terra nullius* in *Western Sahara*, above at pp. 125–6.
[348] Toussaint, *The Trusteeship System*, p. 6.
[349] E.g. Anghie, '"The Heart of My Home"'; Anghie, 'Time Present and Time Past', 275–89; Grovogui, *Sovereigns, Quasi-Sovereigns, and Africans*. On postcolonial approaches to international law, see J. T. Gathii, 'International Law and Eurocentricity' (1998) 9 *European Journal of International Law* 184. Compare Algeria's argument on *terra nullius* in *Western Sahara*, above at pp. 121–3. For a Marxist critique, see J. J. A. Salmon, 'À propos de quelques techniques de l'idéologie juridique appliquée au droit international' in Amato, *Marxism, Democracy and the Rights of Peoples*, pp. 1014–25.

of colonialism from the time of Francisco de Vitoria in the sixteenth century, adaptable to the successive justifications of Christianity and civilization. For these authors, the 'sacred trust' did not well up from eighteenth-century European liberalism, but from early on dissimulated the combination of political and economic incentives and profoundly racist attitudes towards non-European peoples which drove colonialism.[350] In Toussaint's[351] mid-twentieth-century account, the political and economic incentives are disguised in Lord Lugard's enduring idea of the 'dual mandate': the administration of the colonies for the benefit of the native people and the benefit once of the colonial power, now of the world at large. However, it is the racial prejudice that I wish to pursue here.

As Toussaint points out,[352] Burke's 1783 speech anticipates that the trust will cease when it no longer serves its purpose. At the 1926 Imperial Conference, the British government officially recognized that British colonialism was a temporary status leading to self-government.[353] What Toussaint and his contemporaries make less of is the sociological premise informing the determination of when a colony was ready for self-government: the idea that colonial societies worked their way up an evolutionary ladder of development with the highest rung being European society, and that while they could not skip a rung, their progress up the ladder could be speeded by European assistance.[354]

---

[350] It should be noted that alongside the noble motives for the mandate system, Hall stresses that of politically expedient solutions to problems of the balance of power in frontier zones. Hall, *Mandates, Dependencies and Trusteeship*, p. 92.

[351] Toussaint, *The Trusteeship System*, pp. 11–14. See also Hall, *Mandates, Dependencies and Trusteeship*, pp. 33, 97, 105. Toussaint actually identifies two separate principles in this regard: colonial administration for the benefit of the world at large and international accountability. In the Covenant of the League of Nations, 28 June 1919, (1919) 112 BFSP 13, see Art. 22, fifth paragraph (Mandatory power to prevent 'the establishment of fortifications or military and naval bases and of military training of the natives for other than police purposes and the defence of territory' and to secure 'equal opportunities for the trade and commerce of other Members of the League') and Art. 22, seventh paragraph, ninth paragraph (Mandatory to report annually to the Council, which will be advised by a permanent Commission on mandates). In the UN Charter, see Arts. 73(c) (non-self-governing territories) and 76(a), (d) (trust territories) regarding benefit to the world at large and Chapters XI (non-self-governing territories) and XII–XIII (trust territories) regarding international accountability.

[352] Toussaint, *The Trusteeship System*, pp. 14–15.   [353] *Ibid.* p. 15.

[354] The ladder metaphor is used by Hall, *Mandates, Dependencies and Trusteeship*, p. 97 ('a ladder... up which primitive native tribes could climb steadily to the goal of a self-governing people') and by C. J. B. Hurst, *Great Britain and the Dominions. Lectures on the Harris Foundation 1927* (Chicago: University of Chicago Press, 1928), pp. 12–13 (describing the dominions' 'evolution from a position of dependence to one of

Perhaps nowhere was this assumption more obvious than in the institutional form given to trusteeship in the League system of mandate territories. In practice, mandate territories were colonies and territories detached from the defeated Germany and Turkey after World War I and administered, under mandate, by one or more of the victorious powers. Article 22 of the Covenant reads in part:

> To those colonies and territories which, as a consequence of the late war, have ceased to be under the sovereignty of the States which formerly governed them, and which are inhabited by peoples not yet able to stand by themselves under the strenuous conditions of the modern world, there should be applied the principle that the well-being and development of such peoples form a sacred trust of civilisation....
>
> The best method of giving practical effect to this principle is that the tutelage of such people should be entrusted to advanced nations who, by reason of their resources, their experience, or their geographical position, can best undertake this responsibility...
>
> The character of the mandate must differ according to the stage of development of the people, the geographical situation of the territory, its economic conditions and other similar circumstances.[355]

Under Article 22, the mandates were classified as A, B or C according to their stage of development.[356] The A mandates, which included Iraq, Syria and Lebanon, were described as those communities that had 'reached a stage of development where their existence as independent nations can be provisionally recognised subject to the rendering of administrative advice and assistance by a Mandatory until such time as they are able to stand alone'.[357] Whereas the destiny of the A mandates was full independence, the goal for the B mandates was not stated.[358] The C mandates, considered the least likely to be able to stand alone under 'the strenuous conditions of the modern world', were slated for assimilation into the territory of the mandatory state. In the words of Article 22, the C mandates, among which were South West Africa and a number of South Pacific islands, could 'be best administered under the laws of the Mandatory as integral portions of its territory'.[359]

---

freedom from control. These great communities have all the time been climbing a ladder').

[355] LN Covenant, Art. 22.
[356] Q. Wright, *Mandates under the League of Nations* (Chicago: University of Chicago Press, 1930), p. 47.
[357] LN Covenant, Art. 22, fourth paragraph.   [358] *Ibid.*, Art. 22, fifth paragraph.
[359] *Ibid.*, Art. 22, sixth paragraph.

This distinction between mature and immature societies[360] differentiated the concept of trusteeship applied to colonies from the liberal idea that those who possessed political power had a duty to exercise it for the benefit of those subjected to it. The relationship between mandatory power and mandate territory was compared to the guardianship of a minor, with the mandate territory to be educated for self-government: 'a community with a corporate personality – adolescent perhaps, unprepared for immediate independence but capable of organic development... the trust undertaken by the imperial power was... for the development of a ward'.[361] To trusteeship thus was added tutelage. Norman Bentwich, for example, compounded the Anglo-American concept of the trust – 'c'est-à-dire, biens tenus par une personne pour le bénéfice d'une autre dans un certain but, et avec le devoir de rendre compte de la façon dont elle remplit sa charge à un tribunal' ('that is to say, goods held by one person for the benefit of another for a certain purpose and with the duty to account to a tribunal for the way in which he fulfils the charge')[362] – with the civil law concept of the *tutelle* of a minor.[363]

Analysing the 'sacred trust' embodied in the League of Nations mandate system, Judge McNair wrote in the 1950 advisory opinion of the International Court of Justice in *International Status of South-West Africa*:

> Nearly every legal system possesses some institution whereby the property (and sometimes the persons) of those who are not *sui juris*, such as a minor or a lunatic, can be entrusted to some responsible person such as a trustee or *tuteur* or *curateur*. The Anglo-American trust serves this purpose, and another purpose even more closely akin to the Mandates System, namely, the vesting of property in trustees, and its management by them in order that the public or some class of the public may derive benefit or that some public purpose may be served. The trust has frequently been used to protect the weak and the dependent.[364]

In addition to the liberal aim of trusteeship, the chapters of the UN Charter on non-self-governing (Chapter XI) and trust territories (Chapters XII and XIII) also reflect the cultural paternalism of this guardianship or tutelage.[365] In keeping with their role as guardian or tutor,

---

[360] The language of maturity is used, for example, by N. Bentwich, 'Le Système des Mandats' (1929-IV) 29 Hague Recueil 115 at 129–30.
[361] Wright, *Mandates Under the League of Nations*, p. 11.
[362] (Translation mine) Bentwich, 'Le Système des Mandats', 125. [363] *Ibid.*, 130.
[364] *International Status of South-West Africa*, Advisory Opinion, ICJ Reports 1950, p. 128 at p. 149 (Separate Opinion of Judge McNair).
[365] While both non-self-governing and trust territories are treated conceptually as a

states administering non-self-governing territories were responsible for the protection and education of the people.[366] Whereas the Charter requires administering states to develop self-government,[367] it makes no mention of a right of self-determination of peoples.

In contrast, the later Declaration on the Independence of Colonial Peoples (GA Resolution 1514), the international legal manifesto of decolonization, unequivocally gives all colonial peoples the right of self-determination; that is, the right to determine their political status freely and to pursue their economic, social and cultural development freely. Not only does every colonial people have the choice of independence, the choice is theirs immediately. Sweeping aside the discourse of stages of development, the Declaration states: 'inadequacy of political, economic, social or educational preparedness should never serve as a pretext for delaying independence'.[368] In a complete rejection of trusteeship and its racial underpinnings of tutelage, it insists that

> Immediate steps shall be taken, in Trust and Non-Self-Governing Territories or all other territories which have not yet attained independence, to transfer all powers to the peoples of those territories, without any conditions or reservations, in accordance with their freely expressed will and desire, without any distinction as to race, creed or colour, in order to enable them to enjoy complete independence and freedom.[369]

In its 1971 advisory opinion on *Namibia*, the International Court of Justice concluded that developments in international law, culminating in the Declaration on the Independence of Colonial Peoples, had left little doubt that 'the ultimate objective of the sacred trust was the self-determination and independence of the peoples concerned'.[370]

The UN Charter and the Declaration on the Independence of Colonial Peoples thus represent two different approaches to decolonization. When drafted, the UN Charter envisaged self-government as the eventual outcome of the sacred trust. The trust would protect a colonial people while preparing them politically, economically, socially and educationally for self-government. Based on the equality of peoples, the

---

'sacred trust', institutionally they are governed by different systems under the UN Charter. As East Timor is a non-self-governing territory, the discussion here will focus on non-self-governing territories. On trust territories, see Chapter 7 below.

[366] UN Charter, Art. 73(a).   [367] *Ibid.*, Art. 73(b).
[368] Declaration on the Granting of Independence to Colonial Countries and Peoples, GA Res. 1514 (XV) (1960), para. 3.
[369] *Ibid.*, para. 5.
[370] *Namibia (South West Africa)*, Advisory Opinion, ICJ Reports 1971, p. 16 at p. 31.

Declaration and the resolutions that came after it[371] instead demanded the immediate exercise of self-determination, which was assumed to result in independence.

The quandary in *East Timor* was therefore as follows. The Declaration on the Independence of Colonial Peoples and later the Declaration on Friendly Relations, recognized by the International Court of Justice in *Western Sahara* as the source of the right of self-determination in international law,[372] made no room for the idea of trusteeship. They anticipated the immediate exercise of the right of self-determination of peoples. How, especially in a case such as *East Timor*, where the exercise of self-determination was seemingly indefinitely delayed, should the court interpret the ongoing relationship between the administering power and the people of the non-self-governing territory? In particular, did the traditional understanding of the administering power as the better-knowing trustee still govern or had it been replaced by some conception of the administering power as the agent of the people?

The difference between trustee and agent in a similar legal context is captured by the Supreme Court of Canada's discussion in *Guerin v. The Queen*[373] of the fiduciary relationship in Canadian law between aboriginal peoples and the federal government. In *Guerin*, the Musqueam Indian Band had aboriginal title to four hundred acres of land in the City of Vancouver. Under Canadian law, aboriginal title to land was alienable only to the Crown. As a result, any sale or lease to a third party could not take place directly, but had to be carried out by surrender to the Crown, whereupon the Crown acted on the aboriginal people's behalf. The court in *Guerin* found that the Crown's lease of part of the Musqueam land for a golf course violated the Crown's fiduciary duty to the band because Crown officials had promised to lease the land on certain specified terms and then, after surrender, had obtained a lease on different and much less valuable terms. The court described the relationship between the Crown and aboriginal peoples as combining the characteristics of trust and agency:

---

[371] See the principle of self-determination in the Declaration on Principles of International Law Concerning Friendly Relations and Cooperation Among States in Accordance with the Charter of the United Nations, GA Res. 2625 (XXV) (1970), first, second and fourth paragraphs.
[372] See *Western Sahara*, pp. 32–3.
[373] *Guerin v. The Queen*, [1984] 2 SCR 335. For an overview of the fiduciary obligation owed to indigenous peoples in other national legal systems, see D. Pharand, 'Canada's Fiduciary Obligation Under General Principles of Law Recognized in National Legal Systems' in Anaya, Falk and Pharand, *Canada's Fiduciary Obligation*, pp. 116–31.

[While the Crown's fiduciary obligation to the Indians is not technically a trust,] the obligation is trust-like in character. As would be the case with a *trust*, the Crown must hold surrendered land *for the use and benefit of* the surrendering Band... The fiduciary relationship between the Crown and the Indians also bears a certain resemblance to *agency*, since the obligation can be characterized as a duty to act *on behalf of* the Indian Bands who have surrendered lands, by negotiating for the sale or lease of the land to third parties.[374]

The Crown's breach of duty in *Guerin* was therefore by analogy to both trust and agency: it lay both in the Crown's failure to obtain the best possible terms and in its acting without the band's authorization.

Arguments and opinions in East Timor

Having not sought the consent of the people of East Timor before bringing the case,[375] Portugal appealed to the traditional role of the administering power as trustee and additionally to its role as representative of the East Timorese people by virtue of its singular position as administering power.[376] To the first, Australia responded that an administering power no longer in control of a non-self-governing territory did not have automatic standing as trustee for the territory's inhabitants.[377] Capitalizing on Portugal's lack of demonstrated support from the East Timorese people, Australia argued as to the second that Portugal needed to be the people's chosen and authorized representative in the case.[378] In any event, according to Australia, the appropriate dispute-resolution process was not adjudication, which, at best, allowed the people of East Timor to participate only indirectly, but a process of consultation and negotiation which included them directly as one of the parties.[379]

Portugal's claim that it had standing as trustee rested on its modern reinterpretation of the 'sacred trust'. This reinterpretation incorporated the paradigm shift from Charter Article 73 to the right of

---

[374] (Emphasis mine), *Guerin*, 386–7.
[375] *East Timor*, p. 135 (Separate Opinion of Judge Vereshchetin).
[376] Réplique du Gouvernement de la République Portugaise, *East Timor*, pt. II, c. 8, pp. 237–48, paras. 8.01–8.17.
[377] Rejoinder of the Government of Australia, *East Timor*, pt. I, c. 2, s. I, pp. 60–6, paras. 125–44. This response by Australia is not pursued here because the interest of the chapter is in Portugal's duties as the administering power to the people of East Timor, as distinct from its rights vis-à-vis other states.
[378] *Ibid.*, pt. I, c. 2, s. II, pp. 66–8, paras. 145–51.
[379] Counter-Memorial of the Government of Australia, *East Timor*, pt. II, c. 3, s. II, pp. 128–35, paras. 287–305.

self-determination in the Declaration on the Independence of Colonial Peoples and subsequent resolutions.[380] On Portugal's account of the development of self-determination in international law, the Declaration was a watershed.[381] It replaced 'the international control of management by the administering power' envisaged by Article 73 with 'the pure and simple abolition of colonial administration'.[382] In Eduardo Jiménez de Aréchaga's phrase, quoted by Portugal, the Declaration recognized that 'good government is no substitute for self-government'.[383]

By reading the right of self-determination of peoples into Article 73, Portugal actualized[384] the interpretation of the 'sacred trust': the principle of trusteeship applied, but only transitionally, whereas the principle of tutelage was rejected outright.[385] As trustee, Portugal had the duty to act in the interests of the East Timorese people and to promote their well-being.[386] But this duty no longer involved the political, economic and social remaking of the people in the European image. Instead, Portugal had to expedite the exercise of self-determination by the people and, in the interim, preserve the people's resources and sovereignty over their resources.[387]

---

[380] Mémoire du Gouvernement de la République Portugaise, *East Timor*, pt. II, c. IV–V, pp. 79–160, paras. 4.01–5.60.

[381] *Ibid.*, pt. II, c. IV, s. 1(B)(1)(a), pp. 86–92, paras. 4.14–4.23.

[382] *Ibid.*, pt. II, c. IV, s. 1(B)(1)(a), p. 86, para. 4.14 at p. 88, para. 4.18.

[383] *Ibid.*, quoting E. Jiménez de Aréchaga, 'International Law in the Last Third of a Century' (1978-I) 159 Hague Recueil 1 at 103.

[384] The French expression used by Portugal is 'interprétation actualiste'. *Ibid.*, pt. II, c. V, s. 2(B), p. 151, para. 5.46 at p. 153, para. 5. 48. Older provisions of international law are actualized or contemporized by reading in contemporary values. Michael Reisman identifies the court's remarks on the need for actualization as a method of interpretation (he gives as an example *South West Africa – Voting Procedure*, Advisory Opinion, ICJ Reports 1955, p. 67 at p. 77) as one of the procedural steps that the court could take to respond to the anachronistic treatment of indigenous peoples' rights. W. M. Reisman, 'Protecting Indigenous Rights in International Adjudication' (1995) 89 *American Journal of International Law* 350 at 360.

[385] Mémoire Portugais, pt. II, c. V, s. 1(B), p. 128, para. 5.07 at pp. 141–6, paras. 5.29–5.38.

[386] *Ibid.*, pt. II, c. V, s. 1(A), pp. 125–8, paras. 5.01–5.06 ('La qualification de la fonction juridique de la puissance administrante comme "sacred trust"... s'inspire fondamentalement de la conception anglo-saxonne de "trust"' at pp. 127–8, para. 5.05); pt. II, c. V, s. 2(A), p. 148, para. 5.41 ('Les idées de primauté des intérêts des habitants du territoire et de "mission sacrée" signifient que les pouvoirs d'administration sont des pouvoirs fonctionnels, des pouvoirs qui existent comme instrument juridique de satisfaction d'un devoir de gestion d'intérêts étrangers à leur titulaire' at pp. 149–50, para. 5.42).

[387] *Ibid.*, pt. II, c. V, s. 2(B), pp. 151–4, paras. 5.46–5.49; Réplique Portugaise, pt. II, c. VIII, s. 2, p. 238, para. 8.03 at p. 239.

Thus, working from the idea that all peoples are equal and all have the same right to choose their place in the world, Portugal reinterpreted the administering power's duty as to give the people that choice in short order and not to undermine it through political, economic and social engineering. No matter how narrowly this duty is defined, however, it would still seem to be the administering power that decided how best to carry it out. Pending the exercise of self-determination, the people had no right to be consulted by the administering power. In a case before the International Court of Justice, such as *East Timor*, the administering power would speak for the people of a non-self-governing territory, but the people themselves would not speak through it.

In contrast, Portugal's other basis for standing, that as the administering power of East Timor it represented the people of the territory, could be seen as requiring the consent of the people. Instead of treating the non-self-governing status of East Timor as a relic of colonialism, this conception of Portugal's standing presented East Timor as one of those geopolitical oddities where a territorially-based non-state entity had to rely on a particular state, from which it was separate and distinct, to represent it internationally.[388] For example, Portugal maintained that the relationship of Portugal to East Timor was analogous to that of the United Kingdom to the Island of Jersey in the *Minquiers and Ecrehos* case. Jersey and the other Channel Islands belonged to the British Crown, but were not part of the United Kingdom. Historically, they were not colonies. They had a unique status and enjoyed extensive autonomy founded on ancient constitutional conventions. In *Minquiers and Ecrehos*, the disputed groups of small islands and rocks were considered by the UK government to be dependencies of Jersey. In this sense, the United Kingdom in the case represented a separate and distinct political entity that it was uniquely placed to represent.[389] Although Portugal did not elaborate on what was involved in representation, it would arguably require Portugal to consult, if not obtain the consent of, the people of East Timor to the proceedings against Australia. If the meaning of representation was taken this far, then a colonial people would be able to communicate its wishes and views to the court through the administering power.

[388] Mémoire Portugais, pt. II, c. IV, s. 1(C)(I)(b), p. 108, para. 4.51 at pp. 111–12, para. 4.55; Réplique Portugaise, pt. II, c. 8, s. 3, p. 243, para. 8.09 at pp. 243–6, paras. 8.09–8.13.
[389] Réplique Portugaise, pt. II, c. 8, s. 2, p. 238, para. 8.03 at pp. 241–2, para. 8.06; *ibid.*, pt. II, c. 8, s. 3, p. 243, para. 8.09 at p. 246, para. 8.13.

Australia took the idea of representation further, arguing that it had to involve choice of representative as well as consent to the course of action. Australia pointed to evidence that when Portugal withdrew from East Timor in 1975, none of the conflicting local political forces wanted to depend on Portugal as the continuing administering power; one proclaimed independence, while another proclaimed integration with Indonesia.[390] Even though there was, as Portugal's evidence indicated,[391] some East Timorese support for Portugal and the Portuguese case against Australia, it did not amount to a meaningful choice of Portugal as representative. Moreover, Australia contended that the appropriate process for resolving the East Timor dispute was,[392] and was seen by representatives of the East Timorese people to be,[393] direct consultation and negotiation between the people of East Timor, Portugal and Indonesia under the auspices of the United Nations.

In his separate opinion, Judge Vereshchetin began with the fact that although Portugal, the applicant state in *East Timor*, had acted in the name of the people of East Timor, it had not sought their consent before filing the application. He recalled that the court's finding of inadmissibility in *East Timor* was based on Indonesia's right not to be subjected to the court's jurisdiction without its consent.[394] Although there was no similar reference to the people of East Timor in the court's judgment, wrote Judge Vereshchetin, it would be a mistake to conclude that 'the people, whose right to self-determination lies at the core of the whole case, have no role to play in the proceedings'.[395]

While Judge Vereshchetin equated the people of East Timor with the state of Indonesia as necessary third parties, he acknowledged that the ICJ Statute does not give peoples the same access as states to the court.[396] As already discussed, the Statute allows only states to be parties in cases before the court. Without disturbing this limit on standing, Judge

---

[390] Australian Counter-Memorial, pt. II, c. 2, s. II(A), pp. 111–12, para. 242; Australian Rejoinder, pt. I, c. 2, s. II, p. 66, para. 145 at p. 67, paras. 148–9.
[391] Mémoire Portugais, c. I, s. 2(H), pp. 46–8, paras. 1.67–1.72; Réplique Portugaise, Preliminary Part, c. III, s. 3, pp. 36–9, paras. 3.13–3.18.
[392] Note 379 above.
[393] Australian Rejoinder, pt. I, c. 2, s. II, p. 66, para. 145 at p. 68, para. 150.
[394] Technically, the court applied the so-called *Monetary Gold* principle, which interprets the requirement of consent to mean that the court has no jurisdiction where the legal interests of a third state, such as Indonesia, form the very subject-matter of the decision. *Monetary Gold Removed From Rome in 1943 (Italy v. France, United Kingdom and United States)*, ICJ Reports 1954, p. 19.
[395] *East Timor*, p. 135 (Separate Opinion of Judge Vereshchetin). [396] *Ibid.*

Vereshchetin found that Portugal had a 'duty to consult the leaders or representatives of the people before submitting the case to the Court on its behalf'.[397]

In an international order traditionally centred on states, Judge Vereshchetin's starting assumption that peoples could normatively be third parties on a par with states was, by itself, remarkable and indicative of how different international law might look from the perspective of the right of self-determination of peoples.[398] In the context of a state-centred court, his conclusion that a state bringing a case as the administering power of a non-self-governing territory had the duty to consult the people of the territory is similarly significant and follows similarly from viewing the 'sacred trust' through the lens of self-determination.

Judge Vereshchetin's method of interpretation resembled Portugal's in that he read the right of self-determination developed in the Declaration on the Independence of Colonial Peoples into the 'sacred trust' in Article 73 of the Charter.

The United Nations Charter, having been adopted at the very outset of the process of decolonization, could not explicitly impose on the administering Power the obligation to consult the people of a non-self-governing territory when the matter at issue directly concerned that people. This does not mean, however, that such a duty has no place at all in international law at the present stage of its development and in the contemporary setting of the decolonization process, after the adoption of the Declaration on the Granting of Independence to Colonial Countries and Peoples (General Assembly resolution 1514 (XV)).[399]

The difference between Judge Vereshchetin's interpretation and Portugal's interpretation was that Portugal projected only the urgency and the imperativeness of self-determination, whereas Judge Vereshchetin projected the actual meaning. Portugal abbreviated and neutralized the idea of trusteeship in order to guarantee self-determination. Judge Vereshchetin instead infused trusteeship with the essence of self-determination as expressed by the court in *Western Sahara*: 'the need to pay regard to the freely expressed will of peoples'.[400] For him, all

---

[397] *Ibid.*, p. 137.
[398] Compare Klein, 'Multilateral Disputes' (using Antonio Cassese's state-centric 'Westphalian' and diversified 'UN Charter' models of international law to analyse *East Timor*).
[399] *East Timor*, p. 138 (Separate Opinion of Judge Vereshchetin).
[400] *Western Sahara*, p. 33, discussed by Judge Vereshchetin at *East Timor*, pp. 137–8. While *Western Sahara* gives exceptions to the requirement of consultation, Judge Vereshchetin found that none justified Portugal's failure to consult.

administering powers had a duty of consultation, although Portugal, as an administering power that had not been in effective control of the territory for many years, had an even more compelling duty to ascertain and take into account the wishes of the people.[401]

Like the Canadian Supreme Court's interpretation of the fiduciary relationship between aboriginal peoples and the Crown in *Guerin*, Judge Vereshchetin thus gave a new structure to the 'sacred trust' such that the features of the trust, once tied to the indignity of tutelage, were combined with the features of agency. He thereby created the possibility of a colonial people's indirect participation before the court in a case concerning their right of self-determination.[402] The deeper point, which ties into the other cases discussed in this chapter, is the relationship of identity to participation. It was the rejection of international law's image of the child-like native that opened the door to a more participatory structure for the trust. So long as colonial peoples were imagined as backward, it would have been unthinkable for them to be consulted, rather than guided, by the administering power. The duty to consult was only made possible by the recognition of their equality in the right of self-determination.

As Christine Chinkin points out, however, Judge Vereshchetin's conclusion that the *East Timor* case was inadmissible because Portugal did not consult the East Timorese people was 'a double-edged sword for the East Timorese: while it recognises the inappropriateness of proceedings that fail to accord a voice to those most immediately concerned, the outcome is to deny judicial consideration of their situation'.[403] Sensitive to this Hobson's choice, the two dissenting judges, Judge Weeramantry and Judge *ad hoc* Skubiszewski, found the case admissible. Applying the pure principle of trusteeship, Judge Weeramantry found that Portugal's failure to consult the East Timorese people was not a bar to admissibility:

the power given by the Charter under Chapter XI is clearly the power of a trustee. The power derives expressly from the concept of 'a sacred trust', thus

---

[401] *East Timor*, pp. 135–6 (Separate Opinion of Judge Vereshchetin).

[402] This is not to underestimate the resulting problems of agency. Interestingly, Judge Vereshchetin's language is broad enough to suggest that the court itself might have a duty to verify the wishes and views of the people. In addition to his reference to the need for the court to ascertain and take into account the people's wishes, his reference to 'the necessity for the Court to check its [the administering power's] claims by reference to the existing evidence of the will of the people concerned' may contemplate available evidence beyond that presented by the parties. *Ibid.*

[403] Chinkin, 'The East Timor Case', 722.

underlining its fiduciary character. The very concept of trusteeship carries with it the power of representation, whether one looks at the common law concept of trusteeship or the civil law concept of *tutela*. A trustee, once appointed, always carries out his or her duties under supervision, but is not required to seek afresh the right of representation each time it is to be exercised, for that is part and parcel of the concept of trusteeship itself.[404]

But it is difficult to rid the principle of trusteeship of its association with tutelage; that is, to dignify its structure of participation by ignoring the assumptions about identity that traditionally informed it. If Portugal carried out its duties as trustee under supervision, it was under UN and not East Timorese supervision because colonial peoples were not considered ready to make decisions about their own lives. Nor, on the facts of *East Timor*, did Portugal even have the credibility as a representative that might derive from being on the ground and being aware of popular opinion.

To outweigh Australia's objections to jurisdiction and admissibility, Judge Weeramantry invoked 'the high idealism which is the essential spirit of the Charter – an idealism which spoke in terms of a "sacred trust" lying upon the Powers assuming responsibilities for their administration, an idealism which stipulated that the interests of their inhabitants were paramount'.[405] However, a return to the Charter ideals is also a return to the unreconstructed notions of trusteeship, under which a European administering power decided what was in the best interests of a colonial people; and of tutelage, which assumed that the colonial people was too backward to do so.[406]

Presumably to avoid this stereotype, Judge Weeramantry strove to present the purpose of the 'sacred trust' as procedural and the administering power's duties under the trust as conservationist. He identified the underlying philosophy of the UN Charter's system of non-self-governing territories as to avoid leaving the people of these territories defenceless and voiceless in a world order which had not yet accorded them an independent status.[407] The administering power was their voice – indeed, their only voice[408] – in the international community. To deprive them of it, for whatever reason, would be to silence them altogether and thereby defeat the very purpose of the Charter's institutional design.

---

[404] *East Timor*, p. 189 (Dissenting Opinion of Judge Weeramantry).   [405] *Ibid.*, p. 179.
[406] Judge Weeramantry uses the language of trusteeship and tutelage at *ibid.*, pp. 192, 195, 201.
[407] *Ibid.*, p. 179.   [408] *Ibid.*, p. 181.

Judge Weeramantry wrote: 'The deep concern for their welfare, which is a primary object of Chapter XI of the Charter, and the 'sacred trust' notion which is its highest conceptual expression, would then be reduced to futility; and the protective structure, so carefully built upon these concepts, would disintegrate'.[409] The legacy of cultural paternalism in the 'sacred trust' was also downplayed by Judge Weeramantry's portrayal, like Portugal's, of the administering power as a caretaker, its duty being to safeguard the people's sovereignty, including their economic sovereignty, until they freely exercise their right of self-determination.[410]

For Judge Weeramantry, a new account of the trust and the interests it protects, including participation, thus followed from his implicit rejection of international law's traditional picture of the child-like native, whereas what followed from this for Judge Vereshchetin was a new structure of participation for the trust. Judge *ad hoc* Skubiszewski's negotiation of the relationship between identity and participation is somewhat closer to that of Judge Vereshchetin. Against the rules on jurisdiction and admissibility, Judge *ad hoc* Skubiszewski weighed not the Charter ideal of the 'sacred trust', but the more general demands of justice.[411] Whereas Judge Weeramantry's reliance on the Charter's conception of trusteeship established non-consultation as the rule, Judge *ad hoc* Skubiszewski was able to present consultation as the rule[412] and the situation in *East Timor* as an exception. Judge *ad hoc* Skubiszewski characterized *East Timor* as exceptional because the interests of the East Timorese people which Portugal sought to protect in the case were so self-evident as to make consultation of them unnecessary.

---

[409] *Ibid.*, p. 180. See also *ibid.*, p. 192 (stating that Portugal's poor colonial record was irrelevant because a refusal to recognize Portugal's power to protect the East Timorese people, based on its past performance, would leave the people defenceless).

[410] *Ibid.*, p. 184. See also *ibid.*, p. 188 ('the duty of an administering Power to conserve the interests of the people of the territory'). Of course, even the most conservative decision regarding the use of resources involves choices about what to conserve and how, making the case for consultation all the more compelling.

[411] *Ibid.*, pp. 237–8 (Dissenting Opinion of Judge *ad hoc* Skubiszewski).

[412] *Ibid.*, pp. 275, 277. It is possible to distinguish between the East Timorese people's role in bringing the case and the role that they should have played in the negotiation of the Timor Gap Treaty. Although Judge Weeramantry acknowledges no role for the East Timorese people in the context of the case, he did refer in the context of Australia's negotiation of the treaty to the need to consult the administering power *or the people*. *Ibid.*, pp. 199, 222 (Dissenting Opinion of Judge Weeramantry).

During the proceedings, both Parties invoked the interests of the East Timorese people, but they presented us with little or no evidence of what the actual wishes of that people were. Be this as it may, I think that the Court can base itself on certain elementary assumptions: the interests of the people are enhanced when recourse is made to peaceful mechanisms, not to military intervention; when there is free choice, not incorporation into another State brought about essentially by the use of force; when the active participation of the people is guaranteed, in contradistinction to arrangements arrived at by some States alone with the exclusion of the people and/or the United Nations Member who accepted 'the sacred trust' under Chapter XI of the Charter.[413]

Like *Western Sahara* and the EC Arbitration Commission's *Opinion No. 2* on Yugoslavia, the opinions of Judge Vereshchetin, Judge Weeramantry and Judge *ad hoc* Skubiszewski in *East Timor* have proven to be not just about the formula for self-determination, but about judges' efforts to interpret the international law of self-determination impartially such that their judgment would be valid across cultures. In each of the cases, judges were confronted with the partial perspective of international law: its European norm of sovereignty and legality, its individualistic viewpoint, its ladder of development with Europe at the top, and so on. In each of the cases, traditional international law had rendered invisible, insignificant or inferior some dimension of identity important to the marginalized communities involved. Similarly, in each judgment, we find the response of judges in the creative use of some intermediate legal construct – between sovereignty and nothingness – to capture this dimension of identity and thereby help to equalize cultures in international law. In *Western Sahara*, the constructs are *terra nullius*, legal ties and legal entity; in *Opinion No. 2*, nationality; in *East Timor*, the 'sacred trust'. It is this apparent aspiration to represent identity in a way that might resonate with those represented that unites *East Timor* with *Western Sahara* and the Yugoslavia opinion. The particular approach to interpretation is not the same in the judgments, nor is the particular aspect of identity recognized, but the concern with a better picture of identity runs through all three.

In *Western Sahara* and *East Timor*, interpretation is also infused with a concern to equalize cultures through participation, whether in the general development of international law or in the meaning of specific international law concepts. Reliance on schools of thought beyond

---

[413] *Ibid.*, p. 240 (Dissenting Opinion of Judge *ad hoc* Skubiszewski).

Europe as a source of international law in the past, the use of UN General Assembly resolutions as a present source, the doctrine of intertemporal law and the finding that a duty to consult is part of the 'sacred trust' are all examples. Thus what emerges from the judgments discussed in this chapter is a pattern of practices aimed at reducing inequities of contribution as well as depiction.

5 Developing texts

The draft declaration[1] on the rights of indigenous peoples[2] completed by

[1] E.-I. A. Daes, Report of the Working Group on Indigenous Populations on its Eleventh Session, UN Doc. E/CN.4/Sub.2/1993/29 (1993), Annex I. The draft declaration was adopted by the UN Sub-Commission on Prevention of Discrimination and Protection of Minorities (since retitled the Sub-Commission on the Promotion and Protection of Human Rights) by resolution 1994/45. This copy is reproduced at (1995) 34 ILM 541.

[2] The definition of 'indigenous' and the debate over 'populations' versus 'peoples' are discussed below.

For a sampling of the growing literature on indigenous peoples in international law, see P. Aikio and M. Scheinin (eds.), *Operationalizing the Right of Indigenous Peoples to Self-Determination* (Turku/Åbo: Institute for Human Rights, Åbo Akademi University, 2000); S. J. Anaya, *Indigenous Peoples in International Law* (New York: Oxford, 1996); S. J. Anaya, R. Falk and D. Pharand, *Canada's Fiduciary Obligation to Aboriginal Peoples in the Context of Accession to Sovereignty by Quebec* (Papers prepared as part of the Research Program of the Royal Commission on Aboriginal Peoples) (Minister of Supply and Services Canada, 1995); R. L. Barsh, 'Indigenous Peoples in the 1990s: From Object to Subject of International Law?' (1994) 7 *Harvard Human Rights Journal* 33; I. Brownlie, *Treaties and Indigenous Peoples. The Robb Lectures 1991* (Oxford: Clarendon Press, 1992); E. Gayim and K. Myntti (eds.), *Indigenous and Tribal Peoples' Rights – 1993 and After* (Juridica Lapponica No. 11) (Rovaniemi, Finland: Northern Institute for Environmental and Minority Law, 1995); International Centre for Human Rights and Democratic Development, *People or Peoples; Equality, Autonomy and Self-Determination: The Issues at Stake of the International Decade of the World's Indigenous People* (Essays on Human Rights and Democratic Development, Paper No. 5) (Montreal, 1996); B. Kingsbury, ' "Indigenous Peoples" in International Law: A Constructivist Approach to the Asian Controversy' (1998) 92 *American Journal of International Law* 414; W. Kymlicka, 'Theorizing Indigenous Rights' (1999) 49 *University of Toronto Law Journal* 281; M. C. Lâm, *At the Edge of the State: Indigenous Peoples and Self-Determination* (Ardsley, N.Y.: Transnational Publishers, 2000); D. McGoldrick, 'Canadian Indians, Cultural Rights and the Human Rights Committee' (1991) 40 *International and Comparative Law Quarterly* 658; S. Pritchard and C. Heindow-Dolman, 'Indigenous Peoples and International Law: A Critical Overview' (1998) 3 *Australian Indigenous Law Reporter* 473; D. Sanders, 'Self-Determination and Indigenous Peoples' in C. Tomuschat (ed.), *Modern Law of Self-Determination* (Dordrecht: Martinus Nijhoff, 1993), pp. 55–81; C. Scott, 'Indigenous Self-Determination and Decolonization of the International Imagination:

the UN Working Group on Indigenous Populations[3] in 1993 has been described by Robert Williams, Jr. as 'one of the most important encounters occurring on the frontiers of international human rights law'.[4] For Williams and other indigenous commentators, its importance is procedural as well as substantive. The draft is portrayed as responding significantly to the stories told by indigenous peoples about their place in the world and to their arguments about the human rights that must be recognized for them to preserve this place.[5] But Mary Ellen Turpel describes the draft as significant, first and foremost, for the remarkable 'power-sharing of the pen' between the human rights experts who comprised the Working Group and the indigenous peoples and state representatives who took part in its work.[6]

A Plea' (1996) 18 *Human Rights Quarterly* 814; P. Thornberry, *International Law and the Rights of Minorities* (Oxford: Clarendon Press, 1991), pp. 331–82; M. E. Turpel, 'Indigenous Peoples' Rights of Political Participation and Self-Determination: Recent International Legal Developments and the Continuing Struggle for Recognition' (1992) 25 *Cornell International Law Journal* 579; S. H. Venne, *Our Elders Understand Our Rights: Evolving International Law Regarding Indigenous Peoples* (Penticton, B.C.: Theytus Books, 1998); R. A. Williams, Jr., 'The Rights and Status of Indigenous Peoples under International Law During the Classical Era Treaty Period (1600–1840)' (1990) 5 *Law and Anthropology. Internationales Jahrbuch für Rechtsanthropologie* 237; Symposium: Contemporary Perspectives on Self-Determination and Indigenous Peoples' Rights (1993) 3:1 *Transnational Law and Contemporary Problems*.

[3] Although formally known as the Working Group on Indigenous Populations, it is often referred to as the Working Group on Indigenous Peoples.

[4] R. A. Williams, Jr., 'Encounters on the Frontiers of International Human Rights Law: Redefining the Terms of Indigenous Peoples' Survival in the World' [1990] *Duke Law Journal* 660 at 700.

[5] E.g. R. Kuptana, 'The Human Rights of Peoples' (Canadian Bar Association Conference on Aboriginal Peoples in the Canadian Constitutional Context: Application of International Law Standards and Comparative Law Models, Montreal, 28–29 April 1995); D. Sambo, 'Indigenous Peoples and International Standard-Setting Processes: Are State Governments Listening?' (1993) 3 *Transnational Law and Contemporary Problems* 13.

[6] M. E. Turpel, 'Draft Declaration on the Rights of Indigenous Peoples – Commentary' [1994] 1 *Canadian Native Law Reporter* 50 at 50.

On the early efforts of indigenous peoples within the United Nations system, see R. Coulter, 'Les Indiens sur la scène internationale. Les premiers contacts avec l'Organisation des Nations unies (1974–1983)' in *Destins croisés: Cinq siècles de rencontres avec les Amérindiens* (Paris: Albin Michel/UNESCO, 1992), pp. 333–48; D. Sanders, 'Indigenous Peoples at the United Nations: An Overview' [1996] 2 *Canadian Native Law Reporter* 20; F. Wilmer, *The Indigenous Voice in World Politics: Since Time Immemorial* (Newbury Park, Calif.: Sage Publications, 1993). Indigenous peoples have been involved in the interpretation of the International Covenant on Civil and Political Rights, New York, 16 December 1966, in force 23 March 1976, 999 UNTS 171 and International Covenant on Economic, Social and Cultural Rights, New York, 16 December 1966, in force 3 January 1976, 993 UNTS 3 through the informal

The participation of indigenous peoples themselves in the articulation of their rights in international law, including their right of self-determination, differentiates this interpretive forum from the international courts and tribunals in the previous chapter. The UN Working Group integrated indigenous participation into both its credo and its methods.[7] The number of participants in the 1993 session of the Working Group, including observer governments, UN organizations, indigenous nations, organizations and communities, non-governmental organizations, individual experts and scholars, totalled over six hundred.[8] In addition to the nine indigenous NGOs having consultative status with the UN Economic and Social Council,[9] more than one hundred indigenous nations and organizations were represented at the session.[10]

These indigenous participants were outsiders to the institutional system of states as well as to the normative wellspring of international law. And with their participation, this chapter shows, came their challenges to states' and international organizations' *ideas* of their participation. As *East Timor* illustrated, the presence or, in that case, the absence of a group does not speak for itself. It is evaluated against some idea of participation. Judge Vereshchetin found the absence of the East Timorese people and the lack of evidence of their wishes unacceptable because he viewed the structure of participation as having become a hybrid of trust and agency. Judge Weeramantry considered it normal because he accepted the trust structure, although not its traditional implication

submission of comments on the periodic reports required of their state (see e.g. T. Moses, 'The Right of Self-Determination and its Significance to the Survival of Indigenous Peoples' in Aikio and Scheinin, *Operationalizing the Right of Indigenous Peoples to Self-Determination*, pp. 155–77 at pp. 171–6; M. Scheinin, 'The Right to Self-Determination under the Covenant on Civil and Political Rights' in *ibid.*, pp. 179–99 at pp. 191–2) and through the bringing of individual communications under the Optional Protocol to the International Covenant on Civil and Political Rights, New York, 16 December 1966, in force 23 March 1976, 999 UNTS 171.

It should be noted that indigenous groups and organizations have also held their own international conferences, meetings and consultations. This chapter will make reference to some of the resulting texts. See also Anaya, *Indigenous Peoples in International Law*, at pp. 185–91.

[7] See S. J. Anaya, 'Canada's Fiduciary Obligations Toward Indigenous Peoples in Quebec under International Law in General' in Anaya, Falk and Pharand, *Canada's Fiduciary Obligation*, pp. 9–40 at pp. 19, 24; S. Henderson, 'The United Nations and Aboriginal Peoples' in S. Léger (ed.), *Linguistic Rights in Canada: Collusions or Collisions?* (Proceedings of the First Conference, University of Ottawa, 4–6 November 1993) (Canadian Centre For Linguistic Rights, University of Ottawa, 1995), pp. 615–38 at p. 630 (asserting that recent developments in the international law governing indigenous peoples have been shaped by indigenous peoples' participation and articulation of their positions).

[8] Report on Eleventh Session, p. 14.   [9] *Ibid.*, p. 5.   [10] *Ibid.*, pp. 5–6.

of inferiority. Judge *ad hoc* Skubiszewski saw the absence of input from the East Timorese as exceptionally justified by the clear-cut nature of the wrongs done to them. Similarly, this chapter shows how the expert Working Group and the states and indigenous groups who took part in its work differed in their understanding of the process and the roles of the different participants. Through a comparison with the International Labour Organization's conclusion of the 1989 Convention (No. 169) concerning Indigenous and Tribal Peoples in Independent Countries (Convention No. 169),[11] which involved less participation by indigenous peoples, the chapter highlights the relationship between an institution's self-understanding and its receptiveness to input by marginalized groups and, conversely, between those groups' understanding of the institutional process and their receptiveness to its outcome.

Most writers on ILO Convention No. 169 and the Working Group declaration on indigenous rights discuss the drafting of these texts in terms of the different positions taken by states and indigenous peoples on the right of self-determination, and assess the result against these positions. In so far as participation figures in the analysis, it is usually a direct relationship between more indigenous participation in the Working Group process and greater gains for indigenous peoples in the text, or between more participation and greater acceptability. This chapter argues that both the point about causality and the point about legitimacy need to be unpacked. Once we recognize that participation is experienced and processed through an idea of participation, we begin to notice that the speaker's idea and the listener or interpreter's idea are not necessarily the same. And, each's idea is contestable and therefore changeable. It follows that participation is not a straightforward panacea for the democratic deficit of international law, but requires a more complex analysis.

While Robert Williams, Jr. links the progress made in the draft declaration to the diverse forms of discourse allowed in the Working Group, and the ethic of equality and respect between states and indigenous peoples mediated by the Chairperson,[12] he does not examine how the Working Group heard the various kinds of statements made by indigenous participants.[13] It is therefore not surprising that he is somewhat vague

---

[11] Convention (No. 169) concerning Indigenous and Tribal Peoples in Independent Countries, Geneva, adopted by the International Labour Conference on 27 June 1989, in force 5 September 1991, 28 ILM 1382.

[12] Williams, 'Encounters on the Frontiers of International Human Rights Law'.

[13] Compare F. V. Kratochwil, *Rules, Norms and Decisions. On the Conditions of Practical and*

as to whether to credit their impact to the power of outsider narratives or storytelling,[14] to the use of 'rights' talk, or to the leverage of one on the other.[15] This chapter suggests that an institution's sense of its mandate acts as a filter. However free indigenous participants might be to tell their stories in their own voice and in a setting that recognizes their equal worth, the institution's understanding of itself and its task determines how it hears a story. In a technical standard-setting exercise, where the object is to work out the application of general international human rights law to indigenous peoples, both storytelling and 'rights' talk intended to go beyond the existing law would be screened out as irrelevant. Indeed, the institution might well be convinced that its authority depends on remaining neutral and objective and discarding narratives that attempt to create a bond of empathy with the speaker. If the institution views itself instead as a problem-solver in a particular tradition, then participants are accordingly viewed as contributors of information about the problem. While the solution must accommodate their concerns, it need not reflect their perspectives. This would not be true of an institution that understood its role as a mediator charged with reaching a fair balance between indigenous peoples and states. For such a mediator, the measure of the text would be much more its resonance with the different perspectives, as opposed to its grounding in international law or its ability to address the full complex of on-the-ground problems within the institution's normative and organizational framework. Thus, Williams's explanation for the Working Group's success is incomplete because an institutional interpreter's responsiveness to outsider groups depends on her characterization of outsider speech as well as on speech conditions.

Maivân Clech Lâm adds to the explanation the factors of the Working Group members' status as independent experts, their impression that

Legal Reasoning in International Relations and Domestic Affairs (Cambridge: Cambridge University Press, 1989), pp. 181-6 (discussing the different types of third-party decision-makers).

[14] The legal literature on narrative or 'storytelling' shows the pervasive narrative structure of legal discourse. Much of this literature focuses on 'outsider' narratives, meaning stories by members of groups usually subordinated in or excluded from mainstream legal discourse. These 'outsider' narratives both challenge assumptions about such subordinated or excluded groups and expose the partiality of the dominant narrative – which masquerades as universal. See R. Delgado (ed.), *Critical Race Theory: The Cutting Edge* (Philadelphia: Temple University Press, 1995), pp. 37-96.

[15] The same is true of H. E. Dallam, 'The Growing Voice of Indigenous Peoples: Their Use of Storytelling and Rights Discourse to Transform Multilateral Development Bank Policies' (1991) 8 *Arizona Journal of International and Comparative Law* 117.

they were free to craft the declaration as they judged best so long as it was acceptable to states and indigenous peoples alike and the strong commitment of the Working Group Chairperson.[16] But Lâm presents these factors as a combination of givens and chance, whereas this chapter examines them as the stuff of argument and persuasion. The chapter's claim is that to begin to grasp how interpretation might be affected by and legitimated through participation, we need to recognize that participation itself requires interpretation and to develop a more nuanced understanding of how these interpretations of participation operate.[17]

The chapter first introduces broadly the different ideas that states and indigenous peoples[18] had of the ILO and Working Group processes, of the role of the participants in these processes and of the substance of indigenous self-determination. It then turns to a more detailed and technical consideration of how these differences figured in the ILO and Working Group processes and their outcomes.[19]

Competing visions

Like a theory of what international law is, a theory of what a particular international institution does, creates a certain amount and type of

---

[16] Lâm, *At the Edge of the State*, pp. 76–81.
[17] Although not examined here, other types of analysis, such as those of legal process and international institutions, might also prove relevant. Equally, the inquiry into why and how the Working Group on Indigenous Populations proved responsive joins with the discussion in philosophy and political theory on public space, in particular, on ideas of discursive democracy in the face of cultural and gender differences. For an introduction to the political and philosophical discussion on public space, see S. Benhabib, *Situating the Self: Gender, Community and Postmodernism in Contemporary Ethics* (New York: Routledge, 1992), pp. 89–120. Collections include S. Benhabib (ed.), *Democracy and Difference: Contesting the Boundaries of the Political* (Princeton: Princeton University Press, 1996) and R. Bontekoe and M. Stepaniants (eds.), *Justice and Democracy: Cross-Cultural Perspectives* (Honolulu: University of Hawai'i Press, 1997).
[18] As will be seen in the discussion of Convention No. 169 and the draft declaration, respectively, neither the positions taken by states nor those taken by indigenous peoples were monolithic. Nevertheless, both the negotiation of Convention No. 169 and the preparation of the draft declaration were structured by certain basic differences.
[19] It bears emphasis that this chapter's – indeed, the book's – focus on the process of articulation should not be taken to imply that strategic considerations (here, for example, the different legal value or authority of conventions and declarations, some states' lack of engagement with low-level UN drafting exercises) are not important. The attention of this chapter is confined to the interrelation of ideas of text and ideas of context.

discursive space. Was the mandate of the ILO or the Working Group with respect to the interpretation of indigenous rights technical or visionary, standard-setting or constitution-drafting, codification or progressive development?[20] The answer helps shape perceptions of the appropriate discussion, including the degree to which legal norms need be used, the acceptability of policy considerations and the balance of speaking styles.

This point is well illustrated by the self-styled 'impartial comments' of the Comisión Jurídica de los Pueblos de Integración Tawantinsuyana, an indigenous organization, on the 1991 Working Group session:

(a) The organizers/rapporteurs and the representatives of the indigenous organizations were all given the opportunity to express themselves in a democratic manner;
(b) The experiences described by each people and the participating representatives were very useful;
(c) The legal instrument which is being discussed, namely the declaration, is a supranational instrument that will lay the foundation for the next century;
(d) Most of the participants representing their organizations had little legal expertise;
(e) The debate was serious and of a high standard.[21]

For the Comisión, the Working Group was engaged in visionary lawmaking, akin to the drafting of a supranational constitution (comment (c)). Indeed the Comisión suggested that the draft declaration should project the new relationship between nation states and indigenous peoples, and should incline toward new models of legal pluralism.[22] From this forward-looking understanding of the draft declaration, it followed that the discussion need not be exclusively grounded in legal norms. The debate could therefore be described as 'serious and of a high standard' (comment (e)) despite the lack of much legal expertise (comment (d)). Similarly, styles of speaking other than argumentative would be appropriate to the discussion: the narration of experiences was 'very useful'

---

[20] See M. C. Lâm, 'Making Room for Peoples at the United Nations: Thoughts Provoked by Indigenous Claims to Self-Determination' (1992) 25 *Cornell International Law Journal* 603 at 617–18 (contrasting the 'apolitically' technical discourse privileged in the UN specialized agencies, ad hoc committees and working groups with the 'visionary' discourse used by NGOs in the UN). See also C. J. Iorns, 'Indigenous Peoples and Self-Determination: Challenging State Sovereignty' (1992) 24 *Case Western Reserve Journal of International Law* 199 at 224–5, 228–9.

[21] Note by the Secretary-General: Information Received from Non-governmental Organizations, UN Doc. E/CN.4/Sub.2/AC.4/1992/3 (1992), p. 7.

[22] *Ibid.*

(comment (b)). Nevertheless, given the legal form that the document would ultimately take, the Comisión's suggestions identified the need for more participation by indigenous jurists in such capacities as rapporteur and for greater legal expertise in the drafting of the declaration.[23] In contrast, most states were inclined to view the objective of the ILO and the Working Group on Indigenous Populations more as technical standard-setting, which entails a stricter resort to legal norms, narrower range of considerations and less recourse to narrative and storytelling as a style of speaking.[24]

A second set of competing ideas about the ILO and the Working Group involved the roles of participants in the process. For some, the relative absence of indigenous peoples from the ILO's discussion and adoption of Convention No. 169 represented the maximal access possible in the ILO's tripartite structure of government, management and worker representation and was remedied by the Convention's responsiveness to indigenous needs and concerns. For others, the unequal access flawed the ILO as a forum for the determination of indigenous rights and the Convention as a result. Because the Working Group involved indigenous peoples extensively in its work,[25] the difference in views was instead over the expectations raised by their presence. For instance, Denis Marantz, a member of the Canadian government delegation to the Working Group during this time, contrasts the 'true' state view of the Working Group as dominated by the need to secure consensus among

---

[23] *Ibid.*

[24] Compare Lâm, *At the Edge of the State*, p. 82 (presenting the importance of the Working Group on Indigenous Populations to indigenous peoples as analogous to the importance of the General Assembly to the Third World in the early days of decolonization and recalling that Western commentators often criticized the Third World representatives in the General Assembly for 'their lack of positivist legal acumen and derided their aspirational speeches').

[25] This is not to ignore a host of disparities including indigenous groups' access to the Working Group sessions (see e.g. R. L. Barsh, 'Indigenous Peoples: An Emerging Object of International Law' (1986) 80 *American Journal of International Law* 369 at 384, citing allegations of interference with indigenous representatives travelling to Geneva to attend the Working Group's sessions; and M. C. Lâm, 'The Legal Value of Self-Determination: Vision or Inconvenience?' in International Centre for Human Rights and Democratic Development, *People or Peoples*, pp. 79–142 at p. 127, raising the need for more travel funding) and relations and priorities among indigenous groups (see e.g. notes 88–92 below and accompanying text) and between indigenous men and women. (At the 1994 session of the Sub-Commission on Minorities, a member of the Sub-Commission made reference to a group of indigenous women that had contacted a government observer, asserting that they had not dared approach the Working Group out of fear of what the indigenous men might do. UN Doc. E/CN.4/Sub.2/1994/SR.29 (1994), p. 12. See generally Chapter 8, below.)

states with the 'false' indigenous and NGO view of the Working Group as having some autonomous existence or authority.

It is critically important to understand the environment in which indigenous issues are debated by states. It is particularly important to be sensitive to the perspectives of these same states if one wishes to arrive at a multilateral and universal institutionalization of the collective rights of indigenous peoples.

In the UN, the universal application of standards and the acceptance of these by consensus, are fundamental principles for progressing on a corpus of human rights. Because of conflicting value systems and political/economic interests, often the lowest common denominator emerges from the exhaustive process of debate. No rights instruments would have come into existence if all participants to their elaboration had held fast to their highest aspirations.

The impression is often created by indigenous representatives and some observers that multilateral organizations (the UN in particular) are supranational bodies in their own right, empowered to supersede the national authority of the state. Some who press for the eventual acceptance of a declaration on the rights of indigenous peoples would like to see in the UN, an institution independent of the will of states. Misled by this view, many indigenous organizations divert their major lobbying efforts to the UN from the relations that they ought to entertain as a first priority with the governments of the countries from which they come. Some others do so in the hope of circumscribing the powers of states because of their past abuses of power.[26]

On Marantz's account, states saw the Working Group process as bargaining among states, whereas indigenous peoples were inclined to envisage the UN expert body as a third party.

The final set of competing ideas involved the status of a right of secession. During the discussion and drafting of ILO Convention No. 169 and the UN Working Group draft declaration on indigenous rights, this was the most contentious subtext of the successive drafts – and most accurate gauge of their responsiveness to indigenous demands.[27] Governments were vigilant for any terminology that might sanction

---

[26] B. D. Marantz, 'Issues Affecting the Rights of Indigenous Peoples in International Fora' in *People or Peoples*, pp. 9–77 at pp. 14–15.

[27] The sharp normative distinctions drawn in this chapter between the positions taken by indigenous peoples and governments are generally true for states such as Australia, Canada, New Zealand and the United States. At the same time, they are neither accurate nor helpful for many other indigenous peoples. See below, the discussion of ILO Convention No. 169, which covers indigenous and tribal peoples, at note 92 (noting North–South split in indigenous groups' attitudes toward Convention No. 169) and pp. 243–7 generally (discussing the normative implications of Convention No. 169's broad coverage). See also Kingsbury, 'The Asian Controversy'.

It should also be noted that although these distinctions may also hold for the national level, there may be an interplay, or even a contrast, between states' and indigenous peoples' positions at the international and the national levels.

secession. For some governments, the term 'peoples' was unacceptable because it could signify the right-holder of 'self-determination', which, in turn, could signify the right-holder of secession. Many indigenous groups were indignant at the hypocrisy of coded phrases carefully chosen to foreclose that option.[28]

Among those indigenous peoples who argued that indigenous self-determination must mean the right to choose freely any political status, including independence, secession was a matter of principle. The denial of a right to secede was associated with refusal to acknowledge the colonial fact, the historical injustice of conquest or broken treaties on which the modern state rested.[29] These views correspond to a corrective justice account of self-determination:[30] in the case of conquest, as discussed in Chapter 2, a story of wrongful taking; and in the case of treaties, a story of breach of pact.

In contrast, states were inclined to be receptive to equality or the familiarity of minority rights as a basis for group rights for indigenous peoples – stopping short, that is, of secession. Since states' negotiating stands may have involved little more than ritual invocation of normative language or unreflective advocacy of the domestic status quo, it is difficult and perhaps even misleading to generalize or extrapolate further. However, Will Kymlicka's work illustrates the shape that an equality-based argument might take.[31] In outline, Kymlicka's argument proceeds from the idea that cultural membership is a good that should be equally protected for the members of all national groups in a

---

[28] E.g. Statement of Dalee Sambo to the Martin Ennals Memorial Symposium on Self-Determination, March 1993, Saskatoon, Saskatchewan, p. 4 (unpublished).

[29] Compare C. C. Tennant and M. E. Turpel, 'A Case-Study of Indigenous Peoples: Genocide, Ethnocide and Self-Determination' (1990) 59 *Nordic Journal of International Law* 287 at 292 (arguing that the underlying political claim is generally more important to the claimants than the particular rights by which the claim may be expressed).

[30] See S. J. Anaya, 'The Capacity of International Law to Advance Ethnic or Nationality Rights Claims' (1990) 75 *Iowa Law Review* 837, (1991) 13 *Human Rights Quarterly* 403, in W. Kymlicka (ed.), *The Rights of Minority Cultures* (New York: Oxford University Press, 1995), pp. 321–30.

[31] W. Kymlicka, *Liberalism, Community and Culture* (Oxford: Clarendon Press, 1991); W. Kymlicka, *Multicultural Citizenship: A Liberal Theory of Minority Rights* (Oxford: Clarendon Press, 1995). While I draw on *Multicultural Citizenship*, it should be noted that *Multicultural Citizenship*, unlike the earlier *Liberalism, Community and Culture*, supplements an equality argument for indigenous rights with a historical argument. For a review of Kymlicka's revised arguments for indigenous rights from the perspective of indigenous self-determination, see R. Spaulding, 'Peoples as National Minorities: A Review of Will Kymlicka's Arguments for Aboriginal Rights from a Self-Determination Perspective' (1997) 47 *University of Toronto Law Journal* 35.

multinational state. Since decisions in areas such as official languages, political boundaries and the division of powers unavoidably support one culture or another, the majority in a democratic state will always have its language and culture supported, and will always have the legislative power to protect its interests in decisions that affect culture. Kymlicka argues that fairness demands that the same benefits and opportunities should be given to national minorities:

> Group-differentiated self-government rights compensate for unequal circumstances which put the members of minority cultures at a systemic disadvantage in the cultural market-place, regardless of their personal choices in life. This is one of the many areas in which true equality requires not identical treatment, but rather differential treatment in order to accommodate differential needs.[32]

To the extent that indigenous rights derive instead from the acceptance of minority rights in international law, their normative foundation is unclear. Inter-war international law recognized minority rights, but only as the international legal expression of particular political solutions.[33] It therefore left unclear the question of their justification.[34] Some inter-war theorists believed in autonomy for ethnic groups and protection of minorities as palliatives where the ideal of an ethnic nation-state could not be contrived through new borders or population transfer.[35] Then again, during the inter-war period and before, liberal defences of minority rights were also current.[36] The failure of the League of Nations' scheme for minority protection and its role in the outbreak of World War II[37] led to disenchantment with minority rights after the War.[38] The Universal Declaration of Human Rights omitted them[39] and the 1966 International Covenant on Civil and Political Rights included them in a formulation that scarcely acknowledged their

---

[32] Kymlicka, *Multicultural Citizenship*, p. 113.

[33] See Thornberry, *Rights of Minorities*, pp. 113-16. (The common opinion was that the inter-war minority treaties did not create international customary law.)

[34] See J. Crawford, 'The Rights of Peoples: Some Conclusions' in J. Crawford (ed.), *The Rights of Peoples* (Oxford: Clarendon Press, 1988), pp. 159-75 at p. 161.

[35] See e.g. R. Redslob, *Le principe des nationalités: Les origines, les fondements psychologiques, les forces adverses, les solutions possibles* (Paris: Recueil Sirey, 1930), pp. 173-4.

[36] See Kymlicka, *Multicultural Citizenship*, pp. 50-7.

[37] See I. L. Claude, *National Minorities: An International Problem* (Cambridge: Harvard University Press, 1955), pp. 56-69; T. D. Musgrave, *Self-Determination and National Minorities* (Oxford: Clarendon Press, 1997), pp. 55-7.

[38] See Thornberry, *Rights of Minorities*, pp. 113-224; Musgrave, *Self-Determination and National Minorities*, pp. 126-37.

[39] Universal Declaration of Human Rights, adopted 10 December 1948, GA Res. 217A (III) (1948).

collective nature.⁴⁰ Although the post-Cold War proliferation of minority rights instruments testifies to their rediscovery in international human rights law,⁴¹ the tendency is to accept them as a useful vestigial category, without much attention to their *raison d'être*. Such attention as is paid, however, leans toward deriving minority rights from equal rights.⁴²

In short, to the extent that various states supported indigenous rights, they did so on grounds of rights rather than history. It follows that if states were inclined to accept a right to secede, secession would be a last resort in the case of gross and sustained abuses of the group's rights – what Chapter 2 called a remedial view of self-determination – and not at the option of the group as the victim of a historical wrong. Thus the issue of secession that fell to the ILO and the UN Working Group on Indigenous Populations was whether to recognize a right to secede and if so, on what basis.

International Labour Organization

In 1989, the International Labour Organization completed Convention (No. 169) Concerning Indigenous and Tribal Peoples in Independent Countries. This convention revised Convention (No. 107) Concerning the Protection and Integration of Indigenous and Other Tribal and Semi-Tribal Populations in Independent Countries,⁴³ a 1957 ILO convention on the subject which had come under strong criticism for its integrationist orientation.⁴⁴ The two ILO Conventions, now both in

---

⁴⁰ International Covenant on Civil and Political Rights, Art. 27.
⁴¹ See A. Phillips and A. Rosas (eds.), *Universal Minority Rights* (Turku/Åbo and London: Åbo Akademi University Institute for Human Rights and Minority Rights Group (International), 1995) (essays on the 1992 UN Declaration on the Rights of Persons Belonging to National or Ethnic, Religious and Linguistic Minorities; the Organization for Security and Cooperation in Europe (OSCE) and national minorities; minority rights in the Council of Europe; and collection of documents on minority rights including selected cases under Article 27 of the International Covenant on Civil and Political Rights); G. Gilbert, 'The Council of Europe and Minority Rights' (1996) 18 *Human Rights Quarterly* 160 (on the 1995 Council of Europe Framework Convention for the Protection of National Minorities); J. Wright, 'The OSCE and the Protection of Minority Rights' (1996) 18 *Human Rights Quarterly* 190 (on OSCE documents on minorities, especially the 1990 Copenhagen Document).
⁴² Crawford, 'Some Conclusions', p. 161.
⁴³ Convention (No. 107) Concerning the Protection and Integration of Indigenous and Other Tribal and Semi-Tribal Populations in Independent Countries, Geneva, adopted by the International Labour Conference on 26 June 1957, in force 2 June 1959, 328 UNTS 247.
⁴⁴ International Labour Office, Report VI(1). Partial Revision of the Indigenous and Tribal Populations Convention, 1957 (No. 107), International Labour Conference, 75th

force,⁴⁵ are the only international instruments to deal specifically with the rights of indigenous peoples.⁴⁶ As of 2000, fourteen countries had ratified Convention No. 169,⁴⁷ and the Convention has also had significant influence on domestic policies and programmes in some states that have not yet ratified and on the policy guidelines of several international funding agencies.⁴⁸

This part of the chapter traces the controversies over the limited participation afforded indigenous peoples in the adoption of ILO Convention No. 169 and the agreement reached to use the term 'peoples' in the Convention with the express proviso that its use not be construed as implying that indigenous peoples had a right of self-determination or any other rights of peoples at international law. The dampening effect of these procedural and substantive controversies on support for Convention No. 169 demonstrates the problem of insider and outsider perspectives and the difficulty in seeking to bridge them in this institutional context through an approach that is true to the institution rather than to the parties' positions. This part shows that from the ILO's insider perspective on its institutional theory and praxis, Convention No. 169 is intelligible as a gain for the rights of indigenous peoples. Read against the rigid ILO procedures for the adoption of conventions, the limited participation of indigenous peoples represents an achievement. Read in the ILO's tradition of integrated, interactive and empirically-based functionalism, the provisions of Convention No. 169 hold greater promise than their wording might indicate. The Convention is effectively a product not of the ILO's mediation between parties, but of its standard-setting as interested expert. To the extent that the rights in the Convention are thereby true to a procedural and substantive perspective that is too

---

Session (1988), pp. 18–43. See generally R. L. Barsh, 'Revision of ILO Convention No. 107' (1987) 81 *American Journal of International Law* 756.

[45] As of the coming into force of Convention No. 169 on 5 September 1991, a state's ratification of Convention No. 169 amounted automatically to its denunciation of Convention No. 107, and Convention No. 107 ceased to be open to ratification. Convention No. 107 remains in force for those states that have ratified it but not Convention No. 169. Convention No. 107, Art. 36.

[46] Convention No. 107 deals with indigenous, tribal and semi-tribal populations; Convention No. 169 with indigenous and tribal peoples. For convenience, I shall refer generally to indigenous peoples.

[47] Argentina, Bolivia, Columbia, Costa Rica, Denmark, Ecuador, Fiji, Guatemala, Honduras, Mexico, Netherlands, Norway, Paraguay and Peru.

[48] M. Tomei and L. Swepston, *Indigenous and Tribal Peoples: A Guide to ILO Convention No. 169* (Geneva: International Labour Office, July 1996) (with the International Centre for Human Rights and Democratic Development, Montreal), pp. viii–ix, 31–2.

far from or too alien to the outside perspectives of indigenous peoples, indigenous peoples have not supported ratification.

Process

The International Labour Organization is a specialized agency within the UN system, although it is actually older than the United Nations. Created by the Treaty of Versailles in 1919 to abolish the 'injustice, hardship, and privation' which workers suffered and to guarantee 'fair and humane conditions of labour',[49] it was the only major intergovernmental organization to survive World War II and the demise of the League of Nations. The ILO consists of three main bodies: the International Labour Conference, the International Labour Office and the Office's Governing Body. It is the annual International Labour Conference that votes on the adoption of conventions. In accordance with the ILO's 'double-discussion' procedure,[50] two consecutive annual Conferences must consider a convention before it can be adopted.

Much of the ILO's success in adopting and implementing conventions is attributed to its tripartitism, which means that representatives of governments, employers' organizations and workers' organizations participate in all ILO deliberative bodies and activities, including the drafting of conventions and supervision of their implementation.[51] Delegations to the Conference are composed of two government representatives, one employers' representative and one workers' representative, each of whom has a vote.[52] The Governing Body, the executive organ, is also tripartite in composition. The Governing Body meets between the yearly Conferences and determines the agenda for the Conference. In the case of Convention No. 169, the Governing Body convened a Meeting of Experts in 1986 on the revision of the existing Convention. The experts unanimously

---

[49] Constitution of the International Labour Organization (Geneva: International Labour Office, May 1989), Preamble. See generally C. W. Jenks, 'Human Rights, Social Justice and Peace: The Broader Significance of the ILO Experience' in A. Eide and A. Schou (eds.), *International Protection of Human Rights (Proceedings of the Seventh Nobel Symposium Oslo, September 25–27, 1967)* (Stockholm: Almqvist & Wiksell, 1968), pp. 227–60.

[50] Standing Orders of the International Labour Conference, Arts. 34–45 ('Conventions and Recommendations Procedure'), reprinted in International Labour Office, *Constitution of the International Labour Organization and Standing Orders of the International Labour Conference* (Geneva, May 1989).

[51] V. A. Leary, 'Lessons from the Experience of the International Labour Organization' in P. Alston (ed.), *The United Nations and Human Rights: A Critical Appraisal* (Oxford: Clarendon Press, 1992), pp. 580–619 at pp. 584–5.

[52] ILO Constitution, Arts. 3–4.

recommended the Convention's urgent revision and drew particular attention to the need to review its overall integrationist approach and its provisions on land rights.[53] In accordance with the experts' recommendations, the Governing Body added the item to the agenda of the 1988 Conference and thereby set in motion the 'double-discussion' process.[54]

The International Labour Office, the organization's secretariat, plays a central and directive role in this process, beginning with its background 'law and practice' report.[55] The report, which includes a questionnaire, is circulated to governments for their comments. Governments are expected – and, if they have ratified the 1976 Tripartite Consultation Convention,[56] required – to consult representative employers' and workers' associations. In this instance, governments were invited to consult representatives of indigenous peoples as well. Another report by the Office[57] summarizes and analyses the replies received, as well as offering 'proposed conclusions' for discussion at the first of the two successive Conferences to consider the item.[58]

The sequence is repeated between the first and second Conferences: in three separate reports, the Office prepares a draft convention based on the conclusions adopted at the first Conference,[59] summarizes the comments received on this draft[60] and prepares a further draft for discussion.[61] The final text is adopted following discussion at the second

---

[53] Report of the Meeting of Experts, excerpted in International Labour Office, Report VI(1), pp. 100–18. On the Meeting of Experts, see Barsh, 'Revision of ILO Convention No. 107'.

[54] In the case of a partial revision, discussion at only one session of the Conference may be sufficient. Convention No. 169 is technically the partial revision of Convention No. 107, but was subjected to the full double-discussion procedure for adopting conventions.

[55] International Labour Office, Report VI(1).

[56] Convention (No. 144) concerning Tripartite Consultations to Promote the Implementation of International Labour Standards, Geneva, adopted by the International Labour Conference on 21 June 1976, in force 16 May 1978, (1976) 15 ILM 1076.

[57] International Labour Office, Report VI(2). Partial Revision of the Indigenous and Tribal Populations Convention, 1957 (No. 107), International Labour Conference, 75th Session (1988).

[58] International Labour Conference, Provisional Record Nos. 32, 36, 75th Session (1988).

[59] International Labour Office, Report IV(1). Partial Revision of the Indigenous and Tribal Populations Convention, 1957 (No. 107), International Labour Conference, 76th Session (1989).

[60] International Labour Office, Report IV(2A). Partial Revision of the Indigenous and Tribal Populations Convention, 1957 (No. 107), International Labour Conference, 76th Session (1989).

[61] International Labour Office, Report IV(2B). Partial Revision of the Indigenous and

annual Conference.[62] Convention No. 169 was adopted at the 1989 session of the Conference by a vote of 328:1:49.[63]

In the adoption of Convention No. 169, the ILO was concerned that the limitations on access for indigenous groups would jeopardize the relevance and legitimacy of the process. Whereas the ILO structurally incorporates the full participation of employers' and workers' organizations, its rather rigid procedures have not permitted the same degree of participation by non-occupational NGOs.[64] The challenge was articulated by an indigenous adviser to the Canadian workers' delegation.

> This forum is one which is used for bargaining and negotiating to achieve a desired result. But how can you negotiate and bargain over who we are and what our rights are? This is not a normal labour issue concerning which each party gives and takes something of what they want. How can you bargain away something which does not belong to you?[65]

The Meeting of Experts recommended that the ILO take all possible measures to ensure the participation of indigenous representatives in the process leading to the revision of Convention No. 107 and in other ILO activities relating to indigenous peoples.[66] Since neither the Organization's Constitution nor the Standing Orders of the Conference allowed for the formal participation of representatives of indigenous groups in the Conference discussions,[67] the ILO used such flexibility as these documents gave it to include indigenous groups informally.

For the Meeting of Experts itself, the ILO Governing Body included two experts representing NGOs among the sixteen experts appointed: one of the two was from an international organization of indigenous peoples and the other from an organization working for the protection of indigenous peoples.[68] The Governing Body also took the unusual step of

---

Tribal Populations Convention, 1957 (No. 107), International Labour Conference, 76th Session (1989).

[62] International Labour Conference, Provisional Record Nos. 25, 31, 32, 76th Session (1989).
[63] International Labour Conference, Provisional Record No. 32, 76th Session (1989), pp. 17–19.
[64] Leary, 'Lessons from the Experience of the ILO', pp. 585–6.
[65] International Labour Conference, Provisional Record No. 31, 76th Session (1989), p. 9 (Sayers, Workers' adviser, Canada).
[66] Recommendation (d), Report of the Meeting of Experts, p. 118. See also *ibid.*, pp. 104, para. 23; 117, Conclusion 8. The employer experts expressed their reservation on Conclusion 8, apparently on the basis of its possible conflict with the ILO Constitution. ILO Governing Body, 234th Session, ILO Doc. GB.234/5/4 (1986), p. 7.
[67] ILO Governing Body, p. 8.   [68] *Ibid.*, p. 1.

inviting observers from NGOs active in the field of indigenous rights.[69] The Meeting decided to give these observers the right to speak during the sessions, although the experts and representatives of other intergovernmental organizations took priority. The report of the Meeting records that 'many of these participants played an active and useful part in the discussions' – too active a part, it seems, for some experts.[70]

The International Labour Office suggested to governments that in preparing their replies to the questionnaire on revision of the old convention, they consult indigenous peoples in their country as well as the usual employers' and workers' organizations.[71] The governments of Australia, Canada, Finland and Sweden indicated in their replies that they had consulted with indigenous peoples. The government of Peru stated that due to time pressures, it had not been able to hold formal consultations and had relied instead on the views expressed by indigenous peoples in previous consultations.[72] The Canadian indigenous working group's comments were submitted separately by Canada and were treated separately in the Office's summary and analysis of replies to the questionnaire. Responses to the questionnaire received from indigenous and other NGOs were summarized by the Office in an additional document.[73] Six governments, the original four and the governments of Norway and the United States, indicated that they had consulted with indigenous representatives in composing their comments on the first draft of the convention, and the Office stated that it had taken account of the views expressed directly to it by indigenous organizations.[74]

As regards participation in the International Labour Conference, the Standing Orders of the Conference provide that entry to the Conference hall, other than for delegates and their advisers, is restricted to international NGOs with ILO observer credentials and such other international NGOs as have been invited.[75] A number of international groups were accredited and took part in the Conference as observers, although, according to Howard Berman, some of the groups most closely in touch with the needs and aspirations of particular indigenous communities

[69] See Barsh, 'Revision of ILO Convention No. 107', p. 758, n. 13.
[70] Report of the Meeting of Experts, p. 103. See also ILO Governing Body, p. 2.
[71] International Labour Office, Report VI(1), p. 2.
[72] International Labour Office, Report VI(2), p. 2.
[73] Comments Received from Non-Governmental Organisations. Partial Revision of the Indigenous and Tribal Populations Convention, 1957 (No. 107), International Labour Conference, 75th Session (1988), ILO Doc. C.C107/D.65.
[74] International Labour Office, Report IV(2A), p. 2.
[75] ILO Standing Orders, Art. 2(3)(j).

were ineligible because they were local or national, as opposed to international, organizations.[76] Furthermore, the workers allowed representatives from accredited indigenous NGOs to attend the workers' caucus meetings and introduced amendments that coincided with many of the indigenous positions.[77] Finally, indigenous persons took part in the Conference as advisers to various government, employer and worker delegations.[78]

As much of the Conference work is done in committees, participation in committees and other working groups is an important dimension of participation in the Conference. The Standing Orders allowed indigenous representatives, with the permission of the committee's chair and vice-chair, to make or circulate statements to the committees.[79] The Committee on Convention No. 107 at the 1989 Conference agreed that

> international non-governmental organisations would be allowed to make interventions during one hour of the general discussion. They would then be able to make 12 interventions at given moments during the discussion of the text of the draft Convention. The Committee also agreed to adjourn one sitting in order to be able to hear the views of non-governmental organisations which were not international organisations outside of its formal sittings.[80]

Representatives of four international NGOs are on record, for instance, as having made statements to the Committee on the question of land rights.[81] Berman writes that in the result, each indigenous organization with ILO accreditation was given ten minutes to address the Committee following the close of business on the second day of actual deliberations, and the organizations collectively were given the opportunity to make one ten-minute presentation on each category of articles being

---

[76] H. R. Berman, 'The International Labour Organization and Indigenous Peoples: Revision of ILO Convention No. 107 at the 75th Session of the International Labour Conference, 1988' (1988) 41 *International Commission of Jurists: The Review* 48 at 51.

[77] Berman, 'The International Labour Organization and Indigenous Peoples', 51–2. International Labour Conference, Provisional Record No. 31, 76th Session (1989), p. 6 (Venne, representative of the International Work Group for Indigenous Affairs).

[78] See ILO Constitution, Art. 3(2). International Labour Conference, Provisional Record No. 36, 75th Session (1988), p. 3. The American government, employer and worker delegations, for example, each included at least one indigenous adviser. International Labour Conference, Provisional Record No. 31, 76th Session (1989), p. 14 (Kickingbird, Government adviser, US). For a full list, see Berman, 'The International Labour Organization and Indigenous Peoples', 57, n. 9.

[79] ILO Standing Orders, Art. 56(9).

[80] Report of the Committee on Convention No. 107, International Labour Conference, Provisional Record No. 25, 76th Session (1989), p. 2.

[81] *Ibid.*, p. 16.

considered by the Committee.[82] Berman also reports that during the second week of the Committee session, representatives of the National Coalition of Aboriginal Organizations publicly withdrew from the process in frustration.[83] Speaking of the 'sorely inadequate ILO procedures', Sharon Venne, a representative of the International Work Group on Indigenous Affairs, stated that the most critical provisions were negotiated behind closed doors.[84]

For several indigenous representatives who spoke prior to the vote on Convention No. 169, their experience of the process undermined the legitimacy of the Convention. A representative of the Indian Council of South America described the absurdity of watching

> from the observers' seats, deprived as we were of the right to speak or to vote by the regulations and structures of the ILO, the Government and Employers' delegates of a large part of the world (Canada, the United States, Argentina, Brazil, Bolivia and Venezuela) behave like representatives of the old colonial empires which despoiled the Americas, denying us the right to exist.[85]

Another indigenous speaker stated that indigenous peoples did not have to accept Convention No. 169 even if it were the best result that could have been obtained in the ILO context. She suggested that it might have been better to reserve the issues for 'other appropriate forums where time is not limited and input from indigenous peoples' positions are respected and taken into account'.[86] Yet Dalee Sambo maintains that even the 'less than adequate' participation of indigenous peoples had an effect on Convention No. 169, and that the convention offers several important protections.[87]

The general indigenous response to Convention No. 169 has been mixed.[88] The article of the 1992 Indigenous Peoples Earth Charter urging ratification is the only one of the 109 articles with a reservation noted,[89]

---

[82] Berman, 'The International Labour Organization and Indigenous Peoples', 51.
[83] Ibid., 52.
[84] International Labour Conference, Provisional Record No. 31, 76th Session (1989), p. 6.
[85] Ibid., p. 8 (Ontiveros Yulquila, representative of the Indian Council of South America). See also ibid., pp. 6–10; and Berman, 'The International Labour Organization and Indigenous Peoples' generally.
[86] International Labour Conference, Provisional Record No. 31, 76th Session (1989), pp. 9–10 (Sayers, Workers' advisers, Canada).
[87] Sambo, 'Are State Governments Listening?', 19–20. See also Anaya, *Indigenous Peoples in International Law*, pp. 47–9.
[88] D. Sanders, 'Introduction' to International Labour Organization Convention 169 – Concerning Indigenous and Tribal Peoples in Independent Countries [1989] 4 *Canadian Native Law Reporter* 49 at 49.
[89] Indigenous Peoples Earth Charter, adopted at the Kari Oca Conference, 25–30 May

and a 1992 joint written statement of indigenous nations, peoples, and organizations attending the inaugural ceremonies of the International Year of the World's Indigenous People refers only to the need for states to 'consult with indigenous organizations and nations' regarding the ratification of the Convention.[90] In some countries, indigenous groups have reportedly lobbied against the Convention.[91] In others, especially in Central and South America, indigenous groups have been active in pressing for ratification, and there are indications that support for the Convention is growing.[92]

Implicit in criticism of the ILO's tripartite structure and its inability to accommodate indigenous peoples as equal participants is the ideal of direct negotiation with indigenous peoples. But this ideal does not contend with the significant role played by the International Labour Office in the adoption of conventions.[93] In many ways, the standard ILO procedure for adopting conventions resembles not so much three-way bargaining, as standard-setting by the Office with the input of governments, employers and workers.

Consider the mechanics alone of the Office's role in the adoption of Convention No. 169. The Office prepared a working document for the 1986 Meeting of Experts. Once the revision of Convention No. 107 had been placed on the agenda for the 1988 Conference, the Office prepared a background 'law and practice' report, which was circulated to governments on the expectation that they would consult with representative employers' and workers' associations. Of particular significance was the questionnaire contained in the law and practice report, which identified the parts of the old convention for revision. A second report by the Office not only summarized and analysed the replies received to the

1992, in Information Received from Indigenous Peoples' and Non-Governmental Organizations, UN Doc. E/CN.4/Sub.2/AC.4/1994/12 (1994), p. 2, Art. 9.

[90] 1992 Joint Written Statement of Indigenous Nations, Peoples, and Organizations Attending the Inaugural Ceremonies of the 'International Year of the World's Indigenous People', reprinted in (1993) 3 *Transnational Law and Contemporary Problems* 219 at 221.

[91] Venne, *Our Elders Understand Our Rights*, p. 92.

[92] Anaya, 'Canada's Fiduciary Obligations', pp. 22–3. Compare L. Swepston, 'The Adoption of the Indigenous and Tribal Peoples Convention, 1989 (No. 169)' (1990) 5 *Law and Anthropology: Internationales Jahrbuch für Rechtsanthropologie* 221 at 226 (as of 1990, observing a North–South split in indigenous groups' attitudes towards the Convention).

[93] See generally Leary, 'Lessons from the Experience of the ILO', pp. 581–2 (listing the activist ILO Secretariat (the 'Office') among the ILO's lessons for the UN), 613–16 (on the Office). With respect to Convention No. 169, see Berman, 'The International Labour Organization and Indigenous Peoples', 49.

questionnaire, but offered 'proposed conclusions' for discussion at the first of the two successive Conferences to consider the item. Following the first Conference, the Office prepared a draft convention based on the conclusions adopted at the Conference. In two final reports, the Office summarized the comments received on the draft and prepared a further draft for discussion.

Not only does the Office play a central role in the adoption of conventions, its officials consider themselves, according to scholar and former ILO official Virginia Leary, 'not as simple executors of the desires of member States, but rather as collaborators in the pursuit of social justice'.[94] The conviction that they are independent experts, rather than the servants of states, is a legacy of the ILO's history:

> The International Labour Office emerged from World War II as a small staff with a high sense of commitment to building a new world order. The staff members were united by their efforts to survive the debacle of the League of Nations, by the tradition of strong executive leadership, and by their conviction that they had a right to express collectively an independent international viewpoint on the postwar issues of social policy.[95]

Given the Office's control over the shape of Convention No. 169, contact between indigenous groups and the International Labour Office had the potential to compensate in outlook and result for the limited access of indigenous groups to the discussions. But even with equal access, their effectiveness would have depended on the Office's appreciation of the ILO's goals, norms and rules. In Leary's words, 'the Office plays a leadership role in promoting the objectives of the ILO and keeping it "on course" as well as embodying the institutional memory of the Organisation'.[96] As a result, its tendency is to discard, rather than engage with, legal and normative positions it considers incompatible with ILO theory and praxis. This tendency is illustrated by one Office account of the ILO debate on the right of self-determination of indigenous peoples.

> It has been argued that international law would be taking a step backward if the revised Convention failed to recognise the right of these peoples to self-determination and control of all activities which affect them. Others have argued that the recognition of such rights in the revised Convention would seriously limit its prospects for ratification or would lead to the creation of a State within

---

[94] Leary, 'Lessons from the Experience of the ILO', p. 613.
[95] R. W. Cox, 'ILO: Limited Monarchy' in R. W. Cox and H. K. Jacobson, *The Anatomy of Influence: Decision Making in International Organization* (New Haven: Yale University Press, 1974), pp. 102–38 at p. 121, quoted in *ibid.*, p. 615.
[96] Leary, 'Lessons from the Experience of the ILO', p. 613.

a State. Both arguments, however, fail to take into account the characteristics of ILO Conventions, and the requirements of a Convention on this subject.[97]

Whereas this concern for the integrity of ILO conventions reflects the Office's role as an expert engaged in standard-setting for the Organization, the assertion of jurisdiction in Convention No. 169 and concern for its adoption, ratification and implementation point to another role as guardian of the Organization's historical prominence on indigenous issues, its wide relevance and its reputation for effectiveness. In this sense, any authority that standard-setting by the Office might carry due to its expertise is diminished by the perception of its interestedness.

Convention No. 169, like its predecessor, is sometimes regarded as an anomalous, if not suspect, assertion of jurisdiction by the International Labour Organization.[98] Writing in the early 1970s on whether Convention No. 107 was outside the competence of the Organization, Gordon Bennett commented slightingly:

> It is difficult to see how a tribal food-gatherer can be described, by any stretch of the imagination, as the 'systematic', 'habitual', industrial worker with whose welfare alone the I.L.O. is properly concerned. Nor does the primitive ordinarily engage in any 'form of production', if that term is intended to connote the creation of surplus wealth to be exchanged in the market for other goods.[99]

Convention No. 169 is intelligible, however, as the outgrowth of early ILO standard-setting relating to indigenous workers and ILO technical assistance for indigenous peoples. As a historical matter, it was a product of the ILO's long and prominent involvement in indigenous issues.[100] The International Labour Organization as early as 1921 undertook studies on indigenous workers. The work of its Committee of Experts on Native

---

[97] International Labour Office, Report VI(1), p. 89.
[98] For the debate on the ILO's competence to promulgate Convention No. 107, see G. L. Bennett, 'The ILO Convention on Indigenous and Tribal Populations – The Resolution of a Problem of *Vires*' (1972–3) 46 *British Yearbook of International Law* 382.
  With respect to Convention No. 169, compare Report of the Meeting of Experts, p. 106 (the issue of the ILO's competence to deal with the subject of indigenous peoples had been resolved at the time of the original discussion of the issue) with Berman, 'The International Labour Organization and Indigenous Peoples', 49, 56 ('The ILO has sought to maintain an institutional hold on a human rights process that has evolved far beyond its mandate').
[99] Bennett, 'A Problem of *Vires*', 386.
[100] See International Labour Office, Report VI(1), pp. 3–8 and, in slightly more detail, International Labour Office, International Standards and Indigenous and Tribal Populations (unpublished) (Working Document for the 1986 Meeting of Experts on the Revision of the Indigenous and Tribal Populations Convention, 1957 (No. 107)), pp. 4–11.

Labour, established in 1926, laid the groundwork for the Forced Labour Convention,1930(No. 29) and various other conventions more directly concerned with indigenous workers. In 1953, the ILO published *Indigenous Peoples*, a hefty book divided into preliminary definitions and data, living conditions, the place of indigenous workers in the economy, and national and international action. Leading up to Convention No. 107, a Committee of Experts on Indigenous Labour engaged in the detailed study of such problems as the plight of forest-dwelling indigenous peoples.

ILO technical assistance for indigenous peoples included the Andean Indian Programme, which spanned the 1950s, 60s and 70s, and the 1962 Panel of Consultants on Indigenous and Tribal Populations. The goal of the Andean Indian Programme, in accordance with the approach then prevalent in the ILO, was to facilitate the economic, social and political integration of the indigenous peoples of the Andes by improving their living and working conditions. In this vastly ambitious development programme, described as 'inter-agency, multi-sectoral and multi-country', the ILO spearheaded the efforts of the United Nations, the Food and Agriculture Organization (FAO), United Nations (International) Children's (Emergency) Fund (UNICEF), United Nations Educational, Scientific and Cultural Organization (UNESCO) and the World Health Organization (WHO) in Bolivia, Ecuador, Peru, Colombia, Chile, Argentina and Venezuela.[101]

More fundamentally, the ILO's adoption of a convention on indigenous peoples reflects the Organization's philosophy.[102] In defence of the ILO's jurisdiction, Lee Swepston of the International Labour Office maintains that those who see the ILO's mandate as limited to labour in the sense of wage-earning employment fail to grasp the 'complex of activities surrounding the means by which, and the conditions under which, humanity pursues its economic and survival struggle'.[103] Speaking at the first of the two International Labour Conferences to discuss Convention No. 169, a Cherokee adviser to the employers' delegation from the United States argued along similar lines:

So I ask, has the ILO been stretched beyond its mandate in focusing attention on indigenous peoples? Surely not, if its aim is to protect a people's fundamental right to organise. Surely not, if its aim is to prevent discrimination and safeguard

---

[101] International Labour Office, Working Document for the 1986 Meeting of Experts, p. 8.

[102] As will be seen, the ILO's philosophy is central not only to the Organization's re-assertion of jurisdiction in Convention No. 169, but also to the Convention's approach.

[103] Swepston, 'The Adoption of the Indigenous and Tribal Peoples Convention', 222.

precarious human rights. Surely not, if its efforts will result in economic justice and a fair and dignified livelihood for those peoples.[104]

Intimately related to the manifold idea of labour that Swepston implicitly presents is the ILO's 'holistic' or integrated approach to human rights.[105] The ILO has largely avoided the gulf between civil and political rights and economic and social rights institutionalized in the UN system by the two Covenants and their separate implementation mechanisms. The Organization's refusal to sever human rights from social justice is apparent in its 1944 declaration of aims and purposes: 'all human beings, irrespective of race, creed or sex, have the right to pursue both their material well-being and their spiritual development in conditions of freedom and dignity, of economic security and equal opportunity'.[106]

The ILO also invoked its institutional strengths as a reason to act. In the past, the Organization has been accused of being uncooperative and parochial with respect to the UN's drafting of the International Covenants on Human Rights and of demonstrating 'agency imperialism'.[107] Leary justifies the ILO's response as an understandable reluctance to sever the human rights under its jurisdiction from the Organization's remarkably effective system of protection for those rights.[108] She observes, however, that this institutional effectiveness is largely an article of faith, since it is virtually impossible to establish scientifically in such a complex multi-variable world.[109]

Swepston similarly defends the ILO's assertion of jurisdiction in Convention No. 169 on the grounds that the ILO has the technical capacity to adopt conventions, to revise them as needed and to supervise their application.[110] Under the ILO Constitution, member states must submit

---

[104] International Labour Conference, Provisional Record No. 36, 75th Session (1988), p. 22 (Adamson, Employers' adviser and Cherokee American Indian, United States).
[105] Leary, 'Lessons from the Experience of the ILO', pp. 590-4.
[106] Declaration of the Aims and Purposes of the International Labour Organization [the Declaration of Philadelphia], attached as an annex to the ILO Constitution.
[107] J. P. Humphrey, *Human Rights and the United Nations: A Great Adventure* (Dobbs Ferry, N.Y.: Transnational Publishers, 1984), pp. 12, 103. (Humphrey was Director of the UN Human Rights Division during the drafting of the Covenants.)
[108] Leary, 'Lessons from the Experience of the ILO', p. 588.
[109] *Ibid.*, p. 595, citing attempts by the ILO and others: International Labour Office, *The Impact of International Labour Conventions and Recommendations* (Geneva, 1976); E. B. Haas, *Human Rights and International Action: The Case of Freedom of Association* (Stanford: Stanford University Press, 1970); E. A. Landry, *The Effectiveness of International Supervision: Thirty Years of ILO Experience* (London: Stevens & Sons, 1966).
[110] L. Swepston, 'A New Step in the International Law on Indigenous and Tribal Peoples: ILO Convention No. 169 of 1989' (1990) 15 *Oklahoma City University Law Review* 677 at 681; Swepston, 'The Adoption of the Indigenous and Tribal Peoples Convention', 221.

any new or revised convention to their legislature within a certain time period.[111] Once a convention is ratified, and thus binding on the ratifying state, its implementation is subject to regular supervision by an independent body of experts, which can ask specific questions, make recommendations for action, and follow up the action taken. In appropriate cases,[112] a ratifying state can be called before the annual Conference to explain its conduct, and technical assistance can be provided to assist a government in overcoming any barriers to implementation. Swepston cites the ILO practice of supplementing standard-setting with practical technical assistance to the relevant groups as a further reason for the Organization to act in the area of indigenous peoples.[113]

The perception of institutional strength, or effectiveness, also enters into how the final text of Convention No. 169 is read. Sharon Venne warned that its saturation with 'unnecessary qualifications, such as "where appropriate" and "where possible", in respect to government obligations...will make enforcement highly problematic'.[114] In contrast, the Office supports the Convention's mixture of 'goals, priorities and minimal rights'[115] on the assumption that the ILO's supervisory bodies can be trusted to interpret ambiguous and general terms in the Convention,[116] and may gradually increase their expectations of countries under the more aspirational language in the Convention.[117]

See also International Labour Conference, Provisional Record No. 31, 76th Session (1989), p. 12 (Ms Salway, Employers' adviser, United States and member of Lakota people (Sioux)) ('The true value and force of the ILO and these instruments lie in the application of the standards'). For an overview of the supervisory and monitoring procedures for the application of Convention No. 169, see Tomei and Swepston, *A Guide*, pp. 28–30.

[111] ILO Constitution, Art. 19.

[112] For such a case involving Convention No. 107, see D. Sanders, 'The UN Working Group on Indigenous Populations' (1989) 11 *Human Rights Quarterly* 406 at 423–7 (tribal populations in the Chittagong Hill Tracts of Bangladesh).

[113] Swepston, 'A New Step', 681. See International Labour Conference, Provisional Record No. 25, 76th Session (1989), p. 6. (Representative of Four Directions Council recommends Convention be followed by an ILO plan of action including technical assistance.)

[114] International Labour Conference, Provisional Record No. 31, 76th Session (1989), p. 7. See also L. Sargent, 'The Indigenous Peoples of Bolivia's Amazon Basin Region and ILO Convention No. 169: Real Rights or Rhetoric?' (1998) 29 *University of Miami Inter-American Law Review* 451.

[115] Swepston, 'The Adoption of the Indigenous and Tribal Peoples Convention', 227; Swepston, 'A New Step', 689.

[116] Swepston, 'The Adoption of the Indigenous and Tribal Peoples Convention', 231.

[117] See R. L. Barsh, 'An Advocate's Guide to the Convention on Indigenous and Tribal Peoples' (1990) 15 *Oklahoma City University Law Review* 209, especially at 211, 234.

It should be pointed out, however, that the supervisory and monitoring procedures for the application of Convention No. 169 raise the same issues of legitimacy as the procedures for the adoption of the Convention did. Namely, due to the ILO's tripartite structure, indigenous individuals or organizations (unless they are indigenous workers' or employers' associations) must channel comments or more formal complaints and representations through trade unions or employers' bodies.[118]

Substance

The debate over self-determination in the negotiation of Convention No. 169 took the shape of a definitional dispute over whether to replace the term 'populations' in the old convention with the term 'peoples'. At stake was the possibility that the term 'peoples' could be taken to imply recognition of the right of indigenous peoples to self-determination and, further, their right to secede. The initial responses of the Canadian government (Canada) and the indigenous working group (IWG) it consulted give the contours of the debate:

> *Canada.* The term 'populations' should be retained. It is non-pejorative and its use is consistent with the current practice of United Nations bodies and agencies, including the Working Group on Indigenous Populations. The term 'peoples', on the other hand, does not have a clear meaning in international law and could prevent ratification of a revised Convention by some countries. The words 'aboriginal peoples' are used in Canadian law. However, the Government of Canada would, along with many other member States, have strong reservations about supporting the use of the term 'peoples' in an international Convention.
>
> *IWG.* Yes. It is absolutely essential that the distinctiveness of indigenous societies be fully reflected in the terminology of the revised Convention.[119]

Discussions before and during the 1988 session of the International Labour Conference, the first round of the ILO's 'double-discussion' procedure, betrayed little movement on this question of terminology. By the end of the session, there was widespread agreement on an intermediate position: 'peoples' would be used with the proviso that this choice of term should not be taken to express a position on the right of

---

[118] Tomei and Swepston, *A Guide*, pp. 29–30 (also discussing other ways to forward information to the ILO which may be available to indigenous groups in some cases). On the potential of the ILO complaint procedures for addressing indigenous peoples' concerns, see also Anaya, *Indigenous Peoples in International Law*, pp. 161–2.

[119] International Labour Office, Report VI(2), p. 13.

self-determination.[120] Nevertheless, a consensus could not be reached, and the Conference put over the issue until its 1989 session.[121]

In this first round of discussion, the retention of the term 'populations' was supported by the employers' delegates[122] and the delegates of certain governments. Only two of the thirty-two[123] governments that replied to this question on the initial questionnaire – Canada and Ecuador – were recorded as actually favouring 'populations'.[124] While Canada proposed such an amendment during the session, it also introduced an alternative amendment, to the effect that if the term 'peoples' were used, its use would 'not imply the right of self-determination as that term is understood in international law'.[125]

Four of the thirty-two governments offered what the International Labour Office categorized as other than affirmative or negative views. Of the four, Bolivia, in fact, favoured 'populations' outright,[126] the opinion of Saudi Arabia is not quoted, and Australia and Sweden occupied a middle ground. Sweden appears to have hesitated between 'populations' and the qualified use of 'peoples'.[127] In this regard, it is noteworthy that Sweden seconded both the above-mentioned amendments introduced during the session by the Canadian government.[128]

Although they had not answered the question about terminology in their response to the initial questionnaire, the governments of France and India in statements made during the session expressed some doubts about the term 'peoples'.[129]

Proponents of the term 'populations' relied on three types of argument. The uncertainty argument related to both the content of the term 'peoples' in international law[130] and the international legal

---

[120] International Labour Conference, Provisional Record No. 32, 75th Session (1988), p. 6.
[121] Ibid., pp. 6; 24, pt. 1 (proposed conclusions); International Labour Conference, Provisional Record No. 36, 75th Session (1988), p. 24 (adoption of proposed conclusions).
[122] As evidenced by their amendment to that effect; see International Labour Conference, Provisional Record No. 32, 75th Session (1988), p. 5. For the position of the Council of Netherlands Employers' Federations (RCO), see International Labour Office, Report VI(2), p. 13.
[123] Replies were received from fifty-three member states. International Labour Office, Report VI(2), p. 1.
[124] Ibid., p. 12.
[125] International Labour Conference, Provisional Record No. 32, 75th Session (1988), p. 5.
[126] International Labour Office, Report VI(2), p. 12.   [127] Ibid., p. 13.
[128] Notes, International Labour Office (unpublished).
[129] International Labour Conference, Provisional Record No. 32, 75th Session (1988), p. 3.
[130] See e.g. International Labour Office, Report VI(2), p. 13 (Canada's reply); International Labour Conference, Provisional Record No. 32, 75th Session (1988), p. 3 (general discussion).

consequences of recognizing a group as a 'people'.[131] According to the jurisdictional argument, since these issues had not been settled in international law, the use of the term 'peoples' would make, as opposed to reflect, international law. In so doing, the ILO would go beyond its competence in the spheres of economic, social and cultural rights, and trespass on the field of political rights.[132] The pragmatic objection to the term 'peoples' was that it would deter a number of states from ratifying the convention.[133]

Support for the term 'peoples' came from indigenous groups,[134] workers' delegates[135] and a majority of the states that responded to the relevant question on the questionnaire. Of the twenty-six states that responded positively to the substitution, however, Bulgaria,[136] Nigeria[137] and Portugal[138] expressed the view that the use of 'peoples' should be strictly circumscribed.

During the debate, six main reasons emerged for adopting the term 'peoples'. Three of these reasons concerned its implications for identity: 'peoples' reflected the fact that indigenous groups had an identity of their own,[139] 'populations' had degrading overtones because the term indicated merely a grouping or aggregate of individuals,[140] and 'peoples' corresponded to indigenous groups' own view of themselves.[141]

A fourth reason to adopt the term 'peoples' was apparent consistency with the terminology used in other international organizations.[142] The fifth and sixth reasons were contradictory, the fifth being the implied recognition of a right of self-determination,[143] and the sixth that since

---

[131] See e.g. International Labour Office, Report VI(2), p. 13 (replies of Ecuador and the Netherlands RCO); International Labour Conference, Provisional Record No. 32, 75th Session (1988), pp. 3 (Governments of Canada and France in general discussion), 5 (employers). See also International Labour Office, Report VI(1), p. 31.

[132] See e.g. Report of the Meeting of Experts, p. 105.

[133] See e.g. *ibid.*; International Labour Office, Report VI(2), p. 13 (Canada's reply); International Labour Conference, Provisional Record No. 32, 75th Session (1988), pp. 3 (India), 5 (employers).

[134] E.g. International Labour Conference, Provisional Record No. 32, 75th Session (1988), p. 4.

[135] *Ibid.*, p. 5.   [136] International Labour Office, Report VI(2), p. 13.

[137] *Ibid.*   [138] *Ibid.*

[139] Report of the Meeting of Experts, p. 105; International Labour Office, Report VI(2), p. 13 (reply of IWG (Canada)).

[140] Report of the Meeting of Experts, p. 105.

[141] *Ibid.*; International Labour Office, Report VI(2), p. 13 (replies of Gabon and Mexico); International Labour Conference, Provisional Record No. 32, 75th Session (1988), pp. 4 (NGOs), 5 (workers, Nordic Same [sic] Council).

[142] Report of the Meeting of Experts, p. 105; International Labour Office, Report VI(2), p. 13 (replies of Finland and Mexico).

[143] Report of the Meeting of Experts, p. 105.

the ILO's competence and the original convention extended only to economic, social and cultural matters, use of the term 'peoples' could not possibly imply a right of self-determination.[144]

The foundation for a compromise was laid by the International Labour Office already in its initial 'law and practice' report, which assured states that the 'implication [of self-determination] can be avoided... if the term is used to recognise that these groups have an identity of their own and consider themselves to be peoples, but that the implications of the term within the national context of ratifying States must be determined at the national level'.[145] Based on responses to the questionnaire, the Office concluded that the term 'peoples' should be used 'in order to be consistent with the terminology used in other international organizations and by these groups themselves'.[146] Its analysis also advised clarifying that 'the use of the term in this Convention should not be taken to imply the right to political self-determination, since this issue is clearly beyond the competence of the ILO'.[147]

Judging from the Office's written commentary, the Office was neutral on whether indigenous peoples should have a right of self-determination (although indirectly acknowledging that they did not currently have the right). The reasons it gave for supporting the use of 'peoples' turned on the implications for indigenous identity, as well as a more technical interest in standardizing terminology across international organizations. The Office's preference for a qualification on the use of 'peoples' was based on respecting the limitations of the Organization's mandate and, by the very fact of its addressing governments' concerns, working toward the adoption of a convention.

The second round of discussion added little to the substantive debate. In commenting on the draft convention, Brazil, Chile and India, three states that had previously not written on the issue, supported the term 'populations' rather than 'peoples'.[148] The next draft prepared by the Office used 'peoples' with the disclaimer that the term had no 'implications as regards the rights which may attach to the term under other international instruments'.[149]

Shifting their emphasis to criticize the qualified use of 'peoples', various indigenous groups characterized this position as racist and

---

[144] International Labour Conference, Provisional Record No. 32, 75th Session (1988), p. 5 (Inuit Circumpolar Conference).
[145] International Labour Office, Report VI(1), p. 31.
[146] International Labour Office, Report VI(2), p. 105, Conclusion No. 1.
[147] *Ibid.*, p. 14. [148] International Labour Office, Report IV(2A), pp. 8–10.
[149] International Labour Office, Report IV(2B), p. 6, Art. 1(3).

discriminatory because it distinguished between peoples: the fact that a people was indigenous was no reason to deny it the full range of international legal rights of peoples.[150] Another shift in approach was the assertion by some indigenous groups that the recognition of indigenous groups as 'peoples' would not lead to secession.[151]

The final outcome was a proviso worded much like the one proposed by the Office:

1(3) The use of the term 'peoples' in this Convention shall not be construed as having any implications as regards the rights which may attach to the term under international law.

The intention behind the Office's wording was to be neutral on the future development of a right of self-determination for indigenous peoples in international law. The Office reasoned that the omission of any reference to the right of self-determination would eliminate the possibility that the disclaimer might be construed as preventing or impeding the development of such a right.[152] The Committee of the Conference nevertheless approved an explanatory statement:

It is understood by the Committee that the use of the term 'peoples' in this Convention had no implication as regards the right to self-determination as understood in international law.[153]

From the perspective of governments, employers, workers and indigenous peoples, Article 1(3) is a 'compromise' that concedes little to indigenous peoples.[154] Governments (and employers) were not attached to the term 'populations' in and of itself, so these parties conceded little by agreeing to the substitution of the term 'peoples'. Their concern was the right of self-determination, in particular, the right of secession, that might flow from the recognition of indigenous and tribal groups as 'peoples', and this concern had been met by the qualifier in Article 1(3). The qualified use of the term 'peoples' is significant to indigenous peoples (and the workers and others who support them) for, as James Anaya expresses it, 'a certain affirmation of indigenous group identity and

---

[150] International Labour Conference, Provisional Record No. 25, 76th Session (1989), pp. 5 (International Organization of Indigenous Resource Development), 6–7 (Indian Council of South America); International Labour Conference, Provisional Record No. 31, 76th Session (1989), p. 7 (Venne, International Work Group for Indigenous Affairs).
[151] International Labour Conference, Provisional Record No. 25, 76th Session (1989), p. 6.
[152] International Labour Office, Report IV(2A), p. 12.
[153] International Labour Conference, Provisional Record No. 25, 76th Session (1989), p. 7.
[154] See, e.g., International Labour Conference Provisional Record No. 31, 76th Session (1989), p. 7 (Venne, International Work Group for Indigenous Affairs).

corresponding attributes of community'.¹⁵⁵ But it is a recognition of identity as 'peoples' without a corresponding recognition of rights as 'peoples', those rights remaining in the control of the Convention as a whole.

From the perspective of the International Labour Office, however, the approach taken to self-determination in Convention No. 169 is not a lopsided saw-off between the parties; it follows from the requirements of ILO standard-setting and the interests of the Organization. As already seen, the integrity of the Organization and the success of the Convention were among the Office's reasons for uncoupling 'peoples' from self-determination.

If we consider the extent to which the Convention more generally has subscribed to the competing normative visions of states and indigenous peoples – the different world-views behind their differences over self-determination – it is apparent that, here again, the Convention does not subscribe to one of these visions or attempt some pastiche of them. Rather than states' receptiveness to individual and minority rights or indigenous peoples' insistence on corrective justice, the Convention is, above all, true to the ILO's tradition of functionalism: integrated, interactive and empirically based.

For Lee Swepston, who directed the Office's efforts in the adoption of Convention No. 169, the Convention's 'flaws' are intentional:

it contains few absolute rules, but fixes goals, priorities and minimal rights... it sets out basic obligations, leaving the means of action to the national governments concerned. It is full of qualifying and flexibility phrases... its terms are not always capable of immediate application, but are instead goals... These things all describe what the ILO set out to do when it began the procedure.¹⁵⁶

Consistent with the ILO integrated approach to human rights, the Convention combines rights as enforceable minima with social goals as aspirational maxima. The potential of the goals identified in the Convention must be read against the developed ILO system for supervising conventions,¹⁵⁷ the belief being that a government obliged by its ratification of the Convention to carry on a dialogue with the Organization

---

¹⁵⁵ Anaya, 'Canada's Fiduciary Obligations', p. 22.
¹⁵⁶ Swepston, 'The Adoption of the Indigenous and Tribal Peoples Convention', 227; Swepston, 'A New Step', 689–90. Compare International Labour Office, Report VI(1), pp. 89–90 (stating already in 1987 that the Convention 'must establish general guide-lines or promotional measures, as well as specific obligations').
¹⁵⁷ Leary includes the ILO system for supervising conventions among the lessons for the United Nations. Leary, 'Lessons from the Experience of the ILO', pp. 581, 595–612.

will be more susceptible to the promotion of these goals by the ILO.[158] Finally, the Organization's method is primarily empirical: as its history of engagement with issues of indigenous peoples shows, the Organization tends to begin from its observation and cataloguing of common problems, rather than from a particular normative framework.

The application of the Convention signals the ILO's empirical bent. The first two subsections of Article 1 read:

1. This Convention applies to:
   (a) tribal[159] peoples in independent countries whose social, cultural and economic conditions distinguish them from other sections of the national community, and whose status is regulated wholly or partially by their own customs or traditions or by special laws or regulations;
   (b) peoples in independent countries who are regarded as indigenous on account of their descent from the populations which inhabited the country, or a geographical region to which the country belongs, at the time of conquest or colonisation or the establishment of present state boundaries and who, irrespective of their legal status, retain some or all of their own social, economic, cultural and political institutions.
2. Self-identification as indigenous or tribal shall be regarded as a fundamental criterion for determining the groups to which the provisions of this Convention apply.

The different historical experience – and, therefore, potentially different normative argument – of indigenous and tribal peoples is acknowledged by defining them separately, but nothing in the Convention turns on this difference.[160] At the time of Convention No. 107, which distinguishes tribal, semi-tribal and indigenous populations,[161] the attitude of the Conference was summarized as being that the distinction 'affected the theoretical basis for considering their situation, but had little effect on the practical aspects of their existence'.[162]

The ILO approach is thus to work from common problems of living and working conditions. Among the definitional criteria examined in the Organization's 1953 tome, *Indigenous Peoples*, was a 'functional' criterion, that 'instead of attempting to define the Indian first of all and then to apply for his benefit the measures considered appropriate, information

---

[158] Swepston, 'The Adoption of the Indigenous and Tribal Peoples Convention', 224.
[159] As in Convention No. 107, the term 'tribal' is undefined.
[160] See Tomei and Swepston, *A Guide*, p. 5.   [161] Convention No. 107, Art. 1.
[162] International Labour Office, Working Document for the 1986 Meeting of Experts, p. 15, n. 2.

should first be collected regarding the conditions of life of the groups commonly described as indigenous in each country where there is an indigenous problem'.[163]

To some extent, the ILO was locked into its utilitarian definition by the fact that Convention No. 169 revised Convention No. 107.[164] In recommending revision, the Meeting of Experts noted that the earlier convention is intended to apply and has been applied to a wide variety of indigenous and tribal peoples. It covers, for instance, Indians in the Americas, whatever their degree of integration into the national culture; tribal peoples in Asia, including in Bangladesh, India and Pakistan which have all ratified Convention No. 107; and nomadic populations in desert and other regions. The experts from Africa agreed that Convention No. 107 is applicable in Africa, including to relatively isolated groups such as the San or Bushmen, the Pygmies and the Bedouin and other nomadic populations.[165]

To a greater extent, the broad application of Convention No. 169 reflects the ILO's deliberate rejection of a priori normative constructs as the appropriate analytical apparatus, in favour of observed common needs. The Office stated that 'attempts to analyse the historical precedence of different parts of the national population would detract from the need to protect vulnerable groups which in all other respects share many common characteristics, wherever they are found'.[166]

Even where historical precedence could be established, the Office insisted that there also be some present need. It did not consider historical precedence sufficient to define an 'indigenous people' – which it would be from the standpoint of corrective justice. In contrast, the indigenous working group consulted by the Canadian government objected to the requirement that the people in question retain some or all of their social, economic, cultural and political institutions, arguing that some indigenous peoples may have lost these institutions through no fault of their own.[167]

Further, the critical date in the definition of 'indigenous peoples' was generalized from 'the time of conquest or colonisation' to 'the time of conquest or colonisation or the establishment of present state

---

[163] Quoted in *ibid.*, p. 4.   [164] International Labour Office, Report VI(1), p. 32.
[165] Report of the Meeting of Experts, p. 105.
[166] International Labour Office, Report VI(1), p. 32. See also Tomei and Swepston, *A Guide*, p. 5 (the ILO intention *ab initio* 'was to cover a social situation, rather than to establish a priority based on whose ancestors had arrived in a particular area first').
[167] International Labour Office, Report VI(2), pp. 14–16.

boundaries' at the suggestion of Norway.[168] Whereas conquest and colonization encode the wrong central to a historical argument for the rights of indigenous peoples, the phrase 'establishment of present state boundaries' is more neutral and could be seen as diminishing the normative power of the other two.

The provisions on land claims in Convention No. 169 offer another window on the underlying philosophy of the Convention.[169] The background debate is between recognition of the rights of indigenous peoples to the lands they now occupy and restitution of lands of which they have been deprived and to which they lay claim.[170] During the discussion of Convention No. 169, states were critical of proposed wording that could be interpreted as recognizing the rights of indigenous peoples over lands that they had ceased to occupy.[171] Recognition of rights to land currently occupied is usually grounded in traditional occupancy and can be accommodated within many existing systems of property law. Restitution is often sought by indigenous peoples on the basis of prior sovereignty or treaty, thereby posing a fundamental challenge to the state.[172]

An alternative argument for recognition of rights to land and, in some cases, restitution derives from the importance of a land base for the survival and traditional culture of a minority group. This argument is particularly strong for indigenous peoples, whose relationship with the land is central to their spiritual and cultural life.[173] The Office, in its law and practice report, referred to the situation where, their lands

---

[168] International Labour Office, Report IV(2A), p. 13. It was incorporated into the draft convention in International Labour Office, Report IV(2B), p. 6 and appears in the Convention as adopted.

In the first round of discussion, Norway had made a similar suggestion. International Labour Office, Report VI(2), p. 15. A Workers' amendment to this effect was made during the first Session, but was withdrawn. International Labour Conference, Provisional Record No. 32, 75th Session (1988), p. 7.

[169] See generally L. Swepston and R. Plant, 'International Standards and the Protection of the Land Rights of Indigenous and Tribal Populations' (1985) 124 *International Labour Review* 91.

[170] International Labour Office, Working Document for the 1986 Meeting of Experts, p. 38.

[171] E.g. International Labour Office, Report VI(2), pp. 46–9 (Canada and the United States); International Labour Office, Report IV(2A), pp. 34–6 (same countries).

[172] See International Labour Office, Report VI(1), p. 15; International Labour Office, Report IV(2A), pp. 34–5 (Indigenous Peoples' Working Group, Canada); International Labour Conference, Provisional Record No. 25, 76th Session (1989), pp. 16–17; International Labour Conference, Provisional Record No. 31, 76th Session (1989), p. 7.

[173] See e.g. Innu Communication submitted to the UN Secretary-General pursuant to ESC Resolution 1503 (25 March 1990), reprinted in edited form in Tennant and Turpel, 'Genocide, Ethnocide and Self-Determination', 302 at 302–3.

having been fragmented over the course of centuries, the demand of an indigenous people is for 'the restitution of sufficient ancestral land to provide them with a cohesive territory over which they may exercise management and control in accordance with their own traditions'.[174] Restitution of land on the basis of need is thus distinguishable from restitution on the basis of historical claims.

Generally speaking, the provisions on land in Convention No. 169 are not based on historical claims. Article 14(1) recognizes that peoples who traditionally occupy the land have special rights to it, but does not thereby recognize rights over any lands they ever occupied.[175] The first reason given by Swepston for not satisfying indigenous demands for recognition of prior sovereignty is the near certainty that governments would not ratify an instrument that required them to alter their entire legal system.[176]

Swepston's other line of reasoning is that the recognition of prior sovereignty would exclude 'groups, equally disadvantaged and equally exploited, [which] do not necessarily enjoy this temporal priority'.[177] This reasoning highlights the normative implications of the Convention's broad coverage. In choosing to group together indigenous and tribal peoples, the ILO has restricted the approach that can be taken in the Convention to ones that apply equally to both groups. At the same time, it has ensured that the common characteristics and needs seen to unite indigenous and tribal peoples will always be available as basis for the Convention's provisions.

Thus, like the Convention's definition of indigenous and tribal peoples – or because of it – the Convention's provisions on land respond to the perceived commonality of indigenous and tribal peoples' needs; here, their needs for territory. Article 13 obliges governments to respect the special cultural and spiritual importance of territory for indigenous peoples. Article 19(a) acknowledges the importance of a sufficient land base for collective survival: 'National agrarian programmes shall secure to the peoples concerned treatment equivalent to that accorded to other sectors of the population with regard to: the provision of more land for these peoples when they have not the area necessary for providing the

---

[174] International Labour Office, Report VI(1), p. 69.
[175] International Labour Office, Report IV(2A), p. 36.
[176] Swepston, 'A New Step', 697. This is not to say that states may not still have concerns about the Convention's provisions on land. For Canada's concerns, see D. Pharand, 'The International Labour Organization Convention on Indigenous Peoples (1989): Canada's Concerns' in Anaya, Falk and Pharand, *Canada's Fiduciary Obligation*, pp. 132–9 at pp. 133–5, 137–8.
[177] Swepston, 'A New Step', 697.

essentials of a normal existence, or for any possible increase in their numbers'.

While Convention No. 169 is not intended to give rise to new land claims, Article 14(3) requires the establishment of domestic legal procedures adequate to resolve such land claims as might exist. Whereas indigenous peoples may be inclined to read the term 'adequate' as cold comfort, the ILO reads it interactively. In the working document prepared for the Meeting of Experts, the Office stated that requiring a mechanism for settling land claims without specifying the exact mechanism 'would allow the ILO's supervisory bodies to ascertain whether governments are seriously attempting to deal with the difficult questions raised', as is rarely the case.[178]

Although Article 14(3) appears to offer no guidance on how land claims are to be judged, Swepston points to Article 19(a) as 'indicating a dynamic examination within established procedures to determine whether the peoples concerned in fact have any valid claim to given parcels or areas of land, as well as what their needs are in this connection'.[179] Swepston's gloss may mean that a land claim could be reduced by showing that the claimant indigenous people did not need the entire area in order to provide, in the words of Article 19(a), the essentials of a 'normal' existence. Then again, perhaps a land claim could be augmented where the area covered by the claim would still be insufficient to provide, as Article 19(a) puts it, for any possible increase in numbers. In any event, the linking of Articles 14(3) and 19(a) further underscores the pragmatic outlook of the ILO.

Besides land claims, the benchmark of corrective justice in the Convention is the recognition of treaties. On the suggestion of the indigenous working group consulted by the Canadian government, a reference to treaty claims was added to the land claims provision,[180] but was later dropped.[181]

Treaties are mentioned in Article 35, but the position of the term illustrates again the ILO's self-imposed neutrality in matters of political rights. After the 1988 session of the Conference, the Article (then Article

---

[178] International Labour Office, Working Document for the 1986 Meeting of Experts, p. 44.
[179] Swepston, 'A New Step', 703.
[180] International Labour Office, Report VI(2), p. 63. It appears as Article 19 in International Labour Office, Report IV(1), p. 11 and International Labour Office, Report VI(2A), pp. 50–1. It was changed to Article 14(4) in International Labour Office, Report IV(2B).
[181] International Labour Conference, Provisional Record No. 25, 76th Session (1989), p. 19 (Argentina objects to the term 'treaties' in Art. 14(4)).

34) read: 'The application of the provisions of this Convention shall not adversely affect rights and benefits of the (peoples/populations) concerned pursuant to other Conventions and Recommendations, under treaties or international instruments, or under national laws, awards, custom or agreements'.[182] In this formulation, the legal categories are other ILO standards, international law and national law. The grouping of 'treaties' with international instruments potentially recognizes indigenous treaties as being between sovereigns. Canada proposed instead that the categories should be 'Conventions and Recommendations and other international instruments, or under national laws, awards, custom, treaties or agreements', thereby including treaties between states under international law and indigenous treaties under national law.[183] The Office's solution, which was adopted by the Conference, was to make treaties into a separate category in between international and national law.[184] Behind this solution was the Office's concern that the ILO not prejudice the results of studies then being done by the United Nations on the nature of treaties between states and indigenous peoples.[185]

UN Working Group on Indigenous Populations

Unlike the ILO, the UN Working Group on Indigenous Populations is not a full-fledged institution. The Working Group lies at the perimeter of the UN human rights system. It was set up by the Sub-Commission on Prevention of Discrimination and Protection of Minorities (now titled the Sub-Commission on the Promotion and Protection of Human Rights); which, in turn, was created by the Commission on Human Rights; which, in its turn, is a functional commission of the Economic and Social Council. To be adopted, the draft declaration on the rights of indigenous peoples completed by the Working Group in 1993 must work its way inward, toward the centre of the UN human rights system. The Sub-Commission adopted the draft declaration in 1994, and the Commission in 1995 established its own Working Group to elaborate a new draft declaration based on this one.[186]

---

[182] International Labour Office, Report IV(1), p. 16.
[183] International Labour Office, Report IV(2A), pp. 67–8.
[184] International Labour Office, Report IV(2B), p. 26, Art. 35.
[185] International Labour Office, Report IV(2A), p. 68.
[186] Establishment of a Working Group of the Commission on Human Rights to Elaborate a Draft Declaration in Accordance with Operative Paragraph 5 of General Assembly

Whatever the outcome of the Commission's work,[187] however, the 1993 draft declaration of the Working Group on Indigenous Populations is procedurally as well as substantively significant in its own right. James Anaya characterizes it as 'an authoritative statement of norms concerning indigenous peoples on the basis of generally applicable human rights principles' and 'a manifestation of the movement in a corresponding consensual nexus of opinion on the subject among relevant actors'.[188] For Maivân Clech Lâm, the draft declaration also marks a new recognition of the value of participation. As evidence, she points to the access afforded indigenous groups to the Commission's Working Group. What makes this evidence more compelling is that the Commission on Human Rights, unlike the Working Group on Indigenous Populations, is composed of state representatives.[189]

This part of the chapter documents a change in the Chairperson of the Working Group's presentation of the object and nature of the drafting process, moving it closer to indigenous peoples' aspirations for the declaration and understandings of the dynamics of its drafting.[190] The part suggests that this change permitted and ultimately structured the achievement of a right of self-determination in the draft that combined states' and indigenous peoples' ideas of the right and its justifications for secession. That is, the Working Group's responsiveness to the perspectives of indigenous peoples was a function not simply of the exceptional openness and accessibility of this forum throughout, but of the Chairperson's eventual reconception of the process and the place of indigenous peoples in that process.

Process

The Working Group on Indigenous Populations[191] is made up of five individuals drawn from the Sub-Commission,[192] which is a body of

---

Resolution 49/214 of 23 December 1994, CHR Res.1995/32, reprinted in (1995) 34 ILM 535.
[187] To date, see Lâm, *At the Edge of the State*, pp. 70–5.
[188] Anaya, *Indigenous Peoples in International Law*, p. 53.
[189] Lâm, *At the Edge of the State*, pp. 81–2.
[190] Although I do not treat it here, Venne identifies another important shift – from written to oral submissions – prompted by and aimed at recognizing indigenous ideals of participation. Venne, *Our Elders Understand Our Rights*, pp. 147–8, 151.
[191] See generally Sanders, 'The UN Working Group on Indigenous Populations'.
[192] See generally A. Eide, 'The Sub-Commission on Prevention of Discrimination and Protection of Minorities' in Alston, *The United Nations and Human Rights*, pp. 211–64.

independent experts.¹⁹³ While the membership of the Working Group has changed over the course of drafting the declaration on indigenous rights, Erica-Irene Daes was its Chairperson throughout.

The 1982 resolution establishing the Working Group instructed it to 'give special attention to the evolution of standards concerning the rights of indigenous populations, taking account of both the similarities and the differences in the situations and aspirations of indigenous populations throughout the world'.¹⁹⁴ By not specifying how standards would evolve, the resolution left open whether the Working Group's mandate was the passive codification of changing standards in international law or the active development of new standards. Depending on the interpretation given to the Working Group's mandate, the requirement that it take account of indigenous peoples' own aspirations constituted these aspirations as either data to be evaluated or choices to be reconciled with those of states.

Following the Working Group's first draft of principles for the declaration, the Commission on Human Rights passed a resolution¹⁹⁵ in 1986 commending the Working Group for its 'continued broad approach and flexible methods of work',¹⁹⁶ and the participating observer governments, specialized agencies, NGOs, and, in particular, organizations and communities of indigenous peoples for their contributions. The resolution also urged the Working Group to continue its development of international standards 'based on a continued and comprehensive review of developments' in the area of indigenous rights and 'of the situations and aspirations of indigenous populations throughout the world'. As with the earlier resolution, there was a tension between the technical consolidation implicit in 'based on a continued and comprehensive review of developments' and the potential for dialogic innovation in 'aspirations of indigenous populations'.

However ambivalent, these resolutions on the Working Group's mandate made more room for the development of new standards on

---

[193] According to Asbjørn Eide, the requirements of independence and expertise are neither well-defined nor well-policed. *Ibid.*, pp. 212, 252–4.

[194] Study of the Problem of Discrimination Against Indigenous Populations, ESC Res. 1982/34 (1982), para. 2.

[195] Report of the Working Group on Indigenous Populations of the Sub-Commission on Prevention of Discrimination and Protection of Minorities, CHR Res. 1986/27 (1986).

[196] Among the commentators who have noted the exceptional accessibility and openness of the working group process are Barsh ('An Emerging Object', 383), Lâm (*At the Edge of the State*, pp. 80–1), Marantz ('Indigenous Peoples in International Fora', p. 14) and Sanders (D. Sanders, 'Draft Declaration on the Rights of Indigenous Peoples – A Text and a New Process' [1994] 1 *Canadian Native Law Reporter* 48 at 48).

indigenous peoples than did the General Assembly's 1986 resolution on standard-setting in the field of international human rights. A form of 'quality control'[197] for the recognition of new human rights, GA resolution 41/120 read in part

Recalling the extensive network of international standards in the field of human rights...
...

Emphasizing the primacy of the Universal Declaration of Human Rights, the International Covenant on Civil and Political Rights and the International Covenant on Economic, Social and Cultural Rights in this network,
...

Recognizing the value of continuing efforts to identify specific areas where further international action is required to develop the existing international legal framework in the field of human rights...
...

2. *Urges* Member States and United Nations bodies engaged in developing new international human rights standards to give due consideration in this work to the established international legal framework;
...

4. *Invites* Member States and United Nations bodies to bear in mind the following guidelines in developing international instruments in the field of human rights; such instruments should, *inter alia*:

(a) Be consistent with the existing body of international human rights law;
...
(e) Attract broad international support;[198]

Throughout the drafting of the declaration in the Working Group, Resolution 41/120 would be the touchstone for states arguing that the declaration should exhibit strict consistency with existing international human rights instruments or be capable of attracting broad international support.[199]

---

[197] Philip Alston uses the notion of 'quality control' in an article published two years before GA Resolution 41/120 was passed. 'Conjuring Up New Human Rights: A Proposal for Quality Control' (1984) 78 *American Journal of International Law* 607. Alston offers a formal list of substantive requirements for new human rights, much like that in GA Resolution 41/120, but dismisses this approach as unworkable. *Ibid.*, 614–17.

[198] Setting International Standards in the Field of Human Rights, GA Res. 41/120 (1986).

[199] E.g. E.-I. A. Daes, Report of the Working Group on Indigenous Populations on its Fifth Session, UN Doc. E/CN.4/Sub.2/1987/22 (1987), p. 12 (unidentified speaker); Analytical Compilation of Observations and Comments Received Pursuant to Sub-Commission Resolution 1988/18, UN Doc. E/CN.4/Sub.2/1989/33/Add.1 (1989), pp. 5 (Canada), 10 (Sweden); Analytical Compilation of Observations and Comments Received Pursuant to Sub-Commission Resolution 1988/18, UN Doc. E/CN.4/Sub.2/1989/33/Add.3 (1989),

Australia early on summarized the two contending interpretations of the standard-setting process and exemplified the preference of most states:

> it is not clear from the draft itself whether it operates within the framework of existing agreements or whether the draft declaration is conferring additional rights specifically for indigenous peoples and thus going beyond the provisions for minorities in the International Covenant on Civil and Political Rights.
>
> From Australia's perspective, it is clearly the former relationship which the draft declaration should seek to present.[200]

Canada argued that close correspondence to existing international norms would ensure that the declaration's objectives were achievable and acceptable.[201] For Sweden, the risk of straying from established norms was a blurring of concepts and an incoherent system of norms: 'To make indigenous rights individual ones, as for instance minority rights in article 27 of the Covenant... would undoubtedly be the best way of ensuring a clear, coherent and functional normative system in the field of human rights, which would be in accordance with the aims set out in General Assembly resolution 41/120'.[202]

States also understood the Working Group to be engaged in the production of a text precise enough to be easily understood and effectively implemented.[203] Lastly, many expected a text that 'reconciled the points of view of all interested parties, based on a spirit of consensus'.[204]

The conceptions that indigenous groups had of the Working Group's

p. 3 (Japan); E.-I. A. Daes, Report of the Working Group on Indigenous Populations on its Seventh Session, UN Doc. E/CN.4/Sub.2/1989/36 (1989), p. 16 (Government Observer); E.-I. A. Daes, Report of the Working Group on Indigenous Populations on its Ninth Session, UN Doc. E/CN.4/Sub.2/1991/40/Rev.1 (1991), p. 8 (New Zealand, Norway); E.-I. A. Daes, Report of the Working Group on Indigenous Populations on its Tenth Session, UN Doc. E/CN.4/Sub.2/1992/33 (1992), p. 15 (Norway on its own behalf and that of Denmark, Finland and Sweden).

[200] Analytical Compilation of Observations and Comments Received Pursuant to Sub-Commission Resolution 1988/18, UN Doc. E/CN.4/Sub.2/1989/33/Add.1 (1989), p. 2 (Australia).

[201] Analytical Compilation of Observations and Comments Received Pursuant to Sub-Commission Resolution 1988/18, UN Doc. E/CN.4/Sub.2/1989/33/Add.1 (1989), p. 5 (Canada).

[202] *Ibid.*, p. 10 (Sweden).

[203] Report on Ninth Session, p. 8 (New Zealand); Report on Tenth Session, p. 15 (Canada, Denmark, Finland, Norway, Sweden).

[204] E.-I. A. Daes, Report of the Working Group on Indigenous Populations on its Eighth Session, UN Doc. E/CN.4/Sub.2/1990/42 (1990), p. 25. See also Report on Ninth Session, p. 9 (Brazil wants adoption by consensus).

standard-setting function corresponded to the other pole of its mandate: that which required the Working Group to develop standards based on the aspirations of indigenous peoples.[205] Indigenous groups maintained that the draft declaration should not be limited by existing international human rights instruments.[206] Were consistency with the established international legal framework necessary, one NGO representative argued, then a broad notion of consistency should be employed.[207]

Also in contrast to states, a number of indigenous representatives to the Working Group viewed the declaration as a manifesto of the rights of indigenous peoples, with the more detailed provisions on implementing, protecting and enforcing these rights left to a convention.[208] In the words of the Indian Law Resource Center, the declaration should 'declare universal rights for indigenous peoples in broad, ringing and enduring terms'.[209] Finally, indigenous voices in the Working Group tended to speak of the draft declaration as a balance between the aspirations of indigenous peoples and the legitimate interests of states,[210] and were less inclined to insist on consensus.[211]

Over the eight years of drafting the declaration on the rights of indigenous peoples, Chairperson Erica-Irene Daes shifted the process away

---

[205] See e.g. Mary Simon, representing the Inuit Tapirasat of Canada, Inuit Circumpolar Conference (Canada), Grand Council of the Crees (Quebec), Metis National Council, Native Council of Canada, Congress of Aboriginal Peoples, and the International Organization of Indigenous Resource Development, 'Statement on the Occasion of the Inauguration of the "International Year of the World's Indigenous People"', reprinted in (1993) 3 *Transnational Law and Contemporary Problems* 210 at 211.
[206] Report on Seventh Session, p. 17.
[207] Report on Tenth Session, p. 16 (Minority Rights Group).
[208] Report on Fifth Session, p. 13 (unidentified speaker makes reference to a convention); Analytical Compilation of Observations and Comments Received Pursuant to Sub-Commission Resolution 1988/18, UN Doc. E/CN.4/Sub.2/1989/33/Add.1, p. 13 (Indian Law Resource Center); Information Received from Non-Governmental Organizations, UN Doc. E/CN.4/Sub.2/AC.4/1990/3/Add.2 (1990), p. 5 (Indian Law Resource Center).
[209] Analytical Compilation of Observations and Comments Received Pursuant to Sub-Commission Resolution 1988/18, UN Doc. E/CN.4/Sub.2/1989/33/Add.1, p. 13 (Indian Law Resource Center); Information Received from Non-Governmental Organizations, UN Doc. E/CN.4/Sub.2/AC.4/1990/3/Add.2 (1990), p. 5 (Indian Law Resource Center). See also Report on Tenth Session, pp. 15–16 (National Indian Youth Council concerned about use of excessively specific language).
[210] E.g. UN Doc. E/CN.4/Sub.2/1989/33/Add.1, p. 11 (Four Directions Council); E.-I. A. Daes, Report of the Working Group on Indigenous Populations on its Twelfth Session, UN Doc. E/CN.4/Sub.2/1994/30 (1994), p. 14 (Rigobertu Menchu Tum was reported to have stated that the draft declaration, although not responding to all indigenous concerns, constituted a useful and important document.).
[211] Report on Eighth Session, p. 25 (indigenous representative).

from judicious standard-setting by a group of experts with input from interested parties and toward negotiations between the parties as equals mediated by the Chairperson.[212] In an early account of the Working Group's progress on the draft declaration, she drew attention to the guidelines in General Assembly resolution 41/120, including consistency with existing human rights law, and reproduced the resolution as an annex.[213] By the time the Working Group completed the draft declaration in 1993, the declaration had become too radical to satisfy resolution 41/120.[214] Moreover, a description of the declaration given by Daes in 1989 made clear that she had cut the process loose from its moorings in international human rights law and was navigating between the Scylla and Charybdis of the parties' demands: 'The text as it stands now, constitutes a fair balance between the aspirations of indigenous peoples and the legitimate concern of States and, for that reason, seems to be a realistic approach to the issues. It has also been mentioned that substantial changes have to be acceptable to all parties concerned.'[215] In a 1994 comment to the Sub-Commission, Daes indicated that the declaration was not a consensus document: 'The Working Group which, with some 790 participants, was more like a community had agreed on many constructive points but on some matters opinions still differed.'[216]

So long as the Working Group tended to see itself as engaged in standard-setting based on a world-wide review of the legal developments affecting indigenous peoples and of their situations, and in the conservative manner of resolution 41/120, the types of statements made to the Working Group by representatives of indigenous groups would be treated mainly as data for the review and not arguments about what

---

[212] Alston finds that the loose mandates of most UN human rights bodies and their predilection for ad hoc responses mean that there is some capacity to shift from one type of institutional actor to another. P. Alston, 'Appraising the United Nations Human Rights Regime' in Alston, *The United Nations and Human Rights*, pp. 1–21 at p. 5. What is remarkable about the Working Group is that the shift was promoted by peoples, as opposed to states or other more powerful institutional actors.

[213] Report on Fifth Session, p. 12.

[214] E. Gayim, 'The Draft Declaration on Indigenous Peoples: With Focus on the Rights to Land and Self-Determination' in Gayim and Myntti, *Indigenous and Tribal Peoples' Rights – 1993 and After*, pp. 12–45 at p. 37.

[215] First Revised Text of the Draft Universal Declaration on Rights of Indigenous Peoples Prepared by the Chairman-Rapporteur of the Working Group on Indigenous Populations, Mrs. Erica-Irene Daes, Pursuant to Sub-Commission Resolution 1988/18, UN Doc. E/CN.4/Sub.2/1989/33, p. 3.

[216] UN Doc. E/CN.4/Sub.2/1994/SR.29 (1994), p. 12.

standards should be set. Only through reconceiving the process as 'a fair balance between the aspirations of indigenous peoples and the legitimate concerns of states' could indigenous voices have had the impact that they did on the rights in the draft declaration. At the same time, the Chairperson's transformation of herself from expert to mediator could have carried risks for indigenous peoples had she not chosen to treat the balance as 'fair'. As mediator, she might have elected to strike a Realpolitik balance, speaking power to truth instead of truth to power. But Daes exchanged the basis of her authority from her positive law expertise to her ability to reconcile competing demands and normative visions.

Substance

Whereas in discussions of ILO Convention No. 169 the issue of self-determination was confined to the debate over 'populations' or 'peoples', discussions of the UN draft declaration on indigenous rights also engaged the issue of self-determination directly.[217] In the sessions of the UN Working Group on Indigenous Populations, the populations/peoples debate became a debate over 'people' or 'peoples'. For certain states, the danger of 'peoples' in the plural continued to be that the use of the term might implicitly recognize a right of self-determination and, in turn, a right of secession.[218] 'People' in the singular, like 'populations', denoted merely an aggregate of individuals. The third possibility was, as in Convention No. 169, to use 'peoples' with a proviso that explicitly uncoupled 'peoples' from the right of self-determination and thereby from the right of secession. In addition, the term 'self-determination' was, with successive formal and informal drafts, increasingly sprinkled throughout the preamble and operative paragraphs of the declaration. States' willingness to recognize a right of self-determination was largely

---

[217] For a detailed discussion of the debates on self-determination in the Working Group, see also Iorns, 'Challenging State Sovereignty', 204–23.

[218] E.-I. A. Daes, Explanatory Note Concerning the Draft Declaration on the Rights of Indigenous Peoples, UN Doc. E/CN.4/Sub.2/1993/26/Add.1 (1993), p. 2. E.g. D. Marantz, Statement of the Observer Delegation of Canada, Working Group on Indigenous Populations, 10th Session (Geneva, 21 July 1992), p. 6 ('With regard to the use of the term 'peoples', Canada's concern... is linked solely to the self-determination implications of this term in international law: it is not an objection to the term itself'.); Canada's Suggestions on Draft Operative Paragraphs (submitted to the 10th Session of the Working Group, 1992) [undated].

It should be noted that states' positions may have changed since the Working Group completed its draft declaration in 1993.

dependent on decoupling the right of self-determination, in turn, from the right of secession.

By the time that the Working Group produced its final draft of the declaration, a minority of states accepted without reservation a right of self-determination for indigenous peoples.[219] This does not necessarily mean, however, that these states recognized indigenous peoples as having the same right of self-determination as colonial peoples; that is, the right to choose independent statehood, free association or integration with another state, or other political status. Australia's position, for example, was that this right of self-determination had become less and less relevant, and that it could and had to be reconceived for a new age. At the 1992 session of the Working Group, Australia presented its postcolonial conception of self-determination, which recognized the special position of indigenous peoples, as well as guaranteeing their fundamental human rights and their full and genuine participation in the political process. This and later statements to the Working Group give some indication that Australia subscribed to a rights model of self-determination:[220] in its 1992 statement, it proposed the penultimate paragraph on self-determination found in the Declaration on Principles of International Law Concerning Friendly Relations and Cooperation Among States in Accordance with the Charter of the United Nations[221] for inclusion in the draft declaration.[222] As discussed in Chapter 2, this paragraph is considered by some to grant a group the right of external self-determination where that group has been denied a right of internal self-determination (which, on the Australian interpretation, might be a complex of individual and group rights).

For most states, the policy on indigenous peoples was to negotiate an increasing range of options within the framework of the state. Canada, for example, refused to support 'peoples' in the absence of a qualification that the use of the term did not imply a right of self-determination,[223]

---

[219] Report on Eleventh Session, p. 16.
[220] Statement by Mr. Colin Milner on Behalf of the Australian Delegation (Geneva, 24 July 1992) (10th Session of Working Group). See also Report on Eleventh Session, p. 17.
[221] Declaration on Principles of International Law Concerning Friendly Relations and Cooperation Among States in Accordance with the Charter of the United Nations, GA Res. 2625 (XXV)(1970).
[222] See also UN Doc. E/CN.4/Sub.2/1994/SR.29 (1994), pp. 7–8 (Pakistan).
[223] Analytical Compilation of Observations and Comments Received Pursuant to Sub-Commission Resolution 1988/18, UN Doc. E/CN.4/Sub.2/1989/33/Add.1 (1989), p. 4; Information Received from Governments, UN Doc. E/CN.4/Sub.2/AC.4/1990/1/Add.3 (1990), p. 2; Marantz, Statement of the Observer Delegation of Canada, p. 6; Report on Tenth Session, p. 19; Report on Eleventh Session, p. 19.

while simultaneously moving toward an expansive notion of internal self-determination.[224] The Canadian approach was to discard the existing concept of self-determination in international law and to produce a new concept of self-determination within the draft declaration. The existing concept, with its risk of secession, would be jettisoned by severing the use of the term 'peoples' from it and by making plain that any right of self-determination recognized in the declaration was not understood by Canada 'to be a right of self-determination as that term is understood in international law'.[225] Even though the same term would be used, whatever right of self-determination emerged from the drafting of the declaration would be treated by Canada as unconnected to the right of self-determination already established in international law. With respect to the content of the new and distinct right, Canada stated during the 1992 session of the Working Group that it

> is sensitive to the desire of many to exercise control over their own lives and how they are governed. For this reason, Canada supports the principle of self-determination for indigenous people, within the framework of existing states, where there is an inter-relationship between indigenous and non-indigenous jurisdictions that gives indigenous people greater levels of autonomy over their own affairs but that also recognizes the jurisdiction of the state. Canada's understanding of self-determination is that it would be exercised in a manner which recognizes that inter-relationship between the jurisdiction of the existing state and that of the indigenous community, and where the parameters of jurisdiction are mutually agreed upon.[226]

For Canada, the right of self-determination articulated in the draft declaration had to be internal, to recognize that greater autonomy for indigenous communities could modify but not eliminate the jurisdiction of the existing state, and to require agreement on jurisdiction. These requirements remained constant in its position at the 1993 session, at which the reading of the draft declaration was completed.[227] What is different about Canada's position on record at the 1993 session is that whereas Canada had previously been at pains to distinguish any right of self-determination developed in the draft declaration from the traditional right of self-determination in international law, it pointed out that indigenous peoples qualified for the traditional right of self-determination

---

[224] Marantz, Statement of the Observer Delegation of Canada, p. 5; Report on Tenth Session, p. 17; Report on the Working Group on Indigenous Populations on its Eleventh Session. Addendum. Comments by the Government of Canada, UN Doc. E/CN.4/Sub.2/1993/29/Add.1 (1993).
[225] Marantz, Statement of the Observer Delegation of Canada, p. 5.
[226] Ibid.   [227] Addendum. Comments by the Government of Canada.

in international law on the same basis as non-indigenous peoples if they otherwise met the criteria.

To the extent that states articulated a normative basis for their policies on indigenous peoples within the state, it tended to be some understanding of equality or extension of accepted minority rights. Sweden consistently argued:

> The concept of human rights flowed from the idea of the inherent right of each individual. This concept should not become weakened or ambiguous. Therefore, indigenous rights, even when exercised collectively, should be based on the non-discriminatory application of individual rights. He [the observer for Sweden] suggested an approach similar to the one adopted in the Declaration on the Rights of Persons Belonging to National or Ethnic, Religious and Linguistic Minorities.[228]

Venezuela resisted provisions in the draft declaration that it regarded as undermining equality: 'rather than preventing discrimination, the draft declaration tends to increase it by promoting the formation within States of watertight compartments or independent communities'.[229]

Other states identified, as the United States did, both the right of indigenous peoples to 'non-discrimination and equality before the law, and their right to preserve and develop their identity'.[230] Australia initially supported 'the right of indigenous people to be free and equal to all other human beings, to preserve their cultural identity and traditions, and to pursue their own cultural development'.[231] The same normative concerns were present in its subsequent position that self-determination could be realized by 'a system which would guarantee full and genuine participation and fundamental human rights, as well as recognize the special position of indigenous peoples'.[232]

In general, the states that participated in the Working Group[233] were prepared to recognize group-differentiated rights only if they were

---

[228] Report on Eleventh Session, p. 20. Compare Analytical Compilation of Observations and Comments Received Pursuant to Sub-Commission Resolution 1988/18, UN Doc. E/CN.4/1989/33/Add.1 (1989), p. 10 (Sweden's position in 1989 is the same).

[229] Information Received from Governments, UN Doc. E/CN.4/Sub.2/AC.4/1990/1 (1990), p. 14.

[230] Report on the Tenth Session, p. 14.

[231] Analytical Compilation of Observations and Comments Received Pursuant to Sub-Commission Resolution 1988/18, p. 2.

[232] Report on Tenth Session, p. 17.

[233] For other analyses of states' positions in the Working Group, see G. Alfredsson, 'The Right of Self-Determination and Indigenous Peoples' in C. Tomuschat (ed.), *Modern Law of Self-Determination* (Dordrecht: Martinus Nijhoff, 1993), pp 41–54 at pp. 43–5; Marantz, 'Indigenous Peoples in International Fora', pp. 18–21.

referable to equality or, to the extent that this was not subsumed in equality, to the preservation and development of culture. This was put succinctly by India: 'With regard to territorial arrangements, the degree of autonomy appropriate to a given indigenous community had to be judged in the light of what was necessary to maintain its own culture and separate identity, while protecting the rights of other population groups'.[234] If historical claims by indigenous peoples to vast tracts of land were supportable on this type of argument, it would be because the land was demonstrably necessary to their culture and not on the basis of historical entitlement. By and large, states involved in the drafting of the declaration opposed language that might indicate support for historical land claims, notably the use of 'occupy' in the past tense.[235] A number of states also took exception to revisiting the injustices of the international legal doctrine of *terra nullius*, according to which some territories inhabited by indigenous peoples had been considered 'empty lands'.[236]

Throughout the drafting of the declaration, as with ILO Convention No. 169, indigenous participants advocated that the terms 'peoples' and 'self-determination' be used without any reservation.[237] Although

---

[234] UN Doc. E/CN.4/Sub.2/1994/SR.29 (1994), p. 5.

[235] Analytical Compilation of Observations and Comments Received Pursuant to Sub-Commission Resolution 1988/18, UN Doc. E/CN.4/Sub.2/1989/33/Add.1 (1989), p. 24 (Canada); Analytical Compilation of Observations and Comments Received Pursuant to Sub-Commission Resolution 1988/18, UN Doc. E/CN.4/Sub.2/1989/33/Add.3 (1989), p. 7 (Norway); Information Received from Governments, UN Doc. E/CN.4/Sub.2/AC.4/1990/1 (1990), pp. 3, 5 (Argentina); Information Received from Governments: Addendum, UN Doc. E/CN.4/Sub.2/AC.4/1990/1/Add.1 (1990), p. 5 (Australia).

[236] Information Received from Governments, UN Doc. E/CN.4/Sub.2/AC.4/1990/1 (1990), p. 6 (Argentina). See also Information Received from Governments: Addendum, UN Doc. E/CN.4/Sub.2/AC.4/1990/1/Add.1 (1990), p. 6 (Australia), although a reference in the Report on the Tenth Session to what is presumably Australia and the *Mabo* case (*Mabo v. Queensland (No. 2)* (1992), 175 Commonwealth Law Reports 1 (High Court of Australia)) might signal a change. Report on Tenth Session, p. 28.

The Working Group also authorized a study on historical agreements between indigenous peoples and states, which occasioned some controversy in the Working Group. According to Douglas Sanders, this was less because of the normative implications than because the United States and Canada feared that the Cuban rapporteur would use the opportunity to attack the United States and, incidentally, Canada. Sanders, 'The UN Working Group on Indigenous Populations', 409–10.

[237] Report on Fifth Session, p. 14; Report on Seventh Session, pp. 17–18; Report on Tenth Session, pp. 18, 28; Explanatory Note, p. 3; Report on Eleventh Session, p. 18.

The right also appears in a number of declarations of indigenous peoples. E.g. Art. 2, Declaration of Principles Adopted by the Indigenous Peoples Preparatory Meeting, held at Geneva, 27–31 July 1987, in Report on Fifth Session, Annex V; Preamble and Art. 14, Indigenous Peoples Earth Charter; Art. 2, Principles and

secession was not a desirable or viable option for many indigenous peoples, a right of self-determination without a right of secession was criticized as a double standard.[238] Indigenous peoples were peoples and were therefore entitled to the same right of self-determination as other peoples.

Among the indigenous groups taking part in the Working Group, the dominant model of self-determination was historical.[239] Nevertheless, it should not be assumed that illegal taking or breach of pact was the whole of indigenous perspectives on the colonial encounter.[240] Rather, through the idea of corrective justice, a part could be rendered normatively intelligible to international morality. The preamble to the 1992 Indigenous Peoples Earth Charter illustrates the broader indigenous

> Elements of Self-Government, adopted by Inuit delegates, Alaska, 1986, in Notes Submitted by Inuit Circumpolar Conference to UN Meeting of Experts to Review the Experience of Countries in the Operation of Schemes of Internal Self-Government of Indigenous Peoples, Nuuk, Greenland, 24–28 September 1991, UN Doc. HR/NUUK/1991/SEM.1/BP.10 (1991); Preamble, Mataatua Declaration of Cultural and Intellectual Property Rights of Indigenous Peoples, in Information Received from Indigenous Peoples' and Non-Governmental Organizations, UN Doc. E/CN.4/Sub.2/AC.4/1994/12 (1994), p. 12.
>
> [238] E.g. Information Received from Non-Governmental Organizations: Addendum, UN Doc. E/CN.4/Sub.2/AC.4/1990/3/Add.2 (1990), pp. 5–7.
>
> [239] But see Analytical Compilation of Observations and Comments Received Pursuant to Sub-Commission Resolution 1988/18, UN Doc. E/CN.4/Sub.2/1989/33/Add.1 (1989), p. 15 (National Indian Youth Council); and Principles and Elements of Self-Government, adopted by Inuit delegates, Alaska, 1986 (some indication of a rights model of self-determination); Kuptana, 'The Human Rights of Peoples' (status model of self-determination).
>
> [240] For a discussion of the ways in which the Western monopoly on international legal thought has objectified the native and ignored his philosophy and perspective on historical events, see R. Clinton, 'The Rights of Indigenous Peoples as Collective Group Rights', excerpted in Information Received from Non-Governmental Organizations: Addendum, UN Doc. E/CN.4/Sub.2/AC.4/1990/3/Add.1 (1990), pp. 5–9; C. Tennant, 'Indigenous Peoples, International Institutions, and the International Legal Literature from 1945–1993' (1994) 16 *Human Rights Quarterly* 1 at 6–24; L. Little Bear, 'Aboriginal Rights and the Canadian "Grundnorm"' in J. R. Ponting (ed.), *Arduous Journey. Canadian Indians and Decolonization* (Toronto: McClelland and Stewart, 1986), pp. 243–59 at pp. 244–7; R. A. Williams, Jr., *The American Indian in Western Legal Thought: The Discourse of Conquest* (New York: Oxford University Press, 1990).
>
> To the extent that indigenous peoples have participated meaningfully in the drafting of the UN declaration on indigenous rights, it becomes necessary to modify the critique that international law projects onto indigenous peoples a representation that does not correspond to their own. Compare C. Perrin, 'Approaching Anxiety: The Insistence of the Postcolonial in the Declaration on the Rights of Indigenous Peoples' (1995) 6 *Law and Critique* 55 (whose critique of the draft declaration appears to assume no indigenous participation) with Tennant, 'International Legal Literature from 1945–1993' (whose discussion embraces both representation of and resistance by indigenous peoples in contemporary international law).

philosophy that informed indigenous perspectives on historical events:

> We the indigenous peoples walk to the future in the footprints of our ancestors.
>
> From the smallest to the largest living being, from the four directions. From the air, the land and the mountains, the creator has placed us, the indigenous peoples upon our mother the earth.
>
> The footprints of our ancestors are permanently etched upon the lands of our peoples.
>
> We, the indigenous peoples maintain our inherent right to self-determination. We have always had the right to decide our own forms of government, to use our own ways to raise and educate our children, to our own cultural identity without interference.
>
> We continue to maintain our rights as people despite centuries of deprivation, assimilation and genocide.
>
> We maintain our inalienable rights to our lands and territories, to all of our resources – above and below – and to our waters. We assert our ongoing responsibility to pass these on to future generations.
>
> We cannot be removed from our lands. We, the indigenous peoples, are connected by the circle of life to our lands and environments.
>
> We, the indigenous peoples, walk to the future in the footprints of our ancestors.

The preamble tells a story of endurance: indigenous peoples had suffered centuries of colonialism and their rights as sovereign peoples had survived. Many indigenous groups argued that their historical experience was indistinguishable from that of other colonial peoples, whose right of self-determination, including a right of independence, had been recognized in international law. The case was strongly put in a 1992 statement to the Sub-Commission on Minorities by sixteen non-governmental organizations: 'How can there be any Partnership between the World's Indigenous peoples and the non-indigenous when the legacies left by Captain Cook and Christopher Columbus are the invisible, captive, dependent Indigenous minorities of the "New World", who are denied their right of self-determination because they are excluded from the list of peoples and territories which have enjoyed decolonization?'[241]

---

[241] Statement of Concern for the Year of Indigenous Peoples and the Institutionalized Racism That Would Adversely Affect it, signed by sixteen NGOs and directed to the UN Sub-Commission on Prevention of Discrimination and Protection of Minorities, 19 August 1992 (unpublished, on letterhead of National Aboriginal and Islander Legal Services Secretariat). See also M. B. Trask, 'Historical and Contemporary Hawaiian Self-Determination: A Native Hawaiian Perspective' (1991) 8 *Arizona Journal of International and Comparative Law* 77 (arguing that Hawaii is a non-self-governing territory, with the right of self-determination in international law).

In defining colonialism, Rosemary Kuptana, President of the Inuit Tapirisat of Canada, implicitly signalled the principles that constituted a remedy: 'Colonialism is a process of assuming control of other peoples' lands in one own's [sic] self-interest without their consent and without regard to their prior rights.'[242] The principle of consent had to inform the relationship between states and indigenous peoples.[243] It followed that all lands taken from indigenous peoples without their consent had to be restored to them, even lands not 'traditionally occupied' in the strict sense of the words.[244] The international legal doctrine of *terra nullius*, which had been invoked to legalize the acquisition of territory with indigenous inhabitants,[245] had to be, in the words of the Earth Charter, 'forever erased from the law books of States'.[246] Finally, where indigenous peoples did consent, through treaties with the precolonial or postcolonial government, these treaties had to be recognized and respected.[247]

The issue of secession to be resolved in the declaration on the rights of indigenous peoples was thus whether to recognize a right to secede and if so, on what basis. The drafting history shows that to the extent that states supported the text, they did so on grounds of rights. If states were to accept a right of secession – and it is unclear whether any states actually did – consistency suggests that they would consider secession

---

[242] Kuptana, 'The Human Rights of Peoples', p. 5.
[243] E.g., Indigenous Peoples' Preparatory Meeting, Comments on the First Revised Text of the Draft Declaration on Rights of Indigenous Peoples, July 1989, in Information Received From Non-Governmental Organizations: Addendum, UN Doc. E/CN.4/Sub.2/AC.4/1990/3/Add.2 (1990), p. 3; Report on Eighth Session, p. 24; Indigenous Peoples Earth Charter, Art. 7.
[244] Indigenous Peoples' Preparatory Meeting, Comments on the First Revised Text of the Draft Declaration on Rights of Indigenous Peoples, July 1989, in Information Received from Non-Governmental Organizations: Addendum, UN Doc. E/CN.4/Sub.2/AC.4/1990/3/Add.2 (1990), p. 4. See also wording for operative paragraph 16 suggested by Tupay Katari Movement, in Note from the Secretary-General: Information Received from Non-Governmental Organizations, UN Doc. E/CN.4/Sub.2/AC.4/1992/3 (1992), p. 12; Indigenous Peoples Earth Charter, Art. 33.
[245] See Chapter 4 above, *Western Sahara*.
[246] Indigenous Peoples Earth Charter, Art. 36. See also *ibid.*, Art. 6.
[247] Report on Fifth Session, pp. 14, 16; Review of Developments Pertaining to the Promotion and Protection of Human Rights and Fundamental Freedoms of Indigenous Populations; Standard-Setting Activities: Evolution of Standards Concerning the Rights of Indigenous Populations, UN Doc. E/CN.4/Sub.2/AC.4/1989/5 (1989), pp. 5, 9; Indigenous Peoples' Preparatory Meeting, Comments on the First Revised Text of the Draft Declaration on Rights of Indigenous Peoples, July 1989, in Information Received from Non-Governmental Organizations: Addendum, UN Doc. E/CN.4/Sub.2/AC.4/1990/3/Add.2 (1990), p. 3; Report on Ninth Session, p. 9; Indigenous Peoples Earth Charter, Art. 22.

justifiable only as a last resort for severe violations of the group's rights. The Australian government even appeared to raise this model of self-determination by proposing that the Declaration on Friendly Relations language be used in the draft declaration. In contrast, a number of indigenous groups saw the goal of the declaration as, among other things, correcting historical wrongs done to them. On this reasoning, where an indigenous people and their territory were incorporated into the state by force, that people, as the victim, should have the choice of being restored to their prior independence or negotiating more equitable terms of membership in the state. Similarly, in the case where an indigenous people consented to become part of the state by concluding a treaty with the newcomers and the state had since breached the treaty, that people should be able to choose freely between the restoration of their independence and the observance of the treaty.

During the eight years that the UN Working Group on Indigenous Populations prepared the declaration on the rights of indigenous peoples, the document developed from an inoffensive standard-setting exercise to a bold forerunner of the rights of indigenous peoples. The declaration began with a handful of principles developed by the Working Group at its 1985 session. By the time that the Working Group finalized its draft in 1993, the declaration had grown to a nineteen-paragraph preamble and forty-five articles, covering indigenous rights from the right of self-determination to the rights to the repatriation of human remains and protection of vital medicinal plants.

The first set of principles started to compile the individual and minority rights applicable to indigenous peoples in international law.[248] These early principles made no allusion to a right of self-determination, internal or external. Nor did they include any of the rights we now associate with internal self-determination: a right of indigenous peoples to participate in political life and in economic and social decision-making that affects them, or a right of autonomy. The goal of the declaration, as Working Group member Miguel Alfonso Martinez observed in retrospect, 'was to deal with the problem of discrimination against indigenous peoples'.[249] Comprising the equal rights of individuals and minority rights, the principles contained none of the imperatives that would be generated by corrective justice, such as land rights or respect for treaty rights.

---

[248] E.-I. A. Daes, Report of the Working Group on Indigenous Populations on its Fourth Session, UN Doc. E/CN.4/Sub.2/1985/22 (1985), Annex II.
[249] UN Doc. E/CN.4/Sub.2/1993/SR.33 (1994), p. 8.

By 1989,[250] the parts of the declaration on equality and traditionally recognized minority rights had been supplemented with parts on land rights, maintenance and development of traditional ways of life, and political participation and autonomy.[251] Although the term 'self-determination' did not appear in the operative paragraphs of the declaration, the preamble contained a 'saving' provision: 'Bearing in mind that nothing in this declaration may be used as a justification for denying to any people, which otherwise satisfies the criteria generally established by human rights instruments and international law, its right to self-determination.' A provision on honouring treaties with indigenous peoples[252] and some of the provisions on land rights sought to remedy historical wrongs. In particular, paragraph 12 recognized a right of collective and individual ownership of land that has been traditionally occupied, the implication being that the land need not still be occupied by the indigenous group claiming ownership. Paragraph 15 read in part: 'The right to reclaim land and surface resources or where this is not possible, to seek just and fair compensation for the same, when the property has been taken away from them without consent, in particular, if such deprival has been based on theories such as those related to discovery, *terra nullius*, waste lands or idle lands.'

Drafting during the 1990 session of the Working Group took place in three informal drafting groups, each group tasked with revising certain parts of the declaration.[253] The result was to multiply the number of references to 'peoples' and 'self-determination' in the draft.

Among the revisions suggested to the first paragraph of the preamble were 'considering that indigenous peoples...are born free and are equal to all other peoples...in rights'[254] and 'considering indigenous peoples equal to all others in dignity and rights, while recognizing the

---

[250] First revised text, p. 4; also reproduced in Report on Seventh Session, Annex II. For an intermediate draft, see Report on Fifth Session, Annex II.

[251] The final parts deal with dispute resolution and interpretation of the declaration. First revised text.

[252] Paragraph 27 in *ibid*.

[253] Report on Eighth Session, p. 14. Citation will be to the compilation of the Chairperson/Rapporteur's revised text and the suggested revisions by the informal drafting groups and others issued prior to the 1991 session. Draft Declaration on the Rights of Indigenous Peoples: Revised Working Paper Submitted by the Chairperson/Rapporteur, Ms. Erica-Irene A. Daes, Pursuant to Sub-Commission on Prevention of Discrimination and Protection of Minorities Resolution 1990/26, UN Doc. E/CN.4/Sub.2/1991/36 (1991).

[254] Revised Working Paper (1991), p. 5 (Informal Drafting Group I, chaired by Miguel Alfonso Martinez).

right of all peoples...to be different'.²⁵⁵ The effect of the word 'other' or 'others' was to group indigenous peoples with 'peoples'. Along similar lines, it was proposed that 'human groups and peoples' be added to 'human beings' in operative paragraph 2, which recognized the right to be free and equal to all other human beings in dignity and rights.²⁵⁶

One alternative formulation of the saving provision in the preamble seemed to imply that all indigenous peoples had the right of self-determination: 'nothing in this declaration may be used as a justification for denying to any indigenous peoples their right to self-determination'.²⁵⁷ The same drafting group proposed that a paragraph be added to the preamble noting that the International Covenants 'affirm the fundamental importance of the right to self-determination'.²⁵⁸ Most significantly, this group concluded that a new first paragraph on the right of self-determination of indigenous peoples, its wording almost identical to common Article 1 of the Covenants, should be added to the operative portion of the declaration.²⁵⁹ Another drafting group suggested revising one of the recitations in the preamble to include in the right of indigenous peoples to self-determination

> their right freely to determine their present and future relationships with the political, economic and social life of States and that the reaffirmation of said right and of all others enshrined in this Declaration is not to be construed, at present, as in any way limiting their enjoyment of equal rights with citizens of the States in which they currently reside.²⁶⁰

The right of indigenous peoples to determine their relationship with states indicated that they were free to choose their place in the world community, as did the qualification that their enjoyment of equal rights governed their status 'at present' within the state in which they 'currently' resided.

The idea of internal, as opposed to external, self-determination was developed by suggested revisions linking the right of self-determination in the preamble to the 'right to development oriented to the fulfilment of [indigenous peoples'] own spiritual and material needs'²⁶¹ and in

---

²⁵⁵ *Ibid.* (Informal Drafting Group II, chaired by Danilo Turk).
²⁵⁶ *Ibid.*, p. 43 (Informal Drafting Group III, chaired by Erica-Irene Daes).
²⁵⁷ Draft 10th preambular paragraph, in *ibid.*, p. 29 (Informal Drafting Group II, chaired by Danilo Turk).
²⁵⁸ *Ibid.*, p. 37.   ²⁵⁹ *Ibid.*, p. 41.
²⁶⁰ Draft 9th preambular paragraph in *ibid.*, p. 27 (Informal Drafting Group I, chaired by Miguel Alfonso Martinez).
²⁶¹ Draft 7th preambular paragraph in *ibid.*, p. 21.

operative paragraph 20 to the right to design and deliver social and economic programmes affecting indigenous peoples.[262]

None of the changes proposed by the informal drafting groups affected the elements of corrective justice in the provisions on land rights.[263] The drafting group examining the paragraph on treaties with indigenous peoples suggested adding that the treaties must be interpreted 'according to their original intent, pursuant to the principle of *pacta sunt servanda*'.[264]

The 1991 session completed a first reading of the preamble and the operative paragraphs up to paragraph 17 *bis*, resulting in what was seen as a retreat from the text's earlier position on self-determination.[265] The reference to 'peoples' added to the opening paragraph of the preamble was only faintly equated to indigenous peoples. The saving provision in the preamble referred to 'any people', thereby remaining neutral on whether indigenous peoples were 'peoples' under existing international law.[266] Similarly, the preamble noted that the International Covenants affirmed the fundamental importance of the right of self-determination, but made no connection between Article 1 of the Covenants and indigenous peoples.[267] There were no other references to self-determination in the preamble.

The right of indigenous peoples to be equal in rights to all other peoples was now included in the third operative paragraph. More specifically, the right of indigenous peoples to self-determination was established in the first operative paragraph of the draft, but was coded as a right of internal self-determination. By recognizing the right 'in accordance with international law', the paragraph consigned the prospect of external self-determination to the uncertainty and conservatism of state-driven international law in this area. Moreover, the right of indigenous peoples to self-determination was expressed as the right to determine their relationship with the state in which they lived.[268] A

---

[262] Draft operative paragraph 20 in *ibid.*, p. 87.
[263] Draft operative paragraph 12 in *ibid.*, p. 65 and draft operative paragraph 15 in *ibid.*, p. 73.
[264] *Ibid.*, p. 101 (Informal Drafting Group II, chaired by Danilo Turk).
[265] Report on Ninth Session, p. 11.
[266] 14th preambular paragraph, Draft Universal Declaration on the Rights of Indigenous Peoples in *ibid.*, Annex II.
[267] 13th preambular paragraph in *ibid.*
[268] See also 12th preambular paragraph in *ibid.* which mentions the 'right freely to determine their relationship with the States in which they live' without attributing the right to the broader right of self-determination.

prohibition on the violation of territorial integrity was also introduced into the declaration indirectly in a new paragraph that would prevent the declaration from being interpreted contrary to the UN Charter and the Declaration on Friendly Relations.[269] We have seen in Chapter 2, however, that the Charter as interpreted by the Declaration on Friendly Relations could be read as allowing the secession of a group that has been denied any say in its government.

While the provision on treaties was not dealt with in this reading, the provision on reclaiming lands taken away from indigenous peoples without their consent was redrafted to remove the obviously historical slant. The phrase 'in particular, if such deprival has been based on theories such as those related to discovery, occupation, cession, abandonment, *terra nullius*, waste lands or idle lands' was omitted.[270]

Prior to the 1992 session of the Working Group, the Chairperson further altered the right of self-determination in the draft.[271] The indirect (near total) prohibition on the disruption of territorial integrity remained,[272] but the formulation of the right in operative paragraph 1 was made to echo Article 1 of the International Covenants. The phrase 'in accordance with international law' no longer ended the first sentence, thereby limiting the most general expression of the right.[273] Instead, the phrase ran on without punctuation: 'in accordance with international law by virtue of which they may freely determine their political status and institutions and freely pursue their economic, social and cultural development'. The equation was between 'in accordance with international law' and the expression given to the right of self-determination in Article 1 of the International Covenants. While this formulation suggested the full right of self-determination, internal and external, operative paragraph 1 made clear that internal self-determination was more extensive than it had hitherto been in international law. 'An integral

---

[269] After operative paragraph 13 (unnumbered) in *ibid*.
[270] Operative paragraph 16 in *ibid*.
[271] Draft Declaration on Indigenous Peoples: Revised Working Paper Submitted by the Chairperson/Rapporteur, Ms. Erica-Irene A. Daes, Pursuant to Sub-Commission on Prevention of Discrimination and Protection of Minorities Resolution 1991/30 and Commission on Human Rights Resolution 1992/44, UN Doc. E/CN.4/Sub.2/1992/28 (1992).
[272] Now numbered operative paragraph 4 in *ibid*.
[273] Although this limitation existed for the newly added reference to 'peoples' in the first paragraph of the preamble: 'Affirming that all indigenous peoples are free and equal in dignity and rights to all peoples in accordance with international standards, while recognizing...' *Ibid*.

part of this', the paragraph continued, 'is the right to autonomy and self-government'.

The Chairperson also expanded the reference in the preamble to the right of self-determination contained in the International Covenants.[274] Since the preamble said nothing about the application of that right to indigenous peoples, this change, by itself, was simply *trompe-l'oeil*. In conjunction with the changes to the operative paragraph on self-determination, this change strengthened the cautious and circumspect association of the right of self-determination of indigenous peoples with the right of self-determination in the Covenants.

The Working Group completed the first reading of the declaration at its 1992 session.[275] Although the paragraphs remaining for first reading at that session developed the complex of rights associated with internal self-determination, such as the right of autonomy, the term 'self-determination' was not used in the revised text of the paragraphs. The right to claim that states honour treaties with indigenous peoples was modified to include dispute resolution,[276] and an ambiguously placed allusion to original intent was added.[277]

At the 1993 session, the Working Group produced its final draft of the declaration. Prior to the session, the Chairperson had further revised the draft declaration.[278] Among the revisions affecting the right of self-determination[279] were changes to the order of the paragraphs. The paragraph on the right of self-determination was no longer the first operative paragraph. Renumbered as operative paragraph 3, it now followed

---

[274] 14th preambular paragraph in *ibid*.

[275] Report on Tenth Session, Annex I. Revisions to these paragraphs were suggested prior to the session in Revised Working Paper (1992).

[276] This revision was suggested by the Chair already in Revised Working Paper (1991), p. 100.

[277] Operative paragraph 31 in Report on Tenth Session, Annex I.

[278] Draft Declaration on the Rights of Indigenous Peoples: Revised Working Paper Submitted by the Chairperson-Rapporteur, Ms Erica-Irene Daes, Pursuant to Sub-Commission Resolution 1992/33 and Commission on Human Rights Resolution 1993/31, UN Doc. E/CN.4/Sub.2/1993/26 (1993).

 In the Report on the Eleventh Session, there is also a reference to a draft presented during the 1993 session that formed the basis for the further reading of the draft declaration at that session. Report on Eleventh Session, p. 14.

[279] My discussion of the draft declaration thus far has included certain provisions on land claims and treaties, as well as the provisions on self-determination, because the treatment of land claims and treaties is a barometer of the Working Group's receptiveness to a corrective justice model of self-determination. In 1993, the Chairperson took the step of preparing and circulating an explanatory note with her text. As the note gives a more accurate reading of the degree to which corrective justice informs the right of self-determination in the declaration, the discussion does not pursue the treatment of land claims and treaties in the 1993 drafts.

two paragraphs affirming different aspects of the right of indigenous peoples to equality.[280] If self-determination had been moved down in the order of rights, so had its opposite. The reference to compliance with the UN Charter and the Declaration on Friendly Relations had been moved to the end of the declaration, becoming operative paragraph 42.

The paragraph on the right of self-determination (now operative paragraph 3) read:

Indigenous peoples have the right of self-determination, in accordance with international law, subject to the same criteria and limitations as apply to other peoples in accordance with the Charter of the United Nations. By virtue of this, they have the right, *inter alia*, to negotiate and agree upon their role in the conduct of public affairs, their distinct responsibilities and the means by which they manage their own interests.

An integral part of this is the right to autonomy and self-government.

By using 'indigenous peoples' and 'other peoples' in the same sentence, this paragraph recognized that indigenous peoples were peoples and that their right of self-determination was the same as that of any people in international law.[281] To the extent that the ramifications of the right were novel or particular to indigenous peoples, they were spelled out in the second and third sentences.

Corresponding changes were made to a paragraph of the preamble that previously read: 'Believing that indigenous peoples have the right freely to determine their relationships with the States in which they live, in a spirit of coexistence with other citizens'.[282] In the version presented prior to the 1993 session,[283] the words 'in which they live' and 'with other citizens' were omitted, with the effect that relationships with states might not be limited to the domestic framework.

In the draft declaration agreed upon by the members of the Working Group at its 1993 session,[284] the right of self-determination of

---

[280] One of the two lead paragraphs, now operative paragraph 2, had been strengthened by replacing 'have the right to be' with 'are' in the phrase 'Indigenous peoples are free and equal to all other...peoples'.

[281] Similarly, 'all other peoples' has replaced 'all peoples' in the first paragraph of the preamble: 'Affirming that indigenous peoples are equal in dignity and rights to all other peoples.' The change conveys that indigenous peoples are peoples, as opposed to being equal to peoples.

[282] 13th preambular paragraph, in Report on Tenth Session, Annex I.

[283] 13th preambular paragraph, in Revised Working Paper (1993).

[284] Report on Eleventh Session, Annex I. Reproduced as Technical Review of the United Nations Draft Declaration on the Rights of Indigenous Peoples: Addition, UN Doc. E/CN.4/Sub.2/1994/2/Add.1 (1994).

indigenous peoples in Article 3[285] was an exact replica of the right of self-determination of peoples in Article 1(1) of the two International Covenants.[286] Thus indigenous peoples were equated with peoples, and their right of self-determination with the right of self-determination of peoples recognized in Article 1 of the Covenants. This equation was rhetorically reinforced by the addition of a reference to colonization in the preamble.[287] Elsewhere in the preamble, however, new wording suggested that indigenous peoples did not have an unfettered right to determine their relationship with states – which colonies had – but had to determine that relationship in a spirit of 'mutual benefit and full respect' as well as 'coexistence'.[288] The elaboration of forms of self-determination specific to indigenous peoples had been moved from Article 3 to Article 31, which dealt with autonomy or self-government in matters relating to internal and local affairs.

Finally, Article 45, previously operative paragraph 42, provided that nothing in the declaration could be interpreted as authorization for acts contrary to the UN Charter, but no longer referred to the Declaration on Friendly Relations in this connection. The significance of this omission might be that territorial integrity was explicitly made the counterweight to self-determination in the Declaration on Friendly Relations. Then again, the Declaration on Friendly Relations might be read back into the Article as an authoritative interpretation of Charter principles.

The article on self-determination in the Working Group's final draft of the declaration on indigenous rights aligns the right of self-determination of indigenous peoples with the right of self-determination in Article 1(1) of the Covenants. Whereas the formulation of the right and other language used in earlier drafts suggested that the right could be exercised only within the state framework, the limits on the right are not express in the final draft.

Accordingly, over the course of drafting, there was an increasing tendency to read the right of self-determination in the declaration as coming very close to the demands of indigenous peoples. One member of the Sub-Commission on Prevention of Discrimination and Protection of

---

[285] The term 'article' is now used instead of 'paragraph'. Report on Eleventh Session, p. 14.
[286] See Technical Review of the United Nations Draft Declaration on the Rights of Indigenous Peoples: Note by the Secretariat, UN Doc. E/CN.4/Sub.2/1994/2 (1994), p. 7.
[287] Preamble, fifth paragraph, in Report on Eleventh Session, Annex I.
[288] Preamble, twelfth paragraph, in *ibid*.

Minorities remarked negatively that the Working Group's Chairperson, Erica-Irene Daes, 'had been carried away by her commitment to the cause of indigenous peoples',[289] while the Four Directions Council referred positively to the Working Group's 'spirit of growing sympathy for indigenous peoples' aspirations'.[290] Several indigenous representatives were still concerned that the articulation of a right of autonomy or self-government in Article 31 as a specific form in which indigenous peoples could exercise their right of self-determination implicitly excluded secession from their right of self-determination in Article 3.[291] Other indigenous representatives, however, consented to the text on the ground that Article 31 did not limit Article 3.[292]

In a 1993 note on her text,[293] Daes gave a more complex, and non-obvious, reading of the right of self-determination in the declaration. Her reading appeals to indigenous peoples in so far as it finds some right to secede and to states in so far as the main rationale adopts their normative standpoint.

On Daes's analysis, indigenous peoples were 'peoples' for the purposes of self-determination in international law.[294] For those indigenous peoples that also fitted the colonial pattern by satisfying the requirement in GA Resolution 1541 of a 'geographically separate and ethnically or culturally distinct' territory, the right of self-determination included the right to choose independent statehood.[295]

---

[289] UN Doc. E/CN.4/Sub.2/1993/SR.33 (1994), p. 7 (Mr. Saboia). See also Sanders, 'A Text and a New Process', p. 48.

[290] E.g. Written Statement Submitted by Four Directions Council, a Non-Governmental Organization in Consultative Status (Category II), UN Doc. E/CN.4/Sub.2/1993/NGO/20 (1993), p. 1.

[291] Report on Twelfth Session, p. 13.

[292] *Ibid.*, pp. 13–14. See also D. Sanders, 'Developments at the United Nations: 1994' [1994] 4 *Canadian Native Law Reporter* 12 at 13.

[293] Explanatory note.

[294] *Ibid.*, p. 2; E.-I. A. Daes, 'Some Considerations on the Rights of Indigenous Peoples to Self-Determination' (1993) 3 *Transnational Law and Contemporary Problems* 1 at 6. In the final draft, see, for example, the first ('all other peoples'), second ('all peoples'), third ('of peoples') and fourteenth ('all peoples') preambular paras.; Arts. 2 ('all other...peoples'), 3. Report on Eleventh Session, Annex I.

[295] Daes, 'Some Considerations', 5 (referring erroneously to GA Res. 1514). E.-I. A. Daes, 'The Right of Indigenous Peoples to "Self-Determination" in the Contemporary World Order' in D. Clark and R. Williamson (eds.), *Self-Determination: International Perspectives* (New York: St Martin's Press, 1996), pp. 47–57 at p. 50. In the final draft, see, for example, the fifth (reference to colonization) and fifteenth (preserving the existing right of self-determination of peoples) preambular paras. Report on Eleventh Session, Annex I.

For other indigenous peoples, the Declaration on Friendly Relations expressed the limitation on the right of secession. Daes's passages on the right of secession are worth quoting at length:

> [peoples within a state] must try to express their aspirations through the national political system... unless the national political system becomes so exclusive and non-democratic that it no longer can be said to be 'representing the whole people'. At that point, and if all international and diplomatic measures fail to protect the peoples concerned from the State, they may perhaps be justified in creating a new State for their safety and security.... Continued government representativity and accountability is therefore a condition... for continued application of the territorial integrity and national unity principles.
> ...
> The concept of 'self-determination' has accordingly taken on a new meaning in the post-colonial era. Ordinarily it is the right of the citizens of an existing independent state to share power democratically. However, a State may sometimes abuse this right of its citizens so grievously and irreparably that the situation is tantamount to classic colonialism, and may have the same legal consequences. The international community and the present writer discourage secession as a remedy for the abuse of fundamental rights, but, as recent events around the world demonstrate, secession cannot be ruled out in all cases. The preferred course of action, in every case except the most extreme ones, is to encourage the State in question to share power democratically with all groups, under a constitutional formula that guarantees that the Government is 'effectively representative'.[296]

Daes thus adopted a rights model of self-determination, which justified secession as a remedy of last resort for the grievous abuse of a people's right to share power democratically. As a corollary, both the government and the indigenous people concerned had a duty to reach an agreement on power-sharing.[297]

However, Daes gave another reason for sharing power democratically between the government and indigenous peoples, and this reason implied a historical model that was not necessarily consistent with her rights model:

> Furthermore, the right of self-determination of indigenous peoples should ordinarily be interpreted as their right to negotiate freely their status and representation in the State in which they live. This might best be described as a kind of 'belated State-building', through which indigenous peoples are able to join with

---

[296] Explanatory note, pp. 4–5. See also Daes, 'Some Considerations', 6; Daes, 'Contemporary World Order', pp. 52–3. In the final draft, see Arts. 3, 31, 45. Report on Eleventh Session, Annex I.

[297] Explanatory note, p. 5. See also Daes, 'Contemporary World Order', p. 53; Daes, 'Some Considerations', 9.

all the other peoples that make up the State on mutually-agreed and just terms, after many years of isolation and exclusion.[298]

The agreement that Daes described here was intended to rewrite history by acting as the social contract in which indigenous peoples agreed to join the state. She has written elsewhere:

> the principle of territorial security... means that indigenous peoples have defined historical territories – even within the borders of existing States – and the right to keep these territories physically intact, environmentally sound and economically sustainable in their own ways. Here again, I regard this not so much as a special right of indigenousness, as it is a condition indigenous peoples would generally impose on their free incorporation, as peoples, into existing States.[299]

The rights of indigenous peoples in the draft declaration were thus justifiable as what indigenous peoples, standing outside the state, would have imposed as the terms of their membership in the state – had they been free to do so. This idealized historical bargaining situation might or might not produce the same rights as the principles of equality or minority rights. Moreover, on the historical hypothetical, indigenous peoples would have the option of remaining (becoming) independent if no satisfactory agreement could be reached.

If the ILO approach to indigenous self-determination harks back to the functionalism of Judge Dillard and some of the other judges in *Western Sahara*, Daes's approach thus attempts an overlapping consensus reminiscent of Judge Ammoun: both clarifying the right of secession and complicating its normative basis. While she confirmed the dominant forward-looking movement in the international law of self-determination, toward non-historical solutions based on liberal notions of consent and equal rights, she may also have lent support to a movement backward in time – an undoing of historical wrongs done to indigenous groups and a symbolic restoration of them to a past from which they can develop in accordance with indigenous traditions. The difficulty, however, is that the former seems to justify a more limited right of secession than the latter.

While the ILO and the Working Group reached different interpretations of indigenous self-determination, both sought an intermediate approach

---

[298] Explanatory note, p. 5. See also Daes, 'Some Considerations', 8–9; Daes, 'Contemporary World Order', pp. 53–4. In the final draft, see the twelfth preambular paragraph. Report on Eleventh Session, Annex I.

[299] E.-I. A. Daes, 'Dilemmas Posed by the UN Draft Declaration on the Rights of Indigenous Peoples' (1994) 63 *Nordic Journal of International Law* 205 at 208.

that would appeal to both states and indigenous groups. What is sometimes thought to lend the draft declaration broader legitimacy is the more extensive involvement of indigenous groups in the process and the greater gains for them that resulted. The chapter has sought to refine this observation by interposing the indeterminacy of the non-state participation that is increasingly a way of legitimating the creation and application of international law. It has shown that this participation has no single meaning, readily apparent to all. Instead, outsiders and insiders may differ in their view of the process, thereby making contestable the character of the process and the actors. If rhetoric teaches us that argument is bound up with the identity of the speaker, that identity itself becomes arguable. An institutional interpreter of self-determination must therefore constitute its authority persuasively in its interpretation of self-determination. The way that an institutional interpreter constitutes its authority, the chapter has suggested, helps to determine both how it engages the contributions of insiders and outsiders and how this engagement is received by them.

PART III • SELF-DETERMINATION INTERPRETED IN PRACTICE: THE CHALLENGE OF GENDER

6 Women and self-determination in Europe after World War I

In Part II of this book, the judgments, arbitral decisions and other authoritative texts relied on by most authors of the post-Cold War period in their interpretation of self-determination emerged as successive encounters with groups traditionally marginalized in international law: the Muslim world, nomads, ethnic minorities, the colonized, the indigenous. The modern canon of self-determination proved to trace international law's engagement with those on the margins of its culture and their critiques of international law's regulation, narration and exclusion of them. Part III shows that the contest over the application of self-determination in international law has similarly been a place where women have challenged their figuration as unequal members of the self and unequal participants in the process of self-determination.[1] Chapter 6 deals with women's say in the plebiscites held in Europe after

---

[1] Little has been written in international law on women and self-determination as such. Perhaps the only work to look at the effects of self-determination norms on women generally is H. Charlesworth and C. Chinkin, *The Boundaries of International Law: A Feminist Analysis* (Manchester: Manchester University Press, 2000), pp. 151–64, 263–8 and C. Chinkin and S. Wright, 'The Hunger Trap: Women, Food, and Self-Determination' (1993) 14 *Michigan Journal of International Law* 262.

There is, however, growing attention to particular problems of women in international law related to self-determination conflicts. The widespread sexual abuse of women in ethnic self-determination conflicts has resulted in an extensive literature on women and international humanitarian law. See Women's Human Rights Resources, Bora Laskin Law Library, University of Toronto, <http://www.law-lib.utoronto.ca/Diana/human/articles.htm> (visited 16 February 2001). Among the unpublished works on this subject are D. E. Buss, 'Crossing the Line: Feminist International Legal Theory, Rape and the War in Bosnia-Herzegovina' (LLM thesis, University of British Columbia, 1995) and M. Jarvis, 'Redress for Female Victims of Sexual Violence During Armed Conflict: Security Council Responses' (LLM thesis, University of Toronto, 1997). Women's status as refugees in self-determination conflicts has also been treated in the international legal literature. See e.g. C. M. Cervenak, 'Promoting Inequality: Gender-Based

World War I to determine the sovereignty of various disputed border territories and in the right to opt for the nationality of the other sovereign following a plebiscite. The United Nations Charter having included non-discrimination among the basic objectives of the trusteeship system, Chapter 7 attends to UN monitoring of the progress of women's equality in the trust territories as a prescribed part of the territory's preparation for self-determination. In connection with indigenous self-determination, Chapter 8 looks at the limits that the International Covenant on Civil and Political Rights places on a state's power to regulate a woman's status as indigenous where it would not regulate a man's.

As in the previous part of the book, I demonstrate a pattern of responsiveness to the challenge of diversity. Although this is mainly a point about the self-determination cases, I also seek here to contribute to the much-needed larger project of unearthing and examining feminist landmarks in international legal history. While historians have described the international women's suffrage and peace movements[2] and theorists of gender and postcolonialism have critiqued white women's role in empire-building,[3] international lawyers have been slow to examine the relevance of this work for the history of their own discipline. Among international legal historians of the inter-war period, David Kennedy[4]

Discrimination in UNRWA's Approach to Palestine Refugee Status' (1994) 16 *Human Rights Quarterly* 300.

In addition, problems of feminism and nationalism have been treated in other legal literature. See e.g. K. Rittich, 'Recharacterizing Restructuring: Gender and Distribution in the Legal Structure of Market Reform' (SJD thesis, Harvard Law School, 1998); Symposium: Women in Central and Eastern Europe: Nationalism, Feminism and Possibilities for the Future (1994) 5:1 *UCLA Women's Law Journal*. Non-legal works include L. Abu-Lughod (ed.), *Remaking Women. Feminism and Modernity in the Middle East* (Princeton: Princeton University Press, 1998); K. Jayawardena, *Feminism and Nationalism in the Third World* (London: Zed, 1986); C. Kaplan, N. Alarcón and M. Moallem (eds.), *Between Woman and Nation. Nationalisms, Transnational Feminisms and the State* (Durham: Duke University Press, 1999); A. Parker, M. Russo, D. Sommer and P. Yaeger (eds.), *Nationalisms and Sexualities* (New York: Routledge, 1992); D. Ugrešić, 'Because We're Just Boys' in D. Ugrešić, *The Culture of Lies. Antipolitical Essays*, C. Hawkesworth (trans.) (University Park, Penn.: Pennsylvania State University Press, 1998), pp. 113–27; L. A. West (ed.), *Feminist Nationalism* (New York: Routledge, 1997); N. Yuval-Davis and F. Anthias (eds.), *Woman–Nation–State* (New York: St Martin's Press, 1989).

[2] See the sources cited in this chapter.

[3] E.g. A. McClintock, *Imperial Leather: Race, Gender and Sexuality in the Colonial Context* (New York: Routledge, 1995); R. R. Pierson and N. Chaudhuri (eds.), *Nation, Empire, Colony. Historicizing Gender and Race* (Bloomington: Indiana University Press, 1998); L. J. Rupp, 'Constructing Internationalism: The Case of Transnational Women's Organizations, 1888–1945' (1994) 99 *American Historical Review* 1571; V. Ware, *Beyond the Pale: White Women, Racism and History* (London: Verso, 1992).

[4] D. Kennedy, 'The Move to Institutions' (1987) 8 *Cardozo Law Review* 841.

and Nathaniel Berman[5] are exceptional in their inclusion of women as subjects. However, Kennedy and Berman are interested in women's promotion of certain general approaches to international law and international institutions, which is quite different from women's use of those approaches to advance their own equality. Hilary Charlesworth and Christine Chinkin survey the century and a half of women's international activism[6] only to conclude that these efforts 'have had little effect on the substance and process of international law',[7] with the limited exception of the area of international human rights law, most particularly the 1979 Convention on the Elimination of All Forms of Discrimination Against Women.[8] In contrast, Chapters 6 and 7 identify earlier successes for women's equality, gained through the contest over self-determination's meaning in international law.

While recording these victories, Part III also delves into the ideas of identity that both facilitated them and limited or problematized them as victories. Using the relationship between identity and interpretation, specifically the interplay of ideas about women,[9] culture and international law, I explore how the available stock of dichotomies and linkages between dichotomies helped to make some women's interventions readily cognizable and others obscure. Indeed, Chapters 7 and 8 show how representations by a white Western international women's movement, as well as by an anti-colonial resistance, often overwrote further the representations of non-Western women and women of colour. While Charlesworth and Chinkin engage the problems of essentialism and dominance created by Western feminists' imposition of their conceptual frameworks and reform agendas on non-Western women,[10] they deal with these problems more as a challenge for the present than a lens on the past. Unlike the discussion of diverse feminist perspectives in their

[5] N. Berman, 'Modernism, Nationalism, and the Rhetoric of Reconstruction' (1992) 4 *Yale Journal of Law and the Humanities* 351.
[6] Charlesworth and Chinkin, *The Boundaries of International Law*, pp. 14–16. Although p.16 refers to a later discussion of the role of women's groups in the establishment of the United Nations, it is more of a mention.
[7] *Ibid.*, p. 16.
[8] Convention on the Elimination of All Forms of Discrimination Against Women, New York, adopted 18 December 1979, in force 3 September 1981, 1249 UNTS 13.
[9] The difference between the terms 'sex' and 'gender' is worth noting here. 'Sex' refers to a biological distinction between female and male, while 'gender' is a broader term that includes socially or culturally constructed different roles for women and men. Historically, the claims of discrimination discussed in Part III are claims of discrimination on the basis of sex. My analytical perspective, however, is that of gender.
[10] E.g. Charlesworth and Chinkin, *The Boundaries of International Law*, pp. 51–9, 225–9.

contemporary analysis, Charlesworth and Chinkin's historical overview of women's interventions in international law tends to give the impression both of a commonality and of a pattern of failure or, at best, stochastic success.[11] As regards the international law of self-determination, Part III offers a more differentiated and, relatedly, a more critical history of women's participation.

'As a woman, I have no country. As a woman I want no country. As a woman my country is the whole world,' Virginia Woolf wrote in 1930s Britain.[12] The poles of unequal/equal, male/female and national/international that orient her ringing phrases also offer new bearings for the significance of the plebiscites held in Europe after World War I, which are the subject of this chapter, and the movements and metaphors at work in them.

'As a woman, I have no country' alludes to the British laws of the day that deprived women of British nationality on their marriage to a foreigner, as well as excluding them from public life. United by their legal inequality, women in Britain and other countries actively campaigned domestically and internationally for the same right as men to choose their nationality, just as they fought for the same right to vote.

Woolf presents her pledge of indifference – 'As a woman I want no country' – as logical given that England was ready to make her a foreigner if she married a foreigner. But she maintains that even if the laws on nationality treated women and men equally, women would not be nationalists.[13] 'As a woman I want no country' reflects Woolf's contention too that women cannot understand what instinct compels men to take up arms for their country, 'what glory, what interest, what manly satisfaction fighting provides for him'.[14]

While Woolf insists on this commonality of gender,[15] she uses it to proclaim that 'as a woman, my country is the whole world'. In this

---

[11] For Charlesworth and Chinkin, the question raised by history is why international law has not responded to women's concerns, not why it did when it did. *Ibid.*, p. 17.

[12] V. Woolf, *Three Guineas* (1938) in V. Woolf, *A Room of One's Own* and *Three Guineas*, M. Barrett (ed.) (London: Penguin, 1993), pp. 117–365 at p. 234.

[13] Women, Immigration and Nationality Group, *Worlds Apart: Women Under Immigration and Nationality Law*, J. Bhabha, F. Klug and S. Shutter (eds.) (London: Pluto Press, 1985), p. 16.

[14] Woolf, *Three Guineas*, p. 232. It is not clear how much of this Woolf attributes to the essence of women's nature and how much to the effect of socialization. Although Woolf refers to fighting as a male instinct, she also acknowledges it as 'an instinct which is as foreign to her as centuries of tradition and education can make it'. *Ibid.*, p. 233. Her note to this passage offers an example intended to show that 'if sanctioned, the fighting instinct easily develops' in women. *Ibid.*, p. 311, n.15.

[15] Woolf is not uniformly complimentary about feminism in *Three Guineas*. See

resolution of her identity, Woolf resembles the international women's peace movement that emerged during World War I, based on the belief that women's nature caused them to feel a particular moral revulsion at war, and that their role as child-bearers and care-givers gave them a special position in the campaign for peace and internationalism.

Nevertheless, Woolf allows that nationalism is not so easily shed: even 'when reason has said its say, still some obstinate emotion... some love of England dropped into a child's ears by the cawing of rooks in an elm tree, by the splash of waves on a beach, or by English voices murmuring nursery rhymes' may remain.[16] Moreover, in arguing that the discriminatory nationality laws show women to be 'stepdaughters, not full daughters, of England',[17] Woolf perpetuates the idea of their natural belongingness and also, ironically, the analogy of family and state often used to support this discrimination.

This chapter shows that if we orient the interwar plebiscites by ideas of equality and gender, as well as by ideas of the international order, they appear as a milestone for women in the history of self-determination. It also shows, however, that the same bearings locate the related right of option as a stronghold of patriarchy and nationalism.

Collective self-determination

Plebiscites

On a standard account, the significance of the interwar plebiscites[18] lies in their departure from the traditional international law on transfer of territory by giving the population of certain border areas the opportunity to choose between the two states disputing the territory. Traditionally, territory could be acquired by conquest; the consent of its

---

M. Barrett, 'Introduction' in Woolf, *A Room of One's Own* and *Three Guineas*, pp. ix–liii at p. xliii. On the different schools of pre-war and post-war feminism, see generally S. K. Kent, *Making Peace: The Reconstruction of Gender in Interwar Britain* (Princeton: Princeton University Press, 1993).

[16] Woolf, *Three Guineas*, p. 234.   [17] *Ibid.*, p. 277, n.12.

[18] For examples of the renewed interest in internationally held or supervised exercises of the popular will, see Y. Beigbeder, *International Monitoring of Plebiscites, Referenda and National Elections: Self-Determination and Transition to Democracy* (Dordrecht: Martinus Nijhoff, 1994); L. T. Farley, *Plebiscites and Sovereignty: The Crisis of Political Illegitimacy* (Boulder, Colo.: Westview Press, 1986); G. H. Fox, 'The Right to Political Participation in International Law' (1992) 17 *Yale Journal of International Law* 539; G. H. Fox, 'Self-Determination in the Post-Cold War Era: A New Internal Focus?' (1995) 16 *Michigan Journal of International Law* 733; V. Rudrakumaran, 'The "Requirement" of Plebiscite in Territorial Rapprochement' (1989) 12 *Houston Journal of International Law* 23.

inhabitants was not a prerequisite for the transfer of sovereignty from conquered to conquering state. Although plebiscites had been used episodically from the French Revolution onward,[19] by the end of the nineteenth century, they had come to be 'abandoned by diplomats, condemned by the majority of writers on international law, and forgotten by the world at large'.[20]

With World War I, however, plebiscites, and the underlying principle of self-determination, were advocated as the basis for the new frontiers to be drawn by the Peace Conference. At the time, self-determination was not yet recognized as a principle of international law,[21] so its application depended on mustering sufficient political will to give it binding expression in the various peace treaties. In a series of famous speeches from 1916 onward, President Wilson had developed the principle of self-determination as among the imperatives defended by the Allies in the war and among the guides to a just peace. The plebiscites are conventionally depicted as a foothold for Wilson's ideal of liberal self-determination in international law;[22] the imperfect realization of his 1917 pronouncement that 'no right anywhere exists to hand peoples about from sovereignty to sovereignty as if they were property'.[23]

Plebiscites involving Germany were held under the Treaty of Versailles in northern Schleswig,[24] a cattle and dairy-farming area on the border

---

[19] See S. Wambaugh, *A Monograph on Plebiscites with a Collection of Official Documents* (New York: Oxford University Press, 1920). See also J. Mattern, *The Employment of the Plebiscite in the Determination of Sovereignty* (Baltimore: Johns Hopkins Press, 1920).

[20] S. Wambaugh, *Plebiscites Since the World War with a Collection of Official Documents* (2 vols., Washington: Carnegie Endowment for International Peace, 1933), vol. I, p. 3.

[21] See the discussion of the *Aaland Islands* case in Chapter 2 above.

[22] E.g. T. M. Franck, 'The Emerging Right to Democratic Governance' (1992) 86 *American Journal of International Law* 46 at 52–3. Compare the discussion of a consent model of self-determination at pp. 66–7 above.

[23] Address of President Wilson to the American Senate on 22 January 1917, US Congressional Record, vol. 54, pt. 2, 1742, quoted in Wambaugh, *Plebiscites Since the World War*, vol. I, p. 5. It should be noted that President Wilson's conception of self-determination actually involved – some would say confused – several different strands of thought, liberal democracy being only one of them. See e.g. A. Cassese, *Self-Determination of Peoples: A Legal Reappraisal* (Cambridge: Cambridge University Press, 1995), pp. 19–23; M. Pomerance, 'The United States and Self-Determination: Perspectives on the Wilsonian Conception' (1976) 70 *American Journal of International Law* 1.

[24] Treaty of Peace Between the Allied and Associated Powers and Germany, Versailles, 28 June 1919, 225 Consol. TS 188 [Treaty of Versailles], Part III, Arts. 109–114. See Wambaugh, *Plebiscites Since the World War*, vol. I, pp. 46–98 (discussion); vol. II, pp. 3–47 (documentation); Paris Peace Conference (1919–20), *La Paix de Versailles* (Series La Documentation Internationale) (13 vols., Paris: Les Editions Internationales, 1929–39) *Questions Territoriales* (vol. IX, 1939), part 2, pp. 215–315 (documentation).

with Denmark, where a plebiscite had been discussed already in the last century after Denmark had lost Schleswig to Germany;[25] in Allenstein and Marienwerder,[26] two agricultural regions of some strategic importance, disputed with Poland; in Upper Silesia,[27] then one of the richest mining and industrial regions in the world, claimed by Poland; and, after a fifteen-year period of international administration, in the Saar Basin,[28] where the fate of the third most important coalfields in Europe was at stake for Germany and France. Two plebiscites involving Austria were carried out by the Paris Peace Conference: one in the Klagenfurt Basin[29] on the Yugoslav border, of considerable interest to Italy because of the railway links; and the other in Sopron,[30] involving the city and some nearby rural communes on the old Austro-Hungarian frontier. Plebiscites were attempted between Czechoslovakia and Poland over Teschen, Spisz and Orava,[31] and, under League of Nations auspices, between Lithuania and Poland over the city of Vilnius,[32] but were abandoned by the international authority due to the political tension and unrest in the period leading up to the plebiscite. Finally, a plebiscite agreed to by Chile and Peru for Tacna and Arica in the 1883 Treaty

[25] Wambaugh, *Plebiscites Since the World War*, vol. I, pp. 49–51.
[26] Treaty of Versailles, Part III, Arts. 94–97. See Wambaugh, *Plebiscites Since the World War*, vol. I, pp. 99–141 (discussion); vol. II, pp. 48–107 (documentation).
[27] Treaty of Versailles, Part III, Arts. 88–91. See Wambaugh, *Plebiscites Since the World War*, vol. I, pp. 206–70 (discussion); vol. II, pp. 163–261 (documentation).
[28] Treaty of Versailles, Part III, Art. 45–50 and Annex, esp. ch. III of Annex. See generally S. Wambaugh, *The Saar Plebiscite with a Collection of Official Documents* (1940) (Westport, Conn.: Greenwood Press, 1971).
[29] Treaty of Peace Between the Allied and Associated Powers and Austria, St Germain-en-Laye, 10 September 1919, 226 Consol. TS 1 [Treaty of St Germain], Part III, Arts. 49–51. See Wambaugh, *Plebiscites Since the World War*, vol. I, pp. 163–205 (discussion); vol. II, pp. 124–62 (documentation).
[30] Protocol and Additional Article Regarding the Settlement of the Question of Western Hungary, Venice, 13 October 1921, ratified by Austria on 28 December 1921 (ratification not required by the Hungarian constitution), 9 LNTS 203. See Wambaugh, *Plebiscites Since the World War*, vol. I, pp. 271–97 (discussion); vol. II, pp. 261–9 (documentation).
[31] Decision of the Supreme Council of the Principal Allied and Associated Powers, Dated September 27th, 1919, With Regard to the Territory of Teschen (1919), PCIJ Ser. C, No. 4. Documents relating to Advisory Opinion No. 8, p. 116. See Wambaugh, *Plebiscites Since the World War*, vol. I, pp. 142–62 (discussion); vol. II, pp. 107–24 (documentation).
[32] Resolution of the Council of the League of Nations Calling for a Public Expression of Opinion under the Auspices and Supervision of the League, adopted 28 October 1920, reprinted in Wambaugh, *Plebiscites Since the World War*, vol. II, p. 269. See Wambaugh, *Plebiscites Since the World War*, vol. I, pp. 298–330, 547–56 (discussion); vol. II, pp. 269–81 (documentation).

of Ancón[33] was attempted in 1925–6 pursuant to an arbitral award of President Coolidge.[34]

Women's right to vote in the plebiscites

For women, the international plebiscites provided for by the peace treaties are also significant as the first time that women had the right to participate in an international expression of popular sovereignty. Given that the treaties were negotiated when women's suffrage was still the exception,[35] it is remarkable that women were given the vote in all the plebiscites held. The United States and Britain were the only members of the Supreme Council at the 1919 Paris Peace Conference that were within a decade of fully enfranchising women. The Peace Conference took place at the height of the campaign to ratify an amendment to the United States Constitution giving women the vote,[36] and the American suffragist leader Carrie Chapman Catt,[37] president of the National American Woman Suffrage[38] Association (NAWSA) and president and

---

[33] Treaty of Peace and Friendship between Chile and Peru, signed at Ancón, 20 October 1883, 162 Consol. TS 453, Art. 3.

[34] *Opinion and Award of the Arbitrator in the Matter of the Arbitration Between the Republic of Chile and the Republic of Peru, With Respect to the Unfulfilled Provisions of the Treaty of Peace of October 20, 1883, under the Protocol and Supplementary Articles Signed at Washington, July 20, 1922*, 4 March 1925, reprinted in Wambaugh, *Plebiscites Since the World War*, vol. II, p. 282. On the attempted plebiscite in Tacna-Arica, see Wambaugh, *Plebiscites Since the World War*, vol. I, pp. 331–410 (discussion); vol. II, pp. 281–491 (documentation). See also W. J. Dennis, *Tacna and Arica: An Account of the Chile–Peru Boundary Dispute and of the Arbitrations by the United States* (1931) (Hamden, Conn.: Archon Books, 1976).

[35] See A. Winslow (ed.), *Women, Politics, and the United Nations* (Contributions in Women's Studies, No. 151) (Westport, Conn.: Greenwood Press, 1995), App. I, pp. 185–6 (women's right to vote by country and date).

[36] By 1917, twelve American states had given women the vote and a constitutional amendment in 1920 would forbid its denial on the grounds of sex. T. T. Mackie and R. Rose, *The International Almanac of Electoral History* (3rd edn, Washington, D.C.: Congressional Quarterly, 1991), p. 457.

[37] For a biography of Carrie Chapman Catt emphasizing her international work, see J. Van Voris, *Carrie Chapman Catt: A Public Life* (New York: The Feminist Press at The City University of New York, 1987). Other biographies are R. B. Fowler, *Carrie Catt: Feminist Politician* (Boston: Northeastern University Press, 1986); M. G. Peck, *Carrie Chapman Catt: A Biography* (New York: H. W. Wilson Co., 1944).

[38] While this chapter uses the term 'women's suffrage', the movement's originators and early chroniclers used the term 'woman suffrage' to emphasize that suffrage was not an aggregation of individual rights to vote, but, in fact, a group privilege reserved to men. 'Woman suffrage' therefore indicated the need for a new group franchise for women *qua* women. See J. Lind, 'Dominance and Democracy: The Legacy of Woman Suffrage for the Voting Right' (1994) 5 *UCLA Women's Law Journal* 103 at 105, n. 4.

founder of the International Woman Suffrage Alliance (IWSA),[39] was therefore absent from the Peace Conference.[40] By the end of the war, Britain had partially enfranchised women, but would not fully enfranchise them until 1928.[41] The other three members of the Supreme Council, France,[42] Italy[43] and Japan,[44] would not give women the vote until the 1940s. Of the seven states involved in the plebiscites actually held, Austria, Denmark, Germany, Hungary and Poland had extended the franchise to women during or after the war, but France and Yugoslavia were over twenty years away from doing so.[45]

Women themselves were very much part of the spirit of the times that fostered the plebiscites and women's equal participation in them. International women's organizations existed long before the Peace Conference, several international conferences of women were held with the goal of influencing the peace process, and women lobbied the delegations to the Peace Conference on women's rights and other issues concerning the peace treaties and proposed league of nations. White, Western, well educated and well connected,[46] these leaders of the

    Also for reasons of generality, the chapter uses 'suffragist' rather than 'suffragette'. 'Suffragette' was a derogatory nickname coined by the British press and adopted by the militant section of the British women's suffrage movement headed by Emmeline Pankhurst and her daughter Christabel. A. Wiltsher, *Most Dangerous Women: Feminist Peace Campaigners of the Great War* (London: Pandora, 1985), p. xi.

[39] On the International Woman Suffrage Alliance, see generally M. Bosch with A. Kloosterman (eds.), *Politics and Friendship: Letters from the International Woman Suffrage Alliance, 1902–1942* (Columbus, Ohio: Ohio State University Press, 1990). In 1926, the IWSA became the International Alliance of Women for Suffrage and Equal Citizenship, abbreviated as IAW. Ibid., p. 176.

[40] D. Rubinstein, *A Different World for Women: The Life of Millicent Garrett Fawcett* (London: Harvester Wheatsheaf, 1991), p. 254.

[41] Mackie and Rose, *International Almanac*, p. 438.

[42] Winslow, *Women, Politics* (in 1944).   [43] Ibid. (in 1945).   [44] Ibid. (in 1945).

[45] Women had the vote in Austria (1918), Denmark (1915), Germany (1919), Poland (1918). Ibid. Universal suffrage had been achieved in Hungary immediately after World War I, but a period of political change followed with the result that by 1922, women were voting on more restricted terms than men. C. J. C. Street, *Hungary and Democracy* (London: T. Fisher Unwin Ltd, 1923), pp. 185–6, 190–1; A. Nyerges, *Women in Hungary* (Budapest: Pannonia, 1962), pp. 18–19, 21, 34; Van Voris, *Catt: A Public Life*, p. 174.

    Like France, Yugoslavia only gave women the vote in the 1940s. Winslow, *Women, Politics*, App. I, pp. 185–6.

    Four other states would have been involved in the plebiscites had three plebiscites not been abandoned in midstream. Of these additional states, women would shortly have the vote in Czechoslovakia (1920) and Lithuania (1921), but not in Chile (1931) and Peru (1950). Ibid.

[46] While this chapter focuses on what is essentially the white Western liberal women's movement, there were also, for example, a feminist movement within international

international women's movement enjoyed considerable access to the statesmen and diplomats who controlled the peace process.

The issue of women's right to vote in the plebiscites lay at the intersection of the campaign for women's suffrage and the advocacy of the principle of self-determination and plebiscites by the women's peace movement. Even though women's suffrage was not yet assured in any of the states that composed the Supreme Council, the principal Allied leaders at the Peace Conference were well aware of the issue from the national women's suffrage movements. Not only had President Wilson come to support the American women's suffrage movement by this time, but his support has been attributed to propaganda by the militant National Women's Party (NWP) in 1917 that stressed the inconsistency between Wilson's prominent advocacy of democracy abroad and his indifference to women's suffrage at home.[47] As part of this strategy, one banner carried by an NWP picket outside the White House bore the excerpt from Wilson's war message 'We shall fight for the things we have always held nearest our hearts – for democracy',[48] and NWP leader Alice Paul was arrested for carrying a banner with Wilson's Liberty Bond slogan: 'The time has come to conquer or submit'.[49] NAWSA also fastened onto Wilson's wartime aim of democratic self-determination, and the theme of many of Chapman Catt's talks was that the United States had no right to talk about making the world safe for democracy so long as it denied women the vote.[50] Chapman Catt, in the words of one biographer, 'frankly used the war psychology to further her cause'.[51] In the following speech, she characterized women's suffrage as a war measure:

Our nation is engaged in the defense of democracy; the hearts of women would beat more happily if they could feel that our own Government had been true to the standard it proposes to unfurl upon an international field.

---

socialism (see E. C. DuBois, 'Woman Suffrage and the Left: An International Socialist-Feminist Perspective' (March–April 1991) 186 *New Left Review* 20 at 29–34) and an International Council of Women of the Darker Races (see C. Neverdon-Morton, *Afro-American Women of the South and the Advancement of the Race, 1895–1925* (Knoxville, Tenn.: University of Tennessee Press, 1989), pp. 198–201).

[47] S. H. Graham, 'Woodrow Wilson, Alice Paul, and the Woman Suffrage Movement' (Winter 1983–4) 98 *Political Science Quarterly* 665. For the scholarly debate on whether Wilson's contribution to the passage of the Nineteenth Amendment, giving women the right to vote, was motivated by his eventual personal conviction as well as his estimation of political expediency, compare *ibid.* with C. A. Lunardini and T. J. Knock, 'Woodrow Wilson and Woman Suffrage: A New Look' (Winter 1980–1) 95 *Political Science Quarterly* 655.

[48] Graham, 'Woodrow Wilson, Alice Paul', 667.   [49] *Ibid.*, 676.

[50] Van Voris, *Catt: A Public Life*, p. 146.   [51] Peck, *Catt: A Biography*, p. 273.

We speak not so much for ourselves as in defense of our republic, in hope that it will resume its historic place as leader of democracy. *We demand the suffrage by Federal amendment in the United States as a war measure!*[52]

The British leader at the Peace Conference, David Lloyd George, had long been a supporter of the British suffrage movement.[53] Although the French leader, Georges Clemenceau, opposed women's suffrage in France, his opposition has been attributed not to general principle, but to his fear that French women voters would be controlled by the Catholic Church and would therefore not exercise the right to vote freely.[54]

In addition to the political awareness already created by the national women's suffrage movements, women present at the Peace Conference[55] pressed the demand for women's suffrage with the Allied leaders. For example, the diary of Millicent Garrett Fawcett, doyenne of the moderate British suffragists, records her interviews with President Wilson, Prime Minister Clemenceau and a number of other leading figures at the Peace Conference. With Clemenceau she discussed his opposition to women's suffrage; on Wilson she urged a 'people's peace' based on the votes of all the people.[56] French suffragists had organized a conference of suffragists from Allied countries and the United States in parallel to the Peace

---

[52] (Emphasis in original) Quoted in *ibid.*
[53] See S. S. Holton, *Feminism and Democracy: Women's Suffrage and Reform Politics in Britain 1900–1918* (Cambridge: Cambridge University Press, 1986) (although Lloyd George had certain tactical reservations). On these reservations, see J. Grigg, *Lloyd George: The People's Champion, 1902–1911* (London: Eyre Methuen, 1978), pp. 164–9, 294–301; M. Pugh, *Electoral Reform in War and Peace, 1906–18* (London: Routledge & Kegan Paul, 1978), especially pp. 29–44.
[54] See S. C. Hause with A. R. Kenney, *Women's Suffrage and Social Politics in the French Third Republic* (Princeton, N. J.: Princeton University Press, 1984), pp. 97–9, 226, 244. British suffragist leader Millicent Garrett Fawcett had the same impression from her meeting with Clemenceau at the Peace Conference. Rubinstein, *A Different World for Women*, pp. 253–4.
[55] Women's lobbying to be represented on the official delegations to the Paris Peace Conference was unsuccessful. See Resolution 18, adopted by the International Congress of Women at The Hague, 1 May 1915, reprinted in J. Addams, E. G. Balch and A. Hamilton, *Women at The Hague: The International Congress of Women and its Results* (1915) (New York: Garland Publishing Inc., 1971), App. III, p. 150 at p. 158 (urging 'that representatives of the people should take part in the conference that shall frame the peace settlement after the war, and... that amongst them women should be included'); M. L. Degen, *The History of the Woman's Peace Party* (1939) (New York: Burt Franklin Reprints, 1974), p. 210 (resolution of the New York City branch of the Woman's Peace Party calling for men and women representing the ideals of their countries to be appointed to the Peace Conference); Peck, *Catt: A Biography*, pp. 269, 301–2 (Chapman Catt's efforts to have women represented on the American delegation); Van Voris, *Catt: A Public Life*, p. 186 (women in Canada, England and the United States had requested that women be appointed to the treaty delegations).
[56] Rubinstein, *A Different World*, pp. 253–4.

Conference,[57] and a joint delegation from the Conference of Women Suffragists of the Allied Countries and the United States and the International Council of Women (ICW)[58] was heard at the next-to-last meeting of the Peace Conference commission dealing with the part of the peace treaty that would be the Covenant of the new League of Nations. At the 10 April 1919 meeting of the commission, presided over by President Wilson at the Hôtel Crillon,[59] this delegation presented its demands on women's rights. Among them was a demand on suffrage which marshalled the right of self-determination of peoples in support of women's equal right to vote generally and in the plebiscites specifically:

Considérant que le Congrès de la Paix intéresse l'humanité toute entière, les femmes comme les hommes, et que de ce Congrès doit sortir le règne d'une paix durable et la reconnaissance du droit des peuples à disposer librement d'eux mêmes;

Considérant que nul ne peut se croire autorisé à parler au nom des peuples tant que les femmes, qui représentent la moitié de l'humanité, seront exclues de la vie politique des nations;

Considérant que celles des femmes qui sont privées du suffrage sont sans action sur le gouvernement de leur pays; qu'il est profondément injuste qu'elles ne puissent intervenir dans les décisions dont peuvent sortir la guerre ou la paix, décisions qui fixeront un avenir dont elles auront à subir les conséquences sans en avoir pris les responsabilités;

Considérant que, sans être combattantes, elles jouent un rôle essentiel dans les guerres puisque, en donnant leur fils pour la défense de leur pays, elles fournissent ce qu'on a pu appeler le matériel humain;

Considérant d'autre part que les femmes ont, durant la guerre, montré quelle pouvait être la valeur de leur travail et de leur activité sociale;

Considérant que la participation des mères et des épouses au suffrage serait une des meilleurs garanties pour la paix à venir;

[57] J. Alberti, *Beyond Suffrage: Feminists in War and Peace, 1914–28* (London: Macmillan, 1989), p. 88; Rubinstein, *A Different World*, p. 253; C. A. Miller, 'Lobbying the League: Women's International Organizations and the League of Nations' (D. Phil. thesis, University of Oxford, 1992), p. 29; A. Whittick, *Woman into Citizen* (Santa Barbara, California: ABC-Clio, 1979), p. 70.

[58] On the International Council of Women, see generally International Council of Women, *Women in a Changing World: The Dynamic Story of the International Council of Women Since 1888* (London: Routledge & Kegan Paul, 1966).

[59] See 'An Account of the ICW Delegation Received by the Committee for the League of Nations at the Paris Peace Conference in 1919' in P. Rossello, *The Precursors of the International Bureau of Education* (1943), reprinted in *ibid.*, App. 7, 344. Rossello's account gives the list of the Commission members present and the members of the delegation of women. For other communiqués and notes of the meeting, see C. A. Kluyver, *Documents on the League of Nations* (Leiden: A. W. Sijthoff's Uitgeversmaatschappij, 1920), p. 27; D. H. Miller, *My Diary at the Conference of Paris, with Documents* (21 vols., n. p., printed for author by Appeal Printing Co., n. d.), vol. I, p. 238.

Considérant que le statut des femmes a été de tout temps reconnu comme étant le critérium du degré de la civilisation et du libéralisme des États:

Le Conseil International des Femmes et la Conférence des Femmes Suffragistes des Pays alliés et des États-Unis émettent les vœux suivants:

1. Que le bien fondé du principe du suffrage féminin soit proclamé par la Conférence de la Paix et la Ligue des Nations afin qu'il reçoive son application dans le monde entier aussi rapidement que le permettront le degré de civilisation et le développement démocratique de chaque nation.

2. Que dans la consultation populaire qui doit décider de la nationalité d'un État, les femmes soient appelées, comme hommes, à se prononcer sur le sort de leur Patrie.

[Considering that the Peace Conference concerns the whole of humanity, women and men alike, and that from this Conference must issue the reign of a lasting peace and the recognition of the right of peoples to free self-determination;

Considering that no one can consider himself authorized to speak in the name of the people as long as women, who represent half of humanity, are excluded from the political life of nations;

Considering that those women who lack the vote are without a voice in the government of their country; that it is profoundly unjust that they can take no part in the decisions which may give rise to war or peace, decisions that determine a future of which they must bear the consequences without a share in the responsibility,

Considering that without being combatants, they play an essential role in war since by giving their sons for the defence of their country, they furnish what may be called the human *matériel*;

Considering, on the other hand, that women have, during the war, shown what the value of their work and their social activity could be;

Considering that the participation of mothers and wives in the suffrage would be one of the best guarantees for future peace;

Considering that the status of women has always been recognized as the criterion of the degree of civilization and liberalism of states;[60]

The International Council of Women and the Conference of Women Suffragists of the Allied Countries and the United States petition as follows:

1. That the principle of women's suffrage be proclaimed by the Peace Conference and the League of Nations in order that it may be applied throughout the world as soon as the degree of civilization and democratic development of each nation may permit;

2. That in any popular consultation held to decide the nationality of a state, women shall be called upon, equally with men, to express themselves on the fate of their homeland.][61]

---

[60] See Chapter 7 below.
[61] (Translation mine) The 'Memorial of the Women' is reprinted in French in Miller, *My Diary at the Conference of Paris*, vol. VIII, Document 744, p. 173 at pp. 174–5.

The history of the advocacy of women's right to vote in the plebiscites belongs more particularly, however, to the history of the women's peace movement, which developed during the war.[62] Many national women's suffrage organizations devoted their energies to their country's war effort,[63] and the established international women's organizations did not meet for the duration of the war.[64] There were also, however, a number of prominent suffragists in different countries who were opposed to the war, and their initiatives led to the formation of national and international women's committees for peace. The incorporation of women's suffrage into the principle of self-determination, in contrast to the principle of self-determination into the basis for women's suffrage, figured in the feminist pacifism popularized by Emmeline Pethick-Lawrence in her 1914 speaking tour of the United States, the platform of the American Woman's Peace Party established in the wake of her tour, Chrystal Macmillan's proposals for the first International Congress of Women at The Hague in 1915, and the resolutions that emerged from this and the International Congress of Women held in Zurich during the Peace Conference.

The texts contributed by women pacifists to the peace process did not simply add women's equality to the right of self-determination from a different starting point. In these texts, as in the suffragists' texts, women also sought to identify themselves with an idea of the international order which would be furthered by women's suffrage. We have seen how the suffragists strove to associate women with the grit of nationalism

---

According to Carol Ann Miller, the delegation strategically chose not to present a more controversial International Charter of Women's Rights and Liberties. Miller, 'Lobbying the League', p. 22.

[62] See generally Wiltsher, *Most Dangerous Women*. This history has also been told as the history of the Woman's Peace Party, an American women's peace society established in 1915 (Degen, *Woman's Peace Party*); or that of the Women's International League for Peace and Freedom (WILPF), established at the 1919 Zurich International Congress of Women as the successor to the International Committee of Women for Permanent Peace which had emerged from the first International Congress of Women at The Hague in 1915 (G. Bussey and M. Tims, *Women's International League for Peace and Freedom, 1915–1965: A Record of Fifty Years' Work* (London: George Allen & Unwin Ltd., 1965); C. Foster, *Women for All Seasons: The Story of the Women's International League for Peace and Freedom* (Athens: University of Georgia Press, 1989)).

[63] See Hause, *Women's Suffrage*, pp. 191–7 (France); Kent, *Making Peace*, pp. 74–96 (Britain); Rupp, 'Constructing Internationalism', 1588–9 (Britain, France and Germany); Van Voris, *Catt: A Public Life*, pp. 138–41 (United States); Wiltsher, *Most Dangerous Women*, pp. 56–81 (Britain).

[64] On the tensions in the IWSA, see Bosch and Kloosterman, *Politics and Friendship*, pp. 145–73.

and war, as workers who had proved their worth during the war and as mothers who, by giving birth to sons who had fought for their country, had provided the human *matériel* for the war. By pitching in with the war work and arming the nation with their sons, women had earned the right to vote. In contrast, we shall see that the pacifists linked women to an ideal of internationalism and peace. Women, as the custodians of the life destroyed by war, the care-givers to those helpless in its face, the toilers whose patient drudgery had built the home and peaceful industry smashed by war, were particularly inclined toward peace. The extension of the franchise to women would therefore further humanize the governments of the world.

In 1914, Emmeline Pethick-Lawrence,[65] having split with British radical suffragist Emmeline Pankhurst and renounced Pankhurst's resort to violence in the campaign for the vote, embarked on a series of talks and articles[66] in the United States on the theme of women and war.[67] Pethick-Lawrence's feminist pacifism was influenced by the ideology of the women's suffrage movement and also by the Union of Democratic Control's platform for permanent peace.[68] Among the principles of peace formulated by this organization of English liberals and socialists was the principle of self-determination and plebiscites in the peace settlements.[69] To these principles, Pethick-Lawrence added not only women's suffrage, but also the sharing of women in any plebiscite to determine the disposition of territories.[70]

Pethick-Lawrence's agenda for feminist pacifism included the establishment of an international women's movement for constructive peace.[71] In the United States, a first step was taken with the formation

---

[65] See generally E. Pethick-Lawrence, *My Part in a Changing World* (1938) (Westport, Conn.: Hyperion Press, 1976).
[66] F. W. [E.] Pethick-Lawrence, 'Motherhood and War' (1914) 59 *Harper's Weekly* 542; [E.] Pethick-Lawrence, 'Union of Women for Constructive Peace' (1914) 33 *Survey* 230.
[67] See Degen, *Woman's Peace Party*, pp. 31–6; D. Mitchell, *Women on the Warpath: The Story of the Women of the First World War* (London: Jonathan Cape, 1966), pp. 314–15; Wiltsher, *Most Dangerous Women*, pp. 49–53.
[68] Degen, *Woman's Peace Party*, p. 32.   [69] *Ibid.*, pp. 32, 34.
[70] Pethick-Lawrence, 'Motherhood and War'; Pethick-Lawrence, 'Union of Women for Constructive Peace'.
[71] *Ibid.* As did that of Rosika Schwimmer, the Hungarian feminist who lectured on pacifism in the United States at the same time as Pethick-Lawrence, sometimes sharing the stage with her. Degen, *Woman's Peace Party*, p. 33. On Schwimmer, see Wiltsher, *Most Dangerous Women*, especially pp. 43–55 on this period. Wiltsher notes the differences between Pethick-Lawrence's and Schwimmer's pacifism at p. 52. In *Peace and Bread in Time of War* (1945) (New York: Garland Publishing Inc., 1972), pp. 6–7,

of the Woman's Peace Party in 1915,[72] headed by Jane Addams, the social worker who was already a nationally recognized figure in both the women's movement and the peace movement and who would receive the Nobel Peace Prize in 1931.[73] The preamble of the Party's founding platform illustrates the combination of internationalist pacifism[74] with feminism, and the identification of peace with women, that informed the promotion of the principle of self-determination amended by the principle of women's suffrage:

> *We, Women of the United States,* assembled in behalf of World Peace, grateful for the security of our own country, but sorrowing for the misery of all involved in the present struggle among warring nations, do hereby band ourselves together to demand that war be abolished.
>
> Equally with men pacifists, we understand that planned-for, legalized, wholesale, human slaughter is today the sum of all villainies.
>
> As women, we feel a peculiar moral passion of revolt against both the cruelty and the waste of war.
>
> As women, we are especially the custodian of the life of the ages. We will not longer consent to its reckless destruction.
>
> As women, we are particularly charged with the future of childhood and with the care of the helpless and the unfortunate. We will not longer endure without protest that added burden of maimed and invalid men and poverty-stricken widows and orphans which war places upon us.
>
> As women, we have built by the patient drudgery of the past the basic foundation of the home and of peaceful industry. We will not longer endure without a protest that must be heard and heeded by men, that hoary evil which in an hour destroys the social structure that centuries of toil have reared.
>
> As women, we are called upon to start each generation onward toward a better humanity. We will not longer tolerate without determined opposition that denial of the sovereignty of reason and justice by which war and all that makes for war today render impotent the idealism of the race.
>
> Therefore, as human beings and the mother half of humanity, we demand that our right to be consulted in the settlement of questions concerning not alone the life of individuals but of nations be recognized and respected.

  Jane Addams describes Pethick-Lawrence and Schwimmer as influences in the formation of the Woman's Peace Party in the United States.
[72] See Degen, *Woman's Peace Party*, pp. 38–63. The word 'party' is used in the non-political sense of a society. *Ibid.*, p. 11.
[73] For her own account of this time, see Addams, *Peace and Bread*.
[74] Internationalist pacifism aimed not simply at peace, but at a just, or constructive, peace. For internationalist pacifists, the design for a just peace was some combination of democratization, the enhancement of international law and international institutions, and disarmament. See generally Kennedy, 'The Move to Institutions', 878–99. For an appreciation of the American legalists in internationalist pacifism, see F. L. Kirgis, 'The Formative Years of the American Society of International Law' (1996) 90 *American Journal of International Law* 559.

We demand that women be given a share in deciding between war and peace in all the courts of high debate – within the home, the school, the church, the industrial order, and the state.

So protesting, and so demanding, we hereby form ourselves into a national organization to be called the Woman's Peace Party.[75]

A part of this initial platform was 'the further humanizing of governments by the extension of the franchise to women'.[76] The later, more detailed Program for Constructive Peace included the following principle among those 'to insure such terms of settlement as will prevent this war from being but the prelude to new wars': 'No province should be transferred as a result of conquest from one government to another against the will of the people.'[77]

Internationally, the women's peace movement was a result of the International Congress of Women held at The Hague in 1915.[78] In a letter sowing the seeds for this meeting,[79] Scottish feminist Chrystal Macmillan proposed the terms of the peace settlement as the topic. She listed the criteria for the transfer of territory, the democratic control of foreign policy and a number of other terms similar to those being mooted at the time by various organizations devoted to the building of internationalism through the peace settlements.[80] Macmillan wrote that in the suggestion that territory should not be transferred without the consent of the population of the country and the suggestion that foreign policy should be open to discussion and democratic

---

[75] Reprinted in Wiltsher, *Most Dangerous Women*, App. 1, p. 218.

[76] *Ibid.*, p. 219 (point 6).   [77] Reprinted in *ibid.*, App. 1, p. 220 (point II(1)).

[78] See generally Addams, Balch and Hamilton, *Women at The Hague*; Bussey and Tims, *Women's International League for Peace and Freedom*, pp. 17–24; Degen, *Woman's Peace Party*, pp. 64–91; J. Liddington, *The Long Road to Greenham: Feminism and Anti-Militarism in Britain Since 1820* (London: Virago Press, 1989), pp. 87–106; M. M. Randall, *Improper Bostonian: Emily Greene Balch, Nobel Peace Laureate, 1946* (New York: Twayne Publishers, 1964), pp. 152–65; Wiltsher, *Most Dangerous Women*, pp. 82–102.

The resolutions of the International Congress of Women held at The Hague in 1915 are reproduced in Addams, Balch and Hamilton, *Women at The Hague*, App. III, p. 150.

[79] The principal credit for organizing the International Congress of Women goes to the Dutch doctor and suffragist Aletta Jacobs. M. M. Randall, 'Introduction' in Addams, Balch and Hamilton, *Women at The Hague*, pp. 5–15 at p. 7.

[80] In addition to the Union of Democratic Control in England, these included the Anti-Oorlog Raad (Anti-War Council) in The Netherlands; the National Executive Committee of the United States Socialist Party in the United States; the Bund Neues Vaterland and the Deutsche Friedensgesellschaft in Germany; and internationally the 'Minimum Program' of the Central Organization for a Durable Peace and the Ford Peace Expedition. Randall, 'Introduction' in Addams, Balch and Hamilton, *Women at The Hague*, p. 16, n. 2.

control, it was specially important to keep women's suffrage to the fore: 'It is essential to make it clear both nationally and internationally that women are included both in the population and in the democracy.'[81]

Successive generations of historians have alternately dismissed the International Congress of Women held at The Hague in 1915 as naive radicalism and recalled it as courageous visionariness.[82] Belittled in the press as an international ladies' tea party[83] or criticized as the folly of 'Pro-Hun peacettes',[84] the Congress adopted a series of resolutions for a just peace that were later credited with inspiring President Wilson's famous 'Fourteen Points'.[85] Jane Addams recorded that Wilson himself had told her that he considered the resolutions the best formulation he had seen up to that time.[86]

The two broad planks of the Congress platform, that international disputes should be settled by pacific means and that the parliamentary franchise should be extended to women,[87] met in the following resolution on the principles of peace: 'The International Congress of Women, recognizing the right of the people to self-government, affirms that there should be no[88] transference of territory without the consent of the men and women residing therein, and urges that autonomy and a democratic parliament should not be refused to any people.'[89]

[81] Quoted in Wiltsher, *Most Dangerous Women*, pp. 61–2.
[82] Compare Kennedy, 'The Move to Institutions'.
[83] Wiltsher, *Most Dangerous Women*, p. 88 quotes the *Northern Mail*'s 'this amiable chatter of a bevy of well-meaning ladies'.
[84] Randall, 'Introduction', p. 10. Teddy Roosevelt notoriously dubbed the women 'silly and base'. *Ibid.*, p. 9.
[85] Wiltsher, *Most Dangerous Women*, p. 92; Degen, *Woman's Peace Party*, p. 243. For a comparison of Wilson's 'Fourteen Points' with the resolutions of the 1915 Hague International Congress of Women, see Degen, *Woman's Peace Party*, pp. 179–80. (Notably, 'whereas Wilson had called merely for the recognition of the principle of the consent of the governed, the women had demanded a specific logical implication of this principle – woman suffrage'.)
[86] Addams, *Peace and Bread*, p. 59.
[87] 'Some Particulars About the Congress' in Addams, Balch and Hamilton, *Women at The Hague*, App. II, p. 146 at p. 147.
[88] Footnote in original: 'The Congress declared by vote that it interpreted no transference of territory without the consent of the men and women in it to imply that the right of conquest was not to be recognized.'
[89] Resolution 5, adopted by the International Congress of Women at The Hague, 1 May 1915, reprinted in Addams, Balch and Hamilton, *Women at The Hague*, App. III, p. 150 at pp. 152–3.

In a remarkable epilogue, two delegations of women appointed by the Congress[90] travelled from one capital to the next with the purpose of transmitting the resolutions of the Congress, especially a plan for mediation by a conference of neutral states, to belligerent and neutral governments alike.[91] In a manifesto issued by these envoys, they stated that one or the other of the delegations was received by the governments in fourteen capitals: Berlin, Berne, Budapest, Christiania, Copenhagen, The Hague, Havre (Belgian Government), London, Paris, Petrograd, Rome, Stockholm, Vienna, and Washington. They met with the Prime Ministers and Foreign Ministers of the Powers, the King of Norway, the Presidents of Switzerland and the United States, the Pope and the Cardinal Secretary of State. In addition to these thirty-five government visits, the delegations spoke everywhere with members of parliaments and other leaders of public opinion.[92]

The International Congress of Women had already resolved at The Hague in 1915 to hold a congress at the same time as the Peace Conference with the goal of influencing the peace process.[93] This International Congress of Women, held in Zurich in May 1919,[94] had an advance copy of the peace treaty as the basis for its discussions. Strongly critical of the treaty's terms as a betrayal of the principle of

---

[90] Resolution 20, adopted by the International Congress of Women at The Hague, 1 May 1915, reprinted in Addams, Balch and Hamilton, *Women at The Hague*, App. III, p. 150 at p. 159.

[91] For some of the delegates' own impressions, see J. Addams, 'The Revolt Against War' and 'Factors in Continuing the War'; E. G. Balch, 'At the Northern Capitals' and A. Hamilton, 'At the War Capitals' in Addams, Balch and Hamilton, *Women at The Hague*. See also Degen, *Woman's Peace Party*, pp. 92–126; Randall, *Improper Bostonian*, pp. 166–212; Wiltsher, *Most Dangerous Women*, pp. 103–25.

[92] Aletta Jacobs (Holland), Chrystal Macmillan (Great Britain), Rosika Schwimmer (Austro-Hungary), Emily G. Balch (United States), and Jane Addams (United States), Manifesto Issued by Envoys of the International Congress of Women at The Hague to the Governments of Europe and the President of the United States, reprinted in Addams, Balch and Hamilton, *Women at The Hague*, App. IV, p. 160.

[93] Resolution 19, adopted by the International Congress of Women at The Hague, 1 May 1915, reprinted in Addams, Balch and Hamilton, *Women at The Hague*, App. III, p. 150 at p. 158.

[94] See generally Addams, *Peace and Bread*, pp. 152–77; Alberti, *Beyond Suffrage*, pp. 86–8; Bussey and Tims, *Women's International League for Peace and Freedom*, pp. 29–33; Degen, *Woman's Peace Party*, pp. 216–51; Liddington, *The Long Road to Greenham*, pp. 136–8; Randall, *Improper Bostonian*, pp. 258–80; Wiltsher, *Most Dangerous Women*, pp. 200–11.

Some of the resolutions of the International Congress of Women held in Zurich in May 1919 are reprinted in French in Kluyver, *Documents on the League of Nations*, p. 323. In addition, the Congress drew up a Women's Charter which it proposed should be included in the peace treaty. *Ibid.*, p. 323, n. 1.

self-determination and the other principles first framed by President Wilson,[95] the Congress passed a resolution that adherence to the principle of self-determination in territorial adjustments and matters of nationality was among the essential principles omitted from the Covenant of the League of Nations, and the introduction of equal suffrage among the additional principles needed.[96] It also passed a resolution that a clause be introduced into the peace treaty giving women the same voting rights in the plebiscites as men.[97] In addition to telegraphing the first resolution of the Congress, concerning relief from blockade and famine, to President Wilson, who responded sympathetically,[98] the Congress appointed a delegation to take these resolutions to the Peace Conference.[99] Detailing its contact with the Allied leaders at Paris, Jane Addams, president of the delegation, wrote that two of the English members discussed the resolutions with Lord Robert Cecil, she saw Colonel House several times, and the delegation through the efforts of an Italian member was received by Signor Orlando and also had a hearing at the Quai d'Orsay with the French minister of foreign affairs, and with the delegates from other countries.[100]

Given the interventions of women themselves, the question is whether the peace treaties' provision for women's suffrage in the plebiscites reflects the acceptance of the women's arguments that the principle of self-determination should be interpreted consistent with women's equality or the traditional acceptance of the will of the states concerned, as expressed either directly in their proposals for the plebiscites or indirectly in their national laws on suffrage.[101] The plebiscites are clearly a watershed in that they were the first time that women were

---

[95] The resolution of protest is quoted in Addams, *Peace and Bread*, pp. 162–3.
[96] Resolution reproduced in Kluyver, *Documents on the League of Nations*, pp. 323–5.
For specific cases of self-determination in which the women's peace movement took a position, see Liddington, *The Long Road to Greenham*, p. 138 (WILPF and Ireland); Addams, *Peace and Bread*, pp. 55–6 (Woman's Peace Party and the sale of the Virgin Islands from Denmark to the United States); Wambaugh, *The Saar Plebiscite*, p. 237 (WILPF and the conditions for the Saar plebiscite).
[97] Degen, *Woman's Peace Party*, p. 231.
[98] Addams, *Peace and Bread*, pp. 160–2; Degen, *Woman's Peace Party*, pp. 227–8; Wiltsher, *Most Dangerous Women*, pp. 201–2.
[99] Degen, *Woman's Peace Party*, p. 237.   [100] Addams, *Peace and Bread*, p. 164.
[101] The question is whether the primary rationale is liberal feminism or positivism. A concerned state might, of course, propose giving women the right to vote in the plebiscites for reasons of liberal feminism, as opposed to the utility of additional voters or the low number of male voters due to casualties of war.

given the right to participate in an international expression of popular sovereignty. Indeed, Sarah Wambaugh, who authored a magisterial history of plebiscites at the request of the Peace Conference,[102] gives women's suffrage as the first major difference between the pre-war and post-war plebiscites.[103] Women had the vote in all the plebiscites held,[104] as well as all the informal consultations.[105] In addition, the Treaty of Versailles gave women in the Saar Basin the vote during the fifteen-year period of international administration that preceded the plebiscite between France and Germany.[106] But Wambaugh, although she personally supported women's suffrage in the plebiscites on grounds of equality,[107] is careful to present its significance from the dual viewpoint of principle and the effect on the number of voters.[108]

Wambaugh's impression was that the 'principle of woman suffrage in all the plebiscites appears to have been adopted as a matter of course by the Allies at Paris'.[109] This impression is consistent with David Hunter Miller's notes of the official meeting at which the joint delegation of the ICW and the inter-Allied conference of women suffragists presented their demand that in any popular consultation to decide the sovereignty of a territory, women be called upon equally with men to decide the fate of their homeland.[110] Whereas the ICW's account of the meeting records that this demand was 'immediately accepted',[111] which suggests that the women carried their point, Miller's notes read: 'I handed note

[102] 'Fair Vote in Saar is Woman's Task', *The New York Times*, 25 November 1934, s. IV, p. 3.
[103] S. Wambaugh, 'La Pratique des Plébiscites Internationaux' (1927-III) 18 Hague Recueil 151 at 225.
[104] Treaty of Versailles, Art. 109(2) (Schleswig); Art. 88, Annex s. 4 (Upper Silesia); Art. 95 (Allenstein); Art. 97 (Marienwerder plebiscite to conform to the same rules); Art. 49, Annex, c. III, s. 34 (Saar Basin); Treaty of St Germain, Art. 50 (Klagenfurt Basin); Decision of the Commission of Allied Generals for Sopron Regarding the Organization of the Plebiscite for the Sopron Territory, 15 November 1921, Art. III, reprinted in Wambaugh, *Plebiscites Since the World War*, vol. II, p. 265. Women would also have been given the vote in the plebiscite in Teschen, Spisz and Orava. Decision with regard to Teschen, Art. V.
[105] Wambaugh, *Plebiscites Since the World War*, vol. I, p. 477. Notably, women voted in the unilateral consultation held by Poland in Vilnius after the League of Nations plebiscite was abandoned, even though the League Plebiscite Commission had proposed excluding women. See note 150 below.
[106] Treaty of Versailles, Art. 49, Annex, c. II, s. 28.
[107] Wambaugh, *Plebiscites Since the World War*, vol. I, p. 506 (point 18).
[108] Wambaugh, 'La Pratique des Plébiscites Internationaux', 225.
[109] Wambaugh, *Plebiscites Since the World War*, vol. I, p. 477.
[110] See above note 61 and accompanying text.
[111] International Council of Women, *Women in a Changing World*, p. 45.

to President that every referendum had a provision for equal suffrage so far as I had seen the treaties. The President announced this.'[112]

The fact that the Peace Conference had already provided for women's suffrage in the plebiscites may mean that the earlier efforts of the women's movement had been effective. This would seem to have been the case, for example, with Article 7 of the Covenant of the League of Nations, which provided that 'all positions under or in connection with the League, including the Secretariat, shall be open equally to men and women'.[113] E. F. Ranshofen-Wertheimer, a member of the League Secretariat, claimed that Article 7 was already included 'before the feminist pressure groups caught President Wilson's ear'. As evidence, he pointed to the fact that the Commission had adopted Lord Robert Cecil's amendment to this effect two weeks before the meeting when the Commission received the delegation from the ICW and the Conference of Women Suffragists of the Allied Countries and the United States. According to various sources, however, Lady Aberdeen, the head of the delegation, had approached Lord Robert as soon as she learned that the Commission would hear the delegation. She had told him that her main point would be that women should be equally eligible with men to serve in positions under the League, whereupon he volunteered to introduce such a clause himself.[114] Similarly, Jane Addams wrote of governments' reception of the delegations from the 1915 Hague International Congress of Women:

> Our mission was simple, and foolish it may be, but it was not impossible. Perhaps the ministers talked freely to us because we were so absolutely unofficial... We do not wish to overestimate a very slight achievement nor to take too seriously the kindness with which the delegation was received, but we do wish to record ourselves as being quite sure that at least a few citizens in these various countries, some of them officials in high places, were grateful for the effort we made.[115]

While Addams is referring primarily to the prospects for their proposal for mediation, the possibility of persuasion may be more general. According to Emily Balch, 'They were received gravely, kindly, perhaps gladly, by twenty-one ministers, the presidents of two republics, a king, and the Pope. All, apparently, recognized without argument that an expression of the public opinion of a large body of women had every claim to consideration in questions of war and peace.'[116]

---

[112] Miller, *My Diary at the Conference of Paris*, vol. I, p. 238, n. (b).
[113] 28 June 1919, (1919) 112 BFSP 13.   [114] Miller, 'Lobbying the League', p. 23.
[115] J. Addams, 'Factors in Continuing the War', pp. 97–8.
[116] Balch, 'At the Northern Capitals', p. 110.

Addams and Balch however, were, writing for the general public in 1915, when a quietly optimistic account of their peace mission might have furthered its objective. Women writing privately or as the time to influence the peace process was slipping away sometimes betrayed frustration. With respect to the inter-Allied conference of women suffragists and its delegation to the Peace Conference, for example, Margery Corbett Ashby, a delegate from the mainstream British National Union of Women's Suffrage Societies (NUWSS), wrote to Millicent Garrett Fawcett, president of NUWSS and previously a delegate, that it was pointless to send another delegation to continue to press for their demands since the 'men in Paris are under the impression that we have been wonderfully well treated by them and have acquitted ourselves very well'.[117] Of the delegation to the Peace Conference from the International Congress of Women, held later in Zurich, Jane Addams recorded: 'They all received our resolutions politely and sometimes discussed them at length, but only a few of the journalists and "experts" were enthusiastic about them.'[118]

Alternatively, women's suffrage in the plebiscites could be attributed to the fact that women's suffrage was among the conditions for the plebiscite demanded by the Danish, German, Austrian and Hungarian delegations.[119] In the case of the Schleswig plebiscite, the first and in many respects the model for the others,[120] David Hunter Miller's collection of papers on Danish affairs from the peace conference[121] records no controversy over the Danish proposal that women should be allowed to vote.[122] In addition, women's right to vote nationally in several of the

[117] Alberti, *Beyond Suffrage*, p. 89.   [118] Addams, *Peace and Bread*, p. 164.
[119] Wambaugh, *Plebiscites Since the World War*, vol. I, p. 477.
[120] *Ibid.*, vol. I, p. 471; Wambaugh, 'La Pratique des Plébiscites Internationaux', 188–9.
[121] Miller, *My Diary at the Conference of Paris*, vol. X.
[122] At the 6 March 1919 meeting of the Peace Conference's Commission on Danish Affairs, the Minister of Denmark read a note on the method of voting. Procès-verbal No. 5 of the Commission on Danish Affairs, 6 March 1919, reproduced in *ibid.*, vol. X, p. 84 at p. 87. Draft Article II in the note provides for the vote without distinction of sex. Annex III to the procès-verbal of that meeting, reproduced in *ibid.*, p. 91 at p. 91.

This aspect of the suffrage is not commented on and remains unchanged in the procès-verbaux leading to the final report of the Commission to the Supreme Council of the Allies. Procès-verbal No. 6 of the Commission on Danish Affairs, 8 March 1919, Annex (Report on the Danish Claims respecting Slesvig, adopted subject to review by jurisconsults), pt. 2, reproduced in *ibid.*, vol. X, p. 93 at p. 114; Procès-verbal No. 7 of the Commission on Danish Affairs, 10 March 1919, Annex III (Articles Proposed for Inclusion in the Preliminaries of Peace, after review by the jurisconsults), Art. 1(2), reproduced in *ibid.*, vol. X, p. 118 at p. 131; Report (with Annexes) presented to the Supreme Council of the Allies by the Committee on Danish Affairs, Art. 1(2), reproduced in *ibid.*, vol. X, p. 211 at p. 215.

states concerned could be interpreted as a type of indirect consent by those states.

The alternative interpretations of women's right to vote in the plebiscites – the recognition of women as individuals or the acceptance of the will of states – are mirrored in the plebiscite propaganda. Some campaign posters sought to appeal to women as voters, while others used the figure of woman to embody the country or plebiscite region. Posters of the former type sought to appeal in particular to women's interest in their children's welfare. 'Mor! Stem Dansk. Tænk paa mig' ('Mother, vote Danish. Think of me!') read a poster for the Schleswig plebiscite showing a little boy with a Danish flag.[123] In a vignette of German-governed Schleswig prior to the plebiscite, all the more striking for its inclusion in a volume of international documents on territorial questions relating to the Treaty of Versailles, Paul Verrier described a little boy's face as the Danish flag:

Ce gamin que vous rencontrez au long d'un chemin creux, en train de cueillir des noisettes dans les haies, regardez-le: le rouge et le blanc du drapeau danois, du Dannebrog, éclatent sur ses joues avec cette vigueur de contraste que seul arbore le teint des petits Danois. Un maître d'école teuton, agacé de cette protestation silencieuse, empoigna un jour un de ses élèves et lui barra le visage d'une tache d'encre: <<Noir, blanc, rouge, ricanait-il, voilà ton Dannebrog transformé, comme il sied, en tricolore allemand.>>

[This lad that you meet along an empty road, in the process of gathering hazelnuts in the hedges, look at him: the red and white of the Danish flag, the *Dannebrog*, bursts forth on his cheeks with the vigour of contrast that only the complexion of Danish children displays. A Teutonic schoolmaster, irritated at this silent protest, one day grabbed one of his students and crossed his face with a spot of ink: 'Black, white and red,' he sniggered, 'There's your *Dannebrog* transformed, as it should be, into the German tricolour.'][124]

The Danes sent the poster of the little boy to the Polish propaganda committees, which also made wide use of it, modifying the design by hanging an amulet around the child's neck.[125] In a poster for the Klagenfurt Basin plebiscite, a boy entices his sorrowing mother not to vote for Yugoslavia or else he will have to report for duty to King Peter.[126]

[123] Reproduced and translated in Wambaugh, *Plebiscites Since the World War*, vol. I, p. 78.
[124] (Translation mine) 'Le Slesvig: Mémoire de M. Paul Verrier', paper for a 1913 conference at the Ecole des Hautes Etudes Sociales, reprinted in Paris Peace Conference, *Questions Territoriales*, pt. 2, pp. 221–57 at p. 222.
[125] Wambaugh, *Plebiscites Since the World War*, vol. I, p. 79.
[126] Reproduced in Kärntner Landesarchivs under the collaboration of A. Ogris, W. Deuer, B. Felsner, W. Wadl and E. Webernig (eds.), *Der 10. Oktober 1920: Kärntens Tag der*

During the plebiscite campaign in Schleswig, which as German territory was still suffering the effects of the Allied blockade, the Danish committees invited German trade unions to send ailing children to Denmark for a week's outing.[127]

In Henrik Pontoppidan's 1918 poem 'Sønderjylland', the story of Schleswig is told as a fairy tale about a daughter abducted from Denmark.

> Det lyder som et eventyr, et sagn fra gamle dage:
> en røvet datter, dybt begrædt, er kommen frelst tilbage!
> ...
> Velkommen hjem til moders hus, vor søster, hjertenskære!
> så bleg du blev i kæmpens favn, i striden for din ære!
>
> Du sad i bolt og fangejern til spot for vilde drenge,
> seks tusind unge sønners liv var dine løsepenge.
>
> Men du vil ingen sørgefest! Mens tåren øjet brænder,
> du skjuler stolt, hvad ondt du led i hine bøddelhænder.
>
> Du kommer klædt i hvidt og rødt, og smiler os i møde.
> Hil dig, vor moders øjesten, i nytids morgenrøde!
>
> [It sounds like a fairy tale, a legend from olden days:
> an abducted daughter deeply lamented has been rescued and returned!
> ...
> Welcome home to your mother's house, our sister dear!
> how pale you became in the giant's embrace while struggling for your honour!
>
> You sat in chains mocked by wild boys,
> the lives of six thousand young sons were your ransom.
>
> But you don't want mourning while tears are burning in your eyes,
> you proudly hide what you suffered at the hands of your tormentors.
>
> You come dressed in white and red and meet us smiling.
> Hail to you, apple of our mother's eye, at the new dawn.][128]

Selbstbestimmung. Vorgeschichte – Ereignisse – Analysen (2nd rev. edn, Klagenfurt: Verlag des Kärntner Landesarchivs, 1990), p. 121 ('Mutter, stimm' nicht für Jugoslavien – sonst muß ich für König Peter einrücken!').

[127] Wambaugh, *Plebiscites Since the World War*, vol. I, p. 78.
[128] (Translation by H. Knop) H. Pontoppidan, 'Sønderjylland' in 'Ude og hjemme', *Berlingske Tidendes Fotogravure-Udgave*, No. 51 (25 December 1918), p. 3. Pontoppidan shared the Nobel Prize for Literature with fellow Dane Karl Gjellerup in 1917. The poem was made into a Danish song in 1919. When Pontoppidan wrote it, there was

Similarly, in the posters that portray the plebiscite as a story about states, the state or plebiscite region is often represented as daughter, mother, sister or maiden in order to project certain emotions onto the state or the plebiscite region. Simone de Beauvoir maintains that this likening of places to women is a symbolism that corresponds to real emotions felt by many men. Woman, de Beauvoir writes,

> is the soul of such larger groups... as the city, state, and nation. Jung remarks that cities have always been likened to the Mother, because they contain the citizens in their bosom... but it is not only the nourishing soil, it is a more subtle reality that finds its symbol in woman. In the Old Testament and in the Apocalypse, Jerusalem and Babylon are not merely mothers: they are also wives. There are virgin cities, and whorish cities like Babel and Tyre. And so France has been called the 'eldest daughter of the Church'; France and Italy are Latin sisters.[129]

One poster in the Saar plebiscite described by Wambaugh offers a straightforward example of this metaphor: showing 'a grey-haired mother embracing her son, about his feet broken chains and pieces of a frontier post and behind him the smoking chimneys of the Saar, the legend reading, "Deutsche Mutter – heim zu dir"' ("German mother – home to you").[130] More complex examples are the posters bearing nationalist fairy tales, which implicitly make the voter responsible for the fate of the heroine. On a Slovene poster in the Klagenfurt Basin plebiscite, the text accompanying a series of images entitled 'A Tale of Carinthia' reads: 'During the course of centuries the German magpie has stolen from us many a pearl and treasure, among them the golden cradle of Slovenia, our Carinthia. But in an heroic effort the falcon rose from south of the magpie and took the stolen cradle. On the day of the plebiscite the falcon presents the cradle to its sister Slovenia.'[131]

A German poster for the plebiscite in Upper Silesia shows a German Little Red Riding Hood holding a basket of city buildings labelled 'Silesia' away from a hungry wolf with the Polish eagle on its flank. At the top of the poster are her words to the slavering animal:

> both popular momentum and German and Danish support for a plebiscite in Schleswig. The third stanza refers to 'hvad knap vi turde hviske om i krogen mellum venner' ('what we barely dared whisper about in corners among friends') as being 'forkyndes nu på dansk og tysk som løfteord af frænder' ('now proclaimed in Danish and German like words of promise among friends'). On the history of this time, see Wambaugh, *Plebiscites Since the World War*, vol. I, pp. 54–6.
> [129] S. de Beauvoir, *The Second Sex*, trans. and ed. by H. M. Parshley (1953) (New York: Vintage Books, 1989), pp. 177–8.
> [130] (Translation mine) Wambaugh, *The Saar Plebiscite*, p. 253.
> [131] Reproduced and translated in Wambaugh, *Plebiscites Since the World War*, vol. I, p. 187.

> You want my little basket?
> It holds my darling Silesia.
> Undivided it shall stay with me,
> For with you it would become arid and wild.[132]

Perhaps the strongest evidence that these posters consciously relied on stereotypes of women[133] is an Austrian poster in the Sopron plebiscite and the Hungarian poster developed to counter it. In the Austrian poster, a woman holding the shield of Austria knocks on the gates of Ödenburg, crying, 'Macht auf! Die Mutter ist's!' ('Open! Mother is here!').[134] The Hungarian version shows the woman transformed into a man, dressed in red and hiding behind the white mask of Germania, symbol of Austria's Pan-German movement. The Austrian shield now bears the red star of the Communists and partially obscures sacks of meal. 'Open!' reads the caption on the Hungarian poster, 'We have not stolen enough.'[135]

In contrast to the plebiscites held under the peace treaties, women would not have had the right to vote in the plebiscites planned for Vilnius under the League of Nations in 1921[136] and for Tacna-Arica under American President Calvin Coolidge's 1925 arbitral award. The decisions to exclude women from these plebiscites, neither of which ultimately took place, tell us something about the limited success of women's interventions in international law. In the case of the Vilnius plebiscite between Lithuania and Poland, women in Poland protested strongly to Colonel Chardigny, the president of the League of Nations commission that had recommended against women's suffrage in the plebiscite.[137]

---

[132] Reproduced and translated in *ibid.*, p. 228.
[133] In *Nationalism and Sexuality: Respectability and Abnormal Sexuality in Modern Europe* (New York: Howard Fertig, 1985) at pp. 90–113, George L. Mosse argues that the promotion of woman as a symbol of the nation in Europe represented a form of social control through the imposition of a standard type: conformity to that standard served the interests of the nation, while deviance undermined it.
[134] (Translation mine) Described in Wambaugh, *Plebiscites Since the World War*, vol. I, p. 286.
[135] Reproduced and translated in *ibid.*, p. 289.
[136] Based on the Report of the Commission Charged with the Preparation of the Public Expression of Opinion, signed at Warsaw on 17 February 1921 and presented to the Council of the League of Nations on 24 February 1921, reprinted in *ibid.*, vol. II, p. 273 at p. 279 (pt. III). (This Commission is variously referred to as the Plebiscite Commission or the Civil Commission to distinguish it from the International Force or Military Commission responsible for maintaining order in the plebiscite area.) As Wambaugh points out, the Commission's recommendation that women be excluded from the plebiscite had not yet been approved by the Council of the League of Nations when the plebiscite was abandoned, so it is possible that the Council might not have approved it. *Ibid.*, vol. I, pp. 325, 477.
[137] *Ibid.*, p. 325.

According to a snippet in *The Times*, after Chardigny refused to receive a delegation of women who met his train at the Vilnius station to present a petition of protest, the women pelted him with eggs when he appeared in the door of his railway carriage.[138] International women's organizations in Geneva, seat of the League of Nations, also took up the cause of women's right to vote in the Vilnius plebiscite.[139] In the case of the Tacna-Arica plebiscite between Chile and Peru, Coolidge gave the fact that women's suffrage did not exist in either Chile or Peru as a reason to deny women's suffrage in the plebiscite. By this time, however, women had begun working for women's suffrage through the inter-American system.[140] In 1922, a Pan American Conference of Women had been held in Baltimore with the purpose of furthering women's suffrage within the hemisphere,[141] and the International Conference of American States held in Santiago, Chile in 1923, during Coolidge's presidency, had passed a motion on the rights of women in the hemisphere.[142] Sarah Wambaugh, who advised the Peruvian government on the plebiscite, later wrote: 'If the desire is really to ascertain the popular will, women as well as men must be allowed to vote, no matter what the previous custom in the area.'[143]

The decisions to deny women the vote in the plebiscites planned for Vilnius and Tacna-Arica also suggest something about the shape of resistance to women's equality in international law. What is striking about the decisions is their common-sense tone, their air of matter-of-factness. But, as Clifford Geertz argues, common sense is not simply a product of immediate experience, persuasive to all because it is apprehensible by all. Instead, it can more usefully be understood as a cultural system. Common-sense notions, such as rain wets and one ought to come in out of it, are presented as undeniable, something anyone in his right mind should know. Treating common sense as a cultural system, however,

---

[138] 'Commissioner Pelted With Eggs', *The [London] Times*, late edition, 2 April 1921, p. 7b.
[139] Wambaugh, *Plebiscites Since the World War*, vol. I, pp. 325, 477.
[140] For a précis of the initiatives taken by the Consejo Nacional de Mujeres, established in Chile in 1919 and in Peru in 1923, around this time, see International Council of Women, *Women in a Changing World*, pp. 275–6, 283–4.
[141] F. Miller, 'The International Relations of Women of the Americas 1890–1928' (1986) 43:2 *The Americas* 171 at 178–9. The fact that United States Secretary of State Charles Evans Hughes addressed the conference gives some indication of the event's prominence.
[142] *Ibid.*, 180–1. For the resolution, see J. B. Scott (ed.), *The International Conferences of American States, 1889–1928* (New York: Oxford University Press, 1931), p. 244.
[143] Wambaugh, *Plebiscites Since the World War*, vol. I, p. 501. See also Wambaugh, 'La Pratique des Plébiscites Internationaux', 249.

leads us to distinguish the observation that rain wets from the belief that one ought to come in out of it. As Geertz observes, some people may consider it good for one's character to brave the elements. Thus, while home truths present life as their authority, they prove to contain both what life teaches us through the direct apprehension of reality and what we make of these lessons.[144] The reasons given for limiting the Vilnius and Tacna-Arica plebiscites to men not only exhibit the properties that Geertz attributes to common-sense arguments: naturalness, practicalness, thinness, immethodicalness and accessibleness.[145] The plainness of their flaws may also be explained in this way. That is, both decisions rely on a common sense that excludes women from the 'common'; what appears a sensible solution depends upon an idea of sensibleness defined by men.

Sovereignty over Vilnius was among the border issues left unsettled in the Treaty of Versailles, which reserved the right to fix such borders at a later date.[146] In the meantime, the League of Nations had been unable to prevent Vilnius from becoming a battleground between Lithuania and Poland.[147] Eventually, the Council of the League of Nations passed a resolution calling for a plebiscite, its preamble stating that the Council's desire was, above all, to re-establish peace between Lithuania and Poland and noting that both states based their claims to Vilnius on the right of self-determination.[148]

The Council appointed a Plebiscite Commission for Vilnius, headed by Colonel Chardigny, and instructed the Commission to ascertain whether an agreement could be reached between Lithuania and Poland in regard to the procedures for the plebiscite and to notify the Council of the conditions for the plebiscite, 'having regard as far as possible to the points on which both parties have been able to agree'.[149] Although Lithuania and Poland took the common position that women should be allowed to vote in the plebiscite,[150] the Commission rejected this position in its

---

[144] C. Geertz, *Local Knowledge: Further Essays in Interpretive Anthropology* (New York: Basic Books, 1983), pp. 75–6.
[145] Ibid., p. 85.   [146] Treaty of Versailles, Art. 87.
[147] Wambaugh, *Plebiscites Since the World War*, vol. I, pp. 303–8.
[148] Resolution Calling for a Public Expression of Opinion.
[149] Instructions for the Commission Entrusted with the Arrangements for the Taking of a Public Expression of Opinion in the Vilna District, approved by the Council on 1 December 1920, LN Council Minutes, 11th Sess., November–December 1920, annex 129i, reprinted in Wambaugh, *Plebiscites Since the World War*, vol. II, at p. 272.
[150] Report on the Public Expression of Opinion, p. 279. Although women had yet to vote nationally in either Lithuania or Poland, both states had enfranchised women by this time. Wambaugh, *Plebiscites Since the World War*, vol. I, p. 327. Moreover, during

report to the Council, stating that

il faut cependant remarquer que dans le territoire contesté, les femmes n'ayant encore jamais voté, aucun des deux Gouvernements ne peut émettre une opinion sur la façon dont le vote des femmes est susceptible de modifier le résultat du vote où les hommes, seuls, se seraient prononcés. Dans ces conditions et pour réaliser une économie de temps et d'argent, la Commission est d'avis que le droit de suffrage accordé seulement aux hommes pourrait finalement être accepté par les deux Gouvernements.

[it should nevertheless be noted that in the contested territory, women having never voted, neither of the two Governments can express an opinion on the way in which the women's vote is likely to modify the result of a vote where men alone took part. Under these conditions and to save time and money, the Commission is of the view that a right of suffrage accorded only to men could finally be accepted by the two Governments.][151]

Before the Council, Chardigny argued more plainly that it would be 'simpler for the men only to have the right to vote'.[152]

Yet the Commission's recommendation is not even persuasive on its own terms. Since women's suffrage was a point on which Lithuania and Poland agreed and the Council's instructions to the Commission were to have regard 'as far as possible' to the parties' points of agreement, the Commission would arguably have had to convince the Council that women's suffrage was impossible under the circumstances. Yet the Commission's report estimated that registering women voters would add a mere fifteen days to the roughly two hundred days allocated for the plebiscite.[153] It is not entirely inconceivable, however, that fifteen days might have been critical. Not only did the Council's resolution refer to its paramount desire to re-establish peace between Lithuania and Poland,[154] but its instructions to the Commission anticipated that it might 'become impossible to take the public expression of opinion owing... to fighting occurring in the plebiscite area'.[155] Nevertheless, if fifteen days

---

his occupation of Vilnius, the Polish Marshal Pilsudski had issued a proclamation that the inhabitants of Vilnius had the right of self-determination, to be exercised by universal suffrage without distinction of sex. *Ibid.*, p. 303. After the League of Nations abandoned the plebiscite in Vilnius, Poland carried out, under protest from Lithuania, a unilateral consultation in which women voted. *Ibid.*, pp. 548–50.

[151] (Translation mine) Report on the Public Expression of Opinion, p. 279.
[152] LN Council Minutes, 12th Sess., 6th Mtg. (24 February 1921), p. 14.
[153] Report on the Public Expression of Opinion, p. 279 at p. 280 (part VI).
[154] Resolution calling for a public expression of opinion.
[155] Instructions for the Taking of a Public Expression of Opinion in the Vilna District, p. 273.

could therefore have made a difference, it is still significant that the Commission's report did not trouble to spell this out. More important, even if it was necessary to minimize time and expense, the Commission's reasoning is remarkable in its assumption that women's right to vote was so obviously the place to do so.

In addition to saving time and money, the Commission gave as a reason for male suffrage that since women had never voted in either Lithuania or Poland, neither government could predict how the women's vote would modify the result of a men-only vote.[156] Wambaugh described this reason as 'somewhat inconsequential',[157] meaning presumably that the value of individual choice in liberal self-determination is independent of the choice made by an individual or the effect of that individual's choice on the outcome. But the phrasing – 'Dans ces conditions... la Commission est d'avis que le droit de suffrage accordé seulement aux hommes pourrait finalement être accepté par les deux Gouvernements' ('Under these conditions... the Commission is of the view that a right of suffrage accorded only to men could finally be accepted by the two Governments') – indicates that the unpredictability of the women's vote was not intended as an argument for male suffrage per se. Rather, this unpredictability was more likely addressed to the self-interest of the parties and was offered to the League Council as a reassurance that the Commission's reasonable proposal would not be unreasonably rejected by the disputants.

In his arbitral opinion and award on the plebiscite in Tacna-Arica, President Coolidge denied women the vote as follows: 'Women's suffrage does not exist either in Chile or Peru. Neither Party has requested it nor has it been suggested in any of the negotiations between the Parties.'[158] This reasoning might have been internally persuasive, had Coolidge also applied it to other categories of voters. Instead, he concluded that illiterates who owned real property situated in the territory should be allowed to vote despite the fact that both Chile and Peru made the ability to read and write a qualification for voting. Coolidge justified giving this subcategory of illiterates the vote 'in view of the circumstances and of what is understood to be the character of a considerable portion of the population'.[159] As Wambaugh observed crisply, 'if the character of

---

[156] Ironically, the case against women's suffrage domestically was often precisely the opposite: that women's vote would simply follow their husband's or that it would be captive to the Church.
[157] Wambaugh, *Plebiscites Since the World War*, vol. I, p. 324.
[158] *Opinion and Award in the Arbitration Between Chile and Peru*, p. 305.
[159] Ibid.

the population was considered, it is pertinent to call attention to the fact that while only a small part of the inhabitants were illiterate, more than half of the population were women, and that when an exception was made for property it might well have been made for sex'.[160]

Moreover, there were international lawyers writing on plebiscites in this period who distinguished giving women the vote in plebiscites from giving them the vote in domestic elections. In 1920, Paul de Auer wrote:

> The peace contracts give the right of voting without regard to sex. There can be no objection to this, even in States where women have no votes in questions of internal politics. This is supported by the fact that in deciding the question of an annexation a special political training is not necessary. The decision of the question as to whether somebody wants to be Hungarian or Czech, French or German, is easier than that as to whether the happiness of the people is better assured by the liberal or conservative party.[161]

It is possible that President Coolidge's decision to exclude women from the electorate may have been an attempt to strike a balance between Chile and Peru. According to William Dennis, Coolidge's ruling that a plebiscite should be held favoured Chile, while his definition of the electorate favoured Peru.[162] Including women in the electorate would have favoured Peru further, given that the Chilean administration had deported or conscripted many of the Peruvian men in the plebiscite area.[163]

What is common to the decision to deny women the vote in the League of Nations Commission's report on the Vilnius plebiscite and in President Coolidge's arbitral award on the plebiscite in Tacna-Arica is not the arguments used. The Commission rejects the wishes of the parties, whereas Coolidge represents his decision as the acceptance of the parties' wishes. What is shared is the inequality of women visible in the inconsistencies and weaknesses of the reasoning. In the Vilnius plebiscite, the League Commission disregarded the wishes of Lithuania and Poland by excluding women, *even though* its instructions were to have regard 'as far as

---

[160] Wambaugh, *Plebiscites Since the World War*, vol. I, p. 408, n. 1.
[161] P. de Auer, 'Plebiscites and the League of Nations Covenant' (1920) 6 *Transactions of the Grotius Society* 45 at 53–4.
[162] Dennis, *Tacna and Arica*, pp. 213, 215.
[163] Wambaugh, *Plebiscites Since the World War*, vol. I, pp. 359 (loss of Peruvian men), 407 (Peru would certainly have won had women voted); Dennis, *Tacna and Arica*, p. 228 (few Peruvian men remained).

possible to the points on which both parties have been able to agree'. In the Tacna-Arica plebiscite, Coolidge justified the exclusion of women on the ground of the parties' wishes, *even though* he did not apply this ground to illiterates. And if Coolidge's decision to exclude women was an attempt to make his award acceptable to both states, it is significant that he saw the women's vote as the way to do it, just as it was significant that the League of Nations Commission saw the women's vote as the place to save on time and money. What enables both the Commission and Coolidge to present their rulings in such a practical, plain-as-day way is, I suggest, the 'common' sense that women's participation in the exercise of self-determination would be more trouble than it was worth; that is, that women were not really equal members of the self.

Individual self-determination

Right of option

Under the peace treaties, the transfer of territory pursuant to a plebiscite changed the nationality of the inhabitants automatically.[164] When Schleswig was transferred from Germany to Denmark in accordance with the Danish victory in the plebiscite, for example, the Treaty of Versailles[165] provided that its inhabitants *ipso facto* acquired Danish nationality and lost their German nationality. Whereas the plebiscite reflected the right of self-determination of peoples, that is, the right of individuals to decide democratically the sovereignty of their homeland, this automatic change of nationality denied them the right to choose individually the sovereignty under which they would live. 'Puisque le plébiscite est décidé à la majorité des voix,' ('Since a plebiscite is decided by majority vote,') Joseph Kunz wrote, 'un plébiscite sans option de nationalité constitue une oppression de la minorité dissidente.' ('a plebiscite without an option of nationality constitutes an oppression of the dissident minority.')[166]

---

[164] In the case of every transfer of territory, except for that of Alsace-Lorraine, the peace treaties provided that the nationality of the inhabitants would change automatically. J. L. Kunz, 'L'Option de Nationalité' (1930–I) 31 Hague Recueil 107 at 142.

[165] Treaty of Versailles, Art. 112. For other plebiscites, see Treaty of Versailles, Art. 91; Treaty of St Germain, Art. 70. There were no provisions of the Treaty of Versailles dealing with the consequences of the Saar plebiscite for nationality.

[166] (Emphasis in original removed) (Translation mine) Kunz, 'L'Option de Nationalité', 122–3.

The peace treaties therefore gave those individuals whose nationality was affected by the plebiscites the right to opt for the other nationality.[167] In the example of Schleswig,[168] those Germans who were born in Schleswig, but did not automatically become Danish because they were not inhabitants of the territory, had the right to opt for Denmark. Those who, as inhabitants of Schleswig, had automatically become Danish had the right to opt for Germany. The right of option had to be exercised within two years of the change in sovereignty, and those who exercised the right were then required to transfer their place of residence to the state in favour of which they had opted.

While the right of option[169] was better established in international law than the plebiscite,[170] it was also not accepted as custom.[171] It was therefore significant that both the plebiscite and the right of option were used to give the individual some say in the grand designs of the Peace Conference for Europe. By supplementing the right of collective self-determination represented by the plebiscite with a right of individual self-determination, moreover, the option gave a firmer foothold to liberal democracy in international law.[172]

---

[167] A right of option was provided in connection with every transfer of territory under the peace treaties, with the exception of Alsace-Lorraine and Neutral-Moresnet. Kunz, 'L'Option de Nationalité', 143.

[168] Treaty of Versailles, Art. 113. For other plebiscites, see Treaty of Versailles, Art. 91; Treaty of St Germain, Arts. 78–79.

[169] On the right of option generally, see R. Donner, *The Regulation of Nationality in International Law* (2nd edn, Irvington-on-Hudson, N.Y.: Transnational Publishers, 1994), pp. 255–8, 268–77; Kunz, 'L'Option de Nationalité'; D. P. O'Connell, *State Succession in Municipal Law and International Law* (2 vols., Cambridge: Cambridge University Press, 1967), vol. I, pp. 529–36; E. Szlechter, *Les options conventionnelles de nationalité à la suite de cessions de territoires* (Paris: Recueil Sirey, 1948).

[170] Kunz, 'L'Option de Nationalité', 122.

[171] Kunz, 'L'Option de Nationalité', 119, 122; C. L. Gettys, 'The Effect of Changes of Sovereignty on Nationality' (1927) 21 *American Journal of International Law* 268 at 270.

[172] Because the right of option required the individual who exercised the right to emigrate to the state for which he had opted, some publicists of the time saw the right as *demos* in the service of *ethnos*. E. Maxson Engeström wrote that 'le but des traités de paix de 1919–1920 a été d'appliquer purement et simplement ce principe [des nationalités], en réunissant sur le territoire les hommes de même race, de même langue et de même civilisation' (translation mine: 'the goal of the peace treaties of 1919–1920 was to apply this principle [of nationalities] pure and simple in reuniting on the territory the men of the same race, the same language and the same civilization'). E. M. Engeström, *Les Changements de Nationalité d'après les Traités de Paix de 1919–1920* (Paris: A Pedone, 1923), p. 8. Compare the discussion of the European Union Arbitration Commission's *Opinion No. 2* on Yugoslavia, Chapter 4, above.

Collective option

Although a married woman could participate in the process of collective self-determination by voting on an equal footing with men in the plebiscite, she was not an equal participant in the process of individual self-determination that followed. In accordance with the dominant practice of the previous century,[173] the plebiscite provisions of the peace treaties specified a 'collective option',[174] whereby the option of the husband covered that of the wife.[175] If Kunz termed a plebiscite without an option of nationality 'an oppression of the dissident minority', then the collective option was, by the same standard, an oppression of married women.

A series of decisions by the Austrian administrative courts demonstrates the additional frustrations for women caused by a strict interpretation of this collective option. In one case, a woman whose husband had not been heard of in the three years since the end of the war was denied the right to opt for Austria on the ground that so long as she had not been legally divorced, her change of nationality could only be effected through her husband.[176] In another case, the court held that even the husband's express consent to the option of his wife was not sufficient if he himself had not exercised the right to opt.[177]

In the case of the Schleswig plebiscite, the drafting history shows that Denmark proposed a right of option to the Peace Conference's Commission on Danish Affairs, but made no reference to wives.[178]

---

[173] Kunz, 'L'Option de Nationalité', 147.

[174] Treaty of Versailles, Arts. 91, 113; Treaty of St Germain, Arts. 78–9.
 The peace treaties provided for a collective option in connection with every transfer of territory, with the exception of Alsace-Lorraine and those under several treaties concluded with Soviet Russia. Kunz, 'L'Option de Nationalité', 147.

[175] The collective option also covered minor children.

[176] *Kugler v. (Austrian) Federal Ministry for the Interior* (Austrian Administrative Court, 1921), reported in J. R. Williams and H. Lauterpacht (eds.), *Annual Digest of Public International Law Cases, Being a Selection from the Decisions of International and National Courts and Tribunals Given During the Years 1919 to 1922* (London: Longmans, Green and Co., 1932), pp. 220–1 (Case No. 153). For two other Austrian decisions to this effect, see *ibid.*, p. 221 (Note to Case No. 153). The editors venture that these three decisions seem to be in conformity with the collective option in Article 78 of the Treaty of St Germain. *Ibid.*

[177] Austrian Administrative Court, Decision of 29 April 1924, No. 13.529 A, vol. XLVIII (1924), pp. 176, 177, cited in *ibid.*, p. 221 (Note to Case No. 153).

[178] Procès-verbal No. 5 of the Commission on Danish Affairs, 6 March 1919, reproduced in Miller, *My Diary at the Conference of Paris*, vol. X, p. 84 at p. 87.
 In light of the doctrinal disagreement over whether a general right of option signified a collective option or an individual option for married women (see note 181

A collective option covering wives appeared in the Commission's draft articles only after the articles had been reviewed by the jurisconsults,[179] and was unchanged in the Commission's report to the Supreme Council of the Allies.[180]

The alternative of an individual option for married women, which would have given them the same right as men to opt for another nationality, was not unknown to international law. Disagreement over the interpretation of the 1871 Treaty of Frankfurt evidenced that French international legal doctrine, unlike German, read a general right of option in a treaty as giving the wife an individual right of option,[181] and there was some criticism of the collective option in the peace treaties in the post-war French international legal literature.[182] In a 1921 article on nationality in the peace treaties, for example, Niboyet asked whether the collective option had not sacrificed the rights of the woman and cheapened her consent.[183]

For women, the issue of the collective option would logically have been part of the larger issue of the dependent nationality of married women.[184] As of 1910, the nationality of the wife followed the nationality

---

below and accompanying text), it is difficult to know what the Danish position meant and whether the Commission saw itself as departing from Denmark's wishes or specifying them for greater certainty.

[179] Procès-verbal No. 6 of the Commission on Danish Affairs, 8 March 1919, Annex (Report on the Danish Claims respecting Slesvig, adopted subject to review by jurisconsults), pt. 7, reproduced in *ibid.*, vol. X, p. 93 at p. 116 (pt. 7 mentions only children under 18 and is agreed). Procès-verbal No. 7 of the Commission on Danish Affairs, 10 March 1919, Annex III (Articles Proposed for Inclusion in the Preliminaries of Peace, after review by jurisconsults), Art. 4, reproduced in *ibid.*, vol. X, p. 118 at pp. 133–4 (Art. 4 mentions wife).

[180] Report (with Annexes) presented to the Supreme Council of the Allies by the Committee on Danish Affairs, Art. 4 reproduced in *ibid.*, vol. X, p. 211 at p. 218 (mentions wife).

[181] G. Calbairac, *La Nationalité de la femme mariée* (Paris: Recueil Sirey, 1926), pp. 90–1 and authorities cited at p. 91, n. 1; J.-P. Niboyet, 'La Nationalité d'après les traités de paix qui ont mis fin à la Grande Guerre de 1914–1918' (1921) *Revue de droit international et de legislation comparée* 285 at 297–8. Kunz acknowledged this to be the French view, 'L'Option de Nationalité', 126, n.1 (individual option). Contra Kunz, 'L'Option de Nationalité', 126; C. Phillipson, *Termination of War and Treaties of Peace* (London: T. Fisher Unwin Ltd, 1916), p. 298 (collective option).

[182] E.g. Calbairac, *La Nationalité de la femme mariée*; Niboyet, 'La Nationalité d'après les traités de paix'.

[183] Niboyet, 'La Nationalité d'après les traités de paix', 298.

[184] See generally International Law Association, Final Report of the Committee on Feminism and International Law, 'Women's Equality and Nationality in International Law' (2000) (forthcoming in International Law Association, *69th Conference Report*); United Nations, *Convention on the Nationality of Married Women: Historical Background and Commentary*, UN Doc. E/CN.6/389, UN Sales No. 62.IV.3 (1962).

of the husband in all legal systems in the world, with the exception of a few South American states. Upon her marriage to a foreigner, a woman automatically lost her own nationality under the laws of her state and automatically acquired her husband's nationality under the laws of his state.[185] After the war, women's organizations campaigned actively for changes to the domestic laws on nationality and for an international treaty that would guarantee women's equality with men in matters of nationality.[186] The issue had, however, not become a priority by the time of the Peace Conference.[187] The delegation of women from the ICW and

For contemporaneous commentary, see Calbairac, *La Nationalité de la femme mariée*; A. N. Makarov, 'La Nationalité de la Femme Mariée' (1937-II) 60 Hague Recueil 115; Niboyet, 'La nationalité d'après les traités de paix'; T. D. Thao, *De l'influence du mariage sur la nationalité de la femme* (Aix-en-Provence: Editions Paul Roubaud, 1929).

[185] United Nations, *Convention on the Nationality of Married Women: Historical Background*, pp. 3–4.

[186] Shortly after the war, the IWSA drafted a provisional international convention on the nationality of married women, based on the general principle that married women should have the same right as men to keep or change their nationality. Reprinted in International Law Association, *32nd Conference Report* (1923), p. 45. See also C. Macmillan, 'Nationality of Married Women: Present Tendencies' (1925) 7 *Journal of Comparative Legislation and International Law* (3rd Series) 142 at 143 (on the work of ICW, WILPF, IWSA), 152–3 (on the IWSA provisional draft international convention).

Women were active at the 1930 Hague Codification Conference, which was reluctant to go much beyond the practical problems of women's statelessness and dual nationality caused by conflicts between the nationality laws of different states. Makarov, 'La Nationalité de la Femme Mariée', 149–50. The disillusionment of international women's organizations with the resulting Convention on Certain Questions Relating to the Conflict of Nationality Laws, The Hague, 12 April 1930, in force 1 July 1937, 179 LNTS 89 led to the creation of the Women's Consultative Committee on Nationality within the League of Nations. M. O. Hudson, 'The Hague Convention of 1930 and the Nationality of Women' (1933) 27 *American Journal of International Law* 117; Makarov, 'La Nationalité de la Femme Mariée', 154–8; Miller, 'Lobbying the League', pp. 193–209. Nevertheless, there would be no universal convention until the Convention on the Nationality of Married Women, New York, adopted 29 January 1957, in force 11 August 1958, 309 UNTS 65 in 1957.

In contrast, the work of the Inter-American Commission of Women led to the 1933 Convention on the Nationality of Women, Montevideo, 26 December 1933, in force 29 August 1934 (1934) 28 *American Journal of International Law Supplement* 61, which provided that there should be no distinction based on sex as regards nationality. See J. B. Scott, 'The Seventh International Conference of American States' (1934) 28 *American Journal of International Law* 219.

It should be noted that not all international women's organizations supported independent nationality for married women. See Hudson, 'The Hague Convention of 1930', 118; Makarov, 'La Nationalité de la Femme Mariée', 155, n. 4 (International Union of Catholic Women's Organizations).

[187] This is not to say that women had not taken up the issue prior to the Peace Conference. The ICW had advocated independent nationality for married women since 1905. Macmillan, 'Present Tendencies', 143. Women's groups had petitioned the

the Conference of Women Suffragists from Allied Countries and the United States, which appeared before the Peace Conference Commission on the League of Nations, strategically chose not to present a more controversial International Charter of Women's Rights, which included equal nationality rights for married women.[188] At the International Congress of Women held in Zurich during the Peace Conference, the right for a married woman to change or retain her nationality was included among the resolutions,[189] but the resolutions of the Congress to the Peace Conference generally made little impression on the leaders in Paris.[190]

Although the possibility of an individual option for married women seems not to have been discussed at the Peace Conference, such discussion is found in the international legal literature of the period. The justification particular to the collective option hinged on the requirement that the right of option be exercised by way of declaration and perfected by emigration within a certain period of time. An inhabitant of Schleswig made Danish by the transfer of the territory from Germany to Denmark, for example, could declare for his old German nationality, but was then obliged to transfer his place of residence to Germany within twelve months of the declaration.[191] Since a wife's duty, Christian in origin and secularized and codified over

---

British Imperial Conference of 1918. Women, Immigration and Nationality Group, *Worlds Apart*, p. 15; C. Macmillan, *The Nationality of Married Women* (London: Nationality of Married Women Pass the Bill Committee, 1931), p. 9 (quoting the Memorial of Women's Societies throughout the British Empire).

Wartime, however, strained the commitment of women's groups to the idea that a woman's allegiance could not be commanded by the law of nationality. A few years after the war, Chrystal Macmillan would write: 'It is insulting to a woman to assume that she can transfer her allegiance without her consent'. Macmillan, 'Present Tendencies', 144. Yet, during the war, the leaders of the British women's movement were not above the insult of this assumption. For example, Sylvia Pankhurst was angered by the executive decision of the Women's International League, which arose from the International Congress of Women held at The Hague in 1915, to exclude the British-born wives of aliens for fear of controversy. Mitchell, *Women on the Warpath*, p. 286. See also *ibid.*, pp. 285, 323–6. Under the British Aliens Restriction Act, the names of 12,000 women who were aliens by marriage were entered into an Official Register. N. Hiley, 'Counter-Espionage and Security in Great Britain during the First World War' (1986) 101 *English Historical Review* 635 at 646.

[188] Miller, 'Lobbying the League', p. 22.   [189] Wiltsher, *Most Dangerous Women*, p. 202.
[190] See Addams, *Peace and Bread*, quoted in text accompanying note 118 above. See also Bussey and Tims, *Women's International League for Peace and Freedom*, p. 33; Randall, *Improper Bostonian*, p. 268.
[191] Treaty of Versailles, Art. 113. For the other plebiscites, see Treaty of Versailles, Art. 91 ('may'); Treaty of St Germain, Arts. 78–79 ('must').

time,[192] was to follow her husband, it was a practical impossibility for her to opt differently. On this patriarchal expectation, there was no reason to give her a right to opt.

Gaston Calbairac, writing several years after the plebiscites, made the point that the hypotheticals used to demonstrate this practical impossibility reflected their authors' inability to imagine situations resulting from a change in sovereignty in which women might be able to choose a nationality different from their husband.[193] On the hypothesis that the wife had an individual option, Calbairac showed that even if the husband did not opt, the wife could opt and perfect her option without breaking up the household, if her husband were to move abroad for unrelated reasons.[194] Conversely, if the husband did opt, the wife could emigrate with him but retain her nationality by not making the declaration of option.[195] In addition, a married woman who was legally separated would always be in a position to exercise an individual option.[196]

The justification of the collective option also drew on the justification for the dependent nationality of married women more generally in international law.[197] In the international legal discourse on the nationality of women, as in the discourse on the vote, the issue of women's equality was enmeshed not only with images of women, but with the relationship between images of women and images of the international legal order, where these images and their relationship to one another were produced or heightened by the war.[198]

---

[192] On the Christian origins of the rules on women's nationality, see International Law Association, *32nd Conference Report*, p. 31; International Law Association, *33rd Conference Report* (1924), p. 24. But see International Law Association, *32nd Conference Report*, p. 11. The French Civil Code offered an example of the codification of the requirement that a wife follow her husband. A. Weiss, *Manuel de droit international privé* (9th edn., Paris: Recueil Sirey, 1925), p. 164.

[193] Calbairac, *La Nationalité de la femme mariée*, p. 88.   [194] *Ibid.*, pp. 87–8.

[195] *Ibid.*, pp. 88–9. The wife's choice would not be frustrated by the operation of the laws on the nationality of married women because the law did not effect a change in the wife's nationality when the husband changed nationality during the marriage. *Ibid.*, p. 89.

[196] *Ibid.*, p. 90.

[197] Gettys, 'The Effect of Changes of Sovereignty', 273, relying on Phillipson, *Termination of War*, p. 298 (foundation for the collective option in general international law) and Niboyet, 'La Nationalité d'après les traités de paix', 297–8 (with reference to the collective option in the peace treaties); Szlechter, *Les options conventionnelles de nationalité*, p. 338.

[198] Compare Kent, *Making Peace* (showing how in Britain during and after World War I gender was used to construct war, and war, conceived of in gendered terms, then shaped understandings of gender).

The general discourse on the nationality of women was structured, as Germany would put it to the League of Nations in 1932, by the irreconcilable opposition between 'the traditional idea of the civil unity of the family derived from the nature of the marriage union and the union of the family, and also founded on religious principles' and 'the idea of self-determination for women based on principles of individualism'.[199] As applied to nationality, the traditional idea of the unity of the family consisted of two separate propositions.[200] The first proposition was that all members of a family should have the same nationality; the second, that the husband determined that nationality. Whereas the first proposition did not depend on gender, the second relied on a patriarchal notion of the family, entrenched in the law of the period, which gave the husband a privileged status and the power to make decisions affecting the family. What will be seen is that arguments about whether a family should have the same nationality involved the projection of competing visions of the relations between states onto the relations between husband and wife. And, conversely, the projection of the *paterfamilias* onto the state made mutually reinforcing the patriarchal argument that a wife should have the same nationality as her husband because her duty of obedience to her state would otherwise threaten her duty of obedience to her husband, and the xenophobic argument that a wife should have the same nationality as her husband because her loyalty to her state, on the expectation that she was resident in his state, would otherwise create a source of disloyalty within the state.[201]

---

[199] Germany, Letter of 2 July 1932, in Nationality of Women, Observations Submitted by Governments, LN Doc. A.15.1932.V (1932) (Series V.LEGAL; 1932.V.2; Geneva, 23 July 1932), p. 2.

[200] See *Amendments to the Naturalization Provisions of the Constitution of Costa Rica*, Advisory Opinion (Inter-American Court of Human Rights, 1984), 5 *Human Rights Law Journal* 161 at 174; United Nations, *Convention on the Nationality of Married Women: Historical Background*, p. 3.

[201] While the collective option and the nationality of married women more generally provide a rich historical example that has gone unnoticed, other aspects of the state in international law have been analysed as gendered. See H. Charlesworth, 'The Sex of the State in International Law' in N. Naffine and R. J. Owens (eds.), *Sexing the Subject of Law* (North Ryde, NSW: LBC Information Services, 1997), pp. 251–68; Charlesworth and Chinkin, *The Boundaries of International Law*, pp. 124–70; J. B. Elshtain, 'Sovereign God, Sovereign State, Sovereign Self' (1991) 66 *Notre Dame Law Review* 1355; J. B. Elshtain, 'Sovereignty, Identity, Sacrifice' (1991) 58 *Social Research* 545; K. Knop, 'Borders of the Imagination: The State in Feminist International Law' (1994) 86 *Proceedings of the American Society of International Law* 14; K. Knop, 'Re/Statements: Feminism and State Sovereignty in International Law' (1993) 3 *Transnational Law and Contemporary Problems* 293; E. M. Morgan, 'The Hermaphroditic Paradigm of International Law: A Comment on *Alvarez-Machain*' (1992) 21 *Proceedings of the Canadian Council on International Law* 78.

The proposition that a family should have the same nationality harkened back to nationalism and war, while critiques of it looked ahead to internationalism and peace. Those who subscribed to the proposition tended to view international relations as a perpetual power struggle between states. On this view, the attachment of nationality would project the rivalries, tensions and hostilities between states onto a marriage between nationals of different states. Trinh Dinh Thao quoted Varambon's description of the household with two nationalities:

une rivalité de nation à nation, des intérêts opposés entre personnes unies, des affections différentes, des patries diverses, des vœux ennemis pours des pays peut-être en guerre, et cela entre personnes qui ont juré de s'aimer, entre lesquelles tout est commun et qui ne doivent jamais se quitter.

[a rivalry of nation to nation, interests opposed between persons united, different affections, diverse fatherlands, enemy wishes for countries perhaps at war, and this between persons who have sworn to love one another, between whom everything is common and who must never leave one another.][202]

This tendency of a marriage between people of different nationalities to reproduce the antagonism between states was a reason to give spouses the same nationality. Moreover, the conflict between spouses that would otherwise result would, in turn, give rise to conflicts between states as the protectors of the respective spouses.[203]

Contrast this with the vision of marriage between nationals and non-nationals in Calbairac, who argued that the wife should be free to choose her own nationality. Calbairac proceeded from the modern phenomenon of internationalism,[204] which he defined as

---

[202] (Translation mine) Thao, *De l'influence du mariage*, p. 15, quoting from Varambon, *Revue pratique de droit français* (1859), vol. 8, p. 50 (presenting this argument as still enjoying currency).

[203] See *Mackenzie v. Hare* 239 US 299 at 311–12 (1915), relied on by C. C. Hyde, *International Law Chiefly as Interpreted and Applied by the United States* (2 vols., Boston: Little, Brown, and Co., 1922), vol. I, p. 643, n. 4.

[204] Calbairac distinguished between these mixed marriages and the mixed marriages caused by permanent or long-term emigration for economic reasons. This distinction largely tracks class, with the former tending to unite members of a new transnational elite and the latter being between workers in urban industry or the countryside. An exception is marriages between French women and American soldiers during World War I, which he attributed to internationalism. Calbairac, *La Nationalité de la femme mariée*, pp. 9–12.

Calbairac's distinction between the mixed marriage as blueprint for utopian world relations and the more familiar mixed marriage takes on the dimension of 'good' and 'bad' mixed marriages in other arguments for the independent nationality of married women. See Thao, *De l'influence du mariage*, pp. 106 (women nationals who made 'good' marriages to allied soldiers should not be punished by losing their

la compénétration des peuples, des intérêts économiques, des ressources intellectuelles. C'est la substitution à des nations, à des Etats chez qui l'antagonisme des intérêts financiers succède aux antagonismes belliqueux, d'une communauté d'individus, d'intérêts, d'idées qui émanent des points du monde les plus divers. L'internationalisme, c'est l'ensemble des rapports qui existent d'individus à individus appartenant à des Etats différents, rapports économiques, intellectuels, moraux, qui finissent par créer une sorte de mentalité internationale.

[the compenetration of peoples, economic interests, intellectual resources. It is the substitution for nations, for states among which the antagonism of financial interests succeeds the antagonism of belligerents, of a community of individuals, of interests, of ideas which emanate from the most diverse points of the world. Internationalism is the ensemble of relations that exist from individuals to individuals belonging to different States, economic, intellectual and moral relations, that end by creating a sort of international mentality.][205]

Internationalism was thus seen as creating a new environment and a state of mind that lent themselves to the success of mixed marriages, that enabled a man and a woman to give themselves more completely to one another.[206] In the new dawn of internationalism, man and woman came to one another as individuals, free of the old inter-state antagonism. In turn, their very coming together enhanced internationalism, knitting individuals closer together and fostering the empathy necessary to it. War would find only a weak echo in the relationship of mixed marriage, and that relationship would, conversely, discourage war.

Thus, behind the issue of whether a family should have the same nationality lay a vision of the state in the world. And behind the accepted

nationality), 36–40 (women nationals who made 'bad' marriages to immigrant workers from different cultures should be protected from the laws of the husband's state by the retention of their own nationality); Women, Immigration and Nationality Group, *Worlds Apart*, p. 17 (quoting the IWSA journal *Jus Suffragii* on the need to protect through British nationality the large number of British women throughout the Empire who became the wives of men of coloured races).

In the case of women who made a 'bad' marriage to a non-national, the argument that they should be protected through the retention of their nationality projected assumptions of the time about superior and inferior states onto the needs of the woman in a mixed marriage. A similar point is made about the international legal initiatives to outlaw 'white slavery'. D. J. Guy, ' "White Slavery," Citizenship and Nationality in Argentina' in Parker, Russo, Sommer and Yaeger, *Nationalisms and Sexualities*, pp. 201–17 (women as pretexts for defining one nation's sovereignty against another's).

[205] (Translation mine) Calbairac, *La Nationalité de la femme mariée*, p. 12.
[206] *Ibid.*, pp. 13–14.

proposition that a family should, lay the legal and psychological assumption that we are irreducibly of a world of states which are forever competitors, rivals and even enemies.[207]

What permitted international lawyers of the time to derive the further proposition that the husband determined the nationality of the family from the proposition that the family should have the same nationality was the prevailing patriarchal notion of the family. In his manual on private international law, published in 1921, René Foignet wrote:

Il est conforme à l'esprit du mariage que les époux aient la même nationalité. Il est dès lors naturel que la nationalité du mari se communique à la femme.

[It is in conformity with the spirit of marriage that spouses have the same nationality. From that moment, it is natural that the nationality of the husband spread to the wife.][208]

To this, Macmillan objected:

do the supporters of this form of 'unity of the family' really mean any more, by this expression, than 'supremacy of the husband'? If they were to argue that a woman who marries a man and goes to live in his country should take her husband's nationality, and that a man going to settle in his wife's country should, in the same way, automatically take his wife's nationality, the masculine bias of his point of view would be less suspect.[209]

Conversely, the proposition that the family should have the same nationality could be derived from the patriarchal model of the family reflected in the proposition that the husband determined that nationality. As patriarch, the husband was the sole authority in the family. If the wife were the national of a state other than her husband's, her

---

[207] The same assumption informed the argument that independent nationality for married women was undesirable because it would increase the numbers of dual nationals. See International Law Association, 'Women's Equality and Nationality'.

[208] (Translation mine) R. Foignet, *Manuel élémentaire de droit international privé* (6th edn, Paris: Librairie Arthur Rousseau, 1921), p. 80. While Foignet's assumption may reflect a wife's legal duty under the Civil Code to obey the husband and follow him in all his changes of residence (see note 192 above), other French international lawyers maintained that the Code did not apply this duty of obedience to the wife's nationality because the Code accepted that the husband's nationality could change over the course of the marriage without the wife's also changing. The Code's duty of obedience thus reinforced but did not require the patriarchal assumption.

[209] Macmillan, 'Present Tendencies', 145.

duty of obedience to that state, represented by her nationality, would threaten her duty of obedience to her husband. On this reasoning, a wife's acquisition of her husband's nationality was necessary to remove a rival for her obedience.[210]

Proponents of the unity of the family applied similar reasoning to the wife's loyalty to the state. The presence in the state of wives who were non-nationals, the assumption being that wives would live in their husband's state, would contribute to the creation of veritable 'îlots étrangers' ('islands of foreigners') within the state, whereas the state required the loyalty of all those within its borders. It followed that married women must become nationals so as to destroy the presence of these rival sovereigns.[211]

While the patriarchal and the xenophobic arguments may seem separate but parallel, they are connected by the analogy between *paterfamilias* and state historically found in international law and morality.[212] Patriarchy thus naturalized the idea of the state as unmenaced by foreigners, and xenophobia reinforced the idea of the husband as unchallenged in the family. In causal terms as well, it may have appeared likely that the state's interest in security was served if loyalty to husband and state reinforced one another.

In the international legal discourse of the period on the nationality of women, gender and nationalism also combined in opposing pairs of good and bad female stereotypes. As de Beauvoir observed, since 'group symbols and social types are generally defined by means of antonyms in pairs, ambivalence will seem to be an intrinsic quality of the Eternal Feminine. The saintly mother has for correlative the cruel stepmother, the angelic young girl has the perverse virgin.'[213] Although one pair of these female stereotypes was used to justify dependent nationality for married women and the other pair to justify independent nationality, the purveyors of one were as chauvinistic as the purveyors of the other.

---

[210] See Makarov, 'La Nationalité de la Femme Mariée', 166, citing E. Audinet, 'La nationalité française' (1928) *Revue* 30 and F. Pelletier, 'La nationalité de la femme mariée' (thèse de l'Université de Dijon, 1925), p. 9.

[211] (Translation mine) Makarov, 'La Nationalité de la Femme Mariée', 167, citing Pelletier, 'La nationalité de la femme mariée', p. 52 ff.

[212] R. Pound, 'Philosophical Theory and International Law' in *Bibliotheca visseriana; dissertationum ius internationale illustrantium cura Facultatis iuridicæ Lugduno-Batavæ edita* (Lugduni Batavorum: E. J. Brill, 1923), vol. I, pp. 71–90 at pp. 75–80 (analogy in international law of state to *paterfamilias*).

[213] de Beauvoir, *The Second Sex*, p. 254.

The one pair of these female stereotypes – the faithless daughter and the dutiful daughter-in-law – symbolized the view of some supporters of the dependent nationality of married women that women, but not men, could express loyalty or disloyalty to the state through the act of marriage. A state was justified in withdrawing its nationality from a woman who married a non-national because by plighting her troth to a foreigner, she had deserted her own country. A state was justified in extending its nationality to a non-national woman who married a national because by pledging obedience to a national, she had embraced his country as well. Thao traced this nationality regime as it appeared in Articles 12 and 19 of the French Civil Code to France's desire, born of the Revolution, to withdraw favour from individuals who showed their willingness to abandon France and to reward individuals who cast their lot with France.[214]

A state's withdrawal of nationality from a woman who married a foreigner could thus be portrayed as punishment for 'bad' women and its extension of nationality to a foreign woman who married a national as reward for 'good' women. The combined effect of this gendered disciplinary system of dependent nationality and the analogy of state to *paterfamilias* was to symbolize the woman who married a non-national as the faithless daughter rightly disowned and the non-national woman who married a national as the dutiful daughter-in-law fittingly accepted.[215]

The opposing pair of good and bad female stereotypes – the virtuous daughter cruelly banished from the family and the viper-like daughter-in-law clasped to its bosom – embodied an equally chauvinistic opposition to the dependent nationality of married women. The virtuous daughter showed that dependent nationality punished some 'good'

---

[214] Thao, *De l'influence du mariage*, pp. 73–6. Articles 12 and 19 of the French Civil Code were widely copied (Makarov, 'La Nationalité de la Femme Mariée', 118), although this need not mean that their rationale was thereby adopted.

In a 1915 judgment, the Supreme Court of the United States similarly used the idea that a woman's marriage expressed her relationship to the state to reconcile the American law of dependent nationality for married women with the principle of consent to nationality. The Supreme Court held that against the legal background of dependent nationality, a wife must be seen to have consented to her husband's nationality because she voluntarily entered into marriage with notice of the consequences. *Mackenzie v. Hare*, 311–12. See also C. L. Bredbenner, *A Nationality of Her Own. Women, Marriage, and the Law of Citizenship* (Berkeley: University of California Press, 1998), pp. 15–79.

[215] Candice Bredbenner calls them 'prodigal daughters' and 'dutiful wives'. Bredbenner, *A Nationality of Her Own* (title of chapter 2).

women, while the viper-like daughter-in-law showed that it rewarded some 'bad' women. The following example of a virtuous daughter was used in the 1922 US Congressional debate on independent nationality for women and recounted, in equal detail, in some authors of the period: she was

> the daughter of an admiral in the American Navy who was wealthy in property acquired entirely by her family residing in the United States. In the war she had one brother in the American Army and one brother who had enlisted in the French Army before America entered the war. While she was a mere schoolgirl in Switzerland she had married a German who proved to be of no worth and no character. He frittered away all her property, of which he could get possession, and gave her abundant cause for divorce. For this reason she was obliged to take up a separate abode in Switzerland, where she instituted divorce proceedings against her husband. Because he was an officer in the German Army, these proceedings were stayed for the entire period of the war. During the war she went to Hungary, and there busied herself in relief work for the wounded prisoners of the allied armies. The American Alien Property Custodian, in the execution of his duty, seized and held the remainder of her property, consisting of a trust fund in the United States. Reduced from wealth and luxury to absolute poverty, this woman, who had never ceased to be an American at heart, returned to America penniless to appeal to the chivalry of the American Congress to restore her citizenship.[216]

The sense of injustice created by this example comes not just from the woman's patriotism. It also comes from her depiction as the daughter and sister of a family which, father an admiral in the American Navy and brothers eager to fight for freedom, virtually *is* the United States; and as the wife of a man who, as a German army officer, virtually *is* the enemy. The appeal to chivalry is further strengthened by her schoolgirl naiveté and her husband's caddishness. If the point of the example were only that a woman's loyalty to her state might survive her loss of its nationality, then the evidence of her patriotism would have sufficed and the details of her family would have been superfluous. The inclusion of these details suggests that the example also intended to create an image of the virtuous daughter to oppose to the image of the faithless daughter, to invoke Lear's Cordelia against his Goneril and Regan.

---

[216] R. N. Crane, 'Naturalization and Citizenship of Married Women in the United States' (1923) 5 *Journal of Comparative Legislation and International Law* (3rd Series) 47 at 50. Cited also by Thao, *De l'influence du mariage*, pp. 41–2; Calbairac, *La Nationalité de la femme mariée*, pp. 251–2.

The other image of this pair, the viper-like daughter-in-law, is alluded to by a number of international legal scholars writing after World War I. The fear was that foreign women who married nationals and thereby became nationals themselves might be opportunists or – worse – spies.[217] As actual examples of opportunists, Thao cited a well-to-do German woman who married a French shoeshine man, paying him in return a modest pension; and a wealthy and refined young Hungarian woman, devoted to the arts, who married a 74-year-old illiterate stonecutter of French origin.[218] As Macmillan ruefully observed,[219] the spells of spy fever in Britain had made bellicose patriots – Thao called them warmly 'hommes aux sentiments généreux et patriotes' ('generous and patriotic men')[220] – the allies of feminists in the campaign for women's equal right to choose their nationality.

In comparison, Niboyet's discussion of the risk posed by German husbands who acquired French nationality under the articles of the Treaty of Versailles on Alsace-Lorraine[221] is relatively restrained:

Cette disposition dont les intentions sont évidemment pures peut être qualifiée de déplorable. Il y a en effet des conjoints, en particulier des maris allemands, parmi lesquels on peut même compter d'anciens officiers de l'armée active qui sont devenus Français uniquement parce qu'ils avaient épousé des Alsaciennes ou d'autres femmes qui devenaient Françaises par le traité. La France a ainsi hérité de concitoyens parfois dangereux qu'il aurait été bien facile de laisser à leur ancienne nationalité.

[This disposition, the intentions of which were evidently pure, can be described as deplorable. There are in effect spouses, in particular German husbands, among whom one can even count former officers of the active army who have become French uniquely because they had married Alsatian women or other

---

[217] Calbairac, *La Nationalité de la femme mariée*, p. 250; Thao, *De l'influence du mariage*, pp. 54–5, 88. On the myth of the spy-seductress, women spies and spy mania during World War I, see J. Wheelwright, *The Fatal Lover: Mata Hari and the Myth of Women in Espionage* (London: Collins & Brown, 1992), pp. 31–46, 101–28. For an account of women spies in World War I by a former member of the British Naval Intelligence Department and the Secretariat of the War Cabinet, see G. Aston, *Secret Service* (New York: Cosmopolitan Book Corp., 1930), pp. 150–64. More generally, Christopher Andrew gives a darkly comic account of spy mania in England before and during World War I in *Secret Service: The Making of the British Intelligence Community* (London: Heinemann, 1985), pp. 34–85, 174–202.
[218] Thao, *De l'influence du mariage*, p. 55.   [219] Macmillan, 'Present Tendencies', 144.
[220] (Translation mine) Thao, *De l'Influence du Mariage*, p. 100.
[221] Under the Treaty of Versailles, Alsace-Lorraine was treated as a special case.

women who became French under the treaty. France thus inherited sometimes dangerous citizens whom it would have been very easy to leave to their old nationality.]²²²

Niboyet's tone is more measured than that often taken in the equivalent discussion of women: his concern centres on men whose past actions have marked them as loyal to Germany, and his characterization of the danger posed by spouses is qualified.

The examples of the American admiral's daughter and the moneyed young Hungarian woman who married a French stonecutter promoted independent nationality for married women through prevailing ideas of patriotism and womanly virtue, rather than the goal of equality. The comparison indirectly suggested by these examples was between 'good' women and 'bad' women, rather than between women and men. In criticism of the French legal regime of dependent nationality for married women, the comparison between 'good' women who suffered under this regime and 'bad' women who prospered was sometimes even made directly. In one such comparison, the one neighbour, a woman of German origin, married a Frenchman and received maternity benefits, whereas the other neighbour, a French woman, married an immigrant worker and was reduced to charity.²²³ In another, a young woman employed in the public service was unable to continue in her position because she had married a former soldier in the allied armies, whereas the electoral rolls continued to list another young woman who during the war cohabited with a stranger suspected of harbouring anti-French sentiments.²²⁴

The plebiscites held in Europe after World War I are traditionally seen as a turning point in the history of self-determination in international law: although few in number, they symbolized the commitment of the Paris Peace Conference to the principle of self-determination and gave it tangible and lasting effect. This chapter showed that the plebiscites should also be seen as a turning point for women in the history of self-determination. By voting in these plebiscites, women participated in the exercise of self-determination for the first time.

The interpretation given to self-determination by the Peace Conference in the plebiscites offered another instance where self-determination

²²² (Translation mine) Niboyet, 'La Nationalité d'après les traités de paix', 314.
²²³ Thao, *De l'influence du mariage*, pp. 95–6, quoting Sauterand.
²²⁴ *Ibid.*, p. 106, quoting from the introduction of a French legislative initiative.

as an idea and a set of legal concepts to be interpreted served as a vocabulary for marginalized groups to challenge their exclusion from international law and its depiction of them. Despite an increasingly rich feminist history of the women's suffrage and women's peace movements, women have remained virtually invisible in international legal accounts of self-determination after World War I. The chapter sought to make visible the participation of women suffragists and pacifists at the Peace Conference and the ways in which they used the principle of self-determination both to frame the demand that they be given the vote in the plebiscite and to articulate their identity as women relative to the competing narratives of nationalism and internationalism in post-war international law.

Most immediately, the espousal of the principle of self-determination by the leaders at the Peace Conference was a way for women suffragists to introduce women's equality into democracy domestically and internationally, and for women pacifists, who were pioneers in the advocacy of self-determination and plebiscites, to further democracy and women's equality in international law. At its broadest, women's demand for the right to vote in the plebiscites expressed their view of the relationship of gender to nationalism and internationalism, war and peace. Whereas suffragists stressed women's role in war as a reason that they had earned the vote, pacifists argued that women were a moral and social force for peace and their votes would humanize governments.

In contrast to women's right to vote in the plebiscites, the collective option denied married women the right to opt for another nationality following the determination of sovereignty by the plebiscites. As with other challenges to international law by marginalized groups through the interpretation of self-determination, international law thus responded only partially. This chapter showed that in the discourse on the collective option and the nationality of married women more generally, the rhetoric of women's equality combined in a variety of complex ways with the rhetorics of gender and international law. Here, the interrelated narratives of gender and international law that supported the collective option and the dependent nationality of married women proved impossible for women to overcome. At the same time, the assortment of women's allies in the campaign for independent nationality highlights the fact that the achievement of equality in international legal terms need not signal either its deeper acceptance or women's ability to define their identity and relationship to the national and international orders.²²⁵ A married woman's equal right to choose her nationality was consistent, on the one hand, with an internationalism that saw mixed marriages as speeding the end of national antagonisms and, on the other, a nationalist paranoia that the husband's nationality would serve as a cover for temptresses and Mata Haris.

[225] See K. Knop, 'Of the Male Persuasion: The Power of Liberal Internationalism for Women' (1999) 93 *Proceedings of the American Society of International Law* 177.

7 Women and self-determination in United Nations trust territories

As seen in connection with the *East Timor* case in Chapter 4, the idea and the institution of 'trusteeship' have traditionally been the terrain on which the meaning of self-determination for colonial peoples has been worked out in international law. This chapter shows that the responsibility to educate the colonized for self-government or independence that was expressed in the international trusteeship system established by the United Nations Charter after World War II[1] has also been significant as a way for women's groups and, within the UN, the Commission on the Status of Women (CSW) to integrate their vision of equality into colonial self-determination. The reinterpretation of this responsibility in the 1960 Declaration on the Granting of Independence to Colonial Countries and Peoples (Declaration on the Independence of Colonial Peoples) (GA Resolution 1514 (XV)) as a duty to take immediate steps toward self-determination corresponded similarly to the CSW's re-examination of the priority between women's equality and self-determination and, indeed, the very import of equality. Conversely, the status of women in the trust territories was critical in the contest among the UN Trusteeship Council, the states administering trust territories and the local leaders in those territories over the meaning of self-determination.

While this inscription of ideas of gender and decolonization onto the figure of the colonized woman has been explored in feminist and postcolonial studies,[2] it has not informed international law. Yet, this chapter

---

[1] Charter of the United Nations, 26 June 1945, 59 Stat. 1031, 145 BFSP (1943-5) 805 (1953), c. XII-XIII.

[2] For a sample of the non-legal literature on women as figured in colonialism and anti-colonial nationalism, see P. Chatterjee, *The Nation and its Fragments: Colonial and Postcolonial Histories* (Princeton: Princeton University Press, 1993), pp. 116-57; P. Chatterjee, 'The Nationalist Resolution of the Women's Question' in K. Sangari and

demonstrates that from the late 1940s to the early 1970s,[3] the identity of women in the trust territories was, in fact, central to the articulation both of self-determination and of feminism in international law. Individuals, women and part of the people, women in the trust territories encoded competing notions of equality, gender and decolonization.

What has been overlooked by lawyers and non-lawyers alike, moreover, is the fact that women in the trust territories themselves made use of the right to petition the Trusteeship Council. While these *petits récits* made little headway against the battle of grand narratives in the international trusteeship system and the CSW,[4] they mark a place in the history of self-determination for colonial women as participants in its interpretation. They illustrate as well that no single grand narrative engages the range of identities visible in local women's communications of concern.

The first part of this chapter recapitulates the usual history of the development of colonial self-determination in international law, a history that highlights the shift in thinking from the League of Nations Covenant to the UN Charter, and from the Charter to the Declaration

---

S. Vaid (eds.), *Recasting Women: Essays in Colonial History* (New Delhi: Kali for Women, 1989), pp. 233–53; C. Enloe, *Bananas, Beaches and Bases: Making Feminist Sense of International Politics* (rev. edn, Berkeley: University of California Press, 2000), pp. 42–64; M.-A. Helie-Lucas, 'Strategies of Women and Women's Movements in the Muslim World vis-à-vis Fundamentalisms: From Entryism to Internationalism' in O. Mendelsohn and U. Baxi (eds.), *The Rights of Subordinated Peoples* (Delhi: Oxford University Press, 1994), pp. 251–75; K. Jayawardena, *Feminism and Nationalism in the Third World* (London: Zed, 1986); A. McClintock, *Imperial Leather: Race, Gender and Sexuality in the Colonial Context* (New York: Routledge, 1995); A. Parker, M. Russo, D. Sommer and P. Yaeger (eds.), *Nationalisms and Sexualities* (New York: Routledge, 1992); J. J. Pettman, *Worlding Women: A Feminist International Politics* (London: Routledge, 1996), pp. 25–63, 132–6; N. Yuval-Davis and F. Anthias (eds.), *Woman–Nation–State* (New York: St Martin's Press, 1989).

[3] This chapter focuses on the period 1947–72, during which the Commission on the Status of Women considered annually, for the latter half biannually, reports prepared by the Secretary-General on the status of women in trust and non-self-governing territories. The materials considered in the chapter are (1) Commission on the Status of Women annual reports for 1950–72, i.e., 4th-24th sessions; (2) Secretary-General reports for 1950–72 on the status of women in trust and non-self-governing territories, which summarize information from other UN sources, primarily reports submitted by the states administering these territories; (3) petitions to the Trusteeship Council brought by women in trust territories for 1947–53 and by or about women in trust territories for 1953–72; (4) Trusteeship Council resolutions associated with the petitions; (5) Visiting Mission reports for 1950–72, chosen as in (2).

Although (1) and (2) also pertain to non-self-governing territories, the chapter concentrates on trust territories because the existence of (3)–(5) provides a greater range of perspectives on women in trust territories.

[4] Compare J. F. Lyotard, *The Postmodern Condition: A Report on Knowledge*, G. Bennington and B. Massumi (trans.) (Minneapolis: University of Minnesota Press, 1984), p. 27.

on the Independence of Colonial Peoples. The next two parts show the familiar paradigm shifts to be shifts as well in paradigms of equality and self-determination. In comparison to these general lines of debate, the final part looks at the petitions submitted to the Trusteeship Council by women in the trust territories.

Self-determination and the UN trusteeship system

We look to you as our Gods, and hope that we shall not be disappointed.

> Petition to the Trusteeship Council from Six Persons on behalf of the Men and Women of Bagangu-Akum concerning the Cameroons under British Administration[5]

The UN international trusteeship system was structured much like a trust in Anglo-American law.[6] A territory was placed under international trusteeship by agreement and administered by one or more states in accordance with the objectives of international trusteeship in the Charter and the terms of the particular trusteeship agreement. Its administration was supervised principally by the Trusteeship Council, through a combination of the examination of reports from administering states, the consideration of petitions and the dispatching of periodic visiting missions.

The system resembled a trust not only in its institutional design, but also in the conceptual analogy drawn to the guardianship of a minor. The League of Nations international mandate system had applied this analogy to colonies detached from enemy states after World War I and considered to be 'inhabited by peoples not yet able to stand by themselves under the strenuous conditions of the modern world'. Under Article 22 of the League Covenant, the well-being and development of such peoples formed a 'sacred trust of civilisation' and was to be entrusted to those 'advanced nations who, by reason of their resources, their experience or their geographic position' could best undertake the responsibility.[7] The Charter continued the idea of the 'sacred trust' and expanded it to all colonial territories. In addition to the international trusteeship system established by the Charter, Article 73 more broadly required UN members responsible for non-self-governing territories to

---

[5] Petition from Six Persons on Behalf of the Men and Women of Bagangu-Akum Concerning the Cameroons under British Administration (T/Pet.4/51), TCOR, 6th Sess., Annex Vol. 2, Agenda Item 5 (1950), p. 102.

[6] See the discussion of trusteeship at pp. 194–202 above.

[7] Covenant of the League of Nations, Versailles, 28 June 1919, in force 10 January 1920, (1919) 112 BFSP 13.

administer those territories in the best interests of the inhabitants. The UN systems of trust territories and non-self-governing territories broke with the cultural determinism of the League of Nations, however, by requiring the development of self-government or independence for all territories, whereas the League system of mandate territories had envisaged independence only for those territories it classified as sufficiently advanced. In fact, all but one of the territories placed under trusteeship were former mandate territories that, under the classification of mandate territories, were not entitled to independence.

If this interpretation of trusteeship in the Charter represented a certain turning away from the paternalism of the Covenant, its interpretation came to be identified with a second turn: toward the principle of self-determination of colonial peoples. In 1960, the Declaration on the Independence of Colonial Peoples proclaimed the right of all colonial peoples to immediate self-determination. The International Court of Justice wrote in its 1971 advisory opinion on *Namibia* that the Declaration had left 'little doubt that the ultimate objective of the sacred trust was the self-determination and independence of the peoples concerned'.[8]

In total, there were eleven United Nations trust territories, seven in mainland Africa and four island territories in the Pacific. By the early 1960s, the trust territories in Africa had all attained self-government or independence, choosing either to join a neighbouring state or to become a new state. The other trust territories attained independence over the next decades, the Trusteeship Council suspending operation in 1994 with the independence of the last remaining trust territory.[9]

In Africa, Britain administered Togoland, which pursuant to a UN-supervised plebiscite was united with the Gold Coast to form the new state of Ghana in 1957; Cameroons, which was divided in 1961 in accordance with UN-supervised plebiscites in which the northern population chose to join neighbouring Nigeria and the southern population chose to join the neighbouring Republic of Cameroon; and Tanganyika, which after achieving internal self-government became independent in 1961 and later united with Zanzibar to form the United Republic of Tanzania. There was also a French-administered Togoland, which in 1960, following a UN-observed election won by a pro-independence party, became the state of Togo; and a French-administered Cameroons, which became the Republic of Cameroon in the same year. The other two trust territories in Africa were Somaliland under Italian administration,

---

[8] *Namibia (South West Africa)*, Advisory Opinion, ICJ Reports 1971, p. 16 at p. 31.
[9] Trusteeship Council <http://www.un.org/Overview/Organs/tc.html> (visited 3 March 2001).

which, together with the British Protectorate of Somaliland, became the Republic of Somalia in 1960 after an elected legislative assembly had drawn up a constitution for independence; and Ruanda-Urundi under Belgian administration, which following UN-supervised elections held separately in Ruanda and Urundi split into Rwanda and Burundi in 1962. In the Pacific, New Zealand administered Western Samoa until its independence in 1962, pursuant to a UN-supervised plebiscite. Australia, New Zealand and the United Kingdom jointly administered Nauru, which became progressively self-governing from 1965 until its independence in 1968. Australia also administered New Guinea, united administratively with Papua in 1971 to form Papua New Guinea, which achieved self-government in stages and became independent in 1975. The final trust territory was the Pacific Islands under United States administration,[10] which ended when Palau, the last of the trust territory's four administrative units, became independent in 1994.

In practice, the Trusteeship Council supervised the administration of these trust territories in three ways.[11] The primary means of supervision was its consideration of the annual reports prepared by the administering authorities according to a questionnaire formulated by the Trusteeship Council.[12] It also accepted and examined petitions in consultation with the administering authority.[13] The Charter and the Trusteeship Council's rules of procedure placed almost no restrictions on petitions. Petitions had to concern 'the affairs of one or more Trust Territories or the operation of the International Trusteeship System as laid down in the Charter',[14] and petitioners could be 'inhabitants of Trust Territories or other parties'.[15] There were few formalities; a petition might be as

---

[10] Summaries taken from United Nations, *Everyone's United Nations. A Handbook of the Work of the United Nations* (10th edn, New York, 1986), pp. 341–6.

[11] See generally H. D. Hall, *Mandates, Dependencies and Trusteeship* (Washington: Carnegie Endowment for International Peace, 1948); C. E. Toussaint, *The Trusteeship System of the United Nations* (New York: Frederick A. Praeger, 1956).

[12] UN Charter, Arts. 87(a), 88.

[13] *Ibid.*, Art. 87(b). See generally T. J. M. Zuijdwijk, *Petitioning the United Nations: A Study in Human Rights* (New York: St Martin's Press, 1982), pp. 136–54.

[14] Rules of Procedure of the Trusteeship Council, UN Doc. T/1/Rev.6, Rule 76 (rules as amended up to and during 29th session). (Although a revised version of the Rules has since been issued (UN Doc. T/1/Rev.7 (1995)), this version was in force during most of the relevant time period.) The chief restriction was that petitions could not normally be directed against judgments of competent courts of the administering authorities or deal with matters within the competence of the courts, unless the petitions involved a challenge to legislation on the ground of incompatibility with the UN Charter or the Trusteeship Agreement. *Ibid.*, Rule 81.

[15] *Ibid.*, Rule 77.

simple as a letter or a telegram[16] sent to the UN Secretary-General[17] or handed to a visiting mission.[18] The final means of supervision was the periodic visiting missions to the trust territories. Missions were normally composed of two members of the Trusteeship Council representing administering states and two representing non-administering states, and were accompanied by staff and representatives from the local authority. These annual missions rotated between the groups of trust territories in East Africa, West Africa and the Pacific, such that each trust territory was visited once every three years. In addition to reporting generally on conditions in the trust territories, a mission might respond to specific questions asked by the Trusteeship Council.[19]

Equality and self-determination in the UN trusteeship system

If the conception of colonial self-determination in the UN trusteeship system was an advance on the League mandate system, it also stood as a milestone for women. Like the terms of the World War I peace treaties that gave women the right to vote in the plebiscites, the definition of trusteeship in the Charter incorporated women's equality into self-determination. Women delegates and NGOs at the San Francisco Conference had succeeded in having references to human rights inserted into several articles of the Charter,[20] among them the article on the objectives of the trusteeship system. Whereas the only references to human rights in Covenant Article 22 on the mandate system were to the freedoms of conscience and religion, which were subject to the maintenance of public order and morals, and to the prohibition of abuses such as the slave trade, the arms traffic and the liquor traffic, Article 76 of the Charter made encouragement of respect for human rights and

---

[16] *Ibid.*, Rule 79.   [17] *Ibid.*, Rule 82.   [18] *Ibid.*, Rule 84.
[19] D. Rauschning, 'United Nations Trusteeship System' in R. Bernhardt (ed.), *Encyclopedia of Public International Law* (12 vols., Amsterdam: North-Holland, 1983), vol. V, pp. 369–76 at pp. 373–4.
[20] J. Connors, 'NGOs and the Human Rights of Women at the United Nations' in P. Willetts (ed.), *'The Conscience of the World': The Influence of Non-Governmental Organisations in the UN System* (Washington, D.C.: Brookings Institution, 1996), pp. 147–80 at pp. 150–1; M. E. Galey, 'Forerunners in Women's Quest for Partnership' in A. Winslow (ed.), *Women, Politics, and the United Nations* (Contributions in Women's Studies, No. 151) (Westport, Conn.: Greenwood Press, 1995), pp. 1–10 at p. 7; L. Reanda, 'The Commission on the Status of Women' in P. Alston (ed.), *The United Nations and Human Rights: A Critical Appraisal* (Oxford: Clarendon Press, 1992), pp. 265–303 at p. 266; United Nations, *The United Nations and the Advancement of Women 1945–1995* (United Nations Blue Book Series, Vol. VI) (New York, 1995), p. 10.

fundamental freedoms for all without distinction as to sex a basic objective of the trusteeship system.[21] Women could therefore use the administration of trust territories and the Trusteeship Council's supervision of their administration to promote women's equal rights in these territories. Through one such case-study, this part of the chapter compares the model of equality sought by one international women's group with the responses of the main actors in the UN trusteeship system and with the model of equality promoted by trusteeship.

The Fon of Bikom

I am Foin Ndi of all Kom village. I hold undisputed sway over this Bikom Foindom, in other words Bikom (Kom) State. I am the 9th of the dynasty of Kings in Kom. My authority in tribal life, morally, socially, economically and politically is derived from three things – I am the custodian of the tribal lands, I am the rainmaker to aid the crops to grow, and thirdly I am the link between the tribes' dead, the living and the unborn members of Kom.

...

I had and I must still have servants [i.e., wives[22]] in the Kwiiton compound. Without them I am unable to fulfil my duties... My compound... must be cared for as was the custom at the origin. But I do not press that when we have become civilised and adopted modern ways of life the current changes must not come.[23]

The case of the Fon of Bikom[24] concerned a tribal king in the British-administered Cameroons. It originated in a 1947 petition to the Trusteeship Council by the St Joan's Social and Political Alliance, a Catholic women's organization[25] with an active and long-standing interest in

---

[21] There was no equivalent provision for non-self-governing territories.
[22] Reports of the United Nations Visiting Mission to Trust Territories in West Africa, TCOR, 7th Sess., Supp. No. 2, UN Doc. T/798 (1950), p. 37.
[23] Petition from the Fon of Bikom concerning the Cameroons under British Administration (T/Pet.4/36), TCOR, 6th Sess., Annex Vol. 2, Agenda Item 5 (1950), p. 89 at p. 90.
[24] See Visiting Mission to Trust Territories in West Africa (1950), pp. 36–8.
[25] Founded in 1931, the St Joan's Social and Political Alliance had as its objects in unenfranchised countries (1) 'to band together Catholics of both sexes in order to secure for women the parliamentary vote on the same terms as it is, or may be, granted to men'; and (2) 'to secure the political, social and economic equality between men and women and to further the work and usefulness of Catholic women as citizens'. In enfranchised countries, its object was limited to (2). Internationally, the St Joan's Social and Political Alliance was especially involved in the areas of the nationality of married women and the position of African women. League of Nations, *Handbook of International Organisations* (1938), quoted in C. A. Miller, 'Lobbying the League: Women's International Organizations and the League of Nations' (D. Phil. thesis, University of Oxford, 1992), p. 295.

promoting the equality of colonial women.[26] The petition consisted of an article from *The Catholic Citizen*, a publication of the St Joan's Social and Political Alliance. Its title – 'Our African Sisters' – suggests the community felt by the women of the St Joan's Social and Political Alliance with women in the trust territories. The article reprinted from *The Franciscan Missionary Herald* a lurid account of the forcible taking of a thirteen-year-old girl to be the wife of the Fon of Bikom. The day after the Fon's men spotted her grinding corn outside her father's hut, branded her with a red mark on her forehead and stripped her naked,

Papa arrayed in his tribal splendour, sets off for the King's Compound. The girl, nothing but a string of large native seeds round her neck, comes sobbing behind. They come to the King's Compound; guards in Native costume with erect spears, stand on guard. The King, a man of about eighty years, sits on a Native throne, a leopard under his feet. About one hundred of his six hundred wives stand round him in a semi-circle – naked – as is the privilege and custom of the 'King's Own'. The father steps forward, bends his knees so that although bent forward, he is still on his feet, claps his hands three times, then standing upright, drags his daughter forward, throws her on the ground in front of the King, who steps forward, puts his right foot on top of the girl's body which means 'I accept this piece of *Cargo*.' The girl is then taken away by one of the older wives and this poor child will probably be a mother at fourteen years.

Do not think this is just an isolated case. This is the everyday custom of the 'Bekom' tribe of the British Cameroons. The King sends out his 'Chinda' and this is what happens with girls, young children and cattle.[27]

The St Joan's Social and Political Alliance made no comment on this account – presumably persuaded that none was necessary – but its general position is found in a previous petition to the Trusteeship Council. In this previous petition,[28] the Alliance expressed confidence that the Trusteeship Council would be vigilant for sex discrimination, which was inconsistent with the trusteeship system objective of 'respect for human rights and fundamental freedoms for all without distinction as to race,

---

[26] The St Joan's Social and Political Alliance had been interested in the status of 'native' women since the 1930s. It had carried out research on the subject, which it had contributed to the relevant committees of the League of Nations. Miller, 'Lobbying the League', p. 63. In particular, the St Joan's Social and Political Alliance had frequently made representations to the Mandate Commission of the League. Petition from St Joan's Social and Political Alliance, London, W.1 (T/Pet./General/2), TCOR, 1st Sess., Annex 7a, Agenda Item 9, Supplement (1947), p. 153 at p. 153.

[27] Petition, Dated 28 November 1947, from St Joan's Social and Political Alliance (T/Pet.4/2), TCOR, 3rd Sess., Agenda Item 6, Supplement (1948), p. 286 at p. 287.

[28] Petition from St Joan's Social and Political Alliance, London, W.1 (T/Pet./General/2), TCOR, 1st Sess., Annex 7a, Agenda Item 9, Supplement (1947), p. 153.

sex, language or religion'. With this petition was a proposal for the questionnaire that the Charter required the Trusteeship Council to formulate as the basis for the administering authorities' annual reports. The picture of equality that emerges from the Alliance's proposed questionnaire is equal legal status for women, notably in matters of contract, property and inheritance, as well as the eradication of such traditional practices as child marriages, forced marriages, polygamy, dowry or brideprice, inheritance of widows and lending of wives.[29]

Other general petitions from the St Joan's Social and Political Alliance to the Trusteeship Council, submitted after the petition on the Fon of Bikom, were fairly successful in pressing for the implementation of their view of women's equality. In response to a petition proposing that enquiries about child marriages and compulsory marriages be included in the terms of reference for all visiting missions to trust territories,[30] the Trusteeship Council informed the St Joan's Social and Political Alliance that it had included such questions in the provisional questionnaire of the Trusteeship Council and gave the replies of the administering authorities regular attention.[31] Another petition from the St Joan's Social and Political Alliance, on the need for immediate measures to promote the progressive abolition of customs violating the physical integrity of women in the trust territories,[32] led to the Trusteeship Council decision to draw the administering authorities' attention to the question (already included in the Trusteeship Council's questionnaire) and to take up the question during its annual examination of conditions in the relevant trust territories.[33]

In the concrete case of the Fon of Bikom, however, the British administration, the Trusteeship Council[34] and the 1950 Visiting Mission to Trust Territories in West Africa[35] approached the problem of polygamy more

[29] *Ibid.*, pp. 154–6.
[30] Petition from St Joan's International Social and Political Alliance (T/Pet./General/20), TCOR, 4th Sess., Agenda Item 4, Annex (1949), p. 376.
[31] Petition from the St Joan's International Social and Political Alliance Concerning all Trust Territories, TC Res. 76 (IV) (1949).
[32] Petition from St Joan's International Social and Political Alliance (T/Pet./General/22), TCOR, 12th Sess., Annexes, Agenda Item 5, UN Doc. T/L.368 (1953), p. 83.
[33] Petition from St Joan's International Social and Political Alliance, TC Res. 865 (XII) (1953).
[34] Although a few women served on the Trusteeship Council early on as government advisors or alternates or as the representatives of UN specialized agencies, there appears to have been no woman government representative until 1962 (Marthe Tenzer, Belgium). See TCOR, Lists of Delegations Members of Council. See also M. E. Galey, 'Women Find a Place', in Winslow, *Women, Politics, and the United Nations*, pp. 11–27 at p. 11 (under 5%).
[35] The first woman to take part in a visiting mission was Angie Brooks (Liberia), who

managerially, as part of a larger strategy for implementing Western ideas of democracy, equality and modernization in the trust territories prior to the exercise of self-determination.[36] In its observations on the St Joan's Social and Political Alliance petition, the British government began by characterizing the nun who wrote the original story as most likely carried away by an active imagination and a sensationalist fancy. It concluded that she had probably 'for the sake of vividness ... dramatised Bikom custom, using a certain amount of literary licence to make it appear that she was describing an actual incident'.[37] The British government further implied that the encounter with heathen customs might have been too much for a devout Christian: 'It is not surprising that this extraordinary state of affairs, which provides a striking illustration of the strange customs which persist particularly in parts of the Cameroons, is shocking to Christian sentiment.'[38]

As explained in its observations on the St Joan's Social and Political Alliance petition, the general British policy was not to abolish polygamy and other traditional marriage practices outright. During the 1930s, Catholic missionaries in the Bamenda Division attempted to end the polygamy of the Fons by actively encouraging their wives to leave their compounds and then to marry missionary converts. These attempts were largely unsuccessful, since many of the women later returned to the Fons' compounds of their own accord. The Catholic missionaries therefore concluded that the custom was best modified by 'the effect of continuous disapproval of any form of coercion into marriage, deterrent

participated in the 1964 UN Visiting Mission to Trust Territories of the Pacific Islands. Galey, 'Women Find a Place', p. 17.

[36] States administering trust territories recognized women's role as keeper and symbol of tradition. E.g., Commission on the Status of Women, Information Concerning the Status of Women in Trust Territories Contained in Annual Reports by the Administering Authorities, 4th Sess., UN Doc. E/CN.6/138 (1950), p. 14 (United Kingdom regarding Tanganyika); Commission on the Status of Women, Information Concerning the Status of Women in Trust Territories (Report by the Secretary-General), 8th Sess., UN Doc. E/CN.6/235 (1954), p. 20 (France regarding Togoland under French administration).

The corollary of this recognition was the recognition of women as the social group most resistant to progress. E.g., Commission on the Status of Women, Information Concerning the Status of Women in Trust Territories, 7th Sess., UN Doc. E/CN.6/210 (1953), p. 12 (France regarding Cameroons under French administration); Commission on the Status of Women, Information Concerning the Status of Women in Trust Territories (Report by the Secretary-General), 15th Sess., UN Doc. E/CN.6/370 (1960), p. 6 (Trusteeship Council regarding New Guinea).

[37] Observations Submitted by the Government of the United Kingdom on the Petition, Dated 28 November 1947, from St Joan's Social and Political Alliance (T/Pet.4/2), UN Doc. T/178, para. 1.

[38] Ibid., para. 9.

action taken by the Administration if and when cases of coercion are discovered and by the spread of education and Christianity'.[39] The British administration was similarly persuaded that a sudden break with this long-established custom would only harm the Fons' wives themselves and those families entitled to have daughters in the Fons' compounds.[40] Among the people, complete and immediate abolition could lead to strong objection and the superstition that punishment would follow in the form of a dreadful supernatural calamity.[41] The general British policy was therefore 'to achieve a gradual modification of custom and at the same time to ensure that individual hardship or cruelty is prevented'.[42] The British administration pursued only cases of coercion amounting to offences such as child stealing, assault or false imprisonment,[43] while leaving further modification to the 'continued efforts of the missionaries supplemented by the influence and advice of Government officers'.[44] In particular, it appointed a woman education officer to work with women in their homes.

The British response to the St Joan's Social and Political Alliance petition was thus twofold: polygamy was generalized to a problem of culture and acceptable polygamy was distinguished from unacceptable polygamy by the notion of coercion. The responses of the Fon of Bikom, the Kom Improvement Association and the women of Kom mirrored the British response. The petitions of the Fon of Bikom and the Kom Improvement Association, which described itself as 'an organization set up by the Kom people, with the Fon as patron, to seek to exalt and improve Kom in every way possible',[45] characterized the St Joan's Social and Political Alliance allegation as an unjustified interference with Kom custom and an affront to the community as a whole. The 1950 United Nations Visiting Mission to Trust Territories in West Africa, to which the petitions were publicly presented, described their tone as 'one of polite but firm resentment that the name and dignity of their "king" had suffered as a result of what they regarded as incorrect and unjustified allegations and interference with their accepted customs'.[46] Even had there been six hundred wives, the Fon asked in his petition, with reference to the British District Officer (DO) who had come to verify the reported number of wives,

---

[39] *Ibid.*, para. 7.   [40] *Ibid.*, para. 9.   [41] *Ibid.*   [42] *Ibid.*, para. 10.
[43] *Ibid.*, para. 3.   [44] *Ibid.*, para. 10.
[45] Petition from the Kom Improvement Association Concerning the Cameroons under British Administration (T/Pet.4/35), TCOR, 6th Sess., Annex Vol. 2, Agenda Item 5 (1950), p. 88 at p. 88.
[46] Visiting Mission to Trust Territories in West Africa (1950), p. 37.

what fairness is there for the said DO to order an exodus of my X. wives without a refund of dowry? Are these the fundamental principles of the four freedoms and the ends to which the UNO came into being to achieve? Wherein comes the clash of cultures, taking for granted that such a thing existed? Where lies the need for the D.O. who is not Bikom and who knows very little of the cultural progress of Bikom, to force me to abandon my way of life and take his which is entirely unknown to me and not wished for?[47]

In its petition, the Kom Improvement Association equated the insult to the Fon with an insult to 'every Kom citizen'.[48]

While the Fon of Bikom and the women of Kom, in their petition, protested the challenge to their cultural legitimacy, the notion of consent they employed to establish that the Fon's practice of polygamy was legitimate was the same as the British notion of consent. Following the British administration's investigation of the story in the St Joan's Social and Political Alliance petition, the Fon was reported to have willingly returned his only prepubescent wife to her family.[49] Both the annual report of the British administration in 1948 and the report of the 1950 Visiting Mission to Trust Territories in West Africa recorded the Fon's assurances that any of his wives was free to leave the compound, that in fact many had left, and that the remaining wives were there of their own free will. He further undertook only to accept new wives on the basis of their consent.[50] Similarly, the petition by the 'women of Kom' reads:

We the undersigned women of Kom including some of the Foin's wives protest against the wrong news concerning our husbands. We are very happy to live with our husbands. We do not grudge sharing husbands. We live with them happily. 2. We, the Fon's wives live happily with the Fon according to our native law and custom.[51]

The 1950 Visiting Mission to Trust Territories in West Africa, which the Trusteeship Council had charged with pursuing the case of the Fon of Bikom,[52] differed from the British administration in the style

---

[47] Petition from the Fon of Bikom, p. 90.
[48] Petition from the Kom Improvement Association, p. 88.
[49] Observations of the United Kingdom, para. 3. In his petition, the Fon noted that he was also considering libel action in connection with the newspaper story: 'Gentlemen I resent very strongly the...libel and I will seek redress through litigation'. Petition from the Fon of Bikom, p. 89.
[50] Visiting Mission to Trust Territories in West Africa (1950), pp. 37–8.
[51] Petition from the Women of Kom Concerning the Cameroons under British Administration (T/Pet.4/38), TCOR, 6th Sess., Annex Vol. 2, Agenda Item 5 (1950), p. 92.
[52] Petition from St Joan's Social and Political Alliance Concerning the Trust Territory of the Cameroons under British Administration, TC Res. 38 (III) (1948).

of its response. Somewhat breathlessly, the Visiting Mission described 'its strenuous ascent of the mountain near whose summit the Fon of Bikom and his people reside'[53] and the reception it received:

> the aged Fon, now weak and ailing and living most of his days in the semi-darkness of his compound, knew full well the principal purpose of the Mission's visit. So did his people. He and they, and even the women of the Fon's compound, were ready with carefully prepared memoranda.[54]

The Visiting Mission cautioned that Western standards should not be brought to bear on the customs and culture of African peoples, and that these customs must be recognized as deeply rooted. It also identified polygamy as a form of social security for the women under existing economic conditions. Inserted between these two observations, however, was the comment that 'unwholesome' customs should be altered through education. In the end, the Visiting Mission concluded, 'the harmful effects of the practice, and its inability to adapt itself to the needs of a progressive society' outweighed the moral and material importance of polygamy in African culture and necessitated its progressive, but rapid, disappearance.[55] Its recommendations were in substance the British policy of speeding the disappearance of polygamy through establishing and publicizing the right of women and girls to refuse to enter into a forced marriage and to be released from such a marriage, as well as their right to withdraw from a polygamous marriage should they no longer wish to continue as additional wives.[56]

Although the comments of some Trusteeship Council members on the 1947 report of the United Kingdom on the Cameroons under British administration supported outlawing child marriage,[57] the Trusteeship Council's resolution on the St Joan's Social and Political Alliance petition merely condemned the customs of compulsory marriage and child marriage 'as set forth' in the petition, noted the administering authority's policy and expressed confidence that the administering authority would take all appropriate measures to end such practices. The resolution also requested both the administering authority and the next visiting

---

[53] Visiting Mission to Trust Territories in West Africa (1950), p. 37. In contrast to this story of adventure in far-away places, the Visiting Mission elsewhere in the report described a view as having a familiar beauty: 'The panorama seemed to resemble the Lake District of England, so varied is the countryside in its topography and climate.' Ibid., p. 3.

[54] Ibid., p. 37.   [55] Ibid., p. 38.   [56] Ibid.

[57] Report of the Trusteeship Council, GAOR, 4th Sess., Supp. No. 4, Vol. 7, UN Doc. A/933 (1949), p. 14 (Belgium, USSR).

mission to the territory to pursue the situation.⁵⁸ The Trusteeship Council resolved to take no action on the three Kom petitions, noting only that the misunderstanding had arisen from factors beyond its control.⁵⁹

In the case of the Fon of Bikom, the original petition by the St Joan's Social and Political Alliance implicitly raised an issue of women's equal rights. In contrast, the Fon of Bikom and the Kom Improvement Association, on the one hand, and the administering authority, Visiting Mission, and Trusteeship Council, on the other, treated the issue as the interpretation of self-determination: whether the goal of self-determination stood for respect for cultural difference or necessitated its gradual modification. Kom women were the example, *par excellence*, of this interpretive conflict. At the same time, the Fon of Bikom and the United Nations⁶⁰ shared an idea of women's consent. The Fon's assurances that the women in his compound were there of their own free will and that he would only accept new wives on this condition, and the consent expressed by the women of Kom in their petition, showed that both he and the United Nations understood a wife's initial and continuing consent as necessary to a polygamous household. Yet even if a wife's consent could have been meaningfully ascertained in this patriarchal context, there was no evidence that either the British administration or the Visiting Mission had gone beyond the public assurances of consent offered.⁶¹

Equality as promoted by the visiting missions and the administering authorities

To the extent that the United Nations trusteeship system actively promoted the equality of women, the reports of the administering authorities and the Trusteeship Council visiting missions reveal its model of gender equality as Western relations between women and men – which

---

[58] TC Res. 38 (III) (1948).
[59] Question of the Alleged Libellous Nature of the Petition from St Joan's Social and Political Alliance as Raised in Certain Petitions Concerning the Cameroons under British Administration, TC Res. 186 (VI) (1950).
[60] Compare L. Mani, 'Contentious Traditions: The Debate on *Sati* in Colonial India' in Sangari and Vaid, *Recasting Women*, pp. 88–126 (seeing common ground between the British colonial administrators and local male elites in the debate on *sati* (widow-burning) in colonial India).
[61] It is unclear whether the Visiting Mission spoke separately with the Fon's wives or other Kom women. Visiting Mission to Trust Territories in West Africa (1950), pp. 37–8. Compare U. Narayan, *Dislocating Cultures. Identities, Traditions, and Third World Feminism* (New York: Routledge, 1997), pp. 73–7 (discussing Indian feminists' critiques of a woman's consent to *sati* in current-day India).

were far from equal. What emerges from most of these reports is an inability to see either the possibility that gender equality might look different from Western relations between women and men or the possibility that the model they sought to impose encoded the gender hierarchy of their own Western societies.

Belgium's discussion of the Muhutu and Mututsi women in its reports to the Trusteeship Council on Ruanda-Urundi is perhaps the most obvious instance of a failure to consider that women in the trust territories might traditionally enjoy equal social standing.[62] On the one hand, the excerpt from Belgium's report on Ruanda-Urundi considered by the Commission on the Status of Women at its fourth session in 1950,[63] recorded that Muhutu 'women, and especially mothers, are held in high esteem. Whereas in certain parts of Central Africa a woman is regarded as a mere beast of burden, in Ruanda-Urundi, she is almost the equal of her husband.'[64] As for the Mututsi woman, 'she was hardly able to leave the conjugal *rugo* [rugo – group of huts within an enclosure] and could not perform any laborious task. When obliged to accompany her husband on a journey, she was carried in a hammock. In some cases she enjoys great political or social influence.'[65] On the other hand, the report stated, with apparent satisfaction, that 'attendance at school, clinics and religious services has brought Mututsi women out of their retirement'.[66]

---

[62] At least on the face of the reports, this is not uniformly true of administering authorities. See, e.g., Australia's successive reports on New Guinea in Commission on the Status of Women, Information Concerning the Status of Women in Trust Territories Contained in the Annual Reports Made by the Administering Authorities, 4th Sess., UN Doc. E/CN.6/138 (1950), p. 12 ('customs indicate that the worlds of men and women are in a sense different, but that each is important in its own way'); Commission on the Status of Women, Information Concerning the Status of Women in Trust Territories (Report by the Secretary-General), 18th Sess., UN Doc. E/CN.6/427 (1964), pp. 3–4 (explaining why modernization is eroding the equal but different status of women); Commission on the Status of Women, Information Concerning the Status of Women in Trust and Non-Self-Governing Territories (Report by the Secretary-General), 24th Sess., UN Doc. E/CN.6/560 (1972), pp. 6–7 (registering the inequities brought by modernization: 'one sees women hard at work cultivating the subsistence gardens or carrying heavy loads of foodstuffs in string bags slung from their forehead, while on the new highways men drive the lorries of the cash economy').

[63] This discussion draws only on those portions of the administering authorities' reports reproduced in the Secretary-General's reports on women in trust territories submitted to the Commission on the Status of Women.

[64] Commission on the Status of Women, Information Concerning the Status of Women in Trust Territories Contained in the Annual Reports Made by the Administering Authorities, 4th Sess., UN Doc. E/CN.6/138 (1950), p. 13.

[65] Ibid.   [66] Ibid.

The Belgian description of the Mututsi women considered by the Commission on the Status of Women at its seventh session in 1953 suggested irritation at their seeming indolence: 'The proud and haughty Mututsi women as a general rule never left the family compound; they did no manual work except for a little basket-making. They supervised the work of others'.[67] This report noted more generally that the indigenous women of Ruanda-Urundi showed little inclination to give up their customary role of wife and mother, but insisted that this 'apathy' was no reason to neglect the question.[68]

By the CSW's tenth session in 1956, however, the Belgian report on Ruanda-Urundi reflected a sense of progress:

In the past, although women were not barred by law from any occupation by reason of their sex, it was unusual for them to show any desire to depart from their traditional roles as wives and mothers. Attendance at hospitals, clinics and religious services is daily helping to liberate Mututsi women from their traditional seclusion. Education in the schools has awakened the minds and intelligence of girls.[69]

In an account of women in the Pacific Islands considered by the CSW at its thirteenth session in 1958, the United States implicitly presented as progress the gradual disappearance of social structures favouring women. The American administration's report stated that although the adoption of the Western European family structure by the Chamorros of Saipan had made the father the nominal head of the family, the mother continued to exercise the real power and authority. It reported, however, that in the western islands, the matrilineal descent pattern appeared to be moving toward a patrilineal pattern.[70]

If states administering trust territories were often hopelessly Eurocentric in their approach to relations between women and men in these territories, they tended to be equally oblivious to the gender hierarchy

---

[67] Commission on the Status of Women, Information Concerning the Status of Women in Trust Territories, 7th Sess., UN Doc. E/CN.6/210 (1953), pp. 13–14.

[68] Ibid., p. 14.

[69] Commission on the Status of Women, Information Concerning the Status of Women in Trust Territories (Report by the Secretary-General), 10th Sess., UN Doc. E/CN.6/273 (1956), p. 9.

[70] Commission on the Status of Women, Information Concerning the Status of Women in Trust Territories (Report by the Secretary-General), 13th Sess., UN Doc. E/CN.6/338 (1958), p. 21. The same transition from matrilineal to patrilineal systems was noted among some tribes in the Cameroons under British administration. Commission on the Status of Women, Information Concerning the Status of Women in Trust Territories (Report by the Secretary-General), 14th Sess., UN Doc. E/CN.6/352/Add. 1, (1959), p. 6.

in the European model that they sought to implant. In a report by France on its administration of the Cameroons, considered by the CSW at its seventh session in 1953, modern Western housewifery was presented as the key to the liberation of the territory's women: the French administration 'sends domestic science teachers into the villages and, by means of social workers penetrates into the African home; it tries to liberate women from the burden of centuries of male domination'.[71] On one interpretation, the meaning of this statement might be that modern home economics lightened women's daily duties and freed time for other activities, a point which a 1951 visiting mission made about the social welfare centres in Ruanda-Urundi.[72] Given the visiting mission's description of the social welfare centre programme as also 'designed to give indigenous women a new interest in life... by creating a desire for better homes',[73] the alternative interpretation is that Western domesticity was seen as a good in itself. 'Through the rituals of domesticity, increasingly global and more often than not violent, animals, women and colonized peoples were wrested from their putatively "natural" yet, ironically, "unreasonable" state of "savagery" and inducted through the domestic progress narrative into a hierarchical relation to white men.'[74]

The report on the French Cameroons also gives a glimpse of what the French administration imagined gender equality would look like. It recorded that despite young girls tending to be less receptive to civilization than young men, 'young men with diplomas are more and more frequently able to find wives who, if not quite up to their husbands' level, are at least not far below it'. The examples given of those fortunate matches where 'both husband and wife are educated' were teacher and nurse, and journalist and typist.[75]

[71] Commission on the Status of Women, Information Concerning the Status of Women in Trust Territories, 7th Sess., UN Doc. E/CN.6/210 (1953), p. 12.
[72] UN Visiting Mission to Trust Territories in East Africa, 1951, Report on the Trust Territory of Ruanda-Urundi, TCOR, 11th Sess., Supp. No. 2, UN Doc. T/1031 (1952), para. 205.
[73] 1951 Report on the Trust Territory of Ruanda-Urundi, para. 205.
[74] A. McClintock, *Imperial Leather*, p. 35. Although Anne McClintock is writing about colonialism, the policies of the administering authority did not necessarily break with colonial policies. For example, the British representative argued, in observations on Britain's 1947 report on the Cameroons under British administration, that the Charter and Trusteeship Agreements were based very largely on British policy in the colonies. Report of Trusteeship Council, GAOR, 4th Sess., Supp. No. 4, UN Doc. A/933 (1949), p. 9.
[75] Commission on the Status of Women, Information Concerning the Status of Women in Trust Territories, 7th Sess., UN Doc. E/CN.6/210 (1953), p. 12.

Equality and self-determination in the UN Commission on the Status of Women

By insisting on the immediate granting of independence to colonial peoples, the Declaration on the Independence of Colonial Peoples sought the end of trusteeship. This also spelled the end of the interval in which women's equality could be secured through the international trusteeship system, leaving women's rights instead to the newly independent state. By following the discussion of women in the trust territories by the Commission on the Status of Women, this part of the chapter shows that the Declaration on the Independence of Colonial Peoples and the growing diversity of states represented on the CSW created a turning point for women as well.

As this part traces, the idea and institution of trusteeship has been central to the development of the feminist project in the UN. Women's lobbying in San Francisco had succeeded in hitching equality to the wagon of trusteeship. And it was the CSW's consideration of women in the trust territories that led it to focus on the abolition of traditional practices such as dowry, bride-price, *sati* (widow burning) and child marriage. With the reinterpretation of trusteeship in light of the Declaration on the Independence of Colonial Peoples came the complication of the feminist project – a questioning of priorities and a crisis of confidence about advocating the abolition of traditional practices.

From its very inception, the Commission on the Status of Women sought to promote the equal rights of women in the trust territories through the Trusteeship Council. At its first session in 1947, before the Trusteeship Council had even been established, the CSW proposed that it should consult and collaborate with the Trusteeship Council.[76] In 1949, the CSW requested the Secretary-General to transmit to it any information on the status of women communicated in the administering authorities' annual reports on trust territories and non-self-governing territories.[77] The Secretary-General's reports became the CSW's main

---

[76] Commission on the Status of Women, Report on the First Session, UN Doc. E/281/Rev.1 (1947), para. 24, reprinted in United Nations, *The United Nations and the Advancement of Women*, p. 103 at p. 106. See similarly Petition, Dated 18 May 1947, from the International Alliance of Women, London, England, Concerning the Views of the Organization with Regard to the Status of Women on the Work of the Trusteeship Council (T/Pet./General/7), TCOR, 2nd Sess.: 1st Part, Agenda Item 4, Supplement (1947), p. 205 (proposing that a member of the Commission on the Status of Women be specially associated with the Trusteeship Council's work).

[77] Commission on the Status of Women, Report on the Third Session, ESCOR, 9th Sess., Supp. 5, UN Doc. E/1316 (1949), para. 18.

source of information on women in these territories and the basis for its resolutions on the subject. CSW staff also kept Commission members informed of developments in the Trusteeship Council.[78] In 1951, the Economic and Social Council adopted a resolution, at the CSW's request, inviting member states to nominate and the Trusteeship Council to consider appointing women to serve as members of visiting missions.[79] Another of the CSW's interests in the Trusteeship Council's procedures was the inclusion of particular questions on the status of women in the Trusteeship Council questionnaire that served as the basis for the administering authorities' reports to the Trusteeship Council, and the transmission to the CSW of all information received in response to these questions.[80]

The CSW's initial approach to women in trust and non-self-governing territories was much like the liberal feminist approach of the St Joan's Social and Political Alliance and other international women's organizations.[81] Based on the idea of women as equal

---

[78] Galey, 'Women Find a Place', p. 14.
[79] Status of Women in Trust Territories, ESC Res. 385E (XIII) (1951); Status of Women in Trust Territories, CSW Res. E, Commission on the Status of Women, Report on the Fifth Session, ESCOR, 13th Sess., Supp. 10, UN Doc. E/1997/Rev.1 (1951), p. 15.
[80] E.g. Commission on the Status of Women, Report on the First Session, para. 23; Status of Women, ESC Res. 48 (IV) (1947), C. 2; Questionnaire on Trust Territories as It Relates to the Status of Women, ESC Res. 504K (XVI) (1953); Commission on the Status of Women, Report on the Seventh Session, ESCOR, 16th Sess., Supp. 2, UN Doc. E/2401 (1953), p. 9.
[81] See Petition from the International Alliance of Women, Wembley, England (T/Pet./General/1), TCOR, 1st Sess., Annex 7, Agenda Item 9, Supplement (1947), p. 152; Petition, Dated 28 March 1947, from the British Commonwealth League, London, England, Concerning the Terms of the Draft Convention on Social Policy Drawn Up by the International Labour Organisation (T/Pet./General/3), TCOR, 2nd Sess.: 1st Part, Agenda Item 4, Supplement (1947), p. 200; Petition, Dated 18 April 1947, from the Open Door International, Egehoj, Charlottenlund, Denmark, Concerning the Terms of the Draft Convention on Social Policy Drawn Up by the International Labour Organisation (T/Pet./General/4), TCOR, 2nd Sess.: 1st Part, Agenda Item 4, Supplement (1947), p. 201; Petition, Dated 23 April 1947, from the Open Door International, Belgian Branch, Brussels, Belgium, Concerning the Terms of the Draft Convention on Social Policy Drawn Up by the International Labour Organisation (T/Pet./General/5), TCOR, 2nd Sess.: 1st Part, Agenda Item 4, Supplement (1947), p. 203; Petition, Dated 18 April 1947, from the National Union of Women Teachers, South Kensington, London, England, Concerning the Terms of the Draft Convention on Social Policy Drawn Up by the International Labour Organisation (T/Pet./General/6), TCOR, 2nd Sess.: 1st Part, Agenda Item 4, Supplement (1947), p. 204; Petition, Dated April 1947 from the Open Door Council, Buckinghamshire, England, Concerning the Terms of the Draft Convention on Social Policy Drawn Up by the International Labour Organisation (T/Pet./General/8), TCOR, 2nd Sess.: 1st Part, Agenda Item 4, Supplement (1947), p. 206; Petition, Dated 22 May 1947, from the Women's International Democratic Federation, Paris, France, Concerning the Terms of the Draft Convention on Social

individuals,[82] this approach emphasized equality of civil and political rights and the abolition of traditional practices that violated women's physical integrity.

In the early 1950s, the CSW focused its attention on the political rights of women in trust and non-self-governing territories. For example, a 1953 ESC resolution requested the General Assembly and the Trusteeship Council, in collaboration with states administering trust or non-self-governing territories, to take all necessary measures to develop the political rights of women in these territories and requested the Secretary-General to report to the CSW on the steps taken.[83]

The CSW's consideration of the Secretary-General's reports on women in trust and non-self-governing territories also led it to advocate strongly the abolition of such traditional practices as dowry, bride-price, *sati* and child marriage.[84] In 1952, the Economic and Social Council adopted a Commission resolution inviting the Trusteeship Council, in collaboration with the administering authorities, to take immediately all appropriate measures to promote the progressive abolition of customs which violated the physical integrity of women.[85] The CSW reiterated this recommendation on an almost yearly basis.[86] A 1954 GA resolution was more specific; in territories where women were subject to customs, ancient laws and practices regarding marriage and the family inconsistent with the principles of the Charter and the Universal

Policy Drawn Up by the International Labour Organisation (T/Pet./General/9), TCOR, 2nd Sess.: 1st Part, Agenda Item 4, Supplement (1947), p. 207 (all of which concern the failure to specify sex as a ground of discrimination in the ILO draft convention on social policy in non-metropolitan territories); Petition from the International Abolitionist Federation (T/Pet./General/24), TCOR, 15th Sess., Annexes, Agenda Item 4, UN Doc. T/L.547 (1955), p. 97.

[82] See generally Galey, 'Women Find a Place', pp. 15–21; Reanda, 'The Commission on the Status of Women', pp. 275–89; United Nations, *The United Nations and the Advancement of Women*, pp. 13–25.

[83] Political Rights of Women, ESC Res. 504F (XVI) (1953); CSW Res. F, Commission on the Status of Women, Report on the Seventh Session, p. 18. See also Development of Political Rights of Women in Territories Where These Rights are not Fully Enjoyed, GA Res. 731 (VIII) (1953).

[84] Galey, 'Women Find a Place', p. 19; United Nations, *The United Nations and the Advancement of Women*, p. 22.

[85] Deprivation of Women of Certain Essential Human Rights, ESC Res. 445C (XIV) (1952); Status of Women in Trust and Non-Self-Governing Territories', CSW Res. C, Commission on the Status of Women, Report on the Sixth Session, ESCOR, 14th Sess., Supp. No. 6, UN Doc. E/2208 (1952), p. 14.

[86] Galey, 'Women Find a Place', p. 19. See e.g. Customs, Ancient Laws and Practices Affecting the Human Dignity of Women, ESC Res. 547H (XVIII) (1954); CSW Res. H, Commission on the Status of Women, Report on the Eighth Session, ESCOR, 18th Sess., Supp. 6, UN Doc. E/2571 (1954), p. 23.

Declaration of Human Rights, the resolution urged the administering states to take all appropriate measures to abolish such customs, including by ensuring complete freedom in the choice of a spouse, abolishing the practice of the bride-price, guaranteeing the right of widows to the custody of their children and their freedom to remarry, and eliminating completely child marriages and the betrothal of young girls before the age of puberty.[87] In 1962, the General Assembly adopted a Convention on Consent to Marriage, Minimum Age for Marriage and Registration of Marriages which in its preamble recalled the 1954 GA resolution and reaffirmed that states responsible for the administration of trust and non-self-governing territories should take all appropriate measures to abolish customs, ancient laws and practices relating to marriage and the family that were inconsistent with the principles of the Charter and the Universal Declaration of Human Rights.[88]

With the adoption of the Declaration on the Independence of Colonial Peoples in 1960, the CSW's priority shifted discernibly from achieving women's equal rights through the UN decolonization process to advocating immediate decolonization.[89] Representatives from socialist countries on the Commission[90] argued that improvement in the status of women in trust and non-self-governing territories was linked to the immediate granting of independence to these territories; that is, that colonial women's equal rights depended on the exercise of the right of self-determination of colonial peoples rather than the other way around.[91] Seeing the achievement of self-determination and women's

---

[87] Status of Women in Private Law: Customs, Ancient Laws and Practices Affecting the Human Dignity of Women, GA Res. 843 (IX) (1954).

[88] Convention on Consent to Marriage, Minimum Age for Marriage and Registration of Marriages, New York, 10 December 1962, in force 9 December 1964, 521 UNTS 231. See also Recommendation on Consent to Marriage, Minimum Age for Marriage and Registration of Marriages, GA Res. 2018 (XX) (1965).

[89] E.g. Commission on the Status of Women, Report on the Fifteenth Session, ESCOR, 32nd Sess., Supp. No. 7, UN Doc. E/3464 (1961), p. 4; Commission on the Status of Women, Report on the Eighteenth Session, ESCOR, 39th Sess., Supp. No. 7, UN Doc. E/4025 (1965), p. 9.

[90] Western and pro-Western members from Latin America, Asia and the Middle East dominated the CSW in the early years. There were few Eastern European members, and the first African member state, Ghana, was elected in 1962. More African and Asian states joined the CSW in 1966, when its membership reached thirty-two. Galey, 'Women Find a Place', p. 15.

[91] E.g. Commission on the Status of Women, Report on the Seventeenth Session, ESCOR, 36th Sess., Supp. No. 7, UN Doc. E/3749 (1963), pp. 8–9; UN Doc. E/CN.6/SR.387 (1963), p. 9 (Czechoslovakia); UN Doc. E/CN.6/SR.388 (1963), p. 5 (USSR); UN Doc. E/CN.6/SR.415 (1965), p. 12 (Poland); Commission on the Status of Women, Report on

equality as simultaneous rather than sequential, the representative of Guinea presented Guinea's rejection of foreign domination as simultaneous with its women's rejection of male domination.[92] The view that the exercise of self-determination would further women's equality was later reflected in a 1975 GA resolution calling on states 'to promote vigorously wider participation of women in...the elimination of colonialism, foreign occupation, racism, racial discrimination and apartheid...contributing in this way to the creation of the most favourable conditions for the complete elimination of discrimination against women'.[93] This view dominated the drafting, beginning in 1977, of a declaration on women's participation in the struggle against colonialism, racism, racial discrimination, foreign aggression and occupation and all forms of foreign domination.[94]

The CSW position that the exercise of self-determination must take precedence over women's equality assumed that the newly independent states would promote women's equality. 'No, no, my sister,/my love,' the Malawian poet Felix Mnthali wrote in 'Letter to a Feminist Friend',

> first things first!
> ...
> When Africa
> at home and across the seas
> is truly free
> there will be time for me
> and time for you

---

the Nineteenth Session, ESCOR, 41st Sess., Supp. No. 7, UN Doc. E/4175 (1966), p. 47; UN Doc. E/CN.6/SR.446 (1966), pp. 4 (Hungary), 8 (USSR).

[92] UN Doc. E/CN.6/SR.416 (1965), p. 5. See also UN Doc. E/CN.4/SR.446 (1966), p. 11 (UAR representative commenting that the movement for the emancipation of Egyptian women had been closely bound up with the struggle for national independence).

[93] Equality Between Men and Women and Elimination of Discrimination Against Women, GA Res. 3521 (XXX) (1975). See also Women's Participation in the Strengthening of International Peace and Security and in the Struggle Against Colonialism, Racism, Racial Discrimination, Foreign Aggression and Occupation and All Forms of Foreign Domination, GA Res. 3519 (XXX) (1975).

[94] See Women's Participation in the Strengthening of International Peace and Security and in the Struggle Against Colonialism, Racism, Racial Discrimination, Aggression, Occupation and All Forms of Foreign Domination, GA Res. 32/142 (1977) (requesting the Commission on the Status of Women to prepare a declaration on the subject in preparation for the 1980 World Conference of the United Nations Decade for Women) and the subsequent debates in the Commission on the Status of Women. In particular, see UN Doc. E/CN.6/626 (1980), pp. 8 (Byelorussian SSR), 11 (Hungary), 17 (Ukrainian SSR), 19 (USSR), 22, 24 (GDR).

> to share the cooking
> and change the nappies –
> till then,
> first things first!⁹⁵

Experience has shown, however, that the subordination by women of their struggle for equality to the nationalist struggle has not always been rewarded by the new nationalist government in the form of women's equal rights. To the contrary, women's relegation to roles portrayed as traditional has often been central to the new nation's process of self-assertion.⁹⁶

In the 1960s, the CSW also experienced a crisis of confidence over its stance on traditional practices, dropping the subject after a 1964 seminar at which African women asked that they be allowed to deal with the matter.⁹⁷ After 1962, the representation of African states on the Commission led to a questioning of the Westernization of women in the trust territories. In the CSW's discussion of New Guinea in 1966, the representative of Ghana commented that the noticeable adoption of Western habits of child care, dress and etiquette in New Guinea was both interesting and disturbing. She stated that many of the developing countries were coming to realize that the adoption of Western habits, based on European history and tradition, was not always in the best interests of the indigenous people.⁹⁸

Petitions

As objects of discussion, women in the trust territories could be constructed in universal terms, abstract principles and absolute priorities. This final part of the chapter demonstrates that as speakers, they reflected the variation, concreteness and indivisibility of their identities

---

⁹⁵ Quoted in K. H. Petersen, 'First Things First: Problems of a Feminist Approach to African Literature', reprinted in B. Ashcroft, G. Griffiths and H. Tiffin (eds.), *The Post-Colonial Studies Reader* (London: Routledge, 1995), pp. 251–4 at 252–3.
⁹⁶ See e.g. G. Heng, '"A Great Way to Fly": Nationalism, the State, and the Varieties of Third-World Feminism' in M. J. Alexander and C. T. Mohanty (eds.), *Feminist Genealogies, Colonial Legacies, Democratic Futures* (New York: Routledge, 1997), pp. 30–45; A. Mama, 'Sheroes and Villains: Conceptualizing Colonial and Contemporary Violence Against Women in Africa' in Alexander and Mohanty, *Feminist Genealogies, Colonial Legacies, Democratic Futures*, pp. 46–62; Pettman, *Worlding Women*, pp. 136–40; L. Amede Obiora, 'New Skin, Old Wine: (En)Gaging Nationalism, Traditionalism, and Gender Relations' (1995) 28 *Indiana Law Review* 575.
⁹⁷ Galey, 'Women Find a Place', p. 19.   ⁹⁸ UN Doc. E/CN.6/SR.446 (1966), p. 6.

as individuals, women and part of the people. This part looks at their own interventions in international law through their petitions to the Trusteeship Council. The petitions, some sixty in all, are remarkable, first and foremost, as a neglected archive of women's voices from the trust territories. Like most petitions to the Trusteeship Council,[99] these provoked little or no action. But their importance lies, second, in their problematizing of the dominant images of women's identity created by the Trusteeship Council and the Commission on the Status of Women.[100]

In contrast to the separate identities of individual, woman and people produced by separate institutional dialogues within the United Nations, the petitions by native women and native women's groups reflect the coexistence of these identities. The preamble of an early petition from the Comité féminin de l'Union des Populations du Cameroun reads:

---

[99] Zuijdwijk, *Petitioning the United Nations*, p. 144.

[100] My interest here is in comparing the texts on colonial women produced by different UN processes, the petitions being the closest we can come to the testimony of the women themselves. I therefore do not pursue the questions of representation, voice and language that a fuller treatment of the petitions would involve.

As regards issues of representation, the occasional reference to ignorance of the right to petition and to fears about approaching a visiting mission with a petition (e.g. 1951 Report on the Trust Territory of Ruanda-Urundi, p. 11) or, conversely, being forced to submit a petition (e.g., Petition from the Association of the Women of Eséka (T/Pet.5/254), TCOR, 15th Sess., Annexes, Agenda Item 4, UN Doc. T/L.523 (1955), p. 21) alert us to the possibility of distortion. Apart from outright coercion, the subject matters of the petitions suggest that the petitioners tended to represent the indigenous political elites; for example, women complaining of police brutality toward them during a political event or women's branches of national political parties.

Issues of voice and language would include the style in which the petition was originally written and its possible influence by the form which a United Nations petition was imagined to take, and the fact that the Trusteeship Council sometimes based its deliberations on a summary of the original petition. Rules of Procedure of the Trusteeship Council, Rule 85.

Given the limited nature of the discussion, I also bracket a consideration of the petitions in light of two important bodies of literature. The first is the theoretical literature on the meaning to be given to native speech under colonialism. Compare e.g. H. K. Bhabha, 'Signs Taken for Wonders: Questions of Ambivalence and Authority Under a Tree Outside Delhi, May 1817' (1985) 12 *Critical Inquiry* 144 with G. C. Spivak, 'Can the Subaltern Speak?' in C. Nelson and L. Grossberg (eds.), *Marxism and the Interpretation of Culture* (Urbana: University of Illinois Press, 1988), pp. 271–313; 'Subaltern Talk; Interview with the Editors' in D. Landry and G. MacLean (eds.), *The Spivak Reader: Selected Works of Gayatri Chakravorty Spivak* (New York: Routledge, 1996), pp. 287–308. The second body of literature, which would be relevant to the background of these petitions, is the historical literature on this period and the earlier period of colonialism, in particular on the policies of the relevant states.

Considering that women have the same rights as men, and can no longer be kept on one side when it is a question of the political, economic, social and cultural interests of their country;
Considering that the women of the Cameroons are the victims of a policy of contempt aimed at keeping them always in a state of inferiority;
...
Considering that women are suffering under all kinds of disabilities, for instance, the ban on the sale of provisions at places of work to ensure a supply of food for the workers at mealtimes, the need for women doing part-time work at home to procure seamstresses' licenses, the ban on the women of Bamoun selling their maize outside the district, and market raids of all sorts;
Considering that the policy of racial discrimination treats the women of the Cameroons as contemptible creatures who have no right to get served in butchers' shops in the market, in stores or anywhere else before white women and their servants;
...
Considering that the women of the Cameroons have the right and duty to take part in the work of emancipating our country[101]

The petition is remarkable stylistically because it uses the form and the abstraction of a UN resolution, yet weaves in the daily humiliation of seeing white women's servants get the choicer cut of meat at the butcher's, the details of everyday life that rub in the importance of the higher-sounding concepts. Its requests range similarly from equal rights for women – including their economic empowerment through freedom of trade and provision of agricultural machinery to liberate them from hoeing in plantations and extracting palm oil by pounding – to needs such as maternity homes and midwives, to the end of racism and the unification of the Cameroons.

This early petition by the Comité féminin de l'Union des Populations du Cameroun is the only one that appears to include a request for the formal equality demanded by liberal feminists. The few other petitions that dealt with equal rights were concerned with substantive equality for women. One from the Chairman of the local branch of the Union démocratique des femmes camerounaises (UDEFEC) claimed that many Cameroonian women who had one child or no children never voted, whereas the local branch members believed that 'all women, including

---

[101] Petition from the Comité féminin de l'Union des Populations du Cameroun Concerning the Cameroons under French and under British Administration (T/Pet.5/60-T/Pet.4/32), TCOR, 6th Sess., Annex Vol. 2, Agenda Item 5 (1950), p. 278 at p. 278.

women who have never borne children, have the right to vote. However, they have never been able to vote and have no way of making their opinion known.'[102] A petition from the women teachers of Togoland complained about the lack of equal opportunity for girls to continue their education or learn a trade. At the same time, this petition was concerned with the special needs of women, complaining about medical care for pregnant women, nursing mothers and infants, requesting that scholarships be created for girls to study nursing and midwifery abroad.[103] A number of petitions contained requests for better education and medical facilities, most emphasizing the different needs of girls and women.[104]

If the petitions by native women were not preoccupied with achieving a political and civic status formally identical to men's, there were also no petitions that relied in substance on traditional culture. There were, however, petitions not directly related to women that appeared to rely on the traditional authority of the woman petitioner or petitioners.[105]

---

[102] Petition from the Chairman of the Local Branch of UDEFEC of Hikoajom Concerning the Cameroons under French Administration UN Doc. T/Pet.5/L.52 (1955).

[103] Petition from the Women Teachers of Togoland (T/Pet.6/123), TCOR, 7th Sess., Annex, Agenda Item 5, UN Doc. T/L.101 (1950), p. 15.

[104] Petition from Miss Chanapo (T/Pet.4/192), TCOR, 26th Sess., Annexes, Agenda Item 4, UN Doc. T/L.975 (1960), p. 14 (lack of hospitals, no medicines for women in maternity ward, high cost of hospital treatment, virtual absence of public latrines in Victoria division, women required to obtain market permits in order to trade); Petition from the Union démocratique des femmes camerounaises of the Centre at Loum (T/Pet.5/384), TCOR, 16th Sess., Annexes, Agenda Item 5, UN Doc. T/L.613 (1955), p. 69 (inadequate school and dispensary); Petition from the Editorial Board of the Newspaper Femmes camerounaises (T/Pet.5/618), TCOR, 17th Sess., Annexes, Agenda Item 4, UN Doc. T/L.635 (1956), p. 70 (payment of market fees by widows); Petition from Mrs Suzanna Mbetumou (T/Pet.5/894, sect. 3), TCOR, 21st Sess., Annexes, Agenda Item 5, UN Doc. T/L.825 (1958), p. 39 (village dispensary and social worker inadequate, nurses needed who could treat barren women); Petition from the Société des femmes de Bomp (T/Pet.5/894, sect. 11), TCOR, 21st Sess., Annexes, Agenda Item 5, UN Doc. T/L.825 (1958), p. 39 (dispensary offered inadequate maternity care); Petition from the Women of Awatime (T/Pet.6/129-T/Pet.7-109), TCOR, 7th Sess., Annex, Agenda Item 5, UN Doc. T/L.101 (1950), p. 24 (competent European women teachers should be sent to teach more advanced sewing to girls and doctors sent to train girls in nursing); Petition from the Queen Mother Doe Motte of Ho (T/Pet.6/139), TCOR, 7th Sess., Annex, Agenda Item 5, UN Doc. T/L.101 (1950), p. 24 (need for maternity hospital with mobile clinic, lower hospital fees); Petition from Mrs Fatema Barjeeb, Galcaio (T/Com.11/L.4), TCOR, 12th Sess., Annexes, Agenda Item 5, UN Doc. T/L.345 (1953), p. 43 (special room in hospital needed for women, midwife, special school for girls, women teachers); UN Doc. T/C.2/SR.421 (maternity centres).

[105] See, e.g., Petition from the Queen Mother Doe Motte of Ho (T/Pet.6/139), TCOR, 7th Sess., Annex, Agenda Item 5, UN Doc. T/L.101 (1950), p. 24; Petition from Mesdames Adjoavi Edoh, Atissou Amouzou and Others (T/Pet.7/336), TCOR, 12th Sess., Annexes,

The different identity of women and men is reflected in a petition from Mrs A. Emaimelei on behalf of the women of Palau. The petition requested that women be appointed to the judiciary in Palau for the reasons that there was a good deal of immorality and drunkenness[106] and women magistrates would have more influence with women delinquents; male magistrates were responsible for the delays in enforcing the custom that provided for widows; and admission of women to the judiciary would pave the way for their participation in local government.[107]

The petitions on women's rights and needs are also shot through with the injustice of colonialism as manifested in the discrimination against native women relative to European women. A Togoland woman stated that she earned less as a bank cashier than European women doing the same work, and that the administration did nothing to provide employment for educated young Togoland women.[108] A number of petitions from women in the French Cameroons pointed to the differences between maternity care for European and African women.[109] One also protested at 'the use of family allowance funds for the purchase of motor-coaches for white children while their coloured brothers collapse from fatigue as they walk along the roads under the scorching sun'.[110]

Reflecting the identity of women as part of the people seeking self-determination, a number of petitions by native women and women's organizations, in particular from Italian Somaliland and French Togoland, alleged that their lawful political activities had been hampered or punished by the authorities, thereby violating individual rights such

Agenda Item 5, UN Doc. T/L.359 (1953), p. 72 (on behalf of the grandmothers, mothers and wives of the village of Agbétiko, regarding a dispute over succession to the chieftainship).

[106] Mrs Emaimelei was also the author of a petition from the Women of Palau concerning prohibition of the manufacture of alcohol. Petition from the Women of Palau Concerning Prohibition of the Manufacture of Alcohol (T/Pet.10/3), TCOR, 8th Sess., Annexes, Agenda Item 4, UN Doc. T/L.143 (1951), p. 21.

[107] Petition from Mrs A. Emaimelei on Behalf of the Women of Palau (T/Pet.10/9), TCOR, 12th Sess., Annexes, Agenda Item 5, UN Doc. T/L.369 (1953), p. 87.

[108] Petition from Miss Esther Télé Tekoé (T/Pet.7/471), TCOR, 18th Sess., Annexes, Agenda Item 5, UN Doc. T/L.703 (1956), p. 104.

[109] Petition from Miss Annette Eleanore Biyaga (T/Pet.5/368), TCOR, 16th Sess., Annexes, Agenda Item 5, UN Doc. T/L.613 (1955), p. 68; Petition from Mrs Martha Ngo Mayag (T/Pet.5/502), TCOR, 19th Sess., Annexes, Agenda Item 4, UN Doc. T/L.747 (1957), p. 33; Petition from the Editorial Board of the Newspaper Femmes camerounaises (T/Pet.5/618), TCOR, 19th Sess., Annexes, Agenda Item 4, UN Doc. T/L.747 (1957), p. 35; Eighteen Petitions Raising General Problems in the Cameroons under British Administration and the Cameroons under French Administration, UN Doc. T/Pet.4 & 5/L.24 (1958).

[110] Petition from Mrs Martha Ngo Mayag (T/Pet.5/502), TCOR, 19th Sess., Annexes, Agenda Item 4, UN Doc. T/L.747 (1957), p. 33.

as freedom of association or freedom from arbitrary arrest and detention.[111] Even here, the women's choice of detail is interesting: a nursing mother was detained at the police station,[112] a woman with a baby of eight months on her back was arrested on her way to a meeting,[113] the women detained ranged from the very young to the very old and included some pregnant and some sick women.[114]

---

[111] Petition from Mrs Martha Ngo Mayag (T/Pet.5/502), TCOR, 17th Sess., Annexes, Agenda Item 4, UN Doc. T/L.624 (1956), p. 14 (women's petition confiscated during authority's search of Union des populations du Cameroun office); Petition Dated 19 and 27 June 1951 from Togoland Women (Section féminine de l'Unité togolaise) (T/Pet.7/227, T/Pet.7/227/Add.l), TCOR, 9th Sess., Annexes, Agenda Item 4, UN Doc. T/L.220 (1951), p. 46 (electoral irregularities); Petition Dated 8, 12, and 24 July 1951 from Mr Augustino de Souza and from the Section féminine de l'Unité togolaise (T/Pet.7/237, T/Pet.7/237/Add.l, T/Pet.7/237/Add.2), TCOR, 9th Sess., Annexes, Agenda Item 4, UN Doc. T/L.220 (1951), p. 48 (policemen clubbed group of women on pretext that they were violating municipal prohibition on public meetings); Petition from Miss Béatrice Dweggah (T/Pet.7/388), TCOR, 15th Sess., Annexes, Agenda Item 4, UN Doc. T/L.528 (1955), p. 43 and Petition from Mrs Céline Antoinette Mansah (T/Pet.7/389), TCOR, 15th Sess., Annexes, Agenda Item 4, UN Doc. T/L.528 (1955), p. 43 (two women claimed to have been arrested during a discussion on mass education at Juvento information centre at Lomé and arbitrarily detained); Petition from Mrs Christine Shalman (T/Pet.7/394), TCOR, 15th Sess., Annexes, Agenda Item 4, UN Doc. T/L.528 (1955), p. 47 and Petition from Mrs Emilie D. Mensah (T/Pet.7/396), TCOR, 15th Sess., Annexes, Agenda Item 4, UN Doc. T/L.528 (1955), p. 47 (police brutality directed against people attending political or cultural meetings); Petition from Somali Women in Gardo (T/Pet.11/179), TCOR, 11th Sess., Annexes, Agenda Item 5, UN Doc. T/L.269 (1952), p. 22 (members of the Women's Branch of Somali Youth League arrested at party at the League's club and threatened with exile if they were seen in the club again); Petition from Fatima Haj Omar and Others (T/Pet.11/344), TCOR, 12th Sess., Annexes, Agenda Item 5, UN Doc. T/L.340 (1953), p. 24 (complaints by leaders of women members of the Somali Youth League including break-up of peaceful demonstration in which they were involved, police inaction in face of forcible entry by members of pro-Italian party into house of woman League member); Petition from the Somali Youth League, Branch of Gardo (T/Pet.11/419), TCOR, 15th Sess., Annexes, Agenda Item 4, UN Doc. T/L.550 (1955), p. 105 (women members of Somali Youth League arrested and imprisoned seemingly for joining the League, problems with municipal elections); Petitions from the Great Somalia League Women's Association, Dusa Mareb (T/Pet.11/782 and 816), TCOR, 26th Sess., Annexes, Agenda Item 4, UN Doc. T/L.989 (1960), p. 48; (imprisonment of women, request to demonstrate peacefully).

[112] Petition from Mrs Céline Antoinette Mansah (T/Pet.7/389), TCOR, 15th Sess., Annexes, Agenda Item 4, UN Doc. T/L.528 (1955), p. 43 at p. 44.

[113] Petition from Mrs Emilie D. Mensah (T/Pet.7/396), TCOR, 15th Sess., Annexes, Agenda Item 4, UN Doc. T/L.528 (1955), p. 47 at p. 48. In its observations, the Administering Authority dismissed the charges as imaginary, remarking in particular that it was not customary for a woman to attend a public meeting carrying a baby of eight months on her back. UN Doc. T/OBS.7/23, section 5, summarized with petition.

[114] Petitions from the Great Somalia League Women's Association, Dusa Mareb (T/Pet. 11/782 and 816), TCOR, 26th Sess., Annexes, Agenda Item 4, UN Doc. T/L.989 (1960), p. 48.

The distinct identity of women within a people seeking self-determination is also suggested by a series of petitions by women from the French Cameroons. Several petitions presented the special victimization of women by the colonial administration among the reasons for independence.[115] One in particular sheds light on the intersection of sexism and colonialism.[116] The petitioner complained that 'White women everywhere, including the French, receive support when they fight for a cause, but in the Cameroons we have no one to rely on as we struggle for freedom.' She went on to state that Cameroonian women were 'fettered and led about like goats' by the French[117] and, as a result, pregnant women often miscarried, adding that French women were the only women to receive jobs created by new businesses. 'We believe', she concluded her petition, 'that representatives of the great Powers will neither abandon us nor condemn the weaker sex.' In contrast, the members of the Gazelle Women's Club at Vunamami in New Guinea told a visiting mission that

they feared trouble and chaos would result from attaining self-government too quickly. They felt that the Administering Authority should try to unite people, for without unity self-government was premature. Besides this they asked that the Government help to build more women's club houses. They wanted better housing and equipment such as stoves, sewing machines, toilets, etc., so that people would be in a better position to help themselves. Several club members

---

[115] Petition from the Union Démocratique des Femmes Camerounaises, Local Branch of Toumko Manjo Concerning the Cameroons under French Administration, UN Doc. T/Pet.5/88 (1956); Petition from the Libong Local Committee of the Union Démocratique des Femmes Camerounaises Concerning the Cameroons under French Administration, UN Doc. T/Pet.5/1223 (1957); Petition from Mrs Monique Tang Concerning the Cameroons under French Administration, UN Doc. T/Pet.5/1232 (1957); Petition from Mrs Rebecca Tchiasseup Concerning the Cameroons under French Administration, UN Doc. T/Pet.5/L.274 (1957); Petition from Mrs Victoire Tchamambo Concerning the Cameroons under French Administration, UN Doc. T/Pet.5/L.283 (1957); Petition from Mrs Justine Neumbue Concerning the Cameroons under French Administration, UN Doc. T/Pet.5/L.334 (1957); 78 Petitions Raising General Problems Concerning the Cameroons under French Administration, UN Doc. T/Pet.5/L.455 (1958). See also Petition from the Nyagatare Women's League Concerning Ruanda-Urundi, UN Doc. T/Pet.3/L.114 (1961); Petition from Mrs Theresia Nana, President of the Women's Committee of One Kamerun, in Tiko (T/Pet.4/156), TCOR, 23rd Sess., Annexes, Agenda Item 5, UN Doc. T/L.903 (1959), p. 22.

[116] Petition from Mrs Victoire Tchamambo Concerning the Cameroons under French Administration, UN Doc. T/Pet.5/L.283 (1957).

[117] Another petition complained that judicial authorities strip women in the marketplace, seeing this as further proof that 'in the eyes of the French government the Cameroonian women are goats at pasture'. Petition from Mrs Justine Neumbue Concerning the Cameroons under French Administration, UN Doc. T/Pet.5/L.334 (1957).

complained that men were spending too much money on liquor to the detriment of their families.[118]

Even in petitions that advocate independence on non-gendered grounds, the self is usually identified as 'we, the women'. One petitioner requested that the 1955 decree outlawing the Union démocratique des femmes camerounaises be annulled, that United Nations-supervised elections be held and that Cameroonian unity and independence be proclaimed by the winner. Writing as 'we, the Cameroonian people and the women of the Cameroons', she argued that 'whereas it is we women who populate the earth with men it is you UN who take a decision which causes their bloodshed'.[119]

In Chapter 6, we saw that the interwar plebiscites intertwined the history of women's equality with the history of self-determination in international law. In the interpretation given to suffrage, the interpretation of self-determination advanced women's equality. While women were divided over their identity as women and its relationship to nationalism and internationalism, they were not divided over their goals of women's suffrage and independent nationality for married women.

In this chapter, the concept of trusteeship in the UN Charter twisted the strands of women's equality and self-determination together again: equal rights were built into the interpretation of self-determination through trusteeship. But this victory by women during the drafting of the Charter was questioned as a victory for Western women at the expense of the agency of women in the trust territories. Through the petitions of international women's organizations to the Trusteeship Council and the resolutions of the Commission on the Status of Women, Western women sought to impose their liberal feminism on women in the trust territories. In this sense, they were allies of the international trusteeship system at large, which objectified women by projecting onto them

---

[118] UN Visiting Mission to the Trust Territories of Nauru and New Guinea, 1965, Report on New Guinea, TCOR, 32nd Sess., Supp. 3, UN Doc. T/1646 (1965), para. 145, reprinted in Commission on the Status of Women, Information Concerning the Status of Women in Trust Territories (Report by the Secretary-General), 19th Sess., UN Doc. E/CN.6/446 (1965), p. 5.

[119] Petition from Mrs Rachel Ndambouen Concerning the Cameroons under French Administration, UN Doc. T/Pet.5/1465 (1959). See also Petition from Mrs Rebecca Tchoufe Concerning the Cameroons under French Administration, UN Doc. T/Pet.5/1466 (1959); Petition from Miss Rose Aghemetekpon Concerning Togoland under British Administration and Togoland under French Administration, UN Doc. T/Pet.6 and 7/L.65 (1956).

competing versions of nationalism and gender. While later discussions in the Commission on the Status of Women introduced the idea of self-determination as a condition for women's equality, this inversion simply objectified women in nationalism differently. In the final part of this chapter, I used the petitions submitted to the Trusteeship Council by women in the trust territories themselves to highlight both their agency and the complexity of their subjective identity.

8 Indigenous women and self-determination

In *Sandra Lovelace* v. *Canada*,[1] an indigenous woman successfully challenged the provision of the Canadian Indian Act that deprived her of her status as an Indian[2] because she had married a non-Indian man, but would not have done so had it been an Indian man who married a non-Indian woman. This 1981 decision[3] by the United Nations Human Rights Committee is often cited as pitting the equal rights of women against the right of self-determination of peoples,[4] whether defined in terms of culture (the group's right to apply its traditional membership

---

[1] *Sandra Lovelace* v. *Canada* (Communication No. 24/1977, formerly Communication No. R.6/24), GAOR, 36th Sess., Supp. No. 40, UN Doc. A/36/40 (1981), p. 166 (merits). See also *Sandra Lovelace* v. *Canada* (Communication No. 24/1977), Selected Decisions under the Optional Protocol, vol. I (New York: United Nations, 1985), UN Doc. CCPR/C/OP/1, p. 10 (admissibility), p. 37 (interim decision); Response of the Government of Canada (Communication No. 24/1977), GAOR, 38th Sess., Supp. No. 40, UN Doc. A/38/40 (1983), p. 249.

While this chapter draws on the history of *Lovelace*, a full account of the First Nations politics associated with the case is beyond its scope. For an overview, see J. Borrows, 'Contemporary Traditional Equality: The Effect of the *Charter* on First Nations Politics' (1994) 43 *University of New Brunswick Law Journal* 19.

[2] In Canada, the federal Indian Act defines and employs the controversial legal category of 'Indian'. The Constitution Act 1982 uses the term 'aboriginal' to refer to indigenous peoples including the Métis and the Inuit. Accordingly, this chapter refers to 'Indian' and 'aboriginal' in connection with these legal texts. In general contexts, the international legal term 'indigenous' is used.

At the same time, it is important to keep in mind that indigenous women are not homogeneous, whatever the common experience wrought by colonialism and the legal designation 'Indian' or 'non-Indian'. Their linguistic and cultural affiliations may be, for example, Cree, Iroquois or Ojibway.

[3] While the Human Rights Committee technically considers 'communications' and issues 'views', this chapter also uses more generic terminology.

[4] As discussed above in the Introduction at note 52 and accompanying text, *Lovelace* does not raise an issue of self-determination under the International Covenant on Civil and Political Rights (New York, 16 December 1966, in force 23 March 1976, 999

rules) or autonomy (the group's right to set the rules).[5] For those who side with the equal rights of women, the Indian Act raises the same issue as the collective option in the 1919 peace treaties and the underlying principle of dependent nationality of married women: a woman's right to choose her membership in the self – state, nation, people, minority – on the same basis as a man. And, indeed, the Indian Act followed the principle of dependent nationality consistently. Not only did it deprive an Indian woman who married a non-Indian man of her Indian status, it granted Indian status to a non-Indian woman who married an Indian man. From this perspective, Sandra Lovelace simply brought the campaign for women's equal rights, begun by white women in the civilized world[6] and promoted by them elsewhere,[7] to her own primitive community. The resistance she encountered therefore falls into line with the Fon of Bikom and others who asserted their own culture and power of decision against the UN decolonization process.[8]

By starting from Lovelace's own arguments to the Human Rights Committee, much as the last chapter emphasized the petitions from women in the trust territory themselves, this chapter offers an alternative reading of both the arguments and the decision in *Lovelace*. On this reading, Lovelace's claim to equality is not strongly in tension with indigenous self-determination, but rather is in opposition to the changes that colonialism had wrought in indigenous societies. Correspondingly, her arguments may be seen not as prioritizing her identity as a woman, but as reflecting her indigenousness as well. 'Our struggle as Aboriginal women cannot be separated, even for a moment, from our struggle as a people,' Andrea Bear Nicholas has written of Maliseet women like herself and Sandra Lovelace.[9] Moreover, the reading of the *Lovelace* decision developed in the chapter is consonant with this predicament in ways that the usual framing of the decision as an either-or problem is not. We thus find in the decision one of the threads that – this book has argued – run

UNTS 171), but examines an issue of the 'self' also found in the interpretation of self-determination. Moreover, the broader context of *Lovelace* should be understood as the right of self-determination in that many indigenous peoples in Canada assert a sovereignty that would give them the right to independence.

[5] E.g., D. S. Berry, 'Contextualising International Women's Rights: Canadian Feminism, Race and Culture' in C. McGlynn (ed.), *Legal Feminisms: Theory and Practice* (Aldershot, England: Ashgate/Dartmouth, 1998), pp. 119–34; H. Charlesworth and C. Chinkin, *The Boundaries of International Law: A Feminist Analysis* (Manchester: Manchester University Press, 2000), pp. 223–4.

[6] See Chapter 6 above.   [7] See Chapter 7 above.   [8] *Ibid.*

[9] A. Bear Nicholas, 'Colonialism and the Struggle for Liberation: The Experience of Maliseet Women' (1994) 43 *University of New Brunswick Law Journal* 223 at 238.

through the major third-party interpretations of self-determination: the use of an intermediate concept in an attempt to do justice to identity.

Equality

Sandra Lovelace was born and registered as a 'Maliseet Indian'. Under section 12(1)(b) of the Canadian Indian Act, Lovelace lost her Indian status when she married a non-Indian man in 1970.[10] Her loss of status meant that she could not convey Indian status to her children. Her marriage also deprived her of membership in the Tobique band.[11] This, in turn, meant that she was no longer legally entitled to live on the Tobique Reserve in New Brunswick,[12] where she had been living with her parents at the time of her marriage.[13] The loss of her right to possess or reside on reserve lands included the loss of the right to inherit a possessory interest in the land from her parents and the right to be buried on the reserve.[14] At the time of the case, Sandra Lovelace was living on the reserve, but had no right to remain there.[15] Moreover, she did not have her own place to live and, as a non-status Indian, would not have been able to borrow money for housing from the Band Council.[16] In his dissent in *Canada AG v. Lavell*, the 1973 Supreme Court of Canada judgment which found that section 12(1)(b) did not violate the right of equality guaranteed by the Canadian Bill of Rights, Justice Laskin summarized the effect of section 12(1)(b) on Indian women who married non-Indian men as 'statutory banishment'.[17]

In *Lovelace*, the Human Rights Committee considered possible violations of four groups of rights under the International Covenant on Civil and Political Rights: general provisions against discrimination (Articles 2, 3, 26), the right to choose one's residence (Article 12), rights aimed at protecting family life and children (Articles 17, 23 and 24) and the rights of persons belonging to ethnic, religious or linguistic minorities (Article 27).[18] It found that Canada had violated the minority rights guaranteed by Article 27 because Sandra Lovelace had been denied the legal right to live on the Tobique Reserve.[19]

It is striking that although the Committee did not base its views, or based them only weakly, on any of the Covenant articles on sex discrimination, *Lovelace* is often portrayed as a victory for women's equality.

[10] *Lovelace v. Canada* (merits), p. 166.   [11] *Ibid.*, p. 169.   [12] *Ibid.*   [13] *Ibid.*, p. 170.
[14] *Ibid.*, p. 171.   [15] *Ibid.*, p. 170.   [16] *Ibid.*, pp. 170–1.
[17] *Canada AG v. Lavell* (1973), [1974] SCR 1349 at 1386.
[18] *Lovelace v. Canada* (merits), p. 172. Lovelace herself appears to have argued only Articles 2, 3, 23, 26 and 27. *Ibid.*, p. 166.
[19] *Ibid.*, p. 174.

One reason for this impression may be the outcome; the Committee's decision did remedy the effects of the statutory discrimination for Lovelace and helped to speed the amendments that removed much of the discrimination in the statute itself.[20] Another explanation lies in the projection of the expectations of the time onto the decision. Professor Donald Fleming, who assisted Lovelace, recollects that no one he spoke with during the years the case was under consideration anticipated that the Committee would rely on Article 27.[21] The downplaying of this reliance is furthered and, indeed, rationalized by Anne Bayefsky's much-cited commentary on *Lovelace*.[22] Bayefsky argues essentially that we should take *Lovelace* as a decision about women's equality because the Committee *wanted* to say and *should have* said that there had been a violation of Covenant Article 2(1) on non-discrimination, but wrongly concluded that it had no competence to do so.

Bayefsky's argument relies on the fact that at the time of Sandra Lovelace's marriage and loss of Indian status by application of section 12(1)(b) of the Indian Act, the International Covenant on Civil and Political Rights had not yet come into force for Canada.[23] The Human Rights Committee therefore found that it could not rule on the original cause of her loss of status, that is, the Indian Act as applied to her at the time of her marriage, but only on any continuing effects of its application.[24] According to Bayefsky, the Committee limited its decision to Article 27, the minority rights article, because it overcautiously concluded that it also could not consider whether any continuing effects might violate the articles on sex discrimination. Bayefsky implies that had the Committee not felt itself constrained in this way, it would have said what it really wanted to say – and, to her mind, should have

---

[20] *Response of Canada*, pp. 250–3. Amendments to the Indian Act had been contemplated by the federal government throughout the period of *Lavell* and *Lovelace*, but Bill C-31, the package of amendments that ended much of the discrimination in the Act, only came into force in 1985. On the amendments and their effect, see e.g. Borrows, 'Contemporary Traditional Equality', 32–40; P. Macklem, *Indigenous Difference and the Constitution of Canada* (Toronto: University of Toronto Press, 2001), pp. 227–31; W. Moss, 'Indigenous Self-Government in Canada and Sexual Equality Under the *Indian Act*: Resolving Conflicts Between Collective and Individual Rights' (1990) 15 *Queen's Law Journal* 279 at 280–3.

[21] Letter from Professor Donald J. Fleming to the author, 28 May 1999.

[22] A. F. Bayefsky, 'The Human Rights Committee and the Case of Sandra Lovelace' (1982) 20 *Canadian Yearbook of International Law* 244. To similar effect, see C. Jones, 'Towards Equal Rights and Amendment of Section 12(1)(b) of the Indian Act: A Post-Script to Lovelace v. Canada' (1985) 8 *Harvard Women's Law Journal* 195 at 210–11; M. Nowak, *UN Covenant on Civil and Political Rights: CCPR Commentary* (Kehl: N. P. Engel, Publisher, 1993), pp. 70, n. 23; 505.

[23] *Lovelace v. Canada* (merits), p. 168.   [24] *Ibid.*, pp. 172, 174.

said – about the continuing violation. Since the Committee needlessly tied its hands, Bayefsky hints, *Lovelace* can be taken for what it actually meant and ought to have said: that the case was about sex discrimination. She chides the Committee as follows:

> It might, therefore, *have been more accurate* for the Human Rights Committee to have decided that Lovelace was denied the right to enjoy her culture and to use her language in community with other members of her band, in a discriminatory fashion or because she was a woman. In other words, there was a violation of Article 2(1) in relation to the right embodied in Article 27. The Committee, however, was of the view that only by confining the violation to Article 27 could it avoid the problem that loss of Indian status occurred prior to the Covenant coming into force for Canada. It is to be hoped that its use of the Covenant to describe the derogation of rights that results from section 12(1)(b) of the Indian Act *will be more exact* in the upcoming case.[25]

Bayefsky thus uses the problem of timing to read the Committee's decision in *Lovelace* as about women's equality. Her rhetoric of accuracy and exactitude implicitly gives us licence to correct for the Committee's excessive caution in confining itself to Article 27 and to do so by adding Article 2(1), which guarantees respect for all rights in the Covenant without distinction as to sex.

Lovelace's arguments

While Sandra Lovelace did argue that the Canadian Indian Act was contrary to the equality provisions of the International Covenant on Civil and Political Rights, she also disputed the Canadian government's contention that the Act reflected an Indian tradition of patrilineal legal relationships.[26] One of the government's two main justifications for section 12(1)(b) was that it employed the same definition of Indian as Indians themselves did; the Indian Act traced Indian status through the father's line just as Indian tradition was patrilineal.[27] It follows that

---

[25] (Emphasis mine) Bayefsky, 'The Case of Sandra Lovelace', 263. The 'upcoming case' alluded to by Bayefsky is presumably the communication by Paula Sappier Sisson. See Response of Canada, p. 250. There appears to be no record of this case in the UN Human Rights Committee's publications. See also *L. S. N. v. Canada* (Communication No. 94/1981), Selected Decisions of the Human Rights Committee under the Optional Protocol, vol. II (New York: United Nations, 1990), UN Doc. CCPR/C/OP/2, p. 6 (subsequently withdrawn).

[26] *Lovelace v. Canada* (merits), p. 167.

[27] *Ibid*. The Council of the Six Nations factum in *Lavell* supported this position. K. Jamieson, *Indian Women and the Law in Canada: Citizens Minus* (Minister of Supply and Services Canada, 1978), p. 87.

status Indians and 'real' Indians were identical. Moreover, the Canadian government accepted that Indian tradition, or self-definition, was not static and that any change in the law could only be made in consultation with the Indians.[28]

The Canadian government's other main justification was that the special privileges granted to Indian communities, in particular the right to occupy reserve lands, created the need for a definition of Indian. On this justification, the Indian Act did not define all 'real' Indians. The need to protect scarce resources and preserve Indian society and culture meant not all 'real' Indians could live on reserves. Status Indians were the subset of 'real' Indians that were entitled to do so. Indian women who 'married out' lost their status and Indian men did not because non-Indian husbands were in nineteenth-century farming societies and continued to be a much greater threat to reserve land than non-Indian wives.[29]

Lovelace challenged the Canadian government's assertion that indigenous peoples were traditionally patrilineal. Bet-te Paul, one of the women from the Tobique Reserve who encouraged Sandra Lovelace to bring her case to the Human Rights Committee, described what she discovered about Maliseet society when she began digging:

> it was matrilineal... there was a special relationship between the elder women and the young girls. Also, the elder women were the ones to hold places in council and guide the men. We had chiefs, but the elder women were behind the men; they were listened to and held in high respect... The married women looked after the families, and had a say in anything that concerned the community...
> ... The blood comes from the mother, not the father, which is exactly the opposite of what the Indian Act imposed on us.[30]

In her inquiry into the role of women in Maliseet society and how that role had been changed by colonialism, Andrea Bear Nicholas concluded that the

> dispersal of decision-making among both men and women in traditional Maliseet society is certainly confirmed by any knowledge of our culture and history. It shows up in our language, which has no gender. It shows up in our terms of kinship which, for the most part, are precisely the same for maternal relatives as for paternal relatives, indicating a means of reckoning lineage and

---

[28] *Lovelace* v. *Canada* (merits), p. 167.   [29] *Ibid.*
[30] Tobique Women's Group, *Enough is Enough: Aboriginal Women Speak Out*, as told to J. Silman (Toronto: The Women's Press, 1987), p. 226.

relationships that is neither patriarchal nor matriarchal, but bilateral. According to our recently deceased elder, Dr Peter Paul, our people showed a strong tendency toward matrilocality insofar as a husband often took up residence in or near the family of the wife.[31]

For the Maliseet, then, the Indian Act legislated not indigenous custom, but European patriarchy.[32] As the following conversation between Sandra Lovelace and another Maliseet woman illustrates, however, the Maliseet tended to internalize the patriarchy of the Indian Act over time.

> SANDRA [LOVELACE SAPPIER]: [The chiefs] said things like, 'You've made your bed [by marrying a non-Indian], now sleep in it'; 'My (white) wife is an Indian because the law says she is.'
> KAREN [PERLEY]: They *believed*, the government says you're Indian, so you're Indian. Therefore the government tell us we're not Indian, so we're not Indians.
> SANDRA: Then we'd start arguing. Heavy arguments! (laughter) 'I was born an Indian,' that's what I'd tell them.
> KAREN: If they believed that, where is the reason in all of it? Sometimes your own flesh and blood would say, 'You're not an Indian any more. That's the law; that's the Indian Act.' See how law-abiding Native Indian people are? (laughter) So we'd have these chiefs telling us, 'It's our *right* to discriminate.'
> SANDRA: A few chiefs supported us... But most of them are chauvinist. They'd say, 'You're only a woman, so what do you know? Go watch your babies, clean your house.' That's the attitude.[33]

Unlike Lovelace's sex discrimination argument, which measured the definition of the self against the external standard of equality in the Covenant, her invocation of a matrilineal tradition was thus internal to the historical definition of themselves that some indigenous peoples had.[34]

---

[31] (Footnotes omitted) Nicholas, 'Colonialism and the Struggle for Liberation', 229.

[32] For the same assertion with respect to the Shuswap Nation in British Columbia, see *R. L. v. Canada* (Communication No. 358/1989), GAOR, 47th Sess., Supp. No. 40, UN Doc. A/47/40 (1994), p. 358 at pp. 358–9. More generally, see Chapter 7 above at note 70 and accompanying text (administering authorities reporting a transition from matrilineal to patrilineal systems in certain trust territories).

[33] Tobique Women's Group, *Enough is Enough*, pp. 239–40. See also Nicholas, 'Colonialism and the Struggle for Liberation', 235–6. This was also true of other indigenous peoples. Borrows, 'Contemporary Traditional Equality', 27; L. E. Krosenbrink-Gelissen, *Sexual Equality as an Aboriginal Right. The Native Women's Association of Canada and the Constitutional Process on Aboriginal Matters, 1982–1987* (Nijmegen Studies in Development and Cultural Change, vol. VII) (Saarbrücken: Verlag Breitenbach, 1991), p. 83.

[34] E.g. D. A. Grinde, Jr. and B. E. Johansen, *Exemplar of Liberty: Native America and the Evolution of Democracy* (Los Angeles: American Indian Studies Center, UCLA, 1991), pp. 221–33; Jamieson, *Indian Women and the Law in Canada*, pp. 8–13; Native Women's Association of Canada, *Matriarchy and the Canadian Charter: A Discussion Paper* (Ottawa, 1992).

If Sandra Lovelace's assertion that the Indian Act could not be justified as codifying Indian tradition is seen as an identification with indigenous peoples and their process of self-determination, it complicates her position relative to those indigenous peoples who argued that self-determination should take priority over women's equality. Seven years before the Human Rights Committee's decision in *Lovelace*, Jeanette Corbière Lavell and Yvonne Bédard, Ojibway and Iroquois Indians respectively who had lost their status when they married non-Indians, had failed in their equality challenge to section 12(1)(b) under the Canadian Bill of Rights.[35] In the *Lavell* case, the vast majority of indigenous organizations[36] intervened against Lavell and Bédard, for reasons of either strategy or discrimination.[37] *Lavell* also resulted in the formation of the Native Women's Association of Canada, which has since played a major part in advocating equality for indigenous women on the Canadian political and legal scene.

Indigenous women also differed among themselves as to whether their struggle for equality should take priority over the larger movement for indigenous self-government and, furthermore, what form that equality and its guarantees should take. For Sandra Lovelace and the women from the Tobique Reserve who were in the forefront of the campaign

---

Whether Lovelace's strategy was consistent with indigenous culture is a different question. See e.g. T. Isaac and M. S. Maloughney, 'Dually Disadvantaged and Historically Forgotten?: Aboriginal Women and the Inherent Right of Aboriginal Self-Government' (1992) 21 *Manitoba Law Journal* 453 at 464 (using white law means co-opted by white society); Borrows, 'Contemporary Traditional Equality', 43 (adversarialism inimical to First Nations professions of consensus, harmony and respect); Moss, 'Indigenous Self-Government in Canada and Sexual Equality Under the *Indian Act*', 299 (threat of imposition of externally developed norms even if they coincide with internal cultural norms).

[35] Even earlier, Mary Two-Axe Early and other Indian women had brought the problem to the attention of a Royal Commission on the Status of Women. Borrows, 'Contemporary Traditional Equality', 26.

[36] Lavell and Bédard were supported by a few women's organizations, the Native Council of Canada, and Anishnarvbekwek of Ontario Incorporated. The position of the Attorney General of Canada was supported by the Indian Association of Alberta, the Union of British Columbia Indian Chiefs, the Manitoba Indian Brotherhood Inc., the Union of New Brunswick Indians, the Indian Brotherhood of the Northwest Territories, the Union of Nova Scotia Indians, the Union of Ontario Indians, the Federation of Saskatchewan Indians, the Indian Association of Quebec, the Yukon Native Brotherhood, the National Indian Brotherhood (forerunner of the Assembly of First Nations), the Six Nations Band and the Treaty Voice of Alberta Association. *Canada AG v. Lavell*, 1378.

[37] *Native Women's Association of Canada v. Canada*, [1992] 3 Canada Federal Court Reports 192 at 206 (Federal Court of Appeal); Borrows, 'Contemporary Traditional Equality', 26–7; Krosenbrink-Gelissen, *Sexual Equality as an Aboriginal Right*, p. 83.

to change the discriminatory rules on status in the Indian Act, equality had to come before self-government.³⁸ Others maintained that equality could not be disaggregated from the political environment for indigenous beliefs and existence in Canada. Mary Ellen Turpel, for example, objected to any reform to the Indian Act as tampering with an ethically unacceptable piece of colonial legislation.³⁹ 'Before imposing upon us the logic of gender equality (with White men), what about ensuring for our cultures and political systems equal legitimacy with the Anglo-Canadian cultural perspective which dominates the Canadian State?'⁴⁰

In this light, Sandra Lovelace's allusion to matrilineal tradition complicates the criticism that she and the other Tobique women adopted the white feminists' goal of equality over the indigenous goal of self-determination. Eva (Gookum) Saulis, one of the Tobique women, gave an example of white women's misunderstanding of the equal and complementary places of men and women in indigenous society:

[In] old pictures of an Indian family moving from one place to another; you'd see a man walking ahead with his bow and arrow and the woman walking behind with small children, hauling that *travois*. It looks like she's doing all the hard work.

I heard remarks about that by white women, 'I don't want to be your squaw. I don't want to work hard like that.' But there is a reason for why that man walked ahead. It's because he had to protect his family against animals and enemies. It wasn't that the woman walked behind him because she had to do everything. Like when the woman had to look after the family, it was because the men went away to provide for them by trapping or working in the woods. 'Being a squaw' wasn't a worse or unequal thing. Everything had a *purpose*.⁴¹

The Tobique women thus shared with Mary Ellen Turpel and other indigenous women an attention to what they saw as the traditional

---

[38] Tobique Women's Group, *Enough is Enough*, pp. 244 (Sandra Lovelace Sappier), 247 (Shirley Bear). This is not to say that they did not also support self-government. See e.g. *ibid.*, p. 224 (Juanita Perley).

[39] M. E. Turpel, 'Discrimination and the 1985 Amendments to the Indian Act: Full of Snares for Women' (September 1987) *Rights and Freedoms* 6. See also M. E. Turpel (Aki-Kwe), 'Patriarchy and Paternalism: The Legacy of the Canadian State for First Nations Women' (1993) 6 *Canadian Journal of Women and the Law* 174 at 177.

[40] Turpel, 'Patriarchy and Paternalism', 183. See also R. Johnson, W. Stevenson and D. Greschner, 'Peekiskwetan' (1993) 6 *Canadian Journal of Women and the Law* 153 at 159, 170–1 (Winona Stevenson); P. Monture-Angus, *Thunder in My Soul: A Mohawk Woman Speaks* (Halifax: Fernwood Publishing, 1995), p. 229.

[41] Tobique Women's Group, *Enough is Enough*, p. 216. On differences between feminist and indigenous women's perspectives, see, e.g., Monture-Angus, *Thunder in My Soul*, pp. 229–35; Johnson, Stevenson and Greschner, 'Peekiskwetan', 159–60 (Winona Stevenson).

relationship of equality and complementarity between indigenous men's and women's roles.⁴²

Taken together, Sandra Lovelace's arguments to the Human Rights Committee suggest an attempt to present her identity as a woman within the context of colonialism. In contrast, Bayefsky's commentary on *Lovelace* emphasizes and authenticates Sandra Lovelace's complaint as part of the struggle of all women for equality, while minimizing and problematizing Lovelace's claim about the cultural violence of colonialism. Although Bayefsky reproduces the parties' arguments on whether indigenous peoples were traditionally patrilineal in a section of her commentary summarizing the proceedings,⁴³ she cordons them off as a factual dispute in another section entitled 'An Historical Survey'.⁴⁴ By assigning the meaning of women's equal rights to the Human Rights Committee's decision, Bayefsky associates Sandra Lovelace's identity as a woman with the normative and thereby, paradoxically, with the real; and Lovelace's vision of a lost matriarchy with the factual and thereby, paradoxically, with the fictional.⁴⁵ In so doing, moreover, Bayefsky lends support to the indigenous criticism of Sandra Lovelace and other women from the Tobique Reserve as 'white-washed women's libbers'.⁴⁶

Views in Lovelace

If reading *Lovelace* as a decision about women's equality implicitly identifies Sandra Lovelace with women over indigenous peoples, despite

---

⁴² E.g. V. Kirkness, 'Emerging Native Woman' (1987–8) 2 *Canadian Journal of Women and the Law* 408; Monture-Angus, *Thunder in My Soul*, p. 224; T. Nahanee, 'Dancing with a Gorilla: Aboriginal Women, Justice and the *Charter*' in Royal Commission on Aboriginal Peoples, *Aboriginal Peoples and the Justice System: Report of the National Round Table on Aboriginal Justice Issues* (Ottawa: Minister of Supply and Services Canada, 1993), pp. 359–82 at p. 361; Osennontion and Skonaganleh:rá, 'Our World' (1989) 10 (2–3) *Canadian Women's Studies* 7 at 15. Compare Krosenbrink-Gelissen, *Sexual Equality as an Aboriginal Right*, pp. 36–58 (on the contingency of perceptions of the traditional positions of Indian women).

⁴³ Bayefsky, 'The Case of Sandra Lovelace', 247–8.   ⁴⁴ *Ibid.*, 257.

⁴⁵ In *Sawridge Band v. Canada*, [1996] 1 Canada Federal Court Reports 3, the Trial Division of the Federal Court of Canada accepted the anthropological evidence of the defendant's expert, Dr Alexander von Gernet, that lineality itself as a criterion for membership in an aboriginal group 'is merely an artificial construct that confines the notion of "membership" to a particular theoretical abstraction'. According to von Gernet, the decision as to 'which one of a profusion of practices should serve as the "traditional" culture of a twentieth-century society' is inappropriate for an anthropologist to make. At paras. 148–9. The Federal Court of Appeal later ordered a new trial on the ground of a reasonable apprehension of judicial bias. *Sawridge Band v. Canada*, [1997] 3 Canada Federal Court Reports 580.

⁴⁶ Tobique Women's Group, *Enough is Enough*, p. 13.

the predicament of identity reflected in her arguments, such a reading is made more questionable by the Human Rights Committee's apparent avoidance of the binary choice between women's equality and self-determination.

On the most straightforward reading, the Human Rights Committee in *Lovelace* identified Sandra Lovelace with an ethnic, religious or linguistic minority under Article 27 of the Covenant. A minority within the meaning of Article 27 is independent of any definition in domestic law; in this case, the category of 'Indian' under the Canadian Indian Act. Abstracted from the Committee's reasoning in *Lovelace*, the test for membership in a minority group has both an objective and a subjective element, where the latter involves the desire of the individual as opposed to the self-understanding of the group. A minority within the meaning of Article 27 would normally encompass 'persons who are born and brought up on a reserve, who have kept their ties with their community and wish to maintain those ties'.[47] On the Committee's logic, the base definition of a minority is objective (whether being born or socialized as part of an ethnic group) and individual members have only the possibility of ceasing to belong to the group.

Being an ethnically Maliseet Indian who had only been absent from her home reserve for the few years of her marriage, Sandra Lovelace was found to be a person belonging to a minority. As such, she was entitled to the right to enjoy her culture and use her language in community with the other members of that minority. Since the Tobique Reserve was the only place where the relevant community existed, she had effectively lost the right to her culture and language.

The rights in Article 27 are not, however, absolute. This means that while the notion of status Indian was not a valid definition of the Indian minority, it might nevertheless be a valid restriction on who could enjoy the right to live on a reserve. The Canadian government could not decide who was or was not indigenous, but it might be able to justify restricting the enjoyment of any or all of the rights in Article 27 to those indigenous persons whom it chose to call status Indians. Consistent with the Canadian government's protection justification for the Indian Act,[48]

---

[47] *Lovelace* v. *Canada* (merits), p. 173.
[48] But compare Jamieson, *Indian Women and the Law in Canada*, p. 13; Turpel, 'Indian Act: Full of Snares for Women', 6 (disagreeing with protection as the purpose of the Act) with Krosenbrink-Gelissen, *Sexual Equality as an Aboriginal Right*, p. 83 (stating that the constituency of National Indian Brotherhood did perceive the need for protection from an influx of white men on reserves).

status Indians would simply be the subset of Indians entitled to occupy reserve lands.

To be a valid restriction on minority rights, the restriction 'must have both a reasonable and objective justification and be consistent with the other provisions of the Covenant, read as a whole'.[49] It was open to the Committee to find that the gender bias of the restrictions was inconsistent with the provisions of the Covenant on non-discrimination, but it declined to do so, concluding as follows:

> The case of Sandra Lovelace should be considered in the light of the fact that her marriage to a non-Indian has broken up. It is natural that in such a situation she wishes to return to the environment in which she was born, particularly as after the dissolution of her marriage her main cultural attachment again was to the Maliseet band. Whatever may be the merits of the Indian Act in other respects, it does not seem to the Committee that to deny Sandra Lovelace the right to reside on the reserve is reasonable, or necessary to preserve the identity of the tribe. The Committee therefore concludes that to prevent her recognition as belonging to the band is an unjustifiable denial of her rights under article 27 of the Covenant, read in the context of the other provisions referred to.[50]

While the Committee did refer to the equality provisions of the Covenant, in its conclusion as well as its statement of the test,[51] its analysis did not turn on discrimination on the basis of sex. Instead, its conclusion depended on the naturalness and strength of Sandra Lovelace's membership. The Committee seemed to reason that the Canadian government might be able to justify denying the right to live on a reserve to indigenous persons – even where no comparable linguistic and cultural community existed elsewhere – but not to those indigenous persons with a high degree of need for and cultural attachment to the community.

The Human Rights Committee's 1988 decision in *Ivan Kitok* v. *Sweden*[52] reinforces the impression that the Committee saw its conclusion in

---

[49] *Lovelace* v. *Canada* (merits), p. 174.   [50] *Ibid.*

[51] As discussed above, Anne Bayefsky's view seems to be that the Human Rights Committee did not consider the non-discrimination provisions (Articles 2, 3 and 26) in relation to the continuing effects because it concluded that the problem of timing prevented it from doing so. To the contrary, it can be argued that the Committee did not see itself as precluded from considering these provisions, but either found it unnecessary to do so or hinted at their applicability in conjunction with Article 27. For the position that the Committee found it unnecessary, see Australian Law Reform Commission, *The Recognition of Aboriginal Customary Laws* (Report No. 31) (2 vols, Canberra: Australian Government Publishing Service, 1986), vol. I, p. 130, n. 25.

[52] *Ivan Kitok* v. *Sweden* (Communication No. 197/1985), GAOR, 43rd Sess., Supp. No. 40, UN Doc. A/43/40 (1988), p. 221.

Lovelace as a function of the minority self alone. In *Kitok*, Sweden, like Canada, had statutorily defined a subgroup of the ethnic minority and confined to that subgroup the exercise of rights essential to the minority culture. The legislation at issue divided the Sami population of Sweden into reindeer-herding and non-reindeer-herding Sami, with reindeer herding being reserved for Sami who were members of a Sami village (*sameby*). According to the Swedish government, the purpose of the legislation was to restrict the number of reindeer breeders for economic and ecological reasons and to secure the preservation and well-being of the Sami minority.[53] The parties agreed that effective measures were needed to ensure the livelihood of the Sami whose primary income came from reindeer farming and also the future of reindeer breeding, which played an important part in Sami culture.[54] The Committee recognized that legislation designed to protect the rights of the minority as a whole might justifiably restrict an individual member's enjoyment of his culture, and cited the *Lovelace* test of 'a reasonable and objective justification' and 'necessary for the continued viability and welfare of the minority as a whole'.[55] There is no indication in *Kitok* that the opposite results reached in *Lovelace* and *Kitok* are anything other than an application of Article 27. Sandra Lovelace and Ivan Kitok were similarly described: both were ethnically indigenous,[56] had maintained ties with their community and wanted to become full members of it.[57] The distinguishing feature seems to be that Lovelace had suffered the complete deprivation of her right to live on a reserve, whereas Kitok was permitted, albeit not as of right, to graze and farm his reindeer, and to hunt and fish.[58] The Committee singled out Kitok's opportunities to reindeer farm, hunt and fish in concluding that there had been no violation of Article 27.[59]

[53] *Ibid.*, pp. 223, 229. [54] *Ibid.*, p. 229. [55] *Ibid.*, p. 230.
[56] *Ibid.*, p. 221. [57] *Ibid.*, p. 230.
[58] *Ibid.* This distinction may appear shaky, given that in practice Sandra Lovelace continued to live on the reserve. However, Lovelace was in a more precarious position than Kitok. Although Canada stated that the Band Council had made no move to remove Lovelace from the reserve, she maintained that this was only because dissident members of the tribe who supported her cause had threatened to resort to physical violence in her defence. *Lovelace v. Canada* (merits), p. 170. Kitok, in contrast, had a declaration of the Board of the Sami village of Sörkaitum in his favour. *Kitok v. Sweden*, p. 225.

Moreover, Sandra Lovelace would not have been given any financial assistance with housing, whereas Kitok had the economic benefit of hunting and fishing free of charge in the community's pastures. *Lovelace v. Canada* (merits), pp. 170–1; *Kitok v. Sweden*, p. 225.

[59] *Kitok v. Sweden*, p. 230.

Examined through the lens of the minority self, the Human Rights Committee's decision in *Lovelace* has a consistency that it does not have when seen through the lens of equality. Similar to Anne Bayefsky, Manfred Nowak suggests that *Lovelace* involved a violation of Article 3 in conjunction with Article 27, but that 'problems were raised by Canada's discriminatory Indian legislation, which stemmed from the period prior to entry into force of the Covenant'.[60] Even granting the Committee's test for limitations on minority rights,[61] Nowak comments that the relevance of the break-up of Lovelace's marriage is unclear.[62] But if the Human Rights Committee in *Lovelace* understood the minority self partly in terms of maintaining ties with the minority community and understood the limitations on the self even more strongly in terms of emotional need for and cultural attachment to that community, then the break-up of Sandra Lovelace's marriage becomes germane. As the Committee observed, 'after the dissolution of her marriage her main cultural attachment again was to the Maliseet band'.[63] Whatever one may think of the Committee's test or its assumptions about emotional vulnerability, the pertinence of her divorce seems clear.

By basing its views in *Lovelace* on the notion of a minority in international law, the Human Rights Committee avoided the tension between the equal rights of women and the right of self-determination of peoples and, correspondingly, between the need to identify primarily as a woman or as indigenous. The crucial steps in this avoidance were the Committee's distinction between a minority and the state's legal definition of a minority, and its concentration on the latter. The distinguishing of the 'actual' from the legal made room for a 'true' identity, and the focus on the legal shifted the crux of the case from this identity to the limits that the state could place on it. Identity was therefore not

---

[60] Nowak, *CCPR Commentary*, p. 70, n. 23.

[61] Nowak takes exception to the Committee's statement that 'restrictions on the right to residence, by way of national legislation, cannot be ruled out under article 27 of the Covenant. This also follows from the restrictions to article 12(1) of the Covenant set out in article 12(3).' *Lovelace v. Canada* (merits), p. 173. Nowak's position is that the minority rights in Article 27 represent *lex specialis* relative to the general freedoms of religion, association and so on set out in the Covenant. As *lex specialis*, Article 27 is already outside those general freedoms and so cannot be subject to their limitation provisos. Limitations on Article 27 can only come from other Covenant rights (i.e. not the general freedoms already implicated in Article 27) and general limitation clauses. Nowak, *CCPR Commentary*, p. 505.

[62] Nowak, *CCPR Commentary*, p. 505.   [63] *Lovelace v. Canada* (merits), p. 174.

centrally implicated in the Committee's decision. Although the Committee did find that Sandra Lovelace was a member of a minority in the 'actual' sense, the Committee's analysis left open whether the objective aspect of its definition of minority always respected formal non-discrimination or whether it reflected tradition, autonomy or both. We might almost see the Committee as positing the reconciliation of equality and culture in this non-state past or present.[64]

In addition, by framing the problem in *Lovelace* as one of state-imposed limitations, the Committee in effect acknowledged the colonial context because it essentially probed what restrictions could be justified given the scarcity of resources for material and cultural survival that was the legacy of colonialism for indigenous peoples.[65] On this reading of *Lovelace*, the decision structures an inquiry that looks quite different from the 'hard choice' usually posed through the case and that exhibits important continuities with the approaches we have seen in other self-determination cases.

[64] In this connection, it is noteworthy that some cite *Lovelace* as support for indigenous self-definition. E.g. Moss, 'Indigenous Self-Government in Canada and Sexual Equality Under the Indian Act', 294.

[65] Compare C. A. MacKinnon, 'Whose Culture? A Case Note on Martinez v. Santa Clara Pueblo' in C. A. MacKinnon, *Feminism Unmodified. Discourses on Life and Law* (Cambridge, Mass.: Harvard University Press, 1987), pp. 63–9.

Conclusion

For over a century, international lawyers have debated the right of a group to choose its sovereignty. The emergence of new states and self-determination movements after the Cold War has only intensified the disagreement over the status of a right to secede. I have sought in this book to shift the discussion from the articulation of the norm to the inevitable activity of interpretation. Whereas self-determination is routinely analysed as recognizing diversity through statehood, self-government and other forms of political organization, I have argued that the practice of its interpretation also involves and illuminates a more general problem of diversity raised by the exclusion of many of the groups that self-determination most affects from the making and the perspective of the norm.

Distinguishing different types of exclusion and the relationships between them has revealed the deep structures, biases and stakes in the scholarship and decisions on self-determination. This framework of analysis has also revealed – perhaps more surprisingly – that the leading cases have grappled with these embedded inequalities. Through new readings of the cases, challenges by Islamic communities, colonies, ethnic nations, indigenous peoples, women and others to the culture or gender biases of international law have emerged as integral to the interpretation of self-determination historically, as have attempts by judges and other institutional interpreters to meet these challenges.

In this conclusion, I attempt to summarize the pattern of responsiveness found in the cases and to propose why it might be both relevant to the future application of self-determination and instructive for the interpretation of international law generally and perhaps beyond. If the first part of the conclusion is an effort to synthesize, to review the fact and range of these equality-seeking approaches to interpretation, the second part is freer and more speculative. While the territory of the book has been historical, its aim has been to open up what seems like promising ground for normative consideration, and I suggest here what the scope of the promise might be.

Patterns

Almost by definition, groups claiming a right of self-determination have had, up to then, no hand in the development of the norm and its standpoint. Indeed, a group's history of marginalization and discrimination structured on an identity that its members experience as beyond choice and change is often the impetus or justification for its claim to external self-determination. As a consequence of this exclusion, the norm of self-determination and the complex of concepts involved in its application tend, however inadvertently, to disadvantage those who assert it. The liberatory potential of self-determination, whether as an idea or an outcome, can sometimes overcome this problem. More frequently, however, the competing claims of self-determination and the accompanying contest over meaning increase the likelihood that self-determination will not be seen as an impartial norm, impartially interpreted.

By setting aside the prevailing tendencies to assess the interpretation of self-determination as either an exercise in doctrinal pigeon-holing or the furtherance of the proper principle, we can see that a number of the international judgments, arbitral decisions and other authoritative texts show an awareness of the problem of impartiality and a resulting effort to construct a broader justification for their interpretation of self-determination. Through their choice of interpretive method, these judges, arbitrators and others have engaged with the inequalities that I have grouped representationally as identity and participation. They have thereby sought to reconstitute both their own authority and that of international law.

Before I discuss the array of responses, let me reiterate why I think these qualify as such. In arguing that the international adjudication of territorial disputes has failed to recognize the rights of indigenous peoples, Michael Reisman includes *Western Sahara*[1] in the 'pattern of devaluation of indigenous claims'.[2] According to Reisman, although the

---

[1] *Western Sahara*, Advisory Opinion, ICJ Reports 1975, p. 12.
[2] W. M. Reisman, 'Protecting Indigenous Rights in International Adjudication' (1995) 89 *American Journal of International Law* 350 at 356.

International Court of Justice in *Western Sahara* said 'some of the politically correct things', it avoided giving meaningful effect to Morocco's and Mauritania's precolonial territorial claims to Western Sahara based on indigenous theories of law.[3] For him, the court's advisory opinion in *Western Sahara* therefore testifies to the same prejudice as its judgments in the *Gulf of Fonseca*[4] case between El Salvador and Honduras and the *Territorial Dispute*[5] between Libya and Chad, which refused even to consider indigenous rights. Leaving aside Reisman's analysis of *Gulf of Fonseca* and the *Territorial Dispute*, I want to indicate briefly why, unlike Reisman, I see *Western Sahara* as paying more than lip service to cultural difference.[6]

Implicit in Reisman's criticism of *Western Sahara* seems to be that without results, reasons do not much matter. Although he footnotes Judge Dillard's 'more functional, transcultural' approach to interpretation,[7] his main message is that talk is cheap. But while results are important, reasons matter. In particular, they matter because the interpretation of international law reflects and reinforces an idea of the international community it regulates. In so far as it invites scrutiny of any concept in international law, Judge Dillard's approach might well be farther reaching than the acceptance of Morocco's and Mauritania's arguments would have been. 'Indeed, the moment that any set of values, meanings, and material forms comes to be explicitly negotiable, its hegemony is threatened; at that moment it becomes the subject of ideology or counterideology'.[8] This moment in *Western Sahara* has no equivalent in *Gulf of Fonseca* and the *Territorial Dispute*, at least on Reisman's account of the two judgments. Furthermore, talk is not always cheap. Even if, for example, the court's 'narrow' interpretation of *terra nullius* in *Western Sahara* could be dismissed as window-dressing in that case, the *Mabo* case has illustrated the significant practical effect that it can have in the adjudication of indigenous land claims.

---

[3] *Ibid.*, 354–5.
[4] *Land, Island and Maritime Frontier Dispute (El Salvador v. Honduras, Nicaragua intervening)*, ICJ Reports 1992, p. 351.
[5] *Territorial Dispute (Libyan Arab Jamahiriya v. Chad)*, ICJ Reports 1994, p. 6.
[6] In so far as there is a contrast between the self-determination cases and the territorial cases, the question of categorization and its consequences deserves attention. After all, *Western Sahara* could have been treated as a case about territory (as Spain's objections to the court's advisory jurisdiction demonstrate), just as the territorial disputes could have involved self-determination.
[7] Reisman, 'Protecting Indigenous Rights', 355, n. 25.
[8] J. and J. Comaroff, *Ethnography and the Historical Imagination* (Boulder, Colo.: Westview Press, 1992), p. 29.

Finally, Reisman's assumption that a pro-indigenous result would favour Morocco and Mauritania implies that Morocco and Mauritania were the only indigenous peoples in *Western Sahara*, whereas the population of Western Sahara was also indigenous. The trade-off for giving effect to Morocco's and Mauritania's precolonial territorial claims grounded in indigenous theories of international law would have been to dismiss the identity, interests and wishes of the colonial population in that situation and implicitly in many others. My account of *Western Sahara* showed precisely the court's struggle to reconcile the value of identity reflected in the historical referents of *terra nullius*, 'legal ties' and 'legal entity' with the value of participation expressed in the General Assembly's expectation of self-determination as 'the need to pay attention to the freely expressed wishes of the people'. While Reisman as a general matter recognizes the need to test indigenous claims, by which he means historically-based claims, against peremptory norms of international law and especially international human rights norms,[9] he does not analyse *Western Sahara* in this light.

Reisman finds the same cultural bias in *Western Sahara* as in *Gulf of Fonseca* and the *Territorial Dispute* by being more radical in the revamping of international law he desires in *Western Sahara*. His criticism of *Gulf of Fonseca* and the *Territorial Dispute* is based on the demonstration that international law was already capacious enough to accommodate a consideration of indigenous rights. In contrast, Reisman takes the court in *Western Sahara* to task for declining to incorporate indigenous theories of law; that is, to particularize international law. This is not to say that different responses might not be appropriate in different cases, but that some treatment of these different directions that interpretation might take seems necessary to sustain Reisman's criticism of *Western Sahara*. In one of his general recommendations, 'to apply international law in its contemporary acceptance',[10] he makes reference to the court's interpretive technique in earlier cases of 'actualizing' international law by reading contemporary values into older provisions. Yet he does not pursue the fact that what he faults in *Western Sahara* – the court's empty political correctness in acknowledging but not giving effect to indigenous theories of law – stems precisely from the court's awareness that one of its functions is this integration of contemporary normative expectations and demands with older legal formulations.

[9] Reisman, 'Protecting Indigenous Rights', 358–9.   [10] *Ibid.*, 360.

This quick comparison of my view of *Western Sahara* with Reisman's brings out two features of the responses to culture and gender difference visible in the self-determination cases. The first is that the response may be at the level of result, reasons or both, but that a response at the level of reasons in one case may lead to one at the level of results in another. The second feature of these responses is that they yield no single method of interpretation, uniform direction or perfect balance point between identity and participation. While Reisman's analysis of *Western Sahara* is unbalanced, it is hard to say what the right balance would have been. Much of this book's analysis of the cases was aimed at recreating a sense of the enterprise and suggesting why it might aspire to be a larger one than the impromptu task of establishing workable political structures between divided loyalties and conflicting identifications – the task that Martti Koskenniemi proposes.[11] Koskenniemi argues that in the Yugoslavian situation and elsewhere, what is needed is 'greater openness towards locally and regionally idiosyncratic arrangements than is probably allowed under the conceptualisation of these conflicts from the perspective of existing sovereignties'.[12] At a number of moments, international judges, arbitrators and others have indeed shown this openness toward the particular, but while also seeking – almost paradoxically – the ideal of a more universal international law.

The most familiar and the most easily identifiable set of responses in the cases – no less important or powerful for their familiarity – is those based on formal equality. The eventual recognition of men and women, colonizer and colonized, settler and indigenous as likes made it possible to argue that they should be treated alike. As ideas of inferiority were rejected, interpretive arguments for equality grounded in notions of consistency gained in strength.[13] During World War I, for example, fighting for democratic self-determination while denying women the vote, whether nationally or in international plebiscites, became recognizable as hypocrisy. The equality implicit in the right of all colonial peoples to immediate self-determination made problematic the inequality implicit in the trust as even a transitional structure of representation.

---

[11] M. Koskenniemi, 'National Self-Determination Today: Problems of Legal Theory and Practice' (1994) 43 *International and Comparative Law Quarterly* 241 at 269.

[12] *Ibid.*

[13] I have shown elsewhere that consistency was a slipperier argument for women than it now seems in retrospect and did not always correspond to their self-image. K. Knop, 'Of the Male Persuasion: The Power of Liberal Internationalism for Women' (1999) 93 *Proceedings of the American Society of International Law* 177.

In the United Nations Working Group on Indigenous Populations, indigenous peoples came to be treated as equal in status to states. In these and other cases, consistency demanded that equality be read into existing international law.[14]

Beyond formal equality, a number of the cases contended with the structural inequalities between groups. One set of responses sought essentially to maximize the liberal and democratic tendencies of international law. The recognition of all societies as deserving of equal respect led the International Court of Justice in *Western Sahara* to emphasize the room that legal concepts such as *terra nullius* and sovereignty contained for variation among societies and to evaluate the facts accordingly. Similarly, the Conference on Yugoslavia Arbitration Commission in *Opinion No. 2*[15] employed the stock concept of nationality to give legal expression to transnational social identifications, freeing nationality from its traditional association with a right of option resulting in group emigration, on the one hand, and from its association with individual rights, on the other. If these responses reflected liberalism's respect for identity, others stemmed from democratization as the corrective in international law; notably, the court's reliance on General Assembly resolutions to establish a right of self-determination and its consideration of the doctrine of intertemporal law in *Western Sahara*, and the reinterpretation of the role of the administering authority as trustee by some judges in *East Timor*.[16]

Whereas the liberal and democratic responses made full and innovative use of the concepts in question, another set of responses went further in recognizing cultural differences. In particular, a number of the judges in *Western Sahara* acknowledged that the concepts of sovereignty and legality, however much room they left for cultural autonomy, were based on a European model of the state and of law. Any abstracted test would therefore be an abstraction from Europe and European relations.

---

[14] This was not to say, however, that formal equality was fully realized. We need only think back on the men-only vote planned for the Vilnius and Tacna-Arica plebiscites, the man's right to opt for himself and his wife, the European gender hierarchy promoted by the United Nations Trusteeship Council despite the trusteeship system's objective of non-discrimination on the basis of sex (UN Charter, Article 76), and the lesser standing of indigenous organizations relative to the International Labour Organization's three main constituencies in the preparation of ILO Convention (No. 169) Concerning Indigenous and Tribal Peoples in Independent Countries, Geneva, adopted by the International Labour Conference on 27 June 1989, in force 5 September 1991, 28 ILM 1382.

[15] Conference on Yugoslavia, Arbitration Commission, *Opinion No. 2* (1992) 31 ILM 1497.

[16] *East Timor (Portugal v. Australia)*, ICJ Reports 1995, p. 90.

The response on the part of Judge Forster, Judge *ad hoc* Boni and Judge Ammoun was at the level of the facts going to sovereignty: to recognize that the same function could be performed by different facts in different cultural contexts. Judge Dillard spoke instead to the articulation of the concept, questioning whether a function could be used as definitive if it was distinct in one culture, but not in another. Through functionalism, these judges sought to retain a single international law, but to remove its biases through sociological equivalence.

As opposed to cultural difference, a last set of responses attended more to culture perspectives. We might include here Judge Ammoun's interpretive approach of an overlapping consensus between different traditions of thought. Chairperson Daes's explanation of the right of self-determination in the draft declaration on the rights of indigenous peoples[17] similarly draws justifications from more than one vantage point. This amounts to a sort of rebuilding of international law, rather than the particularizing that some might fear in the concern with local authenticity in the *Dubai/Sharjah* boundary arbitration.[18] Yet even *Dubai/Sharjah* might belong with the dictum of the International Court of Justice in the *North Sea Continental Shelf Cases*: 'it is a truism to say that the determination must be equitable; rather is the problem above all one of defining the means whereby the delimitation can be carried out in such a way as to be recognized as equitable'.[19] Whereas the context there was equity and the difference was one of interests as between the various parties rather than one of culture as between international law and the parties, the point may be taken as a point about the fit of judgment and community. In decisions seen as primarily relevant to certain communities, the decision's reception in those communities plays a more significant role. In this last set of responses, we might also include those aimed at equalizing cultural perspectives by restructuring participation. The shift from understanding the Working Group on Indigenous Populations as an expert standard-setting process in which states and indigenous peoples were equal informants to a process in

---

[17] E.-I. A. Daes, Explanatory Note Concerning the Draft Declaration on the Rights of Indigenous Peoples, UN Doc. E/CN.4/Sub.2/1993/26/Add.1 (1993).

[18] *Dubai/Sharjah* Border Arbitration, 19 October 1981, Court of Arbitration (Cahier, Simpson, Simmonds) (1993) 91 *International Law Reports* 543.

[19] *North Sea Continental Shelf Cases (Federal Republic of Germany v. Denmark; Federal Republic of Germany v. Netherlands)*, ICJ Reports 1969, p. 3 at p. 50. See also L. D. M. Nelson, 'The Roles of Equity in the Delimitation of Maritime Boundaries' (1990) 84 *American Journal of International Law* 837 at 853-7.

which they were equal parties is a clear example. Another would be the *Lovelace* case,[20] where the UN Human Rights Committee used the concept of a minority to create a space, separate from the Canadian state's definition of Indian, in which indigenous peoples could engage in their own activity of definition.

Promise

The interest of many international lawyers in extracting a rule on secession from the cases or that of other international lawyers in establishing a better rule through the cases has led to a neglect of the inevitability of interpretation and the challenges it presents. Interpretation is, of course, not the cure-all for secessionist conflict: this study chronicles both successes and failures. But if optimism about finding the rule is misplaced, so too is pessimism about the possibility of persuading deeply diverse and marginalized groups that an interpretation is legitimate and should therefore be complied with. Moreover, the enterprise of interpretation has independent importance as part of reconstructing an international law that has been shaped by colonialism, patriarchy and other forms of exclusion. Recovering a micro-history of such attempts helps by pointing to this as an ideal of judgment more-or-less visible in international judgments, arbitral decisions and other institutional interpretations of self-determination.[21]

By seeing concretely how these judges, arbitrators and others have approached the task, we may be able to imagine and analyse better what judging across difference might look like. This will involve a hard look at the pitfalls as well as the promise of the history that I have presented. If identity and participation name important dimensions of interpretation, they also signal questions that need to be addressed. I raise two here, both of which appear in the writing on self-determination treated in the book. One is the identity-related concern implicit in Judge Gros's declaration in *Western Sahara*: how to take account of a marginalized group's standpoint without simply replacing one stereotype with another. For Judge Gros, the risk of romanticization seemed to argue against the attempt.[22] The other concern, spied in Rosalyn Higgins's

---

[20] *Sandra Lovelace v. Canada* (Communication No. 24/1977, formerly Communication No. R.6/24), GAOR, 36th Sess., Supp. No. 40, UN Doc. A/36/40 (1981), p. 166.

[21] See more generally L. V. Prott, *The Latent Power of Culture and the International Judge* (Abingdon, Oxon.: Professional Books, 1979), pp. 153–90.

[22] Compare R. West, Book Review of *Poetic Justice: The Literary Imagination and Public Life* by M. C. Nussbaum (1997) 95 *Michigan Law Review* 1851.

scholarship on self-determination, is whether all arguments deserve equal respect. Higgins's inclination was to pre-empt the question by an uncharacteristic resort to positivism and thus to authority – an inclination explainable by fears about demagoguery and having truck with positions widely recognized as morally odious. (Indeed, the more complex approach to international law to which she generally subscribes might well be among the available resources for addressing the question.) Based on my discussion of these writers, however, I would maintain that recognizing the validity of the two concerns does not require the acceptance of their responses, rather it identifies some of the directions for future work.

I want to end with the suggestion that the experience of international law, in particular, the experience of self-determination, may prove useful in thinking about legal interpretation in transitional, multinational and plural societies. Whereas the usual inclination among domestic and international lawyers alike is to treat international law as a laggard, struggling to keep up with even the basic requirements for a legal system set by domestic law, here international law may be seen as a fruitful comparison for domestic law.

The very study of international law often begins defensively by raising and attempting to dispose of the question 'Is international law really law?' Even if this question drives international legal scholarship less than it once did, much time is spent in demonstrating how international law compensates for its weaknesses relative to domestic law: giving teeth to international law by maximizing the opportunities for domestic enforcement, honing non-forcible measures and so on. I propose turning this comparison on its head and treating international law as a resource for domestic law.[23] It has been argued that the distinction based on sanctions is overdrawn; that, in fact, domestic law is often served and better served by persuasion. Beyond this, I would suggest that the context of diversity and historical inequality within which persuasion so evidently must operate in international society also exists in many domestic societies. And, if so, then the sense of possibilities that this book has sought to communicate may be relevant beyond the question of secession from which it began.

---

[23] In a different context, see K. Knop, 'Here and There: International Law in Domestic Courts' (2000) 32 *New York University Journal of International Law and Politics* 501.

Bibliography

Abu-Lughod, L. (ed.), *Remaking Women. Feminism and Modernity in the Middle East* (Princeton: Princeton University Press, 1998)
Acton, J. E. E. Dalberg- (First Baron Acton), 'Nationality' (1862) in J. E. E. Dalberg-Acton, *Essays on Freedom and Power* (Glencoe, Illinois: The Free Press, 1948), pp. 166–95
Addams, J., 'Factors in Continuing the War' in J. Addams, E. G. Balch and A. Hamilton, *Women at The Hague: The International Congress of Women and Its Results* (1915) (New York: Garland Publishing Inc., 1971), pp. 82–98
   Peace and Bread in Time of War (1945) (New York: Garland Publishing Inc., 1972)
   'The Revolt Against War' in J. Addams, E. G. Balch and A. Hamilton, *Women at The Hague: The International Congress of Women and Its Results* (1915) (New York: Garland Publishing Inc., 1971), pp. 55–81
Addams, J., E. G. Balch and A. Hamilton, *Women at The Hague: The International Congress of Women and its Results* (1915) (New York: Garland Publishing Inc., 1971)
Adede, A. O., 'Judicial Settlement in Perspective' in A. S. Muller, D. Raič and J. M. Thuránszky (eds.), *The International Court of Justice: Its Future Role After Fifty Years* (The Hague: Martinus Nijhoff, 1997), pp. 47–81
Aikio, P. and M. Scheinin (eds.), *Operationalizing the Right of Indigenous Peoples to Self-Determination* (Turku/Åbo: Institute for Human Rights, Åbo Akademi University, 2000)
Alberti, J., *Beyond Suffrage: Feminists in War and Peace, 1914–28* (London: Macmillan, 1989)
Alexandrowicz, C. H., 'The Afro-Asian World and the Law of Nations (Historical Aspects)' (1968-I) 163 Hague Recueil 125–214
   'Empirical and Doctrinal Positivism in International Law' (1975) 47 *British Yearbook of International Law* 286–9
   'New and Original States: The Issue of Reversion to Sovereignty' (1969) 45 *International Affairs* 465–80

Alfredsson, G., 'The Right of Self-Determination and Indigenous Peoples' in
C. Tomuschat (ed.), *Modern Law of Self-Determination* (Dordrecht: Martinus
Nijhoff, 1993), pp. 41–54
Allison, W. C., 'Self-Determination and Recent Developments in the Baltic
States' (1991) 19 *Denver Journal of International Law and Policy* 625–40
Alston, P., 'Appraising the United Nations Human Rights Regime' in P. Alston
(ed.), *The United Nations and Human Rights: A Critical Appraisal* (Oxford:
Clarendon Press, 1992), pp. 1–21
  'Conjuring Up New Human Rights: A Proposal for Quality Control' (1984)
  78 *American Journal of International Law* 607–21
Amankwah, H. A., 'Self-Determination in the Spanish Sahara: A Credibility Gap
in the United Nations' Practice and Procedure in the Decolonisation
Process' (1981) 14 *Comparative and International Law Journal of Southern Africa*
34–55
An-Na'im, A. A., 'The National Question, Secession and Constitutionalism: The
Mediation of Competing Claims to Self-Determination' in I. G. Shivji (ed.),
State and Constitutionalism: An African Debate on Democracy (Harare: SAPES,
1991), pp. 101–19
Anand, R. P., 'Attitude of the "New" Asian-African Countries Toward the
International Court of Justice' in F. E. Snyder and S. Sathirathai (eds.), *Third
World Attitudes Toward International Law* (Dordrecht: Martinus Nijhoff, 1987),
pp. 163–77
Anaya, S. J., 'Canada's Fiduciary Obligations Toward Indigenous Peoples in
Quebec under International Law in General' in S. J. Anaya, R. Falk and
D. Pharand, *Canada's Fiduciary Obligation to Aboriginal Peoples in the Context of
Accession to Sovereignty by Quebec* (Papers prepared as part of the Research
Program of the Royal Commission on Aboriginal Peoples) (Minister of
Supply and Services Canada, 1995), pp. 9–40
  'The Capacity of International Law to Advance Ethnic or Nationality Rights
  Claims' (1990) 75 *Iowa Law Review* 837–44, (1991) 13 *Human Rights Quarterly*
  403–11, in W. Kymlicka (ed.), *The Rights of Minority Cultures* (New York:
  Oxford University Press, 1995), pp. 321–30
  Indigenous Peoples in International Law (New York: Oxford University Press, 1996)
  'Self-Determination as a Collective Human Right under Contemporary
  International Law' in P. Aikio and M. Scheinin (eds.), *Operationalizing the
  Right of Indigenous Peoples to Self-Determination* (Turku/Åbo: Institute for
  Human Rights, Åbo Akademi University, 2000), pp. 3–18
Anaya, S. J., R. Falk and D. Pharand, *Canada's Fiduciary Obligation to Aboriginal
Peoples in the Context of Accession to Sovereignty by Quebec* (Papers prepared as
part of the Research Program of the Royal Commission on Aboriginal
Peoples) (Minister of Supply and Services Canada, 1995)
Anderson, B., *Imagined Communities: Reflections on the Origin and Spread of
Nationalism* (rev. edn, London: Verso, 1991)

Andrew, C., *Secret Service: The Making of the British Intelligence Community* (London: Heinemann, 1985)

Anghie, A., 'Finding the Peripheries: Sovereignty and Colonialism in Nineteenth Century International Law' (1999) 40 *Harvard International Law Journal* 1–80

'Francisco de Vitoria and the Colonial Origins of International Law' (1996) 5 *Social and Legal Studies* 321–36

'"The Heart of My Home": Colonialism, Environmental Damage, and the Nauru Case' (1993) 34 *Harvard International Law Journal* 445–506

'Time Present and Time Past: Globalization, International Financial Institutions and the Third World' (2000) 32 *New York University Journal of International Law and Politics* 243–90

Arangio-Ruiz, G., 'Human Rights and Non-Intervention in the Helsinki Final Act' (1977-IV) 157 *Hague Recueil* 195–332

Aston, G., *Secret Service* (New York: Cosmopolitan Book Corp., 1930)

Australian Law Reform Commission, *The Recognition of Aboriginal Customary Laws* (Report No. 31) (2 vols, Canberra: Australian Government Publishing Service, 1986)

Balch, E. G., 'At the Northern Capitals' in J. Addams, E. G. Balch and A. Hamilton, *Women at The Hague: The International Congress of Women and its Results* (1915) (New York: Garland Publishing Inc., 1971), pp. 99–110

Barbier, M., *Le conflit du Sahara Occidental* (Paris: Éditions l'Harmattan, 1982)

Barsh, R. L., 'An Advocate's Guide to the Convention on Indigenous and Tribal Peoples' (1990) 15 *Oklahoma City University Law Review* 209–36

'Indigenous Peoples: An Emerging Object of International Law' (1986) 80 *American Journal of International Law* 369–85

'Indigenous Peoples in the 1990s: From Object to Subject of International Law?' (1994) 7 *Harvard Human Rights Journal* 33–86

'Revision of ILO Convention No. 107' (1987) 81 *American Journal of International Law* 756–62

Bartkus, V. O., *The Dynamic of Secession* (Cambridge: Cambridge University Press, 1999)

Baty, T., *The Canons of International Law* (London: Murray, 1930)

Bauböck, R., Citizenship and National Identities in the European Union, Harvard Jean Monnet Working Paper No. 4/97, http://www.jeanmonnetprogram.org/papers/97/97-04.html (visited 11 October 2001)

Bayefsky, A. F., 'The Human Rights Committee and the Case of Sandra Lovelace' (1982) 20 *Canadian Yearbook of International Law* 244–66

Bayefsky, A. F. (ed.), *Self-Determination in International Law: Quebec and Lessons Learned* (The Hague: Kluwer Law International, 2000)

Beaudoin, L. and J. Vallée, 'La reconnaissance internationale d'un Québec souverain' in A.-G. Gagnon and F. Rocher (eds.), *Répliques aux détracteurs de la souveraineté du Québec* (Montreal: VLB Editeur, 1992), pp. 181–205

Becker, T., 'Self-Determination in Perspective: Palestinian Claims to Statehood and the Relativity of the Right to Self-Determination' (1998) 32 *Israel Law Review* 301–54

Bedjaoui, M., 'Article 1 (commentaire général)' in J.-P. Cot and A. Pellet (eds.), *La Charte des Nations Unies* (2nd edn, Paris: Economica, 1991), pp. 23–30

'The Gulf War of 1980–1988 and the Islamic Conception of International Law' in I. F. Dekker and H. H. G. Post (eds.), *The Gulf War of 1980–1988: The Iran–Iraq War in International Legal Perspective* (Dordrecht: Martinus Nijhoff, 1992), pp. 277–99

Towards a New International Economic Order (Paris: UNESCO, 1979)

Beigbeder, Y., *International Monitoring of Plebiscites, Referenda and National Elections: Self-Determination and Transition to Democracy* (Dordrecht: Martinus Nijhoff, 1994)

Benhabib, S. (ed.), *Democracy and Difference: Contesting the Boundaries of the Political* (Princeton: Princeton University Press, 1996)

Benhabib, S., *Situating the Self: Gender, Community and Postmodernism in Contemporary Ethics* (New York: Routledge, 1992)

Bennett, G. L., 'The ILO Convention on Indigenous and Tribal Populations – The Resolution of a Problem of *Vires*' (1972–3) 46 *British Yearbook of International Law* 382–92

Bentwich, N., 'Le Système des Mandats' (1929-IV) 29 *Hague Recueil* 115–86

Beran, H., 'A Liberal Theory of Secession' (1984) 32 *Political Studies* 21–31

'A Philosophical Perspective' in W. J. A. Macartney (ed.), *Self-Determination in the Commonwealth* (Aberdeen: Aberdeen University Press, 1988), pp. 23–35

Berat, L., 'The Evolution of Self-Determination in International Law: South Africa, Namibia, and the Case of Walvis Bay' (1990) 4 *Emory International Law Review* 251–90

Walvis Bay. Decolonization and International Law (New Haven, Conn.: Yale University Press, 1990)

Berman, H. R., 'The International Labour Organization and Indigenous Peoples: Revision of ILO Convention No. 107 at the 75th Session of the International Labour Conference, 1988' (1988) 41 *International Commission of Jurists: The Review* 48–57

Berman, N., '"But the Alternative is Despair": Nationalism and the Modernist Renewal of International Law' (1993) 106 *Harvard Law Review* 1792–903

'The International Law of Nationalism: Group Identity and Legal History' in D. Wippman (ed.), *International Law and Ethnic Conflict* (Ithaca: Cornell University Press, 1998), pp. 25–57

'Legalizing Jerusalem or, Of Law, Fantasy, and Faith' (1996) 45 *Catholic University Law Review* 823–35

'Modernism, Nationalism, and the Rhetoric of Reconstruction' (1992) 4 *Yale Journal of Law and the Humanities* 351–80

'Nationalism "Good" and "Bad": The Vicissitudes of an Obsession' (1996) 90 *Proceedings of the American Society of International Law* 214–18

'A Perilous Ambivalence: Nationalist Desire, Legal Autonomy, and the Limits of the Interwar Framework' (1992) 33 *Harvard International Law Journal* 353–79

'Sovereignty in Abeyance: Self-Determination in International Law' (1988) 7 *Wisconsin International Law Journal* 51–105

Berry, D. S., 'Contextualising International Women's Rights: Canadian Feminism, Race and Culture' in C. McGlynn (ed.), *Legal Feminisms: Theory and Practice* (Aldershot, England: Ashgate/Dartmouth, 1998), pp. 119–34

Bhabha, H. K., 'Introduction' in H. K. Bhabha (ed.), *Nation and Narration* (London: Routledge, 1990), pp. 1–7

'Signs Taken for Wonders: Questions of Ambivalence and Authority Under a Tree Outside Delhi, May 1817' (1985) 12 *Critical Inquiry* 144–65

Bhalla, R. S., 'The Right of Self-Determination in International Law' in W. Twining (ed.), *Issues of Self-Determination* (Aberdeen: Aberdeen University Press, 1991), pp. 91–101

Bibó, I., *The Paralysis of International Institutions and the Remedies: A Study of Self-Determination, Concord Among the Major Powers, and Political Arbitration* (New York: John Wiley & Sons, 1976)

Bieber, R., 'European Community Recognition of Eastern Europe: A New Perspective for International Law?' (1992) 86 *Proceedings of the American Society of International Law* 374–8

Binder, G., 'The Kaplan Lecture on Human Rights: The Case for Self-Determination' (1993) 29 *Stanford Journal of International Law* 223–70

Blay, S. K. N., 'Self-Determination *versus* Territorial Integrity in Decolonization' (1986) 18 *New York University Journal of International Law and Politics* 441–72

Blaydes, L. E., 'International Court of Justice Does Not Find "Legal Ties" of Such a Nature to Affect Self-Determination in the Decolonization Process of Western Sahara' (1976) 11 *Texas International Law Journal* 354–68

Bontekoe, R. and M. Stepaniants (eds.), *Justice and Democracy: Cross-Cultural Perspectives* (Honolulu: University of Hawai'i Press, 1997)

Borrows, J., 'Contemporary Traditional Equality: The Effect of the *Charter* on First Nations Politics' (1994) 43 *University of New Brunswick Law Journal* 19–48

Bosch, M. with A. Kloosterman (eds.), *Politics and Friendship: Letters from the International Woman Suffrage Alliance, 1902–1942* (Columbus, Ohio: Ohio State University Press, 1990)

Bossuyt, M. J., *Guide to the 'Travaux Préparatoires' of the International Covenant on Civil and Political Rights* (Dordrecht: Martinus Nijhoff, 1987)

Bothe, M. and C. Schmidt, 'Sur quelques questions de succession posées par la dissolution de l'URSS et celle de la Yougoslavie' (1992) 96 *Revue générale de droit international public* 811–42

Bowett, D. W., 'The Dubai/Sharjah Boundary Arbitration of 1981' (1994) 65 *British Yearbook of International Law* 103–33

Brass, P. R., 'Elite Competition and Nation-Formation' in J. Hutchinson and A. D. Smith (eds.), *Nationalism* (Oxford: Oxford University Press, 1994), pp. 83–9

Bredbenner, C. L., *A Nationality of Her Own. Women, Marriage, and the Law of Citizenship* (Berkeley: University of California Press, 1998)

Brilmayer, L., 'Secession and Self-Determination: A Territorial Interpretation' (1991) 16 *Yale Journal of International Law* 177–202

  'Secession and Self-Determination: One Decade Later' (2000) 25 *Yale Journal of International Law* 283–6

Brossard, J., *L'accession à la souveraineté et le cas du Québec* (Montreal: Les Presses de l'Université de Montréal, 1976)

  'Le droit du peuple québécois de disposer de lui-même au regard du droit international' (1977) 15 *Canadian Yearbook of International Law* 84–145

Brownlie, I., 'An Essay in the History of the Principle of Self-Determination' in C. N. Alexandrowicz (ed.), *Grotian Society Papers: Studies in the History of the Law of Nations, 1968* (The Hague: Martinus Nijhoff, 1970), pp. 90–9

  'The Rights of Peoples in Modern International Law' in J. Crawford (ed.), *The Rights of Peoples* (Oxford: Clarendon Press, 1988), pp. 1–16

  Treaties and Indigenous Peoples. The Robb Lectures 1991 (Oxford: Clarendon Press, 1992)

Buchanan, A., *Secession: The Morality of Political Divorce from Fort Sumter to Lithuania and Quebec* (Boulder, Colo.: Westview Press, 1991)

Buchheit, L. C., *Secession: The Legitimacy of Self-Determination* (New Haven: Yale University Press, 1978)

Bunting, A., 'Particularity of Rights, Diversity of Contexts: Women, International Human Rights and the Case of Early Marriage' (SJD thesis, University of Toronto, 1999)

Buss, D. E., 'Crossing the Line: Feminist International Legal Theory, Rape and the War in Bosnia-Herzegovina' (LLM thesis, University of British Columbia, 1995)

  'Women at the Borders: Rape and Nationalism in International Law' (1998) 6 *Feminist Legal Studies* 171–203

Bussey, G. and M. Tims, *Women's International League for Peace and Freedom, 1915–1965: A Record of Fifty Years' Work* (London: George Allen & Unwin Ltd., 1965)

Calageropoulos-Stratis, S., *Le droit des peuples à disposer d'eux-mêmes* (Brussels: Emile Bruylant: 1973)

Calbairac, G., *La Nationalité de la femme mariée* (Paris: Recueil Sirey, 1926)

Cartwright, M. G., 'Biblical Argument in International Ethics' in T. Nardin and D. R. Mapel (eds.), *Traditions of International Ethics* (Cambridge: Cambridge University Press, 1992), pp. 270–96

Carty, A., *The Decay of International Law? A Reappraisal of the Limits of Legal Imagination in International Affairs* (Manchester: Manchester University Press, 1986)

Cass, D. Z., 'Re-thinking Self-Determination: A Critical Analysis of Current International Law Theories' (1992) 18 *Syracuse Journal of International Law and Commerce* 21–40

Cassese, A., 'Article 1, Paragraphe 2' in J.-P. Cot and A. Pellet (eds.), *La Charte des Nations Unies* (2nd edn, Paris: Economica, 1991), pp. 39–55

'The Helsinki Declaration and Self-Determination' in T. Buergenthal (ed.), *Human Rights, International Law and the Helsinki Accord* (New York: Universe Books, 1977), pp. 83–110

'The International Court of Justice and the Right of Peoples to Self-Determination' in V. Lowe and M. Fitzmaurice (eds.), *Fifty Years of the International Court of Justice. Essays in Honour of Sir Robert Jennings* (Cambridge: Grotius Publications, 1996), pp. 351–63

International Law in a Divided World (Oxford: Clarendon Press, 1986)

'Political Self-Determination – Old Concepts and New Developments' in A. Cassese (ed.), *UN Law/Fundamental Rights: Two Topics in International Law* (Alphen aan den Rijn: Sijthoff & Noordhoff, 1979), pp. 137–65

'The Self-Determination of Peoples' in L. Henkin (ed.), *The International Bill of Rights. The Covenant on Civil and Political Rights* (New York: Columbia University Press, 1981), pp. 92–113

Self-Determination of Peoples: A Legal Reappraisal (Cambridge: Cambridge University Press, 1995)

'Self-Determination of Peoples and the Recent Break-up of USSR and Yugoslavia' in R. St J. Macdonald (ed.), *Essays in Honour of Wang Tieya* (Dordrecht: Martinus Nijhoff, 1994), pp. 131–44

Castellino, J., *International Law and Self-Determination: The Interplay of the Politics of Territorial Possession with Formulations of Post-Colonial 'National' Identity* (The Hague: Martinus Nijhoff, 2000)

'Order and Justice: National Minorities and the Right to Secession' (1999) 6 *International Journal on Minority and Group Rights* 389–416

Cervenak, C. M., 'Promoting Inequality: Gender-Based Discrimination in UNRWA's Approach to Palestine Refugee Status' (1994) 16 *Human Rights Quarterly* 300–74

Chappez, J., 'L'avis consultatif de la Cour Internationale de Justice du 16 octobre 1975 dans l'affaire du Sahara occidental' (1976) 80 *Revue générale de droit international public* 1132–87.

Charlesworth, H., 'The Sex of the State in International Law' in N. Naffine and R. J. Owens (eds.), *Sexing the Subject of Law* (North Ryde, NSW: LBC Information Services, 1997), pp. 251–68

'Transforming the United Men's Club' (1994) 4 *Transnational Law and Contemporary Problems* 421–54

Charlesworth, H. and C. Chinkin, *The Boundaries of International Law: A Feminist Analysis* (Manchester: Manchester University Press, 2000)

Charpentier, J., 'Les Déclarations des Douze sur la Reconnaissance des Nouveaux Etats' (1992) 96 *Revue générale de droit international public* 343–55

Chatterjee, P., *The Nation and its Fragments: Colonial and Postcolonial Histories* (Princeton: Princeton University Press, 1993)
  'The Nationalist Resolution of the Women's Question' in K. Sangari and S. Vaid (eds.), *Recasting Women: Essays in Colonial History* (New Delhi: Kali for Women, 1989), pp. 233–53
  Nationalist Thought and the Colonial World: A Derivative Discourse (Minneapolis: University of Minnesota Press, 1986)

Chaumont, C., 'Cours général de droit international public' (1970-I) 129 Hague Recueil 333–528
  'Le droit des peuples à témoigner d'eux-mêmes' (1976) 2 *Annuaire du Tiers Monde* 15–31

Chemillier-Gendreau, M., 'La Question du Sahara Occidental' (1976) 2 *Annuaire du Tiers Monde* 270–80

Chen, L.-C., 'Self-Determination and World Public Order' (1991) 66 *Notre Dame Law Review* 1287–97
  'Self-Determination as a Human Right' in W. M. Reisman and B. H. Weston (eds.), *Toward World Order and Human Dignity: Essays in Honor of Myres S. McDougal* (New York: Free Press, 1976), pp. 198–261

Chimni, B. S., *International Law and World Order: A Critique of Contemporary Approaches* (New Delhi: Sage Publications, 1993)

Chinkin, C., 'The East Timor Case (Portugal v. Australia)' (1996) 45 *International and Comparative Law Quarterly* 712–25
  'East Timor Moves into the World Court' (1993) 4 *European Journal of International Law* 206–22

Chinkin, C. and S. Wright, 'The Hunger Trap: Women, Food, and Self-Determination' (1993) 14 *Michigan Journal of International Law* 262–321

Christakis, T., *Le droit à l'autodétermination en dehors des situations de décolonisation* (Paris: La documentation française, 1999)

Clark, D. and R. Williamson (eds.), *Self-Determination: International Perspectives* (New York: St Martin's Press, 1996)

Claude, I. L., *National Minorities: An International Problem* (Cambridge: Harvard University Press, 1955)

Claydon, J. and J. D. Whyte, 'Legal Aspects of Quebec's Claim for Independence' in R. Simeon (ed.), *Must Canada Fail?* (Montreal: McGill-Queen's University Press, 1977), pp. 259–80

Cobban, A., *The Nation State and National Self-Determination* (rev. edn, New York: T. Y. Crowell, 1969)

Cockram, G.-M., *South West African Mandate* (Cape Town: Juta & Co., 1976)

Cohen, R., 'Legal Problems Arising from the Dissolution of the Mali Federation' (1960) 36 *British Yearbook of International Law* 375–84

Comaroff, J. and J., *Ethnography and the Historical Imagination* (Boulder, Colo.: Westview Press, 1992)

Comaroff, J. L., 'Ethnicity, Nationalism and the Politics of Difference in an Age of Revolution' in J. L. Comaroff and P. C. Stern (eds.), *Perspectives on Nationalism and War* (Luxembourg: Gordon and Breach, 1995), pp. 243–76

Condorelli, L., 'Le droit international face à l'autodétermination du Sahara occidental' in G. Amato, A. Cassese, J. Echeverría, V. Gerratana, G. Haupt, L. Matarasso, O. Negt, F. Rigaux, S. Rodotá and A. Soboul (eds.), *Marxism, Democracy and the Rights of Peoples: Homage to Lelio Basso* (Milan: Franco Angeli Editore, 1979), pp. 653–62

Connors, J., 'NGOs and the Human Rights of Women at the United Nations' in P. Willetts (ed.), *'The Conscience of the World': The Influence of Non-Governmental Organisations in the UN System* (Washington, D. C.: Brookings Institution, 1996), pp. 147–80

Coombe, R. J., 'Identifying and Engendering the Forms of Emergent Civil Societies: New Directions in Political Anthropology' (1997) 20 *Political and Legal Anthropology Review* 1–12

Corten, O., 'Le droit à l'autodétermination en dehors des situations de décolonisation, de Théodore Christakis. A propos d'un désormais "classique"' (1999) 32 *Revue belge de droit international* 329–49

Coulter, R., 'Les Indiens sur la scène internationale. Les premiers contacts avec l'Organisation des Nations unies (1974–1983)' in *Destins croisés: Cinq siècles de rencontres avec les Amérindiens* (Paris: Albin Michel/UNESCO, 1992), pp. 333–48

Cover, R., 'Nomos and Narrative' in M. Minow, M. Ryan and A. Sarat (eds.), *Narrative, Violence, and the Law: The Essays of Robert Cover* (Ann Arbor: University of Michigan Press, 1992), pp. 95–172

Cox, R. W., 'ILO: Limited Monarchy' in R. W. Cox and H. K. Jacobson, *The Anatomy of Influence: Decision Making in International Organization* (New Haven: Yale University Press, 1974), pp. 102–38

Crane, R. N., 'Naturalization and Citizenship of Married Women in the United States' (1923) 5 *Journal of Comparative Legislation and International Law* (3rd Series) 47–51

Craven, M. C. R., 'The European Community Arbitration Commission on Yugoslavia' (1995) 66 *British Yearbook of International Law* 333–413

Crawford, J., Book Review of *Self-Determination of Peoples: A Legal Reappraisal* by A. Cassese (1996) 90 *American Journal of International Law* 331–3

  The Creation of States in International Law (Oxford: Clarendon Press, 1979)

  'The General Assembly, the International Court and Self-Determination' in V. Lowe and M. Fitzmaurice (eds.), *Fifty Years of the International Court of Justice. Essays in Honour of Sir Robert Jennings* (Cambridge: Grotius Publications, 1996), pp. 585–605

  Response to Expert Reports of the *Amicus Curiae* (*Reference re Secession of Quebec*, [1998] 2 SCR 217, (1998) 37 ILM 1340), reprinted in A. F. Bayefsky (ed.),

    Self-Determination in International Law: Quebec and Lessons Learned (The Hague: Kluwer Law International, 2000), pp. 153–71

    (ed.), *The Rights of Peoples* (Oxford: Clarendon Press, 1988)

    'The Rights of Peoples: "Peoples" or "Governments"?' in J. Crawford (ed.), *The Rights of Peoples* (Oxford: Clarendon Press, 1988), pp. 55–67

    'The Rights of Peoples: Some Conclusions' in J. Crawford (ed.), *The Rights of Peoples* (Oxford: Clarendon Press, 1988), pp. 159–75

    'Self-Determination Outside the Colonial Context' in W. J. A. Macartney (ed.), *Self-Determination in the Commonwealth* (Aberdeen: Aberdeen University Press, 1988), pp. 1–22

    'State Practice and International Law in Relation to Secession' (1998) 69 *British Yearbook of International Law* 85–117

    State Practice and International Law in Relation to Unilateral Secession (Expert Report for Canadian federal government, *Reference re Secession of Quebec*, [1998] 2 SCR 217, (1998) 37 ILM 1340), reprinted in A. F. Bayefsky (ed.), *Self-Determination in International Law: Quebec and Lessons Learned* (The Hague: Kluwer Law International, 2000), pp. 31–61

Crenshaw, K., 'Demarginalizing the Intersection of Race and Sex: A Black Feminist Critique of Antidiscrimination Doctrine, Feminist Theory and Antiracist Politics' [1989] *University of Chicago Legal Forum* 139–67

Daes, E.-I. A.,'Dilemmas Posed by the UN Draft Declaration on the Rights of Indigenous Peoples' (1994) 63 *Nordic Journal of International Law* 205–12

    'The Right of Indigenous Peoples to "Self-Determination" in the Contemporary World Order' in D. Clark and R. Williamson (eds.), *Self-Determination: International Perspectives* (New York: St Martin's Press, 1996), pp. 47–57

    'Some Considerations on the Rights of Indigenous Peoples to Self-Determination' (1993) 3 *Transnational Law and Contemporary Problems* 1–11

Dallam, H. E., 'The Growing Voice of Indigenous Peoples: Their Use of Storytelling and Rights Discourse to Transform Multilateral Development Bank Policies' (1991) 8 *Arizona Journal of International and Comparative Law* 117–48

Danspeckgruber, W., with A. Watts (eds.), *Self-Determination and Self-Administration: A Sourcebook* (Boulder, Colo.: Lynne Rienner, 1997)

de Auer, P., 'Plebiscites and the League of Nations Covenant' (1920) 6 *Transactions of the Grotius Society* 45–58

de Beauvoir, S., *The Second Sex*, trans. and ed. by H. M. Parshley (1953) (New York: Vintage Books, 1989)

de Montigny, Y., 'Exposé constitutionnel' in Commission sur l'avenir politique et constitutionnel du Québec, *Les avis des spécialistes invités à répondre aux huit questions posées par la Commission* (Document de travail, No. 4) (M. Bélanger and J. Campeau chairs, 1991), pp. 249–68

Degen, M. L., *The History of the Woman's Peace Party* (1939) (New York: Burt Franklin Reprints, 1974)

Delgado, R. (ed.), *Critical Race Theory: The Cutting Edge* (Philadelphia: Temple University Press, 1995)

Dennis, W. J., *Tacna and Arica: An Account of the Chile–Peru Boundary Dispute and of the Arbitrations by the United States* (1931) (Hamden, Conn.: Archon Books, 1976)

Doehring, K., 'Self-Determination' in B. Simma (ed.), *The Charter of the United Nations: A Commentary* (Munich: C. H. Beck, 1994), pp. 56–72

Donner, R., *The Regulation of Nationality in International Law* (2nd edn, Irvington-on-Hudson, N.Y.: Transnational Publishers, 1994)

DuBois, E. C., 'Woman Suffrage and the Left: An International Socialist-Feminist Perspective' (March–April 1991) 186 *New Left Review* 20–45

Dugard, C. J. R., 'The South West Africa Cases, Second Phase, 1966' (1966) 83 *South African Law Journal* 429–61

Duursma, J. C., *Fragmentation and the International Relations of Micro-States: Self-Determination and Statehood* (Cambridge: Cambridge University Press, 1996)

Dworkin, R., *Taking Rights Seriously* (Cambridge, Mass.: Harvard University Press, 1978)

Dyzenhaus, D., 'Law and Public Reason' (1993) 38 *McGill Law Journal* 366–93
  'Recrafting the Rule of Law' in D. Dyzenhaus (ed.), *Recrafting the Rule of Law: The Limits of Legal Order* (Oxford: Hart Publishing, 1999), pp. 1–12

Eastwood, L. S., 'Secession: State Practice and International Law After the Dissolution of the Soviet Union and Yugoslavia' (1993) 3 *Duke Journal of Comparative and International Law* 299–349

Eide, A., 'In Search of Constructive Alternatives to Secession' in C. Tomuschat (ed.), *Modern Law of Self-Determination* (Dordrecht: Martinus Nijhoff, 1993), pp. 139–76
  Possible Ways and Means of Facilitating the Peaceful and Constructive Solution of Problems Involving Minorities, Report to the Sub-Commission on Prevention of Discrimination and Protection of Minorities, UN Doc. E/CN.4/Sub.2/1993/34 (1993)
  'The Sub-Commission on Prevention of Discrimination and Protection of Minorities' in P. Alston (ed.), *The United Nations and Human Rights: A Critical Appraisal* (Oxford: Clarendon Press, 1992), pp. 211–64

Eisner, M., 'A Procedural Model for the Resolution of Secessionist Disputes' (1992) 33 *Harvard International Law Journal* 407–25

Elias, T. O., *Africa and the Development of International Law* (2nd rev. edn, Dordrecht: Martinus Nijhoff, 1988)
  The International Court of Justice and Some Contemporary Problems: Essays on International Law (The Hague: Martinus Nijhoff, 1983)

Elshtain, J. B., 'Sovereign God, Sovereign State, Sovereign Self' (1991) 66 *Notre Dame Law Review* 1355–84
  'Sovereignty, Identity, Sacrifice' (1991) 58 *Social Research* 545–64

Engeström, E. M., *Les Changements de Nationalité d'après les Traités de Paix de 1919–1920* (Paris: A. Pedone, 1923)

Enloe, C., *Bananas, Beaches and Bases: Making Feminist Sense of International Politics* (rev. edn, Berkeley: University of California Press, 2000)

Ergang, R. R., *Herder and the Foundations of German Nationalism* (New York: Columbia University Press, 1931)

Falk, R. A., 'Casting the Spell: The New Haven School of International Law' (1995) 104 *Yale Law Journal* 1991–2008

  'The Relevance of the Right of Self-Determination of Peoples under International Law to Canada's Fiduciary Obligations to the Aboriginal Peoples of Quebec in the Context of Quebec's Possible Accession to Sovereignty' in S. J. Anaya, R. Falk and D. Pharand, *Canada's Fiduciary Obligation to Aboriginal Peoples in the Context of Accession to Sovereignty by Quebec* (Papers prepared as part of the Research Program of the Royal Commission on Aboriginal Peoples) (Minister of Supply and Services Canada, 1995), pp. 41–80

  'The Right of Self-Determination under International Law: The Coherence of Doctrine Versus the Incoherence of Experience' in W. Danspeckgruber with A. Watts (eds.), *Self-Determination and Self-Administration: A Sourcebook* (Boulder: Colo.: Lynne Rienner, 1997), pp. 47–63

  'The South West Africa Cases: An Appraisal' (1967) 21 *International Organization* 1–23

  Testimony Before the Commission d'étude des questions afférentes à l'accession du Québec à la souveraineté, Assemblée Nationale, Journal des débats, No. 24 (4 Feb. 1991), pp. 705–14

Farley, L. T., *Plebiscites and Sovereignty: The Crisis of Political Illegitimacy* (Boulder, Colo.: Westview Press, 1986)

Ferencz, B., *Defining International Aggression. The Search for World Peace: A Documentary History and Analysis* (2 vols., Dobbs Ferry, N.Y.: Oceana Publications, 1975), vol. II

Finkelstein, N., G. Vegh and C. Joly, 'Does Québec Have the Right to Secede at International Law?' (1995) 74 *Canadian Bar Review* 225–60

Finkelstein, N. and G. Vegh, *The Separation of Quebec and the Constitution of Canada* (Background Studies of the York University Constitutional Reform Project, Study No. 2) (North York, Ontario: York University Centre for Public Law and Public Policy, 1992)

Fischer, G., 'Les réactions devant l'arrêt de la Cour Internationale de Justice concernant le Sud-Ouest africain' (1966) 12 *Annuaire français de droit international* 144–54

Flory, M., 'L'Avis de la Cour Internationale de la Justice sur le Sahara Occidental (16 Octobre 1975)' (1975) 21 *Annuaire français de droit international* 253–77

  'La notion de territoire arabe et son application au problème du Sahara' (1957) 3 *Annuaire français de droit international* 73–91

Foignet, R., *Manuel élémentaire de droit international privé* (6th edn, Paris: Librairie Arthur Rousseau, 1921)

Forsyth, M., 'The Tradition of International Law' in T. Nardin and D. R. Mapel (eds.), *Traditions of International Ethics* (Cambridge: Cambridge University Press, 1992), pp. 23–41

Foster, C., *Women for All Seasons: The Story of the Women's International League for Peace and Freedom* (Athens: University of Georgia Press, 1989)

Fowler, R. B., *Carrie Catt: Feminist Politician* (Boston: Northeastern University Press, 1986)

Fox, G. H., 'The Right to Political Participation in International Law' (1992) 17 *Yale Journal of International Law* 539–607

'Self-Determination in the Post-Cold War Era: A New Internal Focus?' (1995) 16 *Michigan Journal of International Law* 733–81

Franck, T. M., 'Clan and Superclan: Loyalty, Identity and Community in Law and Practice' (1996) 90 *American Journal of International Law* 359–83

'The Democratic Entitlement' (1994) 29 *University of Richmond Law Review* 1–39

'The Emerging Right to Democratic Governance' (1992) 86 *American Journal of International Law* 46–91

The Empowered Self: Law and Society in the Age of Individualism (New York: Oxford University Press, 2000)

Fairness in International Law and Institutions (Oxford: Clarendon Press, 1995)

'Fairness in the International Legal and Institutional System' (1993-III) 240 *Hague Recueil* 9–498

'Legitimacy in the International System' (1988) 82 *American Journal of International Law* 705–59

'Opinion Directed at Response of Professors Crawford and Wildhaber' (Additional Expert Report of the *Amicus Curiae*, *Reference re Secession of Quebec*, [1998] 2 SCR 217, (1998) 37 ILM 1340), reprinted in A. F. Bayefsky (ed.), *Self-Determination in International Law: Quebec and Lessons Learned* (The Hague: Kluwer Law International, 2000), pp. 179–83

'Postmodern Tribalism and the Right to Secession' in C. Brölmann, R. Lefeber and M. Zieck (eds.), *Peoples and Minorities in International Law* (Dordrecht: Martinus Nijhoff, 1993), pp. 3–27

The Power of Legitimacy Among Nations (New York: Oxford University Press, 1990)

'The Stealing of the Sahara' (1976) 70 *American Journal of International Law* 694–721

Franck, T., R. Higgins, A. Pellet, M. Shaw and C. Tomuschat, 'L' intégrité territoriale du Québec dans l'hypothèse de l'accession à la souveraineté' in Commission d'étude des questions afférentes à l'accession du Québec à la souveraineté, *Les attributs d'un Québec souverain, Exposés et études*, vol. I (1992), pp. 377–461, translated as 'The Territorial Integrity of Québec in the Event of the Attainment of Sovereignty' in A. F. Bayefsky (ed.), *Self-Determination in International Law: Quebec and Lessons Learned* (The Hague: Kluwer Law International, 2000), pp. 241–303

Franck, T. M. and P. Hoffman, 'The Right of Self-Determination in Very Small Places' (1976) 8 *New York University Journal of International Law and Politics* 331–86

Frankel, L. M., 'International Law of Secession: New Rules for a New Era' (1992) 14 *Houston Journal of International Law* 521–64

Frankel, R. E., 'Recognizing Self-Determination in International Law: Kuwait's Conflict with Iraq' (1992) 14 *Loyola of Los Angeles International and Comparative Law Journal* 359–403

Friedmann, W. G., 'The Jurisprudential Implications of the South West Africa Case' (1967) 6 *Columbia Journal of Transnational Law* 1–16

Frowein, J. A., 'Self-Determination as a Limit to Obligations under International Law' in C. Tomuschat (ed.), *Modern Law of Self-Determination* (Dordrecht: Martinus Nijhoff, 1993), pp. 211–23

Galey, M. E., 'Forerunners in Women's Quest for Partnership' in A. Winslow (ed.), *Women, Politics, and the United Nations* (Contributions in Women's Studies, No. 151) (Westport, Conn.: Greenwood Press, 1995), pp. 1–10

  'Women Find a Place' in A. Winslow (ed.), *Women, Politics, and the United Nations* (Contributions in Women's Studies, No. 151) (Westport, Conn.: Greenwood Press, 1995), pp. 11–27

Gambari, I. A., with M. Uhomoibi, 'Self-Determination and Nation Building in Post-Cold War Africa: Problems and Prospects' in W. Danspeckgruber with A. Watts (eds.), *Self-Determination and Self-Administration: A Sourcebook* (Boulder, Colo.: Lynne Rienner, 1997), pp. 273–82

Gathii, J. T., 'International Law and Eurocentricity' (1998) 9 *European Journal of International Law* 184–211

Gayim, E., 'The Draft Declaration on Indigenous Peoples: With Focus on the Rights to Land and Self-Determination' in E. Gayim and K. Myntti (eds.), *Indigenous and Tribal Peoples' Rights – 1993 and After* (Juridica Lapponica No. 11) (Rovaniemi, Finland: Northern Institute for Environmental and Minority Law, 1995), pp. 12–45

  The Principle of Self-Determination: A Study of its Historical and Contemporary Legal Evolution (Oslo: Norwegian Institute of Human Rights, 1990)

Gayim, E., and K. Myntti (eds.), *Indigenous and Tribal Peoples' Rights – 1993 and After* (Juridica Lapponica No. 11) (Rovaniemi, Finland: Northern Institute for Environmental and Minority Law, 1995)

Geertz, C., *Local Knowledge: Further Essays in Interpretive Anthropology* (New York: Basic Books, 1983)

  'Primordial and Civic Ties' in J. Hutchinson and A. D. Smith (eds.), *Nationalism* (Oxford: Oxford University Press, 1994), pp. 29–34

Gettys, C. L., 'The Effect of Changes of Sovereignty on Nationality' (1927) 21 *American Journal of International Law* 268–78

Ghai, Y., 'Reflections on Self-Determination in the South Pacific' in D. Clark and R. Williamson (eds.), *Self-Determination: International Perspectives* (New York: St Martin's Press, 1996), pp. 173–99

Gilbert, G., 'The Council of Europe and Minority Rights' (1996) 18 *Human Rights Quarterly* 160–89

Glenn, P., 'Persuasive Authority' (1987) 32 *McGill Law Journal* 261–98

Gordon, R. E., 'Some Legal Problems with Trusteeship' (1995) 28 *Cornell International Law Journal* 301–47

Graefrath, B., *Zur Stellung der Prinzipien im Gegenwärtigen Völkerrecht* (Berlin: Akademie-Verlag, 1968)

Graham, S. H., 'Woodrow Wilson, Alice Paul, and the Woman Suffrage Movement' (Winter 1983–4) 98 *Political Science Quarterly* 665–79

Grand Council of the Crees (of Quebec), *Status and Rights of the James Bay Cree in the Context of Quebec's Secession From Canada*, Submission to the United Nations Commission on Human Rights (February 1992)

Gravelle, J. F., 'The Falklands (Malvinas) Islands: An International Law Analysis of the Dispute Between Argentina and Great Britain' (1985) 107 *Military Law Review* 5–69

Gray, C., 'Self-Determination and the Break-up of the Soviet Union' (1992) 12 *Yearbook of European Law* 465–503

Grazin, I., 'The International Recognition of National Rights: The Baltic States' Case' (1991) 66 *Notre Dame Law Review* 1385–1430

Green, L. C., 'South West Africa and the World Court' (1966–7) 22 *International Journal* 39–67

Grigg, J., *Lloyd George: The People's Champion, 1902–1911* (London: Eyre Methuen, 1978)

Grinde, D. A., Jr., and B. E. Johansen, *Exemplar of Liberty: Native America and the Evolution of Democracy* (Los Angeles: American Indian Studies Center, UCLA, 1991)

Gros Espiell, H., Study on Implementation of United Nations Resolutions Relating to the Right of Peoples under Colonial and Alien Domination to Self-Determination, UN Doc. E/CN.4/Sub.2/377 (1976)

Grovogui, S. N., *Sovereigns, Quasi-Sovereigns, and Africans: Race and Self-Determination in International Law* (Minneapolis: University of Minnesota Press, 1996)

Guy, D. J., ' "White Slavery," Citizenship and Nationality in Argentina' in A. Parker, M. Russo, D. Sommer and P. Yaeger (eds.), *Nationalisms and Sexualities* (New York: Routledge, 1992), pp. 201–17

Haas, E. B., *Human Rights and International Action: The Case of Freedom of Association* (Stanford: Stanford University Press, 1970)

Hall, H. D., *Mandates, Dependencies and Trusteeship* (Washington: Carnegie Endowment for International Peace, 1948)

Halperin, M. H., and D. J. Scheffer with P. L. Small, *Self-Determination in the New World Order* (Washington, D.C.: Carnegie Endowment for International Peace, 1992)

Hamilton, A., 'At the War Capitals' in J. Addams, E. G. Balch and A. Hamilton, *Women at The Hague: The International Congress of Women and Its Results* (1915) (New York: Garland Publishing Inc., 1971), pp. 22–54

Hannum, H., *Autonomy, Sovereignty, and Self-Determination: The Accommodation of Conflicting Rights* (rev. edn, Philadelphia: University of Pennsylvania Press, 1996)
   Book Review of *Self-Determination in the New World Order* by M. H. Halperin and D. J. Scheffer with P. L. Small (1993) 33 *Virginia Journal of International Law* 467–71
   'Rethinking Self-Determination' (1993) 34 *Virginia Journal of International Law* 1–69
   'Self-Determination, Yugoslavia, and Europe: Old Wine in New Bottles?' (1993) 3 *Transnational Law and Contemporary Problems* 57–69
   'Synthesis of Discussion' in C. Brölmann, R. Lefeber and M. Zieck (eds.), *Peoples and Minorities in International Law* (Dordrecht: Martinus Nijhoff, 1993), pp. 333–9
Hart, H. L. A., *The Concept of Law* (London: Oxford University Press, 1961)
Hashmi, S. H., 'Self-Determination and Secession in Islamic Thought' in M. Sellers (ed.), *The New World Order: Sovereignty, Human Rights, and the Self-Determination of Peoples* (Oxford: Berg, 1996), pp. 117–51
Hause, S. C. with A. R. Kenney, *Women's Suffrage and Social Politics in the French Third Republic* (Princeton, N.J.: Princeton University Press, 1984)
Helgesen, J., 'Protecting Minorities in the Conference on Security and Cooperation in Europe (CSCE) Process' in A. Rosas and J. Helgesen (eds.), *The Strength of Diversity: Human Rights and Pluralist Democracy* (Dordrecht: Martinus Nijhoff, 1992), pp. 159–86
Helie-Lucas, M.-A., 'Strategies of Women and Women's Movements in the Muslim World *vis-à-vis* Fundamentalisms: From Entryism to Internationalism' in O. Mendelsohn and U. Baxi (eds.), *The Rights of Subordinated Peoples* (Delhi: Oxford University Press, 1994), pp. 251–75
Helman, G. B., and S. R. Ratner, 'Saving Failed States' (Winter 1992–3) *Foreign Policy* 3–20
Henderson, S., 'The United Nations and Aboriginal Peoples' in S. Léger (ed.), *Linguistic Rights in Canada: Collusions or Collisions?* (Proceedings of the First Conference, University of Ottawa, 4–6 November 1993) (Canadian Centre For Linguistic Rights: University of Ottawa, 1995), pp. 615–38
Heng, G., '"A Great Way to Fly": Nationalism, the State, and the Varieties of Third-World Feminism' in M. J. Alexander and C. T. Mohanty (eds.), *Feminist Genealogies, Colonial Legacies, Democratic Futures* (New York: Routledge, 1997), pp. 30–45
Henrard, K., *Devising an Adequate System of Minority Protection: Individual Human Rights, Minority Rights, and the Right to Self-Determination* (The Hague: Martinus Nijhoff, 2000)
Hernández-Truyol, B. E., 'Borders (En)Gendered: Normativities, Latinas, and a LatCrit Paradigm' (1997) 72 *New York University Law Review* 882–927
Higgins, R., 'The International Court of Justice and Africa' in E. Yakpo and T. Boumedra (eds.), *Liber Amicorum Judge Mohammed Bedjaoui* (The Hague: Kluwer Law International, 1999), pp. 343–69

'International Law and the Avoidance, Containment and Resolution of Disputes' (1991-V) 230 Hague Recueil 9-342
'Judge Dillard and the Right to Self-Determination' (1983) 23 *Virginia Journal of International Law* 387-94
'Policy Considerations and the International Judicial Process' (1968) 17 *International and Comparative Law Quarterly* 58-84
'Postmodern Tribalism and the Right to Secession, Comments' in C. Brölmann, R. Lefeber and M. Zieck (eds.), *Peoples and Minorities in International Law* (Dordrecht: Martinus Nijhoff, 1993), pp. 29-35
Problems and Process: International Law and How We Use It (Oxford: Clarendon Press, 1994)
Hiley, N., 'Counter-Espionage and Security in Great Britain during the First World War' (1986) 101 *English Historical Review* 635-70
Hobbes, T., *Leviathan*, C. B. MacPherson (ed.), (London: Penguin, 1968)
Hodge, T., 'The Western Sahara' [1984] *International Commission of Jurists Review* 25-32
Holton, S. S., *Feminism and Democracy: Women's Suffrage and Reform Politics in Britain 1900-1918* (Cambridge: Cambridge University Press, 1986)
hooks, b., *Feminist Theory: From Margin to Center* (Boston: South End Press, 1984)
Howse, R. and K. Knop, 'Federalism, Secession, and the Limits of Ethnic Accommodation: A Canadian Perspective' (1993) 1 *New Europe Law Review* 269-320
Hudson, M. O., 'The Hague Convention of 1930 and the Nationality of Women' (1933) 27 *American Journal of International Law* 117-22
Humphrey, J. P., *Human Rights and the United Nations: A Great Adventure* (Dobbs Ferry, N.Y.: Transnational Publishers, 1984)
Hurst, C. J. B., *Great Britain and the Dominions. Lectures on the Harris Foundation 1927* (Chicago: University of Chicago Press, 1928)
Hyde, C. C., *International Law Chiefly as Interpreted and Applied by the United States* (2 vols., Boston: Little, Brown, and Co., 1922), vol. I
Iglar, R. F., 'The Constitutional Crisis in Yugoslavia and the International Law of Self-Determination: Slovenia's and Croatia's Right to Secede' (1992) 15 *Boston College International and Comparative Law Review* 213-39
Iklé, F. C., *How Nations Negotiate* (New York: Harper & Row, 1964)
International Centre for Human Rights and Democratic Development, *People or Peoples; Equality, Autonomy and Self-Determination: The Issues at Stake of the International Decade of the World's Indigenous People* (Essays on Human Rights and Democratic Development, Paper No. 5) (Montreal, 1996)
International Council of Women, *Women in a Changing World: The Dynamic Story of the International Council of Women Since 1888* (London: Routledge & Kegan Paul, 1966)
International Labour Office, *The Impact of International Labour Conventions and Recommendations* (Geneva, 1976)

International Law Association, Final Report of the Committee on Feminism and International Law, 'Women's Equality and Nationality in International Law' (2000) (forthcoming in International Law Association, 69th Conference Report)
   32nd Conference Report (1923)
   33rd Conference Report (1924)
International Lelio Basso Foundation for the Rights and Liberation of Peoples, Universal Declaration of the Rights of Peoples (Paris: François Maspero, 1977)
Iorns, C. J., 'Indigenous Peoples and Self-Determination: Challenging State Sovereignty' (1992) 24 Case Western Reserve Journal of International Law 199–348
Isaac, T. and M. S. Maloughney, 'Dually Disadvantaged and Historically Forgotten?: Aboriginal Women and the Inherent Right of Aboriginal Self-Government' (1992) 21 Manitoba Law Journal 453–75
Islam, M. R., 'Secession Crisis in Papua New Guinea: The Proclaimed Republic of Bougainville in International Law' (1991) 13 University of Hawaii Law Review 453–75
Jacquier, B., 'L'autodétermination du Sahara espagnol' (1974) 78 Revue générale de droit international public 683–728
Jamieson, K., Indian Women and the Law in Canada: Citizens Minus (Minister of Supply and Services Canada, 1978)
Janis, M. W., 'The International Court of Justice: Advisory Opinion on the Western Sahara' (1976) 17 Harvard International Law Journal 609–21
   'Religion and the Literature of International Law: Some Standard Texts' in M. W. Janis (ed.), The Influence of Religion on the Development of International Law (Dordrecht: Martinus Nijhoff, 1991), pp. 61–84
Jarvis, M., 'Redress for Female Victims of Sexual Violence During Armed Conflict: Security Council Responses' (LLM thesis, University of Toronto, 1997)
Jayawardena, K., Feminism and Nationalism in the Third World (London: Zed, 1986)
Jenks, C. W., 'Human Rights, Social Justice and Peace: The Broader Significance of the ILO Experience' in A. Eide and A. Schou (eds.), International Protection of Human Rights (Proceedings of the Seventh Nobel Symposium Oslo, September 25–27, 1967) (Stockholm: Almqvist & Wiksell, 1968), pp. 227–60
   The Prospects of International Adjudication (London: Stevens & Sons Ltd, 1964)
Jennings, R. Y., 'Closing Address' in C. Brölmann, R. Lefeber and M. Zieck (eds.), Peoples and Minorities in International Law (Dordrecht: Martinus Nijhoff, 1993), pp. 341–7
Johnson, R., W. Stevenson and D. Greschner, 'Peekiskwetan' (1993) 6 Canadian Journal of Women and the Law 153–73
Jones, C., 'Towards Equal Rights and Amendment of Section 12(1)(b) of the Indian Act: A Post-Script to Lovelace v. Canada' (1985) 8 Harvard Women's Law Journal 195–213

Kaplan, C., N. Alarcón and M. Moallem (eds.), *Between Woman and Nation. Nationalisms, Transnational Feminisms and the State* (Durham: Duke University Press, 1999)

Kärntner Landesarchivs under the collaboration of A. Ogris, W. Deuer, B. Felsner, W. Wadl and E. Webernig (eds.), *Der 10. Oktober 1920: Kärntens Tag der Selbstbestimmung. Vorgeschichte – Ereignisse – Analysen.* (2nd rev. edn, Klagenfurt: Verlag des Kärntner Landesarchivs, 1990)

Kedourie, E., *Nationalism* (4th edn, Oxford: Blackwell, 1993)

Kennedy, D(avid), 'Images of Religion in International Legal Theory' in M. W. Janis (ed.), *The Influence of Religion on the Development of International Law* (Dordrecht: Martinus Nijhoff, 1991), pp. 137–46

  'International Law and the Nineteenth Century: History of an Illusion' (1996) 65 *Nordic Journal of International Law* 385–420

  'The Move to Institutions' (1987) 8 *Cardozo Law Review* 841–988

  'A New Stream of International Law Scholarship' (1988) 7 *Wisconsin International Law Journal* 1–49

Kennedy, D(uncan), 'Form and Substance in Private Law Adjudication' (1976) 89 *Harvard Law Review* 1685–1778

Kent, S. K., *Making Peace: The Reconstruction of Gender in Interwar Britain* (Princeton: Princeton University Press, 1993)

Kimminich, O., 'A "Federal" Right of Self-Determination?' in C. Tomuschat (ed.), *Modern Law of Self-Determination* (Dordrecht: Martinus Nijhoff, 1993), pp. 83–100

Kingsbury, B., 'Claims by Non-State Groups in International Law' (1992) 25 *Cornell International Law Journal* 481–513

  '"Indigenous Peoples" in International Law: A Constructivist Approach to the Asian Controversy' (1998) 92 *American Journal of International Law* 414–57

  'Reconciling Five Competing Conceptual Structures of Indigenous Peoples' Claims in International and Comparative Law' in P. Alston (ed.), *Peoples' Rights* (Oxford: Oxford University Press, forthcoming 2001), pp. 69–110

  'Sovereignty and Inequality' (1998) 9 *European Journal of International Law* 599–625

Kirgis, F. L., 'The Degrees of Self-Determination in the United Nations Era' (1994) 88 *American Journal of International Law* 304–10

  'The Formative Years of the American Society of International Law' (1996) 90 *American Journal of International Law* 559–89

Kirkness, V., 'Emerging Native Woman' (1987–8) 2 *Canadian Journal of Women and the Law* 408–15

Kiwanuka, R. N., 'The Meaning of "People" in the African Charter on Human and Peoples' Rights' (1988) 82 *American Journal of International Law* 80–101

Klein, E., 'South West Africa/Namibia (Advisory Opinions and Judgments)' in R. Bernhardt (ed.), *Encyclopedia of Public International Law* (12 vols., Amsterdam: North-Holland, 1981), vol. II, pp. 260–70

Klein, N. S., 'Multilateral Disputes and the Doctrine of Necessary Parties in the *East Timor* Case' (1996) 12 *Yale Journal of International Law* 305–47

Kluyver, C. A., *Documents on the League of Nations* (Leiden: A. W. Sijthoff's Uitgeversmaatschappij, 1920)

Knop, K., 'Borders of the Imagination: The State in Feminist International Law' (1994) 86 *Proceedings of the American Society of International Law* 14–18

  'Here and There: International Law in Domestic Courts' (2000) 32 *New York University Journal of International Law and Politics* 501–35

  'Of the Male Persuasion: The Power of Liberal Internationalism for Women' (1999) 93 *Proceedings of the American Society of International Law* 177–85

  'Re/Statements: Feminism and State Sovereignty in International Law' (1993) 3 *Transnational Law and Contemporary Problems* 293–344

  'The "Righting" of Recognition: Recognition of States in Eastern Europe and the Soviet Union' in Y. Le Bouthillier, D. M. McRae and D. Pharand (eds.), *Selected Papers in International Law: Contribution of the Canadian Council on International Law* (The Hague: Kluwer, 1999), pp. 261–90

Korhonen, O., 'The Place of Ethics of International Law' (1998) 21:80 *Retfœrd* 3–20

Koskenniemi, M., 'National Self-Determination Today: Problems of Legal Theory and Practice' (1994) 43 *International and Comparative Law Quarterly* 241–69

Kovalev, A. A., *Samoopredelenie i ekonomicheskaia nezavisimost' narodov* (Moscow: Mezhdunarodnye otnosheniia, 1988)

Kratochwil, F. V., *Rules, Norms and Decisions. On the Conditions of Practical and Legal Reasoning in International Relations and Domestic Affairs* (Cambridge: Cambridge University Press, 1989)

Krieger, H. (ed.), *East Timor and the International Community: Basic Documents* (Cambridge: Grotius Publication, 1997)

Kristeva, J., *Étrangers à nous-mêmes* (France: Gallimard, 1988)

Krosenbrink-Gelissen, L. E., *Sexual Equality as an Aboriginal Right. The Native Women's Association of Canada and the Constitutional Process on Aboriginal Matters, 1982–1987* (Nijmegen Studies in Development and Cultural Change, vol. VII) (Saarbrücken: Verlag Breitenbach, 1991)

Kunz, J. L., 'L'Option de Nationalité' (1930-I) 31 *Hague Recueil* 107–76

Kuptana, R., 'The Human Rights of Peoples' (Canadian Bar Association Conference on Aboriginal Peoples in the Canadian Constitutional Context: Application of International Law Standards and Comparative Law Models, Montreal, 28–29 April 1995)

Kymlicka, W., *Liberalism, Community and Culture* (Oxford: Clarendon Press, 1991)

  Multicultural Citizenship: A Liberal Theory of Minority Rights (Oxford: Clarendon Press, 1995)

  'Theorizing Indigenous Rights' (1999) 49 *University of Toronto Law Journal* 281–93

Lâm, M. C., *At the Edge of the State: Indigenous Peoples and Self-Determination* (Ardsley, N.Y.: Transnational Publishers, 2000)
  'The Legal Value of Self-Determination: Vision or Inconvenience?' in International Centre for Human Rights and Democratic Development, *People or Peoples; Equality, Autonomy and Self-Determination: The Issues at Stake of the International Decade of the World's Indigenous Peoples* (Essays on Human Rights and Democratic Development, Paper No. 5) (Montreal, 1996), pp. 79–142
  'Making Room for Peoples at the United Nations: Thoughts Provoked by Indigenous Claims to Self-Determination' (1992) 25 *Cornell International Law Journal* 603–22
Landry, E. A., *The Effectiveness of International Supervision: Thirty Years of ILO Experience* (London: Stevens & Sons, 1966)
Lansing, R., *The Peace Negotiations – A Personal Narrative* (New York: Houghton Mifflin Co., 1921)
Lauterpacht, E., C. J. Greenwood, M. Weller and D. Bethlehem (eds.), *The Kuwait Crisis: Basic Documents* (Cambridge: Grotius Publications, 1991)
Leary, V. A., 'Lessons from the Experience of the International Labour Organization' in P. Alston (ed.), *The United Nations and Human Rights: A Critical Appraisal* (Oxford: Clarendon Press, 1992), pp. 580–619
Lévi-Strauss, C., *Structural Anthropology*, C. Jacobson and B. G. Schoepf (trans.) (New York: Basic Books, 1963)
Liddington, J., *The Long Road to Greenham: Feminism and Anti-Militarism in Britain Since 1820* (London: Virago Press, 1989)
Lind, J., 'Dominance and Democracy: The Legacy of Woman Suffrage for the Voting Right' (1994) 5 *UCLA Women's Law Journal* 103–216
Little Bear, L., 'Aboriginal Rights and the Canadian "Grundnorm"' in J. R. Ponting (ed.), *Arduous Journey. Canadian Indians and Decolonization* (Toronto: McClelland and Stewart, 1986), pp. 243–59
Lowe, V., 'The Marginalisation of Africa' (2000) 94 *Proceedings of the American Society of International Law* (forthcoming)
Lunardini, C. A. and T. J. Knock, 'Woodrow Wilson and Woman Suffrage: A New Look' (Winter 1980–1) 95 *Political Science Quarterly* 655–71
Lyotard, J. F., *The Postmodern Condition: A Report on Knowledge*, G. Bennington and B. Massumi (trans.) (Minneapolis: University of Minnesota Press, 1984)
MacCormick, N., 'Rhetoric and the Rule of Law' in D. Dyzenhaus (ed.), *Recrafting the Rule of Law: The Limits of Legal Order* (Oxford: Hart Publishing, 1999), pp. 163–77
Mackie, T. T. and R. Rose, *The International Almanac of Electoral History* (3rd edn, Washington, D.C.: Congressional Quarterly, 1991)
MacKinnon, C. A., 'Whose Culture? A Case Note on Martinez v. Santa Clara Pueblo' in C. A. MacKinnon, *Feminism Unmodified. Discourses on Life and Law* (Cambridge: Harvard University Press, 1987), pp. 63–9

Macklem, P., 'The Impact of Treaty 9 on Natural Resource Development in Northern Ontario' in M. Asch (ed.), *Aboriginal and Treaty Rights in Canada: Essays on Law, Equality, and Respect for Difference* (Vancouver: University of British Columbia Press, 1997), pp. 97–134
  Indigenous Difference and the Constitution of Canada (Toronto: University of Toronto Press, 2001)
Macmillan, C., *The Nationality of Married Women* (London: Nationality of Married Women Pass the Bill Committee, 1931)
  'Nationality of Married Women: Present Tendencies' (1925) 7 *Journal of Comparative Legislation and International Law* (3rd Series) 142–54
Maffei, M. C., 'The Case of East Timor Before the International Court of Justice – Some Tentative Comments' (1993) 4 *European Journal of International Law* 223–38
Maguire, J. R., 'The Decolonization of Belize: Self-Determination v. Territorial Integrity' (1982) 22 *Virginia Journal of International Law* 849–81
Makarov, A. N., 'La Nationalité de la Femme Mariée' (1937-II) 60 Hague Recueil 115–241
Mama, A., 'Sheroes and Villains: Conceptualizing Colonial and Contemporary Violence Against Women in Africa' in M. J. Alexander and C. T. Mohanty (eds.), *Feminist Genealogies, Colonial Legacies, Democratic Futures* (New York: Routledge, 1997), pp. 46–62
Mani, L., 'Contentious Traditions: The Debate on *Sati* in Colonial India' in K. Sangari and S. Vaid (eds.), *Recasting Women: Essays in Colonial History* (New Delhi: Kali for Women, 1989), pp. 88–126
Marantz, B. D., 'Issues Affecting the Rights of Indigenous Peoples in International Fora' in International Centre for Human Rights and Democratic Development, *People or Peoples; Equality, Autonomy and Self-Determination: The Issues at Stake of the International Decade of the World's Indigenous People* (Essays on Human Rights and Democratic Development, Paper No. 5) (Montreal, 1996), pp. 9–77
Marchildon, G. and E. Maxwell, 'Quebec's Right of Secession under Canadian and International Law' (1992) 32 *Virginia Journal of International Law* 583–623
Marks, S., *The Riddle of All Constitutions: International Law, Democracy and the Critique of Ideology* (Oxford: Oxford University Press, 2000)
Mattern, J., *The Employment of the Plebiscite in the Determination of Sovereignty* (Baltimore: Johns Hopkins Press, 1920)
Maurer, B., 'Writing Law, Making a "Nation": History, Modernity, and Paradoxes of Self-Rule in the British Virgin Islands' (1995) 29 *Law and Society Review* 255–86
Mayer, A. E., 'War and Peace in the Islamic Tradition and International Law' in J. Kelsay and J. T. Johnson (eds.), *Just War and Jihad: Historical and Theoretical Perspectives on War and Peace in Western and Islamic Traditions* (New York: Greenwood Press, 1991), pp. 195–226

Mazrui, A. A., 'The African State as a Political Refugee: Institutional Collapse and Human Displacement' [July 1995] *International Journal of Refugee Law* Special Issue 21–36

Mbaye, K., 'Le droit au développement en droit international' in J. Makarczyk, (ed.), *Essays in International Law in Honour of Judge Manfred Lachs* (The Hague: Martinus Nijhoff, 1984), pp. 163–77

McClintock, A., *Imperial Leather: Race, Gender and Sexuality in the Colonial Context* (New York: Routledge, 1995)

McCorquodale, R., 'Human Rights and Self-Determination' in M. Sellers (ed.), *The New World Order: Sovereignty, Human Rights and the Self-Determination of Peoples* (Oxford: Berg, 1996), pp. 9–34

  'Secrets and Lies: Economic Globalisation and Women's Human Rights' (1998) 19 *Australian Year Book of International Law* 73–83

  'Self-Determination: A Human Rights Approach' (1994) 43 *International and Comparative Law Quarterly* 857–85

  (ed.), *Self-Determination in International Law* (Aldershot: Ashgate/Dartmouth, 2000)

McDougal, M. S. and H. D. Lasswell, *Jurisprudence for a Free Society* (2 vols., Dordrecht: Martinus Nijhoff, 1992), vol. I

McDougal, M. S., H. D. Lasswell and W. M. Reisman, 'Theories About International Law: Prologue to a Configurative Jurisprudence' (1968) 8 *Virginia Journal of International Law* 188–299

McDougal, M. S. and W. M. Reisman, 'International Law in Policy-Oriented Perspective' in R. St J. Macdonald and D. M. Johnston (eds.), *The Structure and Process of International Law: Essays in Legal Philosophy, Doctrine and Theory* (Boston: Martinus Nijhoff, 1983), pp. 103–29

McGoldrick, D., 'Canadian Indians, Cultural Rights and the Human Rights Committee' (1991) 40 *International and Comparative Law Quarterly* 658–69

  The Human Rights Committee: Its Role in the Development of the International Covenant on Civil and Political Rights (Oxford: Clarendon Press, 1991)

McWhinney, E., *Judge Manfred Lachs and Judicial Law-Making. Opinions on the International Court of Justice, 1967–1993* (The Hague: Martinus Nijhoff, 1995)

Michalska, A., 'Rights of Peoples to Self-Determination in International Law' in W. Twining (ed.), *Issues of Self-Determination* (Aberdeen: Aberdeen University Press, 1991), pp. 71–90

Mill, J. S., 'Considerations on Representative Government' in J. S. Mill, *On Liberty and Other Essays*, J. Gray (ed.), (Oxford: Oxford University Press, 1991), pp. 205–467

Miller, C. A., 'Lobbying the League: Women's International Organizations and the League of Nations' (D. Phil. thesis, University of Oxford, 1992)

Miller, D. H., *My Diary at the Conference of Paris, with Documents* (21 vols., n. p., printed for author by Appeal Printing Co., n. d.), vols. I, VIII, X

Miller, F., 'The International Relations of Women of the Americas 1890-1928' (1986) 43:2 *The Americas* 171-82

Milton, J., 'Paradise Lost', in J. T. Shawcross (ed.), *The Complete Poetry of John Milton* (rev. edn, New York: Anchor Books, 1971), pp. 249-517

Minh-ha, T. T., *Woman, Native, Other: Writing Postcoloniality and Feminism* (Bloomington: Indiana University Press, 1989)

Minow, M., 'Identities' (1991) 3 *Yale Journal of Law and the Humanities* 97-130
  Making All the Difference. Inclusion, Exclusion and American Law (Ithaca: Cornell University Press, 1990)

Mitchell, D., *Women on the Warpath: The Story of the Women of the First World War* (London: Jonathan Cape, 1966)

Mohanty, C. T., A. Russo and L. Torres (eds.), *Third World Women and the Politics of Feminism* (Bloomington: Indiana University Press, 1991)

Monture-Angus, P., *Thunder in My Soul: A Mohawk Woman Speaks* (Halifax: Fernwood Publishing, 1995)

Moore, J. N., 'Prolegomenon to the Jurisprudence of Myres McDougal and Harold Lasswell' (1968) 54 *Virginia Law Review* 662-88

Moore, M., (ed.), *National Self-Determination and Secession* (New York: Oxford University Press, 1998)

Morgan, E. M., 'The Hermaphroditic Paradigm of International Law: A Comment on *Alvarez-Machain*' (1992) 21 *Proceedings of the Canadian Council on International Law* 78-90
  'The Imagery and Meaning of Self-Determination' (1988) 20 *New York University Journal of International Law and Politics* 355-403

Morsy Abdullah, M., *The United Arab Emirates: A Modern History* (London: Barnes & Noble, 1978)

Moses, T., 'The Right of Self-Determination and Its Significance to the Survival of Indigenous Peoples' in P. Aikio and M. Scheinin (eds.), *Operationalizing the Right of Indigenous Peoples to Self-Determination* (Turku/Åbo: Institute for Human Rights, Åbo Akademi University, 2000), pp. 155-77

Moss, W., 'Indigenous Self-Government in Canada and Sexual Equality Under the *Indian Act*: Resolving Conflicts Between Collective and Individual Rights' (1990) 15 *Queen's Law Journal* 279-305

Mosse, G. L., *Nationalism and Sexuality: Respectability and Abnormal Sexuality in Modern Europe* (New York: Howard Fertig, 1985)

Moynihan, D. P., *Pandaemonium: Ethnicity in International Politics* (New York: Oxford University Press, 1993)

Müllerson, R., *International Law, Rights and Politics: Developments in Eastern Europe and the CIS* (London: Routledge/LSE, 1994)
  'Self-Determination of Peoples and the Dissolution of the USSR' in R. St J. Macdonald (ed.), *Essays in Honour of Wang Tieya* (Dordrecht: Martinus Nijhoff, 1993), pp. 567-85

Murswiek, D., 'The Issue of a Right of Secession – Reconsidered' in
C. Tomuschat (ed.), *Modern Law of Self-Determination* (Dordrecht: Martinus Nijhoff, 1993), pp. 21–39

Musgrave, T. D., *Self-Determination and National Minorities* (Oxford: Clarendon Press, 1997)

Mutua, M. wa, 'Putting Humpty Dumpty Back Together Again: The Dilemmas of the Post-Colonial African State' (1995) 21 *Brooklyn Journal of International Law* 505–36

 'Why Redraw the Map of Africa: A Moral and Legal Inquiry' (1995) 16 *Michigan Journal of International Law* 1113–76

Myntti, K., 'National Minorities, Indigenous Peoples and Various Modes of Political Participation' in F. Horn (ed.), *Minorities and Their Right of Political Participation* (Rovaniemi: Northern Institute for Environmental and Minority Law at the University of Lapland, 1996), pp. 1–26

Nahanee, T., 'Dancing with a Gorilla: Aboriginal Women, Justice and the *Charter*' in Royal Commission on Aboriginal Peoples, *Aboriginal Peoples and the Justice System: Report of the National Round Table on Aboriginal Justice Issues* (Ottawa: Minister of Supply and Services Canada, 1993), pp. 359–82

Nanda, V., 'Self-Determination Under International Law: Validity of Claims to Secede' (1981) 13 *Case Western Reserve Journal of International Law* 257–80

Narayan, U., *Dislocating Cultures. Identities, Traditions, and Third World Feminism* (New York: Routledge, 1997)

Native Women's Association of Canada, *Matriarchy and the Canadian Charter: A Discussion Paper* (Ottawa, 1992)

Nawaz, M. K., 'On the Ways and Means of Improving Research of International Law in India' in S. K. Agrawala, T. S. Rama Rao and J. N. Saxena (eds.), *New Horizons of International Law and Developing Countries* (International Law Association (Indian Branch), 1983), pp. 400–16

Necatigil, Z. M., *The Cyprus Question and the Turkish Position in International Law* (Oxford: Oxford University Press, 1989)

Nedelsky, J., 'Embodied Diversity and the Challenges to Law' (1997) 42 *McGill Law Journal* 91–117

 'Judgment, Diversity and Relational Autonomy,' J. A. Corry Lecture, Queen's University, Canada, October 1995 (unpublished)

Nelson, L. D. M., 'The Roles of Equity in the Delimitation of Maritime Boundaries' (1990) 84 *American Journal of International Law* 837–58

Nesiah, V., 'Toward a Feminist Internationality: A Critique of US Feminist Legal Scholarship' (1993) 16 *Harvard Women's Law Journal* 189–210

Neverdon-Morton, C., *Afro-American Women of the South and the Advancement of the Race, 1895–1925* (Knoxville, Tenn.: University of Tennessee Press, 1989)

Niboyet, J.-P., 'La Nationalité d'après les traités de paix qui ont mis fin à la Grande Guerre de 1914–1918' (1921) *Revue de droit international et de legislation comparée* 285–319

Nicholas, A. Bear, 'Colonialism and the Struggle for Liberation: The Experience of Maliseet Women' (1994) 43 *University of New Brunswick Law Journal* 223–39

Note, "Round and 'Round the Bramble Bush:' From Legal Realism to Critical Legal Scholarship' (1982) 95 *Harvard Law Review* 1669–90

Nowak, M., *UN Covenant on Civil and Political Rights: CCPR Commentary* (Kehl, N. P. Engel, 1993)

Nussbaum, M. C., *Poetic Justice: The Literary Imagination and Public Life* (Boston: Beacon Press, 1995)

Nyerges, A., *Women in Hungary* (Budapest: Pannonia, 1962)

Obiora, L. Amede, 'New Skin, Old Wine: (En)Gaging Nationalism, Traditionalism, and Gender Relations' (1995) 28 *Indiana Law Review* 575–99

O'Connell, D. P., *State Succession in Municipal Law and International Law* (2 vols., Cambridge: Cambridge University Press, 1967)

Ofuatey-Kodjoe, W., *The Principle of Self-Determination in International Law* (New York: Nellen Publishers, 1977)

  'Self-Determination' in O. Schachter and C. C. Joyner (eds.), *United Nations Legal Order* (2 vols., Cambridge: American Society of International Law and Grotius Publications of Cambridge University Press, 1995), vol. I, pp. 349–89

Okafor, O. C., *Re-Defining Legitimate Statehood: International Law and State Fragmentation in Africa* (The Hague: Martinus Nijhoff, 2000)

Oloka-Onyango, J. and S. Tamale, '"The Personal is Political," or Why Women's Rights are Indeed Human Rights: An African Perspective on International Feminism' (1995) 17 *Human Rights Quarterly* 691–731

Opsahl, T., 'The Human Rights Committee' in P. Alston (ed.), *The United Nations and Human Rights: A Critical Appraisal* (Oxford: Clarendon Press, 1992), pp. 369–443

Orentlicher, D. F., 'Separation Anxiety: International Responses to Ethno-Separatist Claims' (1998) 23 *Yale Journal of International Law* 1–78

Osennontion and Skonaganleh:rá, 'Our World' (1989) 10 (2–3) *Canadian Women's Studies* 7–19

Otto, D., 'Subalternity and International Law: The Problems of Global Community and the Incommensurability of Difference' (1996) 5:3 *Social and Legal Studies* 337–64

Panel Discussion, 'Communities in Transition: Autonomy, Self-Governance and Independence' (1993) 87 *Proceedings of the American Society of International Law* 248–66

  'National Sovereignty Revisited: Perspectives on the Emerging Norm of Democracy in International Law' (1992) 86 *Proceedings of the American Society of International Law* 249–71

Parghi, I., 'Beyond Colonialism? Voice and Power in the UN Trusteeship System' (unpublished research paper, Faculty of Law, University of Toronto, 1997)

Paris Peace Conference (1919–20), *La Paix de Versailles* (Series La Documentation Internationale) (13 vols., Paris: Les Editions Internationales, 1929–39) *Questions Territoriales* (vol. IX, 1939)

Parker, A., M. Russo, D. Sommer and P. Yaeger (eds.), *Nationalisms and Sexualities* (New York: Routledge, 1992)

Pearson, L. B., *Diplomacy in the Nuclear Age* (Cambridge, Mass.: Harvard University Press, 1949)

Peck, C. and R. S. Lee (eds.), *Increasing the Use and Effectiveness of the International Court of Justice* (Proceedings of the ICJ/UNITAR Colloquium to Celebrate the 50th Anniversary of the Court) (The Hague: Martinus Nijhoff, 1997)

Peck, M. G., *Carrie Chapman Catt: A Biography* (New York: H. W. Wilson Co., 1944)

Pellet, A., 'L'Activité de la Commission d'arbitrage de la Conférence européenne pour la paix en Yougoslavie' (1992) 38 *Annuaire français de droit international* 220–38

  'L'Activité de la Commission d'arbitrage de la Conférence internationale pour l'ancienne Yougoslavie' (1993) 39 *Annuaire français de droit international* 286–303

  'Note sur la Commission d'arbitrage de la Conférence européenne pour la paix en Yougoslavie' (1991) 37 *Annuaire français de droit international* 329–48

  'The Opinions of the Badinter Arbitration Commission: A Second Breath for the Self-Determination of Peoples' (1992) 3 *European Journal of International Law* 178–81

Perrin, C., 'Approaching Anxiety: The Insistence of the Postcolonial in the Declaration on the Rights of Indigenous Peoples' (1995) 6 *Law and Critique* 55–74

Petersen, K. H., 'First Things First: Problems of a Feminist Approach to African Literature', reprinted in B. Ashcroft, G. Griffiths and H. Tiffin (eds.), *The Post-Colonial Studies Reader* (London: Routledge, 1995), pp. 251–4

Pethick-Lawrence, E., *My Part in a Changing World* (1938) (Westport, Conn.: Hyperion Press, 1976)

Pethick-Lawrence, [E.], 'Union of Women for Constructive Peace' (1914) 33 *Survey* 230

Pethick-Lawrence, F. W. [E.], 'Motherhood and War' (1914) 59 *Harper's Weekly* 542

Pettman, J. J., *Worlding Women: A Feminist International Politics* (London: Routledge, 1996)

Pharand, D., 'Canada's Fiduciary Obligation under General Principles of Law Recognized in National Legal Systems' in S. J. Anaya, R. Falk and D. Pharand, *Canada's Fiduciary Obligation to Aboriginal Peoples in the Context of Accession to Sovereignty by Quebec* (Papers prepared as part of the Research Program of the Royal Commission on Aboriginal Peoples) (Minister of Supply and Services Canada, 1995), pp. 116–31

'The International Labour Organization Convention on Indigenous Peoples (1989): Canada's Concerns' in S. J. Anaya, R. Falk and D. Pharand, *Canada's Fiduciary Obligation to Aboriginal Peoples in the Context of Accession to Sovereignty by Quebec* (Papers prepared as part of the Research Program of the Royal Commission on Aboriginal Peoples) (Minister of Supply and Services Canada, 1995), pp. 132–9

Phillips, A. and A. Rosas (eds.), *Universal Minority Rights* (Turku/Åbo and London: Åbo Akademi University Institute for Human Rights and Minority Rights Group (International), 1995)

Phillipson, C., *Termination of War and Treaties of Peace* (London: T. Fisher Unwin Ltd, 1916)

Pierson, R. R. and N. Chaudhuri (eds.), *Nation, Empire, Colony: Historicizing Gender and Race* (Bloomington: Indiana University Press, 1998)

Pomerance, M., 'The United States and Self-Determination: Perspectives on the Wilsonian Conception' (1976) 70 *American Journal of International Law* 1–27

Pontoppidan, H., 'Sønderjylland' in 'Ude og hjemme', *Berlingske Tidendes Fotogravure-Udgave*, No. 51 (25 December 1918), p. 3

Pound, R., 'Philosophical Theory and International Law' in *Bibliotheca visseriana; dissertationum ius internationale illustrantium cura Facultatis iuridicæ Lugduno-Batavæ edita* (Lugduni Batavorum: E. J. Brill, 1923), vol. I, pp. 71–90

Prager, C. A. L., 'Barbarous Nationalism and the Liberal International Order: Reflections on the "Is", the "Ought", and the "Can"' in J. Couture, K. Nielsen and M. Seymour (eds.), *Rethinking Nationalism* (Calgary, Alta.: University of Calgary Press, 1998), pp. 441–62

Preis, A.-B. S., 'Human Rights as Cultural Practice: An Anthropological Critique' (1996) 18 *Human Rights Quarterly* 286–315

Prévost, J.-F., 'Observations sur l'avis consultatif de la Cour Internationale de Justice relatif au Sahara occidental ("terra nullius" et autodétermination)' (1976) 103 *Journal du droit international* 831–62

Pritchard, S. and C. Heindow-Dolman, 'Indigenous Peoples and International Law: A Critical Overview' (1998) 3 *Australian Indigenous Law Reporter* 473–509

Prott, L. V., *The Latent Power of Culture and the International Judge* (Abingdon, Oxon.: Professional Books, 1979)

Przetacznik, F., 'The Basic Collective Human Right to Self-Determination of Peoples and Nations as Prerequisite for Peace' (1990) 8 *New York Law School Journal of Human Rights* 49–109

Pugh, M., *Electoral Reform in War and Peace, 1906–18* (London: Routledge & Kegan Paul, 1978)

Pullat, R., 'The Restauration [sic] of the Independence of Estonia 1991' (1991) 2 *Finnish Yearbook of International Law* 512–32

Quane, H., 'A Right to Self-Determination for the Kosovo Albanians?' (2000) 13 *Leiden Journal of International Law* 219–27

'The United Nations and the Evolving Right to Self-Determination' (1998) 47 *International and Comparative Law Quarterly* 537–72

Ragazzi, M., 'Conference on Yugoslavia Arbitration Commission: Opinions on Questions Arising from the Dissolution of Yugoslavia: Introductory Note' (1992) 31 ILM 1488–90

Randall, M. M., *Improper Bostonian: Emily Greene Balch, Nobel Peace Laureate, 1946* (New York: Twayne Publishers, 1964)

'Introduction' in J. Addams, E. G. Balch and A. Hamilton, *Women at The Hague: The International Congress of Women and Its Results* (1915) (New York: Garland Publishing Inc., 1971), pp. 5–15

Ranjeva, R., 'Peoples and National Liberation Movements' in M. Bedjaoui (ed.), *International Law: Achievements and Prospects* (Paris: UNESCO/Dordrecht: Martinus Nijhoff, 1991), pp. 101–12

Ratković, R., 'Two Concepts of the National Question in the Serbian Political Doctrine' (1995) 46 (Nos. 1035–6) *Review of International Affairs* 25–8

Ratner, S., 'Drawing a Better Line: Uti Possidetis and the Borders of New States' (1996) 90 *American Journal of International Law* 590–624

Rauschning, D., 'United Nations Trusteeship System' in R. Bernhardt (ed.), *Encyclopedia of Public International Law* (12 vols., Amsterdam: North-Holland, 1983), vol. V, pp. 369–76

Rawls, J., 'The Domain of the Political and Overlapping Consensus' (1989) 64 *New York University Law Review* 233–55

'The Law of Peoples' in S. Shute and S. Hurley (eds.), *On Human Rights: The Oxford Amnesty Lectures 1993* (New York: Basic Books, 1993), pp. 41–82

Raz, J., 'Legal Principles and the Limits of Law' (1972) 81 *Yale Law Journal* 823–54

Reanda, L., 'The Commission on the Status of Women' in P. Alston (ed.), *The United Nations and Human Rights: A Critical Appraisal* (Oxford: Clarendon Press, 1992), pp. 265–303

Redslob, R., *Le principe des nationalités: Les origines, les fondements psychologiques, les forces adverses, les solutions possibles* (Paris: Recueil Sirey, 1930)

Reisman, M., 'Designing and Managing the Future of the State' (1997) 8 *European Journal of International Law* 409–20

Reisman, W. M., 'Protecting Indigenous Rights in International Adjudication' (1995) 89 *American Journal of International Law* 350–62

Renan, E., 'What is a Nation?', M. Thom (trans.) in H. K. Bhabha (ed.), *Nation and Narration* (London: Routledge, 1990), pp. 8–22

Rich, R., 'Recognition of States: The Collapse of Yugoslavia and the Soviet Union' (1993) 4 *European Journal of International Law* 36–65

Riedel, E. H., 'Confrontation in Western Sahara in the Light of the Advisory Opinion of the International Court of Justice of 16 October 1975. A Critical Appraisal' (1976) 19 *German Yearbook of International Law* 405–42

Rigaux, F., *Pour une déclaration universelle des droits des peuples: Identité nationale et coopération internationale* (Lyon: Chronique Sociale, 1990)

Rigo Sureda, A., *The Evolution of the Right of Self-Determination: A Study of United Nations Practice* (Leiden: A. W. Sijthoff, 1973)

Riles, A., *The Network Inside Out* (Ann Arbor: University of Michigan Press, 2000)

Rittich, K., 'Recharacterizing Restructuring: Gender and Distribution in the Legal Structure of Market Reform' (SJD thesis, Harvard Law School, 1998)

Rosas, A., 'Internal Self-Determination' in C. Tomuschat (ed.), *Modern Law of Self-Determination* (Dordrecht: Martinus Nijhoff, 1993), pp. 225–52

Rose, C. M., 'Crystals and Mud in Property Law' in C. M. Rose, *Property and Persuasion: Essays on the History, Theory and Rhetoric of Ownership* (Boulder: Westview Press, 1994), pp. 199–232

Rubinstein, D., *A Different World for Women: The Life of Millicent Garrett Fawcett* (London: Harvester Wheatsheaf, 1991)

Rudrakumaran, V., 'The Legitimacy of Lithuania's Claim for Secession' (1992) 10 *Boston University International Law Journal* 33–60

'The "Requirement" of Plebiscite in Territorial Rapprochement' (1989) 12 *Houston Journal of International Law* 23–54

Rupp, L. J., 'Constructing Internationalism: The Case of Transnational Women's Organizations, 1888–1945' (1994) 99 *American Historical Review* 1571–1600

S., J. G., 'Access of Individuals to International Court of Justice' (1978) 52 *Australian Law Journal* 523–4

Saladin, C., 'Self-Determination, Minority Rights, and Constitutional Accommodation: The Example of the Czech and Slovak Federal Republic' (1991) 13 *Michigan Journal of International Law* 172–217

Salmon, J. J. A., 'A propos de quelques techniques de l'idéologie juridique appliquée au droit international' in G. Amato, A. Cassese, J. Echeverría, V. Gerratana, G. Haupt, L. Matarasso, O. Negt, F. Rigaux, S. Rodotá and A. Soboul (eds.), *Marxism, Democracy and the Rights of Peoples: Homage to Lelio Basso* (Milan, Franco Angeli Editore, 1979), pp. 1014–25

Salmon, J., 'Internal Aspects of the Right to Self-Determination: Towards a Democratic Legitimacy Principle?' in C. Tomuschat (ed.), *Modern Law of Self-Determination* (Dordrecht: Martinus Nijhoff, 1993), pp. 253–82

Salo, J., 'Self-Determination: An Overview of History and Present State with Emphasis on the CSCE Process' (1991) 2 *Finnish Yearbook of International Law* 268–354

Sambo, D., 'Indigenous Peoples and International Standard-Setting Processes: Are State Governments Listening?' (1993) 3 *Transnational Law and Contemporary Problems* 13–47

Sánchez, M. A., 'Self-Determination and the Falklands Islands Dispute' (1983) 21 *Columbia Journal of Transnational Law* 557–84

Sanders, D., 'Developments at the United Nations: 1994' [1994] 4 *Canadian Native Law Reporter* 12–16

'Draft Declaration on the Rights of Indigenous Peoples – A Text and a New Process' [1994] 1 *Canadian Native Law Reporter* 48–9

'Indigenous Peoples at the United Nations: An Overview' [1996] 2 *Canadian Native Law Reporter* 20–4

'Introduction' to International Labour Organization Convention 169 – Concerning Indigenous and Tribal Peoples in Independent Countries [1989] 4 *Canadian Native Law Reporter* 49

'Self-Determination and Indigenous Peoples' in C. Tomuschat (ed.), *Modern Law of Self-Determination* (Dordrecht: Martinus Nijhoff, 1993), pp. 55–81

'The UN Working Group on Indigenous Populations' (1989) 11 *Human Rights Quarterly* 406–33

Sargent, L., 'The Indigenous Peoples of Bolivia's Amazon Basin Region and ILO Convention No. 169: Real Rights or Rhetoric?' (1998) 29 *University of Miami Inter-American Law Review* 451–524

Scarry, E., 'The Difficulty of Imagining Other Persons' in C. Hesse and R. Post (eds.), *Human Rights in Political Transitions: Gettysburg to Bosnia* (New York: Zone Books, 1999), pp. 277–309

Scelle, G., *Précis de droit des gens. Principes et systématique* (Paris: Recueil Sirey, 1932) (Première Partie)

Schachter, O., 'Dag Hammarskjold and the Relation of Law to Politics' (1962) 56 *American Journal of International Law* 1–8

International Law in Theory and Practice (Dordrecht: Martinus Nijhoff, 1991)

'International Law in Theory and Practice' (1982-V) 178 Hague Recueil 9–396

'Micronationalism and Secession' in U. Beyerlin, M. Bothe, R. Hofmann and E.-U. Petersmann (eds.), *Recht zwischen Umbruch und Bewahrung. Festschrift für Rudolf Bernhardt* (Berlin: Springer-Verlag, 1995), pp. 179–86

'The Relation of Law, Politics and Action in the United Nations' (1963-II) 109 Hague Recueil 169–256

Remarks in Panel Discussion, 'McDougal's Jurisprudence: Utility, Influence, Controversy' (1985) 79 *Proceedings of the American Society of International Law* 266–73

'Sovereignty – Then and Now' in R. St J. Macdonald (ed.), *Essays in Honour of Wang Tieya* (Dordrecht: Martinus Nijhoff, 1993), pp. 671–88

'Towards a Theory of International Obligation' (1968) 8 *Virginia Journal of International Law* 300–22

'United Nations Law in the Gulf Crisis' (1991) 85 *American Journal of International Law* 452–73

Scheinin, M., 'The Right to Self-Determination under the Covenant on Civil and Political Rights' in P. Aikio and M. Scheinin (eds.), *Operationalizing the Right of Indigenous Peoples to Self-Determination* (Turku/Åbo: Institute for Human Rights, Åbo Akademi University, 2000), pp. 179–99

Schœnborn, W., 'La nature juridique du territoire' (1929-V) 30 Hague Recueil 85–189

Schwarzenberger, G., *The Inductive Approach to International Law* (London: Stevens & Sons, 1965)

Schwed, A., 'Territorial Claims as a Limitation to the Right of Self-Determination in the Context of the Falklands Islands Dispute' (1983) 6 *Fordham International Law Journal* 443–71

Scobbie, I., 'The East Timor Case: Implications of Procedure for Litigation Strategy' (1991) 9 *Oil & Gas Law and Taxation Review* 273–81

Scott, C., 'Dialogical Sovereignty: Preliminary Metaphorical Musings' (1992) 21 *Proceedings of the Canadian Council on International Law* 267–93

  'Indigenous Self-Determination and Decolonization of the International Imagination: A Plea' (1996) 18 *Human Rights Quarterly* 814–20

Scott, J. B. (ed.), *The International Conferences of American States, 1889–1928* (New York: Oxford University Press, 1931)

  'The Seventh International Conference of American States' (1934) 28 *American Journal of International Law* 219–23

Sellers, M., (ed.), *The New World Order: Sovereignty, Human Rights and the Self-Determination of Peoples* (Oxford: Berg, 1996)

  'Republican Principles in International Law' (1996) 11 *Connecticut Journal of International Law* 403–32

Shahabuddeen, M., 'Developing Countries and the Idea of International Law' in R. St J. Macdonald (ed.), *Essays in Honour of Wang Tieya* (Dordrecht: Martinus Nijhoff, 1994), pp. 721–36

  'The World Court at the Turn of the Century' in A. S. Muller, D. Raič and J. M. Thuránszky (eds.), *The International Court of Justice: Its Future Role After Fifty Years* (The Hague: Martinus Nijhoff, 1997), pp. 3–29

Shaw, M. N., 'Peoples, Territorialism and Boundaries' (1997) 8 *European Journal of International Law* 478–507

Shaw, M., *Title to Territory in Africa: International Legal Issues* (Oxford: Clarendon Press, 1986)

  'The *Western Sahara* Case' (1978) 49 *British Yearbook of International Law* 119–54

Shelton, D., 'The Participation of Nongovernmental Organizations in International Judicial Proceedings' (1994) 88 *American Journal of International Law* 611–42

Simpson, G. J., 'The Diffusion of Sovereignty: Self-Determination in the Post-Colonial Age' in M. Sellers (ed.), *The New World Order: Sovereignty, Human Rights, and the Self-Determination of Peoples* (Oxford, Berg, 1996), pp. 35–69; (1996) 32 *Stanford Journal of International Law* 255–86

  'Judging the East Timor Dispute: Self-Determination at the International Court of Justice' (1994) 17 *Hastings International and Comparative Law Review* 323–47

Sinha, S. P., 'Self-Determination in International Law and its Applicability to the Baltic Peoples' in A. Sprudzs and A. Rusis (eds.), *Res Baltica: A Collection of Essays in Honor of the Memory of Dr. Alfred Bilmanis (1887–1948)* (Leyden: A.W. Sijthoff, 1968), pp. 256–85

Skurbaty, Z., *As If Peoples Mattered: A Critical Appraisal of 'Peoples' and 'Minorities' from the International Human Rights Perspective and Beyond* (The Hague: Martinus Nijhoff, 2000)

Sloan, B., *United Nations General Assembly Resolutions in our Changing World* (Ardsley-on-Hudson, N.Y.: Transnational Publishers, 1991)

Smith, M. A., 'Sovereignty Over Unoccupied Territories – The Western Sahara Decision' (1977) 9 *Case Western Reserve Journal of International Law* 135–59

Smith, T. K., in Panel: 'Self-Determination: The Cases of Fiji, New Caledonia, Namibia, and the Western Sahara' (1988) 82 *American Society of International Law Proceedings* 439–42

Spaulding, R., 'Peoples as National Minorities: A Review of Will Kymlicka's Arguments for Aboriginal Rights from a Self-Determination Perspective' (1997) 47 *University of Toronto Law Journal* 35–113

Spelman, E. V., *Inessential Woman: Problems of Exclusion in Feminist Thought* (Boston: Beacon Press, 1988)

Spivak, G. C., 'Can the Subaltern Speak?' in C. Nelson and L. Grossberg (eds.), *Marxism and the Interpretation of Culture* (Urbana: University of Illinois Press, 1988), pp. 271–313

  'Subaltern Talk: Interview with the Editors' in D. Landry and G. MacLean (eds.), *The Spivak Reader: Selected Works of Gayatri Chakravorty Spivak* (New York.: Routledge, 1996), pp. 287–308

Stein, E., *Czecho/Slovakia: Ethnic Conflict, Constitutional Fissure, Negotiated Breakup* (Ann Arbor: University of Michigan Press, 1997)

Steinhardt, R. G., Book Review (1994) 88 *American Journal of International Law* 831–7

  International Law and Self-Determination (Occasional Paper Series) (Washington, D. C.: Atlantic Council of the United States, November 1994)

Street, C. J. C., *Hungary and Democracy* (London: T. Fisher Unwin Ltd, 1923)

Sunstein, C. R., *Legal Reasoning and Political Conflict* (New York: Oxford University Press, 1996)

Suzuki, E., Book Review (1980) 89 *Yale Law Journal* 1247–59

  'Self-Determination and World Public Order: Community Response to Territorial Separation' (1976) 16 *Virginia Journal of International Law* 779–862

Swepston, L., 'The Adoption of the Indigenous and Tribal Peoples Convention, 1989 (No. 169)' (1990) 5 *Law and Anthropology: Internationales Jahrbuch für Rechtsanthropologie* 221–35

  'A New Step in the International Law on Indigenous and Tribal Peoples: ILO Convention No. 169 of 1989' (1990) 15 *Oklahoma City University Law Review* 677–714

Swepston, L. and R. Plant, 'International Standards and the Protection of the Land Rights of Indigenous and Tribal Populations' (1985) 124 *International Labour Review* 91–106

Symposium: Contemporary Perspectives on Self-Determination and Indigenous
   Peoples' Rights (1993) 3:1 *Transnational Law and Contemporary Problems*
Women in Central and Eastern Europe: Nationalism, Feminism and
   Possibilities for the Future (1994) 5:1 *UCLA Women's Law Journal*
Szasz, P. C., 'Protecting Human and Minority Rights in Bosnia: A Documentary
   Summary of International Proposals' (1995) 25 *California Western
   International Law Journal* 237–310
Szlechter, E., *Les options conventionnelles de nationalité à la suite de cessions de
   territoires* (Paris, Recueil Sirey, 1948)
Tappe, T. N., 'Chechnya and the State of Self-Determination in a Breakaway
   Region of the Former Soviet Union: Evaluating the Legitimacy of
   Secessionist Claims' (1995) 34 *Columbia Journal of Transnational Law* 255–95
Tennant, C. C. and M. E. Turpel, 'A Case-Study of Indigenous Peoples: Genocide,
   Ethnocide and Self-Determination' (1990) 59 *Nordic Journal of International
   Law* 287–319
Tennant, C., 'Indigenous Peoples, International Institutions, and the
   International Legal Literature from 1945–1993' (1994) 16 *Human Rights
   Quarterly* 1–57
Tesfagiorgis, G. H., 'Self-Determination: Its Evolution and Practice by the
   United Nations and its Application to the Case of Eritrea' (1987) 6 *Wisconsin
   International Law Journal* 75–127
Thao, T. D., *De l'Influence du Mariage sur la Nationalité de la Femme*
   (Aix-en-Provence: Editions Paul Roubaud, 1929)
Thierry, H., 'L'Evolution de droit international' (1990-III) 222 Hague Recueil
   9–186
Thornberry, P., 'The Democratic or Internal Aspect of Self-Determination With
   Some Remarks on Federalism' in C. Tomuschat (ed.), *Modern Law of
   Self-Determination* (Dordrecht: Martinus Nijhoff, 1993), pp. 101–38
   International Law and the Rights of Minorities (Oxford: Clarendon Press, 1991)
   'Minorities, Indigenous Peoples, Participation' in F. Horn (ed.), *Minorities and
   Their Right of Political Participation* (Rovaniemi: Northern Institute for
   Environmental and Minority Law at the University of Lapland, 1996),
   pp. 27–50
   'Self-Determination, Minorities, Human Rights: A Review of International
   Instruments' (1989) 38 *International and Comparative Law Quarterly* 867–89
Thouvenin, J.-M., 'L'Arrêt de la CIJ du 30 juin 1995 rendu dans l'affaire du
   Timor Oriental (Portugal c. Australie)' (1995) *Annuaire français de droit
   international* 328–53
Thürer, D., 'Self-Determination' in R. Bernhardt (ed.), *Encyclopedia of Public
   International Law* (12 vols., Amsterdam: North-Holland, 1985), vol. VIII,
   pp. 470–6
Tobique Women's Group, *Enough is Enough: Aboriginal Women Speak Out*, as told
   to J. Silman (Toronto: The Women's Press, 1987)

Tomei, M. and L. Swepston, *Indigenous and Tribal Peoples: A Guide to ILO Convention No. 169* (Geneva: International Labour Office, July 1996) (with the International Centre for Human Rights and Democratic Development, Montreal)

Toussaint, C. E., *The Trusteeship System of the United Nations* (New York: Frederick A. Praeger, 1956)

Trask, M. B., 'Historical and Contemporary Hawaiian Self-Determination: A Native Hawaiian Perspective' (1991) 8 *Arizona Journal of International and Comparative Law* 77–95

Tully, J., *Strange Multiplicity. Constitutionalism in an Age of Diversity* (Cambridge: Cambridge University Press, 1995)

Türk, D., 'Recognition of States: A Comment' (1993) 4 *European Journal of International Law* 66–71

Turp, D., 'Le droit à la sécession: l'expression du principe démocratique' in A.-G. Gagnon and F. Rocher (eds.), *Répliques aux détracteurs de la souveraineté du Québec* (Montreal: VLB Editeur, 1992), pp. 49–68

 'Le droit de sécession en droit international public' (1982) 20 *Canadian Yearbook of International Law* 24–78

 'L'Emergence de nouveaux Etats et le droit des peuples à disposer d'eux-mêmes' (1992) 21 *Proceedings of the Canadian Council on International Law* 25–35

 Expert Testimony before the Commission d'étude des questions afférentes à l'accession du Québec à la souveraineté, Assemblée Nationale, Journal des débats, No. 5 (9 Oct. 1991), pp. 128–42

 'Exposé-réponse (Processus d'accession à la souveraineté)' in Commission d'étude des questions afférentes à l'accession du Québec à la souveraineté, *Les attributs d'un Québec souverain, Exposés et études*, vol. I (1992), pp. 655–86

 'Quebec's Democratic Right to Self-Determination: A Critical and Legal Reflection' in S. H. Hartt, A. L. C. de Mestral, J. McCallum, V. Loungenarath, D. Morton and D. Turp, *Tangled Web: Legal Aspects of Deconfederation* (Toronto: C. D. Howe Institute, 1992), pp. 99–124

 'A Select Bibliography on the Right of Self-Determination of Peoples' in D. Clark and R. Williamson (eds.), *Self-Determination: International Perspectives* (New York: St. Martin's Press, 1996), pp. 391–406

Turpel, M. E., 'The Cultural Non-Homogeneity of Québec: Secessionism, Indigenous Legal Perspectives and Inseparability' in D. Clark and R. Williamson (eds.), *Self-Determination: International Perspectives* (New York: St Martin's Press, 1996), pp. 284–90.

 'Discrimination and the 1985 Amendments to the Indian Act: Full of Snares for Women' (September 1987) *Rights and Freedoms* 6–8

 'Does the Road to Québec Sovereignty Run Through Aboriginal Territory?' in D. Drache and R. Perin (eds.), *Negotiating with a Sovereign Quebec* (Toronto: James Lorimer & Co., 1992), pp. 93–106

'Draft Declaration on the Rights of Indigenous Peoples – Commentary' [1994] 1 *Canadian Native Law Reporter* 50–2

'Indigenous Peoples' Rights of Political Participation and Self- Determination: Recent International Legal Developments and the Continuing Struggle for Recognition' (1992) 25 *Cornell International Law Journal* 579–602

(Aki-Kwe), 'Patriarchy and Paternalism: The Legacy of the Canadian State for First Nations Women' (1993) 6 *Canadian Journal of Women and the Law* 174–92

Ugrešić, D., 'Because We're Just Boys' in D. Ugrešić, *The Culture of Lies. Antipolitical Essays*, C. Hawkesworth (trans.) (University Park, Penn.: Pennsylvania State University Press, 1998), pp. 113–27

United Nations, *Convention on the Nationality of Married Women: Historical Background and Commentary*, UN Doc. E/CN.6/389, UN Sales No. 62.IV.3 (1962)

Everyone's United Nations. A Handbook of the Work of the United Nations (10th edn, New York, 1986)

A Sacred Trust. The Work of the United Nations for Dependent People (1953)

The United Nations and the Advancement of Women 1945–1995 (United Nations Blue Book Series, Vol. VI) (New York, 1995)

Ushakov, N. A., 'Mezhdunarodno-pravovye aspekty obrazovaniia Soiuza SSR' [1972] *Sovetskii Ezhegodnik Mezhdunarodnogo Prava* 11–22

Van Voris, J., *Carrie Chapman Catt: A Public Life* (New York: The Feminist Press at The City University of New York, 1987)

Venne, S. H., *Our Elders Understand Our Rights: Evolving International Law Regarding Indigenous Peoples* (Penticton, B.C.: Theytus Books, 1998)

Verrier, P., 'Le Slesvig: Mémoire de M. Paul Verrier', paper for a 1913 conference at the École des Hautes Etudes sociales, reprinted in Paris Peace Conference (1919–1920), *La Paix de Versailles* (Series La Documentation Internationale) (13 vols., Paris: Les Editions Internationales, 1929–1939) *Questions Territoriales* (vol. IX, 1939), pt. 2, pp. 221–57

Virally, M., 'Panorama du droit international contemporain' (1983-V) 183 Hague Recueil 9–382

'Le rôle des "principes" dans le développement du droit international' in *Recueil d'études de droit international: En hommage à Paul Guggenheim* (Geneva: Faculté de droit de l'Université de Genève & Institut universitaire de hautes études internationales, 1968), pp. 531–54

Wambaugh, S., *A Monograph on Plebiscites with a Collection of Official Documents* (New York: Oxford University Press, 1920)

Plebiscites Since the World War with a Collection of Official Documents (2 vols., Washington: Carnegie Endowment for International Peace, 1933)

'La Pratique des Plébiscites Internationaux' (1927-III) 18 Hague Recueil 151–258

The Saar Plebiscite with a Collection of Official Documents (1940) (Westport, Conn.: Greenwood Press, 1971)

Ware, V., *Beyond the Pale: White Women, Racism and History* (London: Verso, 1992)

Webb, W. T., 'The International Legal Aspects of the Lithuanian Secession' (1991) 17 *Journal of Legislation* 309–30

Weeramantry, C. G., 'Symposium. International Law and the Developing World: A Millennial Analysis. Keynote Address' (2000) 41 *Harvard International Law Journal* 277–86

Weiler, J. H. H., 'To Be a European Citizen: Eros and Civilization' in J. H. H. Weiler, *The Constitution of Europe: 'Do the New Clothes Have an Emperor?' and Other Essays on European Integration* (Cambridge: Cambridge University Press, 1999), pp. 324–57

Weinrib, E. J., 'Aristotle's Forms of Justice' in S. Panagiotou (ed.), *Justice, Law and Method in Plato and Aristotle* (Edmonton, Alta.: Academic Printing & Publishing, 1987), pp. 133–52

Weiss, A., *Manuel de droit international privé* (9th edn, Paris: Recueil Sirey, 1925)

Weller, M., 'The International Response to the Dissolution of the Socialist Federal Republic of Yugoslavia' (1992) 86 *American Journal of International Law* 569–607

West, H. G., 'Creative Destruction and Sorcery of Construction: Power, Hope and Suspicion in Post-War Mozambique' (1997) 20 *Political and Legal Anthropology Review* 13–31

West, L. A. (ed.), *Feminist Nationalism* (New York: Routledge, 1997)

West, R., Book Review of *Poetic Justice: The Literary Imagination and Public Life* by M. C. Nussbaum (1997) 95 *Michigan Law Review* 1851–70

Westbrook, D. A., 'Islamic International Law and Public International Law: Separate Expressions of World Order' (1993) 33 *Virginia Journal of International Law* 819–97

Weston, B. H., R. A. Falk and A. A. D'Amato, *International Law and World Order: A Problem-Oriented Casebook* (St. Paul: West, 1980)

Wheelwright, J., *The Fatal Lover: Mata Hari and the Myth of Women in Espionage* (London: Collins & Brown, 1992)

White, J. B., *Justice as Translation: An Essay in Cultural and Legal Criticism* (Chicago: University of Chicago Press, 1990)

  'Law as Rhetoric, Rhetoric as Law: The Arts of Cultural and Communal Life' (1985) 52 *University of Chicago Law Review* 684–702, reprinted in J. B. White, *Heracles' Bow: Essays on the Rhetoric and Poetics of the Law* (Madison, Wisc.: University of Wisconsin Press, 1985), pp. 28–48

  The Legal Imagination: Studies in the Nature of Legal Thought and Expression (Boston: Little, Brown & Co., 1973)

Whittick, A., *Woman into Citizen* (Santa Barbara, California: ABC-Clio, 1979)

Wildhaber, L., Expert Report (*Reference re Secession of Quebec*, [1998] 2 SCR 217, (1998) 37 ILM 1340), reprinted in A. F. Bayefsky (ed.), *Self- Determination in International Law: Quebec and Lessons Learned* (The Hague: Kluwer Law International, 2000), pp. 63–5

'Territorial Modifications and Breakups in Federal States' (1995) 33 *Canadian Yearbook of International Law* 41–74
Williams, M. S., *Voice, Trust, and Memory. Marginalized Groups and the Failings of Liberal Representation* (Princeton: Princeton University Press, 1998)
Williams, Jr., R. A., *The American Indian in Western Legal Thought: The Discourse of Conquest* (New York: Oxford University Press, 1990)
  'Encounters on the Frontiers of International Human Rights Law: Redefining the Terms of Indigenous Peoples' Survival in the World' [1990] *Duke Law Journal* 660–704
  'The Rights and Status of Indigenous Peoples Under International Law During the Classical Era Treaty Period (1600–1840)' (1990) 5 *Law and Anthropology. Internationales Jahrbuch für Rechtsanthropologie* 237–55
Williams, S. A., *International Legal Effects of Secession by Quebec* (Background Studies of the York University Constitutional Reform Project, Study No. 3) (North York, Ont.: York University Centre for Public Law and Public Policy, 1992)
Wilmer, F., *The Indigenous Voice in World Politics: Since Time Immemorial* (Newbury Park, Calif.: Sage Publications, 1993)
Wilson, J., 'Ethnic Groups and the Right to Self-Determination' (1996) 11 *Connecticut Journal of International Law* 433–85
Wiltsher, A., *Most Dangerous Women: Feminist Peace Campaigners of the Great War* (London: Pandora, 1985)
Winslow, A. (ed.), *Women, Politics, and the United Nations* (Contributions in Women's Studies, No. 151) (Westport, Conn.: Greenwood Press, 1995)
Woehrling, J., 'Les aspects juridiques d'une éventuelle sécession du Québec' (1995) 74 *Canadian Bar Review* 293–329
  'Les aspects juridiques de la redéfinition du statut politique et constitutionnel du Québec' in Commission sur l'avenir politique et constitutionnel du Québec, *Eléments d'analyse institutionnelle, juridique et démolinguistique pertinents à la révision du statut politique et constitutionnel du Québec* (Document de travail, No. 2) (M. Bélanger and J. Campeau chairs, 1991), pp. 1–110
Women's Human Rights Resources, Bora Laskin Law Library, University of Toronto, <http://www.law-lib.utoronto.ca/Diana/human/articles.htm> (visited 16 February 2001)
Women, Immigration and Nationality Group, *Worlds Apart: Women under Immigration and Nationality Law*, J. Bhabha, F. Klug and S. Shutter (eds.), (London: Pluto Press, 1985)
Woods, J. M., 'The Fallacy of Neutrality: Diary of an Election Observer' (1997) 18 *Michigan Journal of International Law* 475–525
Woolf, V., *Three Guineas* (1938) in V. Woolf, *A Room of One's Own* and *Three Guineas*, M. Barrett (ed.) (London: Penguin, 1993), pp. 117–365

Wright, J., 'The OSCE and the Protection of Minority Rights' (1996) 18 *Human Rights Quarterly* 190–205

Wright, Q., *Mandates under the League of Nations* (Chicago: University of Chicago Press, 1930)

Yakemtchouk, R., 'Les républiques baltes en droit international. Echec d'une annexation opérée en violation du droit des gens' (1991) 37 *Annuaire français de droit international* 259–89

Yakpo, E. K. M., 'The African Concept of *Uti Possidetis* – Need for Change?' in E. Yakpo and T. Boumedra (eds.), *Liber Amicorum Judge Mohammed Bedjaoui* (The Hague: Kluwer Law International, 1999), pp. 271–90

Young, C., 'Ethnicity and the Colonial and Post-Colonial State in Africa' in P. Brass (ed.), *Ethnic Groups and the State* (Totowa, New Jersey: Barnes and Noble Books, 1985), pp. 57–93

Young, I. M., *Justice and the Politics of Difference* (Princeton: Princeton University Press, 1990)

Yuval-Davis, N. and F. Anthias (eds.), *Woman–Nation–State* (New York: St Martin's Press, 1989)

Zoubir, Y. H., 'The Western Sahara Conflict: A Case Study in Failure of Prenegotiation and Prolongation of Conflict' (1996) 26 *California Western International Law Journal* 173–213

Zuijdwijk, T. J. M., *Petitioning the United Nations: A Study in Human Rights* (New York: St Martin's Press, 1982)

Index

Aaland Islands, 77-80
  carence de souveraineté, 78
  failure to protect minority rights, 78, 79-80
  peace and security, relevance, 86-7
Africa
  borders, relevance, 20, 55-6, 181
  repression of minorities, 20 n. 60
  resort to ICJ, 113-14
  terra nullius as a concept, 123-4, 125, 154
Algiers Declaration of the Rights of Peoples (1976), 25
analogy. *See also* 'sacred trust' concept
  carence de souveraineté/colonialism, 79 n. 130
  colonization as trespass, 71
  development of rules and, 40-1
  fiduciary relationship with aboriginals/trust, 201-2, 207
  indigenous peoples/overseas colonialism, 40-1
  inter-state/husband/wife relationships, 316-19, 326
  international community/family, 319-20
  international/private law
    autonomy of state/individual, 137
    territory/property, 69, 120
    treaty/contract, 69
  restoration of sovereignty/property, 69
  state/paterfamilias, 316, 320, 321
  state/woman, 302-3
arbitrariness, 68
armed resistance as evidence of 'people', 60-1

Australia, *terra nullius*, whether, 116, 128, 129
autonomy, right to, 76-7, 173-4, 271

Baltic states
  carence de souveraineté, 79
  Soviet occupation as wrongful taking, 70-1, 73
Bangladesh, *carence de souveraineté*, 78-9
borders. *See also* boundary/territorial disputes
  in Africa, 20 n. 60, 55-6, 181
  as definition of 'self', 20
Bosnia-Herzegovina. *See also* Croatia and Bosnia-Herzegovina
  violation of principle of self-determination, *Application of the Genocide Convention*, 109 n. 4
boundary/territorial disputes. *See also* borders; territorial integrity of states; *uti possidetis*
  indigenous claims, ICJ handling of
    Gulf of Fonseca, 375, 376
    Territorial Dispute (Libya/Chad), 375, 376
    Western Sahara, 115, 116-17, 133-5, 374-6, 378-9
  protest, relevance, 153 n. 171
  self-determination issues distinguished, 110 n. 4, 375 n. 6
  sovereignty and, *Dubai/Sharjah*, 150-8

Canada
  fiduciary relationship with aboriginals (*Guerin*), 201-2, 207
  treaty interpretation, 132 n. 77

citizenship
   EU citizenship, 187, 189
   nationality and, 187, 189–90
colonies. See also mandated territories; non-self-governing territories; 'sacred trust' concept; trust territories
   as legal artefact, 62
   basis for designation as 'peoples', 55–7
   definition, 53
      limitation to trust territories and non-self-governing territories, 65
   identity underlying, 55–62
      multiplicity, 65
   'internal'/'external' colonialism distinguished, 40–1
   self-determination. See self-determination, right of
   separate status, 75
Conference on Security and Cooperation in Europe, minority rights, 173
consultation, administering power's right to act without, 162–4, 166 n. 219, 204, 207–8, 209–10
Coolidge, President Calvin. See Tacna-Arica plebiscite
corrective justice. See also human rights
   as justification for secession, 68–73
   conflict with consent of population, 162–3
   equal rights and, 263–74
   indigenous peoples, 221, 244–5, 260, 262–3, 273
      recognition of treaties, 247
      treatment of land claims and treaties, 247, 266, 268 n. 279
   Western Sahara, 158–67
Croatia and Bosnia-Herzegovina
   carence de souveraineté, 79
   recognition, requirements for, 172
   self-determination and, 171–3
   Serbian population in, rights
      autonomy, 173–4
      identity, 173, 174, 181, 185
      self-determination, 173
      to choose nationality, 173
cultural diversity. See interpretation of international law, cross-cultural; marginalization; 'people'/'self'

discrimination
   as justification for secession, 37, 63, 75, 77
dual nationality, Dayton Accords (1995), 189

East Timor
   non-self-governing territory, 199–202
   Portugal's standing, 202–10, 378
   lack of consent, 205
Eastern Greenland, *terra nullius*, 136–7
EC Arbitration Commission on Yugoslavia. See Yugoslavia, EC Arbitration Commission
EC Guidelines on Recognition of New States in Eastern Europe and the Soviet Union, 172–3, 187–8
equality. See also marginalization
   access to international law resources, 10, 41–4, 131 n. 77. See also sources of international law; state practice
   of all affected parties, 5
   application/principle distinguished, 72
   as basis for group rights of indigenous peoples, 221–3, 258–9, 264–5
   as vehicle for development of international law, 377–8
   denial of sovereignty and, 157
   differential treatment, need for, 222
   diversity issues and, 5, 14
   intertemporal law and, 211
   participation in. See also participation in self-determination
      ICJ proceedings, 192–4, 206, 214–15
      ILO, 225–37
      UN Working Group on Indigenous Populations, 213–14, 260 n. 240
   of states, 6
   UNGA resolutions and, 44, 167
   trusteeship system and, 192, 194–211, 377
   women. See also women, equality
      nationality and, 315, 325–6
      self-determination and, 279, 327
      trusteeship system, 332–49
ethics in international law, 48–9
Euronationalism, 105

exclusion. *See* marginalization
expatriation, 178–9

fairness, 30, 83
feminist approaches to international law, 277–81
forcible intervention in support of self-determination, 37. *See also* peace and security; territorial integrity of states

gender/sex distinguished, 279 n. 9
General Assembly
  Convention on Consent to Marriage, Minimum Age for Marriage and Registration of Marriages (1962), 347
  determination of
    entitlement to self-determination, 31
    non-self-governing status, 31
General Assembly resolutions
  32/142 (1977) (women's participation in the strengthening of peace and the struggle against colonialism, etc.), 348 n. 94
  41/120 (guidelines for Working Group on Indigenous Populations), 250–5
  731 (VIII) (political rights of women in territories where not fully enjoyed), 346 n. 83
  758 (VIII) (Cameroons), 12
  843 (IX) (1954) (Status of Women in Private Law: Customs, Ancient Laws and Practices Affecting the Human Dignity of Women), 346–7
  1514 (XV) (Declaration on the Independence of Colonial Peoples), 74–5, 85, 85–6, 112, 159, 165, 200–1, 202–3, 206, 327, 328–9, 330, 344, 347
  1541 (XV), 66, 75, 271
  2625 (XXV) (1970) (Declaration on Friendly Relations), 63, 64, 66, 72, 74–9 88–9, 102, 256, 263, 267, 270
  3521 (XXX) (1975) (Equality of Men and Women and Elimination of Discrimination against Women), 348
  as source of international law, 44, 167, 211, 378

human rights. *See also* corrective justice; discrimination; International Covenants on Human Rights (1966); minority rights
  abuses as ground for secession, 73–86
  democratic government, 105, 187–8
  group rights, 80–2
    concept of self-determination and, 80, 81–2
  holistic approach of ILO, 235
  jus cogens, 177
  'peoples', 58–9
  political and economic rights distinguished, 19–20
  self-determination as, 19–20, 81–6
    EC Arbitration Commission on Yugoslavia, 82, 174–5
    General Comment No. 12 (1984), 23, 81–2
    International Covenants on Human Rights (1966), 82
    UNGA resolution, 41/120 guidelines, 250–5

'identity' underlying self-determination. *See also* minorities; nationality, right to choose; 'people'/'self'; women
  colonial borders and, 20, 55–6, 172, 181
  definition, 4
  equality of states and, 6
  indigenous women (*Lovelace*), 358–72
  interpretive approaches and, 50–1, 89–90, 91–105, 374
  'legal ties' considerations, 133, 157–8, 376
  multiplicity of identities, 189–90
  Serbian population in Croatia and Bosnia-Herzegovina, 173, 174, 181, 185, 188–9
  stereotyping, 3, 6–8, 320–4, 374
Ifni, 162–4
ILO Convention concerning Indigenous and Tribal Peoples in Independent Countries (Convention, 169)
  applicability, breadth of, 243–54
  competence of ILO and, 233–7
  functional approach, 243–4
  ILO Convention Concerning the Protection and Integration of Indigenous and Other Tribal and

ILO Convention (cont.)
    Semi-Tribal Populations in Independent Countries (Convention, 107) and, 223–4
  definition of applicability and, 244
  influence on policy, 224
  land claims, 245–7
  Meeting of Experts (1986), 225–6
  participation in drafting, 215, 219, 378 n. 14
    attempts to include indigenous representatives, 227–30
    consultation with indigenous groups, 226, 228
    formal limitations on, 227, 228–9
    role of Office and, 231–3
  'peoples'/'populations', 224, 237–42
  ratification, 224–5
    indigenous peoples' views on, 224–5, 230–1
  'treaties', 247–8
indigenous peoples. *See also* boundary/territorial disputes, indigenous claims, ICJ handling of
  as 'peoples', 269
  basis for group rights
    equality, 221–3, 258–9, 264–5
    minority rights, 222–3, 258–9
    preservation and development of culture, 258–9
    'rights' approach, 256
  changing perceptions, 9
  defining features
    historical precedence and, 244–5
    own institutions, 244
  international institutions and, 9, 212–74
    ICJ, 193 n. 402
    ILO. *See* ILO Convention concerning Indigenous and Tribal Peoples in Independent Countries (Convention, 169); International Labour Organization (ILO)
    UN Working Group on Indigenous Populations. *See* UN Working Group on Indigenous Populations
  land claims
    consent to taking, relevance, 262, 267
    continuity of ownership, relevance, 264

    historical/need basis distinguished, 245–7, 259
  narratives/historical perspectives, 260–1
  participation
    ICJ, 193 n. 327
    ILO Convention, 169, drafting, 227–30, 231–3, 378 n. 14
    UN Working Group on Indigenous Populations, 214–15, 219 n. 25, 260 n. 240
  recognition of group identity and rights distinguished, 241–2
  self-determination, right of, 220–3, 224, 240–2, 255–74
    corrective justice as justification, 221, 244–5, 260, 262–3, 273
    equality of women and (*Lovelace*), 358–72
    equivalence to that of non-indigenous peoples, 257–8, 271
    freely expressed will, 259–60, 263, 271–3
    internal self-determination, 156–8, 265–6
    International Covenants on Human Rights (1966), 267–8, 270
    right of colonial peoples distinguished, 40–1, 256, 261–2, 270
  treaties
    categorization, 247–8
    recognition, corrective justice and, 247
  treatment in
    draft declaration on the rights of indigenous peoples (1993), 264, 266
    ILO Convention, 169, 247–8
  tribal peoples distinguished, 243
indigenous peoples, draft declaration on the rights of (1993), 212–13. *See also* UN Working Group on Indigenous Populations
  as balance of aspirations and legitimate concerns, 254–5
  as manifesto of indigenous peoples' rights, 218, 250, 253, 263
  as technical standard-setting, 219, 250–2
  equality of indigenous peoples, 264–5
  land claims, 259, 264, 266
  'people'/'peoples', 255–6, 269–70

'rights'/corrective justice divide, 263–74
self-determination, right of, 255–74
  'in accordance with international law', 266–9
  internal self-determination, 265–6
  terra nullius, 259, 262, 267
  treaties, 264, 266
Indigenous Peoples Earth Charter (1992), 260–2
International Court of Justice (ICJ)
  African resort to, 113–14
  'decolonization' of, 114
  participation in proceedings
    advisory proceedings, 194
    alternative sources of information, 194
    Court's duty to ascertain the people's wishes, 207 n. 402
    expert opinions, 194
    indigenous peoples, 193 n. 327
    international organizations, 194
    non-governmental organizations, 194–5
    'peoples', 192–3, 205–8, 214–15
    public international organizations, 193–4
    states, 192–4
  South West Africa cases, differing judicial approaches, 114
  Third World disenchantment, 113–14
International Covenants on Human Rights (1966)
  ILO and, 235
  individual's right to choose ethnic, religious or linguistic community, 169, 174–5, 177
  minority rights, 169, 174–5, 177, 368–9
  'peoples', 58–9
  self-determination issues, 22–3, 58–9, 82, 101–2
  indigenous peoples, 267–8, 270
International Labour Organization (ILO)
  establishment and structure, 225–6
  human rights
    holistic approach, 235, 242–8
    International Covenants (1966), ILO role, 235
  indigenous peoples, competence in respect of, 233–7. *See also* ILO Convention concerning Indigenous and Tribal Peoples in Independent Countries (Convention, 169)
  procedure for adopting and implementing conventions, 225–37
    'double discussion' process, 226–7, 237
    legitimacy of supervisory and monitoring procedures, 236–7
    ratification process, 235–6
    role of Office, 231–3
    tripartite nature, 219, 225–6, 231, 237
international law
  as interpretive process, 21, 33, 177
  as 'lawyers' law', 43–4, 100, 104–5
  as a positive force, 380–1
  democratic deficit, 215
  developing world's acceptance of, 141
  development, 29, 52, 378–80
    consensual approach, 127–8
    equality considerations as vehicle for, 377–8
    'principles' as means of, 38–41
    through practice, 177
    transition from club to inclusiveness, 29, 378–80
    treaty interpretation and, 114
    women's role, 278–80, 350
  ethics. *See* ethics in international law
  'European club' approach, 25, 29
  as 'legal paganism', 38–9
  customary international law and, 44
  Dubai-Sharjah, 116, 140 n. 113
  Gulf of Fonseca, 375, 376
  'legal ties', 117–18, 142–3, 156–8
  right of self-determination and, 158
  role of principles and, 38–41
  'rule'-based approach, 38–41
  sovereignty issues, 133, 150–8, 378–9
  status of women, 341–3
  subjects of international law, 147
  terra nullius, 120–5, 127, 262
  Territorial Dispute (Libya/Chad), 375, 376
  territory as a concept, 69, 119, 134–5
  transition from club to inclusiveness, 29, 378–80
  UNGA resolutions as source of international law and, 44, 211, 378
  Western Sahara, 115, 116–17, 133–5, 374–6, 378–9
feminist approaches, 277–81

international law (cont.)
  inequality of, 14. See also equality
  interpretation. See interpretation of
      international law
  intertemporal law. See intertemporal law
  legitimacy, 82–6, 157–8, 161–2, 167, 274
  lex ferenda, 97
  lex lata, 33, 97
  normative structure, 31 n. 8
  'open-textured', 33
  positivist/policy-oriented approaches, 33, 45–9, 93–105
  social reality as basis, 59–60, 96, 145, 156–7
  sources. See sources of international law
  subjects of. See subjects of international law
  universality, 128 n. 73, 133, 139, 148, 377, 379
  'general international law', 148–9
interpretation of international law and self-determination. See also judicial law-making
  'actualization', 203, 376
  ambiguity/clarity, 97–9
  certainty requirement, 36, 104–5
  contextual approach, 33, 102, 103
  cross-cultural
    Dubai/Sharjah, 151, 156–8, 379
    East Timor, 210–11
    Western Sahara, 14–16, 137–40, 210–11, 375–6, 379
  definition, 4
  integration of classic and contemporary norms, 376
  non liquet, 97
  participation in, 8, 100, 103, 104–5, 129, 161–2, 217. See also participation in self-determination
intertemporal law, 70
  definition, 158, 160
  equality and, 211
  Island of Palmas, 70 n. 84, 160
  legal ties and, 165–6
  Western Sahara, 116–17, 121, 129, 145, 158–67, 378
Islamic law, 133

judicial law-making, 40, 96
jus cogens
  human rights, 177
  minority rights, 174, 177
  self-determination as, 160 n. 193, 177

Kuwait/Iraq conflict
  acquisition of territory by force, 69
  self-determination and, 70 n. 83

land claims
  draft declaration on the rights of indigenous peoples (1993), 259, 264
  ILO Convention, 169, 245–7
League of Nations
  appointments, equality of opportunity, 298
  'sacred trust' and, 196, 197–9, 329–30
'legal ties'
  definition, 15, 112
  Dubai/Sharjah, 150–8
  'European club' approach. See international law, 'European club' approach
  intertemporal law, 165–6
  Minquiers and Ecrehos, 142–3
  Morocco and Mauritania/Western Sahara, 115–16, 118, 132–45, 376
  self-determination and, 112–13, 118, 128–9, 157–8, 162–7, 376
  territorial sovereignty requirement, 132–3, 140, 162
  sovereign, 132–3, 138–41, 144–5
    allegiance/control divide, 151–5, 156–7
    Mauritania/Western Sahara, 144–5
    Western Sahara, 15–16, 112–13, 117–18
legitimacy of international law, 82–6, 157–8, 161–2, 167, 274
  broadening of participation and, 274, 378
legitimization of borders, 171–2

mandated territories, 51, 329–30. See also colonies; 'sacred trust' concept; trust territories
  as 'peoples', 38
  description of system, 198
  paternalistic approach, 198–9, 330
  self-determination, right of, 34
marginalization, 3. See also equality; indigenous peoples; narratives; participation; trust territories; women

acknowledgment of cultural differences and, 140–2
authenticity of community and, 24–5
choice of interpretive theory, 4–5, 9–11
construction of identity, 4–5
exclusion from
  interpretive process, 4–5, 374
  participation in judicial and arbitral proceedings, 192–4, 204–10
redressing, 14–15
representation of marginalized groups, 24–6, 67, 260 n. 240. *See also* women, representation issues
Mauritania, status, 145–50
minorities. *See also* Croatia and Bosnia-Herzegovina, Serbian population in; indigenous peoples; minority rights
Aaland Islands, 78, 79–80
in Africa, 20 n. 60
as 'peoples', 62–3, 84–5, 174
definition
  applicable law, 368–9
  International Covenant on Civil and Political Rights (1966), 368–9
  failure to protect identity as justification for secession, 79–82, 87, 185–6
individual's right to choose ethnic, religious or linguistic community
  as right of expatriation, 178
  as right of option, 178–9, 186
  International Covenants on Human Rights (1966), 169, 174–5, 177
'peoples' entitled to self-determination distinguished, 101–2
EC Arbitration Commission on Yugoslavia, 169
post-World War I, 12–13, 62–3
minority rights. *See also* human rights; minorities; minority rights
as basis for group rights of indigenous peoples, 222–3, 258–9
CSCE, 173
jus cogens, 174, 177
limited role in international law, 222–3
restrictions on, *Lovelace/Kitok*, 369–70, 371–2
Mututsi women, 7, 341–2

narratives. *See also* marginalization
as homologies, 48
coherence, need for, 50, 68
different perspectives, relevance, 12, 46–7
getting the voice right, 23–4
indigenous historical perspectives, 260–1
refashioning, 84–5
representation and, 67
rule/principle distinction and, 45–9
UN Working Group on Indigenous Populations, 215–16, 218–19
Western Sahara, 112–15
women's, 328
nationalism
colonialism and, 55–6
EU citizenship as moderating factor, 187, 189–90
Euro/ethno nationalism distinguished, 105
postmodern tribalism and, 94–5
Serb national question, 167–90
nationality, right to choose, 169, 173
dual nationality. *See* dual nationality
giving rise to cross-border 'nation', 169, 186–90, 378
married women, 280–1, 311–26. *See also* post-WW I right of option *below and* women, nationality of married women
  individual option, Treaty of Frankfurt (1871), 312
  Lovelace compared, 358–9
  plebiscite, following, 309–10
post-WW I right of option, 178–9, 186
  emigration requirement, 310 n. 172, 314–15
  individual, 309–10
  married women
    collective option, 311–15, 325–6
    emigration requirement and, 314–15
  territoriality and, 186–7
  unity of family and, 316–20
non-self-governing territories. *See also* colonies; self-determination; trust territories; women, traditional practices in trust and non-self-governing territories
as 'peoples', 38, 52
consultation

non-self-governing (*cont.*)
    administering power's right to act
        without, 162-4, 166 n. 219, 190-2,
        194-5, 204, 207-8, 209-10
    duty of, 205-7, 209-10
    definition (UNGA resolution, 1541), 75
    determination of status as
        by General Assembly, 31, 52
        by responsible states, 52
        criteria (GA Res, 1541 (XV) (1960)), 52
    East Timor, 200-11, 378
    paternalistic approach, 199-201, 209
    status as requirement for
        self-determination, 31
    UN Charter provisions, 34, 52-3, 99-100,
        199-201, 202-3, 206
    Western Sahara, 111
normative structure in international law,
    31 n. 8

option, right of. *See* nationality, right to
    choose

participation in self-determination. *See also*
    marginalization
    definition, 4
    equality of, 10, 41-4, 105, 379-80
    ICJ proceedings, 192-5, 206, 214-15
    ILO, 225-37
    interpretation of international law, 8,
        13, 100, 103, 104-5, 129, 161-2,
        217
    perceptions of
        outcome, 224-5
        participants' role, 216, 219-20
        role of institution, 217-19
    'public space', 217 n. 17
    UN Working Group on Indigenous
        Populations, 214-15, 260 n. 240
    women's. *See* women, participation
peace and security/self-determination, 82,
    86-90, 183-4. *See also* forcible
        intervention in support of
        self-determination; territorial
        integrity of states
    Aaland Islands, 86-7
    Declaration on Friendly Relations, 88-9
    UN Charter provisions, 87-8
    Vienna Declaration and Programme of
        Action (1993), 89
'people'/'self'. *See also* colonies; indigenous
    peoples; secession by sub-state
        groups; self-determination
    avoidance of term in ILO Convention,
        169 discussion and UN Working
        Group on Indigenous Populations,
        220-1, 237-42, 255-6
    borders as definition of, 20
    cultural minority as, 188
    definition, difficulty, 34, 37-8
    'demos'/'ethnos' concept of the nation
        and, 55-8, 84-5, 92-3, 168-9,
        188
        right of option and, 310 n. 172
    ethnic minorities as, 62-3, 84-5, 174. *See
        also* minorities
    ethno-cultural considerations, 61-2
        Declaration on Friendly Relations, 63
        Greco-Bulgarian Communities, 63
        Western Sahara, 118
    evidence of
        armed resistance, 60-1
        position taken by democratically
            elected government, 60
    general and regional international law
        distinguished, 51 n. 2
    group subject to alien domination
        as category separate from 'colonies',
            64-5
        Vienna Declaration and Programme of
            Action (1993), 65
    Ifni, 162-3
    minorities distinguished, 101-2
    non-colonial territories, 53-4
    non-self-governing territories as, 38, 53,
        55
    population of overseas colony as, 18, 118
    population of sovereign state/territory
        as, 57, 62, 117-19
    right/principle of self-determination,
        relevance, 37-8, 220-1, 224,
        237-42, 256-7
    self-defining, 57-8
        International Covenants on Human
            Rights (1966), 58-9
    trust territories as, 38, 53
    women's role in determining, 13
petitions to Trusteeship Council. *See*
    Trusteeship Council, petitions to
plebiscites post-World War I, 282-4
    nationality, right of option, individual,
        309-10

people's role in determining sovereignty, 13, 281–4
precedents, 281–2
propaganda, 300–3
self-determination and, 324–6
women's right to vote, 12–13, 284–309
  reasons for agreement to, 296–303
principles. *See also* rule/principle distinction
balancing of, 40
certainty of application, relevance, 34, 35–6, 39–41, 44, 48
core/penumbra distinction, 36
deductive/innovative principles distinguished, 39 n. 55
'general principles of law' distinguished, 29 n. 2
legal right distinguished, 33–4
legal/political principles distinguished, 33–4
political influences on, 34
sociological/analytical constructs distinguished, 46
state practice and, 43
subjective nature, 40
private law analogies. *See* analogy

recognition of states
EC Guidelines on Recognition of New States in Eastern Europe and the Soviet Union, 172–3, 187–8
requirements
  democratic government, 187–8
  support of population as a whole, 172
representation issues, 24–6, 67, 204–10, 260 n. 240
women, 279
right of option. *See* nationality, right to choose
rights
  identification of subject, need for, 34
  principles distinguished, 34
Ruanda-Urundi, women's status in, 7, 341–3
rule/policy distinction, 35 n. 29
rule/principle distinction, 29–49, 99
  determination of 'peoples' and, 37–8
  development of international law and, 10, 38–41

equality of participation and, 10, 41–4, 105
international community narrative and, 45–9
relative ease of achieving agreement, 46–8
rules, formulation
by analogy, 40–1
dependence on access to sources, 41–4

'sacred trust' concept, 195, 195–203, 329–30
agency relationship, 201–2, 206–8
East Timor, 192 n. 324, 378
international Status of South-West Africa, 199
League of Nations provisions, 196, 197–9, 329–30
Namibia, 200, 330
rejection in Declarations on the Independence of Colonial Peoples and Friendly Relations, 191–2, 200–1, 203, 206, 327, 328–9, 330, 344
UN Charter provisions, 196, 199–200, 329–30
Saskatoon Statement and Recommendations on Self-Determination (1993), 26 n. 85
secession by sub-state groups, 31, 34, 53–65. *See also* 'people'/'self'
Aaland Islands, 77–80
categories approach, 53–4, 62–5, 68, 80, 89
coherence approach, 53–4, 55–62, 80, 83–5, 89–90
EC Arbitration Commission on Yugoslavia, 176, 179–86
Declaration on Friendly Relations, 76–8, 256, 263, 267
decolonization and
  suggested grounds for distinguishing
    nature of historical grievance, 73
    separate territorial status, 75–6
justification
  abuse of sovereign power, 77–9, 85
  better territorial claim, 72–3
  carence de souveraineté, 34, 38, 78–9
    Aaland Islands, 78
    Bangladesh, 78–9

secession (cont.)
    corrective justice, 68–73, 221, 262–3
    denial of autonomy, 76–7
    denial of political participation, 85–6, 101, 272–3
    discrimination, 63, 75, 77, 84, 102
        systematic political or economic, 37, 81
    failure to protect minority identity, 79–82, 87, 185–6
    failure to respect minority rights, 185
    human rights abuses, 73–86
    Loizidou v. Turkey, 73–4, 77
    non-compliance with principle of self-determination, 18, 75–7
    peace and security considerations, 86–90. *See also* peace and security/self-determination
    rejection by central regime of reasonable proposals for autonomy and minority rights, 37, 81
    requirements/'standards', distinct identity, 37, 61–2, 81
    right of, 18
        analogy with non-self governing territories, 40–1
        as new right, 72
        designation as 'peoples' and, 37–8, 220–1, 224, 237–42, 256–7
        ethnic group, 183
        indigenous peoples, 220–3, 224
            draft declaration on the rights of indigenous peoples (1993), 255–74
        International Covenants on Human Rights (1966) and, 58–9, 101–2
        limitations on exercise, 180–1, 182–4
        Reference re Secession of Quebec, 1, 53
        teleological application, 183–4
        territorial integrity and. *See* territorial integrity of states
    uti possidetis and, 95 n. 21
Security Council resolutions
    660 (1990) (Iraqi invasion of Kuwait), 69 n. 83
    662 (1990), 69 n. 83
    674 (1990), 70 n. 83
'self'. *See* 'people'/'self'
self-determination
    as *jus cogens*, 160 n. 193, 177
    'compliance with principle of', 75–7
    early examples, 148
    equality of women and, 279, 325, 327, 332–49
        Charter provisions, 332–3
        Lovelace, 358–72
    legitimization of borders and, 171–2
    participation and. *See* participation in self-determination
    political and economic manifestations distinguished, 19–20
    revolutionary nature, 13–14
    right/principle dichotomy, 1, 10, 99. *See also* self-determination as principle; self-determination, right of
    subjects of, 6. *See also* 'people'/'self' participation/identity/interpretation and, 4, 8
    UNHRC, jurisprudence, 22–3, 100–1
self-determination as principle, 18, 29
    as ground for interpreting rule, 31
    legal principle, 34
        residual role, 34
    political principle, 33–4
        plebiscites post-WWI, 282, 324–6
    representative government and, 76–7
    right of self-determination distinguished, 34
    universality of UN Charter principle, 31, 85
self-determination, right of. *See also* 'people'/'self'; secession of sub-state groups
    as collective right, 186
    as corrective justice. *See* corrective justice
    as defence against alien domination, 62, 63–5, 72, 100–1, 103
        Declaration on Friendly Relations, 63, 64
        Declaration on the Independence of Colonial Peoples, 64
    as means to achieve democratic government, 184–5
    as restoration of power of determination, 71–2
    as right of 'peoples', 22, 162, 171–2
    competing rights, 170–1

Declaration on the Independence of
    Colonial Peoples, 106, 200–1,
    203, 327, 328–9, 330, 344,
    347
East Timor, 191, 378
erga omnes nature, 191
freely expressed will and, 34, 37, 52,
    66–7, 68, 100–1, 159–60, 256
  as continuing process, 67–8, 100
  competing considerations, 116, 163–4,
    165–7
  Croatia and Bosnia-Herzegovina, 172–3
  Declaration on Friendly Relations, 66
  indigenous peoples, 259–60, 263,
    271–3
  UNGA resolution, 1541(XV), 66, 112
  Western Sahara, 66, 115–16, 117–18,
    206, 376
identity considerations. *See* identity;
    'people'
indigenous peoples. *See* indigenous
    peoples, self-determination,
    right of
internal self-determination, 18–19, 31,
    100–1, 256–8, 265–6. *See also*
    secession by sub-state groups
Kuwait/Iraq conflict, 70 n. 83
mandated territories, 34
non-self-governing territories under UN
    Charter, 34, 52–3, 99–100,
    199–201, 202–3. *See also* secession
    by sub-state groups
  subsequent developments in
    international law, 52, 206
perceived dangers, 7–8
  disintegration, 103–4
  peace and security considerations, 82,
    86–90
requirements/'standards'
  non-self-governing status, 31
  progress in accord with Western
    model, 6–7, 20, 197–9
  reasonableness test, 37–8
'subjugated people', 65
territorial integrity of states and. *See*
    territorial integrity of states
territories not classified as
    'non-self-governing'. *See* secession
    by sub-state groups
trust territories, 34
Serb national question, 167–90

sex/gender distinguished, 279 n. 9
Slovenia, *carence de souveraineté*, 79
sources of international law. *See also* state
    practice
  inter-war minority treaties, 222 n. 33
  judicial and arbitral decisions, 21, 42
  non-European, 210–11
  UNGA resolutions, 44, 167, 211, 378
  Western Sahara, 129
  writings of publicists, distorting effect,
    43–4
sovereignty. *See also* territory
  acquisition rules posited on
    European/non-European
    relationship, 133, 135
  Island of Palmas, 135
  analogy with private law autonomy, 137
  competing claims, 153
  Dubai/Sharjah, 150–8
  effective exercise
    allegiance/control divide, 151–5,
      156–7
    Dubai/Sharjah, 152–3
    Eastern Greenland, 136
    Western Sahara, 137–8
  legal ties and, 132–3, 138–41, 144–5
  population's role in determining
    (post-WWI plebiscites), 13, 281–4
  Status of Eastern Greenland, 135–7
  terra nullius status and, 126–7
  Western Sahara, 133–41, 150
state practice
  bias in recording of, 42–3
    digests and collections, 10, 42–3
    judicial and arbitral decisions, 42–3
  interpretation of principles and, 43
states
  entity without state structures, 146–8,
    157
  as denial of equality, 157
  subjects of international law, 8–9,
    69–70, 129–31, 149, 206
subjects of international law. *See also*
    identity underlying
    self-determination;
    self-determination, subjects of
  active/passive roles distinguished, 8–9
  right of petition, 9
  diversity, 149, 186, 187–9
  Reparations for Injuries, 149–50
  'European club' approach, 147

subjects of international law (cont.)
  'legal entities', Mauritania, 145–50
  states, 8–9, 69–70, 129–31, 149, 206

Tacna-Arica plebiscite, 283–4, 303, 305, 307–9, 378 n. 14
terra nullius
  African concept, 123–4, 125, 154
  consensus approach, 127–8
  draft declaration on the rights of indigenous peoples (1993), 259, 262, 264, 267
  Dubai/Sharjah, 155–8
  Eastern Greenland, 136–7
  European concept, 120–6, 127
  Mabo v. Queensland (No. 2), 116, 128, 129, 375
  sovereignty and, 126–7
  Vattel, 128–9
  Western Sahara, 115–16, 120–9, 375, 378
territorial disputes. See boundary/territorial disputes
territorial integrity of states. See also forcible intervention in support of self-determination; peace and security; uti possidetis
  Croatia and Bosnia-Herzegovina, 170–2
  decolonization, relevance to, 74–5, 162–7
  secession by sub-state groups and, 43
    Declaration on Friendly Relations, 63, 64, 72, 74–6, 102, 267, 270
    Declaration on the Independence of Colonial Peoples, 74–5, 159, 165
    draft declaration on the rights of indigenous peoples (1993), 266–7, 270, 272
  self-determination, compatibility, 37, 72–3, 102–4, 159–60, 187
territory. See also sovereignty
  acquisition by force or wrongful taking as basis of right of self-determination, 70–1
    Baltic states, 70–1, 73
    indigenous peoples, 221, 260, 262, 267
    Iraq invasion of Kuwait, 69
    loss of territory/control distinguished, 71
    recognition as fait accompli, 70
    Western Sahara, 115
  as European concept, 69, 119, 121, 134–5
  as property, 69, 120
  political organization and, 119
  nationality and, 186–7
  terra nullius. See terra nullius
  transfer of populations, 179
treaties. See indigenous peoples, treaties; treaty interpretation
treaty interpretation
  'colonial' treaties
    Canadian practice, 132 n. 77
    ICJ practice, 131 n. 77
  developing international law, relevance, 114
  draft declaration on the rights of indigenous peoples (1993), 266
  object and purpose, 58–9
tribal peoples, 243. See also indigenous peoples
trust territories. See also colonies; mandated territories; 'sacred trust' concept
  as 'peoples', 38
  Canadian government's fiduciary relationship with aboriginals compared 201–2, 207
  establishment and administration, 51–2, 329–32
  petition, right of, 331–2
  supervision, 331–2
  inequality of system, 192, 194–211
  origin in British 'colonial trust', 195–6
  women in, 332–49
    petitions to Trusteeship Council, 328, 349–57
    status as measure of readiness for self-determination, 7
    traditional practices
      CSW attempts to abolish, 344–9
      polygamy/child marriage (Fon of Bikom), 333–40
      UNGA resolution on the Status of Women in Private Law: Customs, Ancient Laws and Practices Affecting the Human Dignity of Women, 346–7
Trusteeship Council
  petitions to, 328, 349–57
    Fon of Bikom (St Joan's Social and Political Alliance), 333–43
    rules of procedure relating to, 331–2
    women's equality and, 328, 349–57
    women's participation in, 328, 349–57

UN Charter
  equality of women under, 332-3
  peace and security considerations, 87-8
  'sacred trust' concept, 196, 199-200, 329-30
  self-determination under, 34, 52-3, 99-100, 199-201, 202-3
  subsequent development of international law and, 52, 206
  universal applicability of principle of self-determination, 31, 84
UN Working Group on Indigenous Populations. *See also* indigenous peoples
  Chairperson's role, 217, 249, 253-5
    expert/mediator distinguished, 254-5
  composition, 249-50
  establishment and competence, 248-9
  factors in successful working, 217, 218-19, 249, 253-5
  mandate, 250
    consolidation/dynamic development options, 250-5
    development of standards based on the aspirations of indigenous peoples, 253
    UNGA resolution, 41/120 guidelines and, 254-5
  objectives, differing perspectives on, 218-20
  participation, 214-15
    difficulties in attending, 219 n. 25
    indigenous women, 219 n. 25
    representation issues, 260 n. 240
UNHRC
  General Comment No. 12 (1984), 23, 81-2
  jurisprudence relating to self-determination, 22-3, 100-1
uti possidetis, 95 n. 21
  as determinant of territorial entity, 171
  EC Arbitration Commission on Yugoslavia, 170-2, 177-82
  internal/external borders, 171
  stability of borders as general principle of international law, 171, 177

Vienna Declaration and Programme of Action (1993), 65, 75 n. 118, 89

Vilnius plebiscite (1921), 303-7, 308-9, 378 n. 14

Wilson, President Woodrow, 13, 57, 84, 282, 296
  women's suffrage and, 286-9
women
  Commission on the Status of Women, 328, 344-9
  equality. *See also* participation *below*
    nationality of married women. *See* nationality of married women *below*
  self-determination and, 279, 325, 327, 332-49
  trusteeship system, 332-49
    imposition of western perceptions, 340-3
    UNGA Res, 843 (IX) (1954), 346-7
    UNGA Res, 3521 (XXX) (1975), 348
    UNGA resolution on political rights of women in territories where not fully enjoyed, 346 n. 83
  international women's organizations, 285-6
  narratives, 328
  nationality of married women
    collective option, 311-15, 325-6
    emigration requirement and, 314-15
    Lovelace compared, 358-9
    Convention on Certain Questions Relating to the Conflict of Nationality Laws (1930), 313 n. 186
    Convention on the Nationality of Married Women (1957), 313 n. 186
    Hague Codification Conference (1930), 313 n. 186
    individual option
      Treaty of Frankfurt (1871), 312
      International Charter of Women's Rights, 314
      International Congress of Women (Zurich) (1919), 314
    unity of the family and, 316-20
  participation
    League of Nations appointments, 298
    Paris Peace Conference and, 13, 285-9, 325

women (cont.)
  petitions to Trusteeship Council, 349–57
  plebiscites
    post-WWI, 12–13, 284–309, 324–6. *See also* plebiscites post-World War I
    right to vote, 12–13, 284–309
    Tacna-Arica, 283–4, 303, 305, 307–9, 378 n. 14
    Vilnius (1921), 303–7, 308–9, 378 n. 14
  UN Working Group on Indigenous Populations, 219 n. 25
peace movement, 290–6
  International Congress of Women (The Hague) (1915), 290, 293–5, 298–9, 314
  International Congress of Women (Zurich) (1919), 290, 295–6
  Woman's Peace Party, 291–3
petitions to Trusteeship Council, 328, 349–57
plebiscite propaganda and, 300–3
representation issues,
    Western/non-Western divide, 279, 356–7
role in
  Convention on the Elimination of All Forms of Discrimination Against Women (1979), 279
  development of international law, 278–80, 350
  establishment of UN, 332
  international human rights law, 279

status
  as measure of readiness for self-determination, 7
  Ruanda-Urundi, 7, 341–3
suffrage, 13, 284–9
  International Woman Suffrage Alliance (IWSA), 284–5
  Paris Peace Conference, 285–9
traditional practices in trust and non-self-governing territories
  Convention on Consent to Marriage, Minimum Age for Marriage and Registration of Marriages (1962), 347
  CSW attempts to abolish, 344–9
  polygamy/child marriage (Fon of Bikom), 333–40
  UNGA resolution on the Status of Women in Private Law: Customs, Ancient Laws and Practices Affecting the Human Dignity of Women, 346–7

Yugoslavia, secession/dissolution, 170 n.228
Yugoslavia, EC Arbitration Commission, 82
  composition, 175
  decolonization approach compared, 181
  criticism of its treatment of international law, 175–86
  lack of coherence, 176, 179–86
  establishment, 167 n. 222
  lex arbitri, 175 n. 250
  uti possidetis, 170–2, 177

For EU product safety concerns, contact us at Calle de José Abascal, 56–1°, 28003 Madrid, Spain or eugpsr@cambridge.org.

www.ingramcontent.com/pod-product-compliance
Ingram Content Group UK Ltd.
Pitfield, Milton Keynes, MK11 3LW, UK
UKHW011948090825
461507UK00005B/107